10.92

THE PRENTICE-HALL SERIES
IN DEVELOPMENTAL PSYCHOLOGY

John C. Wright, editor

Contents

Acknowledgments

Perspectives in Behavior Modification with Deviant Children
includes studies originally published in the following journals:

Journal of Applied Behavior Analysis
Behaviour Research and Therapy
Journal of Experimental Research in Personality
Journal of Abnormal Psychology
Science
Journal of Consulting and Clinical Psychology
Journal of Personality and Social Psychology
Journal of Behavior Therapy and Experimental Psychiatry
Journal of Experimental Child Psychology
Exceptional Children
Journal of the Experimental Analysis of Behavior

52655

Library of Congress Cataloging in Publication Data

LOVAAS, OLE IVAR, comp.
　　Perspectives in behavior modification with deviant
children.

　　(The Prentice-Hall series in developmental
psychology)
　　Includes bibliographies.
　　1. Behavior modification—Addresses, essays,
lectures.　　2. Child psychotherapy—Addresses, essays,
lectures.　　I. Bucher, Bradley D., joint comp.　　II.
Title.　[DNLM: 1. Behavior therapy—In infancy
and childhood—Collected works.　WM420　L896p　1974]
RJ505.B4L68　　　　618.9'28'91　　　　73-18357
ISBN　0-13-657130-1

© 1974 by
Prentice-Hall, Inc., Englewood Cliffs, N.J. 07632

10　9　8　7　6　5　4　3　2　1

Prentice-Hall International, Inc., London
Prentice-Hall of Australia, Pty. Ltd., Sydney
Prentice-Hall of Canada, Ltd., Toronto
Prentice-Hall of India Private Limited, New Delhi
Prentice-Hall of Japan, Inc., Tokyo

Perspectives in Behavior Modification with Deviant Children

Edited by **O. IVAR LOVAAS**
University of California at Los Angeles
and
BRADLEY D. BUCHER
University of Western Ontario

PRENTICE-HALL, INC., ENGLEWOOD CLIFFS, N.J.

Preface

This book brings together a number of recent studies on the treatment of childhood maladaptive behavior. The results of this research are of great practical importance to everyone concerned with the lives of children. The treatment techniques we describe al relate to behavior modification procedures, a form of treatment that appears both powerful and richly instructive. Within a short period of time, behavior modification has produced a technology of considerable social importance.

We have selected papers describing research in a variety of behavior problems and have tried to find those that combine instructive, well-managed research with practicable and useful therapeutic procedures. The book begins with research design since research considerations have formed a most important basis for the work in behavior modification. The research design, perhaps more than any other dimension, serves as a unifying core of all the studies included. The preferred research design in behavior modification has been highly controlled and experimental, and the within-subject design has been relied upon, rather than the more familiar group comparison study. Since the within-subject design is somewhat unfamiliar, the book's first section describes it in some detail.

We have not grouped the papers by traditional diagnostic class nor by method of treatment. A more natural grouping, it seems to us, is according to treatment settings and the behavioral characteristics of the children. Thus "simple" behaviors such as early self-help and social skills are grouped in Section II. More "complex" behaviors such as language are grouped in Section III. Disruptive behaviors treated in the *home* are covered in Section V, and disruptive and poor academic behavior in *school* are grouped in Section VI.

The last section of the book concerns future research. There are many phenomena we do not understand in which future research will provide guidance. One such area is motivation. What are the reinforcers that facilitate children's development? How is it that stimuli become reinforcing? Although it is important, we have not presented any research in this area, since we don't know enough about it. Instead, papers that broaden our understanding of stimulus control, where it seems that we may be making some headway, are included. Stimulus control refers to the child's use and coordination of environmental cues—how behaviors once controlled by one set of cues come to be controlled by another set. When we can help the child respond to new cues, when we can help him to take advantage of the information he possesses, then he is in a better position to master the prodigious feats of learning that society expects of him.

To better understand the implications of these studies on behavior modification and their applications to similar problems, the student should be acquainted with the objective, data-oriented viewpoint and language that characterizes behavior modification. Some students may not have acquired these prerequisites. Some of these considerations will be introduced throughout the book, both in terms of research design and learning theory (largely operant), both of which provide the conceptual basis for behavior modification at the present time. But many students may want a deeper understanding of these issues than we can provide here. Therefore, it may be desirable to supplement this book with an auxiliary source of instruction on operant research methods, results, and terminology. The student may want to familiarize himself with certain basic concepts and laws within learning theory *before* he reads this book. There are several helpful, introductory texts. We were particularly impressed with Fred S. Keller's *Learning: Reinforcement Theory*. Another excellent work is provided by Sidney W. Bijou and Donald M. Baer, *Child Development, Volume I: A Systematic and Empirical Theory*. A slightly more detailed and excellently written book is G. S. Reynolds' *A Primer of Operant Conditioning*.

This collection of readings represents only an interim report. Behavior modification is an area that is developing very rapidly. There remains much to do, and many important issues have hardly been tackled. None are entirely resolved. Challenges and viewpoints from more conventional approaches have been largely unintegrated or ignored. The experimental analysis of child behavior pathology can make no claims for completeness, but it is a very promising beginning.

We wish to thank our colleagues for permitting us to reprint their studies. There is an enormous amount of work and a large diversity of creative skills represented in the papers in the pages to come.

Finally, we wish to express our gratitude to the National Institute of Mental Health, United States Public Health Service, for their support (MH 11440) of our research on childhood schizophrenia. This support has formed a basis for our own research work and has allowed us time to prepare this book.

REFERENCES

BIJOU, S. W. & BAER, D. M. *Child Development, Volume I: A Systematic and Empirical Theory.* New York: Appleton-Century-Crofts, 1961.

KELLER, F. S. *Learning: Reinforcement Theory.* New York: Random House, 1954.

REYNOLDS, G. S. A *Primer of Operant Conditioning.* Glenview, Ill.: Scott, Foresman and Company, 1968.

INTRODUCTION

Behavior modification, the applied experimental analysis of human behavior, has produced some impressive gains in the treatment of deviant behavior during the last ten years. It has offered help in alleviating problems traditionally of concern to the helping professions and has shown promise in helping to solve a much broader range of human problems.

The conceptual basis of behavior modification lies within learning theory, and to understand most of the techniques of behavior modification, one *must* understand modern learning theory. This point has been made by everyone who has written on behavior modification, and we, too, emphasized it in the preface. One must not, however, overlook the fact that certain methodological considerations—considerations of research strategy— have shaped modern learning theory (cf. the chapter on "Behavioristics," in Boring, 1950), just as they have shaped behavior modification. Therefore, to understand what behavior modification is all about one must first understand its research methodology—the experimental analysis of behavior. It would have been impossible for behavior modification to rise so quickly to the forefront of psychological treatments had it not been for its particular research methodology. This experimental analysis is elaborated in the first three chapters, but let us make a brief statement of the problem here.

Basically, all who want to help others are faced with the same problems: the person who needs help shows either a behavioral excess or a deficiency in behavioral development. That is, the person who needs help has either too many contacts with the law, too many suspicions, too much anxiety, too much loneliness, etc. Or, his academic work is deficient, he does not eat well, he does not care for others, etc. If we want to help such a person, our job is to change that person's environment in such a fashion that he can overcome his problem. But before we can change his environment, we must first discern what environmental manipulations will help him. How, then, do we obtain such information?

In the traditional treatment approaches, an attempt to answer this question has been made in part by scrutinizing the person's surroundings for happenings that may be correlated with the onset of, or fluctuations in, the problem behavior. One might observe the actual problem behavior close to real life, as in a school or hospital. In this setting, the nurse or teacher may record day-to-day fluctuations in the person's difficulties and may note the particular features of the person's environment that she feels were present on a particular day. For example, one may note that a child was unusually disruptive in class today and that several unusual events occurred in the child's home the preceding evening. One may hypothesize that those events relate to his poor day in school. Or one might attempt to gain information about what to do by asking about his past—when the problem began, what "significant events" occurred in his life at that time, and so on. In a similar fashion, psychological testing seeks information about the behavior problem as well as about the environment that may have produced the problem.

In this kind of investigation, the investigator (therapist, teacher, etc.) attempts to isolate whatever events affect problems in behavior by observing for the presence or absence of certain environmental events that seem to be correlated with his client's problem. We call such an investigation *correlational,* or *naturalistic-observational,* when it does *not* involve the investigator's active manipulation of suspected causes but *does* involve the description and recording of behavior and the environment in which it occurred.

There is one serious problem associated with this kind of correlational investigation. It concerns *confounding:* too many events are going on in the person's environment (too many variables are operating concurrently) for the data to point out clear–cut, cause–effect relationships. To illustrate this problem, suppose we want to help a five-year-old child to overcome his fear of strangers so that he can enter kindergarten with a fair chance of liking it there. We may begin searching for what to do about his fears by asking the mother when she first noticed that her boy showed these fears. Suppose she answers that it began sometime during the second year of his life, at about the time his sister was born. One may be tempted to infer that it was the presence of the sister that produced the problem. This may or may not be the case; there is no way of knowing. Imagine all the events that take place in a house when a child is born, any one of which could have caused the problem. The mother left him for three days, the father took care of him during that time, and the grandmother came to stay for the first three weeks. The second baby required so much additional housework that the mother lost her social skills, became afraid of strangers, and the boy began to imitate her; or quite unrelated to all this, he took a bad spill outside at that time, and a stranger carried him inside. What is meant by *confounding* variables is that any one of these events (and a host of others) could have caused the boy's problem.

What kind of research procedure could help cut through these kinds of confounding variables? It is generally recognized that confounding can be reduced when the investigator systematically *manipulates* those environmental features that he believes may affect the problem behavior. Such manipulations are usually called *laboratory* or *controlled experimental designs*. In behavior therapy the systematic manipulation of suspected causes is the therapy's most significant characteristic; it is the defining criterion of the *experimental* analysis of behavior. Its prime purposes are the reduction of confounding variables and the isolation of functional (cause-effect) relationships between the person's environment and his behavior. This book is full of illustrations on how to systematically delete and reintroduce (i.e., *replicate*) aspects of a client's environment so as to identify the variables that worsen or improve his behavior. The first three papers deal with the rationale of this procedure; they are important to master. The term *control* of human behavior, a familiar one these days, derives more from its experimental basis than from its social intentions. The research techniques of behavior control are the very techniques that allow us to be more certain about what we are doing to our clients and to identify what is useful, to omit what is not.

There are other defining features in behavior modification work. The term *behavior*, in the experimental analysis of behavior, refers to *socially meaningful behavior*. For reasons that may not be easy to understand, psychologists have often found themselves investigating behavioral "derivatives"—such as psychological test behavior (TAT, Rorschach, etc.) or other symbolic representations of what people do in the real world—"orality" instead of excessive alcohol consumption, "oedipal anxieties" instead of defective sexual functioning. Behavior modification procedures have dealt almost exclusively with the behavior that the client has brought to treatment. Thus, the reader will not find the traditional conceptual language in this book that he is accustomed to seeing in the majority of texts dealing with psychopathology. The conceptual models that have developed within behavior modification depend far more on a language derived from the methodology of experimental behavior analysis than on the traditional language of dynamic psychology. Indeed, the language of the dynamic conceptual model is largely absent from this text. Some may feel this is a loss. The traditional models have a richness of reference and a humanistic emphasis that are not apparent in the language of behavior analysis. However, we prefer a language with clarity and directness, since it provides better guidance for the researcher and leads to the accumulation of usable data. The greatest service the helping professions can offer their clients is the improvement of the effectiveness of the help they provide. We believe experimental behavior analysis offers a promising path to this goal.

If the modification of behavior is our goal, it is clearly of first importance to be able to measure the behaviors toward which our efforts are to be directed. The behaviors to be rated should be exactly specifiable and not difficult to detect. One of the major contributions of experimental behavior analysis to the study of child psychopathology is the recognition of the importance of reliable behavior measurements. It might appear that the problem of measurement would be automatically eliminated in treatment restricted to changes in behavior rather than to changes in such subtle states as cognitive or emotional variables. However, the search for reliable behavioral events has made it quite clear that objective observation of behavior is not a simple task, even when it becomes the subject of detailed study. The child lives in a complex environment, and numerous categories can be devised for his behavior. Behavior seldom divides itself into discrete units. A child in motion moves through event sequences very difficult for another person to assess.

The concern to demonstrate that reliable behavior measures are being gathered is evident throughout this book, and the measures of reliability obtained are not always as high as one might hope for or expect. However, once usable behavior ratings are discovered, it becomes apparent how much has been achieved. Questions about therapeutic effects that earlier could be posed and answered only in nebulous and abstract terms can now be restated in ways that permit clear behavioral validation. Although the restatement of the question of treatment in behavioral terms is not a straightforward translation, the gains in specificity easily offset the losses of connotative reference.

Often when treatment is terminated (reinforcement is withdrawn), or reversal of contingencies is tried, the child's progress may disappear as quickly as it came, to be replaced by the original problem behavior. This phenomenon is called extinction, and it has extensive parallels in animal work. The phenomenon has occasioned a good deal of negative comment about the effectiveness of behavioral treatment, since lasting and generalized treatment effects are certainly desirable. But the fact that some or most behaviors do extinguish should not discourage the behavior modifier. Behavioral permanence is not a given. If behavior is to persist in any specified environment, its presence must be designed into the treatment program. Exactly how to insure long-lasting, generalized change has become of major concern in behavior modification, since it has now been shown that its main treatment variables do make a difference.

There are several approaches available in solving the problems of generalization and endurance of behavior change. Several are discussed and demonstrated in the papers we present in this book. One path would be to rearrange those reinforcers that are already effective (functional) in the child's day-to-day environment. Behavior problems are often the result of improper management by those persons who are effective reinforcers for the child. For example, a child who is given affection and attention for undesirable crying, whining, or tantruming may increase his use of these childish behaviors. Here, it is the child's social environment that seems most in need of modification, and such changes may be evolved by consultation with and training of the child's parents and caretakers and by training his peers.

Sometimes it is difficult to infer that a child's parents reinforce him incorrectly. Even careful observations may suggest that the mother is not deviant in her reinforcement practices, and she may have several other children who function adequately within the same home. In such instances it is possible that the environment has acquired certain deviant reinforcing functions for one child and not for the others. For example, his mother's approval may function as punishment, and her disapproval may be his reward. The mother goes through administering all the right contingencies, but they have the opposite effect for the particular child. In order to observe generalized and long-lasting changes in such cases, the stimulus functions of the child's environment must be changed so that approval and disapproval work the same way for him as they do for other children.

The notion of deviant reinforcement functions can work in other ways. The normal child may have learned something that the deviant child does not know about his environment's resources. Thus, the same reinforcers that maintain acceptable behavior in the normal child fail to reinforce desirable behaviors in the deviant child in the same environment. This consideration leads to another attack on the problems of generalization and persistence of behavior change. One may attempt to give the child the behavioral repertoire that puts him in contact with reinforcers that, although available to him in his normal environment, he is not performing the behaviors to obtain. One may build these new behaviors in special therapeutic environments and then depend on the natural environment to support the behavior gains. For example, the child who does not smile when he meets adults may not do so because he does not know how to smile or how otherwise to get reinforcers. He may be taught to smile, however, and thus obtain access to the reinforcers that adults dispense when they exchange smiles with children. These consequences may then be depended on to maintain smiling permanently in the child's repertoire. No special modification in the natural environment is needed. Sometimes treatment may have as its major purpose the building of more complex behaviors that can place the child in contact with reinforcers that are available only to those who have the skills to get them. Training in social skills, academic behaviors, sports, and the like gives the child access to various reinforcers and ensures the persistence of his new skills.

The use of such training procedures introduces the child to new worlds of reinforcement possibilities and gives the best guarantee of generalized behavior change. Of course, this presupposes that his deficiency was primarily a deficiency in behavioral skills, rather than acquired reinforcement (motivation).

It is possible, however, that the child who does not smile to adults or turn out for athletics fails to do so because the payoff (reinforcement) that maintains these behaviors (the adult approval, competition, whatever) is neutral for him. In this case, one can either build the desired behaviors using artificial experimental reinforcers (such as tokens) and expect quick extinction when the reinforcers are withdrawn; or, one can concentrate on helping the child to acquire the new reinforcers so that he will behave in order to gain approval. Woefully little is known about how to build secondary reinforcers.

We have tried to provide examples of both these approaches to the problem of effective treatment: modifying the stimulus functions of the environment and building new behaviors. The latter has received the major research emphasis up to now. The future efforts of behavior modification research may well focus more on an understanding of how to help children acquire stimulus functions (such as motivations). We, as researchers, also need to understand better what it is about the environment of normal children that can make them so delighted with it.

REFERENCE

BORING, E. G. A *History of Experimental Psychology* (2nd ed.), New York: Appleton-Century-Crofts, 1950.

1

RESEARCH
PROCEDURES

The papers in this section present a rationale for the use of the research design common to most of the papers selected for this book. In this design a single child or a group of children is exposed to a series of experimental conditions. Differences in behavior are determined through the inspection of behavior measures taken frequently in each condition. This research design is not the traditional method of investigating the results of therapeutic treatment. It resembles a study of treatment process rather than of treatment outcome. The latter has customarily been studied through the use of control group designs. However, the control group design has not been used much in behavior modification with children.

Baer, Wolf, and Risley propose the single–subject research design for a context even wider than that of psychotherapy research—the investigation of socially significant problems in applied psychology. The authors emphasize that procedures should be categorized into specific stimulus and response variables. This method of analysis involves concentration on achieving changes in specific behaviors rather than changes in more general client characteristics, as has been customary in more traditional treatment. Objective and specific definition of all variables to be measured is emphasized. This concentration on measurement is intended partly to facilitate the communication of procedures and results to other researcher-therapists—an advantage that should contribute a great deal to the methodology's potential for obtaining usable treatment techniques.

Bijou, Peterson, and Ault present a discussion of research methodology in the context of the field research investigation—one that also encompasses considerably more than treatment of behavior problems. They elaborate some of the points made in the preceding article, reemphasizing the importance of reliable measurement and of the analysis of behavioral events in terms of their environmental concomitants. A number of illustrations of ways to obtain measures on the frequency of interaction is also provided.

These two studies provide a basis for distinguishing between the viewpoints of users of within-subject research design and those of control group research design adherents. Bucher expands on these distinctions—both to point out some problems in the more traditional research methods and to clarify the bases for our own preference for the within-subject research model and for the terminology and measurement appropriate for its use.

DONALD M. BAER
MONTROSE M. WOLF
TODD R. RISLEY
University of Kansas

Some current dimensions
of applied behavior analysis

The analysis of individual behavior is a problem in scientific demonstration, reasonably well understood (Skinner, 1953, Sec. 1), comprehensively described (Sidman, 1960), and quite thoroughly practised (*Journal of the Experimental Analysis of Behavior*, 1957–). That analysis has been pursued in many settings over many years. Despite variable precision, elegance, and power, it has resulted in general descriptive statements of mechanisms that can produce many of the forms that individual behavior may take.

The statement of these mechanisms establishes the possibility of their application to problem behavior. A society willing to consider a technology of its own behavior apparently is likely to support that application when it deals with socially important behaviors, such as retardation, crime, mental illness, or education. Such applications have appeared in recent years. Their current number and the interest which they create apparently suffice to generate a journal for their display. That display may well lead to the widespread examination of these applications, their refinement, and eventu-

Reprinted from *Journal of Applied Behavior Analysis*, 1968, 1, 91–97, with permission of the publisher and the authors. Copyright 1968 by the Society for the Experimental Analysis of Behavior, Inc.

9

ally their replacement by better applications. Better applications, it is hoped, will lead to a better state of society, to whatever extent the behavior of its members can contribute to the goodness of a society. Since the evaluation of what is a "good" society is in itself a behavior of its members, this hope turns on itself in a philosophically interesting manner. However, it is at least a fair presumption that behavioral applications, when effective, can sometimes lead to social approval and adoption.

Behavioral applications are hardly a new phenomenon. Analytic behavioral applications, it seems, are. Analytic behavioral application is the process of applying sometimes tentative principles of behavior to the improvement[1] of specific behaviors, and simultaneously evaluating whether or not any changes noted are indeed attributable to the process of application —and if so, to what parts of that process. In short, analytic behavioral application is a self-examining, self-evaluating, discovery-oriented research procedure for studying behavior. So is all experimental behavioral research (at least, according to the usual strictures of modern graduate training). The differences are matters of emphasis and of selection.

The differences between applied and basic research are not differences between that which "discovers" and that which merely "applies" what is already known. Both endeavors ask what controls the behavior under study. Non-applied research is likely to look at any behavior, and at any variable which may conceivably relate to it. Applied research is constrained to look at variables which can be effective in improving the behavior under study. Thus it is equally a matter of research to discover that the behaviors typical of retardates can be related to oddities of their chromosome structure and to oddities of their reinforcement history. But (currently) the chromosome structure of the retardate does not lend itself to experimental manipulation in the interests of bettering that behavior, whereas his reinforcement input is always open to current re-design.

Similarly, applied research is constrained to examining behaviors which are socially important, rather than convenient for study. It also implied, very frequently, the study of those behaviors in their usual social settings, rather than in a "laboratory" setting. But a laboratory is simply a

---

[1] If a behavior is socially important, the usual behavior analysis will aim at its improvement. The social value dictating this choice is obvious. However, it can be just as illuminating to demonstrate how a behavior may be worsened, and there will arise occasions when it will be socially important to do so. Disruptive classroom behavior may serve as an example. Certainly it is a frequent plague of the educational system. A demonstration of what teacher procedures produce more of this behavior is not necessarily the reverse of a demonstration of how to promote positive study behaviors. There may be classroom situations in which the teacher cannot readily establish high rates of study, yet still could avoid high rates of disruption, if she knew what in her own procedures leads to this disruption. The demonstration which showed her that would thus have its value.

place so designed that experimental control of relevant variables is as easy as possible. Unfortunately, the usual social setting for important behaviors is rarely such a place. Consequently, the analysis of socially important behaviors becomes experimental only with difficulty. As the terms are used here, a non-experimental analysis is a contradiction in terms. Thus, analytic behavioral applications by definition achieve experimental control of the processes they contain, but since they strive for this control against formidable difficulties, they achieve it less often per study than would a laboratory-based attempt. Consequently, the rate of displaying experimental control required of behavioral applications has become correspondingly less than the standards typical of laboratory research. This is not because the applier is an easy-going, liberal, or generous fellow, but because society rarely will allow its important behaviors, in their correspondingly important settings, to be manipulated repeatedly for the merely logical comfort of a scientifically skeptical audience.

Thus, the evaluation of a study which purports to be an applied behavior analysis is somewhat different than the evaluation of a similar laboratory analysis. Obviously, the study must be *applied, behavioral,* and *analytic*; in addition, it should be *technological, conceptually systematic,* and *effective,* and it should display some generality. These terms are explored below and compared to the criteria often stated for the evaluation of behavioral research which, though analytic, is not applied.

Applied

The label *applied* is not determined by the research procedures used but by the interest which society shows in the problems being studied. In behavioral application, the behavior, stimuli, and/or organism under study are chosen because of their importance to man and society, rather than their importance to theory. The non-applied researcher may study eating behavior, for example, because it relates directly to metabolism, and there are hypotheses about the interaction between behavior and metabolism. The non-applied researcher also may study bar-pressing because it is a convenient response for study; easy for the subject, and simple to record and integrate with theoretically significant environmental events. By contrast, the applied researcher is likely to study eating because there are children who eat too little and adults who eat too much, and he will study eating in exactly those individuals rather than in more convenient ones. The applied researcher may also study bar-pressing if it is integrated with socially important stimuli. A program for a teaching machine may use bar-pressing behavior to indicate mastery of an arithmetic skill. It is the arithmetic stimuli which are important. (However, some future applied study could show that bar-pressing is more practical in the process of education than a pencil-writing response.[2])

In applied research, there is typically a close relationship between the behavior and stimuli under study and the subject in whom they are studied. Just as there seem to be few behaviors that are intrinsically the target of application, there are few subjects who automatically confer on their study the status of application. An investigation of visual signal detection in the retardate may have little immediate importance, but a similar study in radar-scope watchers has considerable. A study of language development in the retardate may be aimed directly at an immediate social problem, while a similar study in the MIT sophomore may not. Enhancement of the reinforcing value of praise for the retardate alleviates an immediate deficit in his current environment, but enhancement of the reinforcing value of 400 Hz (cps) tone for the same subject probably does not. Thus, a primary question in the evaluation of applied research is: how immediately important is this behavior or these stimuli to this subject?

Behavioral

Behaviorism and pragmatism seem often to go hand in hand. Applied research is eminently pragmatic; it asks how it is possible to get an individual to do something effectively. Thus it usually studies what subjects can be brought to do rather than what they can be brought to say; unless, of course, a verbal response is the behavior of interest. Accordingly a subject's verbal description of his own non-verbal behavior usually would not be accepted as a measure of his actual behavior unless it were independently substantiated. Hence there is little applied value in the demonstration that an impotent man can be made to say that he no longer is impotent. The relevant question is not what he can say, but what he can do. Application has not been achieved until this question has been answered satisfactorily. (This assumes, of course, that the total goal of the applied researcher is not simply to get his patient-subjects to stop complaining to him. Unless society agrees that this researcher should not be bothered, it will be difficult to defend that goal as socially important.)

Since the behavior of an individual is composed of physical events, its scientific study requires their precise measurement. As a result, the problem of reliable quantification arises immediately. The problem is the same

[2] Research may use the most convenient behaviors and stimuli available, and yet exemplify an ambition in the researcher eventually to achieve application to socially important settings. For example, a study may seek ways to give a light flash a durable conditioned reinforcing function, because the experimenter wishes to know how to enhance school children's responsiveness to approval. Nevertheless, durable bar-pressing for that light flash is no guarantee that the obvious classroom analogue will produce durable reading behavior for teacher statements of "Good!" Until the analogue has been proven sound, application has not been achieved.

for applied research as it is for non-applied research. However, non-applied research typically will choose a response easily quantified in a reliable manner, whereas applied research rarely will have that option. As a result, the applied researcher must try harder, rather than ignore this criterion of all trustworthy research. Current applied research often shows that thoroughly reliable quantification of behavior can be achieved, even in thoroughly difficult settings. However, it also suggests that instrumented recording with its typical reliability will not always be possible. The reliable use of human beings to quantify the behavior of other human beings is an area of psychological technology long since well developed, thoroughly relevant, and very often necessary to applied behavior analysis.

A useful tactic in evaluating the behavioral attributes of a study is to ask not merely, was *behavior* changed? but also, *whose* behavior? Ordinarily it would be assumed that it was the subject's behavior which was altered; yet careful reflection may suggest that this was not necessarily the case. If humans are observing and recording the behavior under study, then any change may represent a change only in their observing and recording responses, rather than in the subject's behavior. Explicit measurement of the reliability of human observers thus becomes not merely good technique, but a prime criterion of whether the study was appropriately behavioral. (A study merely of the behavior of observers is behavioral, of course, but probably irrelevant to the researcher's goal.) Alternatively, it may be that only the experimenter's behavior has changed. It may be reported, for example, that a certain patient rarely dressed himself upon awakening, and consequently would be dressed by his attendant. The experimental technique to be applied might consist of some penalty imposed unless the patient were dressed within half an hour after awakening. Recording of an increased probability of self-dressing under these conditions might testify to the effectiveness of the penalty in changing the behavior; however, it might also testify to the fact that the patient would in fact probably dress himself within half an hour of arising, but previously was rarely left that long undressed before being clothed by his efficient attendant. (The attendant now is the penalty-imposing experimenter and therefore always gives the patient his full half-hour, in the interests of precise experimental technique, of course.) This error is an elementary one, perhaps. But it suggests that in general, when an experiment proceeds from its baseline to its first experimental phase, changes in what is measured need not always reflect the behavior of the subject.

Analytic

The analysis of a behavior, as the term is used here, requires a believable demonstration of the events that can be responsible for the occurrence or non-occurrence of that behavior. An experimenter has achieved an analysis of a behavior when he can exercise control over it. By common laboratory standards, that has meant an ability of the experimenter to turn the behavior on and off, or up and down, at will. Laboratory standards have usually made this control clear by demonstrating it repeatedly, even redundantly, over time. Applied research, as noted before, cannot often approach this arrogantly frequent clarity of being in control of important behaviors. Consequently, application, to be analytic, demonstrates control when it can, and thereby presents its audience with a problem of judgment. The problem, of course, is whether the experimenter has shown enough control, and often enough, for believability. Laboratory demonstrations, either by over-replication or an acceptable probability level derived from statistical tests of grouped data, make this judgment more implicit than explicit. As Sidman points out (1960), there is still a problem of judgment in any event, and it is probably better when explicit.

There are at least two designs commonly used to demonstrate reliable control of an important behavioral change. The first can be referred to as the "reversal" technique. Here a behavior is measured, and the measure is examined over time until its stability is clear. Then, the experimental variable is applied. The behavior continues to be measured, to see if the variable will produce a behavioral change. If it does, the experimental variable is discontinued or altered, to see if the behavioral change just brought about depends on it. If so, the behavioral change should be lost or diminished (thus the term "reversal"). The experimental variable then is applied again, to see if the behavioral change can be recovered. If it can, it is pursued further, since this is applied research and the behavioral change sought is an important one. It may be reversed briefly again, and yet again, if the setting in which the behavior takes place allows further reversals. But that setting may be a school system or a family, and continued reversals may not be allowed. They may appear in themselves to be detrimental to the subject if pursued too often. (Whether they are in fact detrimental is likely to remain an unexamined question so long as the social setting in which the behavior is studied dictates against using them repeatedly. Indeed, it may be that repeated reversals in some applications have a positive effect on the subject, possibly contributing to the discrimination of relevant stimuli involved in the problem.)

In using the reversal technique, the experimenter is attempting to show that an analysis of the behavior is at hand: that whenever he applies a certain variable, the behavior is produced, and whenever he removes this variable, the behavior is lost. Yet applied behavior analysis is exactly the kind of research which can make this technique self-defeating in time. Application typically means producing valuable behavior; valuable behavior usually meets extra-experimental reinforcement in a social setting; thus, valuable behavior, once set up, may no longer be dependent upon the experimental technique which created it. Consequently, the number of reversals possible in applied studies may be limited by the nature of the social setting in which the behavior takes place, in more ways than one.

An alternative to the reversal technique may be called the "multiple baseline" technique. This alternative may be of particular value when a behavior appears to be irreversible or when reversing the behavior is undesirable. In the multiple-baseline technique, a number of responses are identified and measured over time to provide baselines against which changes can be evaluated. With these baselines established, the experimenter then applies an experimental variable to one of the behaviors, produces a change in it, and perhaps notes little or no change in the other baselines. If so, rather than reversing the just-produced change, he instead applies the experimental variable to one of the other, as yet unchanged, responses. If it changes at that point, evidence is accruing that the experimental variable is indeed effective, and that the prior change was not simply a matter of coincidence. The variable then may be applied to still another response, and so on. The experimenter is attempting to show that he has a reliable experimental variable, in that each behavior changes maximally only when the experimental variable is applied to it.

How many reversals, or how many baselines, make for believability is a problem for the audience. If statistical analysis is applied, the audience must then judge the suitability of the inferential statistic chosen and the propriety of these data for that test. Alternatively, the audience may inspect the data directly and relate them to past experience with similar data and similar procedures. In either case, the judgments required are highly qualitative, and rules cannot always be stated profitably. However, either of the foregoing designs gathers data in ways that exemplify the concept of replication, and replication is the essence of believability. At the least, it would seem that an approach to replication is better than no approach at all. This should be especially true for so embryonic a field as behavioral application, the very possibility of which is still occasionally denied.

The preceding discussion has been aimed at the problem of *reliability*: whether or not a certain procedure was responsible for a corresponding behavioral change. The two general procedures described hardly exhaust the possibilities. Each of them has many variations now seen in practice; and current experience suggests that many more variations are badly needed, if the technology of important behavioral change is to be consistently believable. Given some approach to reliability, there are further analyses of obvious value which can be built upon that base. For example, there is analysis in the sense of simplification and separation of component processes. Often enough, current behavioral procedures are complex, even "shotgun" in their application. When they succeed, they clearly need to be analyzed into their effective components. Thus, a teacher giving M & M's to a child may succeed in changing his behavior as planned. However, she has almost certainly confounded her attention and/or approval with each M & M. Further analysis may be approached by her use of attention alone, the effects of which can be compared to the effects of attention coupled with candies. Whether she will discontinue the M & M's, as in the reversal technique, or apply attention with M & M's to certain behaviors and attention alone to certain others, as in the multiple baseline method, is again the problem in basic reliability discussed above. Another form of analysis is parametric: a demonstration of the effectiveness of different values of some variable in changing behavior. The problem again will be to make such an analysis reliable, and, as before, that might be approached by the repeated alternate use of different values on the same behavior (reversal), or by the application of different values to different groups of responses (multiple baseline). At this stage in the development of applied behavior analysis, primary concern is usually with reliability, rather than with parametric analysis or component analysis.

Technological

"Technological" here means simply that the techniques making up a particular behavioral application are completely identified and described. In this sense, "play therapy" is not a technological description, nor is "social reinforcement". For purposes of application, all the salient ingredients of play therapy must be described as a set of contingencies between child response, therapist response, and play materials, before a statement of technique has been approached. Similarly, all the ingredients of social reinforcement must be specified (stimuli, contingency, and schedule) to qualify as a technological procedure.

The best rule of thumb for evaluating a procedure description as technological is probably to ask whether a typically trained reader could replicate that procedure well enough to produce the same results, given only a reading of the description. This is very much the same criterion applied to procedure descriptions in non-applied research, of course. It needs emphasis, apparently, in that there occasionally exists a less-than-precise stereotype of applied research. Where application is novel, and derived from principles produced through non-applied research, as in current applied behavior analysis, the reverse holds with great urgency.

Especially where the problem is application, procedural descriptions require considerable detail about all possible contingencies of procedure. It is not enough to say what is to be done when the subject makes response R_1; it is essential also whenever possible to say what is to be done if the subject makes the alternative responses, R_2, R_3, *etc.* For example, one may read that temper tantrums in children are often extinguished by closing the child in his room for the duration of the tantrums plus ten minutes. Unless that procedure description also states what should be done if the child tries to leave the room early, or kicks out the window, or smears feces on the walls, or begins to make strangling sounds, *etc.*, it is not precise technological description.

Conceptual Systems

The field of applied behavior analysis will probably advance best if the published descriptions of its procedures are not only precisely technological, but also strive for relevance to principle. To describe exactly how a preschool teacher will attend to jungle-gym climbing in a child frightened of heights is good technological description; but further to call it a social reinforcement procedure relates it to basic concepts of behavioral development. Similarly, to describe the exact sequence of color changes whereby a child is moved from a color discrimination to a form discrimination is good; to refer also to "fading" and "errorless discrimination" is better. In both cases, the total description is adequate for successful replication by the reader; and it also shows the reader how similar procedures may be derived from basic principles. This can have the effect of making a body of technology into a discipline rather than a collection of tricks. Collections of tricks historically have been difficult to expand systematically, and when they were extensive, difficult to learn and teach.

Effective

If the application of behavioral techniques does not produce large enough effects for practical value, then application has failed. Non-applied research often may be extremely valuable when it produces small but reliable effects, in that these effects testify to the operation of some variable which in itself has great theoretical importance. In application, the theoretical importance of a variable is usually not at issue. Its practical importance, specifically its power in altering behavior enough to be socially important, is the essential criterion. Thus, a study which shows that a new classroom technique can raise the grade level achievements of culturally deprived children from D− to D is not an obvious example of applied behavior analysis. That same study might conceivably revolutionize educational theory, but it clearly has not yet revolutionized education. This is of course a matter of degree: an increase in those children from D− to C might well be judged an important success by an audience which thinks that C work is a great deal different than D work, especially if C students are much less likely to become drop-outs than D students.

In evaluating whether a given application has produced enough of a behavioral change to deserve the label, a pertinent question can be, how much did that behavior need to be changed? Obviously, that is not a scientific question, but a practical one. Its answer is likely to be supplied by people who must deal with the behavior. For example, ward personnel may be able to say that a hospitalized mute schizophrenic trained to use 10 verbal labels is not much better off in self-help skills than before, but that one with 50 such labels is a great deal more effective. In this case, the opinions of ward aides may be more relevant than the opinions of psycholinguists.

Generality

A behavioral change may be said to have generality if it proves durable over time, if it appears in a wide variety of possible environments, or if it spreads to a wide variety of related behaviors. Thus, the improvement of articulation in a clinic setting will prove to have generality if it endures into the future after the clinic visits stop; if the improved articulation is heard at home, at school, and on dates; or if the articulation of all words, not just the ones treated, improves. Application means practical improvement in important behaviors; thus, the more general that application, the better in many cases. Therapists dealing with the development of heterosexual behavior may well point out there are socially appropriate limits to its generality, once developed; such limitations to generality are usually obvious. That generality is a valuable characteristic of applied behavior analysis which should be examined explicitly apparently is not quite that obvious, and is stated here for emphasis.

That generality is not automatically accomplished whenever behavior is changed also needs occasional emphasis, especially in the evaluation of applied behavior analysis. It is sometimes assumed that application has failed when generalization does not take place in any widespread form. Such a conclusion has no generality itself. A procedure which is effective in changing behavior in one setting may perhaps be easily repeated in other settings, and thus accomplish the generalization sought. Furthermore, it may well prove the case that a given behavior change need be programmed in only a certain number of settings, one after another, perhaps, to accomplish eventually widespread generalization. A child may have 15 techniques for disrupting his parents, for example. The elimination of the most prevalent of these may still leave the remaining 14 intact and in force. The technique may still prove both valuable and fundamental, if when applied to the next four successfully, it also results in the "generalized" loss of the remaining 10. In general, generalization should be programmed, rather than expected or lamented.

Thus, in summary, an *applied* behavior analysis will make obvious the importance of the behavior changed, its quantitative characteristics, the experimental manipulations which analyze with clarity what was responsible for the change, the technologically exact description of all procedures contributing to that change, the effectiveness of those procedures in making sufficient change for value, and the generality of that change.

REFERENCES

Journal of the Experimental Analysis of Behavior. Bloomington: Society for the Experimental Analysis of Behavior, 1957.

SIDMAN, MURRAY. *Tactics of scientific research.* New York: Basic Books, 1960.

SKINNER, B. F. *Science and human behavior.* New York: Macmillan, 1953.

SIDNEY W. BIJOU
ROBERT F. PETERSON
MARION H. AULT
University of Illinois

A method to integrate descriptive and experimental field studies at the level of data and empirical concepts[1]

It is the thesis of this paper that data from descriptive and experimental field studies can be interrelated at the level of data and empirical concepts if both sets are derived from frequency-of-occurrence measures. The methodology proposed for a descriptive field study is predicated on three assumptions: (1) The primary data of psychology are the observable interactions of a biological organism and environmental events, past and present. (2) Theoretical concepts and laws are derived from empirical concepts and laws, which in turn are derived from the raw data. (3) Descriptive field studies describe interactions between behavioral and environmental events; experimental field studies provide information on their functional relationships. The ingredients of a descriptive field investigation using frequency measures consist of: (1) specifying in objective terms the situation in which the study is conducted, (2) defining and recording behavioral and environmental events in observable terms, and (3) measuring observer reliability. Field descriptive studies following the procedures suggested

Reprinted from *Journal of Applied Behavior Analysis*, 1968, 1, 175–91, with permission of the publisher and the authors. Copyright 1968 by the Society for the Experimental Analysis of Behavior, Inc.

---

[1] The formulation presented here was generated from the research conducted under grants from the U.S. Public Health Service, National Institute of Mental Health (M-2208, M-2232, and MH-12067), and from the U.S. Office of Education, Handicapped Children and Youth Branch (Grant No. 32-23-1020-6002, Proposal No. R-006).

here would reveal interesting new relationships in the usual ecological settings and would also provide provocative cues for experimental studies. On the other hand, field-experimental studies using frequency measures would probably yield findings that would suggest the need for describing new interactions in specific natural situations.

Psychology, like the other natural sciences, depends for its advancement upon both descriptive accounts and functional analyses of its primary data. Descriptive studies answer the question "How?". They may, for example, report the manner in which a Bantu mother nurses her child, or the way in which the Yellow Shafted Flicker mates. Experimental studies, on the other hand, provide the "Why?". They might discuss the conditions which establish and maintain the relationships between the mother and infant, between the male and female birds.

It has been claimed that progress in the behavioral sciences would be enhanced by more emphasis on descriptive studies. This may be true, but one may wish to speculate on why descriptive accounts of behavior have been deemphasized. One possibility is the difficulty of relating descriptive and experimental data. For example, a descriptive study of parent-child behavior in the home may have data in the form of ratings on a series of scales (Baldwin, Kalhorn, and Breese, 1949), while an experimental study on the same subject may have data in the form of frequencies of events (Hawkins, Peterson, Schweid, and Bijou, 1966). Findings from the first study cannot reasonably be integrated with the second at the level of data and empirical concepts. Anyone interested in relating the two must resort to imprecise theory or concepts like "permissive mother," "laissez-faire atmosphere," "controlling child," "negativism," *etc.* This practice is unacceptable to psychologists who believe that all concepts must be based on or linked to empirical events.

It is the thesis of this paper that descriptive field studies (which include cross-cultural, ecological, and normative investigations) and experimental field studies can be performed so that the data and empirical terms in each are continuous, interchangeable, and mutually interrelatable.

Barker and Wright (1955) state that one of the aims of their ecological investigations is to produce data that may be used by all investigators in child behavior and development. Their study of "Midwest" and its children (1955) is in part devoted to the development of a method which provides raw material (which they compared to objects stored in a museum) amenable to analyses from different theoretical points of view. There are two considerations which make this doubtful. First, their data consist of "running accounts of what a person is doing and his situation on the level of direct perception or immediate inference" with "minor interpretations in the form of statements *about* rather than descriptions *of* behavior or situations" (Wright, 1967). It would seem that the material they collect would be serviceable only to those who accept non-observables in the raw data defined according to their prescription. Investigators who prefer to define their hypothetical variables some other way or who wish to exclude non-observables will find it difficult to integrate their data with those in the Barker and Wright studies. Second, final data in the form of running narrations cannot readily be transformed into units describing interactions between behavioral and environmental events, such as duration, intensity, latency, or frequency. Any attempt to convert such verbal accounts into one or more of the interactional dimensions would require so many arbitrary decisions that it would be doubtful whether another investigator could even come close to producing the same operations and results.

If, however, frequency-of-occurrence measures of environmental and behavioral events were used in both descriptive and field experimental studies, data and empirical concepts could be made congruous. The measure of frequency is preferable to that of duration, intensity, and latency for several reasons (Skinner, 1953). First, this measure readily shows changes over short and long periods of observations. Second, it specifies the *amount* of behavior displayed (Honig, 1966). Finally, and perhaps most important, it is applicable to operant behaviors across species. Hence, a methodology based on frequency of events would be serviceable for both experimental and descriptive studies of both human and infra-human subjects. This versatility has been illustrated by Jensen and Bobbitt in a study on mother and infant relationships of the pigtailed macaques (Jensen and Bobbitt, 1967).

With the use of frequency measures, the work of the ecological psychologist and the experimental psychologist would both complement and supplement each other. Descriptive studies would reveal interesting relationships among the raw data that could provide provocative cues for experimental investigations. On the other hand, field experimental studies would probably yield worthwhile leads for descriptive investigations by pointing to the need for observing new combinations of behavioral classes in specified situations. Ecological psychologists would show in terms of frequency of events, the practices of a culture, subculture, or an institutional activity of a subculture; experimental investigators working with the same set of data terms and empirical concepts would attempt to demonstrate the conditions and processes which establish and maintain the interrelationships observed.

Before considering the procedures for conducting a descriptive study using frequency measures, it might be well to make explicit three basic assumptions. The first: for psychology as a natural science, the primary data are the observable interactions between a biological organism and environmental events, past and present. These interrelationships constitute the material to be recorded. This means that the method does not include accounts of behavior isolated from related stimulus events ("Jimmy is a rejected child." "Johnny is a highly *autistic* child." "First Henry moved about by making swimming movements, later he crawled, now he can walk with support.") Furthermore, it means that it excludes statements of generalizations about behavior and environmental interactions. ("This is an extremely aggressive child who is always getting into trouble.") Finally, it means that it excludes accounts of interactions between behavioral and environmental events intertwined with hypothetical constructs. ("The preschool child makes errors in describing the water line in a jar because of his undeveloped cognitive structure.")

The second assumption: concepts and laws in psychology are derived from raw data. Theoretical concepts evolve from empirical concepts and empirical concepts from raw data; theoretical interactional laws are derived from empirical laws and empirical laws from relationships in the raw data.

The third assumption: descriptive studies provide information only on events and their occurrence. They do not provide information on the functional properties of the events or the functional relationships among the events. Experimental studies provide that kind of information.

We move on to consider the procedures involved in conducting a descriptive field investigation. They include: (1) specifications of the situation in which a study is conducted, (2) definitions of behavioral and environmental events in observable terms, (3) measurements of observer reliability, and (4) procedures for collecting, analyzing, and interpreting the data. We terminate the paper with a brief illustration of a study for the behavior of a 4-yr-old boy in a laboratory nursery school.

Specifying the Situation in Which a Study Is Conducted

We define the situation in which a study is conducted in terms of its physical and social setting and the *observable events* that occur within its bounds. The physical setting may be a part of the child's home, a hospital or residential institution, a store, or a playground in the city park. It may be a nursery school, a classroom in an elementary school, or a room in a child guidance clinic.

The specific part of the home selected as a setting may consist of the living room and kitchen if the design of the home precludes flexible observation (Hawkins, Peterson, Schweid, and Bijou, 1966). In a hospital it might be the child's bedroom, the dining room, or the day room (Wolf,

Risley, and Mees, 1964). In a state school for the retarded, it may be a special academic classroom (Birnbrauer, Wolf, Kidder, and Tague, 1965); in a regular elementary school, a classroom (Becker, Madsen, Arnold, and Thomas, 1967); and in a nursery school, the schoolroom and the play yard (Harris, Wolf, and Baer, 1964).

During the course of a study, changes in the physical aspect of the situation may occur despite efforts to keep them constant. Some will be sufficiently drastic to prevent further study until restoration of the original conditions (*e.g.*, power failure for several days). Others will be within normal limits (*e.g.*, replacement of old chairs in the child's bedroom) and hence will not warrant disrupting the research.

The social aspect of the situation in a home might consist of the mother and the subject's younger sibling (Hawkins, *et al.*, 1966); in a child guidance clinic, the therapist and the other children in the therapy group. In a nursery school it might include the head teacher, the assistant teacher, and the children (Johnston, Kelley, Harris, and Wolf, 1966).

Sometimes the social situation changes according to routines and the investigator wishes to take records in the different situations created by the changes. For example, he may wish to describe the behavior of a preschool child as he engages in each of four activities in the morning hours of the nursery school: show and tell, music and games, snack, and pre-academic exercises. Each would be described as a field situation and data would be taken in each as if it were a separate situation. The events recorded could be the same for all the activities (*e.g.*, frequency of social contacts), or they could be specific to each depending upon the nature of the activity. They could also be a combination of both (*e.g.*, frequency of social contacts and sum total of prolonged productive activity in each pre-academic exercise).

Major variations in social composition in a home study that would be considered disruptive could include the presence of other members of the family, relatives, or friends. In a nursery school, it might be the absence of the head teacher, presence of the child's mother, or the absence of many of the children. These and other events like them would probably call a halt to data collection until the standard situation is returned.

Temporary social disruptions may take many forms. For example, in the home the phone may ring, a salesman may appear, a neighbor may visit; and in the nursery school it might be a holiday preparation, or a birthday party for a member of the group.

In summary, the physical and social conditions in which an ecological study is conducted is specified at the outset. Whether the variations occurring during the study are sufficient to disrupt data collection depends, in large measure on the interactions to be studied, practical considerations, and the investigator's experience in similar situations in the past. However, accounts of changes in physical and social conditions, whether major or minor, are described and noted on the data sheets.

Defining Behavioral and Stimulus
Events in Observable Terms

In this method we derive definitions of behavioral and stimulus events from preliminary investigations in the actual setting. Such pilot investigations are also used to provide preliminary information on the frequencies of occurrences of the events of interest and the feasibility of the situation for study.

A miniature episode in the life of a pre-school boy, Timmy, will serve as an example. We start with having the observer make a running description of Timmy's behavior in the play yard in the style she would use if she were a reporter for a magazine.

> Timmy is playing by himself in a sandbox in a play yard in which other children are playing. A teacher stands nearby. Timmy tires of the sandbox and walks over to climb the monkeybars. Timmy shouts at the teacher saying, "Mrs. Simpson, watch me." Timmy climbs to the top of the apparatus and shouts again to the teacher, "Look how high I am. I'm higher than anybody." The teacher comments on Timmy's climbing ability with approval. Timmy then climbs down and runs over to a tree, again demanding that the teacher watch him. The teacher, however, ignores Timmy and walks back into the classroom. Disappointed, Timmy walks toward the sandbox instead of climbing the tree. A little girl nearby cries out in pain as she stumbles and scrapes her knee. Timmy ignores her and continues to walk to the sandbox.

To obtain a clearer impression of the time relationships among antecedent stimulus events, responses, and consequent stimulus events, the objective aspects of the narrative account are transcribed into a three-column form and each behavioral and stimulus event is numbered in consecutive order.

> *Setting:* Timmy (T.) is playing alone in a sandbox in a play yard in which there are other children playing. T. is scooping sand into a bucket with a shovel, then dumping the sand onto a pile. A teacher, Mrs. Simpson (S.), stands approximately six feet away but does not attend to T.

Time	Antecedent Event	Response	Consequent Social Event
9:14		1. T. throws bucket and shovel into corner of sandbox.	
		2. . . . stands up.	
		3. . . . walks over to monkeybars and stops.	

Time	Antecedent Event	Response	Consequent Social Event
		4. . . . turns toward teacher.	
		5. . . . says, "Mrs. Simpson, watch me."	
			6. Mrs. S. turns toward Timmy.
	6. Mrs. S. turns toward Timmy	7. T. climbs to top of apparatus.	
		8. . . . looks toward teacher.	
		9. . . . says, "Look how high I am. I'm higher than anybody."	
9:16			10. Mrs. S. says, "That's good, Tim. You're getting quite good at that."
	10. Mrs. S. says, "That's good, Tim. You're getting quite good at that."	11. T. climbs down.	
		12. . . . runs over to tree.	
		13. . . . says, "Watch me climb the tree, Mrs. Simpson."	
			14. Mrs. S. turns and walks toward classroom.
	14. Mrs. S. turns and walks toward classroom.	15. T. stands, looking toward Mrs. S.	
9:18	16. Girl nearby trips and falls, bumping knee.		
	17. Girl cries.		
		18. T. proceeds to sandbox.	
		19. . . . picks up bucket and shovel.	
		20. . . . resumes play with sand.	

Note that a response event (*e.g.*, 5. . . . says, "Mrs. Simpson, watch me.") may be followed by a consequent social event (*e.g.*, 6. Mrs. S. turns toward Timmy.) which may also be the antecedent event for the next response (*e.g.*, 7. T. climbs to top of apparatus.) Note, too, that the three-column form retains the temporal relationships in the narration. Note, finally, that only the child's responses are described. Inferences about feelings, motives, and other presumed internal states are omitted. Even words like "ignores" and "disappointed" do not appear in the table.

On the basis of several such running accounts and analyses a tentative set of stimulus and response definitives are derived and criteria for their occurrence are specified. This material serves as a basis for a provisional code consisting of symbols and definitions. Observers are trained to use the code and are tested in a series of trial runs in the actual situation.

Consider now the problems involved in defining behavioral and stimulus terms, devising codes, and recording events. But first let us comment briefly on the pros and cons of two recording methods.

When discussing the definitions of events and assessing reliability of observers, we refer to observers who record with paper and pencil. In each instance the same could be accomplished by electro-mechanical devices. The investigator must decide which procedure best suits his purpose. For example, Lovaas used instruments to record responses in studies on autistic behavior. He and his co-workers have developed apparatus and worked out procedures for recording as many as 12 responses in a setting. The following is a brief description of the apparatus and its operation (Lovaas, Freitag, Gold, and Kassorla, 1965*b*).

> The apparatus for quantifying behaviors involved two units: an Esterline-Angus 20-pen recorder and an operating panel with 12 buttons, each button mounted on a switch (Microswitch: "Typewriter pushbutton switch"). When depressed, these buttons activated a corresponding pen on the Esterline recorder. The buttons were arranged on a 7 by 14-in. panel in the configuration of the fingertips of an outstretched hand. Each button could be pressed independently of any of the others and with the amount of force similar to that required for an electric typewriter key (p. 109).

An electro-mechanical recording device has certain advantages over a paper-and-pencil system. It requires less attention, thus allowing the observer to devote more of his effort to watching for critical events. Furthermore, instruments of this sort make it possible to assess more carefully the temporal relationships between stimulus and response events, as well as to record a large number of responses within a given period. On the other hand, paper-and-pencil recording methods are more flexible. They can be used in any setting since they do not require special facilities, such as a power supply.

Defining and Recording Behavioral Events

The main problem in defining behavioral events is establishing a criterion or criteria in a way that two or more observers can agree on their occurrences. For example, if it is desired to record the number of times a child hits other children, the criteria of a hitting response must be clearly given so that the observer can discriminate hitting from patting or shoving responses. Or if it is desired to count the number of times a child says, "No", the criteria for the occurrence of "No" must be specified to discriminate it from other words the child utters, and from non-verbal forms of negative expressions. Sometimes definitions must include criteria of loudness and duration. For example in a study of crying behavior (Hart, *et al.*, 1964), crying was defined to discriminate it from whining and screaming and it had to be (a) "loud enough to be heard at least 50 feet away, and (b) of 5-sec or more duration."

The definitions of complex behavioral events are treated the same way. Studies concerned with such intricate categories of behavior as isolate behavior, fantasy-play, aggressive behavior, and temper-tantrums must establish objective criteria for each class of responses included in the category. We shall elaborate on defining multiple response classes in the following discussion on recording behavioral events.

There are two styles of recording behavioral events in field situations: one consists of logging the incidences of responses (and in many situations, their durations); the other of registering the frequencies of occurrences and non-occurrences within a time interval. Sometimes frequencies and their durations are recorded (Lovaas, Freitag, Gold, and Kassorla, 1965b).

Recording the frequencies of occurrences and non-occurrences in a time interval requires the observer to make a mark (and only one mark) in each time interval in which the response occurred. It is apparent that in this procedure the maximum frequency of a response is determined by the size of the time unit selected. If a 5-sec interval were used, the maximum frequency would be 12 per min; if a 10-sec interval were employed, the maximal rate would be six responses per minute, and so on. Thus, in studies with a high frequency of behavioral episodes, small time intervals are employed to obtain high correspondence between the actual and recorded frequencies of occurrences.

There are several approaches to defining and recording single and multiple class responses. One method consists of developing a *specific observational code* for each problem studied. For example, in studies conducted at the Child Behavior Laboratory at the University of Illinois, codes were prepared for attending-to-work behavior, spontaneous speech, and tantruming. The attending-to-work or time-on-task code was employed with a distractible 7-yr-old boy. It included: (1) counting words, (2) looking at the words, and (3) writing numbers or letters. When any of these behaviors occurred at any time during a 20-sec interval, it was scored as an interval of work. In a second study involving a 6-yr-old boy with a similar problem, this code was used with one additional feature: in order for the observer to mark occurrence in the 20-sec interval, the child had to engage in relevant behavior for a minimum of 10 sec. The reliability on both codes averaged 90% for two observers over 12 sessions. (See Section 3 for our method of determining reliability.)

A code for spontaneous speech was developed for a 4-yr-old girl who rarely spoke. Incidences of speech were recorded whenever she uttered a word or words which were not preceded by a question or a prompt by a peer or teacher. Although this class of behavior was somewhat difficult to discriminate, reliability averaged 80% for two observers over 15 sessions.

Tantrum behaviors exhibited by a 6-yr-old boy were defined as including crying, whining, sobbing, and whimpering. The average reliability for this class of behavior was 80% for two observers over 11 sessions.

In contrast to this more or less vocal form of tantrum behavior, a code developed in another study on temper-tantrums centered around gross motor responses of an autistic child (Brawley, Harris, Allen, Fleming, and Peterson, 1968, in press). Here a tantrum was recorded whenever the child engaged in self-hitting in combination with any one of the following forms of behavior: (1) loud crying, (2) kicking, or (3) throwing himself or objects about.

Another method of defining and recording responses is to develop a *general observational code*, one that is inclusive enough to study many behaviors in a given field situation. An example of such a code is the one prepared by the nursery school staff at the University of Washington. In essence, verbal and motor responses are recorded in relation to physical and social events using a three or four track system. Tables 1 and 2 show sample lines from data sheets. Each box represents an interval of 15 sec.

In Table 1, which is a segment of a data sheet for a nursery school girl who changed activities with high frequency, entries were made in the boxes in the top row to indicate occurrences of vocalizations (V). Entries were made in the middle row to shop proximity (P) or physical contact (T) with another person, and in the bottom row to indicate contact with physical objects (E) or with children and whether the interaction was parallel play (A) or shared play (C). Other marks and symbols are added in accordance with the problem studied. For example, each single bracket in Table 1 indicates leaving of one activity and embarking on another. During the 6-min period in which records were taken (24 15-sec intervals),

TABLE 1 Sample line from a data sheet of nursery school girl who changed activities with high frequency

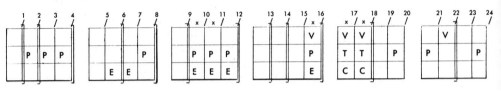

TABLE 2 Sample line from a data sheet of nursery school boy displaying aggressive behaviors

1	2	3	4	5	6	7	8	9	10	11	12	13	14	15	16	17	18	19	20	21	22	23	24	25	26	27	28	29	30
V				V								Ⓥ			V	V	V	V	V		Ⓥ	Ⓥ					V		
P	P			P	P	P	P									P	P	Ⓣ	Ⓣ	P		P	P	P	P	P	P	T	P
C	C			C	C	C	C	C	C	C	A	A	A	A	A	A	A	A	A	A	A	A		A	A	C	C		
				B	B	B	B	B	B	B					B	B	B	B	B	B	B	B	B	B	B	B	B		

the child changed her activity 12 times. During that time the teacher gave approval five times contingent upon her verbal or proximity behavior as indicated by X's above the top line (10, 11, 16, 17, and 18). A tally of the data indicated that she spent most of the 6-min period alone or in close proximity to another child, sometimes on the same piece of play equipment. During three intervals (16, 17, and 18) she talked (V), touched (T), and engaged in physical interaction with another child (C). Even though rate of activity change, and not peer interaction, was the subject of the study, the other data on social behavior provided interesting information: decline in rate of activity change was related to an increase in rate of appropriate peer behavior.

This code can be readily modified to handle more complex interactions. For example, it was used to record the behavior of a nursery school boy who shouted epithets, kicked, and hit other children. Ordinarily these aggressive acts would appear in the record sheets undifferentiated from a non-aggressive interaction. To differentiate them from other behaviors the symbol letter was circled if the behavior met the criteria of an aggressive act. As shown in Table 2, intervals 13, 22, and 23 contain a "V" with a circle, Ⓥ, which indicates aggressive verbalizations, while intervals 19 and 20 contain a "T" with a circle, Ⓣ, which indicates physical "attack" (actual hitting, kicking, or pinching). Another bit of information was incorporated in the recording system. The letter "B" was entered in the fourth row to indicate that the child was playing with or being aggressive to a specific nursery school boy named Bill. This additional notation was made midway in the study when teachers observed that the subject and Bill usually behaved aggressively toward each other. Data collected before this change served as a baseline against which to judge the effects of changing social contingencies. Subsequently, teachers gave approval contingent on nonaggressive interactions between these boys as shown by the X's above intervals 6, 7, 8, 11, 12, 17, 18, 26, 27, and 29.

Another general observational code, tailored for analysis of pupils' behavior in the elementary school classroom, has been devised by Thomas and Becker (1967). Like the nursery school code, it consists of symbols and definitions designed to cover the range of interactions that may take place in the field situation defined by the classroom.

Defining and Recording Stimulus Events

The ease or difficulty of defining a stimulus class is related to its source. It has been pointed out (*e.g.*, Bijou and Baer, 1961) that some stimuli originate in natural and man-made things, some in the biological make-up of the subject himself, and some in the behavior of people and other living organisms. Consider briefly each source in turn.

Defining stimuli from physical things does not pose a difficult problem since physical objects are usually available for all to see. All that is required is that these stimuli be described in the usual physical dimensions of space, time, size, velocity, color, texture, and the like.

Defining stimuli which originate in the biological make-up of the subject is beset with difficulty mostly because of their obscurity under any circumstance and particularly under field conditions. Consider what must be available to an observer if he is to record in objective terms the duration, intensity, or frequency of stimuli involved in a toothache, "butterflies" in the stomach, general bodily weakness, dizziness, and hunger-pangs. Instruments would be needed to make visible all sorts of internal biological events; and for the most part, these are not yet available in practical forms. It seems clear that at present, field methods of research, especially with human beings, are not appropriate for describing biologically anchored variables. Research on these variables must be postponed until it is practical to monitor physiological actions through cleverly designed telemetric devices. But it should be stressed that the exact role of specific biological variables *must* be studied at some time for a thorough functional analysis of psychological behavior (defined here as the interaction of a total functioning biological individual with environmental events).

Defining social stimuli, or stimuli which evolve from the action of people, ranges in difficulty between physical and biological events. This is so because social events, like physical and biological events, must in many instances be described in terms of their physical dimensions, and as is well known, the components of social stimuli can be terribly subtle and complex. For the reader interested in a further analysis of social events within the framework of a natural science, Skinner's discussion is recommended (1953, pp. 298–304).

In field studies, the procedure for defining and recording social stimuli is the same as that for defining and recording response events, since social events are treated as the responses of people in antecedent or consequent relationships to the behavior of the subject. Therefore, the entire previous section on defining and recording behavioral events pertains to defining and recording social events.

Some social stimuli, like response stimuli, may consist of a single class of behavior on the part of an adult or a child and may be recorded on the basis of frequency or its occurrence or nonoccurrence within a time interval. Examples of single-class antecedent stimuli are simple commands and requests, *e.g.*, "Start now," "Gather around in a circle," "Come, let's ride the trikes." Examples of single-class consequent stimuli are confirmations ("Right"), disconfirmations ("Wrong"), approval ("Good") and disapproval ("You play too rough.")

Other social stimuli may be composed of several classes of behavior stemming from one person or several in concert. As in the case of defining multiple response classes, criteria for each subclass in the group may constitute a code. A specific observational code may be developed to describe social events in a specific situation for a specific study. For example, in a study of autistic behavior, adult attention was defined as: "(1) Touching the child; (2) being within two feet of and facing the child; (3) talking to, touching, assisting or going to the child" (Brawley, *et al.* 1968). With such criteria the investigator catalogued the types of behaviors which constituted social interaction involving attention and excluded other stimuli originating in the behavior of an adult in contact with the subject.

General observational codes for social events, like those for response events, have also been devised to study many problems in a general type of field setting. For example, Becker and Thomas (1967) have developed a comprehensive code for recording the teacher's behavior in an elementary classroom situation.

Which classes of behavior-environmental interactions will be selected for study will depend on the purpose of the investigation; the maximum number, however, will be limited by the practical considerations. Studies requiring detailed analyses of many response classes may be planned as a series. The first dealing with grossly defined classes and the others with more and more progressively refined categories. For example, the first study may be concerned with the frequency of social contacts with adults and peers, and the second with specific verbal and motor responses directed to specific adults (teachers and parents) and peers (boys and girls).

Assessing Observer Reliability

Disagreements between observers may be related to inadequacies in (1) the observational code, (2) the training of the observers, or (3) the method of calculating reliability.

The observational code. Problems of defining and recording behavioral and stimulus events have been discussed in Section 2. Observer reliability is directly related to the comprehensiveness and specificity of the definitions in the observational code. Generally it is advisable to devise codes with mutually exclusive event categories, each definition having criteria that do not occur in any other definition.

Training of observers. Even when a code is completely serviceable, two observers may not necessarily record the occurrence of the same event at the same time unless each has been adequately trained in using the code and in controlling his behavior while observing and recording.

For example, training might begin by familiarizing the observer with the tools for recording, *e.g.*, the clipboard, stopwatch, and data sheets. This might be followed by an orientation to the code and exercises in recording behavioral events. A film or video tape of sequences similar to those in the actual situation might be used to provide supplementary experiences.

It is often helpful to have a second observer to record along with the first observer. During trial recordings the observers can indicate to each other the behaviors being scored and uncover misunderstandings regarding the nature of the code or ambiguities in the definition of particular responses. Such a procedure reduces interpretation on the part of the observer and can contribute to an improved code.

Since it is relatively easy for the observers to slip an interval in the course of a long recording session, they should be instructed to note the beginning of certain activities, *e.g.*, story time, snack, nap, *etc.* This allows them to determine easily when they are out of phase with one another. Slips may also result from inaccurate stopwatches. Watches should be periodically tested by starting them simultaneously and checking them a few hours later.

After training on the proficient use of the code the observer might then be given instruction on how to conduct himself while observing and recording. Thus, he might be told how to refrain from interacting with the subject, *e.g.*, ignore all questions, avoid eye-contact, and suppress reactions to the subject's activities as well as those associated with him. He might also be instructed in moving about to maintain a clear view of the subject yet not make it obvious that he is following him.

Method of calculating reliability. The reliability index is to some degree a function of how it is calculated. Suppose we have data from two observers showing the frequency of a class of events taken over 1 hr. Unless the sums obtained by each observer are equal, the smaller sum is divided by the larger to obtain a percentage of agreement. If the sums are identical the reliability index would be 100. This method is often used when the investigator is interested in frequencies *per se*, since the measure obtained gives only the amount of agreement over the total number of events observed. It does not indicate whether the two observers were recording the same event at exactly the same time. Thus, it might be possible that one observer was recording few behaviors during the first half hour and many during the second, while the second observer was doing just the opposite. To ascertain whether this is the case, one could divide the period of observation into small segments and calculate the reliability of each. Agreements over progressively smaller segments give confidence that the observers are scoring the same event at the same time. One may assess the agreement over brief intervals such as 5 or 10 sec. Reliability is calculated by scoring each interval as agree or disagree (match or mismatch) and dividing the total number of agreements by the number of agreements plus the number of disagreements. Note that one may score several agreements or disagreements in an interval if a number of events are being recorded simultaneously as shown in Tables 1 and 2. In this case the interval is broken down according to the number of different events recorded, with each event scored as a match or mismatch.

The reliability index may also be influenced by the frequency of response under study. When a behavior is displayed at a very low rate, the observer will record few instances of occurrence and many of nonoccurrence. In this situation the observers could disagree on the occurrence of the behavior yet still show high reliability due to their agreement on the large number of intervals where no behavior was recorded. A similar problem exists with regard to high-frequency behaviors. Here, however, the observers may disagree on the nonoccurrence of the behavior and agree on occurrence, because of the frequency of the latter. The problem may be resolved by computing not one but two reliability coefficients, one for occurrence and one for nonoccurrence.

In some cases the requirement of perfect matching of intervals may be relaxed slightly. Thus, behaviors recorded within one interval (especially if the interval is short) may also be considered as instances of agreement for reliability purposes. A technique of noncontinuous observing may also increase reliability (O'Leary, O'Leary, and Becker, 1967). In this procedure the observers record for shorter portions of time. For example, instead of taking continuous 10-sec observations, the observer might record for 10 out of every 15 sec, or for 20 out of every 30 sec. During the period in which the observer is not attending to the child, he should be recording the behaviors just observed.

The use of a second observer does not insure high reliability of recording; it is possible for both observers to agree on the scoring of certain events and at the same time be incorrect (Gewirtz and Gewirtz, 1964). Both observers might record some events which should not be noted and ignore others which should. Hence, a third observer might be used on occasion to determine if this possibility exists.

Collecting, Analyzing, and Interpreting Data

Data collection. Final data collection is begun as soon as it is evident that the observers are adequately trained, the field situation is feasible, and the subject has adapted to the presence of the observers.

Whether the investigator collects data during all of the time available for observation or takes time samples will depend upon many factors, including the purpose of the study, the nature of the data, and the practical considerations. Regardless of the frequency with which observations are made, it is recommended that the data be plotted at regular intervals to provide a kind of progress chart. A visual account of the fluctuations and trends can help the investigator make important decisions, *e.g.*, setting up the time for the next reliability evaluation or establishing the termination time for a phase of the study.

Data analysis. Up until now we discussed the investigators' activities in relation to the interactions between the observer and the field events. The investigator was viewed as a critic, watching the observer record the events in a natural ecology. Thus, in the data collection phase of a study the investigator's role is somewhat similar to that of a motion picture director evaluating what the camera is recording in relation to the scene as he sees it. In this section on data analysis and in the next on interpretation, we shall consider what the investigator does, not in relation to the recording equipment and field events, but in relation to the data collected.

Basically, in data analysis the investigator looks at the data collected to "see what is there". Usually he finds that making one or several transformations in the raw data helps him to see more clearly the relationships among the events observed. Transformational procedures might consist of converting the frequency counts into graphic, tabular, verbal, arithmetical, or statistical forms. Exactly which operations he performs on the data will depend on the purpose of the study, the nature of the data, and his theoretical assumptions about what can or cannot be demonstrated by a descriptive field study.

Usually, data analysis begins when data collection ends. However, as noted previously, an investigator might graph the data while the study is in progress. Under these circumstances data analysis might consist of revising and refining the graphs and making other transpositions to show the relationships among the subparts of the data.

Data collected in terms of rate are usually plotted in a graphic form with responses on the vertical axis and time of the horizontal axis. Points on the chart may represent either discrete or cumulative values. Discrete values are the sums or means for each successive session; cumulative values are the sums or means for all previous sessions. Therefore, curves with discrete values might go up, stay at the same level, or go down; cumulative curves might also go up or stay at the same level. Cumulative curves do not go down. A decrease in the frequency of a response is shown in the curve as a deceleration in rate (bends toward the horizontal axis); an increase in frequency as an acceleration (bends toward the vertical axis); a constant frequency as no change in rate; and a zero frequency as a horizontal line.

In most instances graphic presentations are made more meaningful when accompanied by percentage values. In addition, it is often advantageous to show percentages of occurrences in the different conditions and sub-conditions of the field situation.

Viewing the interactions in selected time periods (early morning, and late morning) or around certain events (before and after meal-time) as populations, statistical analyses may be made to assess the nature of and the reliability of differences observed.

Interpretation of findings.   Essentially, interpretation of findings consists of the investigator's statements on what is "seen" in the data together with his conception of their generality. Such statements are the *raison-d'être* of an investigation.

Obviously, an investigator is free to interpret his findings in any way he chooses. The investigator who accepts the assumptions of a natural science approach to psychology seeks to limit his interpretations to empirical concepts and relationships consistent with his observations and the analytical operations made upon the products of his observations. Hence, in a descriptive field study his interpretations would usually consist of a discussion of what was found in the situation with comparisons to other findings obtained under functionally similar conditions. Conclusions on the similarities and differences between his findings and others would be incorporated in his argument for the generality of his findings. Interpretations in an experimental field study would depend on the number and type of manipulations employed and would usually be limited to describing the functional relationships obtained.

Illustrative Study

Using the procedures previously described, a study was undertaken to obtain a descriptive account of a boy in a laboratory nursery school at the University of Illinois. The nursery school curriculum and the practices of the teaching staff of this school were based on behavioral principles (Skinner, 1953, and Bijou and Baer, 1961).

Subject and field situation. The subject (Zachary) was typical of the children in the nursery school in the judgment of the teachers. He was 4.5 yr old, of high average intelligence (Peabody IQ 116) and from a middle socio-economic class family. On the Wide Range Achievement Test he scored kindergarten 3 in reading, pre-kindergarten 5 in spelling, and kindergarten 6 in arithmetic.

The nursery school consisted of a large room, approximately 21 by 40 ft. Evenly spaced along one wall were three doors which led to three adjacent smaller rooms. One of these rooms was a lavatory, the second contained paints, papers, and other equipment, and the third a variety of toys. Nearby was a large table and several chairs used for art activities and snack. Opposite these rooms along the other wall were several tables separated by brightly colored, movable partitions. In these booths, the children worked on academic subjects.

The school was attended by 12 children, six boys and six girls, between 4 and 5 yr of age. The teaching staff consisted of a full-time teacher and an assistant teacher, and depending on the time of day, one to three undergraduates who assisted in administering new programs in reading, writing, and arithmetic.

In general, the morning program was as follows:

9:00–10:00 Art, academic, and pre-academic work
10:00–10:30 Free play
10:30–11:00 Snack
11:00–12:00 Academic work, show-and-tell, and storytime.

A typical morning might begin with art. At this time, 8 to 10 children sat around a large table working with various materials. During this activity each child in turn left the group for 10 to 20 min to work on writing or arithmetic. While engaged in writing or arithmetic the child worked with a teacher in one of the booths. After completing his assigned units of work he returned to his art activity and another child left the group to work on his units of writing or arithmetic. After all the children had participated in these academic subjects, the art period was terminated and was followed by play. During play, the children were free to move about, often spending much of the time in either of the smaller nursery school rooms playing with blocks or other toys. After approximately 30 min of play, the youngsters returned to the large table for a snack of juice and cookies. While eating and drinking they talked spontaneously and informally with their teachers and peers. Following snack time some of the children participated in reading while the others gathered for show-and-tell or storytime. During storytime the children sat on the floor in a group while the teacher read and discussed the story. In show-and-tell, instead of the teacher leading the group, each child had a chance to stand by the teacher in front of the group, and show an object he had brought from home and tell about it. As they did during the art period the children left the group one at a time for a period of reading. Because of variations in the amount of time a child spent on academic subjects, a child did not engage in all of these activities every day.

Behavioral and stimulus events recorded. The behaviors recorded were of two general categories: social contacts and sustained activities. Social contacts included verbal interchanges and physical contacts with children and teachers. Sustained activities involved behaviors in relation to the school tasks. The specific observational code developed for the study is presented in Table 3.

Observation began 3.5 weeks after the start of the school year and covered a 3-hr period in the morning. The observations were taken on 28 school days. The observer sat a few feet from the subject and discretely followed him as he moved from one activity to another in the nursery school room. Every 10 sec the teacher recorded the occurrence or nonoccurrence of events defined in the code. The data sheet was similar to that shown in Table 1; however, only the first and second rows were used.

Observer reliability. The reliability of observation and the adequacy of the behavioral code was evaluated several times throughout the study by having a second observer record stimulus and response events. Reliability was calculated by scoring each interval as a match or mismatch and dividing the total number of agreements by the number of agreements plus disagreements. Four checks on social contacts showed agreements of 75, 82, 85, and 87%. Three checks on sustained activity yielded agreements of 94, 95, and 97%. Thus, average agreement on social contacts exceeded 82% while average agreement of sustained activity exceeded 95%.

Analysis of Data

Social contacts. Data were gathered on Zachary's social behaviors in informal activities of art, play, snack, storytime, and show-and-tell. They will be described and samples of the detailed accounts in art and snack will be presented in graphic form. The youngster's most dominant behavior during the art period, shown in Fig. 1, was talking to others (14% of the time).

Teachers and peers talked with him about equally, an average of 8 and 7% respectively. Physical contacts between Zachary, teachers, and peers were low, around 1 to 2%.

The child's verbal behavior to peers during the play period was higher than in the art period. He talked to his friends on an average of 38%; they talked to him on an average of only 10%. Verbal exchanges with teachers were low (an average of 2.5%). Zachary touched other children 7% of the time on the average and they reciprocated on an average of 3%. Physical contacts with teachers were relatively infrequent.

As in the art and play periods, Zachary's social interactions during snack time, shown in Fig. 2, consisted mostly of talking to his classmates, an average of 21%. They, in turn, talked to him only an average of 7%. During this period the teacher's general commands (instructions addressed to the group) were relatively high, averaging 7% in contrast to the 2% during art and play. Physical contacts with other children were low, as in art and play, about 3%.

Compared to the art, play, and snack periods, Zachary's verbalizations to peers and to teachers were low (8 and 4% respectively), and the number of times he touched children (10%), and children touched him were also relatively low (2%). Storytime had a high frequency of teacher's general commands and statements (average of 73%) since this category was scored when the teacher read and discussed the stories.

In show-and-tell, Zachary's social behavior was similar to that during storytime. He talked to other children 14% of the time and touched them 9% of the time. Zachary physically contacted teachers about 1% of the time and they reciprocated about 3% of the time.

In respect to Zachary's social behavior during the academic periods, these data clearly indicate that the teacher talked to Zachary a great deal during the reading (an average of 69%), writing (an average of 71%), and arithmetic periods (an average of 58%), and the child talked to the teacher with high frequency, particularly in reading (an average of 44%) and arithmetic (an average of 41%). In writing he talked to the teacher only 3% of the time. There were also a few instances in which the teacher touched Zachary and rare occasions in which Zachary interacted socially with other children. Figure 3 is a detailed graphic account of his social behavior during the writing period.

Sustained activity.   For the observer to mark the occurrence of sustained activity, Zachary had to respond in a manner appropriate for a particular school activity. (See second part of Table 3). For example, during art, the child had to be sitting in his chair, facing the art materials and manipulating them during each 10-sec interval. Similar definitions were

TABLE 3 Observational code for describing the behavior of a boy in a laboratory nursery school

Symbol	Definition	Symbol	Definition
	First Row (Social Contacts)		Second Row (Sustained Activity)
◸ (square with diagonal)	S verbalizes to himself. Any verbalization during which he does not look at an adult or child or does not use an adult's or child's name. Does not apply to a group situation.	▣ (square with dot)	Sustained activity in art. S must be sitting in the chair, facing the material and responding to the material or teacher within the 10-sec interval. Responding to the material includes using pencil, paint brush, chalk, crayons, string, scissors or paste or any implement on paper, or working with clay with hands on clay or hands on implement which is used with clay, or folding or tearing paper. Responding to the teacher includes following a command made by an adult to make a specific response. The behavior must be completed (child sitting in his chair again) within two minutes.
⊡ (square with circle)	S verbalizes to adult. S must look at adult while verbalizing or use adult's name.	▣ (square with dot)	Sustained activity in storytime. S must be sitting, facing the material, or following a command given by the teacher or assistant. If the S initiates a verbalization to a peer, do not record sustained activity in the 10-sec interval.
◸ (square with diagonal)	S verbalizes to child. S must look at child while verbalizing or use child's name. If in a group situation, any verbalization is recorded as verbalization to a child.	▣ (square with dot)	Sustained activity in show-and-tell. S must be sitting, facing the material, or following a command given by the teacher. If the S initiates a verbalization to a peer, do not record sustained activity in that 10-sec interval.
S (square with S)	Child verbalizes to S. Child must look at S while verbalizing or use S's name.		
◁ (square with triangle)	Adult verbalizes to S. Adult must look at S while verbalizing or use S's name.		

TABLE 3 (continued)

Symbol	Definition	Symbol	Definition
S	Adult gives general instruction to class or asks question of class, or makes general statement. Includes storytelling.	(square with dot)	Sustained activity in reading. S must be sitting in the chair, facing the material and responding to the material or the teacher within the 10-sec interval.
(horizontally divided box)	S touches adult. Physical contact with adult.	(square with dot)	Sustained activity in writing. S must be sitting in the chair, facing the material and responding to the material or the teacher within the 10-sec interval. Responding to the material includes using the pencil (making a mark), or holding the paper or folder. Responding to the teacher includes responding verbally to a cue given by the teacher.
(vertically divided box)	S touches child with part of body or object. Physical contact with child.	(square with dot)	Sustained activity in arithmetic. S must be sitting in the chair, facing the material and responding to the material or the teacher within the 10-sec interval. Responding to the material or teacher includes using the pencil or eraser or holding the paper or folder or responding verbally to cue.
V	Adult touches S. Physical contact with adult.	(box with diagonal)	Sustained activity did not occur in interval.
T	Child touches S with part of body or object. Physical contact with child.		

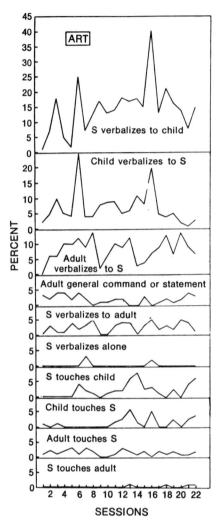

FIGURE 1   Social contact during art.

used for other situations and periods. Given these definitions, the results show a generally high level of sustained activity in all phases of the morning program. Daily rates of sustained activities in art, storytime, and show-and-tell range between 70 and 99% with an average of 89% for art, 95% for storytime, and 88% for show-and-tell. See Fig. 4 for variations from session to session in Zachary's sustained behavior during art. Sustained activity in reading, writing, and arithmetic, range from 90 to 100% over the days observed with an average of 97, 95, and 96% respectively. See Fig. 5 for variations in the child's sustained behavior in writing. Due to

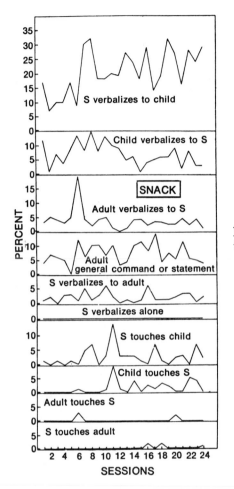

FIGURE 2 Social interaction during snack.

the limited availability of the observer, and the fact that not every activity occurred every day, the number of observations on each activity varied.

DISCUSSION

A descriptive account of the behaviors of a boy during the morning hours in a laboratory nursery school was obtained in terms of the frequency of occurrence of objectively defined stimulus and response events. The account shows rates of changes in social interactions (verbal and physical contacts) and sustained activities during eight periods of the school morning.

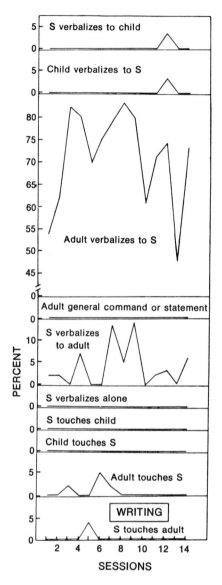

FIGURE 3 Social behavior during writing.

In the informal activities of the nursery school in which the youngster performed on an individual basis, as in art, free play, and snack time, the subject talked to his peers and teachers to a moderate degree. His peers and teachers responded to him verbally to a lesser extent. He talked more than he listened and over the period of the study, his verbal output increased. Physical interactions with peers and teachers in these situations

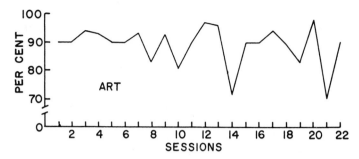

FIGURE 4 Sustained activity during art.

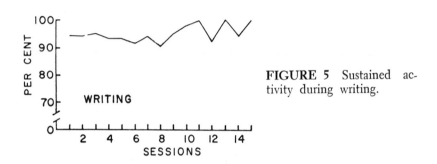

FIGURE 5 Sustained activity during writing.

were at a relatively low level. Finally, the youngster's sustained activity in the art period was high (between 70 and 98%) and became more variable, on a day-to-day basis, during the second half of the study. In the other two informal activities, storytime and show-and-tell, the child participated as a member of a group in which the teacher's verbal behavior was prominent, especially during storytime. In these two situations the child talked to others less, but as in art, free play, and snack time, he talked more than he listened. In storytime and show-and-tell he engaged in some body contacts with peers and teachers, yet his sustained activity on nursery school tasks was high, with a range of 90 to 99% for the former and 70 to 95% for the latter.

In the more structured activities of reading, writing, and arithmetic the teacher's verbal behavior to the child was high and his verbal behavior to her was correspondingly high, particularly in reading and arithmetic. During academic exercises all other social interactions were zero or near zero, and the child's sustained activities were consistently high over days, ranging from 90 to 100% of the time.

The data gathered in this study can serve two main purposes. First, they can provide normative information on behavior in a laboratory preschool. Thus, it might be interesting to compare this child's rates of response obtained in this study after 3.5 weeks of school with his rates during the last month of the school year. It might also be interesting to compare this child's behavior with another child's in the same nursery school. Such a comparison might be especially valuable if someone claimed that the second child's behavior was deviant. In addition, it might be informative to compare this child's behavior with a comparable child in a community-operated nursery school. Second, the data suggest certain relationships between the behavior of the subject, the teacher, and other children. Thus, the investigator might use the data as a baseline for an experimental study in which conditions are manipulated to test for possible functional relationships.

REFERENCES

BALDWIN, A. L., KALHORN, J., and BREESE, F. H. The appraisal of parent behavior. *Psychological Monographs*, 1949, **63**, No. 299.

BARKER, R. G. and WRIGHT, H. F. *Midwest and its children: the psychological ecology of an American town.* New York: Harper & Row, 1955.

BECKER, W. C., MADSEN, C. H., JR., ARNOLD, CAROLE R., and THOMAS, D. R. The contingent use of teacher attention and praise in reducing classroom behavior problems. *Journal of Special Education*, 1967, **1**, 287–307.

BECKER, W. C. and THOMAS, D. R. A revision of the code for the analysis of a teacher's behavior in the classroom. Unpublished manuscript, 1967.

BIJOU, S. W. and BAER, D. M. *Child development: a systematic and empirical theory.* Vol. 1, New York: Appleton-Century-Crofts, 1961.

BIRNBRAUER, J. S., WOLF, M. M., KIDDER, J. D., and TAGUE, CECILIA. Classroom behavior of retarded pupils with token reinforcement. *Journal of Experimental Child Psychology*, 1965, **2**, 219–235.

BRAWLEY, ELEANOR R., HARRIS, FLORENCE R., ALLEN, K. EILEEN; FLEMING, R. S., and PETERSON, R. F. Behavior modification of an autistic child. *Behavioral Science*, 1968, in press.

GEWIRTZ, HAVA and GEWIRTZ, J. L. A method for assessing stimulation behaviors and caretaker-child interaction. Unpublished manuscript, 1964.

HARRIS, FLORENCE R., WOLF, M. M., and BAER, D. M. Effects of adult social reinforcement on child behavior. *Young Children*, 1964, **20**, 8–17.

HAWKINS, R. P., PETERSON, R. F., SCHWEID, EDDA, and BIJOU, S. W. Behavior therapy in the home: Amelioration of problem parent-child relations with the parent in a therapeutic role. *Journal of Experimental Child Psychology*, 1966, **4**, 99–107.

HONIG, W. K. Introductory remarks. In W. K. Honig (Ed.) *Operant behavior: areas of research and application.* New York: Appleton-Century-Crofts, 1966.

JENSEN, G. D. and BOBBITT, RUTH A. Implications of primate research for understanding infant development. *The exceptional child,* Vol. 1, J. Hell-mouth (Ed.), Special Child Publications, Seattle, Washington, 1967.

JOHNSTON, MARGARET S., KELLY, C. SUSAN, HARRIS, FLORENCE R., and WOLF, M. M. An application of reinforcement principles to development of motor skills of a young child. *Child Development,* 1966, **37,** 379–387.

LOVAAS, O. I., FREITAG, G., GOLD, VIVIAN J., and KASSORLA, IRENE C. Experi-mental studies in childhood schizophrenia: analysis of self-destructive be-havior. *Journal of Experimental Child Psychology,* 1965, **2,** 67–84. (*a*)

LOVAAS, O. I., FREITAG, G., GOLD, VIVIAN J., and KASSORLA, IRENE C. Record-ing apparatus and procedure for observation of behaviors of children in free play settings. *Journal of Experimental Child Psychology,* 1965, **2,** 108–120. (*b*)

O'LEARY, K. D., O'LEARY, SUSAN G., and BECKER, W. C. Modification of a deviant sibling interaction pattern in the home. *Behaviour Research and Therapy,* 1967, **5,** 113–120.

SKINNER, B. F. *Science and human behavior.* New York: Macmillan, 1953.

WOLF, M. M., RISLEY, T. R., and MEES, H. L. Application of operant con-ditioning procedures to the behavior problems of an autistic child. *Be-haviour Research and Therapy,* 1964, **1,** 305–312.

WRIGHT, H. F. *Recording and analyzing child behavior.* New York: Harper & Row, 1967.

BRADLEY D. BUCHER
University of Western Ontario

*Problems and prospects for
psychotherapy research design*

PROBLEMS IN EVALUATING
PSYCHOTHERAPY

The usefulness of his therapeutic methods must be a matter of great concern for any psychotherapist. The most valuable techniques to investigate these tools have been the subject of intense study and thought and (perhaps) rather less intense research activity for more than twenty years. Conventional therapists have had to weather continuing criticisms as to the value of their treatment methods and the adequacy of efforts made to investigate those methods. Most of the wide variety of traditional therapeutic techniques now in use were developed at a time when concern as to the effectiveness of treatment had not yet become a critical question. They were elaborated largely on the basis of therapists' observations of their patients' behavior, aided by theoretical inferences and the guidance of accepted authority. The practicing therapist increased his skills largely from feedback obtained from his work. These methods were not in any strict sense experimental.

To distrust the effectiveness of treatments developed in this way casts doubt on the value of the therapist's experience in guiding practice effectively. It may seem odd at first to suppose that such information could not be applied usefully. We learn much of what we know by simple observation, without the aid of controlled experimentation. Touching a hot stove is soon found to be unrewarding, and simple experience suffices. Unfortunately the conventional therapist does not receive information so certainly or so quickly about the results of his treatment. Behavior change does not immediately follow the therapist's intervention. And often what the therapist hopes to change either is not clearly defined or is some intrapsychic process not easily observed. The complexity of the treatment process tends to mask the phenomena that should be investigated.

Such complexity is not unique to psychotherapy. Medical therapeutics, until very recently (Robinson, 1931), has represented a similar technology—one in which the information derived from disease treatment was not effectively utilized. Widely practiced treatments were often useless or positively harmful. Purging and bleeding, for example, were practiced extensively for a wide variety of ailments even into the twentieth century. They cured few or none and killed many. Several factors contributed to medicine's erratic growth. Publication and training were inadequate, social prohibitions hindered surgery and anatomical research, and the waywardness of disease processes often led investigators astray. The voice of authority stood too high, that of research too low. All these factors bear on one point: where feedback from direct experience is inadequate and the problems faced are pressing and real, tactics to deal with the problems may develop that are not only not very effective but may even negatively affect their solution.

In 1952 Eysenck suggested such a possibility for psychotherapy. He challenged the existing evidence that neurosis could be successfully treated through traditional practices. Thus by implication he challenged the theoretical and observational bases of these practices. The resulting uproar has not yet subsided. Even now, however, observation and theory remain the primary modes of validation for most therapeutic viewpoints; and these methods are seen as sufficient guides to practice by many psychotherapists who do not appear to feel a pressing need for controlled research.

THE CONTROL GROUP DESIGN

If earlier and simpler methods of investigating psychotherapy have been inadequate, it becomes important to discover a better method. The group control design, using modern statistical procedures, has been commonly advocated as an alternative to case study and observation. In his review of outcome research Eysenck (1952) concluded that methodological weaknesses in the control group studies then available made them inadequate to establish that psychotherapy was superior to the absence of any explicit treatment. He recommended the continued use of control group designs but with more adequate control procedures, and he cautioned against complacency in using unvalidated treatment procedures. Edwards and Cronbach (1952) also examined this research problem, and they also encouraged use of control group designs; but Cronbach was less sanguine about their potential usefulness. He felt that such designs could not separate the effects of all potential variables, since the immense variety of organismic and situational factors that could affect outcome was too great for group designs to encompass. That is, he felt such designs were inadequate to isolate and determine the influences of specific variables acting in treatment.

Many outcome studies have appeared since Eysenck's original review. Kellner (1967) listed almost one hundred studies that had used control groups or comparisons in some form. Many failed to meet important control criteria. Conclusions that could be drawn from this research were meager. In the light of this research Paul (1967) presented a fresh analysis of the problems of control group investigations. He divided the variables to be studied and controlled into three general classes: client characteristics, therapist characteristics and treatment procedures, and treatment time. The variables that might be included for study under these categories are: any dimensions of the client's personality or his cognitive processes; his behavior and experiences inside and outside of therapy; or any aspect of his past experiences. Also included are any variables derived from the therapy setting, the treatment mode and method of application, and the behavior or personality of the therapist therein. Thus, treatment variables might include such diagnostic or personality classifications of the patient as autistic, dyslexic, phobic, anxious, dependent, etc.; such personality characteristics of the therapist as warm, authoritarian, accepting, etc.; and such summary descriptions of the treatment as behavioral, interactive, psychoanalytic, interpretive, and so on.

Prominent among the variables that have been listed as influential but elusive factors in treatment are those often variously labeled as nonspecific factors, placebo effects, therapy demand characteristics, client expectations, etc. These effects derive from subtle factors in the experimental setting and testing methods and the interactions and attitudes of the participants in therapy. The influence of such variables has been emphasized by Rogers (1957) and by Goldstein, Heller, and Sechrest (1966).

Obviously there is a large number of variables in the above list to be taken into account. Control group designs have been used at several levels of complexity. Those variables that are not the direct object of study somehow must be eliminated as treatment effects that could confuse the interpretation of the experimental results. The simplest design is to compare a group of treated patients with an untreated group. Here, every aspect of treatment is compared, en masse, with its absence. Also, a group may be selected but not contacted; or may be contacted, interviewed briefly, then pre- and post-tested; or it may be exposed to a pseudotreatment or treated by some competing therapy. These various conditions are designed to control for different variables that may be included in such factors as: being interviewed or tested by a therapist, being in the presence of a therapist, being exposed to a plausible sounding treatment program, and so on. An adequate experimental design of the above type must also include certain control procedures. Patients must be randomly assigned to groups, and perhaps matched for various patient characteristics. Therapists may be assigned randomly to treatment conditions, or all therapists may be involved in each group. There also must be reasonable controls over extraneous variables such as treatment time, time spent with the therapist, etc., since such variables may affect the outcome of the various treatments.

Let us now examine how successfully the control group design has met the challenge of exploring the effects of its numerous treatment variables. To begin, note one fundamental requirement of this research. The researcher must say what he has done and what he has found. This requires him to measure and control all relevant treatment variables and to describe these variables well enough for other researchers to replicate the work.

To replicate a study, in the light of Paul's division of the variables in psychotherapy, the experimenter must replicate the relevant variables in each of the three classes—client characteristics, therapist characteristics and treatment procedures, and treatment time. An important difficulty in implementing this very reasonable sounding requirement derives from the diversity of viewpoints psychologists have toward the treatment process: the behaviorist emphasizes overt behavior and observable environment-behavior relationships; the client-centered therapist emphasizes broader therapist and client behavioral characteristics; the more traditional dynamic therapist emphasizes the interpersonal and intrapersonal dynamics in the treatment hour and in the client's early history; and other schools look for other variables. The terms these various schools of therapy use to describe their observations differ enormously, and there is no dictionary to translate the terminology from one to another.

To explore the problem of replication more closely, look first at client variables. The dimensions that may be used to differentiate among or to identify characteristics of persons are so numerous and in many cases so vaguely defined that the experimenter cannot measure all that might be important in predicting response to treatment. These variables include diagnostic labels, behavioral characteristics; social, economic, and educational variables; sex, age, personality characteristics, etc. They could be listed almost endlessly. They are not likely to be noted in experimental reports unless they are of some interest to the experimenter. Even those variables that are reported may not be described clearly. For example, dependency on the therapist, expectation of treatment success, attraction to the therapist, and so on, are imprecisely measurable at best. The development of functional relations between outcome measures and such variables, beyond simple correlational results, seems currently beyond our reach. Finally, many of the client characteristics referred to above vary during treatment; they may be affected by treatment and by other current experiences, so that they can be included only roughly as fixed factors in an experimental design.

The behavior and personality of the therapist constitute a similar wilderness of phenomena. The therapist provides a constantly shifting stimulus for the client, from which much of the client's behavior in therapy is cued. Broadly described therapist variables such as competence, experience, and interpersonal attraction can provide at best summary information about this complex stimulus.

In summary, one crucial aspect in a demonstration of the value of a therapeutic technique—replicability of procedures and results—cannot presently be guaranteed. The concepts guiding psychotherapy are neither well enough defined nor agreed upon to insure that an adequate description of a research procedure has been made. Thus, results in published studies are far more tentative than may be implied by the levels of significance they report. An experimenter may fail to replicate even the most striking result if he does not reproduce crucial client characteristics, therapeutic operations, or therapist characteristics that were either not noticed or not reported in the original work.

We could dispel these worries with little concern if we could point to definable treatment variables that repeatedly had been found to produce strong and consistent effects in a wide range of background conditions, even if the studies did not precisely duplicate the original circumstances. Unfortunately, such strong variables have not been found frequently. In the last of three reviews of outcome studies of conventional forms of psychotherapy with children, Levitt (1971) reaffirmed his earlier conclusion that the studies have not shown positive therapeutic effects. Thus, we are very far from beginning the analysis of techniques with demonstrably powerful effects. For therapy with adults the picture is perhaps somewhat brighter.

AN EXAMPLE FROM RESEARCH
ON TREATMENT OF FEARS

Among all forms of treatment studied in control group research, the systematic desensitization of well-defined fears has been the most consistently successful. The technique has been studied for several kinds of fears and in numerous technical variations. Paul's (1966) study of anxiety about public speaking in college students is an example of the use of the control group design that has been praised widely. This study has been described by Goldstein, Heller, and Sechrest (1966) as a near optimal experiment in psychotherapy. An elaborate effort was made to eliminate, randomize, or control nonexperimental variables. Although the subjects were not children, this research will be examined here in some detail to illustrate the techniques used and to see how well the study solved the problems described above.

A group given systematic desensitization and a group given insight therapy were compared. A third group was given a convincingly presented "attention-placebo" treatment that was not based on an explicit treatment rationale. This "treatment" was intended to seem as valid to the clients as the genuine treatments seemed to the two experimental groups. All groups involved a similar expenditure of treatment and therapist time. There were two altogether untreated control groups: one was given pre- and post-testing as were the experimental groups, and one was tested without actually seeing the experimenters. Temporal variables were controlled over all groups, and stratification and random assignment were used to assign clients to groups. Each of five prominent, eclectic, insight-oriented therapists treated clients from each of the three groups.

Results showed the desensitization group to be the most improved on most of the outcome measures. The attention-placebo and insight groups in general did not differ significantly, and both were superior to the untreated controls. Paul concluded that desensitization was more effective than insight therapy; that all three forms of psychotherapy were more effective than testing and initial interviewing; and that insight and self-understanding, as emphasized in the insight treatment, did not add to the effects of nonspecific factors, since the insight and placebo groups did not differ.

Paul's conclusion seems to be twofold. The obtained differences among groups were attributed to such defining characteristics of the treatments as desensitization, insight therapy, and attention-placebo rather than to differences that might not be related to these descriptive labels. Second, the results were extrapolated to apply to the more general question of comparative treatment effectiveness, beyond the limits set by the situational specifics of the study itself.

If a statistically significant difference between two groups is found in a control group design, the differences can safely be interpreted as due to a specific factor only when that factor has been systematically varied between the groups and when all other factors have been held constant or appropriately randomized. This degree of control requires the weakest statistical assumptions in interpreting the results. Generalization of the results is then valid for that population on which measurements were obtained. Paul's conclusions exceeded these limitations at two points. They failed to take into account possible flaws in the control of inessential factors that may have differed among groups, and they generalized beyond the particular circumstances of the study.

Paul's conclusions presuppose that the group differences he obtained could be attributed to the differences among therapies whose names were attached to his groups: insight, desensitization, and nonspecific effects. If variables not intrinsic to these treatment variations also differed over groups and if these variables affected therapy outcome, this assumption would be compromised. Such possibilities exist in abundance. Consider a variable dependent on therapist behavior during treatment, such as the therapist-client attraction. Although each therapist served in each condition, it may be that this variable does not depend only on therapists as persons. It may depend on some irrelevant features of the techniques by which these particular treatments were carried out that affected the therapist-client interactions. Paul's conclusion implies that therapist-client attraction did not differ over groups or that the differences were intrinsic to the therapies. This is an important assumption, and convincing supporting data are not presented. A search for other therapist variables might be initiated in several directions. The assumption of the design is that differences in skill were constant over groups. It might be questioned whether therapists were equally competent in the various procedures. The therapists were certainly less experienced in behavior modification procedures than in insight-oriented techniques. The presence of these and other factors is implied in some of Paul's post-test assessment measures, such as clients' ratings of therapists' competence and likability, where some differences among treatments were found and some interactions with outcome variables.

Client variables may also have contributed to group differences if they interacted with details of treatment administration or with therapist behaviors. Patient faith or expectation of treatment success was singled out by Paul for special consideration in his design. The attention-placebo group was intended to control for these factors. But patient expectations were not actually equated or randomized over treatments; they were assumed to be equalized by the experimental manipulations designed to make them so. Suitable assessment techniques for such nonspecific variables do not readily suggest themselves, since the manner in which they may affect therapy is not well understood. Control or assessment of such shifty variables presents a very formidable problem, particularly if quite different therapeutic procedures are being compared. Thus, nonspecific variables cannot be discounted as possible influences in the differences between the treatment groups.

The above considerations point up problems of the interpretation of variables that may have influenced the obtained results. One can also question how much the results can be generalized beyond the specific situation and clients. The actual conditions studied represent only a narrow sampling of the potential variations within each treatment class. In desensitization, for example, many technical variations have been tested; and modifications might have produced quite different results. More to the point, modifications of the insight-oriented treatment might have made it more effective. The duration of treatment in this study is not as great as is customary, and it may have been too brief for the potential effects of the more traditional methods to manifest themselves. Comparison among schools of therapy with great flexibility in application should be based on optimal representations of each school if they are known or on a wide sampling of acceptable variations. In the absence of such an inclusive demonstration, an individual study cannot be considered valid for making comparisons of the effectiveness of methods from the different schools.

Other limitations in generalizing the results in Paul's study stem from the narrowness of the behavior problem studied and from the homogeneity of the clients. The limits of generalization beyond the values of the specific treatment parameters of the study can be exceeded only if there are grounds to justify a more general statement—for example, evidence that the relative merit of the treatment procedures does not depend on the specific characteristics sampled in the study. Such evidence is not available here.

In summary, Paul's study may be taken as an example of the relative effectiveness of two techniques of therapy in specific examples, for a specific clientele, and a specific problem, where the limits of useful generalization of the results are not known. It adds to the body of studies testing relative merits of different therapies, and its eminence among them is not denied by any of the criticisms here. But one study does not permit a definitive and general conclusion as to the comparative effectiveness of different therapies. An unflawed study that would permit such a comparison seems hardly possible, due to the problems of specification of relevant variables that have been discussed above. Many comparative studies, no one adequate in itself, would be needed to show convincingly the superiority of one therapeutic technique over another. If such evidence were obtained, it would not have the rigorous inferential character associated with the usual statistical analysis of a control group design. The evaluation of such a body of studies necessarily would be more subjective and unsure. In view of the frequency with which conflicting results appear in the literature, a series of research studies that would convincingly clarify the relative merits of the various schools may not soon appear.

CONTROL GROUP DESIGNS —SUMMARY

In the above analysis we have argued that the defects of Paul's study do not derive from the control group design itself, but from the imprecision in the definitions of the variables the design attempted to evaluate and control. These variables become particularly complex when quite different methods of treatment are being compared as in Paul's study.

A less ambitious use of control group comparisons is possible. This involves the study of variations within a single technique that is otherwise fairly well defined. Such a research design is feasible in systematic desensitization, for example, where the procedure can be controlled fairly precisely and where unstructured interaction between therapist and client can be avoided almost entirely (Linder and McGlynn, 1971; Lomont and Edwards, 1967; McGlynn and Mapp, 1970). This degree of control is not usually available in conventional therapy, because of its interpersonal and interactive nature. Even in desensitization, nonspecific effects cannot be excluded. For example, some procedures may have more face validity to the clients than others, based on their common previous experiences in settings similar to that of therapy.

In some recent desensitization studies, an effort has been made to study nonspecific effects by manipulating variables that *should* influence those effects—instructions, for example. The therapist may give different groups the same treatment but preface the therapy with different preliminary statements (McGlynn, 1971; Lomont and Brock, 1971). These instructions are designed to affect such aspects of the client's behavior or state characteristics as his expectations, attentiveness, cooperation, operant response level, etc., according to the researcher's conceptualization. The use of instructions as a research variable requires that treatment be well defined and involve a minimum of unstructured client-therapist interaction. Thus this method of analysis seems restricted to the relatively low-interaction, behavioral therapies.

Control group designs do not promise a definitive research model for the analysis of variables affecting the outcome of traditional interactive therapies. These variables have not been sufficiently well defined to permit their manipulation and control as the designs require if they are to operate effectively. Due to the unstructured character of traditional treatment methods, it is not clear how greater clarity in the definition of such variables can be obtained. Control group research has been enormously costly and has produced quite limited results. It has not much increased our understanding of the effective variables in psychotherapy; nor, excluding behavior modification, has it resulted in any great modification or improvement in the techniques of treatment. It may be wondered how many, if any, of the major variables studied in the interactional therapies have been found to have clearly strong effects.

WITHIN-SUBJECT DESIGNS

Many commentators have expressed uneasiness as to the inadequacies of control group research procedures in psychotherapy; they have also concluded that these procedures and the conceptual models they have tried to illuminate are not sufficiently exact (Bergin and Strupp, 1970). One attempt to find a new conceptual model has been to analyze the contingencies between specific therapeutic manipulations, therapist behaviors, and client behaviors; to insist on objective measurement and definition of terms, and to control very carefully the therapeutic interaction. The focus of interest is shifted toward the patternings of behavior under control of the environment and away from the presumed permanent or semipermanent environment-free characteristics of the individual. The research model that seems most suitable for the study of behavior within this conceptual model is the within-subject design.

The problems that were examined for control group designs are not automatically eliminated in the within-subject design, since those problems derive partly from the behavioral data that emerge from the treatment process. We must consider these difficulties for within-subject designs without losing sight of therapist, technique, and client variables and of the problems of replicability of procedures and results.

A within-subject experimental manipulation consists of the interposition of an explicit operation or operations on an otherwise constant background. These operations are primarily objective changes in such physical aspects of the situation as the scheduled delivery of reinforcement, discriminative cues, etc. Measurement of relevant client behaviors continues throughout each condition. The operation and the background circumstances may be composites of therapist, client, and technique variables, which should be specified in reporting the treatment procedure. Insofar as possible they should be specified in terms of directly observable behaviors, situational characteristics, and environmental events.

The within-subject design has been used extensively in animal behavior research, and the terminology used to analyze behavioral phenomena within this design is adaptable to the analysis of therapy research data. Analyses of animal behavior under given arrangements of contingencies are also carried over into therapy research. Specific procedures, of course, are not carried over. Humans are not reinforced by rat pellets, and they do not perform by pressing bars. An analogous research procedure requires a translation of the *functions* of the original laboratory procedures, not of the procedures themselves. The researcher following the analogue procedure does so with the mild expectation that a properly constructed functional analogue will produce a behavior change comparable to that in the original study. The value of this translation process can be determined only from research results. Not every attempt at translation will be successful, and often the appropriate translation may be quite uncertain, since the analogue procedure may be based on inaccurate functional analysis or involve inappropriate environmental contingency arrangements.

The functional language of behavioral analysis is more objective and more limited than are the languages used in the more conventional interaction therapies. Therapist variables in this model become specific therapist behaviors or classes of behaviors. The therapist may give verbal instructions and combine these instructions with other actions and environmental manipulations. He may deliver reinforcement through verbal and other physically definable behaviors—touching, smiling, and so on. He may also deliver nonverbal cues to his client—for example, physical guidance in training retarded or psychotic children.

How might one go about translating broad behavioral characteristics into therapist-client behavioral contingencies? For example, how would "warmth" be conceptualized? To translate this characteristic, one might include frequent smiling with a soft tone of voice, an absence of aversive verbal statements, and the use of speech that reinforces the expression of statements about behavior, thoughts, and feelings. The problems in such a translation obviously are not small ones. Perhaps such terms, requiring such translations, are not necessary. It may be preferable to use more clearly translatable behavioral variables *ab ovo* and to abandon those based on broad behavioral classes.

The behavioral researcher tries to eliminate uncontrolled and nonspecifiable therapist interactions as much as he can. Even though the language of behavior analysis is more limited and objective, the phenomenon of therapist behavior is not therefore less complex. Even in a well-controlled setting, therapist characteristics other than experimenter-specified behaviors may influence the client's behavior. These might include the therapist's physical appearance or certain quite subtle behavioral characteristics. The therapist may emit subtle cues that set the scene for the client's reactions to his presence and therapeutic manipulations. Such uncontrolled factors produce variable and uninterpretable outcomes.

Elimination of the therapist or other persons from treatment is not feasible for two reasons. First, disturbed social behavior is an important area of study, and behavior in social contexts must be analyzed. Research on the behavior of teachers in the classroom is an example. Evidence that important variables are under control is the observation that consistent changes in student behavior occur as a function of programmed changes in the teacher's behavior. Similarly, variable or unexpected results signal the absence of control.

For example, it has been discovered that teacher criticism can increase the rate of inappropriate classroom behavior (Thomas, Becker, and Armstrong, 1968). To explain this unexpected result, it has been suggested that criticism from the teacher may affect interaction among the students, cuing or reinforcing inappropriate behavior. In this case, peer interaction might be the crucial determining factor in the unexpected result, and teacher attention would be only indirectly influential. Although all the factors in this supposed chain of effects may be objectively observable, the experimenter may not observe them.

A second reason for retaining the therapist in treatment is to take advantage of his ability to control certain client behaviors. The therapist may feel that his personal interaction with the patient can have a positive effect on treatment outcome by influencing the patient's cooperation. He may also want to use interviewing and personal involvement to obtain information about the patient's behavior patterns and about his response to various potential tactics. Few therapists would wish to dispense with these treatment advantages for the sake of procedural purity and simplicity, and research is necessary to show how such client management tactics are best employed.

The therapist who uses interaction with the client in this way should have definite behavioral goals in mind, so that the effects of his efforts can be objectively assessed. He should structure interaction with his client so as to make use of the cuing and reinforcing properties of his behavior and should conceptualize the interaction in these terms. If he does so, he can draw on analogous research from more controlled settings to guide his procedures. It seems unlikely, however, that this interactional process can be subjected to direct experimental study, since it has not been well enough controlled or described. This problem has already been discussed. The effectiveness of a treatment technique should not, therefore, depend on this interaction, but on more objectively defined procedures in which client-therapist interaction plays only a carefully controlled role. Then the therapist who modifies or augments these more controlled procedures takes a risk that he will introduce new uncontrolled factors. He must hope to gain sufficient flexibility to offset this risk.

To summarize, we have argued that therapist variables can be fairly well controlled using the within-subject design, essentially because the behavioral model does not posit that effective, therapeutic, behavior change requires an extensive interactional model of treatment. This argument accepts the fact that interpersonal interaction is routinely practiced by behavior therapists—just as it is by physicians—to obtain information, provide guidance and correction, and to increase the client's cooperation. We previously reached this conclusion in discussing the use of control group designs for the study of technical variations in desensitization therapy—another noninteractional behavioral treatment.

Client variables remain to be examined. Client variables are also conceptualized in terms of client behavior patterns, as shaped by the client's natural endowment and learning history. Here we must deal with variables that cannot be specified by reporting the experimental manipulations being studied. Yet the client's past experiences seem certain to be important factors in treatment outcome. Clients differ in the reinforcers they will respond to and in the environmental events that control their behavior. Their social responsiveness will be important for many treatment programs. In particular, their tendencies to respond to specific therapist characteristics or manipulations may strongly affect the results of treatment procedures.

To a large extent, individual differences are taken into account by the functional definitions of variables. Terms such as reinforcer and discriminative cue are relational terms—they describe a relation between environmental events and behavioral responses. Thus, treatment procedures requiring certain contingencies to be put into effect do not specify what specific environmental arrangements should be made. The prescription, "The child is to be reinforced for each instance of behavior A," is less specific than the prescription, "The child is to be patted on the head at each instance of behavior A." If behavior A does not increase after head-patting, it may be inferred that this contingency is not reinforcing for this particular child and that some other contingency should be substituted. The first prescription permits, and even demands, this method of analyzing the effects of one's intervention; the second does not.

To aid in this flexible treatment procedure, data are collected throughout treatment so the researcher (or therapist) can continuously observe the relations that occur between the operations performed and their functional effects on the child's behavior. The functional properties of specific therapeutic manipulations may be checked out in preliminary assessment. The researcher does not have to wait until therapy is completed to learn the consequences of a manipulation.

How might one conceptualize the phenomena sometimes attributed to client expectations in the behavioral model? Such phenomena seem likely to be found. Speaking loosely, it is possible in a within-subject research design that the different experimental conditions may appear to have different therapeutic value to the clients. The client's reaction to the therapist's discussion or instructions and treatment manipulations may depend to a degree on the client's prior experiences in similar situations. Behavior modifiers are frequently cautioned to consider expectancies of clients (Valins and Ray, 1967). Resistance to this suggestion comes largely, we believe, from the indefinite way in which these warnings are customarily presented. Client expectations or experimenter demand characteristics are not readily measurable variables. They have that unstructured, unfunctional character that has made control group research so cumbersome and barren, and the importation of such concepts into behavior modification seems to threaten to lead this research into a similar conceptual muddle.

Instead, we should investigate the objective factors that influence the client's response to specific treatment manipulations. Efforts to study the effects of statements to the client about the value of treatment have already been mentioned. It is hardly novel that instructions affect behavior, and instructions in therapy often appear to be influential (Brokovec, 1971; Oliveau, Agras, Leitenberg, Moore, and Wright, 1969). "Expectancy" effects perhaps may be most simply conceptualized in terms of the effects of therapist behaviors on those of the client: greater or lesser cooperation with the therapist's requests to attend to specified internal or external events, to report subjective states accurately, to carry out assignments outside the treatment hour, or even to show up for treatment. The client's cognitions are not necessary factors in this analysis.

It seems too early to judge whether the importance now attributed to client and therapist variables in verbal therapies is also justified for behavior therapy; and whether or not these variables can be redefined or controlled by the sorts of explicit operations suggested above. If they cannot, behavior therapy in the future may become embroiled in investigations of vaguely defined variables and uncertain manipulations. Trends in this direction are noticeable. There are continual attempts to translate behavior therapy terminology into cognitive terms by introducing variables that refer to clients' or therapists' internal perceptions or states. As we have argued throughout this paper, the introduction of variables in this form must be resisted.

Thus, with regard to the effects of client characteristics, we conclude that the behavioral model accompanying the within-subject design aims to translate individual differences into behavioral response measures. If adequate measures are taken, the researcher should be able to discover manipulations that will be effective in achieving the desired behavior change. For the most part, the research that would permit the therapist to act so confidently has not yet been done. In the absence of such a behavioral formulation of the problem of individual client differences, the therapist must remain uncertain about what behavioral variables should be observed and how various client characteristics should be handled.

REPLICABILITY OF RESULTS

We turn now to the second problem discussed for the control group design—the replicability of treatment results over a definable class of clients. As stated earlier, if a therapist attempts to reproduce a reported procedure, he may fail if the original report did not specify some critical feature of the experimental setting, the therapist's behavior, or the client's preexisting behavior tendencies. Such oversights are not unlikely. The small number of subjects in most within-subject studies makes it particularly difficult to recognize the influence of individual differences, which become background variables when only one or two subjects are studied. Differences among therapists in stimulus characteristics and behavior may be unnoticed for similar reasons.

Another problem of replication derives from experimenters' and editors' preference for publication of successful outcomes. Researchers have an understandable tendency not to submit experiments whose results do not fit the original conceptions, and editors may tend to reject them (Sterling, 1959). It is perhaps easier for a researcher to find methodological weaknesses in his work than to conclude that his hypotheses were unsound or his clients in some way unsuitable for the treatment procedure. The consequence of this selectivity is that reported results may give a biased view of the success to be expected for a given technique, even after a number of successful studies have appeared. The extent of this bias in psychological research has not been investigated in any detail, although it is an issue on which comments are frequently made (Gardner, 1966). Presently, only a few behavior therapy techniques have been sufficiently investigated to allow a guarantee as to high predictability of outcome. Generally, the effects of a treatment technique must be inferred from scattered studies with a few cases. Lest one conclude that negative results are quite excluded from the literature, numerous treatment failures have been reported in some areas, such as of smoking or overeating; and patients with multiple phobias have so far shown considerable resistance to treatment. Also, treatment of childhood autism or of retardation has not shown great success if one considers normal functioning the treatment goal.

Studies presenting the results of several replications of a single procedure can help resolve this problem. If such group studies have limited research value, they are important to show the extent of application of a procedure. An experimenter who replicates a technique with different subjects and reports all results gives the reader a better idea of the conditions under which replication can be expected. Studies primarily of work with groups of children in schools have appeared in behavior modification literature, and the results of this work are very impressive. Few serious treatment failures have appeared among them. However, the characteristics of children who do not respond have not been much studied. Reports of well-controlled studies with treatment failures will help define the conditions under which the manipulations are effective and guide specific remedial efforts.

Of course, as we have noted before, if powerful, general, readily detectable behavior changes could be produced through therapeutic technique, detailed concern with research design would become less relevant. It is the failure of interaction therapies to develop and validate such techniques that makes the research question so important. The use of objective behavior outcome measures and contingency analysis has greatly decreased the problems of determining what leads to what in therapy by bringing the intervention and its result closer together and by making both much easier to see. That in itself seems a significant step toward making research simpler, and the improvement of therapy techniques should follow almost inevitably. Behavior modification procedures seem already to have produced such techniques for a number of problems; yet, perhaps no single technique has been so fully validated as to be immune to critical challenge.

The success of within-subject research in behavior modification ultimately may depend on the adequacy of the conceptual model or models followed by the experimenters who use the design. Useful research into a phenomenon so complicated as psychotherapy needs conceptual guidance from results obtained in less complex situations. The conceptual structure derived from human and animal laboratory learning settings provides such models, and our current effort to develop therapeutic methods through behavioral research depends strongly on the adequacy of those models for ordering the manifold phenomena of psychotherapy. The models determine how well the within-subject design will permit the accumulation of useful information. The within-subject design provides a basis of control and observation superior in many ways to that available from control group studies; but that basis does not assure that the experimenter will make the correct observations or discover therapeutically advantageous contingency arrangements. There is no automatic formula for success.

REFERENCES

BERGIN, A. E. and STRUPP, H. H. New directions in psychotherapy research. *Journal of Abnormal Psychology*, 1970, 76, 13–26.

BROKOVEC, T. D. Effects of expectancy on the outcome of systematic desensitization of avoidance behavior. *Behavior Therapy*, 1972, 3, 29–40.

EDWARDS, A. L., and CRONBACH, L. J. Experimental designs for research in psychotherapy. *Journal of Clinical Psychology*, 1952, 8, 51–59.

EYSENCK, H. J. The effects of psychotherapy: An evaluation. *Journal of Consulting Psychology*, 1952, 16, 319–24.

GARDNER, R. A. On box score methodology as illustrated by three reviews of over-training reversal effects. *Psychological Bulletin*, 1966, 66, 416–22.

GOLDSTEIN, A. P., HELLER, K., and SECHREST, L. B. *Psychotherapy and the psychology of behavior change.* New York: Wiley and Sons, 1966.

KELLNER, R. The evidence in favour of psychotherapy. *British Journal of Medical Psychology*, 1967, 40, 341–58.

LEVITT, E. E. Research on psychotherapy with children. In Bergin, A. E. and Garfield, S. L. (Eds.) *Handbook of psychotherapy and behavior change.* New York: Wiley and Sons, 1971.

LINDER, L. H. and McGLYNN, F. D. Experimental desensitization of noise-avoidance following two schedules of semi-automated relaxation training. *Behavior Research and Therapy*, 1971, 9, 131–36.

LOMONT, J. F. and BROCK, L. Cognitive factors in systematic desensitization. *Behavior Research and Therapy*, 1971, 9, 187–96.

LOMONT, J. F. and EDWARDS, J. E. The role of relaxation in systematic desensitization. *Behavior Research and Therapy*, 1967, 5, 11–26.

McGLYNN, F. D. Experimental desensitization following three types of instructions. *Behavior Research and Therapy*, 1971, 9, 367–70.

McGLYNN, F. D. and MAPP, R. H. Systematic desensitization of snake-avoidance following three types of suggestion. *Behavior Research and Therapy*, 1970, 8, 197–202.

OLIVEAU, D. C., AGRAS, W. S., LEITENBERG, H., MOORE, R. C., and WRIGHT, D. E. Systematic desensitization therapeutically oriented instructions and selective positive reinforcement. *Behavior Research and Therapy*, 1969, 8, 27–34.

PAUL, G. L. *Insight vs. desensitization in psychotherapy: An experiment in anxiety reduction.* Stanford: Stanford University Press, 1966.

PAUL, G. L. Strategy of outcome research in psychotherapy. *Journal of Consulting Psychology*, 1967, 31, 109–18.

ROBINSON, V. *The Story of Medicine.* New York: Tudor, 1931.

ROGERS, C. R. The necessary and sufficient conditions of therapeutic personality change. *Journal of Consulting Psychology*, 1957, 21, 95–103.

STERLING, T. D. Publication decisions and their possible effects on inferences drawn from tests of significance or vice versa. *Journal of the American Statistical Association*, 1959, 54, 30–34.

THOMAS, D. R., BECKER, W. C. and ARMSTRONG, M. Production and elimination of disruptive classroom behavior by systematically varying teacher's behavior. *Journal of Applied Behavior Analysis*, 1968, 1, 35–45.

VALINS, S. and RAY, ALICE A. Effects of cognitive desensitization on avoidance behavior. *Journal of Personality and Social Psychology*, 1967, 7, 345–50.

2

BUILDING SELF-HELP
AND SOCIAL SKILLS

The next section deals with methods of helping children to acquire the most elementary kinds of socially desirable behavior: to eat at the table appropriately, not to urinate in bed, to play on playground toys, and so on. Most children learn these behaviors at home, and no expert is required to teach them. Unfortunately some do not learn without such special assistance.

There are several valuable lessons to be gained from the following papers. It is commonplace to assert that children enjoy healthy development when their parents love them and that a good therapist must have concern for his patients. Such views do not include consideration of the concrete actions through which such love and concern find their expression. It is a false and romantic notion that one somehow can raise children by just emanating love to them. When we try to understand what is meant by terms like parent's love and therapist's concern, we want to point out those specific behavior tactics that have a beneficial effect on the development of particular behaviors by the child. Love is manifest in such mundane matters as patting a baby on the back to help him burp, changing his diapers, putting him in a highchair, teaching him to use his fingers to eat cereal, and giving him a whack on the rear when he walks into a busy street. Similarly, to give actuality to the sweeping generalizations that have been written about the value of the therapist-patient interaction, a good therapist must become involved in all the concrete happenings of his patient's life.

We present first the study with retarded children by Barton, Guess, Garcia, and Baer, because it helps us to understand how to teach a behavior that is both elementary and complex—socially acceptable eating. This paper is refreshing in its use of such honest terms as "pigging" to describe messy forms of eating. Good eating behavior, as the authors note, is highly reinforcing to the staff and to the children's parents. Seeing it evokes new hope that these children can make even more progress in other areas.

Buell, Stoddard, Harris, and Baer's study on reinforcing outdoor play in a preschool child also raises the question of what happens to other behaviors when one behavior is altered. The study shows how significant therapeutic changes can occur across several behaviors even though only one behavior is directly treated. These first two studies are concerned with defining the nature of what have been called "response classes." Behaviors in the same response class tend to act as a group when contingencies are attached to some members of their class. Thus, increasing the strength of response A results in changes in response B, C, and D without direct experimental intervention on the latter three responses. The variables affecting the cohesion and differentiation of responses into classes will probably become a most significant focus in behavior modification research in the next several years.

The selection by Lovaas, Freitas, Nelson, and Whalen describes a study on the establishment of nonverbal imitation in autistic children. This work is essentially an efficiency study. Building behavior by successive approximations is a very time-consuming process, and we need to research ways to build behaviors more quickly this way. The study shows how to build imitative behavior and to use this new skill to build other complex behavioral repertoires into the child's day-to-day functioning.

Lovaas, Schaeffer, and Simmons's study on building social behaviors with electric shock is included not so much to demonstrate that one can use shock as a motivator but to try to illustrate that complex effects may take place even when one presents a child with a stimulus that is very simple, at least in physical terms. Pain is used here to build appropriate social stimuli (positive secondary reinforcers), not just to suppress pathological behaviors. Such implementation of shock is an unusual and significant expansion of the usual uses of this stimulus.

Baker's study of symptom substitution concerns itself with a challenge that has been posed to behavior therapists from the very beginning. Can one really work on single behaviors—one at a time—without upsetting the patient's "equilibrium?" If we remove one symptom, does not another replace it—leaving the patient essentially in an untreated state? This has long been an important question, and the study by Baker attempts to deal with it.

There are several ways one can abstract these papers. Perhaps the most important way is according to their methodology. The student should pay particular attention to the use of multiple baseline technique in the Barton, Guess, Garcia, and Baer study; to the use of probes in the study by Buell, Stoddard, Harris, and Baer; and to the use of an *ABA* (or *ABAB*) *design* in the Lovaas, Schaeffer, and Simmons article (where A is baseline and B is the presentation of the treatment variable).

ELIZABETH SPINDLER BARTON[1]
Meanwood Park Hospital, Leeds, England

DOUG GUESS
Kansas Neurological Institute

EUGENE GARCIA
University of Kansas

DONALD M. BAER
University of Kansas

Improvement of retardates' mealtime behaviors by timeout procedures using multiple baseline techniques[2]

Undesirable mealtime behaviors of a hospital cottage of retardates were reduced by contingent timeout procedures applied by ward personnel successively to one undesirable behavior after another, in a multiple baseline design. In some cases the timeout procedure was to remove the subject from the room until the meal was finished; in other cases (depending on the health of the child and the initial rate of the behavior to be reduced), timeout consisted of a 15-sec removal of the child's meal tray. Undesirable behaviors were defined as stealing, using fingers inappropriately, messy use of utensils, and pigging (eating directly with mouth or eating spilled food). Timeout was applied to these behaviors in that order, and in each case led to a marked and useful reduction in the behavior

Reprinted from *Journal of Applied Behavior Analysis*, 1970, 3, 77–84, with permission of the publisher and the authors. Copyright 1970 by the Society for the Experimental Analysis of Behavior, Inc.

---

[1] This study was conducted while the senior author was a member of the Psychology staff of the Kansas Neurological Institute.

[2] The authors are grateful to Mrs. Nellis Shaw, Mrs. Lois Brown, Mrs. Margaret Duffy, Mrs. Florence Watts, Mrs. Arlene Glenn, Miss Stephanie Alexander, Miss Dolores Lowry, and Mrs. Jo Hodison, who served as cottage attendants at various times during this study, and who actually carried out the demanding procedures required by the experimental design. Acknowledgement is also due to Mrs. Linda Vopat, R.N., cottage nurse, for her cooperation and interest.

throughout the group. As these undesirable behaviors were reduced, more appropriate mealtime behaviors emerged: as inappropriate use of fingers declined (under contingent timeout), messy utensil behavior increased; later, as messy utensil behavior declined (under contingent timeout), a defined category of neat utensil behavior increased. Weights of the subjects were monitored steadily throughout the study and showed essentially no change.

Disruptive behavior and undesirable styles of eating are common among severely retarded children, especially in group settings under minimal supervision. Procedures to reduce the frequency of such mealtime behaviors among institutionalized retardates are especially needed. Disruptive eating habits can place an excessive burden on ward attendants (who often find themselves inadequately prepared to deal with these problems), and unaesthetic table manners probably ensure that a retardate will be considered more as an animal and less as a child by those who watch him.

Within recent years, operant procedures have been used to reduce undesirable mealtime behavior, and to train more appropriate eating styles in retarded children. Various forms of mild punishment have been used to reduce inappropriate mealtime behavior, such as timeout from the meal (Hamilton and Allen, 1967), physical restraint (Henricksen and Doughty, 1967), and removing the child's food for short periods of time (Blackwood, 1962; Whitney and Barnard, 1966). An alternative procedure (Lent, 1967), eliminated food stealing by reinforcing non-stealing and removing reinforcers for stealing.

Thus, these studies suggest that mild punishment can be used to improve eating behavior among the severely retarded. However, of the studies reviewed, only one (Lent, 1967) demonstrated experimental control of the treatment (using a reversal technique).

The present study reports a feeding program using timeout techniques in a ward of severely and profoundly retarded children, adolescents, and young adults. The research design involved a multiple-baseline technique (Baer, Wolf, and Risley, 1968) both to demonstrate the function of the timeout variable and to further an analysis of various response components of undesirable mealtime behavior.

Subjects and Setting

The 16 subjects were male residents of a cottage at the Kansas Neurological Institute. Their ages ranged from 9 to 23 yr. All subjects fell within the A.A.M.D. classifications of severely and profoundly retarded. Hand coordination was near normal except for two severely spastic subjects; hearing was normal in all but two, and speech was uniformly absent.

The residents ate their breakfast, lunch, and dinner in two adjoining 12 by 12 ft (3.6 by 3.6 m) dining rooms connected by a 3 by 4 ft (0.9 x 1.2 m) open window in a common wall. Each subject was assigned a regular seat in one of the two rooms, four subjects in each room. Meals were served in two shifts of eight subjects each, the second shift immediately following the first. (These arrangements were initiated specifically for the training program. Previously, residents had their meals as a group in a large room.) Food was placed on the table in cafeteria trays, before the subjects entered. Each tray contained bread, milk, and assorted foods in two or three different dishes. Spoons were provided for all subjects. (Forks were occasionally given as well, but to no more than six of the subjects.) A 6 by 8 ft (1.8 by 2.4 m) bare room approximately 20 ft (6 m) from either dining room was used as a timeout room. From two to four (usually three) cottage attendants were present during these meals.

Observation

Preliminary observation led to the following definitions of mealtime behaviors to be recorded:

1. *Stealing:* removal of food or other object from another resident's tray.
2. *Fingers:* eating food (from a dish) with fingers (excepting use of fingers to hold hamburger buns, bread, rolls, potato chips, celery sticks, and other foods "properly" eaten with fingers).
3. *Messy utensil:* pushing food off dish with utensil, using fingers to place food on utensil, spilling food off utensil or cup en route to mouth, or using utensil with face closer than 2 in. to the dish.
4. *Neat utensil:* use of utensil to eat, excluding those behaviors defined as "Messy Utensil."
5. *Pigging:* eating food spilled on table, floor, clothing, or own tray; and eating food by placing the mouth directly on it (without use of fingers or utensil).
6. *Other behavior:* engaging in behavior not defined above (requesting, being taught to use spoon, appropriate use of fingers, and being timed-out).
7. *No behavior:* absence of gross behavior, *e.g.,* looking about, sitting quietly, chewing or swallowing.

The above seven categories of behavior were mutually exclusive, and functionally exhausted all behavior seen in the situation. Of these seven, three —Stealing, Fingers, and Pigging—were defined as "Disgusting" because of their effect on aides and other spectators.

Observations were made during the noon and evening meals, beginning only when all subjects were seated, and ending when the last subject had finished his meal. Each subject was observed until one of the defined behaviors occurred, or for 10 sec; however, "No Behavior" or "Other Behavior" were recorded for a subject only after 10 sec of observation had failed to produce a different recording. Subjects were observed in turn, starting with the resident who had been seated first and continuing once around the table in clockwise fashion. The observer then recorded the behavior of the subjects seated at the second table, in the same manner; he then returned to observe the first table again. Usually, each subject was observed between six and 12 times per meal. Slow eaters typically were observed more often per meal than fast eaters, who could leave the dining room upon finishing their meal.[3]

From this time-sampling procedure, the percentage of occurrence for each class of behavior was computed for the entire group, by dividing the recorded instances of each class across all subjects by the total number of all recorded observations across all subjects, then multiplying by 100.[4] During seven meals of the study, and at least once during each experimental condition, a second observer made a simultaneous record. Comparison of these two records, subject by subject, and interval by interval, allowed computation of a percentage of observer agreement.

An ongoing daily record of timeouts from meals was kept throughout the experimental conditions by the ward attendants. Body weights of each subject were recorded at monthly intervals.

Procedure

After a baseline condition with no experimentally imposed contingencies, a sequence of timeout conditions was made contingent on the following behaviors in the order listed.

Stealing. The subject was removed from the meal by the cottage attendants and placed in the timeout room immediately following any Stealing response observed by any attendant(s). All subjects removed were placed in this room and kept there for the remainder of the meal. These subjects' trays were removed from the table. In most cases it was sufficient

---

[3] However, near the end of the study, all subjects were encouraged to remain in their seats until everyone had finished his meal, the entire group then leaving the dining rooms as a body. Thus, the final group data of the study are based on nearly equal numbers of observation of each child.

[4] Suppose, for example, that at a given meal 10 children were observed nine times each before leaving the room, four more were observed 10 times each, and two more were observed 11 times each. A total of $10 \times 9 + 4 \times 10 + 2 \times 11 = 152$ observations would have been recorded. If 15 of those observations were "Fingers", then the per cent of occurrence for this category would be $15/152 = 10\%$. The number of subjects contributing to these 15 "Fingers" recordings might have been as low as one or as high as 15, but this number was not reflected in the score, which was intended to display the behaviors of the group as a whole.

merely for the cottage attendant to call a child's name when he was being timed-out, and lead him to the timeout room. It was necessary to pull a few subjects from the dining area to the timeout area, occasionally requiring two cottage attendants.

Fingers. With the preceding timeout condition remaining in effect, each member of one group of 11 subjects was removed from the meal and placed in the timeout room immediately following any Fingers response (timeout from meal). For a second group of five, each subject had his tray removed for 15 sec immediately following Fingers response (timeout 15 sec.). This second group received the 15 sec. timeout because the nursing staff was concerned that timeout from the entire meal might jeopardize these subjects' health. Also, a shaping procedure was initiated for three subjects who had not used utensils previously, two of whom had motor impairments affecting their hand coordination. Special large-handled spoons were given to these subjects.

Messy Utensils. With all the preceding timeout conditions remaining in effect, a 15-sec tray removal immediately followed any instance of Messy Utensils use. The 15-sec. timeout rather than timeout from the meal was used in expectation of many repeated contingencies being necessary to eliminate this frequent behavior.

Pigging. With all the preceding timeout conditions in effect, a 15-sec tray removal immediately followed any Pigging response. Again, the 15-sec timeout was used in the interests of efficiency.

Before each condition, the experimenters met with cottage personnel and identified the specific behavior to be timed-out. The experimenters also served as models for the initial few meals in each condition, working with the cottage attendants to apply the contingencies. A large sign was attached to the wall of the dining area, indicating what contingencies were in effect that day for each subject. Monitoring the attendants' use of these contingencies was accomplished in the course of time-sampling the subjects' behaviors cited for timeout.

Each change in conditions was determined by the overall stability of the data already recorded. Data were collected five days per week during lunch and dinner, but the contingencies described above were in effect during all three meals of each day of each condition, without exception. The study lasted six months.

RESULTS

Inter-observer agreement for each of the seven meals during which observer reliability was assessed ranged from 86 to 95% with a mean of 90%.

Figure 1 represents the percentage of observations of the seven defined classes of mealtime behavior, and the total percentage of the three behaviors defined as "Disgusting" (Stealing, Fingers, and Pigging), for the total group throughout the study. The beginnings of the successive timeout conditions are indicated by vertical lines, with horizontal arrows denoting the temporal span of each condition. Figure 1 shows that each successive condition of timeout led systematically to a decrease in the behavior(s) being manipulated. Thus, Stealing was relatively high during baseline, but it decreased steadily during the timeout procedure until reaching zero. Fingers and Pigging meanwhile remained relatively stable, until timeout for each was imposed; both behaviors fell abruptly and then steadily decreased to near-zero. Messy Utensils remained stable during the Baseline and timeout for Stealing conditions, but a significant increase of this behavior was observed when subjects were timed-out for Fingers. However, timeout for Messy Utensils then produced the usual decrease in this category. Neat Utensils, which had remained consistent throughout the previous timeout manipulations, increased when timeout for Messy Utensils was imposed, gradually replacing Messy Utensils in relative frequency. The percentage of Total Disgusting Behaviors decreased across successive timeout conditions, from a baseline mean of 36% to generally less than 5% during the final meals of the study.

Figure 2 shows the effects of the two timeout conditions imposed for Fingers, and also the percentage of observations for No Behavior and Other Behavior. Both the timeout of 15 sec and the timeout from the meal effectively reduced the relative frequency of Fingers responses; a resulting low level of near-zero was maintained during the final 40 meals of the study.

The percentage of observations in which No Behavior was recorded showed a gradual decline across successive meals of the study. Other Behavior showed a very slight, highly variable increase throughout the study.

Figure 3 tracks the total number of timeouts per day, as recorded by the ward attendants, for successive days of the study. The solid line depicts the number of subjects removed from the meal for Stealing; the broken line represents the number of those 11 subjects who were removed from the meal for Fingers. The number of subjects timed-out for each of these conditions shows an abrupt decrease, which levels off and remains fairly constant for the remainder of the study.

The weights of the 16 subjects participating in the program, measured at monthly intervals during the course of the study, are represented in Fig. 4. The mean weight of the group remained unchanged throughout the six-month period. The child who weighed least at the start of the program (lower limit) showed a slight gain in weight during the study; the child who initially weighed most (upper limit) also gained weight over the six-month period. The subject who lost most during the course of the study

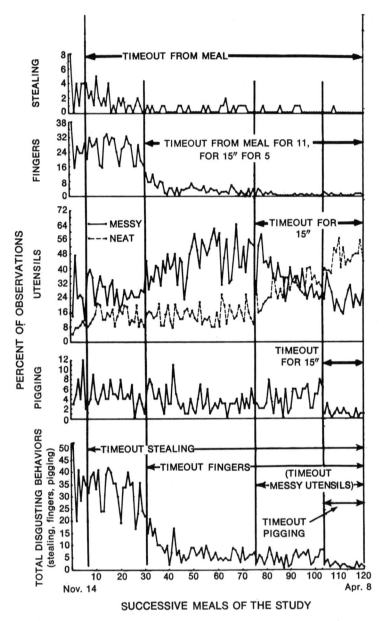

FIGURE 1 Concurrent group rates of Stealing, Fingers, Utensils, and Pigging behaviors, and the sum of Stealing, Fingers, and Pigging (Total Disgusting Behaviors), through the baseline and experimental phases of the study.

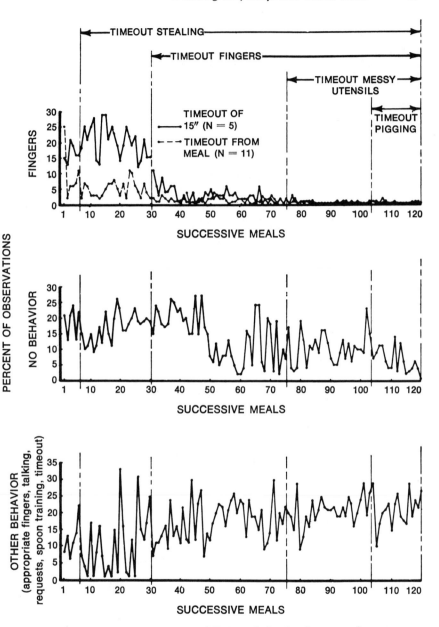

FIGURE 2 Concurrent rates of Fingers behavior for two subgroups of the cottage (representing two forms of timeout), and of No-Behavior and Other-Behavior categories for the total cottage, through the baseline and experimental phases of the study.

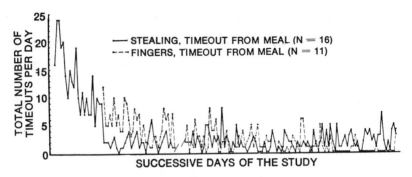

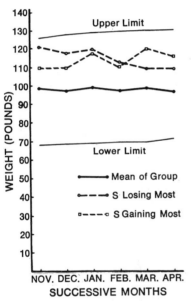

FIGURE 3   Cottage attendants' records of the number of timeouts from the meal required throughout the study.

FIGURE 4   Monthly average and extreme weights of the cottage subjects throughout the study, and the course of weight change for the two subjects showing greatest gain or loss.

(10 lb.) is also compared to the subject gaining the most weight (8 lb.). Neither shift was large.

DISCUSSION

The exact function of the timeout procedure, whether it is a form of simple extinction or a punishing event, remains an area of ambiguity pending further experimental analysis (Leitenberg, 1965; Sherman and Baer,

1969). Nevertheless, accepting Azrin and Holz's (1966) functional definition of a punishing stimulus, the timeout conditions used in the present study can be defined as punishers: the percentage of occurrence of each undesirable behavior was successfully reduced when the timeout contingency was applied to the behavior. Experimental control of the timeout variable was demonstrated through the successive but temporally separated application of the timeout contingency to those behaviors defined as Stealing, Fingers, Messy Utensil, and Pigging. The baseline occurrence of each of these behaviors remained relatively unchanged until that point in time in which the timeout consequence was applied, thus diminishing the possibility that such changes occurred by chance. This "multiple-baseline" technique (Baer, Wolf, and Risley, 1968) is especially useful when the behavior appears to be irreversible or, as in the present case, when reversing the behavior is undesirable.

Further analyses of the data indicate that both the 15-sec timeout and timeout from the entire meal were successful in reducing inappropriate eating behavior. However, an exacting comparison of the two procedures cannot be made from the present design, inasmuch as each timeout contingency was applied to either different behaviors or different subjects. A more accurate comparison of the two procedures would have been possible had both timeout contingencies been alternated across one behavior with the same subjects. For Stealing, however, timeout from the total meal would probably be the more effective contingency, since removal of the child's tray would probably encourage the behavior (at least without prior association as a punishing stimulus for other behaviors).

The continued decrease of each behavior across successive meals indicates that the relative reduction of the behavior may be a cumulative function of the timeout consequence and the length of time it is in effect. As shown in Fig. 1, the timeout contingency usually produced an abrupt deceleration of the behavior, which then continued to decline steadily across meals. From an applied point of view, one might well initiate timeout's for various behaviors more rapidly than in the present study. Similarly, it is likely that each new timeout contingency produces the desired effect more rapidly as a result of cumulative prior timeout conditions. This, again, is difficult to evaluate in the present design, due to the apparent differences in the behaviors under study.

The increase in Messy Utensil (Fig. 1) following timeout for Fingers was an expected change, and represented more appropriate eating behavior among the subjects. Time-out for Messy Utensil was followed by a subsequent decrease in this behavior and a concurrent acceleration in Neat Utensil. Thus, the increase of the desired behavior, Neat Utensil, was obtained without placing a direct contingency on it.

The general decrease in No Behavior across successive meals of the study probably reflects a generally improved mealtime climate where more time was spent by the subjects in appropriate eating behavior. Although data were not available, it was observed that the residents were spending more of their time eating, especially in the slower forms required by Neat Utensil behavior, as the study progressed. (Before the first timeout operation, the subjects tended to eat rapidly before their food was stolen; the remainder of the meal then was spent sitting or engaging in a number of inappropriate behaviors: wandering, head banging, self-stimulation, tantrums, fighting, and throwing of uneaten food.)

The fact that no significant weight losses occurred among the subjects during the study is significant from a practical point of view. (The one subject who lost the most over the six-month period (10 lb) had already been placed on a reduction diet by the medical staff because of overweight.)

It should certainly be pointed out that the cottage attendants were those persons who were primarily responsible for implementing the treatment procedures. Unusually high morale was reported to have been maintained by the cottage personnel over the six-month study period, probably because of the improved eating behavior of the 16 residents. Although the cottage personnel appeared generally disinterested in the graphs depicting progress, they seemed most pleased with favorable comments by parents, other cottage attendants, and other professional staff members. Most likely, however, the simple and straightforward training procedures that enabled them to gain and maintain control over the mealtime behavior of the residents and the very noticeable improvement made by the subjects was largely responsible for the success of the program.

Since results of this study were made available to the institution, three other cottages have implemented similar feeding programs that were initiated and are being maintained by persons other than those participating in the present study.

REFERENCES

Azrin, N. H. and Holz, W. C. Punishment. In W. K. Honig (Ed.), *Operant behavior: areas of research and application*. New York: Appleton-Century-Crofts, 1966. Pp. 380–447.

Baer, D. M., Wolf, M. M., and Risley, T. R. Some current dimensions of applied behavior analysis. *Journal of Applied Behavior Analysis*, 1968, 1, 91–97.

Blackwood, R. O. *Operant conditioning as a method of training the mentally retarded*. Unpublished dissertation, Ohio State University, 1962.

Hamilton, J. and Allen, Patricia. Ward programming for severely retarded institutionalized residents. *Mental Retardation*, 1967, 5, 22–24.

HENRIKSEN, K. and DOUGHTY, R. Decelerating undesired mealtime behavior in a group of profoundly retarded boys. *American Journal of Mental Deficiency*, 1967, 72, 40–44.

LEITENBERG, H. Is time out from positive reinforcement an aversive event? *Psychological Bulletin*, 1965, 64, 428–441.

LENT, J. *Modification of food stealing behavior of an institutionalized retarded subject*. Working Paper #175, Parsons Research Center, 1967.

SHERMAN, J. A. and BAER, D. M. Appraisal of operant therapy techniques with children and adults. In C. Franks (Ed.). New York: McGraw-Hill, 1969. Pp. 192–219.

WHITNEY, LINDA R. and BARNARD, KATHRYN E. Implications of operant learning theory for nursing care of the retarded child. *Mental Retardation*, 1966, 4, 26–29.

JOAN BUELL
University of Oregon

PATRICIA STODDARD
University of Washington

FLORENCE R. HARRIS
University of Washington

DONALD M. BAER[1]
University of Kansas

Collateral social development accompanying reinforcement of outdoor play in a preschool child[2,3]

A 3-yr-old preschool girl with deficits in both motor and social repertoires was socially reinforced by teachers for use of outdoor play equipment, as a contribution to her motor skills and as a tactic to produce increased social contact with other children. Her use of outdoor play equipment, and various examples of her social interaction with both teachers and children were scored in the course of experimental development and analysis of her rate of equipment use. Equipment use increased greatly under the social reinforcement contingency; certain desirable examples of social interaction with other children showed a collateral development; other examples of adult-oriented development remained constant; and one class of undesirable baby-like behavior decreased markedly. Thus, the study provided a picture of what other behavior changes may take place in the course of behavior modification aimed at a single response class.

Reprinted from *Journal of Applied Behavior Analysis*, 1968, 1, 167–73, with permission of the publisher and the authors. Copyright 1968 by the Society for the Experimental Analysis of Behavior, Inc.

———
[1] Research Associate, Bureau of Child Research, University of Kansas.

[2] This research was supported in part by a grant to Donald M. Baer by the National Institute of Mental Health, MH-02208—entitled An Experimental Analysis of Social Motivation.

[3] This research was conducted while the authors were staff members of the Institute of Child Development, University of Washington.

That the preschool teacher should be a notable source of social reinforcement for the children in her class has rarely been doubted. That she can effectively wield this reinforcement as a technique of behavior modification in the service of those children has now been demonstrated in numerous instances (*cf.*, Harris, Wolf, and Baer, 1964; Allen, Henke, Harris, Baer, and Reynolds, 1967; Baer and Wolf, 1968; Hart, Reynolds, Baer, Brawley, and Harris, 1968). These demonstrations uniformly single out a specific class of behavior (a behavior problem for the child studied) and demonstrate that remediation can be produced experimentally. The changes produced are clearly desirable in such cases, and are rarely questioned. However, a persistent question has concerned the possibility of allied behavioral changes in the course of the study. These allied changes are often pointed to as desirable in themselves. Sometimes they are more far-reaching than the behavior originally treated (Baer and Wolf, 1967), and thereby could be seen as the more valuable target of the remediation effort. By contrast, it is sometimes suspected that the allied behavioral changes will represent undesirable developments, due to a surface rather than basic suppression of the child's "real" problem. That is, the new behaviors could represent merely new expressions of the old problem (such that crying, once reduced, might be replaced by, say, thumbsucking).

In the past, little data concerning the actual nature of such allied behavioral changes have been collected objectively. Global observations and impressions have usually testified to the generally desirable character of whatever behavior changes took place, but nothing more specific or precise has been available for close inspection. The present study was designed to provide more objective data, of a reasonably comprehensive nature, concerning the variety and amount of behavioral change that might result, in the course of a behavior modification program aimed at a single specific class of problem behavior. The problem behavior in this case was a lack of both motor play and social repertoires in a 3-yr-old girl; the behavioral setting for remediation was the preschool; and the basic technique applied was social reinforcement.

PROCEDURE

The subject was a strong, attractive 3-yr-old girl, called Polly for this report. Her parents were not native speakers of English, and Polly had spent all of her second year living abroad with them. Presumably as a consequence, her language skills in English, although technically well developed for her age, nevertheless were distinctively strange, by the standards of the usual American audience, and especially so for 3-yr-olds. Thus, it was not particularly surprising to find that Polly participated very little in her preschool program, where she was one of 12 children, the other 11 being normal speakers for their age. In particular, her teachers noted that she showed no cooperative play with the children, never used their names, infrequently touched or spoke to them, and showed only a certain rate of parallel play as her major form of social interaction. She rarely used the outdoor play equipment of the schoolyard. Her behaviors with teachers were frequent, but equally discouraging: she would most often hang on a teacher's coattail and engage in a type of stylized monosyllabic prattling which was clearly a bright imitation of her infant brother's babytalk. No improvement was reported by the teachers after a full month of preschool attendance, and consequently a systematic program of behavior modification was planned.

The essence of this program was to explore a tactic, simple in its basic dimensions but possibly effective in contributing to the totality of Polly's behavior problems. The tactic chosen was to develop Polly's use of outdoor play equipment. It was assumed that if her rate of using such equipment could be increased and maintained, she would very likely be thrown into a steady variety of interactions with her peers, and that from such interactions many useful contributions to her behavioral repertoire could result. To evaluate the extent to which this happened, it was necessary to observe a representative sample of these desired interactions. A set of behaviors reflecting child-oriented and teacher-oriented social behaviors, and equipment use, was defined, as listed in Table 1.

These categories of response were scored by time-sampling. An observer, watching Polly constantly throughout each outdoor preschool session, recorded every 10 sec which of these behaviors, if any, Polly had shown during that 10-sec interval. The observer also recorded teacher response to Polly, whether contingent on these behaviors or offered at other times. Thus, Polly's rate in any behavioral category could be computed as the percentage of 10-sec intervals during which she was observed that she displayed the behavior in question. These rates, expressed as percentages, comprised the basic data of the study.

Observer reliability was checked frequently, mainly because of the unusually large number of categories to be recorded. On three of every five days of each school week, two observers worked as a pair. At the end of each day, their records were compared and a percent-agreement score calculated. Agreement meant that for a given interval of the day, both observers had scored the same behavior as occurring. (Instances in which both observers agreed that nothing had occurred were not counted.) Percent-agreement was calculated as the number of agreements divided by the number of agreements and disagreements combined. Percent-agreement was never less than 85%, and typically exceeded 90%, for each behavior category defined in Table 1. It was thus concluded that observation was

TABLE 1 Definitions of responses under study

Object of response	Type of response	Criteria of response
Teacher	Touching	Polly and teacher in contact, no matter who originated the contact; or both touching the same object, such as holding the same toy.
Child	Touching	Same as for touching teacher, but involving another child instead of teacher.
Teacher	Verbalization	Verbalization within 3 ft of a teacher, either using her name or facing the teacher directly.
Child	Verbalization	Verbalization within 3 ft of a child or within 3 ft of a child and teacher, but not also using teacher's name or facing her directly.
Child	Using Child's Name	Speaking the proximate child's name, or saying "you" to the child directly.
Child	Parallel Play	Playing within 3 ft of another child or at the same recognizable location (*e.g.,* sandbox, table, easel) but *not* sharing material (such as same piece of clay, same jar of paint, *etc.*)
Child	Cooperative Play	Shared play, such as building same structure, taking objects from same container, talking together to coordinate activity, following rules of game, sharing roles in activity such as playing store, *etc.*
Teacher	Baby Behavior	Monosyllabic, repetitive babytalk, babylike hand flapping, hopping from one foot to the other and back repetitively, and speaking incomplete sentences.
Equipment	Play on Outdoor Equipment	Appropriate use of swing, trike, boat, tunnel, log, rocking board, jumping board, ladder box, rocking boat, and climbing frames, with or without another child present on the same equipment.

adequate to the demands of the study, which then proceeded according to the following design.

The experimental design consisted of a baseline period, followed first by reinforcement coupled with an auxiliary technique of "priming", and then by reinforcement without priming. This subsequent period of reinforcement without priming was probed twice, briefly, by periods of noncontingent reinforcement to examine the role of reinforcement in maintaining any behavioral changes that had appeared so far.

Baseline. The baseline period lasted five days, sufficient to demonstrate that the observational categories and techniques of the study were adequate to produce reliable data, and to confirm the teachers' estimate of Polly's behavioral characteristics. During this time, teachers gave Polly random, noncontingent attention as usual. Polly asked to use play equipment only once, requesting that the seesaw be set up. When it was, she then refused to use it. She did show a low rate of spontaneous use of the outdoor play equipment, but never in response to a teacher's invitation, which she invariably answered with "No, I don't want to."

Reinforcement with priming.   Starting on Day 6, teachers began creating an instance of using play equipment outdoors each day, and then reinforcing the behavior created. Referred to here as priming, this technique consisted simply of lifting Polly bodily onto a piece of play equipment once each outdoor session, and holding her there at least 30 sec if necessary. A different piece of equipment was used each successive day. Teachers chose their occasions for doing this by taking advantage of Polly's normal shifts of locale, selecting a piece she had happened to come near at the moment (so long as that piece had not been used for priming on a previous day). Polly was put on equipment whether or not another child was using that equipment, and whether or not she protested (which she did the first three times it occurred). As long as Polly stayed on the equipment, on these as well as on any unprimed occasions, the teacher remained close (within 3 ft or less), watching, touching her as seemed appropriate, smiling and talking about her play, and generally displaying interest, approval, and delight in Polly's activity.

The period of reinforcement with priming lasted nine days (Day 6 to 14), when teachers judged it had served its purpose; it was then supplanted by a period of reinforcement without priming. During this period, in addition to the consistent, continuous reinforcement offered for all forms of equipment play, primed or not, teachers continued their usual practice of giving random, intermittent reinforcement for Polly's other behaviors.

Reinforcement without priming.   Beginning on Day 15, teachers discontinued their daily priming technique. Polly's behavior was reinforced as before if she showed any use of the outdoor play equipment, but she was never lifted or placed on any piece unless she first requested it. Teachers continued to suggest occasionally that she might like to use the equipment ("Polly, would you like a trike?") but urged no further if the invitation were refused. (This had been their standard practice throughout Polly's stay at preschool.) Starting with the fifth day of this period (Day 19), teachers began gradually to make their reinforcement of equipment play more intermittent, stepping a few feet away from Polly between comments (which averaged every 30 sec), and then a few feet more, *etc.* Then, they began staying away longer than 30 sec, gradually lengthening this interval over the days of this and succeeding reinforcement periods of the study. Reinforcement without priming was continued for 27 days, interrupted twice by probes of noncontingent reinforcement.

First probe. After eight days of reinforcement without priming, a five-day probe of noncontingent reinforcement was instituted (Days 23 to 27). During this time, teachers continued (as always) their patterns of intermittent, random reinforcement of various of Polly's activities, as these happened to attract the teachers' attention. Reinforcement for play on outdoor equipment, however, was almost but not quite zero. A five-day probe was judged adequate to show the dependence of the behavior on reinforcement, which accordingly was resumed.

Second probe. Another nine days of reinforcement (Days 28 to 36) followed the first probe. Thereafter, a second four-day probe was initiated (Days 37 to 40), which again was judged sufficiently long to demonstrate the continuing reliance on teacher reinforcement of Polly's outdoor equipment use. Procedures during the second probe were essentially identical to those during the first, with the following exceptions:

Use of outdoor play equipment was never reinforced: if Polly asked to use the equipment, she was simply told that it was all right to do so if she wanted; and teachers consistently reinforced Polly within 20 sec of her leaving any piece of outdoor play equipment.

After the second probe had ended, reinforcement was resumed for a final 10 days (Days 41 to 50) when the study ended as the teachers judged that Polly's total pattern of behavior had improved sufficiently.

RESULTS

Use of outdoor play equipment. Figure 1 shows Polly's rate of using outdoor play equipment, as defined in Table 1. It is clear that the initially low rate of equipment use was markedly increased by reinforcement, changing from approximately 2% during baseline to a near-70% rate by the end of the study. These percentages reflect the time that this equipment was available to Polly, not her total day at preschool. (During indoor times, she of course would not be able to use any of the equipment located in the play yard.)

Figure 1 also displays an effect attributable to the priming technique. When on Day 15 priming was discontinued, Polly's rate of equipment use dropped from its previous rate near 50% of the time available to a notably lower rate approximating 30%. This was apparently a transitory loss, her rate soon recovering its previous near-50% level by the fifth day of this period. Nevertheless, it indicates that a certain amount of Polly's use of equipment was dependent on the one instance which the teachers

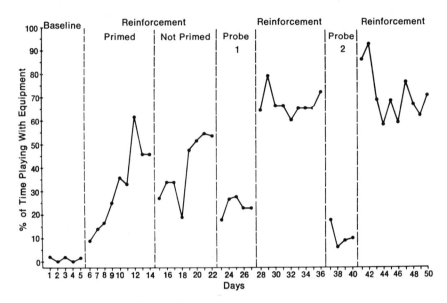

FIGURE 1   The development of outdoor equipment use by priming and reinforcement procedures, probed by noncontingent reinforcement.

prompted each day of the preceding period. The teachers' technique guaranteed only 30 sec of such activity each day. The gradual rise of equipment use during the reinforcement with priming period, coupled with initial loss of rate and its subsequent recovery under reinforcement alone, suggests that the two techniques interacted to produce the initial results, but that reinforcement was certainly basic to the development produced. This is further supported by the clear collapse of Polly's rate of equipment use during the later probes of noncontingent reinforcement.

An interesting observation made by the teachers and confirmed by the observers was that during the reinforcement with priming period, Polly never spontaneously used a piece of play equipment on which she had not previously been primed. Indeed, it was not until the final period of the study that she used a piece of equipment not involved in the priming of the first reinforcement period.

Collateral social development.   Of the behaviors listed in Table 1, some showed no change in the course of the study, some increased, and one decreased. These changes are shown in Fig. 2. Those behaviors which remained constant were primarily teacher-oriented behaviors, specifically touching a teacher or verbalizing to her. However, parallel play remained consistently unstable during the study, too, and this was assumed to be a

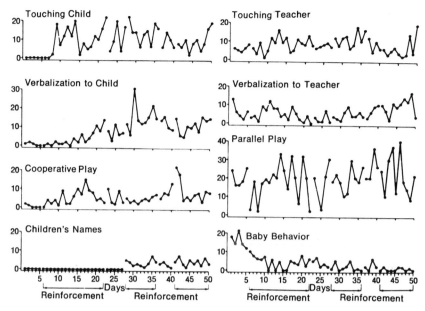

FIGURE 2 Collateral patterns of behavior change accompanying the development of outdoor equipment use.

child-oriented behavior, although one of only rudimentary social significance.

The behaviors which did increase were primarily child-oriented. Specifically, touching or verbalizing to other children, using their names, and engaging in cooperative play with them showed various patterns of increase. Touching children was most prompt in its increase from zero baseline, and was followed closely by a fairly steadily increasing tendency to verbalize to the children touched. Cooperative play also emerged from its near-zero baseline relatively early after reinforcement of equipment play started, and developed slowly but adequately (for 3-yr-old standards) in the course of the next few weeks. The use of other children's names appeared late in the study, but developed to more than adequate levels within a few more days (again, by preschool standards, as exemplified by other children judged quite normal in their social development in such settings).

The one behavior which decreased following reinforcement of equipment use was baby behavior. This category consisted of baby talk, hand-flapping, and hopping responses, appreciated by the teachers as highly accurate imitations of Polly's infant brother, and also of incompleted simple sentences. As the study progressed, baby talk, hopping, and flapping disappeared, leaving an increased frequency of incomplete sentences; presently, however, these too disappeared, leaving a near-zero level of the total response class by the end of the study.

DISCUSSION

The study shows again the clear and powerful role which teacher-supplied social reinforcement can have in developing a selected response class in a preschool child. In this regard, it adds one more behavior class to those already shown sensitive to such analysis. This study also shows, quantitatively and in some breadth, the kinds of behavior changes which may accompany such behavior modification, especially if the behavior chosen for direct modification is a sound tactical choice, in view of the child's total range of behavioral deficit. In this case, the child's basic problems were considered both motor and social. A reasonable tactic, on the face of it, would be to contribute directly to improving the child's motor skill in a sphere—use of outdoor play equipment—where the resulting behavior would tend automatically to create increased social contact with other children. This social contact in itself, if it contained any effective reinforcers for Polly, could be adequate to shape a wide variety of social skills suitable for child-child interaction. The results of this study generally conform with this expectation. Desirable patterns of child-oriented behavior did appear shortly after reinforcement of equipment use was successfully applied, and did continue to develop throughout the periods of the study of equipment use. The developmental curves of these behaviors in general conform only to the initiation of reinforcement at the outset of the study, rather than to its continuing pattern of application in contingent and noncontingent schedules. That appears reasonable, in that this programmed teacher-reinforcement was applied directly only to equipment use, not to the other behaviors under study. Thus, they would have met teacher-reinforcement in the usual way during all phases of the study. More probably, the increasing contact of these behaviors with the demanding contingencies of reinforcement supplied by Polly's peers, now that she was sharing their much-used outdoor play equipment, brought about the desired developments.

Finally, it is encouraging to note that the behavior under study, which might be taken to connote emotional disturbance, autism, regression, or the like, specifically Polly's baby-like repertoire, decreased steadily as the study progressed. Baby-like behavior may have been under more effective extinction during experimental conditions than it had been during the baseline period. The teaching staff, aware of how easy it would be to maintain that behavior by intermittent reinforcement, had from the outset of

Polly's year at preschool attempted to ignore it. Unfortunately, they found themselves failing to do exactly that, from time to time. However, during reinforcement of equipment use, the teachers noted that Polly was most likely to begin her baby performance just when she had stopped playing on equipment; it was of course at exactly these moments that teachers turned away from her, as their assignment was to reinforce equipment play, not its cessation. Thus, a side benefit of the reinforcement procedure may have been an increased efficiency of extinction for the baby-like behaviors.

The priming technique used in this study deserves comment. It was designed to hasten the emergence of equipment use, so that more and more examples of that behavior class would be available for reinforcement. Clearly, it accomplished that. The teachers had wondered whether the use of priming would handicap Polly when priming was later discontinued: would she be able to initiate her own use of the play equipment without teacher assistance? The results show clearly that she was able to do that, with only transitory partial loss of her new rate when priming was discontinued. However, the teachers also noted that not until quite late in the study did Polly show any spontaneous use of a piece of play equipment on which she had not been primed earlier. Thus, priming appears in one sense to have hastened generalization, if it is to be assumed that Polly would not have used any equipment which she was not first acquainted with by teachers. But in another sense, it seems that priming may have restricted generalization, in that Polly would not approach any apparatus she had not previously been primed to use. It is, of course, the same fact of observation which can be interpreted in these two ways. A thorough evaluation of the role of priming in contributing to generalization must remain for future study. In this case, it is clear only that priming can hasten the process of reinforcement, by making available behaviors suitable for reinforcement faster than they would have appeared without priming (according to baseline performance).

REFERENCES

ALLEN, K. E., HENKE, L. B., HARRIS, F. R., BAER, D. M., and REYNOLDS, N. J. Control of hyperactivity by social reinforcement of attending behavior. *Journal of Educational Psychology*, 1967, **58**, 231–237.

BAER, D. M. and WOLF, M. M. The entry into natural communities of reinforcement. Paper read at American Psychological Association convention, Washington, 1967.

BAER, D. M. and WOLF, M. M. The reinforcement contingency in preschool and remedial education. In R. D. Hess and Roberta M. Bear (Eds.), *Early education: current theory, research, and practice.* Chicago: Aldine, 1968. Pp. 119–130.

HARRIS, F. R., WOLF, M. M., and BAER, D. M. Effects of adult social reinforcement on child behavior. *Young Children,* 1964, **20,** 8–17.
HART, D. M., REYNOLDS, N. J., BAER, D. M., BRAWLEY, E. R., and HARRIS, F.
R. Effect of contingent and noncontingent social reinforcement on the
cooperative play of a preschool child. *Journal of Applied Behavior Analysis,* 1968, **1,** 73–76.

O. IVAR LOVAAS
LORRAINE FREITAS
KAREN NELSON
CAROL WHALEN[1]
University of California at Los Angeles

The establishment of imitation and its use for the development of complex behavior in schizophrenic children[2]

This paper presents a procedure for, and data pertaining to, the establishment of non-verbal imitative behavior in schizophrenic children, and the extension of such behavior for therapeutic usefulness into the child's day-to-day functioning.

The program consisted of two parts, the initial part involving the training of imitative behavior on sixty tasks, ranging from the easy to the complex. Training in imitation was analogous to a discrimination training procedure, wherein the children were reinforced (usually with bites of food) for increasingly close approximations to the adult's behavior. The acquisition curves for each of the eleven children who underwent this training were positively accelerated, but their rates of acquisition varied enormously. Upon completion of the initial training of the sixty tasks, the training was extended into socially and intellec-

Reprinted from *Behaviour Research and Therapy*, 1967, 5, 171–81, with permission of the publisher and the authors.

---

[1] Aspects of this paper were presented by Richard Sherman at the Western Psychological Association, Hawaii, and Bijan Guilani at the American Psychological Association, Chicago, 1965.

[2] This research was supported by Grant No. MH-11440 from the National Institute of Health. We wish to express our appreciation for the help of James Q. Simmons, M.D., Chief, The Children's Inpatient Services, The Neuropsychiatric Institute, UCLA.

tually useful behavior, such as personal hygiene, preschool games, drawing and printing, elementary interpersonal skills, etc.

INTRODUCTION

Many children are referred for psychological treatment because they evidence a deficiency in, or failure to develop certain behavior. Thus, some children come for treatment because they show little love, or aggression, or because of below-average school achievement. None of these children show the extreme behavioral deficiencies of the schizophrenic or autistic child. Not only has the schizophrenic child failed in the development of affection, aggression, and intellectual behavior, but in some of these children social behavior is missing altogether. Most often, these children neither speak nor respond when spoken to. They do not play; they do not dress themselves; they are incontinent. In social contacts they behave as if they are blind and deaf. In fact, the behavioral repertoire is often so restricted as to be described completely by three simple categories (a) self-stimulation, which involves stereotyped, repetitive behavior (such as rocking, twirling, spinning); (b) tantrums, including self-destructive behavior (such as head-banging); and (c) vocal output, involving mostly vowels (such as "o, e", screeching, tongue-clicking, etc.).

Traditionally, one has sought to help these children by concentrating on inferred emotional problems which have been hypothesized to block their behavioral development. There are two difficulties associated with this therapeutic approach. First, the traditional therapeutic interventions have not demonstrated their usefulness in helping schizophrenic children. Second, should it be demonstrated that these children suffer from emotional conflicts, there would still be no guarantee of a behavioral change subsequent to resolution of these emotional conflicts. That is, it might be possible to produce a conflict-free, happy child, who still failed to overcome his behavioral deficiencies. It is therefore of some importance to attempt to isolate variables which may help the child overcome his deficiencies.

Observations of the development of normal children suggest that the acquisition of complex behavior is facilitated through imitation of such behavior in adults and peers (cf. Bandura and Walters, 1963). In our treatment program for schizophrenic children at UCLA we have concentrated our efforts on teaching imitative behavior so that rather large new behavioral repertoires could be placed directly at the child's disposal. The more complex the behavior to be acquired, the more useful the imitation training procedure has been. This is particularly true in the case of speech development (Lovaas *et al.*, 1966).

When one works with schizophrenic children one cannot merely provide appropriate models engaging in desired behavior and expect these children to acquire that behavior. With such a procedure one finds that schizophrenic children fail to imitate the attending adult. In fact, the children with whom we have worked have even failed to attend to, or orient toward the adult models; they have behaved as if they were "blind and deaf." Consequently, in the treatment of schizophrenic children, we have been concerned with delineating some conditions under which such children will acquire imitative behavior. We have previously reported on studies designed to teach language through imitation (Lovaas *et al.*, *op. cit.*). In this paper we will report on a procedure whereby schizophrenic children acquire the beginning steps in nonverbal imitation.

The program for the establishment of nonverbal imitation consists of two phases: first, the establishment of generalized nonverbal imitative behavior, or what some may refer to as the establishment of imitative tendencies or capacities, and second the use of this newly established imitative behavior to facilitate the social and intellectual development of schizophrenic children. The procedures used to meet these two objectives, and the results obtained in each case will be described in the two following sections.

THE ESTABLISHMENT OF NONVERBAL IMITATION

Method

In brief, the method pertaining to the establishment of nonverbal imitation involves a set of successive discriminations. In these steps, the children were positively reinforced (rewarded) for closer and closer approximations to the attending adult's behavior. Stated differently, through non-verbal imitation training the behavior of one person gradually becomes the stimulus for similar behavior in another person. We argue that imitation was established when the child responded with imitative behavior upon the first presentation of a novel response by the attending adult.

Specifically, the procedure was as follows. We constructed an initial pool of about sixty behavior items or tasks, ranging from the easy to the complex. Some of the easier responses involved appropriate play with simple toys, such as pegboards and xylophones. These toys were selected with two criteria in mind: first, we hoped that they might possess some reinforcing value for the child, should he play with them appropriately, and that they did not demand a great deal of effort for appropriate play. Secondly, appropriate play with these toys presented both auditory and visual cues which we hoped might facilitate the child's attention to them. Inattention appears to be one of the largest initial difficulties to be found in working with schizophrenic children. Finally, we hoped that, in addition to building imitative behavior by the use of these toys, we might teach the children some appropriate play which would replace their typical inappropriate behavior with objects, such as mouthing.

From the use of these toys, we progressed to more complex tasks which involved the child's attention to more subtle and complex cues. The complexity can be illustrated in our use of coloured block forms. Two blocks would be placed before the child and a successful response on his part would require merely the use of position cues; that is, he would be required to match the adult's behavior in picking up the right versus the left block. Later the child would be forced to respond to other attributes of the blocks, such as shape or color. Following successful performance of these relatively simple responses, the task would be made more complex by requiring that the child respond to two or more attributes simultaneously; for example, that he select the large, red triangle. An even more complex phase of this task involved the use of the sequential cues, in addition to the familiar size, shape, and color attributes. For example, the child might be required to choose the large, red triangle, the small blue square, and the small green circle, *in that order*.

Some tasks were selected because they required that the child attend to a particular bodily movement of the adult in order to imitate appropriately. Once again, the initial tasks in this category were those which involved auditory as well as visual cues; for example, hand clapping. Subsequent tasks increased in difficulty in that they required progressively more attention and discrimination on the child's part. Standing up, raising one's hand and smiling are examples of progressively more difficult bodily responses. Finally, all the tasks were alternated in order to ensure that the child was actually imitating the adult's behavior, and not merely emitting a previously reinforced response.

This initial pool of tasks or behavior can be grouped into categories which we have labeled one-, two-, and three-way discriminations. In a one-way or simple discrimination the child was required to attend to and match a simple bodily action (standing up, pointing) or to manipulate a single object when that object alone was present (such as dialing a telephone). A two-way discrimination involved matching the adult's behavior in relationship to objects or behavior which differed in two stimulus dimensions (picking the red versus the green crayons, or placing a ball in a cup versus putting it in a bowl). Three-way discriminations are the same as the previous ones except that the child will have to attend to three or more cues (he has to pick one crayon from crayons differing in color as well as size; for example, a little red crayon).

The training was carried out on a 1-hr, 5-day-a-week basis. We trained a particular behavior until the child was judged to have mastered or failed it. The criterion for mastery was set at five consecutive matches of the adult's behavior by the child. On the other hand, if he failed to show any improvement on five consecutive trials, the child was judged to have failed that task. Any response which was failed was introduced again 2-5 weeks later in the training, until it was eventually mastered.

The training procedure relied very heavily on initial prompting and continuous food reinforcement for correct behavior, and subsequent fading of prompts and shifts to partial reinforcement. Specifically, the procedure can be described as follows. E (the attending adult) would engage in a particular behavior (the training or discriminative stimulus). If the child did not exhibit (match) this behavior within 5 sec, E would prompt the response. In other words, E would do whatever was necessary and convenient for the child to complete the response. Most often, prompts consisted of physically moving the child through the desired behavior. For example, if the adult demonstrated the placement of a ball in a cup, and the child failed to imitate this behavior upon its first presentation, E would take the child's hand with the ball and move it towards the cup, and by releasing his grip on the child's hand, cause the ball to fall within the cup. On subsequent trials, E would fade the prompt, i.e. gradually remove his active participation in the child's response. For example, E might gradually lessen his hold on the child's hand, then merely touch the child's hand, then his elbow, then his shoulder, and finally only emit the behavior to be imitated. It appears that this procedure causes the child's behavior to shift in its stimulus control; initially controlled by the prompt, the behavior later comes under the control of the adult's modeling behavior.

Reinforcement was given in the form of small bites of the child's food, such as pieces of Sugar Flakes, a breakfast cereal. As learning progressed, evidenced by the fact that the child might occasionally emit an approximation to the current response without prompts, food reinforcement was withheld for prompted behavior and only delivered contingent upon unprompted behavior. This step is a rather important one in the training, since continual reinforcement for prompted behavior probably would prevent a shift into imitative responding.

The use of food as reinforcement apparently "forces" the child to behave correctly. We have observed that some children would not acquire new responses unless it was impossible for them to survive without the new learning, i.e. unless their sustenance was contingent upon the new learning. Stated differently, social rewards, such as attention and approval, which effectively control the behavior of most individuals were inadequate during these early stages of learning. The child not only did not learn, but became very uncooperative and tantrumous.

Results

A total of 11 children, all diagnosed as schizophrenic or autistic, and ranging in age from 4 to 13 yr, have been exposed to the nonverbal imitation training program. In each of the eleven cases, the child has acquired generalized nonverbal imitation (i.e. the child will imitate at least ten of the last twenty tasks, from the pool of sixty, without prompts). The acquisition curves for these various children all have the same form: they are characterized by an increase in the rate of acquisition of new behavior over trials. The amount of time which is required to teach generalized nonverbal imitation varies enormously from one child to another. We have seen children who have mastered the sixty behavior items within 1 week and others have required 3–4 months of more intensive training. We are uncertain about the reasons underlying these large individual differences.

We will present the detailed data on the first two children who were exposed to this training program. Chuck and Bill, each six years of age at the onset of the study, had been diagnosed as autistic by the Department of Child Psychiatry at the University of California at Los Angeles. They were extremely disturbed children, having been refused treatment by others or terminated because of failure to respond to treatment. Chuck was particularly engrossed in self-stimulatory behavior, such as rocking, spinning, and flapping his arms at the wrists. Billy would engage in vicious tantrum behavior, such as feces smearing, biting himself or banging his head, biting and scratching attending adults, etc. Neither child was toilet trained. Neither evidenced any appropriate play behavior. Neither had any form of speech, nor responded appropriately when spoken to. They were essentially without any form of social behavior except for the apparently socially directed tantrums.

Data on the imitation training of Bill is presented in Figure 1. The ordinate shows the number of SD's (Discriminative stimuli, trials or adult responses) required for mastery of a given imitative behavior. The abscissa shows the tasks in order of their presentation. The three lines on the graph represent the three groups of tasks discussed earlier called one-way, two-way, and three-way discriminations. As can be observed, the first exposure to imitation required a large number of presentations to be mastered. Furthermore, the first half of the imitation training is characterized by great fluctuation in the number of trials to mastery. The fluctuations are attributable to the introduction of new kinds of tasks which required that the child focus his attention upon new sets of relevant stimuli. For example, in shifting from color to shape cues (selecting the large triangle rather than the red one), the child required additional training in order to succeed. The latter part of the nonverbal imitation training is characterized by both increased speed of mastery as well as more stable performance. It should be noted that toward the end of training several tasks were imitated at

their first presentation, never requiring a prompt. Perfect performances of
this type were achieved despite the fact that the imitation tasks become
more complex as training progressed. Each new task served as a test of the
generalization of imitative behavior. Since successful imitation occurred on
the first presentation of many of these tasks, it is apparent that generalized
nonverbal imitation was established.

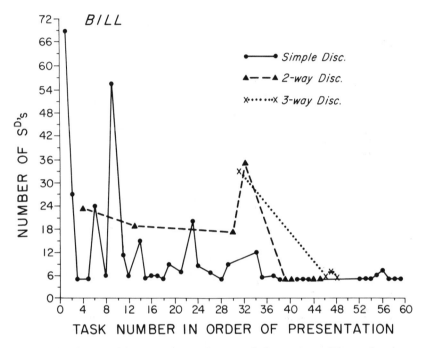

FIGURE 1   Bill's acquisition of non-verbal imitation. The ordinate
shows the number of trials (SD's, adult responses) required for the
child's mastery. The abscissa shows the tasks in order of their presentation. The three lines correspond to one-, two-, and three-way discrimination tasks.

Tasks which were failed at the first presentation and reintroduced
later are not shown in this figure due to the nature of the figure. A task
introduced and failed was always brought to mastery later in training, but
the record of its mastery is not comparable to the record of a task mastered
during its first introduction. Since the number of tasks failed is very low in
number (not exceeding thirteen for any one child), and since these were
mastered in no more than fifteen trials at their second introduction, they
do not alter the essential trends of the figure presented here.

Figure 2 presents the results of this training for the other boy, Chuck.

As can be observed, there are no essential differences in Chuck's and Bill's performance; the above description is as accurate a characterization of Chuck's performance as it is of Bill's.

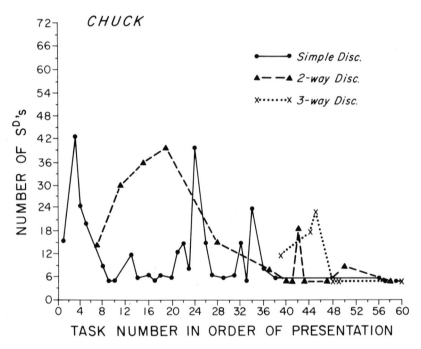

FIGURE 2   Chuck's acquisition of nonverbal imitation. The ordinate shows the number of trials (SD's, adult responses) required for the child's mastery. The abscissa shows the tasks in order of their presentation. The three lines correspond to one-, two-, and three-way discrimination tasks.

Tests for the Role of Reinforcement in Maintaining Imitation

To check the importance of reinforcement as a variable in building and maintaining imitative behavior, reinforcement was withheld after the performance of a particular imitative response which had been previously reinforced. The withdrawal of reinforcement should help to establish its importance in the maintenance of imitation, and may help to answer the question of whether the mere opportunity is sufficient to produce the effect achieved. For therapeutic reasons, only one response was extinguished (placing a ball in a cup).

The extinction sessions began after Bill and Chuck had been in imitation training for 2 months. Two sessions were run per day, separated by a 10-min outdoor play period. A massed-extinction paradigm was employed. At the start of each session, E gave five responses which the child was reinforced for imitating. E then continued to make these responses every 10 sec, but withheld all reinforcement for imitation. Once the child had failed to respond in five consecutive trials, the session was terminated. Extinction sessions were run until the child failed to respond at all within a given session. The number of sessions conducted and the number of imitative responses per session served as the extinction record for each child.

The extinction data are presented in Fig. 3. The ordinate presents the number of adult responses (trials, discriminative stimuli) required in each session before the child failed to imitate on five consecutive trials. The abscissa represents the number of extinction sessions. Inspection of the figure shows a very similar change in the imitative behavior of both boys: an initial increase in the number of responses, followed by a gradual drop over trials until the final session when no imitative responses occurred, except those which were reinforced. It is concluded, therefore, that reinforcement delivered for correct imitative behavior, with reinforcement-

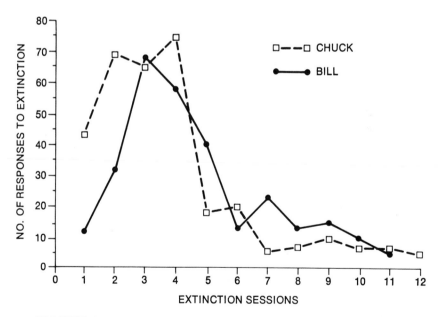

FIGURE 3 Extinction of nonverbal imitation for Bill and Chuck. Ordinate shows the number of trials (SD's, adult responses) required in each session before the child failed to imitate on five consecutive trials. The abscissa represents the number of extinction sessions.

withdrawal for incorrect behavior is necessary for the maintenance of imitation, at least at this early stage of training. The mere provision of a model is not sufficient to maintain imitation in these children. These data are very similar to those obtained by Baer and Sherman (1965) while testing for the effect of reinforcement-withdrawal on the imitative behavior of normal children.

It is unlikely that one will observe the effect of reinforcement-withdrawal, as given in Fig. 3, in all behavior. We now have data which demonstrate that the child will not cease performing certain tasks, regardless of how long the extinction sessions are run. Swimming, and many kinds of games, such as hide-and-seek, which we also introduce through imitation, lock into the child's repertoire on a permanent basis and do not require extrinsic reinforcement for their maintenance. In other words, imitation can be used to establish certain behavior which then shows no signs of losing its strength despite reinforcement-withdrawal. We do not believe that this means that imitation functions independently of reinforcement, but rather that some behavior, such as swimming, is so inherently reinforcing for children of certain ages that they do not require extrinsic reward. In a sense, these behavior patterns provide their own reinforcers for their maintenance.

EXTENSION OF IMITATION TO SOCIAL AND INTELLECTUAL BEHAVIOR

Having established the beginning of imitative behavior in the preceeding sixty tasks, we used this training as a base on which to build and expand socially and intellectually useful behavior. The procedure consisted of first bringing the new behavior under imitative control, and then shifting the stimulus control from that of the attending adult's behavior to a more appropriate context, such as a verbal command. For example, we might first teach a child the mechanics of toothbrushing through imitation, and subsequently bring this behavior under the control of stimuli such as "it's time to brush your teeth," or a temporal cue such as after breakfast.

As we extended the program into new areas of behavior, the responses did not always emerge on the first presentation of that behavior by the attending adult. The extension of the program into useful behavior sometimes required additional training in imitation, over and beyond the first sixty tasks. This additional training was mandatory despite the fact that the first sixty tasks were selected to *facilitate* further imitation, i.e. to give the children experience with a wide variety of behavior, and demand their attention to numerous and diverse cues. It is difficult to ascertain exactly how much imitative behavior the child is capable of at the termination of the sixty tasks. An exact test of this learning involves a more thorough exploration of generalization than that attempted in this project. The children definitely did not engage in the extensive kind of imitation which is denoted by terms such as "introjection" or "identification." For example, we failed to observe that the boys imitated the male adults' masculine behavior, or that the girls imitated their appropriate sex-role behavior without additional training.

In this extension of our program we delineated five groups of apparently useful skills and the mastery of a few rudimentary tasks in each group became our immediate training goal. We set up tasks in areas of (a) personal hygiene and self-help, e.g, washing hands, brushing hair, and making beds; (b) games and learning to follow rules, e.g., playing tag, kick ball, tether ball; (c) appropriate sex-role behavior, e.g. gardening, pounding nails, and doing exercises for the boys, and preparing simple snacks, curling hair, and ironing clothes for the girls; (d) drawing and printing; and (e) certain nonverbal components of interpersonal communication as may be involved in greetings, e.g. smiling and head-nodding, arm-waving, facial expressions of anger, etc.

For each of these more complex tasks, there are a number of dimensions along which learning and eventual mastery proceed. The child can learn to put his clothing on more quickly, more carefully, and so on, and each of these improvements may depend on the mastery of a number of subskills, such as manipulating buttons and discriminating right-side-out from wrong-side-out. Hence, the comprehensive scoring system which we used for simple imitative training was not appropriate in this second phase of training. Instead, we kept a record of the amount of time spent training each behavior, and a running verbal and pictorial account of how well the child was able to perform a given behavior. Thus, while recognizing the difficulty of always keeping accurate quantitative data on complex behavior, we were able to obtain a record which would be sufficient to indicate how well this particular training procedure compares to others.

We can best illustrate the use of nonverbal imitation in teaching complex behavior by presenting our procedure for teaching these children how to draw and our use of this skill in adding to the child's play behavior. Let us consider the third child who was trained in this program, Pamela. Pamela was 9 yr old and, except for the fact that she was echolalic, had striking similarities to the first two children, Chuck and Bill. That is, Pamela was profoundly disturbed, as evidenced by the fact that she had been in intensive psychoanalytic treatment for 4 yr, between the ages of two and a half and six and a half, accompanied by two and a half years of inpatient residential treatment. No improvement resulted from this extensive treatment. When she was seen by us, she was completely engrossed in self-stimulatory behavior. Bizarre and grotesque movements of her body, crossing of her eyes, protruding her tongue, etc. occupied her for as much as 99 per cent of the day. She was as severely regressed an autistic child as one might encounter.

Surprisingly enough, Pamela's acquisition on the first sixty tasks was so rapid that not much can be learned by plotting it in figure form. With two or three prompts on each of the first twenty tasks Pamela showed essentially no further need of prompting.

At this stage, Pamela was introduced to an extension of the nonverbal imitation which involved the establishment of skills in drawing. This behavior was sufficiently different from the initial program as to require additional imitation training. At the beginning of training S was encouraged to trace with a crayon directly over E's pencil marks. Later S was required to copy rather than trace, i.e. to draw her figure on another place than the one used by E. E graded the new material in very small steps, starting first with single horizontal lines to be copied, later with double horizontal lines, then with vertical lines, double vertical lines, lines which intersected, intersected to make triangles or squares and eventually making box figures. Later S was trained to imitate a drawing of small animals and plants, and eventually larger and more complex objects, such as dolls, houses and trains.

The beginning of imitative drawings can be seen in Fig. 4. E denotes experimenter, S denotes subject, and P denotes prompt, which means that E would guide S's hand with a crayon through the appropriate movement or provide for tracing. The sessions are labeled 1 through 9, the numbers representing about every hundredth trial. The left hand side of Fig. 5 shows the progression of training to representation of common every-day objects, such as a flower. This flower is made in color where the child is required to imitate the use of red, yellow, orange, blue, green, etc.

Once Pamela had learned the necessary components involved in imitative drawing, the control of this behavior was shifted from imitation of the adult's behavior to new stimuli, such as "draw me a picture." Here, the adult's behavioral example became a prompt and the new (verbal) environmental context served as the discriminative stimuli. In the same manner as before, the prompt was faded and the newly acquired behavior brought under control of a more appropriate stimulus context. These contexts can be extremely varied and include, in addition to the request of the adult, the sight of objects in her environment, either in concrete form or representation, as in magazine pictures.

Some of the play skills established were used to train Pamela to occupy her free time with appropriate play behavior rather than pathological behavior such as self-stimulation. Although Pamela had mastered several play skills through imitation (drawing and coloring, solving puzzles, cutting out pictures) and was able to do these things in response to verbal

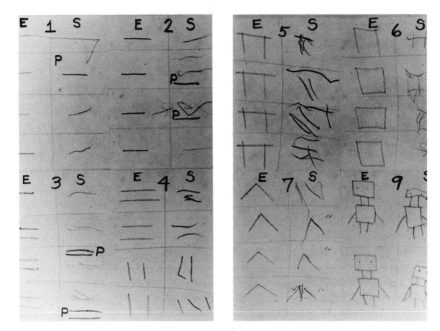

FIGURE 4 Beginning of imitative drawing for Pamela. The sessions are labeled 1 through 9, the numbers representing about every hundredth trial. E denotes experimenter's drawing, S the child's, and P denotes prompt (E's direct assistance of S's response).

commands, as well as in response to a model, she had always done them in the presence of an attending adult and when alone reverted to drifting inattention or self-stimulation. Therefore, we began training her to continue these activities when no adult was present. Her training was approached in the following manner. E first gave her instructions to complete some simple tasks ("draw a man" or "finish the puzzles"), then left her by herself for a few minutes. If the task was completed upon E's return, she was reinforced. In gradual steps, the number and complexity of tasks required and time allowed her to complete them were increased. During this time, E would occasionally leave her alone with play materials (coloring book, paper, scissors, picture magazines and puzzles), with *no* instructions. On these occasions, Pamela was observed through a one-way mirror, and the session continued as long as she used the materials appropriately. If she remained unoccupied with any one of the objects for a total of 5 min, or if she engaged in pathological behavior (such as self-stimulation) for a total of 15 sec she was removed from the room and the session was terminated. The record of the amount of time Pamela remained in the room alone and the activities engaged in during this time demonstrate the improvement in Pamela's independent play as the training progressed. Characteristic examples from this record are presented below.

> *May* 10. S remained occupied with objects for 15 min. Was removed from room after 20 min. Thirteen minutes were spent coloring on paper. Two minutes looking at magazine.
>
> *June* 25. S stayed in room for 21 min. Two short incidents of self-stimulation. Was removed after second one. S occupied self almost exclusively with colors and coloring book. Talked to herself about pictures in book.
>
> *July* 6. In room for 34 min. Looked at magazine. Talked about pictures. Related pictures to things outside. Some drawing—mostly of trains. Showed good detail here, included tracks and smoke. Was removed finally for inactivity.
>
> *July* 10. Was removed after 36 min for inactivity. She spent the entire time coloring, drawing, and coloring circles of different colors on paper. Started self-stimulation (looking at her hand) once, but stopped immediately.
>
> *August* 6. S remained in room 45 min. Was taken out because of self-stimulation. She had been inattentive for a total of 5 min and showed occasional hints of facial grimaces. Used paper in novel way today, held it up high and watched it float to floor. She had observed Ricky doing this the previous day. Occupied self this way during last 4 min. Otherwise spent time coloring and drawing. Returned to coloring when adult appeared to remove her.

The right half of Fig. 5, the train, shows Pamela's drawings during one of the sessions when she was alone. The train is a spontaneous drawing, instead of being drawn in relationship to a similar figure present at that time.

In short, although Pamela had evidenced no appropriate play behavior prior to training but instead was engrossed in self-stimulation, after 1 yr of training in nonverbal imitation, consisting of less than 3 hr a week, she demonstrated a preference for engaging in appropriate play rather than in pathological behaviors. Although it took some effort to teach Pamela how to draw, it is apparent that once she had learned this behavior she was capable of gaining enjoyment from it, as a normal child would be.

It is appropriate at this point to present Ricky's acquisitions in this part of our program. Ricky, a 7-yr-old autistic boy, was the fourth child who was seen in this program. He had many of the same features of Pamela, with the exception of some appropriate play behavior at the onset of treatment (such as filling a water bucket, putting blocks in container, etc.) At the end of one year of training, 3–4 hr a week, Ricky was able to make his bed, brush his teeth, and dress himself. He could play basketball, including dribbling and shooting of the baskets. He would play kick-

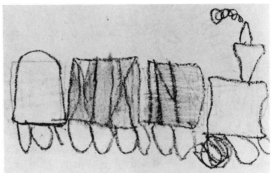

FIGURE 5 On the left side is presented Pamela's drawing of flowers in imitation. The right side shows her last stage in drawing, without model or prompt.

ball and serve as a batter and pitcher in a baseball game. He could cut pictures from magazines, and color in books. He could do puzzles intended for children up to about the age of 8. He could draw and appropriately color pictures of planes, trains, houses, "tall buildings," trees, flowers, mountains, grass, cars, boats, the ocean, fish, roller coaster, etc. He was beginning to learn to draw a familiar object from memory. He could play some simple paper-and-pencil games, such as tic-tac-toe, and simple board games, using marker and dice.

By the use of imitation, we have been able to teach the children a number of behavior patterns which seem virtually impossible to train otherwise. The procedure outlined above has the advantage that it works. Other investigators report similar success with similar procedures. In particular, our study has extensive overlap with that of Metz (1965). Our findings are consistent with those reported by Baer *et al.* (1965) who trained imitative behavior in profoundly retarded children. The procedures are similar to those employed by Hewett (1965) and Lovaas *et al.* (1966) for the establishment of imitative behavior in previously mute schizophrenic children.

The apparent power of these reinforcement procedures does not imply that all the antecedents of imitation have been isolated, or that imitative behavior has reached an optimal level with these children. There are still serious restrictions on the extent of generalized imitation after 1 yr of training. Furthermore, we are not certain about the extent to which the imitative behavior will be maintained without extrinsic reinforcement. Presumably, in normal children, imitative behavior improves over time, without the use of extrinsic reinforcers.

REFERENCES

BAER, D. M. and SHERMAN, JAMES (1964) Reinforcement control of generalized imitation in young children. *J. exp. child Psychol.* (1965) 1, 37–49.

BAER, D. M., PETERSON, R. F. and SHERMAN, J. A. (1965) Building an imitative repertoire by programming similarity between child and model as discriminative for reinforcement. Paper read at Society for Research in Child Development, Minneapolis.

BANDURA, ALBERT and WALTERS, R. H. (1963) *Social Learning and Personality Development.* Holt, Rinehart & Winston, New York.

HEWETT, F. M. (1965) Teaching speech to an autistic child through operant conditioning. *Am. J. Orthopsychiat.* 35, 927–936.

LOVAAS, O. I., BERBERICH, J. P., PERLOFF, B. F. and SCHAEFFER, B. (1966) Acquisition of imitative speech in schizophrenic children. *Science* 151, 705–707.

METZ, R. J. (1965) Conditioning generalized imitation in autistic children. *J. exp. Child Psychol.* 2, 389–399.

O. IVAR LOVAAS
BENSON SCHAEFFER
JAMES Q. SIMMONS
University of California at Los Angeles

Building social behavior
in autistic children
by use of electric shock[1]

Three experimental investigations were carried out on two five-year-old identical twins diagnosed as childhood schizophrenics by using painful electric shock in an attempt to modify their behaviors. Their autistic features were pronounced; they manifested no social responsiveness, speech, nor appropriate play with objects. They engaged in considerable self-stimulatory behavior, and in bizarre, repetitive bodily movements. They had not responded to traditional treatment efforts.

The studies show that it was possible to modify their behaviors by the use of electric shock. They learned to approach adults to avoid shock. Shock was effective in eliminating pathological behaviors, such as self-stimulation and tan-

Reprinted from *Journal of Experimental Research in Personality*, 1965, *1*, 99–109, with permission of the publisher and the authors.

[1] This study was supported by a grant from the National Institute of Health (HD 00938). The authors express their gratitude to Professor Donald M. Baer of the University of Washington for his help in the design and report of these studies. They are also indebted to Gilbert Freitag, M. I. Kinder, and B. D. Rubenstein for their assistance in carrying out Study 1. Finally, we acknowledge the cooperation of the Staff at the Children's Unit, Department of Child Psychiatry, Neuropsychiatric Institute, U.C.L.A. The substance of these studies was presented in a paper to the American Psychological Association, September, 1964, Los Angeles.

107

trums. Affectionate and other social behaviors toward adults increased after adults had been associated with shock reduction.

Psychological or physical pain is perhaps as characteristic in human relationships as is pleasure. The extensive presence of pain in everyday life may suggest that it is necessary for the establishment and maintenance of normal human interactions.

Despite the pervasiveness of pain in daily functioning, and its possible necessity for maintaining some behaviors, psychology and related professions have shied away from, and often condemned, the use of pain for therapeutic purposes. We agree with Solomon (1964) that such objections to the use of pain have a moral rather than a scientific basis. Recent research, as reviewed by Solomon, indicated that the scientific premises offered by psychologists for the rejection of punishment are not tenable. Rather, punishment can be a very useful tool for effecting behavior change.

There are three ways pain can be used therapeutically. First, it can be used directly as punishment, i.e., it can be presented contingent upon certain undesirable behaviors, so as to suppress them. This is perhaps the most obvious use of pain. Second, pain can be removed or withheld contingent upon certain behaviors. That is, certain behaviors can be established and maintained because they terminate pain, or avoid it altogether. Escape and avoidance learning exemplify this. The third way in which pain can be used is the least well known, and perhaps the most intriguing. Any stimulus which is associated with or discriminative of pain reduction acquires *positive* reinforcing (rewarding) properties (Bijou and Baer, 1961), i.e., an organism will work to "obtain" those stimuli which have been associated with pain reduction. The action of such stimuli is analogous to that of stimuli whose positive reinforcing properties derive from primary positive reinforcers.

These three aspects of the use of pain can be illustrated by observations on parent-child relationships. The first two are obvious; a parent will punish his child to suppress specific behaviors, and his child will learn to behave so as to escape or avoid punishment. The third aspect of the use of pain is more subtle, but more typical. In this case, a parent "rescues" his child from discomfort. In reinforcement theory terms, the parent becomes discriminative for the reduction or removal of negative reinforcers or noxious stimuli. During the first year of life many of the interactions a parent has with his children may be of this nature. An infant will fuss, cry, and give signs indicative of pain or distress many times during the day, whereupon most parents will pick him up and attempt to remove the discomfort. Such situations must contribute a basis for subsequent meaningful relationships between people; individuals are seen as important to each other if they have faced and worked through a stressful experience together. It may well be that much of a child's love for his parents develops in situations which pair parents with stress reductions. Later in life, the normal child does turn to his parent when he is frightened or hurt by nightmares, by threat of punishment from his peers, by fears of failure in school, and so on.

In view of these considerations, it was considered appropriate to investigate the usefulness of pain in modifying the behaviors of autistic children. Autistic children were selected for two reasons: (1) because they show no improvement with conventional psychiatric treatment; and (2) because they are largely unresponsive to everyday interpersonal events.

In the present study, pain was induced by means of an electrified grid on the floor upon which the children stood. The shock was turned on immediately following pathological behaviors. It was turned off or withheld when the children came to the adults who were present. Thus, these adults "saved" the children from a dangerous situation; they were the only "safe" objects in a painful environment.

STUDY 1

The objectives of Study 1 were (1) to train the children to avoid electric shock by coming to E when so requested; (2) to follow the onset of self-stimulatory and tantrum behaviors by electric shock so as to decrease their frequency; and (3) to pair the word "no" with electric shock and test its acquisition of behavior-suppressing properties.

Method

Subjects. The studies were carried out on two identical twins. They were five-years old when the study was initiated and were diagnosed as schizophrenics. They evidenced no social responsiveness; they did not respond in any manner to speech, nor did they speak; they did not recognize each other or recognize adults even after isolation from people; they were not toilet trained; their handling of physical objects (toys, etc.) was inappropriate and stereotyped, being restricted to "fiddling" and spinning. They were greatly involved in self-stimulatory behavior, spending 70 to 80 per cent of their day rocking, fondling themselves and moving hands and arms in repetitive, stereotyped manners. They engaged in a fair amount of tantrum behaviors, such as screaming, throwing objects, and hitting themselves.

It is important to note, in view of the moral and ethical reasons which might preclude the use of electric shock, that their future was certain institutionalization. They had been intensively treated in a residential setting by conventional psychiatric techniques for one year prior to the present study without any observable modification in their behaviors. This failure in treatment is consistent with reports of other similar efforts with such children (Eisenberg, 1957; Brown, 1960), which have suggested that if a schizophrenic child does not have language and does not play appropriately with physical objects by the age of three to five, then he will not improve, despite traditional psychiatric treatment, including psychotherapy, of the child and/or his family.

Apparatus. The research was conducted in a 12 × 12-foot experimental room with an adjoining observation room connected by one-way mirrors and sound equipment. The floor of the experimental room was covered by one-half inch wide metal tapes with adhesive backing (Scotch Tape). They were laid one-half inch apart so that when the child stepped on the floor he would be in contact with at least two strips, thereby closing the circuit and receiving an electric shock. A six-volt battery was wired to the strips of tape via a Harvard Inductorium. The shock was set at a level at which each of three Es standing barefoot on the floor agreed that it was definitely painful and frightening.

The Ss' behavior and the experimental events were recorded on an Esterline Angus pen recorder by procedures more fully described in an earlier paper (Lovaas *et al.*, 1965). The observer could reliably record both frequency and duration of several behaviors simultaneously on a panel of push-buttons. A given observer recorded at randomly selected periods.

Pre-shock Sessions. The Ss were placed barefoot in the experimental room with two Es, but were not shocked. There were two such pre-experimental sessions, each lasting for about 20 minutes. The Es would invite the Ss to "come here" about five times a minute, giving a total of approximately 100 trials per session. The observers recorded the amount of physical contact (defined as S's touching E with his hands), self-stimulatory and tantrum behavior, the verbal command "come here," and positive responses to the command (coming to within one foot of E within five seconds).

First Shock Sessions. The two pre-experimental sessions were followed by three shock sessions distributed over three consecutive days during which Ss were trained, in an escape-avoidance paradigm, to avoid shock by responding to E's verbal command according to the pre-established criterion. In the escape phase of the training, consisting of fifty trials, the two Es faced each other, about three feet apart, with S standing (held, if necessary) between them so that he faced one of the Es, who would lean forward, stretch his arms out, and say "come here." At the same time shock was turned on and remained on until S moved in the direction of this E, or, if S had not moved within three seconds, until the second E pushed S in the direction of the inviting E. Either type of movement of S toward the inviting E immediately terminated the shock. The S had to walk alternately from one E to the other.

In the avoidance sessions which followed, shock was withheld provided S approached E within five seconds. If S did not start his approach to the inviting E within five seconds, or if he was not within one foot of E within seven seconds, the shock was turned on and the escape procedure was reinstated for that trial.

During these avoidance sessions Es gradually increased their distance from each other until they were standing at opposite sides of the room. At the same time they gradually decreased the number of cues signaling S to approach them. In the final trials, Es merely emitted the command "come here," without turning toward or otherwise signaling S.

Shock was also turned on if S at any time engaged in self-stimulatory and/or tantrum behaviors. Whenever possible, shock was administered at the onset of such behaviors. Shock was never given except on the feet; no shock was given if S touched the floor with other parts of his body. In order to keep S on his feet, shock was given for any behavior which might have enabled him to avoid shock, such as beginning to sit down, moving toward the window to climb on its ledge, etc.

Extinction Sessions. The three shock sessions were followed by eleven extinction sessions distributed over a ten-month period. These sessions were the same as those in the previous sessions, except that shock and the command "no" were never delivered during this period.

The Second Shock Sessions. Three additional sessions terminated Study 1. In the first of these, S was brought into the experimental room and given a two-second shock not contingent upon any behavior of S or E. This was the only shock given. In all other respects these final sessions were similar to the preceding extinction sessions.

Procedure for Establishing and Testing "No" as a Secondary Negative Reinforcer. During the first shock sessions, shock had been delivered contingent upon self-stimulatory and/or tantrum behaviors. Simultaneous with the onset of shock Es would say "no," thereby pairing the word "no" and shock. The test for any suppressing power which the word "no" had acquired during these pairings was carried out in the following manner. Prior to the shock sessions, Ss were trained to press a lever (wired to a cumulative recorder) for M & M candy on a fixed ratio 20 schedule. The sessions lasted for ten minutes daily. A stable rate of lever-pressing was achieved by the twelfth session, at which Es tested the word "no" for suppressing effects on the lever-pressing rate. The E delivered the "no" contingent upon lever-pressing toward the middle of each session, during three sessions *prior* to the shock sessions, and during three sessions *subsequent* to the shock sessions, i.e., after "no" had been paired with shock.

Results and Discussion

Figure 1 gives the proportion of time Ss responded to Es' commands (proportion of Rs to S^Ds). As can be seen, in the two preshock sessions Ss did not respond to Es' commands. During the first three shock sessions (Shock I), Ss learned to respond to Es' requests within the prescribed time interval and thus avoided shock. This changed responsiveness of Ss to Es' requests was maintained for the subsequent nine months (no shock sessions). There was a relatively sudden decrease in Ss' responsiveness after nine months, i.e., the social behavior of coming to E extinguished. One non-contingent shock, however, immediately reinstated the social responsiveness (Shock II), suggesting that Ss responded to it as a discriminative stimulus for social behavior.

The data on Ss' pathological behaviors (self-stimulation and tantrums) and other social behaviors (physical contacts) are presented in Fig. 2. Prior to shock, pathological behaviors occurred 65–85 per cent of the time; physical contacts were absent. Shock I suppressed the pathological behaviors immediately, and they remained suppressed during the

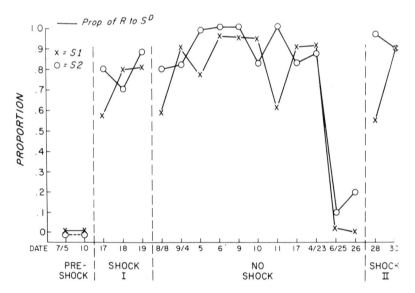

FIGURE 1 Proportion of time Ss responded to E's commands—proportion of Rs to S^Ds.

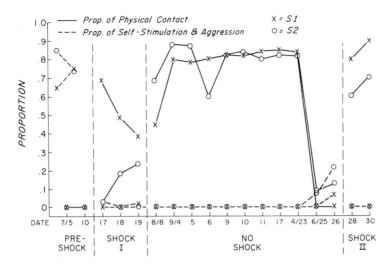

FIGURE 2 Proportion of self-stimulation and tantrums (pathological behaviors) and physical contact (social behavior).

following eleven months. In addition, social behaviors replaced the pathological behaviors. This change was very durable (ten to eleven months), but did eventually extinguish. One non-contingent shock reinstated the social responsiveness and suppressed the pathological behaviors.

The data on the acquisition of "no" as a negative reinforcer are presented in Fig. 3. The records of bar-pressing for candy are presented as cumulative curves. The word "no" was presented contingent upon a bar-pressing response three sessions before and three sessions subsequent to shock, i.e., before and after the pairing of "no" with shock. The cumulative curves of the session immediately preceding and the session following shock to S1 is presented. The curves for the other sessions, both for S1 and S2, show the same effects. It is apparent upon inspection of Fig. 3

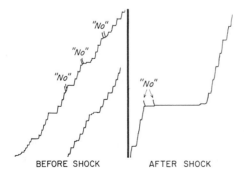

FIGURE 3 Lever-pressing for candy as cumulative response curves; effect of "no" on lever-pressings by S1 before and after "no" was paired with shock.

that the word "no" had no effect upon S1's performance prior to its pairing with shock, but that after such pairing it suppressed the bar-pressing response.

Observations of Ss' behaviors in the experimental room indicated that the shock training had a generalized effect; it altered several behaviors which were not recorded. Some of these changes took place within minutes after the Ss had been introduced to shock. In particular, they seemed more alert, affectionate, and seeking of E's company. And surprisingly, during successful shock avoidance they appeared happy. These alterations in behavior were only partially generalized to the environment outside the experimental room. The changes in behaviors outside were most noticeable during the first fourteen days of the shock training, after which Ss apparently discriminated between situations in which they would be shocked and those in which they would not. According to their nurse's notes, certain behaviors, such as Ss' responsiveness to "come here" and "no" were maintained for several months, while others, such as physical contact, soon extinguished.

These observations formed the basis for the subsequent two studies. In Study 2 a more objective assessment of the changes in Ss' affectionate behavior toward adults was made, and a technique for extending these effects from the experimental room to the ward was explored. In Study 3 a test was made of any reinforcing power adults might have acquired as a function of their association with the termination of shock.

STUDY 2

Study 2 involved two observations. One attempted to assess changes in Ss' affectionate behavior to E who invited them to kiss and hug him. The other observation was conducted by nurses who rated Ss on behavior change in seven areas (given below). Both observations incorporated measures of transfer of behavior changes to new situations brought about by the use of the remote control shock apparatus. Both observations were conducted immediately following the completion of Study 1.

The "Kiss and Hug" Observations. These observations consisted of six daily sessions. Three of the sessions (3, 5, and 6) are referred to as shock-relevant sessions. Sessions 3 and 5 were conducted in the experimental room where Ss had received shock during avoidance training. Three sessions (1, 2, and 4) are labeled control sessions. They took place in a room sufficiently different from the experimental room to minimize generalization of the shock effect. The last shock-relevant session (session 6) was conducted to test the changes produced by remotely controlled shock.

This session was conducted in the same room as the previous control sessions. However, immediately preceding the session Ss received five shock-escape trials, similar to those of Study 1. The shock was delivered from a Lee-Lectronic Trainer.[2] The S wore the eight-ounce receiver (about the size of a cigarette pack) strapped on his back with a belt. Shock was delivered at "medium" level over two electrodes strapped to S's buttock.

In order to minimize the effects of a particular observer's recording bias, two observers alternated in recording Ss' behavior. Each observer recorded at least one shock session. The sessions lasted for six minutes each. Every five seconds E would face S, hold him by the waist with outstretched arms, bow his head toward S, and state "hug me" or "kiss me." The E would alternate his requests ("hug me," "kiss me") every minute. The observer recorded (1) embrace (S placing his arms around E's neck), (2) hug and kiss (S hugging E cheek to cheek or kissing him on the mouth), (3) active physical withdrawal by S from E when held by the waist, and (4) E's requests.

Results

Since Ss' behaviors on the test were virtually identical, their behaviors were averaged. The data are presented in Fig. 4. During the control sessions (sessions 1, 2, and 4) the proportion of time that Ss embraced, or hugged and kissed E was extremely low. Rather, they withdrew from him. During the shock-relevant sessions (sessions 3, 5, and 6) Ss' behavior changed markedly toward increased affection. In a situation where they had received shock-avoidance training they responded with affection to E and did not withdraw from him. The fact that this affectionate behavior maintained itself in session 6 demonstrates that the remotely controlled shock can produce transfer of behavior change to a wide variety of situations.

Nurses' Ratings. The nurses' ratings were initiated at the completion of the "kiss and hug" sessions. Four nurses who were familiar with Ss but unfamiliar with the experiment, and did not know that shock had been used, were asked to complete a rating scale pertaining to seven behaviors: (1) dependency on adults, (2) responsiveness to adults, (3) affection seeking, (4) pathological behaviors, (5) happiness and contentment, (6) anxiety and fear, and (7) overall clinical improvement. The scale was comprised of nine points, with the midpoint indicating no change. The nurses were asked to indicate whether they considered S to have changed (increased or decreased) in any of these behaviors as compared to S's be-

[2] Lee Supply Co., Tucson, Arizona.

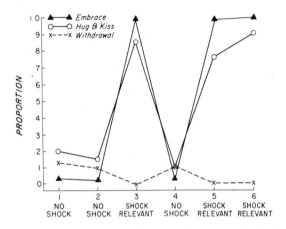

FIGURE 4   Social reactions of Ss as a function of shock presentations. The "no shock" sessions (1, 2, 4) were run in a room where Ss had not been shocked. ["Shock" sessions (3, 5) were conducted in a room in which Ss had received shock-avoidance training. The last "shock" session (6) was conducted in the same room as the "no shock" sessions, but Ss had received remote controlled shock.]

haviors the preceding day or morning. The ratings were obtained under two conditions: (1) an experimental condition in which S, wearing the remote control unit on his belt underneath his clothing, was introduced to the nurses who "casually" interacted with him for ten minutes. S was not shocked while with the nurses, but he had been given a one-second, non-contingent shock immediately prior to his interaction with the nurses; (2) a control condition, which was run in the same manner as the experimental condition, except that S had no shock prior to the ratings.

The nurses rated changes in Ss under both conditions. They were not counter-balanced. The ratings from the control conditions were subtracted from the ratings based on the experimental conditions. The difference shows an increase in the ratings of all behaviors following the shock treatment, except for pathological behaviors and happiness-contentment, which both decreased. Only the ratings on dependency and affection seeking behaviors increased more than one point.

STUDY 3

Study 3 showed the degree to which the association of an adult with shock reduction (contingent upon an approach response of the children) would establish the adult as a positive secondary reinforcer for the children. Increased resistance to extinction of a lever-pressing response producing the sight of the adult was used to measure the acquired reinforcing power of the adult.

The study was conducted in two parts. The first part constituted a "pre-training" phase. During this period the children were trained to press a lever to receive M & Ms and simultaneously see E's face. Once this response was acquired, extinction of the response was begun by removing the candy reinforcement, S being exposed only to E's face. The second part of the study constituted a test of the reinforcing power E had acquired as a result of having been associated with shock reduction. This association occurred when, immediately preceding several of the extinction sessions of the lever-press, Ss were trained to come to E to escape shock. The change in rate of responding to obtain a view of E during these sessions was used as a measure of E's acquired reinforcing power.

Method

Study 3 was initiated after the completion of Study 2. It was conducted in an enclosed cubicle, four feet square, in which E and S sat separated by a removable screen. A lever protruded from a box at S's side. Lever-pressings were recorded on a cumulative recording. An observer (O) looking through a one-way screen recorded the following behaviors of S as they occurred: (1) vocalizations (any sound emitted by S), and (2) standing on the chair or ledge in the booth. The latter measures were taken in a manner similar to that described in Study 1. These additional measures were obtained in an attempt to check on the possibility that an eventual increase in lever-pressing for E might be due to a conceivable "energizing" effect of shock, rather than to the secondary reinforcing power associated with shock reduction. This rationale will be discussed more fully below.

The first ten were labeled *pre-training* sessions. In each, a fifteen-minute acquisition preceded a twenty-minute extinction of the lever-pressing response. During acquisition S received a small piece of candy and a five-second exposure to E (the screen was removed momentarily, placing E's face within S's view) on a fixed ratio 10 schedule. During extinction, S received only the five-second exposure to E on the same schedule as before. Both Ss reached a stable rate of about 500 responses during the first acquisition session.

The ten pre-training sessions were followed for S1 by nine *experimental* sessions. In these experimental sessions S never received candy. The sessions consisted only of a twenty-minute extinction period. An S's performance during the last extinction session of pre-training, labeled Session 1 in Fig. 5, served as a measure of the pre-experimental rate of lever-pressing. Electric shock was administered before the 2nd, 7th, and 9th experimental sessions, as follows: S was placed facing E in the room out-side the cubicle. Shock was administered for two to four seconds, at which point E would tell S to "come here." S would invariably approach E and shock would be terminated. The E would then comfort S (fondle and stroke him) for one minute. This procedure was repeated four times. Im-mediately following this procedure, S was placed within his cubicle. E would repeat S's name every five seconds. On the fixed ratio 10 schedule, the screen would open and E would praise S ("good boy") and stroke him.

The experimental treatment of S2 was identical to that of S1 with the following exceptions: (1) S2 received only seven experimental sessions; (2) shock preceded sessions 2, 6, and 8; (3) E did not call S2's name while he was in the cubicle; and (4) E was only visually exposed to S2 (E did not stroke or praise S2).

Results and Discussion

The Ss' lever-pressing behavior is presented in Fig. 5 as cumulative curves. The last extinction curve from the pre-training is labeled one. This curve gives the rate of lever-pressing in the last extinction session preceding E's association with shock reduction. The upward moving hatchmarks on the curves show the occasions on which E was visually presented to S. The heavy vertical lines labeled shock, show shock-escape training preceding sessions 2, 7, and 9 for S1, and sessions 2, 6, and 8 for S2.

There was a substantial increase in rate of lever-pressing accompanying

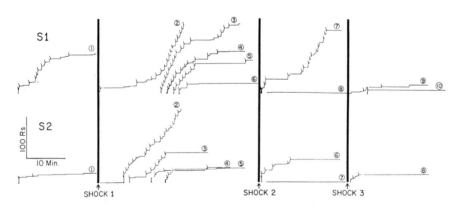

FIGURE 5   The Ss' lever-pressing behavior for E as function of E's association with shock reduction. [Curve labelled "1" is the last ex-tinction curve from the pretraining. Shock preceded sessions 2, 7, and 9 for S1, and sessions 2, 6, and 8 for S2. The upward moving hatch-marks on the curves indicate occasions at which E was visually pre-sented to S].

shock-escape training for both Ss. The curves also show the extinction of this response. The extinction is apparent in the falling rate between shock sessions (e.g., sessions 2 through 6 for S1 show a gradual decrease in rate of responding). A similar extinction is also manifested over the various shock sessions, i.e., the highest rate was observed after the first shock training, the next highest after the second shock training, and so on. The Ss' performances were very systematic and orderly.

Data based on the two additional measures, vocalization and standing on the chair or ledge, are presented in Table 1. The entries in the column labeled O1 can be compared to those in column O2. These data indicate that there was a high degree of agreement between the two observers rating amount of vocalizations of Ss. The O2's ratings were based on tape recordings taken from Ss while in the booth. It was physically impossible to have a second O assess the reliability of O1's ratings of climbing. However, because of the ease of recording such behavior it was judged unnecessary to check on its reliability. The agreement between Os on vocalizations was judged adequate for the purposes of this study.

TABLE 1   Per cent of total time engaged in vocalization and climbing

Session	Shock	S1 Vocal. 01	S1 Vocal. 02	S1 Climb. 01	S2 Vocal. 01	S2 Vocal. 02	S2 Climb. 01
1		49		0	27		96
2	S1 and S2	19	19	0	27		0
3		47		0	20		20
4		25		32	23		0
5		18		65	26	29	0
6	S2	22	23	97	22		0
7	S1	22	23	33	23	23	0
8	S2	22		83	22		0
9	S1	11		0			
10		13		75			

If the increase in lever-pressing behavior was correlated with an increase in the two additional behaviors, then it might not be that shock-escape training had led to an increase in behavior toward people *per se*. Rather, it might have led to an "arousal" of many behaviors, asocial as well as social. As Table 1 shows, the two additional measures showed no systematic relationship to the shock-escape sessions for S2. In the case of S1 there is some possibility of *suppression* of vocalization and climbing subsequent to shock-escape sessions (sessions 2, 7, and 9). It is unlikely, then, that shock-escape training involving other people can be viewed simply as activating many behaviors; rather, such training selectively raised behavior which yielded a social consequence.

Thus it is concluded that this increase in behavior toward E subsequent to shock-escape training came about because E was paired with shock reduction, thereby acquiring reinforcing powers. This conceptualization is consistent with the findings of Studies 1 and 2, both of which demonstrated an increase in social and affectionate behaviors. The findings are similar to those reported by Risley (1964) who observed an increase in acceptable social behavior (eye-to-eye contact) in an autistic child to whom E had administered electric shock for suppression of behaviors dangerous to the child. The data are also consistent with the results of studies by Mowrer and Aiken (1954) and Smith and Buchanen (1954) on animals which demonstrated that stimuli which are discriminative for shock reduction take on secondary positive reinforcing properties. It is to be noted, however, that the data from the studies reported here also fit a number of other conceptual frameworks.

An apparent limitation in these data pertains to the highly situational and often short-lived nature of the effects of shock. This had definite drawbacks when one considers the therapeutic implications of shock. It is considered, however, that the effects of shock can be made much more durable and general by making the situation in which shock is delivered less discriminable from situations in which it is not. The purpose of the present studies was to explore certain aspects of shock for possible therapeutic use. Therefore, only the minimal amount of shock considered necessary for observing reliable behavior changes was employed. It is quite possible that the children's responsiveness to adults would have been drastically reduced if shock had been employed too frequently. It is worth making the point explicitly: a certain use of shock can, as in these studies, contribute toward beneficial, even therapeutic, effects; but it does not at all follow that a more widespread use of the same techniques in each case will lead to even better outcomes. Indeed, the reverse may be true. Recent studies with schizophrenic children in our laboratory have shown, tentatively, that non-contingent shock facilitates performance of a well-learned task; however, such shock interferes with learning during early stages of the acquisition of new behaviors.

Certain more generalized effects of shock training, even though not recorded objectively, were noticed by Es and ward staff. First of all, Ss had to be trained (shaped) to come to E to escape shock. When shock was first presented to S2, for example, he remained immobile, even though adults were in the immediate vicinity (there was no way in which Ss could have "known" that Es presented the shock). This immobility when hurt is consistent with observations of Ss when they were hurt in the playyard, e.g., by another child. But after Ss had been trained to avoid shock successfully in the experimental room, their nurses' notes state that Ss would come to the nurses when hurt in other settings.

*E*s had expected considerable expression of fear by *S*s when they were shocked. Such fearful behavior was present only in the beginning of training. On the other hand, once *S*s had been trained to avoid shock, they often smiled and laughed, and gave other signs of happiness or comfort. For example, they would "mold" or "cup" to *E*'s body as small infants do with parents. Such behaviors were unobserved prior to these experiments. Perhaps avoidance of pain generated contentment.

In their day-to-day living, extremely regressed schizophrenic children such as these *S*s rarely show signs of fear or anxiety. The staff who dealt with these children in their usual environments expressed concern about the children's lack of worry or anxiety. There are probably several reasons why children such as these fail to demonstrate anxiety. It is possible that their social and emotional development has been so curtailed and limited that they are unaffected by the fear-eliciting situations acting upon a normal child. For example, they do not appear to be afraid of intellectual or social inadequacies, nor are they known to experience nightmares. Furthermore, by the age of three or four, like normal children, these children appear less bothered by physiological stimuli, and unlike the small infant, are rather free of physiological discomforts. Finally, when these children are brought to treatment, for example in a residential setting, there is much effort made to make their existence maximally comfortable.

If it is the case, as most writers on psychological treatment have stated, that the person's experience of discomfort is a basic condition for improvement, then perhaps the failure of severely retarded schizophrenic children to improve in treatment can be attributed partly to their failure to fulfill this hypothesized basic condition of anxiety or fear. This was one of the considerations which formed the basis for the present studies on electric shock. It is important to note that the choice of electric shock was made after several alternatives for the inducement of pain or fear were tested and found wanting. For example, in the early work with these children we employed loud noise. Even at noise levels well above 100 decibels we found that the children remained unperturbed particularly after the first two or three presentations.

It seems likely that the most therapeutic use of shock will not lie primarily in the suppression of specific responses or the shaping of behavior through escape-avoidance training. Rather, it would seem more efficient to use shock reduction as a way of establishing social reinforcers, i.e., as a way of making adults meaningful in the sense of becoming rewarding to the child. The failure of autistic children to acquire social reinforcers has been hypothesized as basic to their inadequate behavioral development (Ferster, 1961). Once social stimuli acquire reinforcing properties, one of the basic conditions for the acquisition of social behaviors has been met. A more complete argument supporting this thesis has been presented elsewhere

(Lovaas *et al.*, 1964). A basic question, then, is whether it is necessary to employ shock in accomplishing such an end or whether less drastic methods might not suffice. In a previous study (Lovaas *et al.*, 1964) autistic children did acquire social reinforcers on the basis of food delivery. However, the necessary conditions for the acquisition of social reinforcers by the use of food were both time-consuming and laborious, and by no means as simple as the conditions which were necessary when we employed shock reduction.

REFERENCES

Bijou, S. W., and Baer, D. M. *Child Development: a systematic and empirical theory.* New York: Appleton-Century-Crofts, 1961.

Brown, Janet L. Prognosis from presenting symptoms of preschool children with atypical development. *American Journal of Orthopsychiatry*, 1960, 30, 382–390.

Eisenberg, L. The course of childhood schizophrenia. *American Medical Association Archives for Neurology and Psychiatry*, 1957, 78, 69–83.

Ferster, C. B. Positive reinforcement and behavioral deficits of autistic children. *Child Development*, 1961, 32, 437–456.

Lovaas, O. I., Freitag, G., Gold, V. J., and Kassorla, I. C. A recording method and observations of behaviors of normal and autistic children in free play settings. *Journal of Experimental Child Psychology*, 1965, 2, 108–120.

Lovaas, O. I., Freitag, G., Kinder, M. I., Rubenstein, D. B., Schaeffer, B., and Simmons, J. Q. Experimental studies in childhood schizophrenia—Establishment of social reinforcers. Paper delivered at Western Psychological Association, Portland, April, 1964.

Mowrer, O. H., and Aiken, E. G. Contiguity vs. drive-reduction in conditioned fear: temporal variations in conditioned and unconditioned stimulus. *American Journal of Psychology*, 1954, 67, 26–38.

Risley, Todd. The effects and "side effects" of the use of punishment with an autistic child. Unpublished manuscript, 1964. Florida State University.

Smith, M. P., and Buchanen, G. Acquisition of secondary reward by cues associated with shock reduction, *Journal of Experimental Psychology*, 1954, 48, 123–126.

Solomon, R. L. Punishment. *American Psychologist*, 1964, 19, 239–253.

BRUCE L. BAKER
Yale University

Symptom treatment and symptom substitution in enuresis[1]

This study explored the hypotheses that (a) Aspects of the therapist-patient relationship are responsible for successful behavior therapy; and (b) substitute problems will arise following remission of symptoms. Thirty enuretic children were treated either by a conditioning method or by methods devised to duplicate its motivational aspects. Adjustment measures on the enuretic Ss and control children were obtained independent of treatment. Conditioning was superior to other methods, suggesting that successful treatment was not based solely on the therapist-patient relationship. Subsequent to treatment, test measures did not indicate a decline in adjustment; on several measures, significant improvement was found.

Reprinted from *Journal of Abnormal Psychology*, 1969, 74, 42–49, with permission of the author. Copyright 1969 by the American Psychological Association, and reproduced by permission.

[1] Based on a dissertation submitted to the faculty of the Graduate School of Yale University in partial fulfillment of the requirements for the PhD degree. The author wishes to thank Michael Kahn, his major advisor, and Fred D. Sheffield and Sidney J. Blatt, who served on his Advisory Committee. The author also wishes to thank Gilda Hymer for obtaining the schoolroom measures, and Irving H. Frank, Phillip Morse, and Ragaa Mazen for judging drawings. The conditioning devices were generously provided by Sears, Roebuck and Co.

Two questions are frequently posed to the behavior therapist. First, what are the total effects of treatment on the individual? Traditional psychiatry (e.g., Freud, 1959) views maladjustive behavior as a sign that there is an underlying disorder, and warns that even if a problem can be removed by a nondynamic therapy a relapse or another new problem will follow, since the basic causes have not been treated. This "symptom substitution" hypothesis is probably the principal theoretical reason why many clinicians hesitate to use behavior therapy. Yet while the vast majority of behavior-therapy follow-up reports indicate that no new problems have arisen following successful treatment (e.g., Baker, Kahn, & Weiss, 1968; Lang & Lazovik, 1963; Lazarus, 1961, 1963; Wolpe, 1961), there has been no well-controlled study of this hypothesis.

Second, why does behavior therapy work when it does? Although behavior therapists stress the role of the learning paradigm in treatment, the learning theory upon which some of these methods are based has been criticized as outmoded (Breger & McGaugh, 1965). It seems possible that behavior therapy's success might be attributed to other aspects of the treatment, such as the therapist's enthusiasm, the kind of therapist-patient relationship which behavior-therapy methods establish, and the demands implicit in a "scientific" treatment.

The present study was concerned with both of the above questions. Behavior-therapy methods were employed to treat enuresis in children, and special attention was directed toward the efficiency of conditioning relative to other methods, and the changes in adjustment immediately following cure.

Bed-wetting seems a particularly appropriate disorder for research into the questions posed. Improvement can be accurately assessed, and the point of complete symptomatic relief is attainable and well defined. Also, traditional psychiatric conceptions of enuresis as a symptom of emotional disturbance (summarized in Mowrer, 1950) are quite different from the behavior therapist's view of enuresis as an isolated habit deficiency in the great majority of cases (e.g., Lovibond, 1964). Although the conditioning treatment of enuresis has been reported to be quite effective by many investigators (summarized in Lovibond, 1964), it is still not widely used, in part because of the symptom-substitution concern. For example, Sperling (1965) has recently written: "The removal of the symptom of enuresis, without providing other outlets for the child, leads to a replacement by other symptoms . . . [p. 30]." The few studies which have investigated this question of adjustment following cure (Baller & Schalock, 1956; Behrle, Elkin, & Laybourne, 1956; Biering & Jespersen, 1959; Lovibond, 1964) are inconclusive, however, because they were poorly (or not at all) controlled, for the most part lacked quantified measures, and did not assess change independent of the therapy.

The present study separated the treatment of enuresis and measurements of adjustment, so as to avoid the subtle forms of experimenter bias (Rosenthal, 1966) and demand characteristics (Orne, 1962) which continue to haunt practically all therapy-outcome studies. Measures of adjustment were taken by another *E* in the enuretic child's school, and these measures were taken under the guise of an entirely different research project.

METHOD

Subjects

The Ss were 90 elementary school children—30 enuretics and 60 controls. Two control Ss of the same sex as the enuretic *S* were selected randomly from each enuretic *S*'s classroom.

The enuretic Ss were obtained primarily in response to a newspaper article describing the project and inviting participation. A preliminary phone interview obtained the child's name, address, age, school and grade, and information about the enuresis. Also, the parent's report that in the family physician's opinion there was no organic problem was a prerequisite for being included. The enuretic sample consisted of 10 girls and 20 boys, with a median age of 8 yr. and a range from 6 to 12 yr. All but 4 of the children had been wetting since birth, and more than half were wet 7 nights a week.

Apparatus

The conditioning units used two foil pads, with holes in the top pad, separated by an absorbent sheet, and placed under S's lower bed sheet. The pads were connected to a white plastic box which contained two 6-v. batteries, a sensitive relay, and a buzzer. Within seconds after the child began to wet, a circuit was completed and the buzzer sounded. The buzzer continued to sound until S got out of bed and shut it off.

The "gadgetry" device, used in the subsequent treatment of four waiting-list Ss, consisted of a bulletin board for a star chart, a container for stars, and a wind-up alarm clock, all mounted on a white wooden stand.

Procedure

The 30 enuretic Ss were arranged in triads according to the data obtained in the phone interviews, and 1 S was randomly assigned to each of three experimental conditions. Ten children were placed immediately in behavior therapy with a conditioning device (Group C). Ten children were concurrently given a wake-up treatment designed to duplicate all features of the conditioning treatment except the conditioning procedure (Group WU). Ten children were placed on a waiting list to begin treatment in the near future (Group WL). The Group WL families were scheduled for a brief home interview, in which E obtained further information about the child's enuresis.

Treatment

All treatment was carried out in the child's home. In the first visit, E told S's parents that he was investigating both the process of cure and the changes which follow a child's becoming dry. Parents were asked to be particularly attentive to any changes in their child—especially new problems—both during and after treatment.

Group C. The E explained the operation of the conditioning device and encouraged the child to practice setting it up himself. The S was kept on the device until he had 14 consecutive days dry; the device was then taken off the bed but left in the house for an additional 14 days, after which S was designated as dry. If a child was not dry (or much improved) after 50 reinforcements (buzzer sounds), he was designated a failure. If a child later relapsed, he was begun again on the device when possible.

Group WU. The wake-up treatment was similar to the routine prescribed by many pediatricians, but with emphasis on regularity and thorough awakening (adapted from Smith, 1948). A fixed time was chosen before S usually wet, and the parents were told to awaken S every night at this time; the best time evolved during treatment. It was stressed that the child must be wide awake before going to the bathroom. When S had been dry for a week, he was not awakened for several nights during the next week. If he was dry on these nights, he was put on a new schedule whereby he would only be awakened the 2 nights following a wet night.

Otherwise, treatment was the same for conditioning and wake-up children. All parents aided the child in getting up at night and kept daily records of progress; all children kept progress records with star charts. Every child was visited at home once a week and phoned once a week by the author to review progress and offer suggestions. Parents in both groups were generally very cooperative in keeping records and appeared to be adequately following the treatment routine.

Group WL. Approximately 10 wk. after the original interview, E phoned the 10 waiting-list families. One S in Group WL had become dry and another S had not been examined medically after repeated requests;

consequently, these 2 Ss were not begun in treatment. To explore some peripheral hypotheses, the remaining 8 waiting-list Ss were now treated in the following way.

It seemed possible that the conditioning method might be effective because E brings a "gadget" into the home, thus in some way increasing the child's motivation. To obtain pilot data on this question, four Ss were placed in wake-up treatment, but were also brought the gadget described above, with instructions to place it beside the bed and to set the alarm clock at the time designated for awakening. The other four Ss received the same conditioning treatment as the original Group C.

Also, as an exploratory means of assessing the importance of the therapist's presence, there were two levels of contact with E, full and partial. Two Ss in each group received the same amount of contact with E as Group C and Group WU Ss had received (full contact: one visit and one phone call each week). The remaining Ss received only half as much contact with E (partial contact: a visit one week, a call the next week, etc.).

Measures of Adjustment

Parent measures. Parents were periodically asked whether they had observed any changes in their child, and they completed two rating scales, both before treatment began and several weeks after treatment was terminated. The Adjective Check List (ACL) was adapted from a scale used by Sarason, Davidson, Lighthall, Waite, and Ruebush (1960) and included 20 items designed to assess personality attributes such as confidence, anxiety, and responsibility. The scale included the 12 Sarason items which could readily be scored for adjustment and 8 new items. Items were presented in the form (Sad 321 123 Cheerful), and parents were asked to select the word which better typified S and to indicate the extent (a little, definitely, very much) by circling one number. The Behavior Problem Record (BPR) was a checklist of 26 specific childhood problems; the first 15 items were a scale devised by Lovibond (1964) in his work with enuresis, and the last 11 were added by the author. Many of the problems in the BPR have been associated with enuresis in the psychiatric literature or have been suggested as possible new symptoms if enuresis is removed without treating an underlying cause (e.g., fire-setting, thumbsucking, temper outbursts).

Teacher ratings. The enuretic Ss in the study were distributed throughout 23 public schools and 2 parochial schools; since no two enuretic Ss happened to be in the same classroom, 30 teachers were involved in the ratings. From each enuretic S's class list, two other children of the same sex were randomly selected as controls.

Although E initially contacted the superintendents and principals, all contacts with the teachers and all testing of the children were performed by another E (E_2). The research was presented to the teachers as a study of creativity. No mention ever was made of bed-wetting. Teachers were told that their class and these children had been selected at random. The E_2 explained that many of the hypotheses in the project would be biased if the teachers were made aware of them, but that after the data were all gathered she would welcome the chance to meet with the teachers and explain more fully the project and how their work fit into it. Thus, only when the study was completed did teachers learn of the enuresis treatment and their relation to it.

The teachers were given a 67-item rating form for each of the three children. Each item was to be rated on a scale of either 1–5 or 1–7. Most of the items were taken from the Devereux Elementary School Rating Scale (Spivack & Swift, 1966) and the Devereux Child Behavior Rating Scales (Spivack & Levine, 1964). Both scales had been factor analyzed, and in devising the teachers' rating form items were drawn from each of the factors. These factors represented either aspects of school behavior (e.g., academic anxiety, dependence on the teacher for learning) or personal maladjustment (e.g., social aggression, fears, inability to delay). Since most of the items were stated negatively and measured "problems," new items were added exploring such things as creativity, happiness, confidence, responsibility, maturity, and capacity for play. Items were stated in terms of overt behavior, and teachers were asked to compare S's current behavior with that of other children his age.

Teachers were asked to complete these questionnaires three times throughout the year. Test I was just before treatment began for the enuretic S, Test II was about 10 wk. later, and Test III about 12 wk. after Test II.

Child measures. At these same times, the enuretic child and one of the two control children in each class were tested by E_2, who was not aware of the specific hypotheses being investigated and did not know which child was enuretic. It was announced to the class that E_2 wanted to find out some things about elementary school children and that two names had been picked "out of a hat." The test battery began with the Draw-A-Person and Draw-Your-Family Tests and included four TAT cards (not to be reported here) and a self-report questionnaire in two parts: (*a*) the Self-Image Questionnaire, a 16-item scale designed by the author to measure feelings which might arise from being enuretic and including positively and negatively stated items such as, "My parents are very happy with me," and "I often do things I wish I had never done"; and (*b*) the Neurotic Inventory, a 20-item scale measuring neurotic problems devised and employed with enuretics by Lovibond (1964) and including items such as, "I worry quite a bit about things which might happen," and "Most of the time I feel down in the dumps." Items in both scales were presented verbally to S as "things which boys [girls] I know have said," and S was asked if he was like that child. (E.g., "Bob said: I get a lot of headaches. Are you exactly like Bob? Somewhat? Not at all?")[2]

Neither the parents of tested Ss nor Ss themselves had any knowledge of the relationship between this school testing and treatment; if parents inquired at school about the testing, they too were told that their child was in a creativity study of randomly selected children.

After the final testing it was necessary to determine which of the control Ss happened to be enuretic. The E phoned the parents of the control Ss requesting that they complete a questionnaire about their child. Parents were sent the same questionnaire which the parents of enuretic Ss had filled out, except that two additional items were added to the BPR: bedwetting and daytime wetting.

RESULTS

Reliability and Intercorrelation of the Scales

Table 1 shows the Spearman-Brown corrected split-half reliabilities of the questionnaire measures for Test I and the test-retest coefficients. These reliabilities are satisfactory for questionnaires of this type. Drawing variables requiring subjective judgment were scored independently by the author and another judge, with Test I interjudge reliabilities ranging from .43 to .95. For analyses of drawing variables, an average of the two judges' ratings was used.

Comparison of Enuretics and Controls on Pretreatment Measures

Enuretics and controls did not differ significantly on any item in the self-report scales, any factor in the teachers' ratings, or either total score. None of the specific drawing variables in either the Draw-A-Person or Draw-Your-Family Tests differentiated enuretics from controls. Also, two clinical psychologists making blind judgments of enuretic-control pairs of drawings

---

[2] After the first testing, it seemed that some Ss might be responding defensively to the questionnaire scales, and the need for a defensiveness measure was realized. Hence, the D scale employed by Sarason et al. (1960) was administered to most Ss in Test II and to all Ss in Test III.

TABLE 1   Spearman-Brown corrected split-half reliabilities of the questionnaires for test I and test-retest reliabilities

Scale	Corrected r	Tests I-II[a]	Tests I-III
Children's neurotic inventory	.94	.80	.70
Children's self-image questionnaire			
Negative items[b]	.79	.74	.67
Teachers' rating form	.85	.86	.83
Adjective check list			
Mother	.89	.87	—
Father	.83	.92	—
Behavior problem record			
Mother	.89	.62	—
Father	.93	.71	—

[a]*For the child and teacher measures, there was an average of 10 wk. between Tests I and II and an average of 22 wk. between Tests I and III. For the parent measures, the questionnaire completed just before treatment was correlated with the measure following treatment, yielding only one coefficient.*

[b]*The positive self-image items were unreliable and did not correlate with the negative items or other measures; consequently, only the negative items were considered.*

were unable to identify the enuretics' drawings any better than chance expectation.

Treatment

Figure 1 summarizes the results of the first 10 wk. of treatment. There was a sizable initial drop in wetting frequency from the prelevel to the first 2 wk. of treatment for both treatment groups. Following this, the conditioning group frequency decreased over the 10-wk. period, while the frequency of wetting in wake-up Ss remained essentially unchanged. This Conditions × Weeks interaction was significant at $p < .05$ ($F = 2.54$, $df = 4/72$) by a Lindquist (1956) Type I analysis of variance of the treatment data (excluding the prelevel). Comparing the number of wet nights in Weeks 1–2 and Weeks 9–10, a second-order t test found the improvement in Group C to have been significantly greater than in Group WU ($t = 2.89$, $df = 18$, $p < .01$). These results indicate that the two conditions produced differential effects over time. By Weeks 9–10, the conditioning group was wetting significantly less than the wake-up group ($t = 1.70$, $df = 18$, $p = .05$).[3]

An interview with waiting-list families an average of 10.6 wk. after E's

---

[3] In evaluating treatment differences, it is important to note that Group WU Ss had the aid of being awakened during the night until they had progressed sufficiently

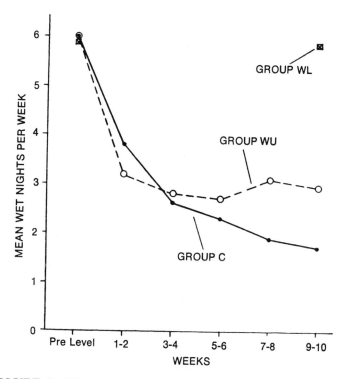

FIGURE 1 Mean number of wet nights a week over the first 10 wk. of treatment for Groups C, WU, and WL.

first visit found the reported mean frequency of wet nights unchanged. During this period, one Group WL S had become dry, but his previous frequency had been only 2 wet nights a week, the lowest in the study, and his decrease was offset by two Ss whose frequency increased. Contrasting the number of wet nights in the previous 3 wk. with the comparable 3 wk. for Group C and Group WU (Weeks 8–10 of treatment), the mean number of wet nights for Group WL ($\overline{X} = 17.7$) was significantly greater than either the mean for Group C ($\overline{X} = 5.5$; $t = 4.30$, $df = 18$, $p < .001$) or the mean for Group WU ($\overline{X} = 9.3$; $t = 3.21$, $df = 18$, $p < .01$).

The improvement during the first 8 wk. of subsequent conditioning or "gadgetry" treatment for the waiting-list children was analyzed by an analysis of variance. While the conditioning treatment was more effective

to be left on their own, whereas Group C Ss did not. The implication is that Group WU Ss appear to be more improved than was actually the case. For example, six Group WU Ss had improved sufficiently to be left on their own some nights. The mean percentage of wetting was 22.5 on nights when they were awakened and 38.5 on nights when they were not awakened ($t = 2.51$, $df = 5$, $p < .03$).

than the gadgetry control, this difference was not statistically significant. (The Ss with the gadget did no better than previous wake-up Ss, but Ss on conditioning did not do as well as previous conditioning Ss.) Children who had been seen less frequently (partial contact) showed more improvement than Ss who received full contact, though this difference was not statistically significant.

Treatment summary. In all, 14 Ss were begun on the conditioning device; of these, 11 attained initial arrest. Fourteen Ss were begun in wake-up conditions; of these, 2 attained initial arrest. Ten Ss who had shown little improvement were switched to conditioning, and 7 subsequently became dry.

Of the 30 enuretic Ss, then, 1 became dry without treatment, 1 was not begun in treatment, and 1 was terminated before treatment could be completed. Of the remaining 27 Ss, 74% were "cured" (dry for at least a period of 1 mo.), and an additional 15% were "very much improved" (dry for at least a 2-wk. period and wetting less than 1 night a week). During the follow up, which averaged 6 mo., 4 cured Ss relapsed, although 2 of these who were retreated became dry again.

Changes Following Treatment

Parents' interviews and questionnaires. It is important to note in assessing the results of parents' measures that changes similar to those reported for enuretic Ss might also have been reported for control Ss if such comparable measures were available. In addition, parents' measures may reflect a desire to please E. It was for these reasons, of course, that independent school measures were taken on both enuretic and control Ss.

The most frequently reported observation of parents was the child's happiness at becoming dry. Many children were able for the first time to sleep overnight with friends or relatives or to go to summer camp; three boys immediately joined the Boy Scouts. Children were reported to be venturing into new activities, taking more responsibility, and becoming more autonomous. For instance, parents made such statements as, "She seems able to do things for herself"; "He started a paper route"; "Now she's cooking, sewing, reading."

While most parents reported that they had observed no new problems, several parents did report a new problem at some time. One boy defecated in his pants several times immediately following treatment. Another began to depend more on his mother to make decisions for him. A third boy developed an "eyeblink." None of these proved to be lasting, and each seemed to arise from specific new stresses, although it is not possible to say if they had any relation to the treatment.

Both mothers and fathers of cured Ss indicated improvement in adjustment on the ACL and the BPR. Combined parents' scores on the ACL showed a mean improvement of 3.5, significant at $p = .002$. Combined parents' scores on the BPR showed a mean improvement (decrease in reported problems) of -2.8, significant at $p = .05$.

School measures. Test II afforded a measure of changes which occurred either during treatment or immediately thereafter. There was an average of 10 wk. from Test I to Test II, at which time 17 Ss were judged improved (wetting less than half their original frequency). There was an average of 22 wk. from Test I to Test III. By Test III, 13 Ss were cured, and another 8 Ss were very much improved (wetting once a week or less). Children designated as cured had not been wetting for an average of almost 3 mo.

Teacher ratings. Change scores were determined for total teachers' ratings from Test I to Test II; enuretics were divided into "improved" and "unimproved" and compared with each other and with their controls. For Test I to Test III comparisons, enuretics were classified as cured, very much improved, or slightly improved and compared with their respective controls. None of the mean change scores, nor the differences between them, approached statistical significance; teachers showed a high degree of consistency in their ratings, and mean change scores were small. Change scores on only 3 of the 24 factors significantly differentiated cured enuretics from their controls, with cured enuretics increasing significantly more ($p < .05$) in academic anxiety, drive for academic success, and unethical behavior.[4]

Children's self-report questionnaires. There was a general downward trend (fewer reported problems) on the questionnaires from Test I to Test II. The direction of changes for enuretics and controls is shown in Table 2. While treatment was in progress or only recently terminated, enuretic Ss who had shown improvement in bed-wetting reported fewer problems than previously. This improvement compared favorably with changes shown in questionnaire scores for both unimproved enuretic Ss and control Ss.

In analyzing changes from Test I to Test III, special attention was given to Ss designated as cured,[5] as these Ss would be most likely to evi-

---

[4] Actually, cured enuretics only increased somewhat in drive for academic success and unethical behavior, but controls decreased in score on these variables, resulting in the significant difference. However, there was a large Test I difference for these Ss on these factors, and even after the above changes the control Ss still scored higher than enuretics.

[5] One cured S and his control could not be tested a third time due to lack of cooperation from the school. The control of another cured S had moved away, so this pair was not included. In all, then, there were 11 cured-control pairs.

TABLE 2   Direction of change in questionnaire scores from test I to test II

Questionnaire	Improved enuretics	Unim- proved enuretics	Controls
Neurotic inventory[a]			
Increase	0	3	10
Same	0	3	1
Decrease	17	7	19
Self-image questionnaire[b]			
Increase	2	4	6
Same	1	1	1
Decrease	14	8	23

Note. — Decrease indicates improvement (fewer reported problems).
[a]$\chi^2 = 15.19, p < .01.$
[b]$\chi^2 = 2.14, p > .10.$

dence adverse changes according to the symptom-substitution hypothesis. On the Neurotic Inventory, no cured S reported more problems, and on the Self-Image Questionnaire only one S increased in score. The mean improvement for cured enuretics was greater than the mean improvement for their controls on both the Neurotic Inventory ($t = 1.49$, $df = 20$, $p = .08$) and the Self-Image Questionnaire ($t = 1.79$, $df = 20$, $p < .05$). Combining the questionnaires, the mean improvement from Test I to Test III for cured enuretics ($\overline{X} = -15.6$) was significantly greater than for their controls ($\overline{X} = -6.4$) at $p = .03$ ($t = 1.93$, $df = 20$).[6]

There were no questionnaire items on which cured and very much improved enuretics showed a significant change for the worse or their controls improved more than the enuretic Ss. Cured and very much improved enuretics improved significantly more than did the controls ($p < .05$) on the following items: "I'm always being scolded or punished by someone"; "I've often been punished for nothing"; "I often feel sick in the stomach"; "Most of the time I feel down in the dumps."

Drawings.   Scoring of specific variables on the Draw-A-Person and Draw-Your-Family Tests failed to reveal significant changes. A total score was derived for each S on the former, based on conceptions in the drawing literature (e.g., Machover, 1951; Mazen, 1963) of what constitutes an improvement in adjustment. To weight each variable equally, only the sign of change was considered. Signs of a shift toward better adjustment were an increase in number of body parts, size of the person, number of colors

---

[6] One explanation for this decrease would be increased defensiveness. Since no D-scale scores were available for Test I, the only change which could be analyzed was from Test II to Test III. The defensiveness scores were fairly stable, and the changes did not differentiate cured enuretics and controls.

used, appropriateness of colors, amount of clothing, smile and movement, and a decrease in erasures, pressure, distortion, bizarreness, paper chopping, transparency, stick figures, drawing side views, drawing the opposite sex, and negative affect. Cured enuretics showed a mean improvement ($\overline{X} = 1.36$, $p = .06$) and differed significantly from their controls who showed a slight worsening ($\overline{X} = -1.45$; t, second-order difference $= 2.29$, $df = 20$, $p = .02$).

Also, two clinical psychologists with the diplomate and 15 and 30 yr. of experience in therapy and diagnosis were asked to evaluate the Draw-A-Person Test drawings for expressions of maladjustment. Each of the 30 enuretic and 30 control Ss was randomly assigned a number between 1 and 60, and each S's three drawings (Tests I, II, and III) were randomly ordered in one of the six possible permutations. Judges were told the age, race, and sex of each child and were to rank order the three drawings with respect to overall adjustment. In assessing the drawings, then, a judge knew neither which drawings had been done by enuretic and nonenuretic Ss nor the order in which they had been drawn.

In this type of analysis, differences between groups are reflected in the slope of the curves connecting mean ranks across testings. As seen in Figure 2, for each judge the mean ranks for the cured enuretics decrease across the three tests, whereas the control slope is essentially flat. The improvement in adjustment rank from Test I to Test III for cured enuretics was significant for both Judge 1 ($t = 3.81$, $df = 10$, $p = .002$) and Judge 2 ($t = 2.36$, $df = 10$, $p = .02$). When this Test I–Test III change score for cured enuretics was compared with a similar score for their controls, the second-order t test showed that improvement in adjustment for cured enuretics

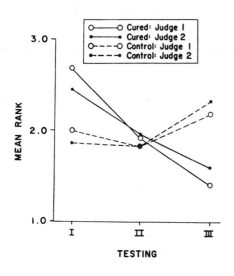

FIGURE 2 Judges' ranks of overall adjustment in Draw-A-Person Test drawings; mean ranks for each judge are plotted over the three testings for cured enuretic Ss and their control Ss. (Lower ranks indicate better adjustment.)

was significantly greater than for controls—for Judge 1, $p = .007$ ($t = 2.72$, $df = 20$) and for Judge 2, $p = .004$ ($t = 2.88$, $df = 20$).

DISCUSSION

The present study suggests, then, that it is extremely doubtful that the successful conditioning treatment of bed-wetting can be explained as some kind of "transference cure," based on only the therapist-patient relationship and the motivation which it engenders. The wake-up procedure was not as effective as the total behavior-therapy treatment, despite an equal amount of therapist contact. These findings are similar to those of Lang and Lazovik (1963), Lazarus (1961), Paul (1966), and Davison (1968) who contrasted systematic desensitization to other methods with equal therapist contact.

Another approach to this question of the relative importance of the therapist and his technique is to withdraw the therapist to some extent and to see if treatment becomes less effective. The exploratory findings indicated that treatment is just as effective with less therapist contact, a result consonant with the fact that many parents buy conditioning devices and cure their child's enuresis with no professional help at all.

The measures of adjustment did not show a worsening in adjustment subsequent to treatment; rather, other improvements were found. Children were reported to be happier, less anxious, and more grown-up, assuming responsibility and venturing into new activities. The changes on childrens' self-report items about punishment suggest that the cure may have had beneficial effects on the parent-child relationship or at least the child's perception of it. Finally, the drawings showed a dramatic improvement in what might be termed "self-image."

Whereas enuresis is considered to be a symptom of emotional disturbance by many clinicians, traditional predictions about treatment and subsequent adjustment for such symptoms were not upheld. This might suggest that the symptom-substitution hypothesis is untenable and that neurotic symptoms, in the traditional dynamic sense, can be removed with equanimity despite the psychological gains they afford. Perhaps in those cases where treatment succeeds, the benefits derived from being dry outweigh such "primary gains." On the other hand, it is possible that new symptoms did not arise because bed-wetting is simply a habit deficiency rather than an expression of, and outlet for, internal conflict. In any case, the dangers of a direct treatment of enuresis seem to have been overstated, and similar research on other classical disorders might be of considerable value in further understanding the symptom-substitution issue and the more basic question of symptom formation.

REFERENCES

BALLER, W., & SCHALOCK, H. Conditioned response treatment of enuresis. *Exceptional Child*, 1956, **22**, 233–236.

BEHRLE, F. C., ELKIN, M. T., & LAYBOURNE, P. C. Evaluation of a conditioning device in the treatment of nocturnal enuresis. *Pediatrics*, 1956, **17**, 849–855.

BIERING, A., & JESPERSEN, I. The treatment of enuresis nocturna with conditioning devices. *Acta Paediatrica*, 1959, **48** (Monogr. Suppl. No. 118), 152–153.

BREGER, L., & McGAUGH, J. L. Critique and reformulation of "learning-theory" approaches to psychotherapy and neurosis. *Psychological Bulletin*, 1965, **63**, 338–358.

DAVISON, G. C. Systematic desensitization as a counterconditioning process. *Journal of Abnormal Psychology*, 1968, **73**, 91–99.

FREUD, S. On psychotherapy. (Orig. publ. 1904) In, *Collected papers of Sigmund Freud*. Vol. 1. New York: Basic Books, 1959.

KAHN, M., BAKER, B. L., & WEISS, J. M. Treatment of insomnia by relaxation. *Journal of Abnormal Psychology*, 1968, **73**, 556–558.

LANG, P. J., & LAZOVIK, A. D. Experimental desensitization of a phobia. *Journal of Abnormal and Social Psychology*, 1963, **66**, 519–525.

LAZARUS, A. A. Group therapy of phobic disorders by systematic desensitization. *Journal of Abnormal and Social Psychology*, 1961, **63**, 504–510.

LAZARUS, A. A. The results of behavior therapy in 126 cases of severe neurosis. *Behavior Research and Therapy*, 1963, **1**, 69–80.

LINDQUIST, E. F. *Design and analysis of experiments in psychology and education*. Boston: Houghton Mifflin, 1956.

LOVIBOND, S. H. *Conditioning and enuresis*. Oxford: Pergamon Press, 1964.

MACHOVER, K. Drawings of the human figure. In H. Anderson & G. Anderson (Eds.), *An introduction to projective techniques*. Englewood Cliffs, N. J.: Prentice-Hall, 1951.

MAZEN, R. Comparative study of the drawings of normal and disturbed children. Unpublished manuscript, Yale University, 1963.

MOWRER, O. H. *Learning theory and personality dynamics*. New York: Ronald Press, 1950.

ORNE, M. T. On the social psychology of the psychological experiment with particular reference to demand characteristics and their implications. *American Psychologist*, 1962, **17**, 776–783.

PAUL, G. L. *Insight versus desensitization in psychotherapy*. Stanford: Stanford University Press, 1966.

ROSENTHAL, R. *Experimenter effects in behavioral research*. New York: Appleton-Century-Crofts, 1966.

SARASON, S. B., DAVIDSON, K. S., LIGHTHALL, F. F., WAITE, R. R., & RUEBUSH, B. K. *Anxiety in elementary school children*. New York: Wiley, 1960.

SMITH, S. *The psychological origin and treatment of enuresis.* Seattle: University of Washington Press, 1948.

SPERLING, M. Dynamic considerations and treatment of enuresis. *Journal of the American Academy of Child Psychiatry,* 1965, 4, 19–31.

SPIVACK, G., & LEVINE, M. The Devereux Child Behavior Rating Scales: A study of symptom behaviors in latency age atypical children. *American Journal of Mental Deficiency,* 1964, 68, 700–717.

SPIVACK, G., & SWIFT, M. The Devereux Elementary School Rating Scale: A study of the nature and origin of achievement related to disturbed classroom behavior. *Journal of Special Education,* 1966, 1, 71–90.

WOLPE, J. The systematic desensitization treatment of neuroses. *Journal of Nervous and Mental Disease,* 1961, 132, 189–203.

3

BUILDING
LANGUAGE BEHAVIORS

Most children acquire language without special assistance, but we know little about how they do it. It is a "natural phenomenon," and knowledge of the process has not been needed. Unfortunately, some children do not learn to talk on their own. To help them, we are beginning to study how language is acquired. Some people have guessed that language is determined by essentially innate factors—that it has been, in a sense, programmed into the organism's nervous system at birth. Others feel that language is determined by environment, that it is chiefly experience that teaches us speech. The benefits of more explicit knowledge about language acquisition may well be widely shared. After all, language is very essential in human life; it is perhaps the most unique characteristic of human behavior and contributes in a major way to human thought and achievement.

One of the most demanding tasks for psychology—and one of the most rigorous tests of a theory of man's behavior—would be the building of language in children who either had no language at all or who were deficient in their language repertoires. This section includes a set of papers that deal with this problem. It is important to recognize that the application of psychological learning principles to the understanding of how language is acquired is a very recent phenomenon. Considering just how recent a phenomenon that application is, the learning approach to the solution of this problem is quite promising.

Let us briefly examine a behavioristic view on language acquisition. The child who acquires language must learn two things. First, he must acquire certain response differentiations or behavioral topographies—that is, the differentiated vocal output that produces verbalizations like "mama," "baby," "I see," and so on. If that were all the child could do, his behavior would exist without "meaning"; the behavior could be described as merely imitating or parroting. Infants typically pass through such a stage of imitating the utterances of others. Some psychotic and brain-damaged children come close to this in instances of echolalic speech, in which they tend to echo fairly precisely the speech they hear. For the child who is mute, however, one must supply him with this behavioral topography through detailed training.

Even though a child can sound out words and sentences, he may not use them for the specific purposes that are intended. He does not know what his utterances mean. What do we mean when we say the child must learn what language means? His verbal productions, like any other behaviors, are without meaning if they are not tied to appropriate stimulus contexts or if they lack appropriate stimulus functions. One may approach the problem of teaching meaning in two ways. We may gradually teach the child what stimulus conditions, external or internal, are appropriate contexts for the occurrence of particular utterances. Secondly, we may teach him what stimulus functions the utterances themselves should possess—that is, what further verbal or nonverbal behavior, in himself or others, these utterances may elicit.

In this section we provide examples of both kinds of learning: the acquisition of behavioral topography and the acquisition of stimulus function. The first selection is a study by Lovaas, Berberich, Perloff, and Schaeffer on the acquisition of imitative speech in mute children. In working with mute children, it soon became apparent that it was impossible to build the kind of elaborate response repertoire the child needs by shaping vocal behavior through successive approximations. Although we had been successful over several months of training in shaping a word like "mama," it took an almost equal amount of effort to shape the word "daddy"; and when we had obtained the second word, we lost control over the first. Clearly, we needed a more efficient way to place the complex behavioral topography of language at the child's disposal. It appears that normal children learn language topographies by imitating their parents and later their peers. We wanted to use this learning procedure, but the children we worked with did not imitate others. So our first task became one of teaching them how to imitate.

The way to teach imitation that we eventually found is described in this article. The training procedure is essentially discrimination training. We delivered reinforcement contingent upon the child's responding in a manner that resembled the responses of the adults around him. Imitation, then, is a discrimination in which the response resembles its stimulus— either in its topography (clasping hands) or in the environmental manipulation it achieves (putting a block in a box).

Once the child can imitate, one begins the enormous task of making this behavior relevant, or functional, in the child's day-to-day life. The paper by Risley and Wolf on establishing functional speech in echolalic children is addressed to this problem. There are many fine features in this article. Their work does not point out how much skill a behavior modifier needs to shape a complex behavior like speech in a psychotic child. Observing Wolf and Risley shaping a child is a very impressive sight. Like a sculptor who creates a beautiful object from undifferentiated clay, a good behavior modifier shapes beautiful behavior from formless activity.

Hart and Risley's study on their work in enriching the language of culturally disadvantaged children has several important implications. Despite the fact that we systematically aim to educate our children and have done so for thousands of years, relatively little is known objectively about how one should proceed in preparing children for school, or once they come to school, what the best training procedures are to apply there. The Hart and Risley study represents a beginning step in extending the vocabulary of children who typically are judged by the school system to be deficient in language development. In general, the use of the procedures of behavior modification research, as well as the application of its conceptual framework, could have vast implications for the way in which we try to help children to function successfully and happily.

Wheeler and Sulzer's study on training a verbal response form represents one of the early studies in an area that has become very active in the last few years. The study aims to build a complex language form using operant training procedures. It points to a better understanding of how syntax may be acquired. Critics of behavioristic approaches to language have insistently argued that certain aspects of language, such as sentence form, are too complex to be adequately handled through learning principles and training methods. The Wheeler and Sulzer study is a beginning effort that strongly suggests that the environment can, in fact, shape such complex linguistic forms. What is particularly encouraging about this is the fact that when the environment can be manipulated to produce complex behaviors, there is hope for the children we now label deficient.

The last study by Risley and Hart shows some interesting relations between language and behavior. Certainly the child who can talk can deal more effectively with his social environment. But what about the role that language has in controlling the child's own behavior? To put it differently, what help, in the form of direction and solutions, does language give to the child who uses it? There have been several theoretical and empirical approaches to this problem. An advantage of the study by Risley and Hart lies in the explicitness with which they designed their tests. The question they raise is perhaps the most important one to raise about language, and the student should become familiar with the way in which they go about trying to answer it.

O. IVAR LOVAAS
JOHN P. BERBERICH
BERNARD F. PERLOFF
BENSON SCHAEFFER
University of California at Los Angeles

Acquisition
of imitative speech
by schizophrenic children[1]

Two mute schizophrenic children were taught imitative speech within an operant conditioning framework. The training procedure consisted of a series of increasingly fine verbal discriminations; the children were rewarded for closer and closer reproductions of the attending adults' speech. We found that reward delivered contingent upon imitation was necessary for development of imitation. Furthermore, the newly established imitation was shown to have acquired rewarding properties for the children.

With the great majority of children, the problem of teaching speech never arises. Speech develops within each child's particular environment without parents and teachers having to know a great deal about how it occurs. Yet, in some children, because of deviations in organic structure or prior experience, speech fails to develop. Children with the diagnosis of

[1] Study supported by grants from Margaret Sabl of Los Angeles. We express appreciation to James Q. Simmons and the staff at the Children's Unit, Neuropsychiatric Institute, University of California, Los Angeles.

childhood schizophrenia, especially autistic children, often show little in the way of speech development (1). The literature on childhood schizophrenia suggests two conclusions regarding speech in such children: first, that the usual treatment setting (psychotherapy) in which these children are placed might not be conducive to speech development (2); and second, that a child failing to develop speech by the age of 5 years remains withdrawn and does not improve clinically (2). That is, the presence or absence of speech is an important prognostic indicator. It is perhaps obvious that a child who can speak can engage in a much more therapeutic interchange with his environment than the child who has no speech.

The failure of some children to develop speech as a "natural" consequence of growing up poses the need for an increased knowledge of how language is acquired. A procedure for the development of speech in previously mute children would not only be of practical importance but might also illuminate the development of speech in normal children. Although several theoretical attempts have been made to account for language development, the empirical basis for these theoretical formulations is probably inadequate. In fact, there are no published, systematic studies on how to go about developing speech in a person who has never spoken. We now outline a procedure by which speech can be made to occur. Undoubtedly there are or will be other ways by which speech can be acquired. Furthermore, our procedure centers on the acquisition of only one aspect of speech, the acquisition of vocal responses. The development of speech also requires the acquisition of a context for the occurrence of such responses ("meaning").

Casual observation suggests that normal children acquire words by hearing speech; that is, children learn to speak by imitation. The mute schizophrenic children with whom we worked were not imitative. Thus the establishment of imitation in these children appeared to be the most beneficial and practical starting point for building speech. The first step in creating speech, then, was to establish conditions in which imitation of vocal sounds would be learned.

The method that we eventually found most feasible for establishing verbal imitation involved a discrimination training procedure. Early in training the child was rewarded only if he emitted a sound within a certain time after an adult had emitted a sound. Next he was rewarded only if the sound he emitted within the prescribed interval resembled the adult's sound. Toward the end of training, he was rewarded only if his vocalization very closely matched the adult's vocalization—that is, if it was, in effect, imitative. Thus verbal imitation was taught through the development of a series of increasingly fine discriminations.

The first two children exposed to this program are discussed here. Chuck and Billy were 6-year-old in-patients at the Neuropsychiatric Institute at UCLA. These children were selected for the program because they did not speak. At the onset of the program, vocal behavior in both children was restricted to occasional vowel productions with no discernible communicative intent. These vowel sounds occurred infrequently, except when the children were tantrumous, and did not resemble the pre-speech babbling of infants. In addition, the children evidenced no appropriate play (for example, they would spin toys or mouth them). They engaged in a considerable amount of self-stimulatory behavior such as rocking and twirling. They did not initiate social contacts and became tantrumous when such contact was initiated by others. They evidenced occasional self-destructive behavior (biting self, head-banging, and so forth). Symbolic rewards such as social approval were inoperative, so biological rewards such as food were substituted. In short, they were profoundly schizophrenic.

Training was conducted 6 days a week, 7 hours a day, with a 15-minute rest period accompanying each hour of training. During the training sessions the child and the adult sat facing each other, their heads about 30 cm apart. The adult physically prevented the child from leaving the training situation by holding the child's legs between his own legs. Rewards, in the form of single spoonsful of the child's meal, were delivered immediately after correct responses. Punishment (spanking, shouting by the adult) was delivered for inattentive, self-destructive, and tantrumous behavior which interfered with the training, and most of these behaviors were thereby suppressed within 1 week. Incorrect vocal behavior was never punished.

Four distinct steps were required to establish verbal imitation. In step 1, the child was rewarded for all vocalizations. We frequently would fondle the children and we avoided aversive stimulation. This was done in order to increase the frequency of vocal responses. During this stage in training the child was also rewarded for visually fixating on the adult's mouth. When the child reached an achievement level of about one verbal response every 5 seconds and was visually fixating on the adult's mouth more than 50 percent of the time, step 2 of training was introduced.

Step 2 marked our initial attempt to bring the child's verbal behavior under our verbal control in such a manner that our speech would ultimately stimulate speech in the child. Mastery of this second step involved acquisition of a temporal discrimination by the child. The adult emitted a vocal response—for example, "baby"—about once on the average of every 10th second. The child was rewarded only if he vocalized within 6 seconds after the adult's vocalization. However, any vocal response of the child would be rewarded in that time interval. Step 3 was introduced when the frequency of the child's vocal responses within the 6-second interval was three times what it had been initially.

Step 3 was structurally similar to the preceding step, but it included the additional requirement that the child actually match the adult's vocalization before receiving the reward. In this and in following steps the adult selected the verbalization to be placed in imitative training from a pool of possible verbalizations that had met one or more of the following criteria. First, we selected vocal behaviors that could be prompted, that is, vocal behaviors that could be elicited by a cue prior to any experimental training, such as by manually moving the child through the behavior.

An example of training with the use of a prompt is afforded in teaching the sound "b". The training would proceed in three stages: (i) the adult emitted "b" and simultaneously prompted the child to emit "b" by holding the child's lips closed with his fingers and quickly removing them when the child exhaled; (ii) the prompt would be gradually faded, by the adult's moving his fingers away from the child's mouth, to his cheek, and finally gently touching the child's jaw; (iii) the adult emitted the vocalization "b" only, withholding all prompts. The rate of fading was determined by the child; the sooner the child's verbal behavior came under control of the adult's without the use of the prompt, the better. The second criterion for selection of words or sounds in the early stages of training centered on their concomitant visual components (which we exaggerated when we pronounced them), such as those of the labial consonant "m" and of open-mouthed vowels like "a." We selected such sounds after having previously found that the children could discriminate words with visual components more easily that those with only auditory components (the guttural consonants, "k" and "g," proved extremely difficult and, like "l" and "s," were mastered later than other sounds). Third, we selected for training sounds which the child emitted most frequently in step 1.

Step 4 was a recycling of step 3, with the addition of a new sound. We selected a sound that was very different from those presented in step 3, so that the child could discriminate between the new and old sounds more easily. To make certain that the child was in fact imitating, we randomly interspersed the sounds of step 3 with the sound of step 4, in a randomized ratio of about 1 to 3. This random presentation "forced" (or enabled) the child to discriminate the particular sounds involved, in order to be rewarded. There was no requirement placed upon the child in step 3 to discriminate specific aspects such as vowels, consonants, and order of the adult's speech; a child might master step 3 without attending to the specific properties of the adult's speech. Each new introduction of sounds and words required increasingly fine discrimination by the child and hence provided evidence that the child was in fact matching the adult's speech. All steps beyond step 4 consisted of replications of step 3, but new sounds, words, and phrases were used. In each new step the previously mastered words and sounds were rehearsed on a randomized ratio of 1 to 3. The next step was introduced when the child had mastered the previous steps—that is, when he had made ten consecutive correct replications of the adult's utterances.

One hour of each day's training was tape-recorded. Two independent observers scored the child's correct vocal responses from these sessions. A correct response was defined as a recognizable reproduction of the adult's utterance. The observers showed better than 90 percent agreement over sessions. When the child's correct responses are plotted against days of training, and the resulting function is positively accelerated, it can be said that the child has learned to imitate.

The results of the first 26 days of imitation training, starting from introduction of step 3, have been plotted for Billy (Fig. 1). The abscissa denotes training days. The words and sounds are printed in lower case letters on the days they were introduced and in capital letters on the days they were mastered. It can be seen that as training progressed the rate of mastery increased. Billy took several days to learn a single word during the first 2 weeks of the program, but a single day to master several words during the last 2 weeks. Chuck's performance was very similar to Billy's.

After 26 days of training both children had learned to imitate new words with such ease and rapidity that merely adding verbal responses to

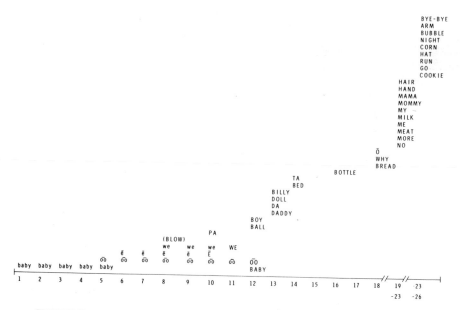

FIGURE 1 Acquisition of verbal imitation by Billy. The abscissa denotes training days. Words and sounds are printed in lower case letters on the days they were introduced, and in capital letters on the days they were mastered.

their imitative repertoire seemed pointless. Hence the children were then introduced to the second part of the language training program, wherein they were taught to use language appropriately.

The imitation training took place in a rather complex environment, with many events happening concurrently. We hypothesized that it was the reward, given for imitative behavior, which was crucial to the learning. To test this hypothesis, the adult uttered the sounds as during the training and the children received the same number of rewards as before. However, the rewards were contingent upon time elapsed since the last reward, regardless of the child's behavior.

The data show a deterioration in imitation behavior whenever rewards are shifted from response-contingent to time-contingent delivery. It is concluded, therefore, that reward immediately following correct, imitative behavior (and withholding of reward following incorrect responding) is a crucial variable in maintaining imitative behavior in these children. The same finding has been reported by Baer and Sherman (3) who worked with imitative behavior in normal children.

Since the child was rewarded whenever he responded like the adult, *similarity* was consistently associated with food. Because of such association, similarity should become symbolic of reward. In other words, imitative behavior, being symbolic of reward, should eventually provide its own reward (Baer and Sherman, 3). To test this hypothesis, both children were exposed to Norwegian words which they were unable to reproduce perfectly when first presented. The adult simply stated the Norwegian word and the child always attempted to repeat it; no extrinsic rewards were delivered. However, occasionally the child was presented with English words which the adult rewarded when correctly imitated. This procedure was necessary to maintain the hypothesized symbolic (learned) reward function of imitation.

The children improved in the imitation of the Norwegian words over time. It is as if they were rewarded for correct behavior. In view of the data pointing to the need for rewards in maintaining imitative behavior, and in the absence of extrinsic rewards, we would argue that the reward was intrinsic and a function of the prior imitation training. There is one implication of this finding which is of particular interest for therapeutic reasons: children may be able to acquire new behaviors on their own. (This finding contrasts with the frequent stereotype of a conditioning product, namely, that of an automaton unable to function independently.)

Currently, three new schizophrenic children are undergoing the same speech training program as Billy and Chuck. After 3 days of training, one of these children achieved a level of imitative behavior similar to that shown by Billy and Chuck after 26 days. It should be pointed out that schizophrenic children are a very heterogeneous group with respect to their speech histories and symptomatology in general, and that Billy and Chuck had failed in development to a profound degree. Insofar as one works with such a diverse population, it is likely that numerous procedures could be helpful in establishing speech.

REFERENCES

1. B. RIMLAND, *Infantile Autism* (Appleton-Century-Crofts, New York, 1964).
2. J. BROWN, *Amer. J. Orthopsychiat.* **30**, 382 (1960).
3. D. BAER and J. SHERMAN, *J. Exp. Child Psychol.* **1**, 37 (1964).

TODD RISLEY
MONTROSE WOLF
University of Kansas

Establishing functional speech
in echolalic children[1]

This paper is a summary of research by the authors in the development of speech in echolalic children. The procedures are based on operant behavior-modification techniques such as: (1) shaping and imitation training for the development of speech; (2) fading in of new stimuli and fading out of verbal prompts to transfer the speech from imitative control to control by appropriate stimulus conditions; and (3) extinction and time-out from reinforcement for the reduction of inappropriate behavior in conjunction with the differential reinforcement of appropriate responses which are incompatible with the inappropriate behavior.

INTRODUCTION

Echolalia

". . . autistic children usually do learn to talk, sometimes very well, but their speech fails to follow the normal patterns. Often prominent in their

Reprinted from *Behaviour Research and Therapy*, 1967, 5, 73–88, with permission of the publisher and the authors.

---
[1] This work was partially supported by PHS grant HD00870-04 and OEO contract KAN CAP 670694/1 to the Bureau of Child Research, University of Kansas.

150

speech is a compulsive parroting of what they hear called echolalia. They pick up a phrase, a name, a snatch of song, or even a long verse, and repeat it endlessly" (Stone and Church, 1957).

The sporadic and usually inappropriate imitation of words, phrases and snatches of song, is observed in many deviant children. Although this behavior pattern is generally associated with the diagnosis of emotional disturbance or autism, it is also a frequently observed behavior pattern of children diagnosed as retarded or brain-damaged. The procedures described in this paper have been developed from work with echolalic children with almost every conceivable diagnosis. Indeed, the records of each of these children usually contained diagnoses of retardation and brain-damage as well as autism, each label applied to the same child by a different diagnostician. For our procedures, the diagnostic classification of the child is largely irrelevant. The presence or absence of echolalia is the important predictor of the ease of establishing more normal speech in a deviant child.

In alleviating any deficit in behavior, the most time-consuming task is the teaching of new topographies of behavior. When a child's repertoire does not include a particular behavior and the child cannot be taught by conventional means, training can be carried out by the behavior modification technique called *shaping*. This procedure involves the long and intricate process of reinforcing behaviors which resemble (although, perhaps only remotely) the desired terminal behavior, and then, in successive steps, shifting the reinforcement to behaviors which more and more closely resemble the terminal behavior. When the terminal response is obtained, the response can then be shifted to imitative control by *imitation training*.

Imitation training involves reinforcing a response made by the child only when it immediately follows the same response made by the therapist. The child's response may already have existed in his echolalic repertoire or it may have been shaped into a high probability response. The therapist can shift the response to imitative control by reinforcing it when it occurs after the presentation of an identical modeled stimulus or *prompt*. In this manner large units of previously randomly occurring behavior can be brought under imitative control. Once a child accurately imitates most words, phrases, and sentences, then any topography of verbal behavior (i.e. any word, phrase, or sentence) can be produced when desired by presenting the child with the prompt to be imitated.

Echolalia, then, is of significance to the therapist, for, since the echolalic child already has verbal responses, the arduous task of shaping them is unnecessary. Once the child's responses are brought under imitative control, so that, for example, he says "that's a cow" when the therapist has just said "that's a cow," the only remaining step is to shift the control of his responses to the appropriate stimuli, so that, for example, he says "that's a cow" to a picture of a cow. This shift to naming is made by *fading out* the imitative prompt in gradual steps as described in detail below. In this manner the responses acquire their appropriate "meanings." Thus, the procedures for establishing functional speech in echolalic children are relatively simple and produce appropriate speech rapidly, in contrast to the procedures which have been used in establishing speech in nonecholalic speech-deficient children (e.g. Lovaas, 1966: Risley, 1966).

GENERAL PROCEDURES

The authors developed the procedures summarized in this paper while working with children with echolalic speech. The general methodology was initially developed in the course of dealing with the behavior problems of an autistic child named Dicky (Wolf, Risley and Mees, 1964). We will review his case before describing the more refined procedures which evolved from it.

Our contact with Dicky began 4 yr ago when he was 3½ yr old. He had been diagnosed as autistic and had been institutionalized previously for a 3-month period. Prior to this he had been diagnosed variously as psychotic, mentally retarded, and brain-damaged. Dicky had a variety of severe problem behaviors, and lacked almost all normal social and verbal behavior. His verbal repertoire was quite bizarre though not atypical of children diagnosed as autistic. He was echolalic, occasionally exactly mimicking in form and intonation bits of conversation of the staff. He sang songs, "Chicago," for example. He emitted a variety of phrases during tantrums, such as "Want a spanking," and "Want to go bye-bye" but none of his verbal behavior was socially appropriate. He never made requests, asked questions, or made comments. Although he mimicked occasionally, he would not mimic when asked to do so.

Our training began with the attendant presenting, one at a time, five pictures approximately 3 x 4 in. in size, of a Santa Claus, a cat, etc. The attendant would prompt, for example, "This is a cat. Now say cat." After she had gone through all five pictures, she would mix their order and go through them again. Just as Dicky occasionally mimicked the speech of other people, he would occasionally mimic the attendant by saying "This is a cat," or "Now say cat." On those occasions the attendant would say, "Good boy" or "That's right," and give him a bite of his meal. As a result Dicky began mimicking more frequently, until after about a week he was mimicking practically every prompt in addition to almost everything else the attendant said during the session.

However, during this time Dicky was not looking particularly closely at the pictures. Instead, he twisted and turned in his seat. So an *anticipation procedure* was introduced, where anticipating the correct response would result in a reinforcer sooner than if he waited for the prompt. The attendant would present the picture for a period of several seconds before giving the prompt. Gradually, Dicky began looking at the pictures and saying the phrases in the presence of the pictures without the prompts. In 3 weeks he did this in the presence of about ten pictures. We then introduced picture books and common household objects which he learned with increasing ease. At the same time temporally remote events were taught in the following manner. Dicky would be taken outside and swung or allowed to slide and then brought back inside and asked: "What did you do outside?" and then after a few seconds given a prompt. Imitations and finally the correct answers were followed by a reinforcer.

He was taught the answers to other questions such as, "What is your name?" and, "Where do you live?". The question would be asked and, if after a pause he had not answered, the prompt would be given and the correct response reinforced.

After several weeks of training, Dick's verbal repertoire was markedly expanded, although he still had several verbal anomalies, such as imitating the question before answering and reversing his pronouns, e.g. he would ask for a drink by saying, "You want some water." Dicky was released from hospital 7 months after our contact began. The training was continued by his parents, and after about 6 months he was using pronouns appropriately and was initiating many requests and comments, although he still was making frequent inappropriate imitating responses. After attending the Laboratory Preschool at the University of Washington for 2 yr, his verbal skills had developed to the point that he was ready for special education in the public school.

Dicky's verbal behavior now resembles that of a skilled 5-yr old. This means that since his operant training his rate of language development has been approximately normal. This probably has been the result of the diligent efforts of his parents and teachers to provide an environment which reinforced his verbal behavior. However, now the naturally occurring rewards of verbal behavior (see Skinner, 1957, for a discussion of these) appear to be the most important factors in maintaining and expanding his verbal repertoire.

These procedures for developing speech were subsequently refined in the course of working with the following echolalic children.

Pat was a blind 12-yr-old boy who has been recently institutionalized with the diagnosis of childhood autism. He had previously been enrolled in a school for the blind, but had been dropped from the program due to his disruptive behavior and general lack of progress.

Billy was a 10-yr-old boy who had been institutionalized for several years with the diagnosis of childhood autism.

Carey was a 7-yr-old boy who lived at home although he had been diagnosed variously as autistic, retarded, and brain-damaged, and institutionalization had been recommended. He had attended a day-school for special children during the previous 2 yr, but had been dropped due to a general lack of progress.

Will was an 8-yr-old boy who had been institutionalized for 2 yr with the diagnosis of severe retardation and brain-damage. He was not considered to be trainable and had been placed on a custodial ward.

The Physical Arrangement

To work most efficiently with a deviant child, particularly one with disruptive behaviors, the speech training should be carried out in a room containing as few distractions as possible. In our training room, we usually have only chairs for the child and teacher, a desk or table between them, and a small table or chair next to the teacher on which to place the food tray. Such an arrangement is shown in Fig. 1.

In a room where the child may reach for, throw, or destroy many items, turn on and off light switches and climb on furniture, the therapist may inadvertently train the child to engage in these behaviors, since they must be attended to by the therapist. For some children with high rates of tantrums and disruptive behavior, the rooms have been entirely cleared except for the chairs and tables which have been secured to the floor.

The Reinforcer

Certain consequences of a behavior will increase the frequency of that behavior. Those consequences, which are technically termed reinforcers, are usually events which are commonly described as important, significant, or meaningful for the particular child. With normal children, attention and praise can be used as consequences to strengthen behavior (Harris *et al.*, 1964). Such sophisticated social consequences often are only weak positive reinforcers for a severely abnormal child. For this reason food must often be relied upon as a reinforcing consequence for modifying speech and other behaviors of deviant children.

The ideal food reinforcer is one which the child particularly "likes", many bites of which can be eaten, and which cannot be readily "played with". We have found that the food reinforcer which best satisfies these criteria is ice cream or sherbet. It is generally a favorite food of children, it can be eaten in quantity, and it disappears rapidly from the mouth. Many other foods have been used, such as sugar coated cereals (Captain Crunch, Fruit Loops), TV dinners, peanut butter sandwiches, and regular meals. Bites of food are given to a child on a spoon or fork. Each bite is small, which allows large numbers of responses to be reinforced before the child becomes satiated.

A small portion of the food (e.g. ¼ teaspoon of ice cream) is placed on the spoon, (Fig. 1A). The spoon is held directly in front of the therapist's face. As a child will tend to look at the food, this procedure ensures that he will be looking toward the therapist's face. The therapist then waits until the child's glance shifts from the spoon to his face and reinforces this by quickly presenting the stimulus for the child to imitate (Fig. 1B). As the sessions progress, a child will tend to look at the food less and at the therapist's face more, and the position of the spoon can then gradually be varied to suit the convenience of the therapist. The same procedure is used later in the program to train a child to attend to pictures or objects, except that, in that case, the spoon is held behind the items.

When the child responds appropriately, the therapist *immediately* says "Good" or "That's right," while extending the spoon of food to the child. This verbal statement serves to bridge the time between the appropriate response and the presentation of the food, and makes the reinforcement contingencies more precise. To save time, the food on the spoon is placed directly in the child's mouth by the therapist (Fig. 1C).

The effectiveness of the food reinforcer can be increased by mild food deprivation of about half a day. For example, when training sessions are held around noon, the mother or institutional staff are told to provide the child with only a very light breakfast, such as a glass of juice and a vitamin pill. Similar instructions involving lunch are given to caretakers of children for sessions later in the day.

For the most rapid and significant changes in deviant children the necessity of using powerful extrinsic reinforcers, made more effective by sufficient deprivation, *cannot be overemphasized.* (Examples showing the importance of the food reinforcers in the treatment of two children will be presented later.)

The Elimination of Disruptive Behavior

Most deviant children exhibit behavior which is incompatible with the behavior involved in speech training. With echolalic children the most usual disruptive behavior is repetitive chanting of songs or TV commercials, inappropriate imitation of the experimenters, comments, and, frequently, temper tantrums whenever the reinforcer is withheld. The frequency of this behavior must be reduced before notable progress can be made in establishing functional speech. Systematic extinction procedures, in conjunction with reinforcement of appropriate responses incompatible with the disruptive behaviors, have usually been sufficient to eliminate these behaviors.

Mild disruptive behavior in the therapy situation (such as leaving the chair, autistic mannerisms, mild temper tantrums, repetitive chanting, or

FIGURE (1a)

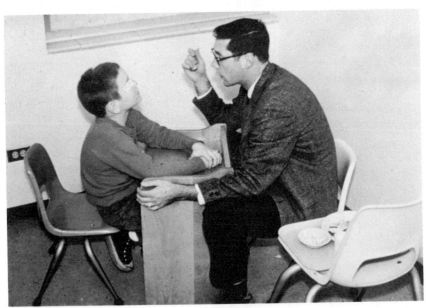

FIGURE (1b)

FIGURES 1 a–c These three pictures illustrate the physical arrangement of the therapy room, and the method of presenting the food reinforcers.

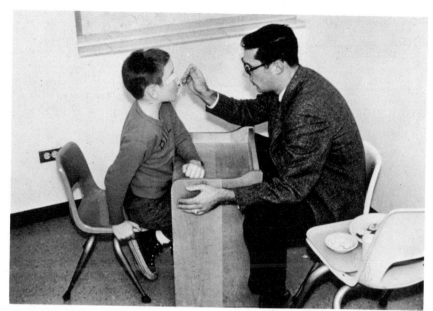

FIGURE (1c)

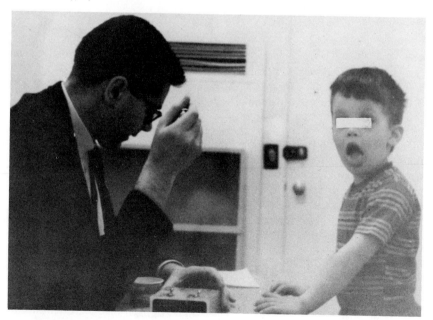

FIGURE 2 An illustration of a therapist extinguishing disruptive behavior by looking away from a child contingent upon disruptive behavior.

inappropriate imitation) can usually be eliminated by removing all possible positive reinforcers for these behaviors. Once the child spends at least some of the session sitting quietly in the chair and has come into contact with the reinforcers, the experimenter should simply look away from the child whenever mild disruptive behavior occurs (Fig. 2). When the child is again sitting silently in his chair, the experimenter reinforces this by attending to him and proceeding with the session. (This procedure is technically termed *time-out from positive reinforcement*.)

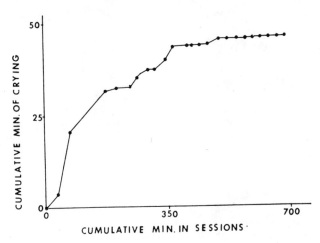

FIGURE 3   The elimination of temper tantrums (crying) of Carey. (Each dot represents the end of a session.)

The temper tantrums of a child (Carey) were eliminated as a consequence of these procedures (Fig. 3). The duration of crying systematically declined from an average of 16 min/hr in the first three sessions to an average of 20 sec/hr in the twenty-fourth to twenty-sixth sessions of these conditions.

The procedures were also effective in reducing the frequency with which a child (Carey) inappropriately imitated and repeatedly chanted the verbal statement "Very good", which accompanied the food reinforcer (Fig. 4). During the four sessions in which this behavior was recorded, the rate declined from 3.4 to 0.12/min. By the eighth session this behavior was almost totally absent.

Where disruptive behaviors are at high strength or experimental conditions are such that these behaviors are inadvertently reinforced, a more rigorous time-out procedure may be necessary. This procedure involves both extinction of the undesirable behavior and the removal, for a period

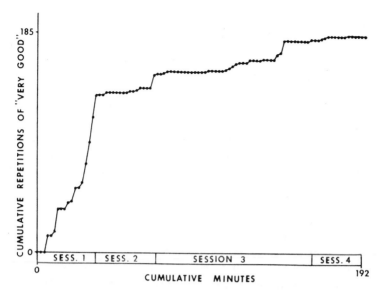

FIGURE 4 The elimination of Carey's inappropriate repeating the statement "very good", which accompanied the food reinforcer. Whenever the child would say "very good" the therapist would look away for approximately 5 sec. Each dot corresponds to the 2 min of session time.

of time, of the possibility of *any* behavior being reinforced. Whenever an instance of disruptive behavior occurs, either the therapist leaves the room (with the food tray), or the child is removed to an adjacent room. The therapist re-enters or the child is allowed back in the therapy room only after both (1) a set time period had elapsed (e.g. 10 min) and (2) the child had not engaged in the disruptive behavior for a short period of time (e.g. 30 sec).

Dick's severe temper tantrums accompanied by self-destructive behavior were eliminated by this procedure (Fig. 5). The severity of the

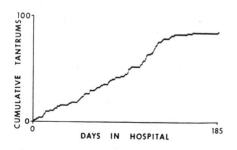

FIGURE 5 The elimination of Dick's temper tantrums. The child was isolated in his room for 10 min contingent upon each tantrum, after which time he was allowed to leave the room following 30 sec of silence. Each dot represents one day.

tantrums, which necessitated their rapid elimination, also made the tantrums difficult for observers to ignore. It appeared highly likely that the attendants who were working with the child, while attempting to simply ignore (extinguish) the tantrums, would feel compelled to "stop the child from hurting himself" whenever the self-destructive behavior became severe. If this had occurred, they would have been, in effect, differentially reinforcing the more extreme forms of self-destructive behavior thereby increasing the problem.

To avoid this, the child was isolated in a room whenever temper tantrums occurred. This *time-out* procedure resulted in a gradual decline in the severity of the tantrums (which is not reflected in Fig. 5, as only the frequency of tantrums was recorded) and finally a complete cessation of tantrums.

The effectiveness of either of these procedures is dependent upon the strength of the positive reinforcer which is being withheld. This is another important reason for using the strongest reinforcers possible. When only weak positive reinforcers (such as M&M's with a non-food-deprived child) are used, not only will the progress in speech be slow, but disruptive behavior will be persistent.

The Establishment of Control over Imitation

Although echolalic children do imitate words and phrases, usually this imitation is sporadic and cannot be consistently evoked. Imitation must reliably occur immediately after a word or phrase prompt is presented before significant advances in speech can be made.

Reliable and immediate imitation can be obtained by systematic reinforcement of imitation. The therapist presents a given word every 4–5 sec. Whenever the child says this word he is reinforced. Initially the probability of imitation can be somewhat increased by varying the intonation, pitch level and loudness of the word presented; however, this procedure should be deleted as soon as the child is reliably repeating the word.

Systematically reinforcing an imitated word will increase the frequency with which the child imitates that word, but it may also increase the frequency of non-imitative repetitions of the word. Other verbal utterances such as phrases or snatches of song may also increase and should be extinguished. The therapist should wait until the child is silent before again presenting the word to be imitated. In this manner only *imitation* is being reinforced.

When the child is frequently imitating the word (5–6 times/min), extraneous behavior should be extinguished and attending to the therapist reinforced by presenting the word to be imitated only when the child is sitting quietly, looking at the therapist. As the probability of immediate imitation is greater when the child is looking at the therapist, this procedure, which increases the proportion of attending, increases the number of immediate imitations.

When the child is reliably and immediately imitating the first word, a new word is introduced, and the above procedure is repeated. The two words are then alternately presented. When the child is reliably imitating both words, new words are presented interspersed with the two original words. Usually by the second or third word, a general imitative response class will have been established, i.e. the child will then reliably and immediately imitate any new word.

Figure 6 shows the establishment of control over a child's (Carey) imitation. From the start of session 2 the word "train" was repeated by the experimenter. The child imitated this word once early in the session, and was reinforced. Sixteen minutes later, during which time he was intermittently having tantrums, he again imitated "train" and was reinforced. After this the rate of imitating the word rapidly increased. Three other words, "flower," "car" and "airplane," were then introduced, and the child imitated each of them on the *first* presentation as well as on each subsequent presentation. Thus, in approximately 30 min, control was established over the child's imitative speech.

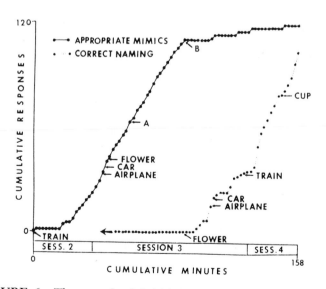

FIGURE 6 The record of initial rate of appropriate imitations (mimics) and correct naming of objects by Carey (see text). Each dot represents 2 min of session time.

The Transition from Imitation to Naming

Naming involves the emission of the appropriate verbal response in the presence of some stimulus object. After imitative responses occur. with high probability and short latency following each verbal prompt, stimulus control is shifted from the verbal prompts (imitation) to appropriate objects and pictures (naming).

Once reinforcement for imitation has produced a high probability of successful imitation of the verbal prompt alone, a picture or object is presented together with the verbal prompt, and the child is reinforced for imitating the name. Then the imitative prompt is faded out, while the child continues to receive reinforcement for saying the object's name.

The therapist holds up an object (if necessary holding the spoonful of food behind it) and says, "What is this?" When the child looks at it, the therapist immediately prompts with the object's name. The child is reinforced for imitating the prompt. When the child is reliably looking at the object without the food being held behind it, the time between the question "What is this?" and the prompt is gradually lengthened to more than 5 sec. If after several trials the child continues to wait for the presentation of the verbal prompt, a *partial prompt* is given, for example, "Trr" for train. If the correct response does not occur within about 5 sec more, the complete prompt is then presented. A correct response is followed by a social consequence such as "right" or "good", and the partial prompt is immediately repeated. A correct response to the partial prompt results in a bite of food.

When the child begins saying the name when only the partial prompt is presented, the therapist continues the above procedure but begins to say the partial prompt more softly. The loudness of the partial prompt is varied according to the child's behavior. When the child fails to respond to a partial prompt and the complete prompt is presented, the next partial prompt is given more loudly. When the child correctly responds to the partial prompt, the next partial prompt is given more softly. This continues until the therapist only "mouths" the partial prompt and then, finally, discontinues it altogether as the child responds to the object and the question "What is this?" with the name of the object.

Throughout this procedure, whenever the child inappropriately imitates the question "What is this?", a time-out is programmed, i.e. the object is withdrawn and the therapist looks down at the table. After 2 or 3 sec of silence by the child, the therapist looks up and continues the procedure.

The transition from imitation to naming with one child (Carey) is illustrated in Fig. 6. From point A in Fig. 6, the pictures of the four objects were held out one at a time, and the child was required to look at them before the therapist said the name. The child quickly began attending to the pictures. The therapist's presentation of the words had been discriminative for the child to imitate and be reinforced. The increased proportion of attending indicated that the word presentations themselves had become reinforcers.

Just before B in Fig. 6, the therapist began delaying naming the picture, requiring a longer period of attending by the child, so that he would be more likely to name the picture instead of imitating the therapist. At B the child began to tantrum during an especially long delay. The therapist merely sat quietly looking down at the table. The tantrum gradually subsided and the therapist again held up the picture (the flower). The child attended to the picture and promptly named it. After this he named the picture with increasing speed with each presentation.

The picture of the airplane was re-introduced. The child immediately said "Car." The therapist said, "No, airplane." The child mimicked this and correctly named the picture when it was immediately re-presented. The remaining two pictures were then re-introduced, and the child correctly named each after a single prompt. After this he correctly named the four pictures when each was presented. Next, a new object, a cup, was presented. After imitating only two prompts, the child correctly named it and continued to name it correctly when it was presented interspersed with the original four pictures. Thus, by the end of the third session a small naming vocabulary had been established.

The following two examples demonstrate the role of food reinforcers in the maintenance of appropriate naming behavior. During the first five training sessions with Will, reliable imitation and then appropriate naming had been developed. The reinforcer involved a variety of edibles, such as ice cream, Coke, and M&M's.

The contribution of the food reinforcer was investigated by reversing the relationship between the naming behavior and the reinforcer. About a third of the way through the sixth session, the procedure was changed so that the child was reinforced only when he *did not* correctly name a picture for 10 sec. This procedure is technically termed *differential reinforcement of other behavior* (DRO) because any behavior except one particular response, in this case naming, is reinforced. As can be seen in Fig. 7, the naming responses dropped from about 8/min to zero. After 45 min, when no naming responses were being made, the procedure was changed back so that naming responses were again the only responses being reinforced. The rate of naming quickly increased to approximately the same rate as during the first part of the session. These results show the power of the reinforcer over the occurrence and accuracy of Will's naming behavior.

Once a reliable rate of naming had been developed with Carey the procedure was changed in that ice cream was given on a non-contingent basis. Instead of giving him bites of ice cream after each correct response,

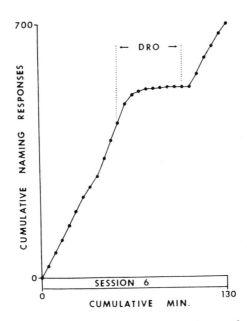

FIGURE 7   A cumulative record showing the results of changing the food reinforcement contingency on Will's rate of correct naming. During the sixth session a DRO contingency (see text) was introduced for 9 min and Will's rate of naming decreased to zero. When the original food reinforcement contingency was reinstated the behavior increased to its pre-DRO rate.

he was given the spoon and the bowl of ice cream and allowed to eat at his own rate. Pictures continued to be presented. He was still asked to name them, and when he named them correctly he was praised. The rate of correct naming dropped immediately from approximately 8 to 3/min and then stabilized at about 2/min (Fig. 8). When the ice cream was again presented only after correct naming responses, the rate immediately increased to approximately 10 responses/min.

To summarize, Carey's results show that after naming responses have been acquired, it may be possible to maintain them (although at a lower rate) with a weak reinforcer such as praise alone, but, as shown in the case of both the children the more powerful food reinforcer maintained a much higher and more steady rate of appropriate behavior.

The Expansion of the Naming Vocabulary

After the child has been taught to name several pictures or objects, naming any new picture or object can be quickly established. However, the child often will not correctly name an item at the beginning of the next daily

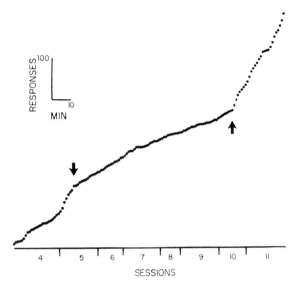

FIGURE 8 A cumulative record showing the effects of Carey receiving bites of ice cream independent of his picture naming responses. For the first session and a half in Fig. 8 Carey was fed a bite of ice cream after each correct response. At the first arrow Carey was allowed to feed himself ice cream independent of his naming responses. At the second arrow the food reinforcers were again made contingent upon correctly naming the pictures. Each dot represents a 1-min period.

session or subsequent to learning other new items in the same session. A new response cannot be considered to be added to a child's naming vocabulary until he can name an item when it is presented again after other items have been learned, and following a passage of time. This is accomplished by gradually changing the context in which the item is presented. After a child is consistently naming new items on repeated presentations, a previously learned item is presented. When the child names the old item he is reinforced and the new item is presented again. When the child is reliably naming a new item when it follows one presentation of any of several previously taught items, two, then three, then four old items are presented between each presentation of the new item. (The well-established naming of old items need be reinforced only intermittently with food to maintain accuracy and short latencies.) When the child is reliably naming a new item under these conditions, another new item is introduced. When an item is reliably named the first time it is presented in several subsequent sessions, it can be considered to be a member of the child's naming vocabulary; only occasional reviews in subsequent sessions are needed to maintain it.

Figure 9 shows the increasing naming vocabulary of Pat, a blind echolalic boy, who was taught to name common household objects which were placed in his hands. An item was considered to be "learned" when the child correctly named it on its first presentation in three successive sessions.

Carey's naming vocabulary was expanded under two reinforcement conditions. The items to be named were pictures (line drawings) of various objects. Two 10-min sessions a day were held, with separate pictures for each session. In one of the sessions each day, the reinforcer was praise ("That's right, very good") and a bite of ice cream, whereas praise alone was used in the other session. Several pictures were repeatedly presented in a random order during each session. New pictures were added when the child was consistently naming all the pictures used during a session. A picture was considered to be learned when the child correctly named it the first time it was presented, three sessions in a row. It would then be retired until ten subsequent pictures had been learned, at which time it would be presented again to test for recall.

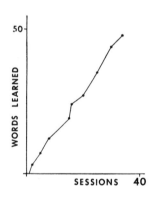

FIGURE 9 A cumulative record of Pat's learning to name objects correctly. The name of an object was recorded as "learned" when Pat named it correctly the first time it was presented in three successive sessions.

While the child learned to name 50 per cent more pictures when both praise and ice cream were used as reinforcers (——, Fig. 10), his naming vocabulary was significantly expanded when praise was the only reinforcer (----, Fig. 10). Furthermore, items were recalled equally well whether they had been reinforced with praise only or with both praise and ice cream (histogram, Fig. 10). However, following this evaluation, since only one session per day could be held, the more effective reinforcer, a combination of ice cream and praise, was used throughout the remaining sessions. Approximately one new word per session was established with this reinforcer (. . . ., Fig. 10).

Just as Fig. 8 demonstrates that established naming can be maintained (although at a lower rate) with praise as the only reinforcer, Fig. 10 shows that when a child can readily be taught to name new items with food reinforcers his naming vocabulary can then be significantly expanded (al-

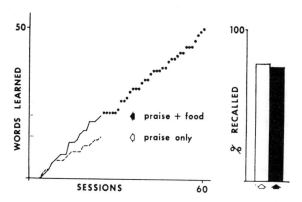

FIGURE 10 Records of the number of pictures which Carey learned to name and later recalled in daily sessions under two reinforcement conditions, praise alone ("that's right" or "very good") and both praise and food (bites of ice cream). A picture was considered to be learned when the child named it when it was first presented in three successive sessions. A picture was considered to be recalled when the child correctly named it when it was re-presented after ten subsequent pictures had been learned.

though at a lower rate) when only social reinforcers of the type available in a "normal" environment are used.

The authors consider it necessary to use strong reinforcers such as food to establish the initial instances of appropriate mimicking and naming behavior and to eliminate disruptive behavior in a reasonable period of time. However, it appears that once disruptive behaviors have been eliminated and some appropriate mimicking and naming have been established, these appropriate behaviors can be maintained and expanded by the systematic use of social reinforcers. This does *not* imply that food deprivation and food reinforcers should then be discontinued. The magnitude of a child's speech deficits and the value of a therapist's and of a child's time require the utilization of those procedures which will produce the greatest gains in the shortest time. The strongest reinforcers or combination of reinforcers available should be used in the therapy sessions so long as large behavioral deficits exist. However, social reinforcers outside the therapy sessions can generally be relied upon to maintain and expand the behaviors established in the sessions.

The Establishment of Phrases

Once naming is established, the response units can be expanded to phrases and sentences. In most cases this expansion occurs without explicit training. In those instances where multiple word units have to be taught, the procedure is the same as in teaching individual words, i.e. mimics of the phrases are reinforced until the phrases are consistently imitated. Then the control is shifted to the appropriate circumstances itself, by introducing partial prompts which are gradually faded out. In this case, the partial prompts are the first word or words of the phrase.

At first, phrases such as "That's a————," or "I want————" are taught, using the child's newly acquired naming vocabulary. Then more varied phrases are taught, such as answering the appropriate questions with "My name is————," "I live at————," "I am————years old," "My sisters' names are————and————."

Food reinforcers are used to build the initial responses, but, once established, the opportunity to obtain some natural consequence can usually maintain the behavior. For example, for Carey the comment, "Out (or in) the door," was maintained by opening the doors to and from the therapy room. The therapist would say, "Out the door," and when the child would mimic this, the door would be opened.

After several trials on succeeding days, the therapist began introducing a partial prompt, saying only, "Out," and the child continued to say, "Out the door." The partial prompt was then gradually faded out until the therapist put his hand on the door knob and looked at the child, and the child said, "Out the door." The therapist gradually faded in the appropriate controlling stimulus—the question, "Where are you going?" This was presented by at first mumbling it softly as they approached the door and then increasing the volume on succeeding trials. Whenever the child inappropriately imitated the question "Where are you going?" the therapist repeated the question at a lower volume and followed it with a loud partial prompt: "Where are you going? OUT." On succeeding trials the partial prompt, "Out," was then decreased in volume until the child responded to the closed door and the question, "Where are you going?" with the response "Out the door."

The same procedure was used to establish appropriate answers to the question, "Where are you going?", such as "Up the stairs," "Down the hall," or "In the car." In each case, the reinforcer which maintained appropriate answering was simply being allowed to proceed up the stairs, down the hall, and so on. In this manner the child came to make appropriate verbal comments about his environment. Once such simple comments have been learned, the child tends to generalize the grammatical form with appropriate substitutions. One example of such establishment and generalization, which could be termed "generative speech," resulted from a procedure used with Carey. On many occasions at home, this child would chant a word or short phrase over and over, with gradually increasing volume which terminated in piercing shrieks and crying. For example, while standing by the couch, he would repeat "Sit down, sit down." His parents could terminate this by responding in any way, e.g. "Yes, Carey," "O.K., sit down," "You can sit down if you want to," "Be quiet." The parents were requested to record these instances of stereotyped chanting, and also to send him to his room for 5 min whenever the chanting developed into shrieking and crying. This decreased the occurrences of the shrieking (———— Fig. 11), but did not decrease the frequency of the stereotyped chanting episodes (. . . . Fig. 11). The therapist decided to change the form of this behavior, rather than attempt to eliminate it, as it contained elements of appropriate social behavior.

The parents were instructed to turn away from the child when he chanted. One parent (e.g. the father) would then call out the name of the other parent ("Mommy"), and when the child would mimic this the mother would attend to him and "Yes, Carey." The first parent would then say a complete sentence ("I want to sit down, please."). When the child would mimic this, the other parent would respond accordingly ("Oh, you want to sit down. Well, you can sit down right here."). On subsequent occasions the verbal prompts were faded out. Finally, the parents withheld reinforcement by looking away until the child called their names, and they would wait while looking at him until he gave the complete sentence before responding to his request. This procedure was begun at the arrow in Fig. 11. The stereotyped chanting soon decreased to zero as the child began to indicate more appropriate requests such as "Mommy, I want to sit down, please", or "Daddy, I want a drink of water, please."

The grammatical structure of "(name), I want ————, please," after being established with several people's names and many different requests in the home began to generalize to new people and new requests. One recorded instance of this occurred in the therapy sessions. Prior to the start of each session, when Carey was seated in the room, the therapist would spend some time setting up the tape recorder. During this time the child would usually start chanting "Ice cream, ice cream" softly. When the therapist was ready, he would turn to the child and say, "What do you want?" to which the child had been taught to answer "I want some ice cream." Prior to one session, after the grammatical form of requests mentioned above had been established at home, the child was, as usual, chanting "Ice cream, ice cream" while the therapist threaded the tape recorder. He suddenly stopped and after a pause, said "Mr. (therapist's name), I want some ice cream, please." Most of the elements of this sentence had been established in the therapy sessions, e.g. "Hello, Mr. (therapist's name)," and "I want some ice cream," but they had always been given as responses to specific stimuli, (e.g. "Hello, Carey" and "What do you want?") However, the particular grammatical structure of "(Name), I want ————, please," had only been taught in the home.

Carey's extension of his home training exemplifies our general obser-

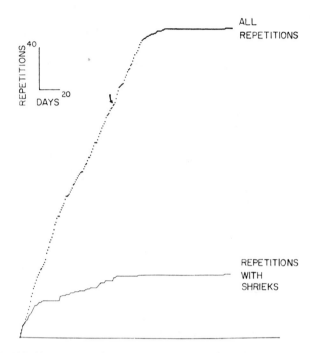

FIGURE 11   A cumulative record of episodes of repetitious chant-ing by Carey at home. From the onset, he was sent to his room for 5 min whenever he began shrieking during one of those episodes. At the arrow his parents began establishing appropriate speech behavior which was incompatible with chanting. Each dot represents one day.

vation that once rudimentary generative speech and grammatical structure have been established they will tend to generalize broadly, often with ap-propriate substitutions.

OTHER CONSIDERATIONS

The Generalization of Appropriate Speech

The term "generalization" can refer to the *phenomenon* of the occurrence of appropriate behavior under other than the original training conditions or it can refer to the *procedure* used to establish this occurrence.

While newly acquired appropriate speech often will "spontaneously" generalize widely, the therapist need not passively rely on this phenomenon. He can, instead, set out to extend the occurrence of the behavior to other situations by systematically reinforcing appropriate speech under a variety of conditions. The child can be systematically trained to respond appropriately to a variety of individuals, including members of his family and other caretakers, and in a variety of situations, such as at home, in the family car, and in the therapist's office. Once appropriate speech has been established in the therapy sessions, the child's parents can be present during occasional sessions and the child reinforced for responding appropriately to their questions. Whenever a new word has been established in a therapy session, the therapist can continue to ask for, and reinforce the appropriate use of this word after the formal session, for instance, while walking around the building. The therapist can also conduct therapy sessions in the child's home, teaching the child to name household objects.

Generalization training can be facilitated by initially selecting words and phrases to be taught which can be appropriately asked for frequently during the day, e.g. "car" is better than "zebra," and which are immediately functional in the child's environment, e.g. "I want a cookie."

Perhaps the most effective means of generalizing the appropriate use of speech is to train the parents or caretakers to use the therapeutic procedures. They can then take advantage of naturally-occurring events during the day to generalize appropriate speech to a wide variety of situations, as well as to establish new speech in appropriate contexts.

The Usefulness of Data in Therapy

The gathering of continuous data throughout the course of therapy can be valuable in many ways. For example, it can provide objective information about the long term course of therapy. Behaviors followed over a long period of time, as described in this paper, often reveal an orderliness which is not clear from the day-by-day observations. Gradual changes can be discerned in spite of large daily fluctuations, as in the instance of the rate of Carey's shrieking (Fig. 11). The frequency of the shrieks decreased in a manner which was orderly overall even though some of the individual days (sometimes several consecutive days) showed considerable variability.

A second use of data is in the analysis of the functions of therapeutic procedures. An *experimental probe* is usually necessary if the therapist wants to isolate the variables responsible for a behavioral change. Isolation is accomplished by keeping all of the therapeutic conditions the same except one. If varying this condition produces a reliable change in the data, which disappears when the condition is reversed to its pre-experimental value, then the importance of the variable has been established. Sidman (1960) has discussed in detail strategies and considerations for research with individual subjects. Probe experiments of the above type were described in this paper. For example, the role of the food reinforcement contingency in Will's progress in naming was evaluated (Fig. 7). Its importance was dramatically demonstrated when the DRO procedure was interjected into a session. A similar probe experiment, in a slightly different manner and over a longer period of time, demonstrated the function of the food reinforcement in Carey's rate of naming pictures (Fig. 8).

The easiest of data-gathering methods is to use a tape recorder to record all of the sessions. The therapist or an assistant can replay tapes from previous sessions and count the frequencies of various responses (e.g. correct imitations) or the durations of certain behaviors (e.g. temper tantrums, inappropriate chanting). Tapes of earlier sessions are particularly useful for gathering data about behavior that was not originally thought to be of interest.

A multi-pen event recorder can be used if the therapist is certain in advance of the classes of behavior that he will want to record. A bank of push-button switches can be wired from the therapist's table to the recorder so that durations and frequencies of responses can be recorded by the therapist and/or by an independent observer.

A pencil and paper can always be used to take simple frequencies. Duration of a specific behavior can be recorded during each session with a stop watch.

Such data and probe experiments enable the therapist to give a more complete and objective description of his procedures and their effects to others, including colleagues who are also interested in developing a more effective technology of speech modification through a systematic analysis of speech modification procedures.

CONCLUSIONS

This paper indicates that functional verbal behavior can be developed from rudimentary imitative behavior by established behavioral techniques. We have outlined procedures which were effective in establishing functional speech in echolalic children. However, the procedures as they are described here should not be taken as fixed and unchanging. The developing strength of behavioral technology lies in the continued refinement of its procedures.

Acknowledgements. The teachers who played particularly important roles in Dicky's speech development were Florence Harris, Margaret Johnston, Eileen Allen, Nancy Reynolds and Thelma Turbitt. Will's data was collected by Jacquelyn Raulerson and Thomas Dillon under the senior author's supervision. We are indebted to Stephanie Stolz, Nancy Reynolds and Betty Hart for critical readings of the manuscript.

REFERENCES

HARRIS, F. R., WOLF, M. M. and BAER, D. M. (1964) Effects of adult social reinforcement on child behavior. *Young Child.* **20**, 8–17.

LOVAAS, O. I. (1966) A program for the establishment of speech in psychotic children. In (Ed. WING J. K.) *Childhood Autism.* Pergamon Press, Oxford.

RISLEY, T. R. (1966) The establishment of verbal behavior in deviant children. Unpublished dissertation, University of Washington.

SIDMAN, M. (1960) *Tactics of Scientific Research.* Basic Books, New York.

SKINNER, B. F. (1957) *Verbal Behavior.* Appleton-Century-Crofts, New York.

STONE, J. L. and CHURCH, J. (1957) *Childhood and Adolescence.* Random House, New York.

WOLF, M. M., RISLEY, T. R. and MEES, H. I. (1964) Application of operant conditioning procedures to the behavior problems of an autistic child. *Behav. Res. & Therapy* **1**, 305–312.

BETTY M. HART
TODD R. RISLEY
University of Kansas

Establishing use of descriptive adjectives in the spontaneous speech of disadvantaged preschool children[1]

From observer records, a count was made for each child, in a group of disadvantaged children in an experimental preschool, of usage and acquisition of descriptive adjectives, with and without noun referents. Procedures were sought which would effectively modify the low rates of adjective-noun combinations in the everyday language of all the children. Time in school, intermittent teacher praise, and social and intellectual stimulation were not effective in changing the low rates of using adjectives of size and shape. Group teaching effectively increased rates of using color- and number-noun combinations in the group-teaching situation, but was ineffective in changing rates of usage in the children's "spontaneous" vocabularies. By operating directly on the children's language

Reprinted from *Journal of Applied Behavior Analysis*, 1968, 1, 109–20, with permission of the publisher and the authors. Copyright 1968 by the Society for the Experimental Analysis of Behavior, Inc.

[1] This study is based upon a thesis submitted by the senior author to the Department of Human Development in partial fulfillment of the requirements for the Master of Arts degree. The authors express appreciation to Nancy Reynolds, Dianetta Coates, and Maxine Preuitt for their able assistance in all aspects of the study. This research was supported by Grants (HD 03144) from the National Institute of Child Health and Human Development and (CG-8474) from the Office of Economic Opportunity, Headstart Research and Demonstration to the Bureau of Child Research and the Department of Human Development at the University of Kansas.

174

in the free-play situation, making access to preschool materials contingent upon use of a color-noun combination, significant increases in such usage were effected in the spontaneous vocabularies of all the children. Preschool materials apparently functioned as powerful reinforcers. Though traditional teaching procedures were effective in generating adjective-noun combinations in that restricted situation, it was only through application of environmental contingencies that color names as descriptive adjectives were effectively and durably established in all the children's spontaneous vocabularies.

Reflected in the national concern for the scholastic retardation of culturally deprived children is the contemporary conviction that the sources of academic failure are primarily environmental rather than genetic (Bijou, 1963). That the environment of the culturally deprived child can, and should, be changed, is not an issue; rather the questions are ones of defining and producing those environmental changes which will generate academic success. The present consensus is that the behavior most correlated with public school success is verbal behavior, skill in language (Weikart, 1966). As opposed to the linguistically skillful and academically successful middle-class child, the culturally deprived child is characterized as having a language environment which is both "restricted" in terms of range and detail of concept (Hess and Shipman, 1965), and rich in forms of expressive speech which are not used in middle-class-oriented school books and systems (Riessman, 1962). Thus, programs for the development of language skills, the core of all preschool programs for culturally deprived children, seek to give the children educationally appropriate forms of speech, and to enrich their descriptive vocabularies. In such programs the children are directly taught, for instance, the appropriate use of adjectives of color, number, size, shape, etc., and the preschool environment is arranged so that they will use them in conversation and narration. That is, "knowing" —the ability to respond correctly when asked—is not considered sufficient; the criterion for "skill" is usage, spontaneous emission as functional language in everyday situations.

There is general agreement concerning what should be taught to culturally deprived children but considerably less agreement about how to teach it most effectively. Many methodologies have been employed, with varying degrees of success (Weikart, 1966). The urgency of the problem, and the need for practical solutions has led, however, for the first time in the long history of preschool education, to empirical evaluation of the effectiveness of traditional teaching procedures. Such evaluation has frequently resulted in pervasive restructuring of the preschool environment in order to achieve the behavioral goals set for the culturally deprived child (Bereiter and Engelmann, 1966). Most important, it has resulted in introducing into the time-honored preschool program those procedures which experimental research has demonstrated to be effective in teaching children.

Research has repeatedly demonstrated that a child's behavior can be modified by its consequences. Such demonstrations have been made in a multiplicity of settings; in the laboratory (Lindsley, 1966), in institutions (Wolf, Risley, and Mees, 1964; Lovaas, Freitag, Kinder, Rubenstein, Schaeffer, and Simmons, 1966), in preschools (Harris, Wolf, and Baer, 1964; Brown and Elliot, 1965), in the classroom (Zimmerman and Zimmerman, 1962), in the clinic (Wahler, Winkel, Peterson, and Morrison, 1965), and in the home (Allen and Harris, 1966). The behaviors so modified have included verbal (Risley and Wolf, 1967), motor (Johnston, Kelley, Harris, and Wolf, 1966), social (Allen, Hart, Buell, Harris, and Wolf, 1964), and academic behaviors (Wolf, Giles, and Hall, 1968; Birnbrauer, Wolf, Kidder, and Tague, 1965). The general principles of reinforcement, which were the basis of all of the above-mentioned studies, were also the basis of the present study. That is, the present investigation involved: defining an observable terminal behavior, the use of descriptive adjectives during free play; devising a method of recording and measuring important categories of spontaneous verbal behavior; and manipulating the consequences of the children's use of language, the presentation of social reinforcement and access to materials contingent on a specified form of verbal behavior. The effectiveness of these procedures is evaluated in terms of the behavioral goals defined, and compared to the effectiveness of traditional preschool procedures in the attainment of these goals. The implications of the study thus relate not only to the problem of cultural deprivation, but to preschool practice in general.

METHOD

Setting and Subjects

The study was conducted at the Turner House preschool of the Juniper Gardens Children's Project in Kansas City, Kansas, and involved 15 children, all Negroes, from a lower class community, selected from large families with extremely low incomes. There were eight boys and seven girls in the group, all aged from 4 to 5 yr. The average IQ, as measured by the Peabody Picture Vocabulary Test, was 79.

The preschool sessions were 3 hr long, from 8:30 to 11:30 A.M., five days per week. The daily program was: breakfast, then free play indoors, then group time, then free play outdoors, followed by story time at the end of the morning. During indoor and outdoor free play the children could interact with materials and with other children in one or more of the unstructured activities normally provided in the preschool program, *e.g.*, blocks, painting, sand play, *etc.* Most, but not all, materials were available to the children during free play; items such as water and paint were dispensed by teachers.

Breakfast, story time, and group time were teacher-structured situations. At group time, eight or fewer children sat on a rug with a teacher who formally presented stimuli for identification and description. Children were called on individually by the teacher, and were presented with a food snack and teacher praise for correct responses. The classes of responses reinforced at group time were first, identification of pictures and objects, then description of objects in terms of color, and finally description of objects in terms of number. Stimuli for a given class of responses, such as identification, were presented daily at varying levels of difficulty for several months, until all children in the group had attained a certain criterion of response accuracy.

Procedures

Recording. At group time throughout the year an observer recorded on a check sheet whether each response of each child in the group was designated by teacher feedback to the child as "right" or "wrong".

During four periods within the school year, daily samples were taken of children's verbalizations during free play. A sample was recorded by one of four observers, who moved with the child being observed from one activity to another, and for 15 min wrote down in longhand "everything" the child said. Two observers recorded throughout the school year; the third was replaced by the fourth observer for two months in mid-year (February and March).

Each child in the group was assigned for observation approximately every other day during the periods of sampling; roughly two observations were made indoors for every one made outdoors because of the sequence of the preschool program. Observation was discontinued whenever free play ended; therefore samples were occasionally of less than 15 min when, for example, outdoor play was curtailed by rain, or a child was removed from the group for a test. Usually a given child was assigned for observation to each of the observers in turn. This was done to minimize the development of any observer bias concerning a given child, and to distribute the writing load of high-rate verbalizers *versus* low-rate.

The sampling periods were:

(1) 7 days (August 31–September 9; days 3 through 9 of school).
(2) 18 days (October 3–October 26; days 25 through 42 of school).

(3) 10 days (December 12–December 23; days 71 through 80 of school).

(4) 99 days (January 17–June 9; days 91 through 189 of school).

From the samples were extracted for each child lists of vocabulary entries in the classes of nouns, verbs, and adjectives. Only certain categories of adjectives were counted: size, color, number, and shape, *i.e.*, the descriptive categories usually directly taught in preschool programs. Within each of the categories of descriptive adjectives (color, number, size, and shape) separate counts were made for:

(1) All adjectives of that category. Every use of an adjective in each of the four categories was counted regardless of the context in which it appeared, *i.e.*, whether or not it was followed by a noun, or was used with a verb. The categories of descriptive adjectives thus counted were defined as:

   All color adjectives: *e.g.*, "red", "red one", "red paint".

   All number adjectives: *e.g.*, "one", "two blocks", "three billion" (counted as a single number), "one-two-three" (counted as three numbers).

   All size adjectives: *e.g.*, "big", "little one", "He is big", "long time".

   All shape adjectives: *e.g.*, "round", "square one", "round circle".

(2) All adjective-noun combinations of that category. Every use of an adjective in each of the four categories was counted *only* if it was followed by a noun. The categories of descriptive adjectives so counted were defined as:

   All color-noun combinations, as "red paint".

   All number-noun combinations, as "two blocks".

   All size-noun combinations, as "long time".

   All shape-noun combinations, as "round circle".

(3) All new adjective-noun combinations of that category. Every use of an adjective in each of the four categories was counted for a given child only if it was followed by a noun and that combination of adjective and noun had never been recorded in any previous sample on that child. The categories of descriptive adjectives so counted were defined as:

   New color-noun combinations.

   New number-noun combinations.

   New size-noun combinations.

   New shape-noun combinations.

Thus, for example, if an observer recorded a child's having said, "I want red paint", and the adjective-noun combination *red paint* had never appeared in any prior sample on that child, it would be listed as a new color-noun combination (in addition to being counted as another use in all color adjectives and in all color-noun combinations).

Periodic reliability checks were taken among the three observers (the third and fourth observers were considered, over the year, as a single observer). Periodically, two or more observers were assigned to observe the same child at the same time, each observer recording independently all that child's verbalizations during a given 15-min period. In addition, a volunteer observer made once-weekly reliability checks, in the same manner, with one or more of the regular observers; this volunteer had almost no contact with either the teachers, the other observers, or any changes in preschool conditions. From the two or more records obtained, all instances of adjective usage in any of the four categories of color, number, size, and shape, were totaled. The record of Observer 1 was always taken as standard, whenever she and any other observer recorded on the same child. When Observers 2 and 3 took reliability checks together the record of that observer who had taken the majority of samples on the given child was taken as standard. Product-moment correlations of the reliability of the total adjective usage over samples was calculated for the regular observers in relation to one another, and for the volunteer observer in relation to the three regular observers.

Baseline. From the beginning of the school year, teachers attended to children when they heard them use descriptive adjectives during free play. The appropriate use of such adjectives was thus followed intermittently by teacher approval, and incorrect use was followed intermittently by teacher correction. If the adjective used was part of a request for a material, the child almost always obtained the object requested; no differential attention was given for use of adjective-noun combinations. The observer samples of the children's verbalizations during free play, however, revealed continuously low rates of use of all descriptive adjectives, whether of color, number, size, or shape. Teachers hypothesized that the limited use of these adjectives might be due to limited repertoires of appropriate labels. Therefore it was decided to systematically teach adjectival labels, starting with colors.

Baseline: color naming at group time. Beginning on day 103 of school, colors were presented every day at group time. The number of colors presented simultaneously was gradually increased from the initial three up to nine, but the manner of presentation remained essentially the same. In presenting each color, the teacher first named each object of that color (*i.e.,* "The car is red"), and placed it with others of the same color. Then she indicated, or had a child indicate, one object in a group and name it and its color (*i.e.,* "The car is red"). Every time a child correctly identified both an object and its color, the teacher praised him and passed him a snack. A complete sentence was always required; if a child named the correct color without naming the object, the teacher praised him and told him he was right, and then asked for the complete sentence before passing him a snack.

Thus, in the group-time situation, teachers prescribed the terminal form of the behavior which they hoped to see in the free-play situation, that is, color-noun combination. Only by requiring that the referent for an adjective be named can a teacher be (fairly) certain that a child has made an appropriate discrimination. Subsequently, a teacher can judge the extent to which a child is forming a concept of a given property (such as "redness") only on the basis of that child's verbal behavior of attributing that property ("red") to a variety of objects ("apple", "car", etc.). When a child merely names the property ("red") or names the property with an indefinite word such as "one" ("the red one"), the teacher must make an assumption concerning the referent, and thus guess both that the child is making a discrimination and that he is forming a concept.

At group time, while presenting colors in the general manner described above, the teacher employed various levels of prompts in order to ensure each child's giving a correct response each time he was called on to name an object and its color. The level of prompt was adjusted to each child's need for such prompts, and every time a new color was introduced, the teacher dropped back, for the whole group, to the more obvious levels of prompts. In the most obvious prompt, the teacher gave the child the correct response immediately before the question, *i.e.*, "The car is red. What color is the car?". In less obvious prompts, the teacher asked a child to name a color and then if he hesitated, mouthed the color word, or gave its initial sound; often, she asked a child to name the color of an object which another child had named correctly immediately before.

Throughout the period of naming colors at group time, any color naming during free play was attended to by teachers, whether the child specified a referent for the color named or not. The teacher praised the child who named a color and told him he was right if this were the case, or corrected him and then praised his repetition of the appropriate color name.

After two months (50 school days) of naming colors daily at group time, seven of the 15 children were reliably naming nine colors in that situation (red, yellow, blue, green, purple, orange, brown, white, and black). The other eight children were being presented only six colors at group time (red, yellow, blue, green, purple, and orange).

During this time, the children's rate of using color adjectives in the free-play situation showed no general change; however, teachers did note on two occasions late in this period sudden and marked increases in color naming by several children in the free-play situation. Both of these occasions involved a teacher dispensing vari-colored pegboard materials to children who, in order to obtain a specific item, had to ask for it by color. This procedure, of a teacher withholding materials until they were requested by a color-noun combination, appeared effective, at least on these occasions, in generating use of such combinations by children in the free situation.

Materials contingent on color naming. It was decided to apply this procedure throughout the preschool situation, and have teachers withhold materials until children asked for them by a color-noun combination. Therefore, beginning on day 153 of school, all of the children in the group could obtain a snack outdoors and certain materials and equipment indoors and out only if they named the desired object and described it by its color. Outdoor items such as trikes, wagons, balls, and shovels were not placed outside the storage shed as usual; rather, a child wanting to use them had to ask a teacher for them and employ an appropriate color-noun combination. A child desiring a snack from the basket held by the teacher had to ask, not for a snack or a cookie, but for a "brown" cookie (if the cookies were of that color), or a "yellow" banana. Indoors, items such as dress-up clothes in the doll house, pegboard materials, parquetry blocks, toy animals, and cars, *etc.*, all had to be named by a color-noun combination before a child was allowed to use them. These materials were not removed from the children's reach; rather, when a child approached one of these materials, a teacher put her hand on the material the child was reaching for. During the first three days of the procedure, the teacher prompted the desired behavior, asking the child, "What do you want?", and then, if the child named the object without naming its color, the teacher asked, "What color of a . . . . . .?", and supplied the color name if the child either did not respond or responded incorrectly. After the third day teachers no longer prompted; if a child asked for an object without naming its color, or reached for certain objects, the teacher simply put her hand on the object and looked expectantly at the child until he named the object and its color.

Certain materials such as paint and water, which had never been freely available to children, were dispensed only when asked for by color-noun combination, the teacher being "too busy" to attend to requests stated in any other form. The water which children regularly used to "cook" in the doll house was colored with food coloring, so that children had to specify the color or colors of water they wanted to use.

This procedure was continued for 19 days. Throughout, teachers praised every use of color adjectives. Whenever a child asked for a material by naming its color, the teacher verbalized her approval simultaneously with either dispensing the material to him or removing her hand so that he could take the object he had asked for. Spontaneous use of color adjectives on occasions unrelated to the contingency (*i.e.,* occasions other than those when the child "wanted something") were also praised; praise for such usage was given whether or not the child named a noun referent for the color.

Five days after introducing the requirement for naming colors in free play, the naming of colors at group time was discontinued for those seven children reliably discriminating all nine colors, and naming objects by number (counting) was substituted. A second group of eight children continued to have colors presented at group time; children moved from this group into the number-naming group as soon as they had demonstrated mastery of all nine colors. At the end of the school year 10 children were naming objects by number at group time and four children were naming objects by color at group time. One child was sick for the last month of school.

Materials not contingent on color naming. When stable changes were noted in all of the children's spontaneous vocabularies of color adjectives, the contingency of naming colors to obtain materials in the free-play situation was removed. This was done in order to evaluate whether the use of color-noun combinations during free play was maintained solely by the contingencies presented by teachers. Thus, from the 172nd to the 189th and final day of school, all requirements for color naming during free play were discontinued; children were given snack and materials whenever they asked for them either with a noun alone or with an adjective-noun combination. None of the materials ordinarily made available in the free-play situation were withheld by teachers. The consequences of color naming were essentially those which existed during the first baseline period. That is, correct color naming in the free situation was followed intermittently by teacher approval and usually by obtaining an object (if the color name was part of a request for a material). Incorrect naming of a color was followed intermittently by correction from a teacher, and often by obtaining an object (whatever object the teacher assumed the child to be requesting).

RESULTS

Recording

Reliability checks taken periodically over the year by having two observers simultaneously record the behavior of a given child yielded the following product-moment correlation coefficients between observers for the total number of descriptive adjectives of color, number, size, and shape used by all the children in the group:

Observer 1—Observer 2   0.96
Observer 1—Observer 3   0.99
Observer 2—Observer 3   0.86

The correlation between the volunteer observer and all of the three regular observers was 0.89.

Since most of the children were rotated for observation among the three observers, the correspondence of observations taken by the different observers during each of the four conditions provides another assessment of reliability. Figure 1 (top) shows the correspondence of observations taken by the three observers on all children in the group during each experimental condition. In each of the conditions the total number of color adjectives used per sample hour, and the total number of color-noun combinations used per sample hour for all children, as recorded by each observer, is shown. The bottom of Fig. 1 shows the correspondence of observations of a single child taken by the three observers on different days during each experimental condition. This child, whose individual data are plotted in Fig. 3, is the median child in the group (number 8 in Table 1) in terms of overall rate of using color adjectives across all conditions; he is representative of the group also in terms of correspondence between observers in each condition.

Baseline

Figure 2 shows the average rate of use of descriptive adjectives of color, number, and size per sample hour by all the children during each of the four experimental conditions of the study. In each case, the white bar (all adjectives) includes the black bar (adjective-noun combinations). Use of adjectives of shape was not graphed, since the total was only 19 instances over the whole year for the whole group.

During the first baseline (102 school days), the average use of all color adjectives was 0.5 per sample hour, with a range from 0 to 2.3 per sample hour. Table 1 presents the exact rates per sample hour for each child in the group. The average rate of all color-noun combinations was 0.2 per sample hour, the highest rate being one color-noun combination used per sample hour by one child, the lowest rate zero per sample hour by 10 children. The average rate of new color-noun combinations (those not previously recorded for the given child) was 0.1 per sample hour (range 0 to 0.7 per sample hour). Average use of all number adjectives was 3.4 per sample hour (range 0 to 8.8) with average use of all number-noun combinations at 0.5 per sample hour (range 0 to 1.4). All size adjectives were

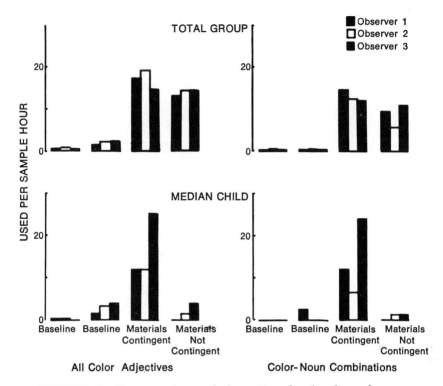

FIGURE 1 Correspondence of observations by the three observers across conditions for the total group and for the representative median child. Top shows the correspondence of observations taken by each of the three observers on all the children in the group during each experimental condition. Bottom shows the correspondence of observations on a single child taken by the three observers on different days during each experimental condition.

used at an average rate of two per sample hour (range 0.9 to 7.5); all size-noun combinations were used at an average rate of 1.5 per sample hour (range 0 to 7.1). Thus, the rates of using descriptive adjectives as a class were low, and rates of naming colors were considerably lower than rates of naming number and size attributes. For a third of the children, use of a color adjective had never been recorded during five months of school. No trend toward increased use of descriptive adjectives was observed for any of the children.

Figure 3 shows use of color adjectives by the child (child 8, Table 1) with the median overall rate across all experimental conditions. For this child only two instances of usage of a color adjective had been recorded during the first baseline period, and there were no instances of color adjectives used with a noun.

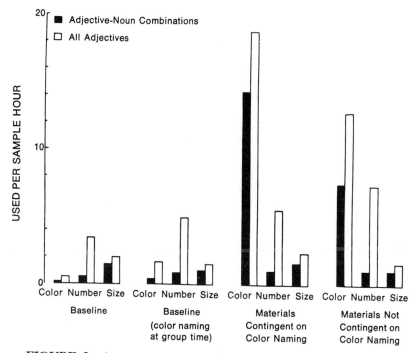

FIGURE 2   Average use per sample hour of descriptive adjectives of color, number, and size for a group of 15 children. The first baseline was from the first to the 102nd day of school. The second baseline (color naming at group time) was from school day 103 through 152. The condition of access to materials contingent on color-naming was from school days 153 through 171. From school days 172 through 189 materials were no longer contingent on color naming. All samples were of approximately 15 min.

Baseline: Color Naming at Group Time

During the 50-school-day period of naming colors at group time, the group average for use of all color adjectives increased to 1.8 per sample hour. The range was from 0 (for two children) to 4.2 color adjectives used per sample hour. The average rate of using all color-noun combinations rose from 0.2 to 0.4 per sample hour; the range was from a low of zero comparable to the first baseline condition to a high of 1.2 as compared to the high of 1.0 per sample hour during the first baseline condition. New color-noun combinations were used at an average rate of 0.3 per sample hour (range 0 to 0.9). The average rate of using all number adjectives rose from 3.4 to 4.9 per sample hour (range 0.5 to 14.7), and all number-noun combinations were used at an average rate of 0.9 per sample hour (range 0 to 3.2).

TABLE 1   Use of color adjectives per sample hour

Child	Baseline — All color	Baseline — All color-noun	Baseline — New color-noun	Baseline (color naming at group time) — All color	Baseline (color naming at group time) — All color-noun	Baseline (color naming at group time) — New color-noun	Materials contingent on color naming — All color	Materials contingent on color naming — All color-noun	Materials contingent on color naming — New color-noun	Materials not contingent on color naming — All color	Materials not contingent on color naming — All color-noun	Materials not contingent on color naming — New color-noun
* 1.	1.1	1.0	0.7	2.0	0.0	0.0	46.7	30.0	1.0	5.0	5.0	1.1
* 2.	1.3	0.0	0.0	2.2	0.4	0.4	8.2	5.4	2.9	54.5	33.1	6.8
3.	0.4	0.1	0.1	1.3	0.2	0.2	23.3	17.4	8.9	25.6	7.8	1.1
* 4.	0.0	0.0	0.0	3.0	0.3	0.3	33.5	30.5	13.0	13.0	12.0	1.0
5.	1.3	0.7	0.4	3.1	1.2	0.6	25.7	24.5	1.0	0.7	0.0	0.0
6.	0.2	0.0	0.0	0.8	0.2	0.2	31.2	15.9	7.7	15.0	15.0	4.5
7.	0.5	0.0	0.0	4.2	0.9	0.9	7.5	2.2	2.2	3.1	3.1	2.1
* 8.	0.3	0.0	0.0	3.1	0.4	0.2	18.2	15.3	7.7	2.2	1.1	1.1
* 9.	0.2	0.0	0.0	3.3	0.6	0.6	15.9	13.6	3.6	2.2	1.7	1.7
10.	0.1	0.1	0.1	0.0	0.0	0.0	29.2	25.0	12.3	11.8	3.2	1.4
*11.	0.0	0.0	0.0	0.6	0.0	0.0	8.9	8.4	3.2	21.6	16.3	4.5
*12.	0.0	0.0	0.0	0.5	0.5	0.5	11.1	11.1	4.8	10.8	3.8	2.3
13.	0.0	0.0	0.0	1.3	0.6	0.6	2.1	2.1	2.1	3.8	0.8	0.8
14.	0.0	0.0	0.0	0.0	0.0	0.0	2.5	2.5	2.5	8.7	1.3	0.7
*15.	2.3	0.5	0.4	1.1	0.3	0.3	14.5	9.3	3.1	Not in school		
Average	0.5	0.2	0.1	1.8	0.4	0.3	18.6	14.2	5.1	12.7	7.4	1.9
Range: High	2.3	1.0	0.7	4.2	1.2	0.9	46.7	30.5	13.0	54.5	33.1	6.8
Low	0.0	0.0	0.0	0.0	0.0	0.0	2.1	2.1	1.0	0.7	0.0	0.0

These average increases in use of number adjectives, in which no training was given, were as great as the increases in use of color adjectives; the rate of using color adjectives during this period was most comparable to the average rate of using size adjectives (1.5 per sample hour, range 0 to 5.6) in which, like number adjectives, no training had been given. Thus, it is not demonstrated that the increased use of color adjectives during this condition was affected by the group time procedures.

Figure 3 shows an increased rate of spontaneous usage of color adjectives in the free-play situation by the child with the median rate. The increase however, was entirely in color adjectives used without a succeeding noun, a form which did not correspond to the behavioral goal (color-noun combinations) set by the teachers. This child was among the seven children who had demonstrated mastery of nine colors by the end of the second baseline condition. Table 1, however, shows that increased color naming was not restricted to those children (marked by asterisks) who had mastered naming of all nine colors at group time. It can be seen that the greatest increase in color naming was by a child (7) who was not yet correctly naming nine colors at group time. There seemed to be little conti-

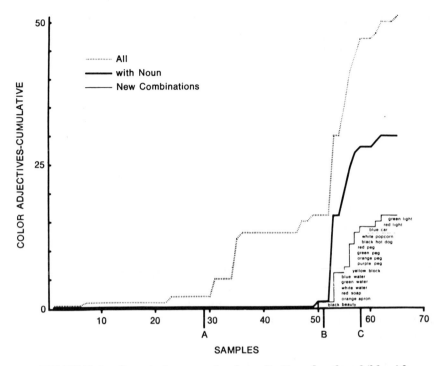

FIGURE 3 Cumulative use of color adjectives by the child with the median rate. The dotted line shows use of all color adjectives; the solid line shows use of all color-noun combinations. New color-noun combinations are printed in above the samples in which they were first recorded. Samples 1–6 were taken during days 3–9 of school. Samples 7–21 were taken during days 25–42 of school. Samples 22–26 were taken during days 71–80 of school. Samples 27–65 were taken during days 91–189 of school. All samples were of approximately 15 min. Baseline is samples 1–29. At A the naming of colors at group time was begun. At B access to materials was contingent on use of color-noun combinations. At C materials were not contingent on color naming.

nuity between "knowing" colors, as demonstrated at group time, and "using" them in the free situation.

Materials Contingent on Color Naming

During the 19 days when access to snack and materials was contingent upon use of a color-noun combination, there was a marked increase in such usage. As can be seen in Fig. 2, the average use of all color adjectives rose to 18.6 per sample hour (ranging from 2.1 to 56.7). The average rate of using all color-noun combinations was 14.2 per sample hour (range 2.1 to 30.5). In contrast, the use of number and size adjectives during this period showed little change from the preceding periods; average use of number adjectives was 5.5 per sample hour while size adjectives were used on an average of 2.1 per sample hour.

During the second baseline condition, only 22% of color adjectives were followed by noun referents. When obtaining an object required naming the object and its color, 75% of the color adjectives used were followed by a noun. The marked rise in new color-noun combinations (to an average of 5.1 per sample hour) can be seen in Fig. 4; more than a third of the objects named by color during the condition of making materials contingent on color-naming constituted new color-noun combinations.

Table 1 shows the changes in rate for individual children during this experimental condition. Though the magnitudes of the increases vary, the increase in use of color adjectives can be seen to be general across the group. The new color-noun combinations, as they appear in Fig. 3 for the representative median child, indicate usage of a variety of color names, applied to a variety of objects, in most cases appropriately. The onset of this behavior among the children during this experimental condition permitted an empirical assessment of the extent of their knowledge of the different colors.

Materials Not Contingent on Color Naming

During the 18 days after the contingencies for color naming were removed, the overall rate of using all color adjectives decreased to an average of 12.7 per sample hour. The rate of using all color-noun combinations decreased to an average of 7.4 per sample hour; that is, 58% of colors named were followed by the name of an object referred to. Though both of these rates show declines from the condition of making materials contingent on color naming, they are well above the rates during either the first or second baseline conditions, indicating that once the behavior was generated in the free-play situation it tended to be maintained, at least in some children. Table 1 shows that there was more inter-subject variation when materials were no longer contingent on color naming, than in any prior condition. The highest rates of color naming, 54.5 per sample hour for all color adjectives used and 33.1 per sample hour for all color-noun combinations used, were higher than during the condition of making materials contingent on color naming; the lowest rate, zero per sample hour for all color-noun combinations, was at the level of the first baseline.

The overall rate of new color-noun combinations was 1.9 per sample hour (see Fig. 4), with the highest rate 6.8 per sample hour for one child and the lowest rate zero for one child. That is, even after the contingency

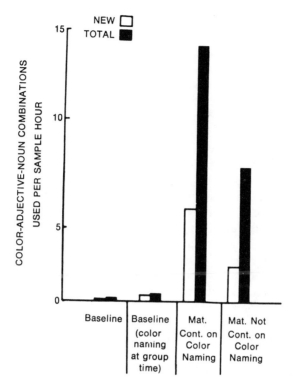

FIGURE 4 Average new and all color-noun combinations used per sample hour for a group of 15 children. The conditions were: baseline, (color naming at group time), materials contingent on color naming, and materials no longer contingent on color naming.

was removed, one quarter of all the color-noun combinations employed were new combinations.

Figure 2 shows that even with an overall decrease the rates of using color adjectives were markedly higher than the rates of using adjectives of size and number. Average use of size adjectives continued at approximately the same rate as during the first baseline condition: 1.6 per sample hour. All number adjectives were used at an average rate of 7.3 per sample hour.

DISCUSSION

This study demonstrated that traditional preschool methods were ineffective in modifying the children's spontaneous speech. These methods assume, as it was assumed by teachers in this study, that what is "known" will be "used", given the appropriate stimulus conditions. Thus, in the usual preschool during and after teaching a skill in a group situation, teachers arrange stimuli in the free situation—a variety of sizes, colors, and shapes of materials, for instance, and social attention and approval—so as to foster usage in that situation of the skill trained in the group situation. The present study gives evidence that, despite this usual arrangement, such usage in the free situation seldom occurred. An examination of the group and free-play stimulus situations, however, indicates that they may have been so dissimilar as to make transfer between them difficult and hence unlikely.

The verbal behavior reinforced in the group situation was of the form: noun-verb-adjective ("the car is red"). This form, in which the adjective stands alone as predicate adjective rather than as a modifier, is the form called for by the stimulus question, "What color is this (car)?". There is no simple stimulus question in English which necessarily calls for a response form in which an adjective, such as a color name, modifies a noun: the question, "What is this?", calls for a noun response ("a car") rather than, necessarily, for a modified noun ("a red car"). In group teaching, prompting the response form of a modified noun concurrently with prompting color responses, while feasible, is rarely done in traditional preschool practice.

For descriptive speech to be "spontaneous", however, the stimulus situation controlling the behavior cannot be a direct question concerning an object. Rather, the stimulus situation must involve an object plus the necessity (not provoked by a question) of singling out that object from one or more other objects. This is the function of descriptive language. Most children come into contact with this function casually, over time, both inside and outside of preschools, and often even before they "know" the precise meaning of the descriptive language used. Since the children in the present study were termed "culturally deprived", an appellation indicating that their environment was in some way deficient in the stimulus conditions conducive to the development and maintenance of complex language skills, it seemed contradictory to teach them a skill such as color naming and then rely on unsystematic environmental events to make that skill functional. Rather, the environment was deliberately structured so that the children would come into contact with the function of descriptive adjectives: the stimulus situation which hopefully would control some rate of the behavior outside of school was created on a massive scale inside of school when access to materials was made contingent on naming them by color.

That the behavior continued in some strength after the contingencies were removed seems to indicate that once color description was generated, there were enough "natural" contingencies in the preschool situation to maintain it. Even after removal of the contingency, children did obtain an object when they asked for it by color; though teachers discriminated the removal of the contingency, not all of the children may have done so. By the end of the contingency period teachers were rarely withholding materials in the obvious manner of the beginning of that period; rather, most of the children were spontaneously naming the color of the object whenever they requested an object from a teacher. This verbal topography was the one most regularly and promptly reinforced. Even after removal of the contingency for color naming this was probably often the case.

There are two implications of this study for preschool practice. The first is that of creating for children a functional environment where the contingencies for pre-academic behavior approximate those applied to such behavior in the "beyond-preschool" environment. The teachers in this study felt, in fact, that the whole process of teaching colors could have been more efficiently and painlessly done by making access to materials contingent on color naming even before the children knew the names of any colors. Prompting and reinforcing in the free situation was little different than that done at group time, except that children did not have to wait for their "turn", and teachers were able to make use of reinforcers such as materials in the free-play situation. The generalization from free-situation naming to test-situation naming seemed more easily made, perhaps because the spontaneous response form is appropriate to both stimulus situations.

The second implication is that preschool materials may function as reinforcers for many children, and for some children may be even more powerful than the social reinforcement and/or food presented in the preschool situation. Some of the children in the present study appeared to teachers to have "really learned" colors only when required to name them in connection with objects they wanted to use; these were the children whose behavior in the group time situation was not well controlled by the praise and food presented there (for neither of which they were deprived, at least in the preschool environment). As reinforcers, materials are not only inherent in the preschool, but are uniquely appropriate to the development of descriptive vocabulary since they are the same class of reinforcers which maintain the behavior in everyday situations.

REFERENCES

ALLEN, K. EILEEN and HARRIS, FLORENCE R. Elimination of a child's excessive scratching by training the mother in reinforcement procedures. *Behaviour Research and Therapy*, 1966, **4**, 79–84.

ALLEN, K. EILEEN; HART, BETTY M., BUELL, JOAN S., HARRIS, FLORENCE R., and WOLF, M. M. Effects of social reinforcement on isolate behavior of a nursery school child. *Child Development*, 1964, **35**, 511–518.

BEREITER, C. and ENGELMANN, S. *Teaching disadvantaged children in the preschool.* Englewood Cliffs: Prentice-Hall, 1966.

BIJOU, S. W. Theory and research in mental (developmental) retardation. *Psychological Record*, 1963, **13**, 95–110.

BIRNBRAUER, J. S., WOLF, M. M., KIDDER, J. D., and TAGUE, CECILIA E. Classroom behavior of retarded pupils with token reinforcement. *Journal of Experimental Child Psychology*, 1965, **2**, 219–235.

BROWN, P. and ELLIOTT, R. Control of aggression in a nursery school class. *Journal of Experimental Child Psychology*, 1965, **2**, 103–107.

HARRIS, FLORENCE R., WOLF, M. M., and BAER, D. M. Effects of adult social reinforcement on child behavior. *Young Children*, 1964, **20**, 8–17.

HESS, R. D. and SHIPMAN, VIRGINIA C. Early experience and the socialization of cognitive modes in children. *Child Development*, 1965, **36**, 869–886.

JOHNSTON, MARGARET K., KELLEY, C. SUSAN; HARRIS, FLORENCE R., and WOLF, M. M. An application of reinforcement principles to development of motor skills in a young child. *Child Development*, 1966, **37**, 379–387.

LINDSLEY, O. R. Experimental analysis of cooperation and competition. In T. Verhave (Ed.), *The experimental analysis of behavior*. New York: Appleton-Century-Crofts, 1966. Pp. 470–501.

LOVAAS, O. I., FREITAG, G., KINDER, M. I., RUBENSTEIN, B. D., SCHAEFFER, B., and SIMMONS, J. Q. Establishment of social reinforcers in two schizophrenic children on the basis of food. *Journal of Experimental Child Psychology*, 1966, **4**, 109–125.

RIESSMANN, F. *The culturally deprived child.* New York: Harper & Row, 1962.

RISLEY, T. and WOLF, M. Establishing functional speech in echolalic children. *Behaviour Research and Therapy*, 1967, **5**, 73–88.

WAHLER, R. G., WINKEL, G. H., PETERSON, R. F., and MORRISON, D. C. Mothers as behavior therapists for their own children. *Behaviour Research and Therapy*, 1965, **3**, 113–124.

WEIKART, D. P. Results of preschool intervention programs. Paper presented at the symposium on the Education of Culturally Disadvantaged Children, University of Kansas, 1966.

WOLF, M. M., GILES, D. K., and HALL, R. V. Experiments with token reinforcement in a remedial classroom. *Behaviour Research and Therapy*, 1968, **6**, 51–64.

WOLF, M. M., RISLEY, T. R., and MEES, H. L. Application of operant conditioning procedures to the behavior problems of an autistic child. *Behaviour Research and Therapy*, 1964, **1**, 305–312.

ZIMMERMAN, ELAINE H. and ZIMMERMAN, J. The alteration of behavior in a special classroom situation. *Journal of the Experimental Analysis of Behavior*, 1962, **5**, 59–60.

ANDREW J. WHEELER
BETH SULZER[1]
Southern Illinois University

Operant training and generalization of a verbal response form in a speech-deficient child

A subject who spoke essentially in "telegraphic" English, leaving out most articles and auxiliary verbs, was trained to use a particular sentence form that included the articles and verbs to describe a set of standardized pictures. The subject used the trained sentence form to describe the trained pictures, and in addition, use of the sentence form generalized to sets of untrained and novel stimuli. When the trained sentence form was changed, the subject used the new form to describe both training and generalization stimuli. When the original correct form of response was retrained, the subject once again used the trained sentence form to respond to both training and generalization trials.

The problem of training complex language in speech-deficient children is a long-standing one. Recent literature contains many examples of training of relatively simple verbal responses: use of descriptive adjectives (Hart

Reprinted from *Journal of Applied Behavior Analysis*, 1970, 3, 139–47, with permission of the publisher and the authors. Copyright 1970 by the Society for the Experimental Analysis of Behavior, Inc.

[1] The authors wish to thank Steven M. Andes and Bernard H. Salzberg for technical assistance. Valuable critical suggestions were offered by Mrs. Gretchen Walters and Drs. E. S. Sulzer and B. L. Hopkins.

and Risley, 1968); use of the plural morpheme (Guess, Sailor, Rutherford, and Baer, 1968); correct use of personal pronouns and prepositions (Lovaas, 1969); increased frequency of continuous speech (Salzinger, Salzinger, Portnoy, Eckman, Bacon, Deutsch, and Zubin, 1962); imitation, labelling, and simple answers to questions (Risley and Wolf, 1964), and many studies cited by Peterson (1968) on imitative verbal behavior. Little work has been done, however, on developing complex forms of verbal responding, such as the development of syntax or sentence structure, including the correct use of articles, appropriate verb endings, and word order. A possible reason for the paucity of experimental studies on complex language is the difficulties encountered when trying to observe and reliably measure such responses. The present study attempts to demonstrate a procedure for the training of complex language, to show the generalizability of the acquired complex response, and to present a reliable measuring system for the use of a particular sentence form.

Although linguistic development has been an area of concern for some time, according to Guess *et al.* (1968), most recent efforts have focused primarily on theory with few attempts to analyze language development functionally. Linguists have made use of the concept of "generative" language to account for the fact that an organism exhibits ". . . more behavior exemplifying the dimensions of his experience than that experience has taught directly to him." (Guess *et al.*, 1968, p. 297). To the behavioral psychologist, the linguist's use of generative language is probably analogous to the terms generalized or functional response classes. A generalized response class exists when all responses in the class show an effect of a manipulation (*e.g.* extinction or differential reinforcement) which is made in relation to only a few members of the class. If this is indeed the case, then environmental intervention could have a great effect upon the development of generative language. By analyzing generative language in terms of functional response classes, the growing body of knowledge and techniques available to behavioral psychologists can be brought to bear on the analysis of the development of normal language as well as upon the modification of problem language behavior (Salzinger, 1968).

Several studies have appeared in the recent literature in which imitative responses seem to form functional response classes (Baer, Peterson, and Sherman, 1967; Metz, 1965; Lovaas, Berberich, Perloff, and Schaeffer, 1966; Peterson, 1968; Brigham and Sherman, 1968). In these studies, several responses were reinforced while, typically, a few never-reinforced responses were interspersed. The general findings seemed to be that the nonreinforced responses improved along with the reinforced ones. When a manipulation, such as extinction or differential reinforcement of other responses (DRO) was made on the previously reinforced responses, a decrement in responding was seen with all responses, thus apparently demonstrating a functional response class.

Much of language other than imitative responses can be at least theoretically analyzed in terms of the response class model. In addition to attacking some of the applied problems mentioned above, the present study was very similar to the Guess *et al.* (1968) analysis of morphology, but with the analysis applied instead to syntax. In the present study, a subject who spoke essentially in "telegraphic" English, leaving out most articles and auxiliary verbs, was trained to use a particular sentence form that included the articles and verbs to describe a set of standardized pictures. The basic training consisted of combining labels that had already been present in his repertoire, in order to teach him the use of grammatically correct sentences, all of which included subjects, predicates, and objects. The training procedure used was a chaining paradigm similar to that used by Risley and Wolf (1967). An attempt was also made to demonstrate the generalization of this form of response to a set of pictures that were never trained or reinforced, demonstrating the development of a functional response class or generative language.

METHOD

Subject

Tod was an 8-yr-old boy who had previously been echolalic, and had carried various diagnostic labels: brain damage, autism, and retardation. After 2 yrs of speech training, Tod was no longer echolalic, and he had gained a verbal repertoire consisting mostly of a large number of one-word tacts, simple mands, and some fragmentary answers to questions. He had never been observed to use a complete sentence of the type trained in this study and had very little spontaneous speech. While he was no longer echolalic, imitative responses could easily be occasioned with the appropriate discriminative stimuli (S^Ds). Such S^Ds, for example, might have consisted of the experimenter instructing Tod to repeat or the experimenter assuming a particular tone of voice. Simultaneous with the study, Tod was attending a special education class where activities included training in academic skills and social skills, and some informal language training.

Setting

The study was conducted in a large therapy room connected via one-way mirror and intercom to an observation area. Tod and the experimenter sat facing each other, next to a large table on which were kept some of the reinforcers and objects to be used in the study. Other reinforcers were scattered about the room within Tod's sight but out of his reach.

Materials

The stimuli consisted of thirteen 7 by 9-in. (17.8 by 22.8 cm) picture cards from Levels #P and #3 of the Peabody Language Development Kit (American Guidance Service Inc., 1967). Appropriate descriptions of the 13 pictures used, along with their numbers, are shown on the sample data sheet in Table 1. Seven of the cards, which could be adequately described by a particular form of sentence, Form I, were selected for use throughout all experimental phases. A Form I sentence was defined as including the article "the" followed by a noun subject, followed by a verb phrase consisting of the auxiliary verb "is", followed by a present participle, followed by an object phrase consisting of the article "the" and a noun object. Each sentence was thus divided into three components. The subject phrase ("the man") was the initial component, the verb phrase ("is smoking") was the middle component, and the object phrase ("the pipe") was the terminal component.

A second sentence form, Form II, was also defined. Form II consisted of the same key words presented in the same order as in Form I, but omitting the article "the" and the verb "is". Thus, an example of a perfect Form I response is, "The man is smoking the pipe". For the same stimulus card, a perfect Form II response is, "Man smoking pipe".

Of the seven cards selected, five (P-4, P-6, A-3, A-6, and A-7) were used for training. The training cards were selected on the basis that a

TABLE 1   Sample data sheet

	Response		
Card #	Initial	Middle	Terminal
P-1	The baby	is taking	a (the) bath
P-2	The boy	is putting on	his (the) shirt
P-4	The man	is smoking/is sitting	a (the) pipe/in the chair
P-5	The lady (woman)	is talking	on the telephone
P-6	The lady (woman)	is washing	the dish
P-7	The girl	is combing	her (the) hair
P-11	The man	is riding	on the tractor
P-18	The teacher (lady)	is writing	on the chalkboard
A-3	The boy	is emptying	the garbage (can)/the trash
A-6	The boy	is painting	a (the) picture
A-7	The girl	is opening	the window
A-19	The girl	is swimming	in the water
A-21	The boy	is washing	the car

Form I sentence would be an appropriate description of each. Two cards (P-7 and A-21) were selected for generalization trials on the same basis, but with an additional criterion. The additional criterion was that without any training Tod had emitted the key words in response to the presentation of the cards. Key words for these two cards were: boy, girl, combing, washing, hair, and car. The reason for this additional criterion was that there was never to be any prompting or reinforcement given for responses to these two cards, and if the form of response was to generalize, the necessary vocabulary would have to be already present in Tod's repertoire. The remaining six cards, the test cards, were to be presented only during the first baseline phase of the experiment and during the last part of the final phase. This was done in order to test for generalization to stimuli to which Tod had relatively little exposure. Four of these cards were of a slightly different form than the others. They ended in a prepositional phrase rather than in a direct object.

Scoring

Scoring of responses was done on the data sheet shown in Table 1. The sentence was divided into three components with a score of one point possible in each component, giving a possible total of three points per sentence. The correct Form I responses are shown on the data sheet. As Tod responded to each presentation of a card, each component was marked as correct if his response conformed to the Form I response shown. In order to receive a point for any component, all articles and endings had to be present and key words correct. Any omission (*e.g.*, "The man/smoking/the pipe") or error in key word resulted in the loss of a point for that component only (the middle one in this case). Per cent correct for either form of response per session was tabulated by dividing the number of points earned by the number of points possible during that session. Since cards were presented twice per session, the per cent correct for each session was based on a total of 30 possible points for the training cards and 12 possible points for the generalization cards. The six test cards, when used, were presented only once per session, and thus per cents for these cards are based on 18 possible points each session. Per cent correct Form I responses were tabulated throughout the experiment. On the five cards ending in a prepositional phrase, scoring was the same as for the other cards, except that a point was given for the terminal component only if Tod said the prepositional phrase the way it appears on the sample data sheet.

All scoring of responses was done directly on the data sheets by the experimenter. Seven reliability checks were made during the first and second baseline phases, during the first and third Train Form I phases, and during the Train Form II phase. Three of the checks were taken by an observer scoring simultaneously with the experimenter from behind the one-way mirror. The other four checks were made from an audio tape of the session by a third observer. Reliabilities were calculated by dividing the number of agreements by the total number of components scored. There were 60 components when the test cards were being used, and 42 components when these cards were not used. The three live checks yielded agreements of 88, 94, and 90%. The tape checks yielded agreements of 97, 95, 98, and 100%.

Procedure

The experimental manipulations took place during the first 10 min of each 30-min speech training session. Sessions were held four days a week. Other tasks taking place during the sessions included training in the use of pronouns and prepositions, and teaching answers to personal identity and social amenities questions, and recall of morning activities and events. Reinforcement during all types of training consisted of the immediate presentation of tokens (poker chips). When four tokens were accumulated, Tod was allowed to count them out into the experimenter's hand in order to gain access to one of several toys in the room, have something to eat, or be tickled or rocked by the experimenter. Each back-up reinforcement period lasted for 30 sec, after which work was resumed.

Baseline. During the first four sessions, all 13 cards shown in Table 1 were presented in the order shown. The experimenter presented each card by holding it up and saying only, "What do you see?" No other instructions were given and no reinforcement was available.

Train Form I. During these five sessions, Tod was trained to use the Form I response on the five training cards. The Form I response was treated as a three-component chain. The correct completion of each component was the S^D for the beginning of the next, and completion of the terminal component resulted in the delivery of reinforcement. Thus, following the S^D, "What do you see?" if Tod failed to use Form I in any component of his response, he was stopped and given an imitative prompt for the missed component. He was then required to emit the Form I response before he was allowed to go on to the next component or to receive reinforcement. Reinforcement always occurred after the terminal component was completed, whether prompts had been used or not. However, each component of the response was scored correct only if it occurred without prompting. Thus, an example of a typical training sequence might have proceeded as follows: The experimenter: "What do you see?" Tod: "The man/smoking," The experimenter: "Is smoking," Tod: "Is smoking/ the pipe." The experimenter: "Good" (delivers token). Such a sequence would have received a score of two points, one each for the initial and terminal components. No shaping by successive approximations was ever used in the training. Imitative control over Tod's verbal responses was good enough that an imitative prompt delivered after a wrong response, as in the above example, reliably occasioned the correct response. Because this imitative control was so good, it was also never necessary to move the delivery of reinforcement forward in the chain of responses. From the beginning of training, reinforcement was always delivered after completion of the entire chain immediately following the terminal component. In the early stages of training, of course, extensive prompting was necessary, but the scoring system allows for reflection of the prompting in the data. As the procedure was set up, every time a card was presented, a full correct response occurred, sometimes prompted and sometimes not prompted.

The two generalization cards were presented throughout this phase, but without any prompting or reinforcement. Thus, baseline conditions were maintained with these two cards throughout the phase. During each session, the five training cards were presented in the order shown in Table 1. This was followed by the presentation of the two generalization cards. Then, the whole sequence was repeated for a second set of trials.

Baseline repeated.   For the next six sessions the original baseline conditions were reinstituted for all seven cards.

Train Form I repeated.   For the next seven sessions there was a return to the original Train Form I conditions for the five training cards, with no change in conditions for the two generalization cards.

Train Form II.   The next five sessions consisted of training the Form II response to the five training cards. Here Tod was prompted, and reinforcement was delivered, for leaving out all articles and auxiliary verbs. Except for the form of response, the training procedure was the same as during Train Form I. There was no change in conditions during this phase for the generalization cards.

Train Form I repeated.   The final phase of the experiment, lasting 11 sessions, was a return to the original Train Form I conditions for the training cards with no change for the generalization cards. In addition, during Sessions 35, 36, and 37, the six cards that had not been presented since the original baseline were presented as a post-test without any prompting or reinforcement.

RESULTS

Figure 1 shows the per cent correct for the Form I response to both training and generalization stimuli through all phases of the experiment. With

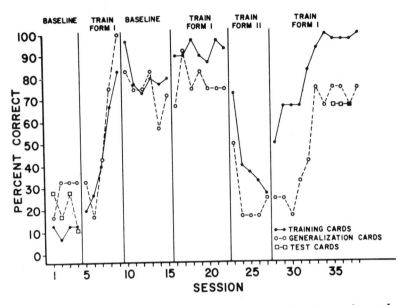

FIGURE 1 Per cent correct Form I responding for six experimental conditions. Form I is the long form of response, *e.g.*, "The man is smoking the pipe."

both training and generalization cards, correct Form I responses progressed from a range of 7% to 33% during baseline to 83% and 100% respectively by the fifth session of Train Form I. The next two manipulations, however, produced little effect. The Train Form II manipulation produced a large and rapid drop in the use of Form I response, but recovery of the use of Form I on both training and generalization cards was rapid upon return to the Train Form I condition. From the end of the second baseline onwards, Form I responding on the generalization cards was consistently lower than that on the training trials, although it had originally been higher during the first baseline. For the six test cards, performance improved substantially as evidenced by the mean of 21% Form I responses during baseline and the mean of 67% Form I responses at the end of the experiment. Table 2 shows the mean per cent correct for the

TABLE 2 Mean per cent correct in each component for test cards during baseline and last train form I condition.

Component	Baseline	Train Form I
Initial	0	72
Middle	0	89
Terminal	58	39

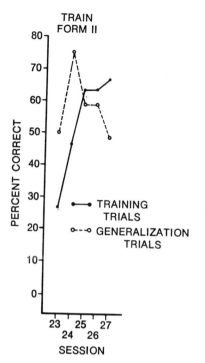

FIGURE 2 Per cent correct Form II responding in Train Form II. Form II is the short form of response, *e.g.,* "Man smoking pipe."

individual components of these test cards during the two conditions. As can be seen from the table, Tod never made a correct response for the first two components during baseline, but at the end of the experiment most of the correct responding occurred in these two components, while errors increased somewhat in the terminal component.

Figure 2 shows the acquisition of the Form II response during Train Form II, while Figure 1 showed the decrease in Form I responding. Although Forms I and II are mutually exclusive, these two response forms are not exhaustive. Other errors, such as incorrect verb forms, would lower the per cent correct for both forms of response. For instance, if Tod said for card #P-4, "Man/smoke/pipe," the middle component would have been incorrect for Form II as well as for Form I. Thus, the acquisition of Form II responding could not be inferred from Figure 1. Per cent Form I responses emitted during the last session of the second Train Form I manipulation was 93% and 75% respectively for training and generalization cards. Therefore, per cent use of Form II during that session could have been no greater than 7% and 25% respectively, given mutually exclusive forms of response. The 25% and 50% respective levels of Form II responding on training and generalization cards in the first session of Train Form II represent a considerable rise in the use of this form over what had obtained in the previous session. During the five sessions of Train Form II, correct Form II training card responses increased steadily, but the generalization cards showed a rise and subsequent decrease in the use of the Form II response. As was noted above, however, the level of Form II responding on the generalization cards, despite its variability, was considerably higher than it had been under the previous experimental condition.

In Figure 1, the components of the sentence are averaged, thereby in some cases cancelling out the effects of changes in individual components. Figure 3 breaks these down and shows per cent correct Form I responding by component. The data show large variations from component to component during any given manipulation. In the generalization trials, the use of Form I in the middle component is consistently higher than in the initial component. The initial component in turn is consistently higher than the terminal component. In the training trials there is no obvious ordering of components by per cent correct Form I responding. The terminal component shows the least variability from manipulation to manipulation, maintaining a high stable level of correct Form I responding regardless of experimental phase. It was in the terminal component also that the generalization trials showed the least effect of the manipulations. From the middle of the second baseline to the end of the experiment, Form I responding in the generalization trials seldom varied from 50% in the terminal component. The other two components show much clearer effects of the manipulations in both training and generalization trials. The middle and initial components accounted for most of the effects seen in Fig. 1. While Fig. 1 showed little change in Form I responding in generalization trials from second baseline to second Train Form I, some change is evident on these trials in the middle and initial components in Fig. 3.

DISCUSSION

The results of this study demonstrated that a complex verbal response could be trained in a speech-deficient child. The response was measured with an acceptable level of reliability, and the response generalized to untrained and novel stimuli. The large reversal and concurrent acquisition of Form II during Train Form II demonstrated that the training procedures, a combination of chaining, imitative prompting, and differential reinforcement, were the crucial factors in the development of the response. The generalization responses showed many of the same variations as the training responses, but generalization responding was consistently at a lower level of accuracy than training responding for most of the experiment. One reason for the comparatively lower level of generalization responding was that some consistent error patterns that were never corrected developed in these

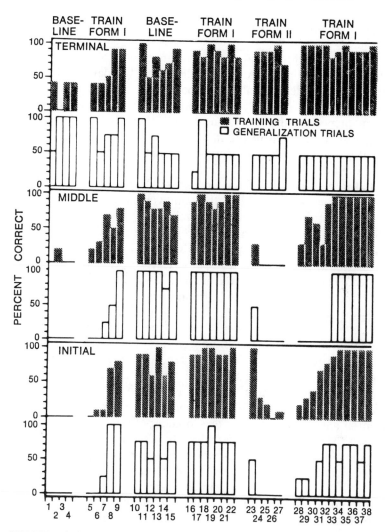

FIGURE 3 Per cent correct Form I responding by component for six experimental conditions.

trials. For instance, on card #P-7, Tod almost always said, "The girl is combing *my* hair." This response caused a point to be lost in the terminal component, the primary reason for the low level of accuracy in this component shown in Fig. 3. Another possibility is that Tod formed a discrimination between reinforced and unreinforced stimuli, since the cards were always presented in the same order and the same cards were always reinforced. This possibility, however, would have worked against the results obtained, and thus would not seem to detract from the significance of these results.

Changes in training and generalization card responses corresponded throughout the manipulation made in the study. The data on the test cards offered further evidence that the response did generalize to stimuli to which Tod had had relatively little exposure. Since some of the test cards ended in prepositional phrases, one could argue that earlier preposition training had contributed to the improvement shown in Fig. 1. However, examination of the individual component data demonstrated that all of the improvement occurred in the first two components. The terminal component, the one containing the prepositional phrase, actually showed a decrement in performance. Thus, the improvement on the test cards could in no way be attributed to preposition training.

Since the response was rapidly developed to stimuli with which training had been given and to stimuli with which no training had been given, it can be said that a functional response class or generative language had developed. The training involved no new vocabulary for Tod, only the way in which the words already in the repertoire were combined. Thus, it was the form of the response, or syntax, that was trained, and the response class that developed was not a new set of labels for the stimuli but a new combination of old labels. As can be seen from Fig. 3, during baseline Tod never had emitted an entire Form I sentence. During the last phase of the experiment, he emitted several Form I sentences in response to training, generalization, and test cards.

Whereas Guess et al. (1968) demonstrated the role of imitation and differential reinforcement in the development of a morphological response, the present study extended the analysis to a syntactic response. As Guess et al. point out, such a demonstration does not show that all generative language develops in the manner that it developed in the present experiment. Such an experiment is of primary value in demonstrating the feasibility of producing generative language with the techniques presented. Perhaps the most significant point to be gained from the present study, and from earlier studies analyzing language in terms of functional response classes, is that every response that is eventually learned does not have to be directly trained.

REFERENCES

American Guidance Service, Inc. *Peabody language development kits.* Circle Pines, Minn., 1967.

Baer, D. M., Peterson, R. F., and Sherman, J. A. The development of imitation by reinforcing behavioral similarity to a model. *Journal of the Experimental Analysis of Behavior,* 1967, **10**, 405–416.

BRIGHAM, T. A. and SHERMAN, J. A. An experimental analysis of verbal imitation in preschool children. *Journal of Applied Behavior Analysis,* 1968, **1,** 151–160.

GUESS, D., SAILOR, W., RUTHERFORD, G., and BAER, D. M. An experimental analysis of linguistic development: the productive use of the plural morpheme. *Journal of Applied Behavior Analysis,* 1968, **1,** 297–306.

HART, B. and RISLEY, T. Establishing use of descriptive adjectives in the spontaneous speech of disadvantaged preschool children. *Journal of Applied Behavior Analysis,* 1968, **1,** 109–120.

LOVAAS, O. I. (Technical Director). *Behavior modification: teaching language to psychotic children.* 16 mm-sound; New York: Appleton-Century-Crofts, 1969.

LOVAAS, O. I., BERBERICH, J., PERLOFF, B., and SCHAEFFER, B. Acquisition of imitative speech by schizophrenic children. *Science,* 1966, **151,** 705–707.

METZ, J. Conditioning generalized imitation in autistic children. *Journal of Experimental Child Psychology,* 1965, **2,** 389–399.

PETERSON, R. F. Some experiments on the organization of a class of imitative behaviors. *Journal of Applied Behavior Analysis,* 1968, **1,** 225–235.

RISLEY, T. R. and WOLF, M. M. *Experimental manipulation of autistic behaviors and generalization into the home.* Paper delivered at the American Psychological Association Convention, Los Angeles, 1964.

RISLEY, T. R. and WOLF, M. M. Establishing functional speech in echolalic children. *Behavior Research and Therapy,* 1967, **5,** 73–88.

SALZINGER, K. On the operant conditioning of complex behavior. In J. M. Shlien (Ed.), *Research in Psychotherapy,* Vol. III. Washington, D. C.: American Psychological Association, 1968, pp. 122–129.

SALZINGER, S., SALZINGER, K., PORTNOY, S., ECKMAN, J., BACON, P., DEUTSCH, M., and ZUBIN, J. Operant conditioning of continuous speech in young children. *Child Development,* 1962, **33,** 683–695.

TODD R. RISLEY
BETTY HART
University of Kansas

Developing correspondence
between the non-verbal
and verbal behavior
of preschool children[1]

Correspondence was developed between children's non-verbal and verbal behavior such that their non-verbal behavior could be altered simply by reinforcing related verbal behavior. Two groups of six children each were given food snack at the end of the day: for reporting use of a specific preschool material during free play (procedure A); and then only for reports of use which corresponded to actual use of that material earlier that day (procedure B). Initially, procedure A alone had little or no effect on the children's use of materials. Procedure B resulted in all of the children in one group actually using a specific material, and after repeating procedures A and B with this group across a series of different materials, procedure A alone was sufficient to significantly increase use of a specific material. Correspondence between verbal and non-verbal behavior was produced such that, in this group of 4-yr-old disadvantaged Negro children,

Reprinted from *Journal of Applied Behavior Analysis*, 1968, 1, 267–81, with permission of the publisher and the authors. Copyright 1968 by the Society for the Experimental Analysis of Behavior, Inc.

[1] This work was supported by a grant (HD 03144) from the National Institute of Child Health and Human Development to the Bureau of Child Research and the Department of Human Development, University of Kansas. The authors wish to acknowledge the vital roles performed by our head teacher, Nancy Reynolds; our observers, Maxine Preuitt, Ella Murphy, and Diane West; and our secretary, Cordelia McIntosh, in this study.

206

"saying" controlled "doing" 22 or more hours later. In the second group, procedure B initially did not increase the use of a specific material; rather, the children's reports decreased so as to correspond to the intermittent use of the material. It appeared from subsequent procedures with this group that maintenance of a high level of reporting was crucial to the saying-then-doing correspondence seen in the first group.

It is frequently assumed that what a person says he has done or will do relates to what he actually has done or will do. Much of psychotherapy —even the new "behavior" therapy—is based on the assumption that reorganizing and restructuring a patient's verbal statements about himself and his world will result in a corresponding reorganization of the patient's behavior with respect to that world. Similarly, education, in addition to teaching specific skills, strives to inculcate social attitudes—that is, verbal behaviors about the standards of society and the citizen's role in that society—which, it is hoped, will lead to behaviors that correspond to the verbalization of these attitudes.

Since this assumption of a correspondence between verbal and nonverbal behavior is necessary for much of its affairs, society is concomitantly concerned with maintaining that correspondence. The procedures which are advocated and used for producing and maintaining such correspondence largely involve the punishment of verbal behavior which does not correspond to non-verbal behavior. But punishment applied to verbal behavior which does not correspond to *socially desirable* non-verbal behavior should serve to produce correspondence by suppressing the report of the socially desirable behavior to the level of the occurrence of that desirable behavior itself. More beneficial to society might be the production of correspondence by increasing socially desirable behavior to the level of verbal report. If such correspondence were then generalized, desirable non-verbal behavior could be increased simply by increasing related verbal behavior: significant alterations in non-verbal behavior in other settings could be produced by modifying verbal behavior in restricted and convenient settings such as the classroom or the therapist's office.

Investigations of the existence of such a generalized relationship between verbal and non-verbal behavior in preschool children have been made by Lovaas (1961, 1964) and Sherman (1964). In these studies, reinforcement procedures were applied to the modification of verbal behavior alone; little increase in related non-verbal behavior resulted. The purpose of the present study was to develop training procedures which would be sufficient to produce generalized correspondence between verbal and non-verbal behavior in preschool children, such that non-verbal behavior might be modified by reinforcing verbal behavior alone.

METHOD

Settings and Subjects

Twelve children, seven boys and five girls, in a half-day experimental preschool located in a depressed area of Kansas City, Kansas, served. All were 4- to 5-yr old Negroes from large families with low incomes. School lasted for approximately 3 hr. As soon as the children arrived at school at about 9 A.M. they were served cereal and milk or juice for breakfast. After 30 min of free play indoors and 15 to 20 min of music and rhythms, the children had a snack of fruit and cookies or sandwiches before going outside for 30 min of free play. The remainder of this snack was eaten on coming back inside, just before going home. At this time (approximately 12:00 noon) the children sat on two separate rugs, in two groups of six children with one teacher each. Each teacher asked her group: "What did you do that was good today?", and then, for about 10 min, responded to the children's answers while serving the food. Whenever a child was passed the snack baskets, he helped himself to as much food as he wanted or as much as he could hold in both hands. The data on verbal behavior presented in this study were taken during this last snack period. The data on non-verbal behavior were taken during the indoor free-play period, 1.5 hr earlier.

Recording.   For each group of six children, an observer recorded in longhand everything said by each child. A third observer took an independent record to determine the reliability of the recording system. She alternated between the two groups, similarly recording in longhand everything said by each child. Approximately halfway through the school year, this third observer took reliability checks on each of the two regular observers only once a week (*i.e.*, only every other week on each given observer); the other four days of the school week she alternated between the two groups and recorded everything said by the teacher to the children.

The children's use of materials during indoor free play was recorded by the teachers, who each day noted the time a child began and finished using a given material. Each of the three observers also noted times of using materials by those children whom they were observing in the course of collecting 15-min verbalization samples during free play for another study.

EXPERIMENT I

Procedures

Baseline.   For the first 15 days (Days 1 to 15) of school, each teacher presented the question: "What did you do that was good today?" to the six children on her rug, and then responded socially to all ensuing verbalizations from the children. Content of the children's verbalization was never differentially reinforced during these 15 days.

For the first five days of baseline, in order to assess operant levels of rate and content of speech among the groups, snack was non-contingent: the teacher held out the snack baskets to each child whether he verbalized or not. Then for the next five days, with food still non-contingent, teachers prompted verbal responses in order to increase the rate of verbalization in the group as a whole. Prompting consisted of asking the question: "And what did you do that was good today?" more than once, and addressing it directly to a specific child. Usually the teacher presented the snack basket to the child simultaneously with asking the question. All verbalizations were responded to socially as before with approval, comments, a further question, or repetition of what the child said. Then, so that teachers in subsequent stages of the experiment would be able to present reinforcement immediately upon a response, snack was made contingent on hand-raising during the last five days of baseline. The children were prompted to raise their hands; when a child's hand was raised, the teacher praised him, simultaneously offering him snack, and then asked what he had done that was good that day. The child was encouraged to take snack whether he verbalized or not; the teacher waited about 30 sec for a response and then turned to another child. Again, all verbalizations were responded to socially by the teacher, with no differential reinforcement for content.

Reinforcement of content. For the next 24 days (Days 16 to 40) each child was given snack and social approval contingent upon raising his hand and verbalizing that he had interacted with a specific preschool material. In one group (Group A) verbalizing use of blocks was reinforced; in the other group (Group B) verbalizing use of paint was reinforced. That is, the teacher in Group A reinforced with snack and praise any positive statement containing both the words "I" and either "blocks" or any form of the verb "to build"; the teacher in Group B reinforced all positive statements containing both "I" and any form of "paint" used either as a noun or a verb. The teacher responded minimally to any other statements made by the children ("mmhumm", "yes", head nod).

On the first day of reinforcing content, teachers twice prompted the desired response, by saying to the group: "What did you do that was good today? Did anyone build with blocks (paint)?" at the same time looking directly at a child who had done so. As soon as a child verbalized use of the specified material, the teacher, while holding out the snack basket, praised him enthusiastically and repeated his verbalization several times with emphasis on the name of the material used. After the first day, no more prompts were given.

The form of the verbal behavior which initially resulted from thus reinforcing content tended to be stereotyped: the children said either: "I painted" or "I built with the blocks", with very little elaboration. It was thought that the lack of effect on actual use of these materials during free play might be due to this stereotypy; therefore, during the ensuing 19 days (Days 21 to 40) of reinforcing content, teachers required elaboration of a statement of use of a material before presenting a child with snack. The teachers prompted elaboration by asking: "What did you paint?" when a child merely said, "I painted", or "What did you build?" when a child said he had played with the blocks. The final (reinforced) statement from a child had thus to contain some description of what he might have done with a material as well as the reference to himself ("I") and to the material ("paint" or "blocks/build"). Accuracy of description was never differentially reinforced: a child was given snack and teacher praise and comments for his elaborated report whether or not it described what he had actually built or painted.

The teacher in Group B was stationed in the painting area in a small side room during the morning free-play period. She dispensed paint and paper and other needed materials to children, approved appropriate use of materials and hung finished paintings on a drying rack near the rug on which Group B had snack at the end of the day. The teacher in Group A was stationed in the block area in the main room during the morning free-play period. She praised appropriate use of blocks and other materials available in this area. These area assignments remained in effect throughout the study. Thus, while reinforcing with snack at the end of the day verbal behavior for describing painting or block building, teachers were also giving social approval for the behavior itself (as for many other behaviors) if it occurred during the morning free-play period. This 30-min play period, which ended approximately 90 min before the end-of-the-day snack time, was the children's only opportunity to use these materials during the school day.

Reinforcement of correspondence. Next, only those statements of use of a material which corresponded to actual use of that material were reinforced with snack. For the next 27 days (Days 40 to 67), a child in Group B was presented snack for saying "I painted" only if he had actually used paint during the morning free-play period. The teacher confirmed the child's report of having painted ("You really did") and pointed out the picture, hanging on the drying rack, which he had made. At the same time, a child in Group A was presented snack for saying, "I built with blocks" only if he had actually used blocks during the morning free-play period. At the end of free-play, the teacher had each child who used blocks put two blocks on a separate shelf where they remained until the end of the day. Then the teacher in Group A, as she presented a child's snack, confirmed that child's report of having used blocks, ("You really did") and pointed out the two blocks on the shelf nearby. In both groups, if a child stated that he had used the material, but had not actually done so that day, the teacher said: "You didn't really, though, did you?", and either went on to another child whose hand was raised, or, if the child verbalized something else he had done, responded socially to that statement. Thus, the teacher responded socially to all children if they raised a hand, but presented snack only for a statement of use of a material that corresponded to actual use of that material.

Results

Recording. The results of Exp. 1 are graphed in Fig. 1. The data graphed as "said" (the dotted line) were taken from the observers' long-hand records of everything said by each child during the end-of-day snack period. Each child of the number present in the observed group was counted if he was recorded as saying the reinforced content ("I" plus some form of "paint" or "block/build") one or more times; the percentage of each group who "said" blocks or paint was then derived. Percentages were graphed, rather than actual numbers of children, because of occasional absences among the groups. Reliability between each of the observers and the third (alternating) observer was calculated in terms of the total instances of occurrence or non-occurrence of the behavior (whether a given child said, or did not say, on a given day, "blocks/build" or "paint" one or more times) recorded by each of the prime observers which were also recorded by the third observer when the two were observing together. The agreement between the third observer and the observer in Group A was 97%; between the third observer and the observer in Group B the agreement was 95%.

The data graphed as "did" (solid line) in the lower portion of Fig. 1 (Paint) were taken entirely from the records kept by the teacher in Group B, who noted time spent painting by each child who entered her area during the indoor free-play period. The data graphed (solid line) in the upper portion of Fig. 1 (Blocks) were, beginning at the heavy solid lines, taken from the records kept by the teacher in Group A, who noted the time spent by each child using the materials in the block area. The data graphed with the light solid line in Fig. 1, (Blocks) were taken from the 15-min sample records of the three regular observers. These observers, while recording all a given child's verbalizations for 15 min, noted every material used and the time span of its use by that child in that 15 min. Only half of the children, rotated from day to day, were so observed during the indoor free-play period; therefore, these observer records constitute a sampling of the group's use of materials. The portion of Fig. 1 (Blocks) in which the heavy

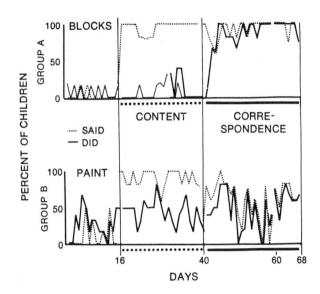

FIGURE 1 Percent of children who reported use (said) and who actually used (did) blocks (Group A) and paint (Group B). During the condition labelled CONTENT, reports of the use of blocks (or paint) were reinforced whether or not the children had actually used that material that day. During the condition labelled CORRESPONDENCE, reports of the use of blocks (or paint) were reinforced *only* if the children had actually used that material that day.

and light solid lines overlap compares the number of children who "did" blocks as recorded by the teacher (heavy solid line) and by observer sampling (light solid line). With both groups throughout this study, the specific child whom an observer designated as using blocks and/or paint in every case was among those children recorded by teachers as using that material that day.

In Fig. 1 the data points for the number of children who "did" use a material are offset at changes in conditions: that is, Day 16 is both the last day of baseline on "doing" and the first day of reinforcement of content for "saying", and Day 40 is both the last day of reinforcement of content on "doing" and the first day of reinforcement of correspondence for "saying". This is because snack time followed indoor play each day, such that when conditions changed at snack time, any effects on the percentage of children engaging in the reported activity would not be seen until the next day.

Baseline. The data shown indicate that more of the children in Group A may actually have used blocks during the baseline period than are represented in Fig. 1 (Blocks); however, these data indicate, as well, that the number was not large. The median percentage of children reporting using blocks was 0%; only two children reported using blocks (once each) during this period. During baseline the median percentage of painting was 20% of the children in Group B per day. While the median percentage of reporting having painted was 0%, the actual instances were higher than those of reporting use of blocks; on only three days however, did the number reporting correspond to the number who actually painted.

Reinforcement of content. When snack was contingent on verbalizing use of blocks or paint, the number of children who "said" the reinforced content rose to a median of 100% in both groups, and remained at 80 to 100% (except for Day 28 in Group B) throughout this condition. No reliable effect on use of the corresponding materials was correlated with this increase in verbal behavior. The number of children in Group A who used blocks during the indoor free-play period remained at baseline level of 0-2 (0 to 33%, 0% median) per day; the percentage of children in Group B who painted rose somewhat, initially, to a median of 50% per day, a number which, in the course of this experimental condition, gradually decreased to a median of 33% per day.

Reinforcement of correspondence. When snack was made contingent on correspondence between the verbal report and the non-verbal behavior, the number of children in Group A who used blocks during the indoor free-play period rose to correspond to the 80 to 100% of the group that reported such use. The median percentage of both saying and doing was 100%. In Group B on the other hand, the number of children reporting painting declined (to a median of 40%) to correspond to the 25% (median) of the children who had actually painted. On only three occasions during this condition did a child who had actually used the materials on a given day fail to so report, once in Group A, and twice in Group B. The divergence in effect between the two groups took place after the eighth day of reinforcing correspondence; at first, the trend of the non-verbal behavior corresponding to the verbal behavior was upward both in Group B and in Group A. On the eighth day, however, only two children painted, and on the tenth day, none. Subsequently, few children in Group B reported painting unless they had done so, and the number of children painting varied from one to four each day (median 23%), a number slightly lower than during the condition of reinforcing content.

When an effect on actual use of the materials was seen, the relevance of the presence during the snack period of the materials themselves (the pictures painted and the two blocks on the shelf) was tested by interchanging the rugs the two groups were seated on. Being out of sight of the materials they were reporting having used did not alter the near-100% level and correspondence of the verbal and non-verbal behaviors of the children in Group A, and was correlated with a slight increase in the number of children in Group B who painted and correspondingly so reported each day.

Discussion

In both groups, the initial reinforcement of content (*i.e.*, when the children were given snacks for saying they used a material whether they actually had or not) produced a marked effect on the percent of children who reported (said) such use. But only a slight increase was noted in one of the groups in the percent of children who actually did use the materials. This slight increase in the number of children who painted may be a weak effect of the verbal conditioning procedures comparable to that found by Lovaas (1961, 1964) and Sherman (1964): one child in Group B who had not painted for the six previous days painted on each of the four days subsequent to first receiving snack for the verbalization of having painted. More probably however, the increased rate of painting should be attributed to adventitious reinforcement of correspondence between the verbal behavior and the actual use of paint. Two of the three children who had painted on the day that reinforcement of content was begun had painted only six and two times previously; one of these two children subsequently painted every day for the next 10 days, and the other child painted on 31 out of the next 33 days.

The reinforcement of correspondence (*i.e.*, when the children were given snack for saying they had played with the material only when they actually had played with the material) in both groups produced a high degree of correspondence between their verbal and non-verbal behaviors. However, the two groups differed in the manner in which this correspondence was reached. In Group A, this correspondence was a result of a sudden marked increase (from 0 to 100%) in the number of children who played with the material during the free-play time 90 min before the occasion for reinforced reporting. In Group B, this correspondence was a result of a cessation of reporting on the part of those children who had not actually played with the material during the free-play period. The effect in Group A could be characterized as demonstrating the control of reinforcing the children's verbal behavior during group time on their non-verbal behavior during the free-play period on the following day. The effect in Group B could be characterized as the children discriminating (differentially responding on the basis of) their own non-verbal behavior during the preceding free-play time on the same day.

A factor that may have contributed to the difference in effects in Groups A and B was the difference in response requirements for using paint and for using blocks. In order to use blocks, a child had only to ask for, and be handed one (or two) which he could stack on the floor and then put up on the shelf. In order to use paint, on the other hand, a child had to emit a fairly long chain of responses in order to acquire an apron, paint, brushes, and paper, before he could arrive at a "painting". In addition, painting was done in a side room rather than in the main preschool room where most other activities (including breakfast and block play) were located.

A second question concerned the discriminative properties of putting two blocks on the shelf: though the exchange of areas between the groups on Day 61 demonstrated that it made no difference whether the materials were within view at snack time, the original placement of the blocks on the shelf may have functioned in some way to reinforce play with blocks (for instance, as a token "guarantee" that snack would be forthcoming later).

These two questions were investigated in Exp. II, in the course of replicating Exp. I in Group A.

A third question concerned the marked decline in verbal behavior in Group B to the level of the occurrence of the non-verbal behavior. With this decline, any stimulus properties of reinforcing the verbal behavior which might have contributed to actual use of the corresponding material were present much less frequently at snack time: there was little "saying" for "doing" to correspond to. While the reporting of those children who had not painted on a given day was no longer reinforced with snack, it produced the teacher's comment: "You really didn't though, did you?" During the last 18 days of reinforcement of correspondence, children in Group B who had not painted that day rarely reported having done so more than once at the outset of snack time; after the teacher responded: "You didn't really though, did you?" to that statement, these children talked of other activities (and were responded to socially by the teacher when they did so). Thus, under the reinforcement of correspondence procedures, the low rate of painting resulted in a condition in which punishment as well as extinction could have produced the observed decline in reporting.

Experiment III investigated the function of the food snack in maintaining reporting and the function of the teachers' comments in reducing reporting, in the course of replicating Exp. I in Group B.

Table 1 presents the number of days in each experimental condition for Group A and Group B, the material of reported use, and the contingency for food reinforcement in that condition.

EXPERIMENT II

Experiment II was designed to investigate whether repeated replication of Exp. I in Group A (reinforcement of content followed by reinforcement

TABLE 1   Table of conditions

	Material	Reinforce	Days
Group A (N = 6) Baseline			15
Exp. I	Blocks	Content Correspondence	24 28
Exp. II	Paint	Content Correspondence	12 17
	Blocks	Content Correspondence	13 13
	Keg	Content	6
	Tower	Content Correspondence	4 4
	Books	Content Correspondence	1 1
Group B (N = 6) Baseline			15
Exp. I	Paint	Content Correspondence	24 28
Exp. III	Paint	Content Correspondence	29 15
	Blocks	Content	9
+ teacher comments		Content	7
− teacher comments		Correspondence	10
+ teacher comments		Correspondence	5

of correspondence) would result, in time, in the children's verbal behavior beginning to control their non-verbal behavior, such that "saying" would lead to "doing".

Procedures

Preschool conditions, recording and experimental procedures were identical to those in Exp. I.

In order to replicate Exp. I, and at the same time investigate the role of the type of non-verbal response, the children in Group A were, beginning on the sixty-eighth day of school, given snack and social approval for verbalizing use of paint. No prompts were given: the teacher simply waited until one of the children verbalized that he had painted that day. After 12 days of reinforcing content, on Day 80, the children were given snack only if their verbal behavior corresponded to their non-verbal behavior (*i.e.*, if they had actually painted that day). As in Exp. I, the teacher confirmed the child's report as she presented snack ("That's right, you really did"), or disconfirmed it ("You didn't really though, did you?"); she responded socially to all other verbalizations.

On Day 97, after 17 days of reinforcing correspondence in painting (when the children reliably both painted and reported painting), the teacher in Group A returned to giving snack contingent upon only verbal behavior of the content "I played with the blocks". Thirteen days later, on Day 110, she began giving snack for correspondence between the verbal behavior at snack time and actual play with blocks during indoor free play that morning. All conditions, at snack time and during free play, were similar to those in the last seven days of Exp. I except that the children were not instructed to place two blocks on the shelf at the end of block play.

On Day 123, after 13 days of reinforcing correspondence (when the children reliably both played with blocks and reported it), the teacher in Group A began giving snack for the verbal behavior "I played with the kitty-in-the-keg". No actual use of the material was required, and the teacher neither confirmed nor disconfirmed the reports. (The kitty-in-the-keg was a small nest of barrels, a Montessori-type manipulative toy.) Since no child had played with the keg on the first day of reinforcement of content, the teacher prompted the response by asking: "What else did you play with in the block area?" such that the children, in the course of naming all the materials available in that area, eventually named the keg.

Six days later, on Day 129, the children in Group A were given snack for verbalizing use of the nesting tower (another Montessori-style manipulative toy). No prompts, confirmations, or disconfirmations were given and no actual use was required. On Day 133, the first day after fewer than five of the six children actually used the nesting tower during free play, the teacher began giving snack contingent on correspondence between the verbal behavior and the non-verbal behavior.

After four days, on Day 137, the children in Group A were given snack for verbalizing use of a book. The response was not prompted. The following day, the teacher gave snack only to children whose verbal behavior corresponded to their non-verbal behavior (those who had looked at a book during indoor free play). This move directly to reinforcing correspondence was made in order to offset the formation of a discrimination that the correspondence contingency never followed immediately upon the contingency for content.

Results

The third observer recorded with the regular observer during the snack period every other day (a total of six days) at the beginning of Exp. II; after the eighty-second day of school she observed with the regular observer on varying days of the week once every two weeks (a total of eight days). On all 14 of these days, agreement between the two observers, calculated in the same way as in Exp. I, was 100%. Checks of all the observers' records of the use of materials by given children on given days in every case confirmed the teachers' records of those children's use of that material that day.

The results of Exp. II are graphed in Fig. 2. The data are graphed in the same way as those in Fig. 1: "said" (the dotted line) represents the percentage of the children in the group recorded in the verbatim observer

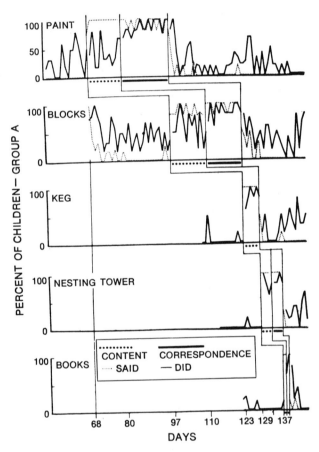

FIGURE 2 Percent of children in Group A who reported use at snack time (said) and who actually used (did) during free play paint, blocks, kitty-in-the-keg, nesting tower, and books. The dotted line below each x-axis indicates reinforcement of content; the solid line below each x-axis indicates reinforcement of correspondence.

records as verbalizing the reinforced content one or more times, and "did" represents the percentage of children in the group who used the given material, as noted by the teacher in the area. The data points for "did" are offset at changes in conditions, as in Fig. 1. Since they are typical, only the 15 days of baseline immediately before the condition of reinforcing content are shown in Fig. 2 for each material except blocks, where all days are shown subsequent to those shown in Fig. 1.

During the 15 days of baseline on painting, no child in Group A verbalized use of paint, while a median of 33% of the children actually painted. When snack was contingent on verbalizing use of paint, the number of children who reported painting increased to 100% of the group and remained there for 11 days. The number of children in the group who actually used paint increased slightly to a median of 40%. When snack was made contingent upon correspondence between the report and use of the material, both use of paint and reporting its use stabilized at a median of 100% of the group. The increase in painting to five or six out of the six children in Group A each day after snack was made contingent on correspondence, indicates that the difference between the tasks, block play and painting, could not in itself account for the difference between Group B and Group A in Exp. I.

Over the 29 days of reinforcing content and then correspondence in painting, the median percentage of children in Group A verbalizing use of blocks returned to the baseline level of zero. The use of blocks during this period declined to a median of 33% of the children per day. When the children were again given snack contingent on verbalizing use of blocks, 80 to 100% (median, 83%) of the children described use of blocks on the next 13 days. On the fourth day of thus reinforcing content, all six of the children used blocks during indoor free play; on subsequent days, four and five children used blocks (median, 67%). On three of the days of reinforcing content, all of the children who received reinforcement for the verbal content of "blocks", had used the blocks; that is, correspondence was in fact often reinforced when the contingency was for content only. The increase in the average number of children "doing" each day produced by this reinforcement of content (blocks) was greater than that produced by reinforcement of content (paint).

When correspondence between the verbal and non-verbal behavior was reinforced with snack, the average number of children using blocks rose to five to six each day (median, 83%) to match the number reporting such use (median, 100%). This correspondence took place sooner than it had in Exp. I: only on the sixth day of reinforcing correspondence in Exp. I did all of these children use blocks; in Exp. II all of the children used blocks during free play on the third day of reinforcing correspondence. After this first 100% day, the subsequent numbers of children using and reporting blocks each day in Exp. I and II are comparable at five to six children per day. Since the two blocks were not put up on the shelf in the correspondence condition of Exp. II, as they were in Exp. I, such placement was shown to be, at least on replication, not necessary for the effect on block play.

On the second day after reinforcement of reporting use (content) of the kitty-in-the-keg, 80% of the children in the group played with this material during indoor free play, as opposed to the one child during the preceding 13 days of baseline. The number of children using the keg remained at 80 to 100% (median, 83%) on the four subsequent days. With 100% of the children reporting the use of this material, only two children were given snack (once each) on these four days when their non-verbal behavior did not correspond to their verbal behavior. On the first day after reinforcing the verbal behavior, "I played with the nesting tower", all six of the children in Group A engaged in the non-verbal behavior, whereas only one of them had used the nesting tower (once) during the prior 15 days. The number of children using the nesting tower during free play declined (by one child each day) over the next two days. When snack was made contingent on correspondence, the number of children using the nesting tower returned to 100% after two days. The first day after reinforcing the verbalization of looking at a book, four of the six children asked for books during free play indoors, whereas only two children had done so during the previous 10 days. All six of the children looked at a book the next day, after correspondence had been reinforced at snack time. In all cases, when the reinforcement contingency was shifted to reporting a new material, the percent of children who used and reported the previous material declined systematically, approaching the baseline level.

Discussion

Experiment II shows that, over time, "saying" did lead to "doing" for most of the children in Group A: verbal behavior on the prior day controlled non-verbal behavior (the selection of a play material) on the following day. Across the last four materials, four to six of the children in Group A used each material in turn, in Exp. II, when only the verbalization of use of that material was reinforced with snack. On four occasions, all of the children used a material during free play subsequent to being reinforced for just saying they used it. In these circumstances, correspondence was in fact being reinforced, though the requirement was only of content. It may be that an observed correlation between verbal and non-verbal behavior in everyday situations occurs as a result of some such process: that correspondence between verbal and non-verbal behavior is "accidentally" reinforced, by a reinforcer scheduled not for correspondence, but for either the verbal content or the non-verbal behavior alone, or even for an unrelated behavior.

EXPERIMENT III

Concurrent with Exp. II, Exp. III was conducted with Group B. Recording procedures and preschool conditions were unchanged from Exp. I. The first purpose of Exp. III was to replicate Exp. I in Group B through a reversal to the condition of reinforcement of content in order to increase the verbal behavior, to be followed once again by reinforcement of correspondence.

Procedures

Beginning on the sixty-eighth day of school, after 28 days of reinforcing correspondence in Exp. I, the children in Group B were given snack for verbalizing use of paint whether they actually used it that day or not. The teacher responded socially to the children as she had during the prior condition of reinforcement of content: she approved a child's verbal behavior while offering snack, and responded socially to any other comments made by the children, but neither confirmed nor disconfirmed any child's report of using paint.

After 29 days, on Day 97, when all the children were again reporting use of paint, and actual use was comparable to use during the first condition of reinforcement of content, reinforcement of correspondence was reintroduced. Children were given snack only when their verbal behavior at snack time corresponded to their non-verbal behavior during indoor free play. As in the prior condition of reinforcement of correspondence, the teacher confirmed a child's report while offering snack ("You really did"), or disconfirmed his report by saying: "You didn't really, though, did you?". Any other comments made by children were socially responded to by the teacher as before. Snack was contingent on correspondence for the next 15 days.

In the course of replicating the effects with a new material, an attempt was made to separate the role of the teacher's comments on the reporting from that of food presentation. Beginning on the Day 112 of school, the children in Group B were given snack for reporting use of blocks. The criteria for reinforcible verbal behavior were the same as in the previous conditions of reinforcing content: a positive statement of use containing both "I" and the name of the material. The behavior was not initially prompted. All statements on the part of the children were responded to socially by the teacher, but snack was given only for statements of use of blocks. No comments on block play were made by the teacher.

After 10 days of reinforcing content in the same manner as in the two prior conditions of reinforcement of content, teacher confirmation or disconfirmation of the child's verbal behavior (as previously presented only in the condition of reinforcement of correspondence) was introduced into the condition of reinforcement of content. However, snack continued to be given for all verbalizations of use of blocks. The teacher said (instead of her usual general statement of approval): "That's right, you really did" as she offered snack to a child who had actually used blocks; if the child had not used blocks that day, she said as she offered snack: "You didn't really, though, did you?". All other statements by children were responded to socially by the teacher as in prior conditions.

Seven days later on Day 129, conditions were changed to the reinforcement of correspondence. Snack was presented for reporting use of blocks only if blocks had actually been used during indoor free play that day. However, no differential social response was made to the verbalization. The teacher neither confirmed nor disconfirmed a child's report: she said "mmmhmm" to all statements of use of blocks, but offered snack only to those children who had actually used the material.

After 10 days, while snack was still contingent on correspondence, the differential social response was reintroduced: the teacher again said, as she presented snack to a child whose report of block play corresponded to actual use of the material that day: "That's right, you really did". To a child who reported block play without having actually used blocks, the teacher responded: "You didn't really, though, did you?". Any statements other than reports of block play were socially responded to as in all prior conditions.

Results

The third observer recorded with the regular observer in Group B every other day (a total of six days) at the beginning of Exp. III; after the eighty-second day of school she recorded with the regular observer on varying days of the week once every two weeks (a total of six days). Over the 12 days that reliability checks were made, the inter-observer agreement that each child did or did not verbalize the reinforced content on that day was 98%: there was one disagreement on one child on Day 112. The third observer's records, taken on the other four days of each week after the eighty-second day of school in every case confirmed the description of the social responses given by the teacher to children across the succeeding conditions of Exp. III. Checks of all the observers' records of the use of materials by given children on given days also in every case confirmed the teachers' records of those childrens' use of that material that day. Reliability was taken on one day in each of the conditions during reinforcement of reporting use of blocks; the inter-observer agreement on the number of times per snack time each child verbalized use of blocks was 96%.

The results of Exp. III are graphed in Fig. 3. The dotted line, "said", represents the percent of children in the group recorded in the observer records as verbalizing the reinforced content one or more times, and the solid line, "did", represents the percentage of children in the group who used a given material, as recorded by the teacher in the area. The data points for "did" are offset at changes in conditions, as in Fig. 1 and 2. The first day of "said" (paint) in Fig. 3 coincides with the final day (Day 68) of "did" in Fig. 1.

On the first seven days after the reversal to reinforcement of content

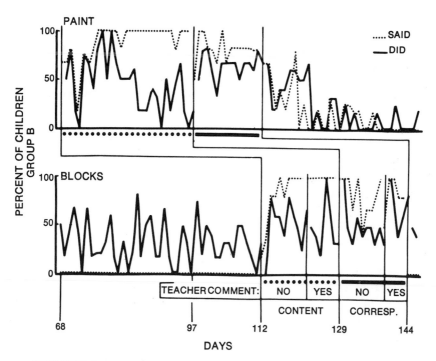

FIGURE 3   Percent of children in Group B who reported use (said) and who actually used (did) paint and blocks. Teacher comments (confirmation: "You really did," when a child reporting use of blocks had actually used blocks during free play that day, or disconfirmation: "You didn't really though, did you?" when a child reporting use of blocks had not actually used them that day), were not presented (NO) during the first part of the CONTENT and CORRESPON-DENCE conditions (blocks) but were presented (YES) during the second part of these two conditions.

in Group B, the correspondence of the verbal behavior to the non-verbal behavior was very similar to that of the prior condition of reinforcement of correspondence; it was nine days before all six children again reported painting. This increase to 100% reporting preceded by one day a similar increase in the non-verbal behavior; on two days (77 and 79 in Fig. 3) every child in the group painted, the first occurrences of 100% "doing" in the entire course of the experiment in Group B. Thereafter, while the number reporting painting remained at 100%, the number of children actually painting gradually decreased to the Exp. I baseline level of a median of 18%. It was not until the eighteenth day of again giving snack for the verbal behavior alone, that each of the children in the group had at least once reported painting without actually having engaged in painting.

When correspondence was again required, the initial effect was comparable to that in Exp. I: on the first day a drop in the number of children who reported painting, followed in succeeding days by an increase in both the non-verbal and the verbal behavior, and then by subsequent decline in verbal behavior to correspond approximately to the non-verbal behavior. Perhaps due to additional strengthening in the second condition of reinforcement of content, the verbal and non-verbal behaviors did not decline in Exp. III as much as they had in Exp. I: rather, they stabilized with a median of 83% of the children regularly reporting, while a median of 67% of the children were actually painting each day. When the criterion for reinforcement was shifted to another material on Day 112, the percentage of children either painting or reporting painting slowly declined to medians of 0%.

When the children in Group B were given snack for verbalizing use of blocks the number of children who reported such use, zero during baseline, increased to 100%. Actual use of blocks during indoor free play, which during baseline was at a median of 33% of the children per day, increased somewhat to a median of 60% during reinforcement of content. As can be seen in Fig. 3, there was no further trend toward correspondence. While the overall number of children using blocks actually declined somewhat to the baseline median of 33% per day when the teacher added confirmation or disconfirmation of each child's report while still reinforcing content, reporting remained at 100% of the group.

Actual use of blocks increased to 100% of the children on the day after reinforcement of correspondence was introduced without teacher confirmation or disconfirmation but stabilized at 50% of the children per day. The number of children reporting use of blocks decreased until, on the sixth day of this condition, only those two children who had played with blocks during indoor free play that morning reported having done so, an effect similar to that seen with this group in Exp. I (paint) and Exp. III (paint). The number of children reporting rose, however, on the subsequent days such that on Day 138 it was again 100%.

As seen upon the two prior introductions of the requirement of correspondence at snack time (for paint), when teacher confirmation-disconfirmation was added to the presentation of snack for reporting block play, the number of children so reporting dropped on the first day of the condition, and then rose again on the second day. Subsequently, the number of children reporting remained at 80 to 100%. Actual use of blocks increased to a median of 60% in this condition, but due to the end of the school year, there are not enough data points to evaluate this trend adequately.

Figure 4 shows for each condition in Fig. 3 (blocks), the average number of times per day per child that block play was reported by those children who had actually used blocks that day, and by those children who had not used blocks. It can be seen that during reinforcement of content only, children reported use of blocks equally often whether they had actually played with the blocks or not: 2.5 times per child per snack time.

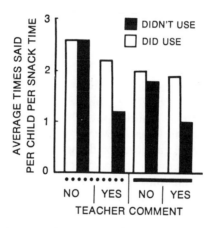

FIGURE 4   Average times use of blocks was reported in Group B per child per snack time by those children who had actually used blocks (open bar) and by those children who had not actually used blocks (solid bar) during free play.

When, while still presenting snack for content only, the teacher added confirmation or disconfirmation of the child's report, the rate of reporting by those children who had actually used blocks remained at twice or more per day, while reporting by children who had not used blocks dropped to a little more than once per day. Confirmation did not increase the rate of reporting. On the other hand, the child who reported: "I played with the blocks", and received snack plus the teacher's response: "You didn't really though, did you?", seldom reported block play again that day. Disconfirmation by the teacher appeared, thus, to reduce the rate per child of reporting within snack time, even though it did not reduce the per cent of children so reporting at least once each day.

The presentation of snack alone for correspondence, without teacher confirmation or disconfirmation, led to a decrease in the number of children reporting (Fig. 3) but to an increase in rate of reporting by those children who had not used blocks (Fig. 4). Of the children who had not used blocks and therefore received no snack, those who reported did so nearly as often as did the children who were receiving snack: about twice per snack time, a rate more comparable to that when snack was presented for just the verbal behavior. Those children who continued reporting when they had not actually used the materials were those whose rates of reporting were not sensitive to differential food reinforcers alone.

When teacher confirmation or disconfirmation was added to the contingency for correspondence, the rate of reporting by children who had not used blocks again decreased to once per child per snack time. The twice-per-snack-time average reporting rate for children who had used blocks that day did not change.

Discussion

Reinforcing verbal reporting alone, which (after eight days) produced 100% of the children reporting, was followed by an increase in the percentage of children actually painting to 100% on two days, a level never previously reached with this group. However, with continued reinforcement of verbal reporting alone, the level of doing subsequently declined, producing the discrepancy between the percentage of children reporting and the percentage of children doing previously seen with these children in the comparable condition in Exp. I. Reinforcing again on the basis of correspondence between verbal and non-verbal behavior again produced a level of correspondence similar to that seen with this group in the comparable condition in Exp. I: the percent of children reporting dropped somewhat to correspond to the percent actually using the material. However, the level of non-verbal behavior increased markedly, such that a greater number of children in this group were both doing and saying than in Exp. I. The decline in the number of children actually using paint when the reinforcement contingency was shifted to another material indicates the function of the reinforcement contingencies in maintaining the use of paint in the preceding condition.

The investigation of the role of the teacher's comments in producing the correspondence in this group, particularly the role of disconfirmation ("You didn't really, though, did you?") in producing the drop in percent of children reporting, revealed that whereas this variable apparently functioned as a mild punishing stimulus, it did not account for the drop in percent of children verbally reporting. Although the teacher's disconfirmation was functional in reducing the rate of a child (who had not actually used the reported material) repeatedly reporting the use of the material during snack time, it did not affect the probability of his similarly reporting during snack time on the following day. Differential food reinforcement was apparently the functional variable in producing this drop in verbal behavior. In the correspondence condition, the correlation between reinforcement for reporting and a child's actually having engaged in the non-verbal behavior was apparently sufficient to produce at least an initial decline in reporting. The role of the teacher's comments could probably best be characterized as additional discriminative stimuli specifying the contingencies for reinforcement. In the absence of differential food reinforcement, the teacher's comments had no discernible effect either on reducing the percent of children reporting or in increasing the percent of children actually using the material.

GENERAL DISCUSSION

By the end of this study, several of the children in Group B and all of the children in Group A were clearly emitting non-verbal behavior under the control of the stimulus of differential reinforcement for verbal behavior 22.5 hr (and even 60 hr over weekends) earlier. The present training procedures had developed a generalized correspondence between the verbal and non-verbal behaviors of these children such that their temporally remote non-verbal behavior could be modified by simply reinforcing their verbal behavior. With these children the correspondence between verbal and non-verbal behavior appeared to be a functional sequence of differential reinforcement of verbal behavior affecting non-verbal behavior such that differential reinforcement of "saying" led to "doing". The remaining children in Group B (and all of the children in Group B in the earlier portions of the study) conversely were clearly demonstrated to be differentially responding verbally on the basis of the discriminative stimulus of their own non-verbal behavior 1.5 hr earlier. In this case, differential reinforcement of saying served to bring the children's verbal behavior under the discriminative control of their own non-verbal behavior such that "doing" led to "saying" and "not-doing" led to "not-saying". Even in this group, there were times (*e.g.* during the second reinforcement of content with paint on Days 77 and 79) when saying did lead to doing for all subjects.

The increase in the number of children who engaged in the non-verbal behavior during the second correspondence condition (paint), as compared with the first correspondence condition in Group B, indicates that with a continuation of the sequence of reinforcing content and then reinforcing correspondence (with either the same or new materials) as was carried out with Group A, it is likely that for all the children in Group B the effect seen in Group A of saying leading to doing would have been produced. Except on the initial day of the first correspondence condition for each group, the teachers did not mention the materials which were the basis for differential reinforcement. The children's own verbal behavior appeared to acquire stimulus properties such that their own (or other children's) reports served as instructions for them.

To produce a reliable saying-doing correspondence between verbal and non-verbal behavior, several conditions may have been initially critical. The "difficulty" or probability of occurrence of the non-verbal behavior may have contributed to the differential effect between Group A and Group B in Exp. I, even though later in the study it was shown not to be functional. The token placement of two blocks on the shelf and the teacher's confirmation may have initially served as functional discriminative stimuli to "bridge" the considerable time span involved in the study and to make explicit the reinforcement contingencies. These factors which were not necessary in the later stages of the experiment for saying to lead to doing, may have been critical, especially in combination, to the initial effect. The food reinforcer, which was demonstrated to be critical in producing the effect, was not dependent upon any discernible level of food deprivation, as it was delivered less than 1 hr after the second meal of the children's 3-hr preschool day. In this study, involving disadvantaged Negro preschool children, the non-verbal behavior "directed" by the children's own verbal behavior was performed the next day almost 24 hr after the verbal behavior occurred, and the reinforcement of correspondence between verbal and non-verbal behavior took place 1.5 hr after the occasion for the non-verbal behavior. The characterization of members of this population as unable to plan ahead or delay gratification (Mischel, 1958), if at all true, appears not to apply at age four.

REFERENCES

Lovaas, O. I. Interaction between verbal and nonverbal behavior, *Child Development*, 1961, **32**, 329–336.

Lovaas, O. I. Control of food intake in children by reinforcement of relevant verbal behavior, *Journal of Abnormal and Social Psychology*, 1964, **68**, 672–678.

Mischel, W. Preference for delayed reinforcement: an experimental study of a cultural observation. *Journal of Abnormal and Social Psychology*, 1958, **56**, 57–61.

Sherman, J. A. Modification of non-verbal behavior through reinforcement of related verbal behavior. *Child Development*, 1964, **35**, 717–723.

4

FEARS IN CHILDREN

The emotional experience of the disturbed child has traditionally been a major concern in his treatment. Terms referring to emotions are numerous and commonplace; and it is natural to infer, from their high frequency in literature and speech, that they are important psychological constructs. The child is assumed to display his feelings through his behavior: resentment, timidity, insecurity, love, tension, inadequacy, joy, hostility, excitement, anxiety, and so on. The sensitive therapist or parent tries to recognize and respond to the underlying emotion.

Terms referring to emotion, however, have an elusive character. Their use as descriptive terms often serves to give the illusion that an explanation for an observed behavior is being offered, when in fact the behavior is simply being labeled. For example, it is common to say that a child cries because he is disturbed, hurt, or fearful. But the line of inference could easily be the reverse—that he is upset because he is crying. Underlying emotional states are not directly observable, and inferences from the behavior to its determining state do not seem useful unless the inferred condition or state can be tied to other observable behavioral and environmental events. For example, if reference to a state variable such as "fear" is to be made useful, it seems necessary to show that the use of this variable reconciles or integrates behavioral and environmental events more effectively than could be done otherwise. Thus, a child who is afraid may cry, become incontinent, throw things, refuse food, or strike adults. The mutual relations among these behaviors show the value of an integrating construct that might be labeled "fear." Similarly, fear may be related to several specific environmental conditions such as loss of love or pain. These relations give status to the inferred concept, "fear," as a summarizing descriptive term. But such terms as yet have been empirically difficult to define.

The problem is not simply academic. Treatment procedures have been affected greatly by inference of underlying states and by the assumed relations between these states and environmental events. Caretakers commonly infer that a child who cries is anxious or disturbed; and an anxious child should be comforted, understood, and reassured. Here the alleviation of the emotional state is of major concern, and this state is assumed to depend primarily on the events that preceded it. More psychologically elaborate arguments often tend to similar conclusions. But research indicating how emotional states are acquired or modified in humans is far rarer than this treatment emphasis would appear to warrant. For example, controlled research to modify human pathological fear is of quite recent origin, dating primarily from the work of Wolpe in the 1950s.

The papers presented here deal with behaviors that usually are taken to indicate anxiety or fearfulness. They represent therapeutic studies of the events that accompany expressions of "fearful" behavior and of the modification of such fears through changes in these events, or contingencies. They do not all take the same view of the usefulness of "fear" as a conceptualization of the behavior under treatment. They all do proceed, however, on the assumption that alleviating the child's "fearful" behavior can best be achieved by bringing the child into an increasingly close relationship with the feared objects or events. Treatment may include use of the following: positive rewards for approach behavior toward the avoided objects or events; attachment of mildly aversive contingencies to the "fearful" behaviors; or gradual presentations of approximations of the "feared" situations to a relaxed or entertained child.

The technique for reduction of fear that is most commonly chosen in behavior therapy is called systematic desensitization. It has been used extensively with adults but much less frequently with children. Systematic desensitization resembles counter-conditioning. However, it is not exactly analogous, since it involves, for example, use of symbolic presentations of fear-producing stimuli. Obler and Terwilliger present a modified version of this technique that appears usable with both young retardates and normal children. Their procedure differs from systematic desensitization in several ways. However, desensitization is only one variation of many similar techniques that have been tried in the elimination of fears in humans and animals. There is strong evidence that some of these other modifications can also produce successful outcomes.

Bandura, Grusec, and Menlove's classic paper presents a procedure derived largely from human research that has shown how a child's observation of the behavior of a model may lead him to perform similar behavior. They demonstrate that fearful behavior may be reduced through this process of observational learning and speculate about the learning variables that produce its effectiveness. Imagine the social implications that are implied in their research. Treatment much like that reported in their article could be presented readily on television, making this medium a therapeutic agent.

Ayllon, Smith, and Rogers produce a treatment procedure for school phobia that is also based on learning research. They do not treat the problem as one of eliminating a classically acquired emotional response, but more simply as one of increasing the rate of a low rate behavior—attendance at school. They propose that the child's avoidance of school is a response intended to provide access to the greater rewards obtainable outside. Further, they hypothesize that the "emotional" behaviors that identify the avoidance as phobic are simply the effective operant behaviors that give access to this more rewarding state of affairs. Thus they emphasize controlling the consequences of the behavior rather than its antecedents. It is interesting to note that their procedure might also be derived from the assumption that the phobic behavior was evinced by fearfulness, since the procedure includes gradual exposure of the child to the "feared" school setting in a manner similar to systematic desensitization. The learning data on which these various procedures are based are more robust than the conceptual models that have been derived to explain them.

MARTIN OBLER
ROBERT F. TERWILLIGER
New School for Social Research

Pilot study on the effectiveness of systematic desensitization with neurologically impaired children with phobic disorders

A modified version of Wolpe's systematic desensitization therapy involving direct confrontation with the fear-inducing stimulus was attempted with neurologically impaired children with phobic symptoms. Two hypotheses were tested: (a) A nonverbal therapeutic technique not requiring motivation will produce successful symptom reduction for these children, and (b) awareness of therapeutic procedure is not necessary for successful results. Both hypotheses were confirmed. The implications of these results for further research on systematic desensitization therapy were discussed.

Certain traditional psychotherapies have operated on the theoretical assumption that patient-therapist interaction is a necessary prerequisite in the modification of undesirable behavior (Wolberg, 1954). Elaborate verbal exchange is assumed to be the mechanism through which modification occurs. The patient-therapist exchange focuses on behavior conflicts con-

Reprinted from Journal of Consulting and Clinical Psychology, 1970, 34, 314–18, with permission of the authors. Copyright 1970 by American Psychological Association, and reproduced by permission.

232

fronting the patients from present and past experiences. The role of the therapist is crucial in accomplishing a modification of the conflicting behavior. He uses the patient's free associations, transference projections, and countertransference responses as his tools (Freud, 1965). Without a therapist as an interpreter of the conflicting experiences, modification of the undesirable behavior would not occur.

In recent years, a large number of clinical investigations have deviated from the assumptions of the above model. One method of treatment employed by Wolpe (1958), systematic desensitization, has been effective in reducing undesirable responses in adults (Rachman, 1967). Recent clinical evidence has supported its successful use with monophobias (Wolpe, 1962a, 1962b), delinquency (Zimmerman & Zimmerman, 1962), enuresis (Lang & Melamed, 1969; Werry, 1966), maladaptive rage and anxiety (Bandura, 1961), etc. Moreover, Wolpe (1962a, 1962b) describes a treatment procedure in which a medical student was substituted for the ongoing therapist with no disruption occurring in the treatment of a phobic disorder. No apparent patient resistance occurred because of the transfer in therapists. Lazarus and Rachman (1957) report data indicating that a change of therapist enhanced treatment success by reducing the negative associations to a particular therapist.

Systematic desensitization therapy, based on Wolpe's reciprocal inhibition theory, requires little verbal capacity or treatment motivation.[1] A short examination of the theoretical assumptions demonstrates the logic of the above position. The theory assumes that maladaptive, fearful responses may be eliminated by the presentation of some other response presumably antagonistic to the fearful one. Whether the therapist uses muscle relaxation, classical conditioning of a neutral response, or operant reinforcement as a presumed fear antagonist, the "counterbalancing" principle of the therapy remains the same. By simply developing a counteracting response to the original fear-producing stimulus, we condition a reduction in the fear response. A patient may cognitively perceive the connection between the counteracting response and the fear-producing stimulus, but it is not a necessary requirement. With adults, Wolpe uses muscle relaxation as the conditioned response, but any reinforcement producing the same results could just as easily be substituted. Instead of developing a muscle relaxation schedule, the therapist and patient might develop a touch reminder schedule. Each time the patient feels the onset of fear, he automatically responds with the conditioned response of touching himself to remind him of the inappropriateness of this reaction. When the original

---

[1] Wolpe has extensively developed this theory in numerous studies he has conducted. The most elaborate description of the theory remains his original work, *Psychotherapy by Reciprocal Inhibition* (1958).

fear-producing stimulus no longer elicits a fear response, the therapy moves to a new stimulus previously established on a hierarchy of low-intensity to high-intensity fear responses. Relaxation or reminder responses are thus hypothesized to become effective in reducing the strength of the unconditioned stimulus. Furthermore, response generalization is hypothesized to occur and effectively operate in the patient's real-life situations (Wolpe, 1958).

The application of traditional therapeutic techniques to the treatment of childhood disorders has had to face the problem of the relatively low verbal ability of children (Freud, 1965). This has been met by various play therapy techniques among others (Subotnick, 1966). However, these more traditional techniques depend on attacking the "causes" of the disorder for their effectiveness. This approach assumes that somehow, the child develops insight or awareness into the nature of his problem. Furthermore, this insight requires some form of transference or intense interpersonal relationship with the therapist (Subotnick, 1966). If the disturbance becomes severe enough—as in the case of neurological impairment—it may become increasingly difficult to arrive at this requisite state of awareness due to the patient's loss of verbal and abstract ability. Thus, as Eysenck (1952) and Rachman (1965) have suggested, there would be limits to the effectiveness of traditionally oriented therapies in the case of severe emotional or neurological disturbances.

The behavior therapy techniques, rather than attacking the presumed causes of the disturbance, attack the symptoms themselves. These techniques make no assumptions about the necessity of awareness of a transference relationship. This factor alone would suggest the desirability of applying these techniques to the severely disturbed child. While various attempts have been made to apply behavior therapy techniques to children, there have been very few attempts to use the specific technique of systematic desensitization described above (Ferster & Simons, 1966; Lovaas, Freitag, Gold, & Kassarla, 1965). However, the literature which exists does suggest that systematic desensitization could be an effective technique in the treatment of phobias in children (Jensen & Wamach, 1967; Lazarus, 1958). Rachman (1965) further points out that its use with severe chronic and neurologically impaired persons is limited but promising. He suggests broadening the use of systematic desensitization to these populations.

This study was conducted to further test the validity of applying systematic desensitization to the treatment of severely disturbed children, specifically to a population hitherto unstudied—neurologically impaired children. It would appear that systematic desensitization, which attempts to attack symptoms directly without requiring any great verbal skill or abstract ability on the part of the patient, would be very well suited to the treatment of a population of neurologically impaired children.

METHOD

Subject Selection

Thirty emotionally disturbed, neurologically impaired children were selected to participate in the study. They were drawn from a population of 150 children diagnosed as having minimal brain dysfunction with severe monophobic disorder. The monophobic disorder was one of two types: either (*a*) phobia regarding the use of a public bus or (*b*) phobia regarding the sight of a live dog. The Ss having both phobias were excluded from the study. The diagnoses were supplied by the clinic currently servicing the children medically.[2] Fifteen Ss were selected at random for the treatment condition (E group) and exposed to a modified version of the Wolpe desensitization method developed by the authors. The remaining 15 Ss served as controls (C group) and were matched with E group Ss for age, sex, intelligence, and phobic diagnosis. Each E group S was matched with an individual therapist by placing the names of all therapists in a bowl with corresponding numbers for each S. A number and name were selected simultaneously, with the chosen pair remaining together throughout the 10-week period of treatment.

Therapist Training

All 15 therapists were college graduates having no previous training or experience with neurologically impaired children or psychotherapeutic techniques. They were trained by the authors to apply a modified version of the Wolpe method and were instructed not to deviate from the training procedures throughout the course of treatment. The training consisted of two five-hour sessions during a two-week period, in which they were intensively instructed in how to dispense the rewards in attempting to decondition the monophobia. Each therapist was remunerated at the rate of $5 per five-hour session.

Design

Therapist and S met for the first time at the initial therapy session. Each session consisted of a five-hour weekly meeting over a 10-week period. Treatment consisted of exposing each S to the fear-inducing stimulus as it

[2] The authors wish to thank the New York Association for Brain Injured Children, Brooklyn Chapter, for making available the Ss for the research as well as the appropriate diagnostic material. In addition, partial funding for the pilot study was given through their auspices.

appeared in his everyday life. Typically, in desensitization therapy, the patient is asked to imagine the stimulus without actually being exposed to it. The reinforcement then occurs by teaching him to relax in the face of the imagined stimulus. With the relatively nonverbal, unimaginative Ss, this procedure was out of the question. The modification developed by the authors placed S in direct confrontation with the fear-producing stimulus, but with the therapist acting as a buffer between the two. That is, the therapist protected S from intense anxiety emerging from exposure to the real phobic stimulus, and rewarded him by approval for successful tolerance of it.

Prior to exposure to the real phobic stimulus, Ss were asked to look at pictures or models of the fear-inducing stimulus (bus or dog). This eliminated the need for S to imagine the stimulus. Cooke (1966) showed that actual exposure to the fear-inducing stimulus was more effective than merely imagining the stimulus. When S's behavior indicated a tolerance of the picture or model, he was then exposed to the actual fear-producing stimulus (bus or dog). The therapist continuously rewarded S through encouragement for moving closer and closer to the object. Eventually, Ss were able to move up the scale to more anxiety-producing stimulus (e.g., touching the bus or dog). At this point, S was given the option of exposure to the stimulus without the presence of the therapist. A new reward was offered at this time which included toys, books, pets, and candy chosen by S at an earlier session with the therapist.

These rewards were dispensed immediately at the time of successful completion of the defined task (e.g., talking to the bus driver, putting a token in the box, staying in the room with a dog). If an S overcame the phobia prior to completion of the tenth session, he continued to be reinforced by the therapist for his success. Successful handling of the fear-inducing stimulus was considered to be its generalization to S's daily life without the presence of the therapist. This was measured by a parent report scale administered to all E and C group members prior to and at the completion of the treatment period.

It should be clear that the technique used in this study differs from the traditional systematic desensitization technique in four ways: (a) There is no training in relaxation involved in this study.[3] (b) There was no attempt to ask S to develop a hierarchy of anxiety-producing situations to then be treated from the least to the most severe. In effect, a hierarchy was used, but it was determined arbitrarily by the E. (c) It was assumed that reinforcement per se was sufficient to bring about removal of the phobic symptom. No assumption about a link between the autonomic nervous system and relaxation was required or made. (d) There was no

---

[3] This is contrary to Lamont and Edwards' (1967) finding that relaxation training is necessary for successfully reducing phobias.

requirement or demand made of the S to indicate verbally the experience of lowered anxiety. Only overt behavioral manifestations were used, with the therapist making the judgment as to whether or not anxiety had been lowered and tolerance of the fear-producing stimulus shown.

Measurement of Treatment Success—Aware and Unaware Subjects

As indicated earlier, the authors' contention was that intellectual awareness of treatment procedure is not a necessity for insuring success in treatment. Measurement of treatment awareness, it was assumed, might be reflected in S's IQ score (based on the Wechsler Intelligence Scale for Children). An arbitrary cutoff point (a score of 75) was established as the critical value. Those Ss with scores below a 75 IQ were assumed to be minimally aware of treatment procedures, while those above 75 were considered more likely to be aware. The assumption that IQ is highly correlated with awareness was based on the observable behavior of those Ss with an IQ score below 75. These Ss appeared oblivious to most stimulation in their immediate environment, and were extremely detached and relatively indifferent to the influence of others on them. The intelligence test was administered to each S prior to selection for placement in the E and C groups. Ten E and nine C Ss scored above 75. There were, therefore, five minimally aware E Ss and six minimally aware C Ss (Table 1). The authors recognize the arbitrary nature of selecting an IQ score as a measure of treatment awareness. However, it appears reasonable that a child with an IQ score below 75 functions on a level of very limited awareness and could therefore be used as a standard for a minimum likelihood of awareness of treatment procedures.[4]

The basic measure for treatment effectiveness was a parent rating scale administered to each S's parents prior to and at the completion of treatment. The scale consisted of 10 questions concerning the child's functioning in society, 1 of which tapped the critical phobic behavior. This question was as follows:

Bus Phobia: A. Has your child recently been able to ride a bus? 0—No. 1—Yes, when accompanied by another person. 2—Yes, completely on his own.

Dog Phobia: B. Has your child recently been able to touch a dog? 0—No. 1—Yes, with the help of another person. 2—Yes, completely on his own.

The remaining questions dealt with S's functioning in school, with peers, etc., and were included to prevent a favorable response by parents desiring

---

[4] The authors are currently developing a more refined technique for determining an S's awareness of treatment.

TABLE 1 Comparison of IQ scores, age, and parent rating for treated and untreated subjects

		Treated			Untreated	
Subjects	Age	IQ	Score at completion of treatment	Age	IQ	Score at completion of treatment
Unaware						
1	7-1	66	2	7-3	67	0
2	9-5	65	1	9-3	68	0
3	9-6	71	1	9-8	64	0
4	10-2	50	2	10-7	73	1
5	10-5	68	2	10-5	57	0
6				9-3	60	0
Aware						
1	10-1	85	1	10-0	86	0
2	12-0	80	2	11-9	81	0
3	9-3	115	2	9-3	146	0
4	7-6	107	2	7-8	106	0
5	9-4	96	2	9-6	94	1
6	10-3	79	1	10-6	81	0
7	11-1	102	1	10-7	103	1
8	9-2	95	1	9-4	96	0
9	10-3	97	2	10-5	95	0
10	11-4	99	1			

TABLE 2 Proportion of success of at least "1"

IQ group	Treated	Untreated
Below 75	5/5	1/6
Above 75	10/10	2/9
Total	15/15	3/15

their child's continued participation in the program. The parents were not aware of the purpose of the research and assumed that their child attended a weekly recreation program. The parent rating was used as the best measure of treatment success on the belief that a person close to a phobic patient is in a good position to observe any reduction of symptoms that generalize to his daily life. All Ss received a 0 rating on an administration of the rating scale made prior to treatment.

RESULTS

The after-treatment measure for both groups appears in Table 1. A score of 1 indicates a reduction in the phobic system sufficient to insure S's ability (as reported by the parents) to ride a bus or touch a dog with the help

TABLE 3   Proportion of success of at least "2"

IQ group	Treated	Untreated
Below 75	3/5	0/6
Above 75	5/10	0/9
Total	8/15	0/15

of another person. A score of 2 indicates this ability without any need for assistance. Each S in the treated condition (E group) received at least a "1" on his parent's rating and in a great many cases a "2" rating. The corresponding C group, on the other hand, showed a disproportionately small increase in "1" ratings and no "2" ratings at all. Table 2 shows that the proportion of successes of at least "1" for treated Ss was significantly higher than for untreated Ss. The critical ratio value for the difference in proportions was 4.4 which is significant at the .00003 level. Table 3 indicates the proportion of successes of at least "2." The critical ratio value for the difference in proportions was 3.3 which is significant at the .0005 level, again an indication of the superiority of the treatment condition in reducing phobic disturbances.

For behavior changes rated as "1," Table 2 indicated 100% success for both high- and low-IQ treatment groups, thereby indicating no difference in treatment success due to conditions of "awareness." For rating "2," Table 3 yields a critical ratio of .04, further demonstrating no difference between "awareness" conditions.

DISCUSSION

The results indicate that treated Ss were significantly affected by the modified systematic desensitization method. Control group Ss, on the other hand, showed no significant change in reduction of their phobic symptoms. The S's intellectual ability, presumably indicating the possibility of his awareness of being treated, did not affect the results. This lack of difference is interesting considering the fact that severely neurologically impaired children often receive no treatment because of their presumed lack of motivation and concomitant unawareness (Johnson & Myklebust, 1969). Systematic desensitization in its modified form appears to overcome this difficulty, at least for children suffering from specific dog and bus phobias.

The method of treatment employed in this study was designed for specific phobic disorders. However, its application to other childhood disorders would be a relatively simple task. The identification of the fear-inducing stimulus would be followed by the development of a hierarchy of conditions under which the stimulus appears in the patient's life. Fear-antagonist responses would then be introduced conjunctively with the appropriate reinforcement schedule. Recent studies have demonstrated the effective use of systematic desensitization on such disorders as simple autism, enuresis, etc. (Jones, 1968; Myers, 1968), in which the child is often unable to talk about his illness.

Further research seems suggested by several aspects of this study: (*a*) a comparison of the effectiveness of trained versus untrained therapists in the use of systematic desensitization; (*b*) additional modification of the technique as a function of the nature of the symptoms treated, for example, possible treatment of paranoid schizophrenia by exposure to interpersonal interactions inducing suspiciousness; (*c*) determination of what acts as a reward in the therapeutic setting; and (*d*) the assessment of S awareness and its necessity in the successful application of systematic desensitization.

REFERENCES

BANDURA, A. Psychotherapy as a learning process. *Psychological Bulletin*, 1961, 58, 143–157.

COOKE, G. The efficacy of two desensitization procedures: An analogue study. *Behaviour Research and Therapy*, 1966, 4, 17–24.

EYSENCK, H. J. The effects of psychotherapy: An evaluation. *Journal of Consulting Psychology*, 1952, 16, 319–324.

FERSTER, C. B., & SIMONS, J. Behavior therapy with children. *Psychological Record*, 1966, 16, 65–74.

FREUD, A. *Normality and pathology in childhood*. New York: International Universities Press, 1965.

JENSEN, D., & WAMACH, M. G. Operant conditioning techniques applied in the treatment of an autistic child. *American Journal of Orthopsychiatry*, 1967, 37, 30–34.

JOHNSON, E. J., & MYKLEBUST, H. R. *Learning disabilities*. New York: Grune & Stratton, 1969.

JONES, H. G. The behavioral treatment of enuresis nocturna. In H. J. Eysenck (Ed.), *Behavior therapy and the neuroses*. New York: Pergamon Press, 1968.

LAMONT, J. F., & EDWARDS, J. The role of relaxation in systematic desensitization. *Behaviour Research and Therapy*, 1967, 5, 11–25.

LANG, P. J., & MELAMED, B. G. Case report: Avoidance conditioning therapy of an infant with chronic remination vomiting. *Journal of Abnormal Psychology*, 1969, 74, 1–9.

LAZARUS, A. A. New methods in psychotherapy: A case study. *South African Medical Journal*, 1958, 33, 660–663.

LAZARUS, A. A., & RACHMAN, S. The use of systematic desensitization in psychotherapy. *South African Medical Journal*, 1957, 31, 934–939.

LOVAAS, O. I., FREITAG, G., GOLD, V., & KASSARLA, I. Experimental studies in childhood schizophrenia: Analysis of self-destructive behavior. *Journal of Experimental Child Psychology*, 1965, **2,** 67–84.

MYERS, V. The treatment of two phobic patients on the basis of learning principles. In H. J. Eysenck (Ed.), *Behavior therapy and the neuroses.* New York: Pergamon Press, 1968.

RACHMAN, S. The current status of behavior therapy. *Archives of General Psychiatry*, 1965, **13,** 418–423.

RACHMAN, S. Systematic desensitization. *Psychological Bulletin,* 1967, **74,** 93–103.

SUBOTNICK, L. Transference in client-centered play therapy. *Psychology,* 1966, **3,** 2–17.

WERRY, J. The conditioning treatment of enuresis. *American Journal of Psychiatry,* 1966, **123,** 226–229.

WOLBERG, L. R. *The technique of psychotherapy.* New York: Grune & Stratton, 1954.

WOLPE, J. *Psychotherapy by reciprocal inhibition.* Stanford: Stanford University Press, 1958.

WOLPE, J. The experimental foundations of some new therapeutic method. In A. J. Bachrach (Ed.), *Experimental foundations of clinical psychology.* New York: Basic Books, 1962. (a)

WOLPE, J. Isolation of a conditioning procedure as the crucial psychotherapeutic factor: A case study. *Journal of Nervous and Mental Disorders,* 1962, **134,** 316–329. (b)

ZIMMERMAN, E. H., & ZIMMERMAN, J. The alteration of behavior in a special situation. *Journal of Experimental Behavior,* 1962, **5,** 59–60.

ALBERT BANDURA
JOAN E. GRUSEC
FRANCES L. MENLOVE
Stanford University

Vicarious extinction
of avoidance behavior[1]

This experiment was designed to investigate the extinction of avoidance responses through observation of modeled approach behavior directed toward a feared stimulus without any adverse consequences accruing to the model. Children who displayed fearful and avoidant behavior toward dogs were assigned to 1 of the following treatment conditions: 1 group of children participated in a series of brief modeling sessions in which they observed, within a highly positive context, a fearless peer model exhibit progressively stronger approach responses toward a dog; a 2nd group of Ss observed the same graduated modeling stimuli, but in a neutral context; a 3rd group merely observed the dog in the positive context, with the model absent; while a 4th group of Ss participated in the positive activities without any exposure to either the dog or the modeled displays. The 2 groups of children who had observed the model interact nonanxiously with the dog displayed stable and generalized reduction in avoidance behavior and differed significantly in this respect from children in

Reprinted from *Journal of Personality and Social Psychology*, 1967, 5, 16–23, with permission of the authors. Copyright 1967 by the American Psychological Association and reproduced by permission.

---
[1] This research was supported by Public Health Research Grant M-5162 from the National Institute of Mental Health.

The authors are indebted to Janet Brewer, Edith Dowley, Doris Grant, and Mary Lewis for their generous assistance in various phases of this research.

242

the dog-exposure and the positive-context conditions. However, the positive context, which was designed to induce anxiety-competing responses, did not enhance the extinction effects produced through modeling.

Recent investigations have shown that behavioral inhibitions (Bandura, 1965a; Bandura, Ross, & Ross, 1963; Walters & Parke, 1964) and conditioned emotional responses (Bandura & Rosenthal, 1966; Berger, 1962) can be acquired by observers as a function of witnessing aversive stimuli administered to performing subjects. The present experiment was primarily designed to determine whether preexisting avoidance behavior can similarly be extinguished on a vicarious basis. The latter phenomenon requires exposing observers to modeled stimulus events in which a performing subject repeatedly exhibits approach responses toward the feared object without incurring any aversive consequences.

Some suggestive evidence that avoidance responses can be extinguished vicariously is furnished by Masserman (1943) and Jones (1924) in exploratory studies of the relative efficacy of various psychotherapeutic procedures. Masserman produced strong feeding inhibitions in cats, following which the inhibited animals observed a cage mate, that had never been negatively conditioned, exhibit prompt approach and feeding responses. The observing subjects initially cowered at the presentation of the conditioned stimulus, but with continued exposure to their fearless companion they advanced, at first hesitantly and then more boldly, to the goal box and consumed the food. Some of the animals, however, showed little reduction in avoidance behavior despite prolonged food deprivation and numerous modeling trials. Moreover, avoidance responses reappeared in a few of the animals after the normal cat was removed, suggesting that in the latter cases the modeling stimuli served merely as temporary external inhibitors of avoidance responses. Jones (1924) similarly obtained variable results in extinguishing children's phobic responses by having them observe their peers behave in a nonanxious manner in the presence of the avoided objects.

If a person is to be influenced by modeling stimuli and the accompanying consequences, then the necessary observing responses must be elicited and maintained. In the foregoing case studies, the models responded to the most feared stimulus situation at the outset, a modeling procedure that is likely to generate high levels of emotional arousal in observers. Under these conditions any avoidance responses designed to reduce vicariously instigated aversive stimulation, such as subjects withdrawing or looking away, would impede vicarious extinction. Therefore, the manner in which modeling stimuli are presented may be an important determinant of the course of vicarious extinction.

Results from psychotherapeutic studies (Bandura[2]) and experiments with infrahuman subjects (Kimble & Kendall, 1953) reveal that avoidance responses can be rapidly extinguished if subjects are exposed to a graduated series of aversive stimuli that progressively approximate the original intensity of the conditioned fear stimulus. For the above reasons it would seem advisable to conduct vicarious extinction by exposing observers to a graduated sequence of modeling activities beginning with presentations that can be easily tolerated; as observers' emotional reactions to displays of attenuated approach responses are extinguished, the fear-provoking properties of the modeled displays might be gradually increased, concluding with interactions capable of arousing relatively strong emotional responses.

If emotion-eliciting stimuli occur in association with positively reinforcing events, the former cues are likely to lose their conditioned aversive properties more rapidly (Farber, 1948) than through mere repeated nonreinforced presentation. It might therefore be supposed that vicarious extinction would likewise be hastened and more adequately controlled by presenting the modeling stimuli within a favorable context designed to evoke simultaneously competing positive responses.

The principles discussed above were applied in the present experiment, which explored the vicarious extinction of children's fearful and avoidant responses toward dogs. One group of children participated in a series of modeling sessions in which they observed a fearless peer model exhibit progressively longer, closer, and more active interactions with a dog. For these subjects, the modeled approach behavior was presented within a highly positive context. A second group of children was presented the same modeling stimuli, but in a neutral context.

Exposure to the behavior of the model contains two important stimulus events, that is, the occurrence of approach responses without any adverse consequences to the performer, and repeated observation of the feared animal. Therefore, in order to control for the effects of exposure to the dog per se, children assigned to a third group observed the dog in the positive context but with the model absent. A fourth group of children participated in the positive activities, but they were never exposed to either the dog or the model.

In order to assess both the generality and the stability of vicarious extinction effects, the children were readministered tests for avoidance behavior toward different dogs following completion of the treatment series, and approximately 1 month later. It was predicted that children who had observed the peer model interact nonanxiously with the dog

---

[2] A. Bandura, "Principles of Behavioral Modification," unpublished manuscript, Stanford University, 1966.

would display significantly less avoidance behavior than subjects who had no exposure to the modeling stimuli. The largest decrements were expected to occur among children in the modeling-positive context condition. It was also expected that repeated behavioral assessments and the general disinhibitory effects of participation in a series of highly positive activities might in themselves produce some decrease in avoidance behavior.

METHOD

Subjects

The subjects were 24 boys and 24 girls selected from three nursery schools. The children ranged in age from 3 to 5 years.

Pretreatment Assessment of Avoidance Behavior

As a preliminary step in the selection procedure, parents were asked to rate the magnitude of their children's fearful and avoidant behavior toward dogs. Children who received high fear ratings were administered a standardized performance test on the basis of which the final selection was made.

The strength of avoidance responses was measured by means of a graded sequence of 14 performance tasks in which the children were required to engage in increasingly intimate interactions with a dog. A female experimenter brought the children individually to the test room, which contained a brown cocker spaniel confined in a modified playpen. In the initial tasks the children were asked, in the following order, to walk up to the playpen and look down at the dog, to touch her fur, and to pet her. Following the assessment of avoidance responses to the dog in the protective enclosure, the children were instructed to open a hinged door on the side of the playpen, to walk the dog on a leash to a throw rug, to remove the leash, and to turn the dog over and scratch her stomach. Although a number of the subjects were unable to perform all of the latter tasks, they were nevertheless administered the remaining test items to avoid any assumption of a perfectly ordered scale for all cases. In subsequent items the children were asked to remain alone in the room with the animal and to feed her dog biscuits. The final and most difficult set of tasks required the children to climb into the playpen with the dog, to pet her, to scratch her stomach, and to remain alone in the room with the dog under the exceedingly confining and fear-provoking conditions.

The strength of the children's avoidant tendencies was reflected not only in the items completed, but also in the degree of vacillation, reluctance, and fearfulness that preceded and accompanied each approach response. Consequently, children were credited 2 points if they executed a given task either spontaneously or willingly, and 1 point when they carried out the task minimally after considerable hesitancy and reluctance. Thus, for example, children who promptly stroked the dog's fur repeatedly when requested to do so received 2 points, whereas subjects who held back but then touched the dog's fur briefly obtained 1 point. In the item requiring the children to remain alone in the room with the dog, they received 2 points if they approached the animal and played with her, and 1 point if they were willing to remain in the room but avoided any contact with the dog. Similarly, in the feeding situation children were credited 2 points if they fed the dog by hand, but a single point if they tossed the biscuits on the floor and thereby avoided close contact with the animal. The maximum approach score that a subject could attain was 28 points.

On the basis of the pretreatment assessment, the children in each nursery school were grouped into three levels of avoidance behavior, with the corresponding scores ranging from 0 to 7, 8 to 17, and 18 to 20 points. There were approximately the same number of children, equally divided between boys and girls, at each of the three avoidance levels. The subjects from each of these groups were then assigned randomly to one of four conditions.

Treatment Conditions

Children who participated in the *modeling-positive context* condition observed a fearless peer model display approach responses toward a cocker spaniel within the context of a highly enjoyable party atmosphere.

There were eight 10-minute treatment sessions conducted on 4 consecutive days. Each session, which was attended by a group of four children, commenced with a jovial party. The children were furnished brightly colored hats, cookie treats, and given small prizes. In addition, the experimenter read stories, blew large plastic balloons for the children to play with, and engaged in other party activities designed to produce strong positive affective responses.

After the party was well under way, a second experimenter entered the room carrying the dog, followed by a 4-year-old male model who was unknown to most of the children. The dog was placed in a playpen located across the room from a large table at which the children were seated. The model, who had been chosen because of his complete lack of fear of dogs, then performed prearranged sequences of interactions with the dog for approximately 3 minutes during each session. One boy served as the model for children drawn from two of the nursery schools, and a second boy functioned in the same role at the third school.

The fear-provoking properties of the modeled displays were gradually increased from session to session by varying simultaneously the physical restraints on the dog, the directness and intimacy of the modeled approach responses, and the duration of interaction between the model and his canine companion. Initially, the experimenter carried the dog into the room and confined her to the playpen, and the model's behavior was limited to friendly verbal responses ("Hi, Chloe") and occasional petting. During the following three sessions the dog remained confined to the playpen, but the model exhibited progressively longer and more active interactions in the form of petting the dog with his hands and feet, and feeding her wieners and milk from a baby bottle. Beginning with the fifth session, the dog was walked into the room on a leash, and the modeled tasks were mainly performed outside the playpen. For example, in addition to repeating the feeding routines, the model walked the dog around the room, petted her, and scratched her stomach while the leash was removed. In the last two sessions the model climbed into the playpen with the dog where he petted her, hugged her, and fed her wieners and milk from the baby bottle.

It would have been of interest to compare the relative efficacy of the graduated modeling technique with bold displays of approach behavior from the outset. However, pretest findings showed that when modeled displays are too fear provoking, children actively avoid looking at the performances and are reluctant to participate in subsequent sessions. The latter approach would therefore require additional procedures designed to maintain strong attending behavior to highly aversive modeling stimuli.

Children assigned to the *modeling-neutral context* condition observed the same sequence of approach responses performed by the same peer model except that the parties were omitted. In each of the eight sessions the subjects were merely seated at the table and observed the modeled performances.

In order to control for the influence of repeated exposure to the positive atmosphere and to the dog per se, children in the *exposure-positive context* group attended the series of parties in the presence of the dog with the model absent. As in the two modeling conditions, the dog was introduced into the room in the same manner for the identical length of time; similarly, the dog was confined in the playpen during the first four sessions and placed on a leash outside the enclosure in the remaining sessions.

Children in the *positive-context* group participated in the parties, but they were never exposed to either the dog or the model. The main purpose of this condition was to determine whether the mere presence of a dog had an adverse or a beneficial effect on the children. Like the third condition, it also provided a control for the possible therapeutic effects of positive experiences and increased familiarity with amiable experimenters, which may be particularly influential in reducing inhibitions in very young children. In addition, repeated behavioral assessments in which subjects perform a graded series of approach responses toward a feared object without any aversive consequences would be expected to produce some direct extinction of avoidance behavior. The inclusion of the latter two control groups thus makes it possible to evaluate the changes effected by exposure to modeling stimuli over and above those resulting from general disinhibition, direct extinction, and repeated observation of the feared object.

Posttreatment Assessment of Avoidance Behavior

On the day following completion of the treatment series, the children were readministered the performance test consisting of the graded sequence of interaction tasks with the dog. In order to determine the generality of vicarious extinction effects, half the children in each of the four groups were tested initially with the experimental animal and then with an unfamiliar dog; the remaining children were presented with the two dogs in the reverse order.[3] The testing sessions were separated by an interval of 1½ hours so as to minimize any transfer of emotional reactions generated by one animal to the other.

The unfamiliar animal was a white mongrel, predominantly terrier, and of approximately the same size and activity level as the cocker spaniel. Two groups of 15 children, drawn from the same nursery-school population, were tested with either the mongrel or the spaniel in order to determine the aversiveness of the two animals. The mean approach scores with the spaniel $(M = 16.47)$ and the mongrel $(M = 15.80)$ were virtually identical $(t = .21)$.

Follow-Up Assessment

A follow-up evaluation was conducted approximately 1 month after the posttreatment assessment in order to determine the stability of modeling-induced changes in approach behavior. The children's responses were tested with the same performance tasks toward both animals, presented in the identical order.

After the experiment was completed, the children were told that,

---

[3] The authors are especially indebted to Chloe and Jenny for their invaluable and steadfast assistance with a task that, at times, must have been most perplexing to them.

while most dogs are friendly, before petting an unfamiliar dog they should ask the owner. This precautionary instruction was designed to reduce indiscriminate approach behavior by children who were in the modeling conditions toward strange dogs which they would undoubtedly encounter.

Measurement Procedure

The same female experimenter administered the pretreatment, posttreatment, and follow-up behavioral tests. To prevent any possible bias, the experimenter was given minimal information about the details of the study and had no knowledge of the conditions to which the children were assigned. The treatment and assessment procedures were further separated by the use of different rooms for each activity.

In order to provide an estimate of interscorer reliability, the performances of 25% of the children, randomly selected from pretreatment, posttreatment, and follow-up phases of the experiment, were scored simultaneously but independently by another rater who observed the test sessions through a one-way mirror from an adjoining observation room. The two raters were in perfect agreement on 97% of the specific approach responses that were scored.

A dog's activity level may partly determine the degree of fear and avoidance exhibited by the children; conversely, timorous or unrestrained approach responses might differentially affect the animals' reactivity. Therefore, during the administration of each test item, the animals' behavior was rated as either passive, moderately active, or vigorous. The raters were in perfect agreement in categorizing the dogs' activity levels on 81% of the performance tests.

Changes in children's approach-response scores across the different phases of the experiment, and the number of subjects in each treatment condition who were able to carry out the terminal performance task served as the dependent measures.

RESULTS

The percentages of test items in which the animals behaved in a passive, moderately active, or vigorous manner were 55, 43, and 2, respectively, for the model-positive context group; 53, 44, and 2 for children in the model-neutral context condition; 52, 45, and 3 for the exposure-positive context group; and 57, 41, and 2 for the positive-context subjects. Thus, the test animals did not differ in their behavior during the administration of performance tasks to children in the various treatment conditions.

Approach Responses

Table 1 presents the mean increases in approach behavior achieved by children in each of the treatment conditions in different phases of the experiment with each of the test animals.

The children's approach responses toward the two dogs did not differ either in the posttreatment assessment ($t = 1.35$) or in the follow-up phase ($t = .91$) of the study. Nor were there any significant effects ($t = 1.68$) due to the order in which the test animals were presented following completion of the treatment series. A t-test analysis also disclosed no significant change ($t = 1.50$) in mean approach scores between measurements conducted in the posttreatment and the follow-up phases of the experiment. Moreover, analysis of variance of the posttreatment scores revealed no significant Treatment × Dogs ($F = 2.15$) or Treatment × Order ($F = .30$) interaction effects. The data were therefore combined across phases and test animals in evaluating the major hypotheses.

TABLE 1   Mean increases in approach responses as a function of treatment conditions, assessment phases, and test animals

	Treatment conditions			
Phases	*Modeling — positive context*	*Modeling — neutral context*	*Exposure — positive context*	*Positive context*
Post-treatment				
Spaniel	10.83	9.83	2.67	6.08
Mongrel	5.83	10.25	3.17	4.17
Follow-up				
Spaniel	10.83	9.33	4.67	5.83
Mongrel	12.59	9.67	4.75	6.67
Combined data	10.02	9.77	3.81	5.69

An analysis of covariance, in which adjustments were made for differences in initial level of avoidance, was computed for mean approach responses performed by children in the various groups. The results reveal that the treatment conditions had a highly significant effect on the children's behavior ($F = 5.09$, $p < .01$). Tests of the differences between the various pairs of treatments indicate that subjects in the modeling-positive context condition displayed significantly more approach behavior than subjects in either the exposure ($F = 9.32$, $p < .01$) or the positive-context ($F = 8.96$, $p < .01$) groups. Similarly, children who had observed the model within the neutral setting exceeded both the exposure ($F = 6.57$, $p < .05$) and positive-context groups ($F = 4.91$, $p < .05$) in approach behavior. However, the data yielded no significant differences between either the two modeling conditions $(F = .04)$ or the two control groups $(F = .76)$.

Within-Group Analysis of Approach Responses

The approach scores obtained by the different groups of children in pre-experimental and subsequent tests are summarized graphically in Figure 1. Within-group analyses of changes between initial performance and mean level of approach behavior following treatment disclose significant increases in approach behavior for children in the modeling-positive context group $(t = 7.71, p < .001)$ and for those who observed the modeling performance within the neutral setting $(t = 5.80, p < .001)$. Although the positive-context group showed an increment in approach behavior $(t = 5.78, p < .001)$, children who were merely exposed to the dog in the positive context achieved a small, but nonsignificant $(t = 1.98)$, reduction in avoidance responses.

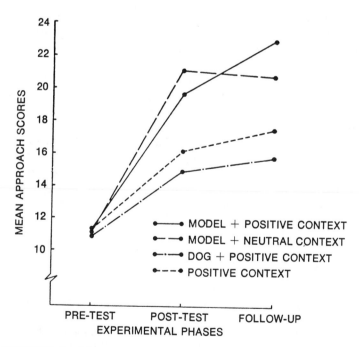

FIGURE 1 Mean approach scores achieved by children in each of the treatment conditions on the three different periods of assessment.

Terminal Performances

Another measure of the efficacy of modeling procedures is provided by comparisons of the number of children in each condition who performed the terminal approach behavior at least once during the posttreatment assessment. Since the frequencies within the two modeling conditions did not differ, and the two control groups were essentially the same, the data for each of the two sets of subgroups were combined. The findings show that 67% of the children in the modeling treatment were able to remain alone in the room confined with the dog in the playpen, whereas the corresponding figure for the control subjects is 33%. The χ^2 value for these data is 4.08, which is significant beyond the .025 level.

Within the control groups, the terminal performances were attained primarily by subjects who initially showed the weakest level of avoidance behavior. The differences between the two groups are, therefore, even more pronounced if the analysis is conducted on the subjects whose pretreatment performances reflected extreme or moderately high levels of avoidance behavior. Of the most avoidant subjects in each of the two pooled groups, 55% of the children in the modeling conditions were able to perform the terminal approach behavior following the experimental sessions, while only 13% of the control subjects successfully completed the final task. The one-tailed probability for the obtained $\chi^2 = 4.74$ is slightly below the .01 level of significance.

The relative superiority of the modeling groups is also evident in the follow-up phase of the experiment. Based on the stringent criterion in which the most fearful task is successfully performed with *both* animals, a significantly larger number of children in the modeling conditions (42%) than in the control groups (12%) exhibited generalized extinction ($\chi^2 = 4.22$, $p < .025$). Moreover, not a single control subject from the two highest levels of avoidance behavior was able to remain alone in the room confined in the playpen with each of the dogs, whereas 33% of the most avoidant children in the modeling conditions successfully passed both terminal approach tasks ($\chi^2 = 4.02$, $p < .025$).

DISCUSSION

The findings of the present experiment provide considerable evidence that avoidance responses can be successfully extinguished on a vicarious basis. This is shown in the fact that children who experienced a gradual exposure to progressively more fearful modeled responses displayed extensive and stable reduction in avoidance behavior. Moreover, most of these subjects were able to engage in extremely intimate and potentially fearful interactions with test animals following the treatment series. The considerable degree of generalization of extinction effects obtained to the unfamiliar dog is most likely due to similar stimulus properties of the test animals. Under conditions where observers' avoidance responses are extinguished to a single animal, one would expect a progressive decrement in approach behavior toward animals of increasing size and fearfulness.

The prediction that vicarious extinction would be augmented by presenting the modeling stimuli within a highly positive context was not confirmed, although subjects in the latter condition differed more significantly from the controls than children who observed approach behavior under neutral conditions. It is entirely possible that a different temporal ordering of emotion-provoking modeling stimuli and events designed to induce anxiety-inhibiting responses would facilitate the vicarious extinction process. On the basis of evidence from conditioning studies (Melvin & Brown, 1964) the optimal treatment procedure might require repeated observational trials, in each of which aversive modeling stimuli are immediately followed by positively reinforcing experiences for the observers. These temporal prerequisites depend upon the abrupt presentation and termination of the two sets of stimulus events that cannot be readily achieved with live demonstrations. It would be possible, however, to study the effects of systematic variations in the temporal spacing of critical variables if modeling stimuli were presented pictorially. Apart from issues of economy and control, if pictorial stimulus material proved equally as efficacious as live modeling, then skillfully designed therapeutic films could be developed and employed in preventive programs for eliminating common fears and anxieties before they become well established and widely generalized.

Although children in both the exposure and the positive-context groups showed some increment in approach behavior, only the changes in the latter group were of statistically significant magnitude. Apparently the mere presence of a dog had some mild negative consequences that counteracted the facilitative effects resulting from highly rewarding interactions with amiable experimenters, increased familiarity with the person conducting the numerous tests of avoidance behavior, and any inevitable direct extinction produced by the repeated performance of some approach responses toward the test animals without any adverse consequences. As might be expected, the general disinhibitory effects arising from these multiple sources occurred only in the early phase of the experiment, and no significant increases in approach behavior appeared between the posttreatment and follow-up assessments.

The data obtained in this experiment demonstrate that the fearless behavior of a model can substantially reduce avoidance responses in observers, but the findings do not establish the nature of the mechanism by which vicarious extinction occurs. There are several possible explanations of vicariously produced effects (Bandura, 1965b; Kanfer, 1965). One interpretation is in terms of the informative value of modeling stimuli. That is, the repeated evocation of approach responses without any adverse consequences to another person undoubtedly conveys information to the observer about the probable outcomes of close interactions with dogs. In the present study, however, an attempt was made to minimize the contribution of purely cognitive factors by informing children in all groups beforehand that the test animals were harmless.

The nonoccurrence of anticipated aversive consequences to a model accompanied by positive affective reactions on his part can also extinguish in observers previously established emotional responses that are vicariously aroused by the modeled displays (Bandura & Rosenthal, 1966). It is therefore possible that reduction in avoidance behavior is partly mediated by the elimination of conditioned emotionality.

Further research is needed to separate the relative contribution of cognitive, emotional, and other factors governing vicarious processes. It would also be of interest to study the effects upon vicarious extinction exercised by such variables as number of modeling trials, distribution of extinction sessions, mode of model presentation, and variations in the characteristics of the models and the feared stimuli. For example, with extensive sampling in the modeled displays of both girls and boys exhibiting approach responses to dogs ranging from diminutive breeds to larger specimens, it may be possible to achieve widely generalized extinction effects. Once approach behaviors have been restored through modeling, their maintenance and further generalization can be effectively controlled by response-contingent reinforcement administered directly to the subject. The combined use of modeling and reinforcement procedures may thus serve as a highly efficacious mode of therapy for eliminating severe behavioral inhibitions.

REFERENCES

BANDURA, A. Influence of models' reinforcement contingencies on the acquisition of imitative responses. *Journal of Personality and Social Psychology,* 1965, 1, 589–595. (a)

BANDURA, A. Vicarious processes: A case of no-trial learning. In L. Berkowitz (Ed.), *Advances in experimental social psychology.* Vol. 2. New York: Academic Press, 1965. Pp. 1–55. (b)

BANDURA, A., & ROSENTHAL, T. L. Vicarious classical conditioning as a function of arousal level. *Journal of Personality and Social Psychology,* 1966, 3, 54–62.

BANDURA, A., Ross, D., & Ross, S. A. Vicarious reinforcement and imitative learning. *Journal of Abnormal and Social Psychology,* 1963, 67, 601–607.

BERGER, S. M. Conditioning through vicarious instigation. *Psychological Review*, 1962, **69**, 450–466.

FARBER, I. E. Response fixation under anxiety and non-anxiety conditions. *Journal of Experimental Psychology*, 1948, **38**, 111–131.

JONES, M. C. The elimination of children's fears. *Journal of Experimental Psychology*, 1924, **7**, 383–390.

KANFER, F. H. Vicarious human reinforcement: A glimpse into the black box. In L. Krasner & L. P. Ullmann (Eds.), *Research in behavior modification*. New York: Holt, Rinehart & Winston, 1965. Pp. 244–267.

KIMBLE, G. A., & KENDALL, J. W., JR. A comparison of two methods of producing experimental extinction. *Journal of Experimental Psychology*, 1953, **45**, 87–90.

MASSERMAN, J. H. *Behavior and neurosis*. Chicago: University of Chicago Press, 1943.

MELVIN, K. B., & BROWN, J. S. Neutralization of an aversive light stimulus as a function of number of paired presentations with food. *Journal of Comparative and Physiological Psychology*, 1964, **58**, 350–353.

WALTERS, R. H., & PARKE, R. D. Influence of response consequences to a social model on resistance to deviation. *Journal of Experimental Child Psychology*, 1964, **1**, 269–280.

TEODORO AYLLON
D. SMITH
M. ROGERS
Georgia State University

Behavioral management
of school phobia[1]

In an 8-year-old Negro child diagnosed as suffering from school phobia the problem was re-defined as zero or low probability of school attendance. The implementation of techniques for increasing the probability involved getting the child's mother to withdraw the rewards of staying at home. Then a home-based motivational system was used to reinforce school attendance and refusal to attend school resulted in punishment. School attendance was generated quickly and maintained even after the procedures were withdrawn a month later. No "symptom substitution" was noticed either by the parents or the school officials within the 9 months of follow-up. An additional important finding was that when the child's school phobia was used to produce aversive consequences on the mother it immediately led the mother to find a "natural" way to rectify her child's psychiatric condition.

Reprinted from *Journal of Behavior Therapy and Experimental Psychiatry*, 1970, 1, 125–38, with permission of the publisher and the authors. Additional information and related research can be found in *The Token Economy: A Motivational System for Therapy and Rehabilitation* by T. Ayllon and N. H. Azrin, published by Appleton-Century-Crofts, 1968.

---
[1] A portion of this paper was read at the Southeastern Psychological Association, New Orleans, 1969. We thank Dr. L. L'Abate for the use of material from psychodiagnostic evaluations. We also acknowledge our deep appreciation to Dr. Joseph Zimmerman and Dr. Zal Newmark for their critical reading of the manuscript.

256

The most widely accepted approach to neurosis is the psychoanalytic one. The phobic object is said to serve as a symbol of some danger that is extremely real to the patient and whose origins are attributed to early childhood. Concern for the underlying dynamics of school phobia has resulted in provocative speculations. For example, sometimes the cause of the child's fear of school is traced to "an unrealistic self-image" (Leventhal and Sells, 1964). More often the mother is blamed for the child's school phobia as she is said to displace her own hostility onto the school (Coolidge, Tessman, Waldfogel and Miller, 1962). It has also been suggested that the hostile impulses of sado-masochistic school personnel toward school phobics leads them to re-enact in the school setting the sado-masochistic relationship alleged to exist between mothers and their children (Jarvis, 1964). Unfortunately, such hypotheses have not led to standardized techniques for its treatment.

An alternative approach to school phobia is that of Wolpe's systematic desensitization technique. The pioneering work of Wolpe constitutes the first effective translation of the conditioning techniques of Pavlov and Hull to therapeutic procedures. Indeed, Wolpe's systematic desensitization technique marks a departure from methods used up to 1958 which was when his book *Psychotherapy by Reciprocal Inhibition* appeared in print.

The effectiveness of this approach, unlike the psychoanalytic one, has received empirical validation (Garvey and Hgrenis, 1966; Lazarus, Davidson and Polezka, 1965; Patterson, Littleman and Hensey, 1964). The impact of Wolpe's work has been such that even when modifications of his work have been explored, such as Patterson's (1965) use of M & M's to reinforce responses to the hierarchy of stimuli presented to the phobic child or Lazarus and Abramovitz's (1962) use of so-called "emotive imagery," the conceptual rationale and procedural details remain those advanced by Wolpe (1958).

A complementary approach to school phobia may now be available through the use of operant techniques. In dealing with "emotional" or behavioral problems this approach tries to determine through observation and experimentation the particular environmental event likely to be responsible for the behavior. The rationale for an operant approach to school phobia, however, requires that the condition or diagnosis of school phobia be behaviorally redefined. Indeed irrespective of the interpretation to be attached to school phobia the major feature of this condition is immediately accessible to observation: the child's attendance at school. School phobia, therefore, can be redefined behaviorally as an observable event of low frequency or probability of occurrence. Two major methodological advantages are obtained by such a redefinition. First, frequencies and rates of behavior constitute the data of a large body of experimental research. Techniques to increase or decrease rates of behavior initially developed in the laboratory (Skinner, 1938; Ferster and Skinner, 1957) have been successfully extended to the treatment of pathological behaviors in clinical settings (Ayllon and Michael, 1959; Isaacs, Thomas and Goldiamond, 1960; Ayllon and Haughton, 1964; Wolf, Risley and Mees, 1964; Ayllon and Azrin, 1965; Ayllon and Azrin, 1968b).

The second advantage of redefining school phobia as a low probability behavior is that it immediately suggests what the relevant target for treatment is, namely reinstatement of school attendance. Our strategy then was to apply such behavioral procedures to the analysis and modification of school phobia.

It should be recognized that while a legitimate target of treatment may be self-understanding, growth, and insight, these are important only insofar as they are presumed to facilitate the behavioral change from not going to school to normal school attendance. The observable datum, school attendance, then is a legitimate if not the only relevant treatment objective for school phobia. Another objective of the behavioral intervention reported here was to bypass treatment in a clinical situation or in a therapist's office since success in such situations would still have to generalize into the school situation for the success to be relevant to the problem. Therefore, our attempt was to treat the phobia in the environment where it survived. In this manner if our strategy succeeded there would be no school phobia and the problem of generalization would simply not arise.

BACKGROUND

The Child

The subject of this study was Valerie, an 8-year-old Negro girl from a low income area. In the second grade she had exhibited episodes of gradually increasing absences from school until she stopped going to school in that grade and this continued on into the third grade.

The Family

She had three siblings, a sister who was 9 and two brothers ages 6 and 10. None of her siblings had a history of school phobia. Her father was periodically employed as a construction worker and her mother worked as a cook in a restaurant. Both had high-school level educations.

School Phobia

Valerie held an above average school attendance in kindergarten and the first grade. She started skipping school only gradually in the second grade and finished that year with 41 absences. According to school records, Valerie attended no more than the first 4 days of school in the third grade. During her 4 days of attendance, her mother reported that Valerie refused to go to school. Whenever the mother attempted to take her to school, Valerie threw such violent temper-tantrums, screaming and crying, that it was nearly impossible to move her from the house.

Finally, the mother took Valerie to a number of specialists, including a school counselor, a medical specialist and a social worker. All these professionals offered extensive advice. The mother reported that the advice took several forms: "Ignore the behavior and it will go away"; "Give her plenty of praise and affection"; and "Punish her severely if she refuses to go". Unfortunately, none of this advice worked and Valerie continued to stay away from school.

Val, according to the mother's reports, had much trouble going to sleep and lay awake during much of the night. Val had no friends except for one cousin to whom she felt close. Children did not seek her nor did she seem interested in playing with children at school or in the neighborhood. According to the teacher's reports, when Val did attend school she was as quiet as a mouse in class and simply stood and watched at recess but would not join the games and activities. As the mother became convinced that Valerie had "something wrong with her nerves" she took her to the local hospital so that she could get some "pills for her nerves." Valerie was evaluated by the pediatric staff and her case diagnosed as school phobia.

Diagnostic Test Results

Several diagnostic psychological tests were administered to Valerie while her case was being presented at the local hospital. The test results were as follows:

> Valerie demonstrated a consistent variability in her overall functioning. Her problem-solving, visual–manual skills (WISC Performance IQ = 78) are considerably below her near average verbal-expressive abilities (WISC Verbal IQ = 90). Within her verbal skills, she ranges from a defective level of functioning in comprehension of social situations and in her fund of information to an above normal level of functioning in her ability to think abstractly. Within her performance skills, she also demonstrated variability (DAP IQ = 87; Peabody IQ = 76). Valerie's variable

functioning is due to an extreme inability to concentrate, since on perceptual tasks not requiring concentration she performed at a normal level (Frostig Perceptual Quotient = 98). Emotionally, Valerie's inability to concentrate is related to her extreme fears—especially her fears about men. The only way she can cope with men is to see them as dead. The inconsistency in her functioning seems to be related to the amount of concentration required by various tasks—such as classroom activities. To handle such stressful situations, she is likely to withdraw by not performing.

Social Intake Evaluation

A social intake evaluation was also done at the pediatric clinic. Excerpts of this evaluation indicated that "when the mother tried to accompany Valerie to school, even as far as getting on the bus with her, as they approached the school, Valerie would become very stiff, begin shaking, screaming and hollering. When Valerie was asked about this, she stated that she was afraid to go to school, that when she went to school she thought about the time she was molested." This was a reference to an incident which took place when the child was 4 years old. According to Valerie's mother, a boy had "played with Valerie's 'private parts'." Neither the extent of this incident nor any physical evidence could be obtained at the time of its occurrence. After the child had been diagnosed, as suffering from school phobia, the mother was advised that the nature of Valerie's difficulties required long-term psychiatric treatment. Since the cost of such treatment was beyond the family means, the mother was left with the understanding that she should resign herself to living with the problem. Quite by accident, one of the authors of this paper was visiting the pediatric facility where Valerie's case was being discussed for the benefit of interns in pediatrics and child psychiatry. It was then that a suggestion was made by the senior author (T.A.) to attempt a behavioral treatment of Valerie's school phobia.

METHODOLOGY

Behavioral Strategy

The behavioral approach to school phobia requires that it be broken down into three major components.

First of all there is the matter of response definition. The relevant dimension, insofar as the school, parent and child are concerned is that of school attendance. Thus, we can define school phobia as a low or near zero level of school attendance. This definition enables us to specify what the target behavior is for a treatment program. If the rate of going to school is low, our aim then is to increase it and maintain it, hopefully under the conditions that obtain in the "natural" setting of the school environment. The next component involves the matter of consequences or reinforcement for staying away from school. These consequences must be examined as they affect the child and the behavior of those living with her. Finally, there is the issue of redesigning the consequences provided by the environment so as to minimize the probability of skipping school while maximizing the probability of attending school.

To identify the relevant environmental consequences responsible for the child's refusal to attend school, the child's behavior was directly observed and recorded by trained assistant-observers. The initial step was to attempt to quantify the dimensions of the relevant behaviors in the three primary environments of the child: (1) home, (2) a neighbor's home (where she was cared for) and (3) school.

The systematic observational schedule that was conducted each day on a minute-by-minute basis started at 7:00 A.M. and ended at 9:00 A.M. The sampling of observations was conducted for 10 days at home and for 3 days at the neighbor's house. Behavioral observations and procedures designed to reinstate school attendance were implemented by two assistant observers. One observer (M.R.) conducted the prompting-shaping procedures and participated in the observations at the neighbor's apartment. The second observer (D.S.) was responsible for giving instructions to the mother and conducted the observations at Valerie's home. Once the child returned to school as a consequence of the procedures applied, the observations were extended to include the child's behavior at school and on the way to and from school.

Valerie's behavior at home.   The observations in the home revealed that Valerie was sleeping an average of 1 hr later than her siblings in the morning, although according to the mother she retired at the same time as they, between 9:00 and 10:00 every night. Her mother had long abandoned any hope of Valerie's going to school and simply allowed her to sleep until she awoke, or until it was time for the mother to leave for work at 9:00 A.M. The mother would usually leave for work approximately 1 hr following the departure of the siblings who left for school at 8:00 A.M.

Except for a few occasions when the mother made breakfast for the children they frequently fixed their own food. Valerie was given no preferential treatment, and was never asked what she would like for breakfast if she slept late. Upon arising, Valerie spoke an average of 14 sentences to the siblings, an average of 10 sentences to her mother and only two sentences to her father. The mother averaged one request each morning asking Valerie to go to school. Physical interaction such as touching, holding or other aggressive or affectionate behavior occurred seldom with her siblings and not at all with her father. On the other hand, Valerie typically followed her mother around the house, from room to room, spending approximately 80 per cent of her time within 10 ft of her mother. During these times, there was little or no conversation. When the mother left for work, she would take Valerie to a neighbor's apartment. On every observational occasion, when the mother left the neighbor's apartment to go to work, Valerie would immediately leave and follow the mother. This behavior of quietly following her mother at a 10-ft distance occurred on each of the 10 days of baseline observations. Each time this occurred, the mother would look back and see Valerie, stop and warn her several times to go back, all of which had no effect on Valerie. When the mother began walking once more, Valerie continued to follow at a 10-ft distance, with no verbal response of any type. Also, it was noted that on three occasions that the mother resorted to punishing Valerie with a switching for following, Val would cry quietly but would make no effort to return home until the mother took her back to the neighbor's apartment. Once the mother left again for work, Valerie would continue to follow at about twice the distance, or 20 ft, behind the mother. This daily scene was usually concluded with the mother literally running to get out of sight of Valerie so that Valerie would not follow her into traffic.

Valerie's behavior at the neighbor's apartment. Valerie was observed at the neighbor's apartment for 3 days during which the observer had no interaction with Val but remained nearby recording whatever behavior occurred. During this time Val watched the observer at times but made no effort to interact in any way.

At the neighbor's apartment, Val was free to do whatever she pleased for the remainder of the day. Val showed little interest in television or radio, preferring to be outdoors unless it was raining. If she had to stay inside she pored over a mail order toy catalogue. Very rarely did the neighbor spend time interacting with Val. The few times she did it was after Val's mother had left for work and Val was still crying.

Outdoors, Val found many ways to entertain herself. The observer watched while she played with a jump rope, exploded caps and found a dozen different ways to play with play-dough. If she ran out of things to play with, Val amused herself by hopping on one foot, jumping, running and turning in circles. In addition, Val had some money and at some time during the day made a trip to the corner store where she bought candy, gum or soft drinks.

Val was the only school age child at the neighbor's house and children from toddlers to kindergarten age sought her attention. She was somewhat aloof, but occasionally joined their play. In short, her day was one which would be considered ideal by many grade children—she could be outdoors and play as she chose all day long. No demands of any type were made on Val by anyone and she had the status of being the eldest among the children.

Valerie's behavior in school. Two visits were made to the school to get acquainted with the principal and teachers and to gather information from them about Val's past school performance, work attitude and social adjustment. Copies were obtained of the official records of Val's attendance for kindergarten, 1st grade, 2nd grade, and the current year (3rd grade). The records showed Val's attendance to have been above average during kindergarten and first grade but that absences had increased each quarter during the second grade; 1st quarter, 1; 2nd quarter, 7; 3rd quarter, 13; and fourth quarter, 20, for a total of 41 absences for the year. Excuses had been illness, oversleeping or missing the bus. Scholastic achievement had been normal or average until absences became numerous. Val, it was reported, had never cried or asked to go home. While described as shy, quiet and rather apathetic, Val had never given the impression that she was unhappy or afraid.

The Behavioral Assessment

The evaluation of Valerie's behavior at home, at the neighbor's apartment and finally at school suggested that Valerie's school phobia was currently maintained by the pleasant and undemanding characteristics of the neighbor's apartment where Val spent her day after everyone had left home in the morning.

Rather than speculating on the "real" causes or etiology of the phobia itself our initial strategy was to determine the feasibility of having Val return to school by some prompting-shaping procedure (see Ayllon and Azrin, 1968a, for rationale and empirical basis for this procedure). Once this was done it would then be possible to provide for some pleasant experience associated with being in school in order to maintain her school attendance. To design the prompting-shaping procedure it was necessary first to assess Valerie's existing behaviors that had a component relation to the target behavior. Indeed, if attending school were to be meaningful, Valerie had to show sufficient interest to go to school voluntarily and consistently. In addition, she had to be prepared to work with school materials and perform academic work. To determine the presence or absence of these component behaviors, first one assistant (M.R.) took a coloring book, crayons, a set of arithmetic flash cards and other academically related items to the neighbor's apartment. While at the neighbor's apartment, she prompted Val to make the appropriate academically related responses to the stimuli. Val responded appropriately to the academic material and contrary to expectations, she did not panic, "freeze," or become at all upset when exposed to academically related material. The next objective was to assess the difficulties associated with leaving the neighbor's apartment. Therefore, the next probe was for the observer to invite Val for a car ride after both had worked on academically related activities. Val offered no resistance and went with the observer for a car ride and later had a hamburger on the way home.

This behavioral assessment assured us (1) that a prompting-shaping procedure could start by taking Val directly to school rather than in gradually increasing steps; (2) that she would do academic work once in the classroom. The next step was to develop the desired response chain eventuating in Valerie's attendance at school. It must be remembered that Val stayed alone with her mother after her siblings left for school at about 8:00 A.M. She remained with her mother until she left for work at 9:00 A.M. If staying with the mother alone was the reinforcing consequence that maintained her refusal to go to school, we reasoned, withdrawal of this consequence might lead Valerie back to school. Before we could try such a procedure, however, it was necessary to determine the probability of Valerie remaining in the classroom once she returned to school. That was in effect the objective of the first procedure. Additional procedures were subsequently implemented to achieve the target behavior.

Specific Procedures and Results

Table 1 shows all procedural stages as well as their behavioral effects. The target behavior of voluntary and consistent (100 per cent) school attendance was achieved in less than 2 months. Four distinct procedures were designed and implemented only after observing and recording their specific effects on Valerie's voluntary school attendance.

Procedure 1. Prompting-shaping of school attendance. Our plan was to manage to have Valerie visit the school at a time when school was almost over for the day. By having the child go to school for a short time only to be dismissed for the day along with the rest of the pupils we attempted to use the "natural" contingencies of the school to maintain Valerie's presence in school. Permission was obtained from the teacher to bring Val to school for the last hour of the school day and for the assistant to remain in the classroom with her. The plan was to arrive at school progressively earlier until the child's presumed fears were extinguished at which time she would then initiate voluntary school attendance. The first day of this procedure the assistant (M.R.) told Val, about 1:30 P.M., that they would be going to school and that she would stay with Val. Val's eyes widened but she offered no resistance. They drove to school, arriving 1½ hr before closing time and holding hands tightly, went to the third grade classroom. Val was given a desk and the assistant sat nearby until the day was over. The teacher, in a very natural manner, greeted Val and gave her some classroom material. Val immediately started doing some school work. On the way out of school the assistant found Val's siblings. To maximize the probability of Val's getting approval from her siblings, associated with the school, the assistant gave Val some candy to share with the siblings and left her to walk home with them.

The following day, the procedure was repeated except that the assistant left Val in the classroom about 10 min before school was out. Again, the teacher worked with Val just as naturally as if she had been attending all day long. The assistant before leaving the classroom instructed Val to meet her siblings and reassured her that they would wait for her to walk home with them. The next day the time of arrival was moved up so that Val spent 2 hr in school. By now Val had attended the third grade for a total of 4 hr. On the basis of her classroom performance the teacher came to the conclusion that Val was too far behind to catch up with her third grade classmates. Therefore, after careful consideration and discussion the school principal decided to place her in a second grade class to insure her learning the material she had missed during her prolonged absence from school. Again, the cooperation of the new second grade teacher was obtained to allow Val to keep going to school at rather unusual hours, about 2–3 hr before the end of the school day.

The next day Val was taken to the second grade class for the first time. She gave no evidence of being upset with the shift from classrooms. On succeeding days Val was taken earlier each day. By the time Val was arriving in school at 9:30 A.M. the assistant had gradually decreased her own time in the classroom from the initial 1½ hr to 5 min. Each day the assistant left a sack containing some small prize like a children's magazine, a few pieces of candy, etc., with the teacher to be given to Val when school was over. On the 8th day of this procedure Val left home with her siblings and went to school without the assistant for the first time. The teacher praised her and the assistant went to school and told Val how happy she was that Val had come to school by herself.

On the next day Val stayed home until her mother left for work. As usual she was then taken to the neighbor's apartment. The assistant picked her up and took her to school where she spent the remaining 4½ hr of the school day. The prompting-shaping procedure was discontinued at this time to allow for further behavioral evaluation. For the next 6 days she remained at home when her siblings went to school and, just as before, the mother took Val to the neighbor's apartment as she left for work.

Figure 1 shows the day-to-day behavior of Val under procedure 1. The

TABLE 1 Procedural and behavioral progression during the treatment of school phobia

Temporal sequence	Procedure	Valerie's behavior
Baseline observations Day 1-10	Observations taken at home and at the neighbor's apartment where Val spent her day.	Valerie stayed at home when siblings left for school. Mother took Val to neighbor's apartment as she left for work.
Behavioral assessment Day 11-13	Assistant showed school materials to Val and prompted academic work.	Val reacted well to books; she colored pictures and copied numbers and letters.
Behavioral assessment Day 13	Assistant invited Val for a car ride after completing academic work at neighbor's apartment.	Val readily accepted car ride and on way back to neighbor's apartment she also accepted hamburger offered her.
Procedure 1 Day 14-20	Taken by assistant to school. Assistant stayed with her in classroom. Attendance made progressively earlier while assistant's stay in classroom progressively lessens.	Val attended school with assistant. Performed school work. Left school with siblings at closing time.
Day 21	Assistant did not take Val to school.	Val and siblings attended school on their own.
Procedure 1 Day 22	Val taken by assistant to school.	Val attended school with assistant. Performed school work. Left with siblings at school closing time.
Return to baseline observations Day 23-27	Observations taken at home.	Val stayed at home when siblings left for school. Mother took Val to neighbor's apartment as she left for work.

TABLE 1 (continued)

Temporal sequence	Procedure	Valerie's behavior
Procedure 2 Day 28-29	Mother left for work when children left for school.	Val stayed at home when children left for school. Mother took her to neighbor's apartment as she left for work.
Procedure 3 Day 40-49	Taken by mother to school. Home-based motivational system.	Val stayed at home when siblings left for school. Followed mother quietly when taken to school.
Procedure 4 Day 50-59	On Day 50, mother left for school *before* children left home. Home-based motivational system.	Siblings met mother at school door. Val stayed at home.
	After 15 min of waiting in school, mother returned home and took Val to school.	Val meekly followed her mother.
	On Day 51, mother left for school *before* children left home.	Val and siblings met mother at school door.
	On Day 52, mother left for school before children left home.	Siblings met mother at school door. Valerie stayed at home.
	After 15 min of waiting in school, mother returned home and physically hit and dragged Valerie to school.	Valerie cried and pleaded with her mother not to hit her. Cried all the way to school.
	On Day 53-59, mother left for school before children left home.	Val and siblings met mother at school door.
Fading procedure Day 60-69	Mother discontinued going to school before children. Mother maintained home-based motivational system.	Val and siblings attended school on their own.
Fading procedure Day 70	Mother discontinued home-based motivational system.	Val and siblings attended school on their own.

267

prompting-shaping procedure demonstrated that Val could go to school and stay all day without running away, causing disturbance in the classroom, or displaying any behavior that might suggest undue fear or panic. Just as significant, Val's behavior in school indicated that the "natural" reinforcing consequences provided at school were adequate to keep her there once she engaged in the first activity of a complex behavior chain including getting up on time, washing, dressing, leaving the house and going to school. True, this procedure reinstated Valerie's school attendance but failed to maintain it. The problem then was how to provide sufficient motivation to insure her leaving for school. At this point it became necessary to examine and re-design the social consequences provided at home for Valerie's refusal to attend school.

Procedure 2. Withdrawal of social consequences upon failure to attend school. As mentioned before, Val stayed with her mother for 1 hr daily right after her siblings had gone to school. The objective here was to eliminate such a social consequence for staying away from school. Therefore, procedure 2 involved instructing the mother that she was casually to inform all the children the night before that she was going to leave for work *at the same time they left for school.* When additional questions were asked, she was to reply that her working hours had been changed. Valerie

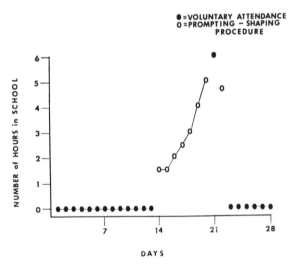

FIGURE 1 Valerie's school attendance both when she was escorted to school during the prompting-shaping procedure, and when she went on her own. Each dot represents the actual duration of her stay in the class room per day. The start of Procedure 1 is indicated by the gap between day 13 and day 14.

gave no verbal or physical reaction to this announcement when it was given. Nothing else was changed. The children were treated the same as on previous occasions. One of the assistant-observers, who had had no interaction with Val, was in the house making standard observations the day the new procedure 2 was initiated and during subsequent intervention. The mother left for work along with the siblings but Val refused to go. Therefore, she was taken to the neighbor's apartment. This procedure was continued for 10 days during which Val did not attend school and was taken to the neighbor's apartment. In addition, Val increased her "following behavior" when the mother left for work. Valerie followed at a distance of 3–6 ft behind the mother. When Valerie was punished by her mother she invariably dropped back to about 8–10 ft and continued following her mother. As there were no other observable effects on Valerie's behavior at the end of 10 days, this procedure was terminated. In effect, we had spent over 20 days trying various procedures and we were now back to the original behavior pattern: Val did not go to school and was taken to the neighbor's apartment. As soon as the mother started to leave for work Val followed her despite her mother's efforts to discourage her.

Procedure 3. Prompting school attendance combined with a home-based motivational system. Despite the fact that Val appeared to have remained unchanged as ever through the various procedures, it was clear from results of procedure 1 that she could return to school through a prompting-shaping procedure. The problem was one of maintaining that attendance for any length of time. To find a solution, it was required that we find some source or sources of reinforcement to be used at home contingent on school attendance. Val's mother described some of the things Val liked most. Among these were having her cousin stay overnight with her, soda pop, chewing gum, and ice cream. Therefore, the strategy for designing the new procedure included the prompting-shaping procedure that previously resulted in Val's return to school and a motivational system designed to reinforce Valerie for attending school. This time, the mother rather than an assistant, was to use the prompting procedure. In addition and to facilitate implementation of the motivational system, a large chart with each child's name and the days of the week was given to the mother. She announced that a star would signify one day of going to school on a *voluntary* basis and was to be placed on the appropriate spot by each child at the end of each day. Five stars would equal perfect attendance and would result in a special treat or trip on the weekend. In addition to the above, each child who went to school on a voluntary basis would receive, each day, three pieces of a favorite candy. If anyone had to be taken to school (non-voluntary attendance), the reward was only one piece of candy. It was felt to be important to attach some reward value to the school attendance even if, in the beginning, attendance was not voluntary. The occasion of putting up stars, handing out rewards and verbal praise was to be made into a special event each evening when the mother returned home. When Valerie did not leave with the other children to go to school in the morning, the mother was to leave the house 15 min later taking Valerie with her to school. No excuses were to be tolerated with the exception of sickness. Since previously Valerie had used the excuse of being sick to avoid going to school, this time the mother was given a thermometer and taught to use it to decide whether or not Valerie was ill. If the thermometer reading was above 100, the mother would then be justified in allowing Val to stay home. This procedure resulted in Valerie's mother taking her to school daily for 10 consecutive days. Once, Valerie stated she was sick but since her temperature was within the normal range, her mother took her to school. Procedure 3, just as procedure 1, resulted in Valerie attending school but it failed to initiate Valerie's going to school on her own. In analyzing the procedure carefully, it seemed that what was happening was that the mother taking Valerie personally to school was perhaps adventitiously reinforcing and thus maintaining her refusal to go on her own. After the other children had left for school, the mother in a very matter-of-fact fashion, asked Valerie to get ready to go to school with her. On the way to school, Valerie and the mother appeared quite natural and even after 10 days of this procedure there was no particular irritation or apparent inconvenience experienced by Valerie or by her mother. It should be pointed out here that prior to the present intervention, Valerie would kick and scream and simply refused to go to school even when her mother attempted to take her by force. The results of procedure 3 suggested that the natural consequences for school attendance plus the motivational system employed here increased the probability of Val's going to school escorted, but it failed to prompt her going to school voluntarily. Procedure 4 was designed to introduce a mild aversive consequence for the mother if Val failed to go to school. In addition, the motivational system used in procedure 3 was maintained.

Procedure 4. The effects of aversive consequences on the mother. Procedure 4 involved having the mother get ready for work and leave the house 10 min *before* the children left for school. She was to inform all the children that she had to go to work much earlier but wanted to see that they got to school on time, so she would meet them at school each morning with a reward. This procedure was designed to have a two-fold effect: one, to prompt the behavior on Valerie's part of voluntarily leaving for school with her siblings and to provide reinforcement through the mother upon arrival at school. If Valerie failed to arrive at school with her siblings, the mother had to return home and escort Valerie to school. Since the school was about a mile away from home, Val's failure to go to school required that her mother walk back home a mile and then walk another mile to school—this time with Valerie in tow, for a total of 3 miles walking. By having Valerie's behavior affect her mother's directly, it was hoped that this procedure would in effect have the mother become more actively interested in conveying to Val the importance of going to school. On the first day of this procedure 4, Val behaved just as she had throughout the previous ones: she remained at home after everyone, her mother and later the siblings, had left for school. The mother met the siblings at school, gave them a bit of candy and then waited for Val to come to school. Following the previous instructions she remained at the school door for 15 min before going back home to find Val. Once there she very firmly proceeded to take Val by the hand and with hardly any words between them, they rushed back to school. Val did not protest and quite naturally followed her mother into school. After a few minutes Val's mother left school for work. That evening, the mother rewarded each child with praise and candy for going to school. She gave stars to the siblings and placed them on the board made for that purpose. She also gave Val a piece of candy and noted that she could not get a star since Val had not attended school on her own. The children's reaction to the stars and praise seemed one of excitement. Val, however, appeared somewhat unsure of what was happening. The second day of procedure 4, Val got up along with her siblings, dressed, fixed herself some breakfast, and left for school with her siblings. When they arrived at school they met their mother who was waiting for them. The mother was obviously pleased with Val to whom she gave candy along with the siblings. At the end of the school day, the children again were praised at home and given stars by the mother on the special board that hung in the kitchen. Val appeared very interested particularly when the mother explained to her that if she collected 5 stars she would be able to exchange them for the opportunity to have the cousin, of whom Val was very fond, spend a night with her. The next day, Val remained at home after the mother and the siblings had left for school. Again, the mother waited for 15 min in school. Then she returned home. As it was raining, it was a considerable inconvenience for Val's mother to have to go back home. Once she reached home she scolded Val and pushed her out of the house and literally all the way to school. As Val tried to give some explanation the mother hit her with a switch. By the time they arrived at school, both were soaking wet. That evening, Val received some candy but no stars as she had not gone to school on her own. This was the last time Val stayed away from school. The next day she went to school along with her siblings. The mother met the children at the school door and genuinely praised them for their promptness. That evening, Val received a star along with candy and was praised by the mother in front of the siblings.

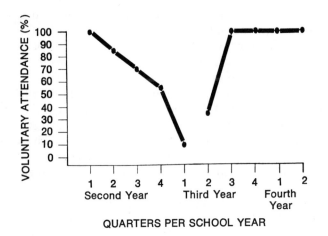

FIGURE 2 Valerie's voluntary school attendance. Each dot represents the percentage of voluntary attendance per school quarter (45 days). The behavioral intervention was initiated during the second quarter of the third year of school.

Within 5 days Val had accumulated enough stars to exchange them for the opportunity to have her cousin stay overnight with her. She appeared in very good spirits and seemed to enjoy her cousin's visit. The next school day, Val got up with her siblings, washed, dressed, fixed herself some breakfast cereal, and left for school with them. When they arrived at school they were met by their mother, who again praised them, gave them some candy, and then the children went to their respective classrooms while the mother went off to work. Val and the children continued attending school without any difficulty, even after one aspect of the procedure was withdrawn: namely, the mother waiting for them at school. The home-based motivational system was maintained in force for 1 month and withdrawn at that time. Still, Val and the children continued attending school unaffected by the withdrawal of these formal procedures.

To gain perspective on the dimensions of the school phobia presented here it is necessary to look at Val's overall school attendance per quarter (45 days each quarter). Figure 2 shows that Val went from 95 per cent school attendance to 10 per cent within 5 quarters. This 10 per cent represented the first 4 days of the fifth quarter after which she quit going to school for the remainder of the quarter. The present behavioral intervention was conducted during the latter part of the 6th quarter. The net result was that Val's overall attendance in the 6th quarter increased from 10 to 30 per cent. The next quarter, the 7th, her overall attendance increased from 30 to 100 per cent. A follow-up for the next 3 quarters indicates that Val had maintained this perfect attendance.

Follow-up

Inquiries were made of Valerie's parents and teachers at 6 and 9 months subsequent to Valerie's return to school. Their comments can be subsumed under school and home evaluation. Finally a psychodiagnostic evaluation was also obtained.

School Evaluation

Val's academic progress is shown by her current grades. While previously she was an average C student, she now has A's and B's. Her teacher remarked that Val is well-behaved in class and helpful to the teacher. While she is pleased to volunteer for small errands and clean-up duties to assist the teacher, she has also shown sufficient skills to be chosen as the school guide for a new girl admitted into her classroom. Val's specific duties as guide consisted of showing and explaining to the new girl the various school facilities such as the school cafeteria, the library, the gym and so on. The teacher was particularly impressed with Val's performance as a guide because the new girl came from Germany and asked more detailed questions than is usually the case for a standard transfer student. Her newly developed social skills appeared to have impressed the Brownie Scouts to extend a cordial invitation for Valerie to join their group. Valerie was thrilled with the prospect and after requesting permission from her mother she joined the Brownies. Every Tuesday afternoon after class she attends the group's meeting which is held in the school. After the meeting she walks home with her girl friends.

A few months after Val resumed normal school attendance an incident took place that suggests the strength of her newly-acquired fondness for school. She was waiting for the school bus when another child snatched her money changer from her, took her bus money and ran away. Instead of crying and returning home, Val ran all the way to school since she did not want to be late.

Home evaluation. Val no longer complains of feeling sick, tired in the morning nor does she suffer from insomnia. She goes to bed about 8:30 P.M. daily with her siblings and gets up at 7:00 A.M. Valerie now fusses and hurries her siblings to finish dressing in the morning in time to go to school. She brings her math and spelling work home to show her mother. The mother very naturally praises her child as she does her other children. Whereas previously Valerie had been rather apathetic in school, she now takes pride in her work there and likes to discuss things she is learning.

Eight months after Val resumed school attendance the mother initiated divorce proceedings against her husband. This situation introduced a definite strain into the home family relations. Still, Val appeared sufficiently motivated to continue attending school without any disruption in her academic or social progress.

Neither the mother nor the school teachers have noticed any other maladaptive behavior or possible "symptom substitution" since the child resumed normal school attendance. On the contrary, the mother as well as Valerie's teachers were very impressed with the astounding change in her behavior and the promise it now offers for her future both academically and socially.

Psychodiagnostic evaluation. Because Valerie's school phobia was initially presented and diagnosed in the psychiatric unit of a pediatric department at a large urban hospital, the formal procedures for case referral included a psychodiagnostic evaluation prior to and following treatment given to the child.

The conclusion now arrived at by the examiner is interesting!

> Her emotional development is characterized by deviations in the area of maturity and aggression. Her reality testing is marred by an extreme concern over sexuality and men, whom she sees as attacking, ever fighting animal-like creatures. On the basis of the recent results, without considerations to results previous to behavioral management, it would seem that the school phobia may have been treated successfully, but it has not meant anything to this girl.

DISCUSSION

A child diagnosed as suffering from school phobia was cured within 45 days through the combined use of behavioral analysis and techniques. The term *cured* is used here purposely since the functional characteristics of school phobia are straightforward: chronic absence from school. Therefore, reinstating the child's school attendance constitutes the only relevant criterion of successful cure.

The therapeutic intervention reported here is characterized by the following features:

(1) Definition of the psychiatric problem is made in terms of behavioral dimensions. The observable and measurable dimension of school

phobia is the child's frequency of school attendance. Hence this is the datum "par excellence" in the treatment of school phobia.

(2) Evaluation of the treatment objective is made in terms that are amenable to direct observation and measurement. Since the treatment objective was defined as reinstatement of voluntary school attendance, it was easy to evaluate the effectiveness of the behavioral intervention. The psychodiagnostic evaluation illustrates the dangers involved when evaluation of a treatment is on a non-behavioral basis: Speculation on personality factors often are given importance at the cost of minimizing the observable behavioral changes.

(3) The behavioral intervention is conducted in the very environment where the individual's behavior is to be displayed. Hence, rather than working in a clinic or hospital situation, the emphasis is on utilizing behavioral techniques right in the field environment to which any clinic-based therapeutic efforts must generalize for these efforts to be successful.

(4) Description of the procedures used here is also consistent with the stress on directly observable and measurable dimensions. The above provides a self-corrective method for approaching psychiatric problems in general. Each of the several procedures used here gave empirical quantitative information that enabled us to revise each procedure in the light of its effects on the child's behavior. This ongoing, step-by-step self-corrective evaluation is particularly critical for developing effective and inexpensive methods of treatment.

One other finding here was that the use of differential consequences for attending school was more effective than the use of either positive reinforcement or negative reinforcement (punishment) alone. It must be pointed out that during the baseline observations, the mother was observed hitting the child with no change in her refusal to attend school. Also during procedure 2, she was observed hitting the child again without any effect on her refusal to attend school. Similarly, Valerie's refusal to attend school continued when positive reinforcement was made available for going to school escorted by her mother (procedure 3). However, when school attendance was reinforced by the mother immediately at the school door, and at home with an incentive system that made use of the child's own motivation, while refusal to attend school was punished, it took but a few days to reinstate normal school attendance.

Why should punishment have worked this time? A parsimonious explanation of this finding lies in the fact that procedure 4 combined punishment for staying away from school with positive reinforcement for voluntary school attendance. Valerie's mother had used punishment previously but no positive reinforcement for going to school. These findings are consistent with those obtained by Holz, Azrin and Ayllon (1963) under more controlled conditions. In that study, they found that one of the most efficient methods for eliminating an undesirable response of mental patients was to schedule punishment for the undesirable response and concurrently, reinforcement for an alternative competing response.

An important procedural innovation introduced here was arranging the child's refusal to attend school to affect the mother's own behavior. When procedure 3 required that she take Valerie to school she did so without ever appearing inconvenienced by it. It was only when Val's refusal to go to school resulted in her mother having to walk from the school back home and then again back to school that the aversive properties of the procedure led to the mother finding a "natural" way of putting an end to such inconvenience. Only twice did she have to be inconvenienced. The second time her reaction was such as to convince Valerie that it would be easier to go to school with her siblings. The aversive properties of the procedure set up an escape-avoidance type of behavior in the mother that led Val to prevent such occurrences in the future by attending school.

REFERENCES

AYLLON, T. and AZRIN, N. H. (1965) The measurement and reinforcement of behavior of psychotics. *J. exp. Analysis Behav.* 8, 357–383.

AYLLON, T. and AZRIN, N. H. (1968a) Reinforcer sampling: a technique for increasing the behavior of mental patients. *J. app. Behav. Anal.* 1, 13–20.

AYLLON, T. and AZRIN, N. H. (1968b) *The Token Economy: A Motivational System for Therapy and Rehabilitation.* Appleton-Century-Crofts, New York.

AYLLON, T. and HAUGHTON, E. (1964) Modification of the symptomatic verbal behavior of mental patients. *J. Behav. Res. & Therapy* 2, 87–97.

AYLLON, T. and MICHAEL J. (1959) The psychiatric nurse as a behavioral engineer. *J. exp. Analysis Behav.* 2, 323–334.

COOLIDGE, J., TESSMAN, E., WALDFOGEL, S. and WILLER, M. (1962) Patterns of aggression in school phobia. *Psychoanal. Study Child* 17, 319–333.

FERSTER, C. B. and SKINNER, B. F. (1957) *Schedules of Reinforcement.* Appleton-Century-Crofts, New York.

GARVEY, W. P. and HGRENIS, J. R. (1966) Desensitization techniques in the treatment of school phobia. *Am. J. Orthopsychiat.* 36, (1), 147–152.

HOLZ, W., AZRIN, N. H. and AYLLON, T. (1963) Elimination of behavior of mental patients by response-produced extinction. *J. exp. Analysis Behav.* 6, 407–412.

ISAACS, W., THOMAS, J. and GOLDIAMOND, I. (1965) Application of operant conditioning to reinstate verbal behavior in psychotics. *Case Studies in Behavior Modification.* (Eds. L. P. ULLMANN and L. KRASNER), pp. 69–72. Holt, Rinehart & Winston, New York.

JARVIS, V. (1964) Countertransference in management of school phobia. *Psychoanalyt. Q.* **33** (3), 411–419.

LAZARUS, A. and ABRAMOVITZ, A. (1962) The use of 'emotive imagery' in the treatment of children's phobias. *J. men. Sci.* **180** (453), 191–195.

LAZARUS, A., DAVIDSON, G. and POLEFKA, D. (1965) Classical and operant factors in the treatment of a school phobia. *J. abnorm. Psychol.* **70** (3), 225–229.

LEVENTHAL, T. and SELLS, M. (1964) Self-image in school phobia: *Am. J. Orthopsychiat.* **34** (4), 685–695.

PATTERSON, G. R. (1965) A learning theory approach to the treatment of the school phobic child. *Case Studies in Behavior Modification.* (Eds. L. P. ULLMANN and L. KRASNER), pp. 279–285. Holt, Rinehart & Winston, New York.

SKINNER, B. F. (1938) *The Behavior of Organisms: An Experimental Analysis.* Appleton-Century-Crofts, New York.

WOLF, M., RISLEY, T. and MEES, H. (1965) Application of operant procedures to the behavior problems of an autistic child. *Case Studies in Behavior Modification* (Eds. L. P. ULLMANN and L. KRASNER), pp. 138–145. Holt, Rinehart & Winston, New York.

WOLPE, J. (1958) *Psychotherapy by Reciprocal Inhibition.* Stanford University Press, Stanford.

5

PROBLEMS IN PARENTAL CONTROL

Undesirable behavior in the home is one of the most common problems that bring parents with their children to treatment. The problems are most frequently of a mild sort that do not lead to hospitalization; but the parents and the child become estranged and miserable, and the functioning of the home is disrupted. If the problem is not treated effectively, serious consequences may result: the child may acquire seriously demaging behaviors; he may fail to acquire important social and manipulative skills; or he may be hospitalized as emotionally disturbed.

Parents universally consider it desirable to influence their children's behavior in some ways. They may become discouraged and punitive if their efforts are unsuccessful. In this section we present research showing that parents can be taught to apply behavior modification principles at home, allowing them to be helpful in the role of therapist. They even may be able to manage previously serious and persistent problems through fairly simple techniques. Most commonly the treatment aims to establish an environment at home through which the desired behaviors become more rewarding for the child than the undesired alternatives.

The use of parents as therapists and of the home as the treatment focus are novel and instructive features of behavior modification work. A variety of approaches for training parents and developing treatment programs is illustrated in the five papers collected here. Conferences with the parents during an office hour may not be a particularly efficient approach. Instead these researchers have set up training courses for parents; they make home visits, monitor progress through assistants, have extensive telephone contact, and otherwise intervene actively to design detailed modifications of parental and child behaviors. These tactics are based on the assumption that the home is the natural locus for behavior control and the parents are the child's proper controlling agents. That a child's misbehavior can be controlled in a clinic or hospital is of limited practical utility. Treatments must be shown to work in the environment where the child must live.

Hall, Cristler, Cranston, and Tucker use multiple baseline techniques to show changes in behavior of children both at home and at school. The authors' discussion of the use of this design is particularly instructive. The use of students to record study behavior and promptness of attendance is an unusual feature.

Wahler presents a technique designed to obtain compliance with parental instructions and to reduce unwanted aggression and other disruptive activity. His method, like the others, involves the discriminating use of the parents' greater power to reinforce their children's behavior or to prevent it from occurring without penalty. This use of superior power may excite some concern in many people, especially in this age made sensitive to the significance of youthful rebellion. They may not be much relieved to learn that the child and the parents appear to be happier when the struggle for power has been resolved in the parents' favor. Like any other powerful controlling principle, the parents' potential control over their children's behavior can be used for many purposes, including those that will not serve the child's interests. However, the cases in this paper illustrate situations in which the failure of the parent to exert control seems potentially more damaging than helpful to the child.

The paper by Stuart deals with behavioral contracts. In a behavioral contract a person agrees to perform a certain behavior for a specific reinforcer. Stuart's contracts involve a complex set of contingencies with little explicit shaping and numerous behavioral changes to be established quickly in a variety of contexts. Mann's contracts have more of the elements of shaping. They specify a target behavior, the necessary steps to get there, and the reinforcers to back up the shaping. In each instance, the subject understands and agrees to the procedures. The use of behavioral contracts is increasing in adult-child relationships for managing difficult interactions, for example, in managing teachers' and parents' expectations of study behavior, requiring compliance with demands for obedience, and so on. We include Stuart's paper on contracts since it seems to be such an important step in certain adult-child interactions even though it includes no data attesting to its effectiveness. Mann's study does not deal with children (the subjects were college students), but it does contain data.

The paper by Phillips is the first in a series of studies of "pre-delinquent" boys in a homelike environment. This is one of many publications that are emerging from the Kansas group (Wolf, Fixsen, Timbers, etc.) who initiated "Achievement Place." They report results that must be rated as extraordinarily successful. It appears that the delinquent behaviors of youths such as these can be controlled effectively through the use of a token system like that managed here in their own community—away from prisons and jails. It introduces the notion of "professional parents" for children who are too much to handle for their natural parents. The social significance of this research may be very great. The degree to which this high degree of control can be relaxed to resemble the controls that operate in more normal homes is an exciting question for future study.

R. VANCE HALL
CONNIE CRISTLER
SHARON S. CRANSTON
BONNIE TUCKER
University of Kansas

Teachers and parents as researchers using multiple baseline designs[1]

Two teachers and a parent used three basic multiple baseline designs to investigate the effects of systematic reinforcement and punishment procedures in the classroom and at home. (1) A fifth-grade teacher concurrently measured the same behavior (tardiness) in three stimulus situations (after morning, noon, and afternoon recesses). Posting the names of pupils on a chart titled "Today's Patriots" was made contingent on being on time after the noon recess, then successively also the morning and afternoon recesses. Tardiness was reduced to near zero rates at the points where contingencies were applied. (2) A high school

Reprinted from *Journal of Applied Behavior Analysis*, 1970, 3, 247–55, with permission of the publisher and the authors. Copyright 1970 by the Society for the Experimental Analysis of Behavior, Inc.

[1] This research was supported in part by the National Institute of Child Health and Human Development (HD-03144-03, Bureau of Child Research and Department of Family Life, University of Kansas). The authors are indebted to Linda Warwick, a student in the fifth-grade class of Highlands School, Mission, Kansas, who served as second observer in the Patriots' Chart experiment; to Susan Helmsing, a student at Shawnee Mission North High School, who independently scored papers in the French class experiment; and to Jessica Shellman, who acted as a reliability observer in the home study experiment. The authors are also indebted to Donald M. Baer, Montrose M. Wolf, Larry Doke, and Joseph Spradlin for comments and suggestions regarding the manuscript.

282

*teacher recorded the same behavior (daily French-quiz grades) of three stu-
dents. She then successively applied the same consequences (staying after
school for individual tutoring for D and F grades) for each student. At the
points where the contingency was applied, D and F grades were eliminated.
(3) A mother concurrently measured three different behaviors (clarinet practice, Campfire project work, reading) of her 10-yr-old daughter. She successively
applied the same contingency (going to bed early) for less than 30 min spent
engaged in one after another of the behaviors. Marked increases in the behaviors were observed at the points where the contingency was applied.*

In a number of studies employing systematic reinforcement procedures to modify academic behaviors of pupils, a traditional experimental-
group control-group research design has been incorporated to evaluate the
effects of the programs (*e.g.,* Wolf, Giles, and Hall, 1968; Clark, Wolf,
Lachowicz, 1968; Ward and Baker, 1968). In these studies, the progress of
a group whose behaviors were exposed to systematic reinforcement procedures was compared to the progress of a control group that was not
exposed to the procedures.

On the other hand, in many studies involving systematic reinforcement procedures, a reversal experimental design was employed (*e.g.,* Hall,
Lund, and Jackson, 1968; Hall, Panyan, Rabon, and Broden, 1968;
Thomas, Becker, and Armstrong, 1968; Madsen, Becker, and Thomas,
1968). In these studies, the progress of an individual subject or of a group
was compared under successive baseline and reinforcement conditions.
First, baseline observations were made to establish the pre-reinforcement
level of performance; then, reinforcement procedures were instituted. Once
a change in level of performance had been demonstrated, a brief return
was made to baseline conditions. When the behavior returned to the baseline level, reinforcement procedures were employed once more to see if the
level of performance achieved in the first reinforcement phase could be
replicated.

Baer, Wolf, and Risley (1968) suggested the desirability of using another research strategy, called a multiple baseline, as an alternative to the
reversal design in applied research. The multiple baseline design involves
the measurement of several behaviors over time so that several baselines
are established. Then, a behavior modification procedure is applied to one
of the behaviors until a change is demonstrated in that behavior; then, the
same procedure is applied to a second behavior, later to a third, and so
forth. If the various behaviors change markedly at the point when the
procedure is introduced, a strong inference of causal relationship is established. To date, very few studies reported have used the multiple baseline
research strategy, although Hart and Risley (1968) employed a multiple

baseline design in their study of preschool language acquisition and Barrish, Saunders, and Wolf (1969) used a multiple baseline design in studying the effects of group contingencies, first during math period and then during reading period, to decrease talking-out and out-of-seat behaviors in a fourth-grade classroom.

The present studies illustrate the use of three basic types of multiple baseline designs: across situations, across individuals, and across behaviors. The studies are also of interest because in each case a teacher or parent acted as the experimenter and the prime observer. Most studies carried out in classrooms and homes have relied completely on outside observers and experimenters. Procedures that allow teachers and parents to act as observers and experimenters will more likely be used than those requiring extensive outside personnel.

EXPERIMENT I

Subjects and Setting

Twenty-five fifth-grade students from upper-middle-class families in the suburban area of Shawnee Mission, Kansas served as subjects. As a part of their daily routine, the 16 boys and nine girls in the class were allowed to go to the restroom and to visit the drinking fountain after recesses. Although most pupils returned to class without undue delay, there were usually a few pupils after each recess who returned a minute or two after class had resumed. This disrupted class and annoyed the teacher.

Observation

The teacher, who was enrolled in a university course on management of classroom behavior, acted as the primary observer. She began recording the number of pupils who were late in returning to class after the morning, noon, and afternoon recesses. The teacher closed the classroom door 4 min after the first pupil entered the hallway outside the classroom on his way to the restroom after recess. Any pupil who entered the classroom after the door closed was counted as being late. The teacher chose a pupil who was always prompt to make a simultaneous record of the number of late pupils. The correspondence of the teacher and pupil records was 100% on all 59 days of the study, except for the first, second, third, tenth, and seventeenth days. On each of these days, there was a difference of one in the number of late pupils recorded. The percentage of agreement of the records on days when the counts differed was computed by dividing the lesser tally of late pupils by the greater and multiplying by 100. The mean percentage of agreement for the study was 99%.

Experimental Phases and Results

Baseline or no-chart phase.   Records were kept of the number of pupils who were late returning to the room after the noon, morning, and afternoon recesses. No contingencies were in effect for being late after the noon recess during the first 13 days of recording. No contingencies were in effect for being late after the morning recess during the first 21 days of recording; and no contingencies were in effect for being tardy after the afternoon recess through the first 27 days of the experiment. Thus baselines of varying length were established. The median number of pupils late after the noon recess during this baseline phase was eight, while the median number late after both the morning and afternoon phases was four. (See Fig. 1)

Patriots Chart part.   Before the experiment, the class had been reading a series of patriotic books about the history of America. In the books, the children of the American colonists helped find powder for the soldiers, went on secret missions, carried messages for the colonists, *etc.* The class discussed how exciting it must have been to live in those days. They discussed how they could be patriots as children living in the 1960s. One suggestion was that if they obeyed class rules they were good citizens and, therefore, patriots. As part of their unit on patriotism, they had a class program in which they acted out some of the stories they had read and told how children today could be patriotic. Since patriotism seemed to have become so important, the teacher decided that for a pupil's name to be included in a list of students' names entitled "Today's Patriots" would probably be a reinforcing event.

On the morning of the fourteenth day, the teacher introduced a "Today's Patriots" list which was to be posted on the bulletin board before the close of school each day. The teacher told the class that if they were inside the classroom before the door was closed after the noon recess, their names would be placed on the "Today's Patriots" chart. Nothing was said about the morning or afternoon recesses. As seen in Fig. 1, the number of pupils late after the noon recess under the Patriots' Chart condition decreased dramatically, while the number of those late after the morning and afternoon recesses remained essentially unchanged.

On the morning of the twenty-second day, the children were told they must be in the room before the door was closed after the morning as well as the noon recess in order to have their names placed on the Patriots' Chart. Nothing was said about the afternoon recess. As shown in Fig. 1, under these conditions the number of pupils late at noon remained at zero; the number of late pupils after the afternoon recess remained at essentially the same level, perhaps slightly lower.

On the twenty-eighth day, the pupils were told that they had been excellent patriots but that beginning that day they must be in the class-

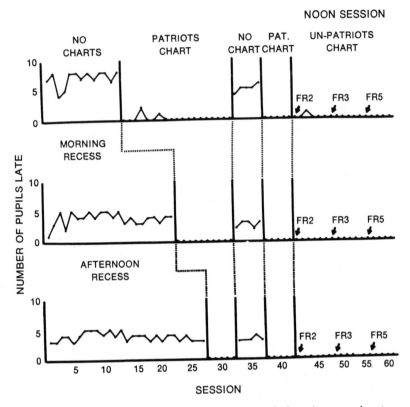

FIGURE 1 A record of the number of pupils late in returning to their fifth-grade classroom after noon, morning, and afternoon recess. *No Charts*—baseline, before experimental procedures. *Patriots' Chart*—posting of pupil names on "Today's Patriots" chart contingent on entering class on time after recess. *No Chart*—posting of names discontinued. *Patriots' Chart*—return to Patriots' Chart conditions. *Un-Patriots' Chart*—posting of names on "Un-Patriots'" chart contingent on being late after recess (FR 2) every two days, (FR 3) every three days, and (FR 5) every five days.

room by the time the door was closed after all three recesses in order to be listed as a patriot. Under these conditions no pupils were recorded as being late after any of the recesses.

No chart phase. After five days in which no pupil was late after any recess, a reversal phase was instituted as a further check on the function of the chart as a reinforcer for being on time. On the thirty-third day, the pupils were told they had done so well and had such a perfect record of being patriots that the teacher thought she no longer needed to post any names. She stressed that she knew she could count on them to continue being patriots. Then, nothing more was said and no lists were posted during the week. As seen in Fig. 1, there was a return of late behavior.

Return to Patriots' Chart phase. On the thirty-eighth day, the pupils were told that because some pupils were again returning to class late, the Patriots' Chart would be posted once more and that pupils must be on time after all recesses in order to have their names listed. As shown in Fig. 1 there was an immediate return to perfect promptness after recess.

Un-Patriots' Chart phase. Up to this point, whenever the Patriots' Chart condition was in effect, names were listed on a continuous reinforcement schedule, that is, every day. On the forty-third day, however, the pupils were told that "Today's Patriots" would be posted at various times, rather than every day. They would not know how often the list would be posted but were encouraged to keep a prompt record so that their names would be on it whenever it was.

In the course of the discussion, one of the pupils suggested that the names of those who were late should be posted rather than those who were on time. Other pupils agreed that this would be a good plan, stating as their reason that it was hard to find one's own name on the list because there were so many on it. Others suggested a larger chart that would be easier to see. Finally, the matter was put to a vote. The pupils voted to list those who were late and suggested it be called the "Un-Patriots' " Chart, adapted from the commercial for the "Un-Cola."

Through the remainder of the experiment, an intermittent schedule was followed in posting the "Un-Patriots' " Chart. Initially, it was posted every other day. Since the pupils were required to have a perfect record between postings, they were on a fixed ratio (FR 2) schedule. Beginning on the forty-ninth day, the chart was posted every third day (FR 3) and in the last week of the experiment it was not posted until the end of the week (FR 5). (As can be seen in Fig. 1, except for one pupil who was late at noon on the third day of the unpatriots' phase, there was a zero rate of being late after recess).

EXPERIMENT II

Subjects and Setting

Three tenth grade students in a French II class met daily for 45 min at Shawnee Mission North High school in Shawnee Mission, Kansas. When the study was initiated, these students, two boys and a girl, had been receiving grades that were primarily Ds and Fs on quizzes given three to four times a week. These quizzes were given at the beginning or end of the class period to determine whether the pupils had studied the homework assignment the previous night or to see if they had paid attention in class that day.

Before the study, the teacher had talked with each of the students concerning their low test scores and encouraged them to make an effort at better performance. She reported having tried applying contingent verbal praise when one of them did well on a quiz as well as writing "good" or other remarks (in French) on their test papers. Contingent verbal praise had also been used to reinforce correct oral responses during recitation in class. These attempts had not been effective in increasing quiz performance.

Observation

The teacher, who was enrolled in a course on management of classroom behavior, acted as the experimenter and primary observer. Letter grades were assigned the quizzes according to the following scale: A=92 to 100% correct; B = 84 to 91%; C = 72 to 83%; D = 64 to 71%; F = 63% or below. As a check on the reliability of scoring, the teacher had an outstanding student score the quizzes independently. The agreement in scoring by the two was 100%.

Experimental Phases and Results

Baseline phase. Quiz scores were recorded and graphed for all three pupils during the baseline phase when no special contingencies were being applied. Baseline conditions were in effect for 10 days for Dave, 15 days for Roy, and 20 days for Debbie. Figure 2 presents a record of their grades. Dave's median grade for 10 baseline quizzes was F. On a four-point scale (A = 4, B = 3, C = 2, D = 1, F = 0) his mean grade point was 0.4. Roy's median grade for 15 baseline quizzes was also F and his grade on a four-point scale was 0.7. Debbie's median for 20 baseline quizzes was F and her grade point was 0.4

After-school tutoring for low grades phase. At the close of class after the tenth quiz had been given, the teacher informed Dave that because he seemed to be having trouble understanding his French lessons, beginning with the next quiz, whenever he earned a score of D or F, he would be required to come in after school and she would work with him until he knew the lesson well. After these conditions were instituted, Dave's median grade was an A and his grade-point average on the four-point scale was 3.6. He received no Ds or Fs on any of the 15 quizzes given.

Nothing was said to Roy until after the fifteenth quiz had been given, at which time the same contingency for D and F grades was put

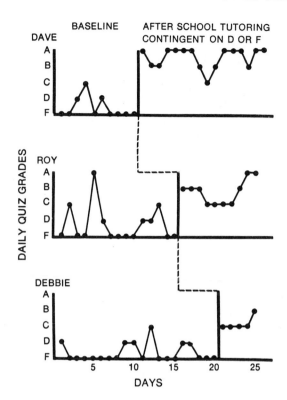

FIGURE 2 A record of quiz score grades for three high school French-class students. *Baseline*—before experimental procedures. *After School Tutoring Contingent on D and F Grades*—pupils required to stay after school for tutoring if they score D or F on daily quizzes.

into effect. Roy's median grade for this phase was B, and his grade point increased to 2.8. He received no D or F grades.

Tutoring after school following quiz grades of D or F was instituted for Debbie after the twentieth class quiz. Debbie's median grade for the five days after experimental conditions were begun was C. Her grade point was 2.2 and, like Dave and Roy, she received no Ds or Fs.

EXPERIMENT III

Subject and Setting

The subject for this experiment was Lisa, a 10-yr-old normal, active, fourth-grade girl. Among her extra-curricular activities were music lessons on the clarinet and membership in a Campfire Girl troop. During the weeks of this study, cold weather confined the subject indoors after school for all but a few minutes of play outdoors each day. In order for her to earn ceremonial honor beads in an upcoming Campfire "ceremonial" she needed to complete several projects. She also had six book reports due before Christmas vacation. Her regularly scheduled clarinet practice time was 30 min per day. The press of these activities caused the girl's mother to ask that she spend 30 min per activity during the after-school and evening hours during the four weeks before Christmas vacation. (Immediately after the study, the requirements for study and working on Campfire projects were reduced).

Observation

The girl's mother, who was enrolled in a university course on management of classroom behavior, acted as the experimenter and primary observer. A stopwatch was used to time all three behaviors. Time spent practicing on the clarinet was measured from the time the first note was sounded until the subject announced she had finished. Time spent getting the clarinet out and putting it away after practice was not counted as part of the practice session. Since the Campfire Girl projects included a variety of activities, time spent on them was measured after Lisa had explained to her mother what she was going to do, had gathered all needed materials and work actually commenced. Reading time was recorded from the time Lisa was seated at a table with her library book open until she closed the book. No time was deducted for occasional pauses when she looked away from the book to "day-dream". As long as the book was open and she was seated at the table in front of it, reading time was recorded.

A classmate of the experimenter came to dinner once a week, and participated in evaluating the reliability of the observation procedures. The classmate would arrive about the same time the children returned from school and would stay until the last task was completed. She used a second stopwatch and observed from a different vantage point than that of the mother. For example, she would sit in the living room to observe Lisa who was reading at a table in the kitchen. Although she could observe Lisa, she could not see Lisa's mother who was also in the kitchen working. Neither was able to hear the click of the other's stopwatch. For purposes of this study it was decided to round off all time measures to the nearest minute. If less than 30 sec showed on the stopwatch, they were not counted. If more than 30 sec showed, another whole minute was added. Under these conditions, agreement between the observers was 100% throughout the study. Data were recorded four evenings a week on Monday, Tuesday, Wednesday, and Friday.

Experimental Phases and Results

Baseline. Before baseline, Lisa was told that she was to spend 30 min each evening on each of the three projects, clarinet practicing, Campfire honors, and book-report reading. Lisa agreed that to do so was necessary if she were to finish her projects on time. Lisa was instructed that her activities were being timed during the baseline phase. Figure 3 presents the records of the number of minutes Lisa spent engaged in clarinet practice, Campfire work, and book-report reading.

Lisa's mean baseline for time spent in clarinet practice was 13.5 min per day. Her mean time spent in Campfire work was 3.5 min per day, and her mean time spent in reading for book reports was 11 min per day.

Bedtime contingent on clarinet practice. At the beginning of the second week, Lisa was told that she would have to go to bed 1 min earlier than her regular bedtime on Monday, Tuesday, Wednesday, and Friday

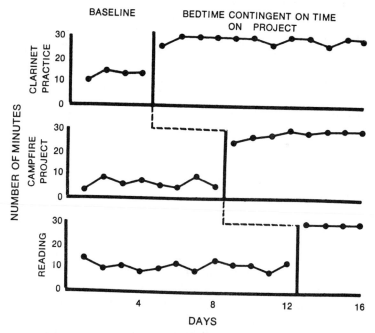

FIGURE 3 A record of time spent in clarinet practice, Campfire honors project work, and reading for book reports by a 10-yr-old girl. *Baseline*—before experimental procedures. *Early Bedtime Contingent on Less Than 30 Min of Behavior*—1 min earlier bedtime for each minute less than 30 engaged in an activity.

for each minute less than 30 min that she spent practicing her clarinet. Under these conditions, she practiced 26 min the first day and 30 min a day thereafter. Her mean duration of practicing for the entire phase increased to 29 min per day. Campfire work averaged 3.75 min per day. Book-report reading remained at the baseline duration of 11 min per day.

Bedtime contingent on clarinet practice and Campfire work.   At the beginning of the third week, Lisa was told that she had not been spending enough time on her Campfire projects. Therefore, she would have to go to bed 1 min early for each minute less than 30 min that she worked on her Campfire projects as well as 1 min early for each minute less than 30 she practiced her clarinet. When bedtime was made contingent on both clarinet practicing and Campfire project work, Lisa spent adequate amounts of time engaged in both of these behaviors. The mean duration of practicing the clarinet remained at approximately 29 min per day and Campfire work increased to about 28 min per day. Book-report reading remained at the relatively short duration of 11.5 min per day.

Bedtime contingent on clarinet practice, Campfire work, and reading. At the beginning of the fourth week, Lisa was told she would be required to go to bed 1 min early for each minute less than 30 that she spent reading for her book reports. The contingencies for clarinet practice and for Campfire work were also still in effect. Thus, when bedtime was made contingent on engaging in all three behaviors, Lisa's mean time practicing was 29 min, time spent working on Campfire projects was 29.75 min, and time spent reading was 30 min. The mean duration of all three activities was 1 hr and 28.75 min, compared to a mean duration of only 28 min during the first baseline week.

DISCUSSION

Multiple Baseline Designs

The three present studies provide examples of three basic types of multiple baseline studies. When Baer *et al.* (1968) suggested the use of the multiple baseline technique, they did not differentiate the various types of multiple baselines that are possible. More recently, however, Risley and Baer (in press) have suggested that at least three different multiple baseline designs are possible in investigating the behavior of individual subjects. We suggest that these multiple baseline designs apply equally well to the behavior of groups if the behavior of the group members is summed or averaged, and the group is treated as a single organism. Such an application is illustrated in Exp. I.

One approach Risley and Baer (in press) suggested, involves obtaining baselines of two or more behaviors of the same individual and introducing experimental procedures to one of the behaviors after the other, causality being demonstrated if the behaviors change successively at the point where experimental procedures were applied and not before. Few such multiple baseline studies have been published, although Schwarz and Hawkins (in press) used such a tactic to explore the effects of contingencies on number size, face touching, posture, and voice loudness in a sixth-grade girl. Risley and Hart (1968) used the multiple baseline design with a group in their investigation of language in groups of poverty area preschool children. The experiment carried out by Lisa's mother (Exp. III) was a very clear example of this type of multiple baseline design. Three of Lisa's behaviors were measured. The same contingency was applied successively to each of the behaviors and at the points where the contingency was placed in effect, significant changes in rate were observed.

The second multiple-baseline design suggested by Risley and Baer (in press) was to measure concurrently the same behavior of several individuals in the same situation. After obtaining these baselines, experimental procedures could be applied successively to the behavior of one after another of the individuals. Few examples of this tactic in applied school settings have been reported; however, Revusky (1967) suggested a statistical treatment for analyzing data in such experiments. The second experiment in which the senior-high French students successively earned better grades on daily quizzes after the consequence of staying after school to be helped was invoked for the first, second, and third student, is an example of the use of this type of multiple baseline design.

The third type of multiple baseline tactic suggested by Risley and Baer (in press) was to measure the same behavior of a single individual concurrently in different stimulus situations. In the classroom, these stimulus situations could involve at least the five major dimensions of time, type of activity, identity of teacher, location, and composition of student group. (It could also, of course, vary in a multitude of other dimensions.)

The Barrish, et al. (1968) study is an example of this design applied to a classroom group. In their study, baselines of talking-out and being out-of-seat behavior were obtained during math and reading periods. Contingencies were then applied, first during math, then during reading. Thus, the stimulus situations differed in at least two major dimensions: time and type of activity. This is seen in the fact that reading period came after math period and in the fact that reading and math are by definition different types of activity. The location, the teacher, and the composition of the student group remained constant, as both math and reading were taught in the same self-contained classroom.

The classroom study in which the names of pupils who were on time were posted on the Patriots' Chart is an example of this third kind of multiple baseline. In this case, however, the stimulus situation varied along one major dimension only, that of time. In all three measurement situations (noon, morning, and afternoon), the same group of pupils was returning to the same classroom and teacher after the activity of recess. The location of the classroom and its relationship to the playground, washrooms, hallways, *etc.* remained constant. Thus, the only apparent change in stimulus situations was associated with whether it was the morning, noon, or afternoon recess.

Instructional Control

It should be pointed out that in each of the three present experiments, in which clear and dramatic effects were observed, the subjects were under good instructional control.

In each study, whenever the teacher or the parent announced a new experimental condition there was an immediate change in behavior directly related to the announced change in condition. This instructional control suggests that in all three cases the subjects had learned that when the teacher or parent announced conditions that would lead to a given consequence, the consequences would indeed follow. Thus, verbal cues from adults had become discriminative stimuli for consequences. (In other words, when the teacher or parent said something they "knew she meant it!".) That instructional control is dependent on consequences, however, is dramatically illustrated in the Patriots' Chart study by the reversal procedure phase. Here, the teacher specifically asked pupils to continue being on time although she removed the Patriots' Chart contingency. Since tardiness increased, it can be seen that even though the teacher had previously shown strong instructional control when her statements promised consequences, instructional control was relatively weak when it was not accompanied by consequences.

Effective Consequences

The data also indicated that the consequences chosen were effective. In the high school French class, it was of special interest to note that the three students never came in contact with the consequence, yet it served to produce marked changes in their performance. In this case, avoidance behavior was observed. Such behavior was not too surprising in Dave's instance because he was athletic and staying after class to study French would have interfered with football turnouts. The results found with Roy and Debbie indicated, however, that staying after school to receive help may be a punishing consequence for many pupils. It would be a mistake to conclude that this would be true in all cases. In Lisa's case, having to go to bed earlier than usual was also shown to be an effective consequence, one that would not be surprising to any parent of a pre-teen son or daughter.

It was a little more surprising, however, that the Patriots' Chart proved as effective as the data indicated. It is probable that many other teachers have tried the posting of names on a chart as a means of reinforcing desired classroom behavior. In most cases, the behavior of concern has probably been something other than returning to class on time after recess and the charts have probably been labelled "Today's Citizens", or "Our Good Workers", or some designation other than "Today's Patriots". Essentially, however, the tactics and aims have been the same. These other teachers may or may not have had successes equal to those achieved in this study, and at least some will be surprised at the present results, as was the teacher who conducted the study. She did not expect the degree of control effected by her procedures. Therefore, mention should probably be made of several important factors that may have contributed to the success achieved and would be important considerations for anyone trying to replicate the results. The fact that this technique proved so effective with this particular class may have been related to the rather extensive study by the students of the unit on patriotism. Reading stories about patriots, class discussions, and other such activities may have contributed to the reinforcing function served by listing pupils as "Today's Patriots".

Discriminating Conditions

Another factor that may have been related to the success of these studies is that the subjects were able to discriminate clearly when experimental conditions were in effect. In the cases of the French pupils and Lisa, it is not surprising that the necessary discriminations were made. In the case of the Patriots' Chart study, however, since the stimulus situations for noon, morning, and afternoon recesses were ostensibly similar in most dimensions, it would seem that there would have been near-maximum possibility for generalization of tardiness behavior from one recess to another. As shown in Fig. 1, however, no generalization occurred and pupils continued to be tardy at recesses other than those for which contingencies were in effect. Thus, pupils were able to make discriminations as to reinforcement or non-reinforcement from the stimuli available that were associated with the various recesses, even though it would seem that the stimulus dimensions of all three after-recess situations were very much the same.

Carrying out Consequences

Two final factors related to both instructional control and discrimination conditions were that in all three studies, the pupils were told that the teacher (and in Lisa's case, the mother) was keeping an accurate record and they did experience the consequences every time that the teacher said they would. Thus, the relationship between the instructions and the consequences was consistent.

Teachers and Parents as Experimenters

Perhaps the most important aspect of these studies, beyond their illustration of three multiple baselines as a research tactic, is the fact that they were carried out by teachers and parents. As previously mentioned, most research reported up to now has employed skilled researchers with outside observers. These studies demonstrate, however, that teachers and parents can carry out important and significant studies in natural settings using resources available to them. In doing so, they demonstrated that systematic behavioral analysis procedures can be successfully employed by teachers and parents using resources and contingencies readily available in school and home settings.

It should perhaps be emphasized once more, however, that had not the experimenters chosen consequences that were effective, had the behaviors been less clearly specified, had the experimenters been less precise in carrying out the measurement and reinforcement procedures, it is improbable that such dramatic results would have been obtained. Others who attempt similar programs should attend to all of these factors if they expect to achieve a similar degree of control.

REFERENCES

BAER, DONALD M., WOLF, MONTROSE M., and RISLEY, TODD R. Some current dimensions of applied behavior analysis. *Journal of Applied Behavior Analysis*, 1968, **1**, 91–97.

BARRISH, HARRIET H., SAUNDERS, MURIEL, and WOLF, MONTROSE M. Good behavior game: effects of individual contingencies for group consequences on disruptive behavior in a classroom. *Journal of Applied Behavior Analysis*, 1969, **2**, 119–124.

CLARK, M., LACHOWICZ, J., and WOLF, MONTROSE M. A pilot basic education program for school dropouts incorporating a token reinforcement system. *Behaviour Research and Therapy*, 1968, **6**, 183–188.

HALL, R. VANCE; LUND, DIANE, and JACKSON, DELORIS. Effects of teacher attention on study behavior. *Journal of Applied Behavior Analysis*, 1968, 1, 1–12.

HALL, R. VANCE; PANYAN, MARION; RABON, DELORIS, and BRODEN, MARCIA. Instructing beginning teachers in reinforcement procedures that improve classroom control. *Journal of Applied Behavior Analysis*, 1968, 1, 315–322.

HART, BETTY M. and RISLEY, TODD R. Establishing use of descriptive adjectives in the spontaneous speech of disadvantaged preschool children. *Journal of Applied Behavior Analysis*, 1968, 1, 109–120.

MADSEN, CHARLES H., JR., BECKER, W. C., and THOMAS, D. R. Rules, praise, and ignoring: elements of elementary classroom control. *Journal of Applied Behavior Analysis*, 1968, 1, 139–150.

REVUSKY, S. H. Some statistical treatments compatible with individual organism methodology. *Journal of Experimental Analysis of Behavior*, 1967, 10, 319–330.

RISLEY, TODD R. and BAER, DONALD M. Operant conditioning: "Develop" is a transitive active verb. In B. Caldwell and H. Ricciuti (Eds.), *Review of child development research*, volume III: *Social influence and social action*. (*In press*)

RISLEY, TODD R. and HART, BETTY M. Developing correspondence between the non-verbal and verbal behavior of preschool children. *Journal of Applied Behavior Analysis*, 1968, 1, 267–281.

SCHWARZ, MICHAEL L. and HAWKINS, ROBERT P. Application of delayed conditioning procedures to the behavior problems of an elementary school child. In R. Ulrich, J. Stachnik, and J. Mabry. *Control of human behavior*, vol. II: *From cure to prevention*. Glenview, Illinois: Scott, Foresman. (*In press*)

THOMAS, D. R., BECKER, W. C., and ARMSTRONG, M. Production and elimination of disruptive classroom behavior by systematically varying teacher's behavior. *Journal of Applied Behavior Analysis*, 1968, 1, 35–45.

WARD, MICHAEL and BECKER, BRUCE. Reinforcement therapy in the classroom. *Journal of Applied Behavior Analysis*, 1968, 1, 323–328.

WOLF, MONTROSE M., GILES, DAVID K., and HALL, R. VANCE. Experiments with token reinforcement in a remedial classroom. *Behaviour Research and Therapy*, 1968, 6, 51–64.

ROBERT G. WAHLER
University of Tennessee

Oppositional children: a quest for parental reinforcement control[1]

The present study attempted to examine changes in parental reinforcement value as a function of parental use of timeout and differential attention. Subjects were two children classified by their parents as highly oppositional to parental requests or commands. Results showed that the children's oppositional behavior varied predictably with the presence and absence of parental use of timeout and differential attention. As expected, parental reinforcement value for the children was higher during treatment periods than during baseline periods.

A recent longitudinal study by Robins (1966) specified childhood behavior patterns that appear to predict serious psychiatric disturbances in adults. Essentially, this study showed that young children who display

Reprinted from *Journal of Applied Behavior Analysis,* 1969, 2, 159–70, with permission of the publisher and the author. Copyright 1969 by the Society for the Experimental Analysis of Behavior, Inc.

---

[1] This study was supported in part by research grant MH 13914-01 from the National Institute of Mental Health. Thanks are due to Michael Thomas, Larry Ventis, Norman Teeter, and Aaron Botbyl for their service as observers in this study.

frequent "antisocial" behavior tend to exhibit similar behaviors as adults, to the point that they are likely to be labeled sociopathic.

Antisocial behavior as defined by Robins included a variety of behaviors, such as truancy, lying, and stealing. Of greater interest to the present study, however, was the finding that many of these "antisocial" children had parents who were quite lax in providing discipline and supervision. The children tended to be quite oppositional to social requirements and their parents were unable or unwilling to cope with the problem. Robins attests to the importance of such disciplinary problems by describing instances in which strict or adequate discipline for some of these children decreased the probability that they would develop adult sociopathic disorders.

The importance of developing effective treatment techniques for antisocial children is certainly illustrated by the Robins study. Many of these children oppose requirements set by their parents, their schools, and their communities in general; if one were to focus treatment on any single broad aspect of their behavior, that behavior would probably be defined as oppositional or negativistic. Thus, if their oppositional tendencies could be modified early in life, chances of later psychiatric problems might be reduced greatly.

From the standpoint of reinforcement theory, the modification of oppositional child behavior presents some interesting practical and theoretical problems. Most reinforcement theorists assume that a child's deviant behavior is supported by appropriately contingent attention provided by the child's parents, his teachers, his peers, *etc.* In other words, one might assume that these people are sources of positive reinforcement for the child and that the sources are responsible for maintaining the child's deviant behavior. Thus, extended observation of the child and members of his immediate social community should reveal roughly consistent attention contingencies for the deviant behavior. Furthermore, manipulation of these contingencies should produce predictable effects on the child's deviant behavior. That is, frequency counts of his deviant behavior should decrease when the contingencies are absent and increase when the contingencies are present. A number of investigations (*e.g.*, Hawkins, Peterson, Schwied, and Bijou, 1966; Harris, Wolf, and Baer, 1964) have provided clear support for these predictions; parents and teachers can be trained to utilize their positive reinforcement power to produce dramatic therapeutic changes in deviant child behavior.

Although these "contingency shifting" procedures have been shown to be effective in modifying several types of deviant child behavior, they have been markedly ineffective in dealing with oppositional behavior, at least as far as parent-child interactions are concerned. The author (Wahler, 1968) studied five families containing extremely oppositional children. In this study, efforts were made to eliminate parental attention contingencies for the children's oppositional behavior, while maintaining the contingencies for cooperative behavior. Figure 1 presents a summary of the findings: although the parents became differentially attentive to their children's cooperative behavior, frequency counts of oppositional behavior were unchanged from the baseline. Fortunately, a timeout procedure proved effective in obtaining therapeutic results. In this procedure, the parents were instructed to isolate their children (in their bedrooms) immediately after oppositional behavior occurred, and to continue their social approval after cooperative behavior. As Fig. 1 indicates, dramatic and rather stable changes occurred in the children's behavior.

The failure to obtain therapeutic changes through the simple contingency shifting procedure could have been due to several factors. One of these factors—the question of parental reinforcement value—was chosen as the focus of the present study. Conceivably, the contingency shifting

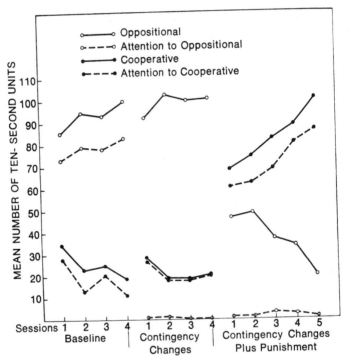

FIGURE 1 Mean number of oppositional and cooperative behaviors and their parental attention contingencies. Means are based on the behavior of five parent-child cases. All observations were made during 20-min clinic playroom sessions, held once a week.

procedure was ineffective because the parents themselves were not reinforcing to the children. To carry this contention further, perhaps the
timeout procedure produced changes in parental reinforcement value; perhaps the stability of the children's cooperative behavior during follow-up
was due to the increased reinforcement power of the parents' social attention. The only bases for this assumption were two frequently reported observations: (1) the children appeared to approach their parents more
frequently during the treatment and follow-up sessions than during the
baseline sessions; (2) although parental use of the timeout procedure was
infrequent during follow-up, the children's cooperative behavior remained
at a stable level.

The present study further investigated oppositional child behavior.
Specifically, the study was designed to answer some of the preceding questions concerning parental reinforcement value.

METHOD

Subjects, Apparatus, and Observers

The subjects were two early elementary school-age boys and their parents.
In both cases, the parents sought psychological help because of their children's oppositional behavior. Both sets of parents reported marked difficulties in getting their children to obey parental requests or commands; they
described their children as "stubborn", "negativistic", and "headstrong".
In both cases, all observations and experimental manipulations were carried out in the children's homes.

Recordings of child and parent behaviors were obtained through a
behavior checklist similar to one described by Hawkins *et al.* (1966). The
method essentially required an observer to make coded checks for the occurrence of a behavior class and its stimulus contingencies within successive
10-sec intervals; any occurrence of a class, regardless of its duration during
an interval, was scored as a single unit.

All observers were sophisticated in the use of operant techniques and
natural science principles of observation. Approximately half of the data
were collected by single observers who were, unfortunately, aware of the
sequence of procedural steps involved in the study. However, at periodic
intervals, reliability checks were made by procedurally naive observers.

General Procedure

Several of the initial home sessions were used to adapt the subject and his
parents to the observer's presence and to obtain written records of parent-

child interactions. These records were analyzed in the following way: the child's responses were grouped into classes on the basis of physical or functional similarities among the separate responses. For example, screaming and crying were considered together because of their generally similar physical characteristics; the child's behavioral failures to obey parental commands, although physically dissimilar, were considered together because of their relationship to common stimulus events, namely parental commands. Parental behaviors occurring immediately after a child response class were considered as a single stimulus class, labeled Parent Social Attention.

Observer reliability and baseline observations.   When behavior and stimulus classes were formulated, efforts were made to obtain frequency counts of selected classes. The previously described paper and pencil checklist was now utilized for all remaining sessions. Each observation session was 40 min in length.

Three classes of child behavior were recorded in this study: oppositional and cooperative behavior were defined in a functional sense as specific responses following parental requests or commands. When a parental request or command was presented to the child, observers scored his future behavior as either oppositional or cooperative, depending on whether or not the instruction was followed. In order for one unit of cooperative behavior to be scored, the child had to comply with the instruction for a full 10 sec. Thus, any period of non-compliance during a 10-sec interval resulted in that interval being scored as oppositional. Observers continued to score the child's behavior into these two categories until he completed the parental requirement or until a new parental request or command was presented; oppositional or cooperative scoring was then considered in light of the new parental instruction.

Social approach behavior was also defined functionally, in this case as verbal or physical behavior that clearly involved the child's parents. In addition, this category required that the behavior not be parent-initiated. For example, talking to a parent, physical contact with a parent, and playing with a parent were all considered instances of social approach behavior as long as the behavior was not immediately preceded by some parental action involving the child. Once this category was scored, it was also scored in future intervals if the child-parent interaction continued. If the interaction stopped for a full interval, future interactions, in order to be scored as social approach behavior, had to be child-initiated.

Two classes of parent behavior were recorded: parental social attention was considered a single stimulus class, composed of the behavior of either or both parents. Any verbal or physical behavior that clearly involved the child was scored into this category as long as it closely followed a category of his behavior (within the same or the following 10-sec interval). The principal parental behaviors composing this category included talking to the child, physical contact with him, and non-verbal play. The parental behaviors of eye contact and looking at the child were also initially scored into this category, but observer reliability problems required that they be omitted.

Parental instructions were scored because of their function in defining the child's oppositional behavior. Any requests or commands were scored into this stimulus category. Before all observation sessions, the parents were told to provide instructions for their child. The instructions presented were taken from a list of household chores that the parents considered aversive to their child (*e.g.*, carrying out the garbage, picking up the newspapers). The parents were also told to feel free to use instructions to terminate undesirable behaviors (*e.g.*, jumping on the couch). During the baseline sessions, these were the only directions given to the parents.

After reliability check sessions, an agreement or disagreement was tallied for each 10-sec interval and the percentage of agreements for the observers was computed for each response and stimulus class. Observer reliability was evaluated for half the sessions within each baseline and experimental period; agreement percentages were always better than 90%, undoubtedly due to the simple nature of the classes. Baseline observations were continued until frequency counts of all behavior and stimulus classes appeared stable across sessions. At that point, the experimental procedures were initiated.

Timeout and contingency changes. After the baseline sessions, the parents were instructed in the use of a combination timeout and differential attention program. They were told to isolate their children (in their bedrooms) immediately following the occurrence of oppositional behavior. The children were to remain isolated for approximately 5 min unless they exhibited undesirable behaviors such as screaming or crying; if these behaviors occurred, the children were to remain in isolation until the behavior terminated. The parents were told also to be especially sensitive to their children's cooperative behavior, regardless of when it occurred. Any occurrence of cooperative behavior was to be immediately followed by parental approval, administered in any manner the parents desired. The parents were also told to keep a daily record which listed the number of timeouts used per day.

The above instructions were provided after the parents were given a brief explanation of reinforcement theory. Marked emphasis was placed on the importance of rigid adherence to the treatment procedures. In fact, the parents were told to think of themselves as mechanical reinforcement and punishment dispensers, operable by specific actions of their children.

Parental training in the above techniques was carried out just before an observation session. The length and number of training sessions varied considerably for the two sets of parents involved in this study. For the first set, only four training sessions were required and these varied from 30 to 65 min (including timeout periods). The second set of parents required seven sessions, which varied from 30 to 105 min (including timeout periods).

During the training sessions (as in the observation sessions), the author told the parents to provide instructions for their child. The instructions presented were again taken from a list of household chores that the parents considered aversive to their child. After an instruction was delivered, the "trainer" was careful to note the child's behavior as either oppositional or cooperative, to note parental social attention contingencies, and to note the promptness of the timeout technique. Whenever a timeout was administered, the trainer and parents used the 5-min timeout period to discuss problems in the application of the procedure. A training session was concluded when observer records revealed prompt timeouts (within 10 sec after oppositional behavior) and correctly contingent parental attention.

A 40-min observation session followed the training sessions. These sessions were characterized by two features: (1) the observers no longer interacted with the parents and, (2) the parents used the differential attention technique *only*. The elimination of timeout during the observation sessions was based on a decision to maximize the child's opportunity to produce oppositional behavior during the sessions. Given such conditions, one could evaluate not only the proportion of parental instructions followed, but also the child's readiness to follow them (as reflected in total number of oppositional units and the latencies between parental instructions and cooperative behavior). If the parents had been permitted to use timeout, and to use it correctly, oppositional behavior would have been restricted to one 10-sec unit per instruction; thus, the possibility of a latency measure of oppositional behavior would have been eliminated.

Experimental demonstrations of parental control. As later data will show, the parents were able to implement the treatment procedures, and implementation was followed by predictable changes in the children's behavior. At this point, experimental sessions were scheduled to assess the role of the treatment procedures in producing the results that were recorded.

Experimental tests were conducted by instructing the parents to resume their baseline contingencies for the child's behavior. After several of these sessions, all parents were instructed to resume the timeout and differential attention program. These instructions were in effect for the duration of the study.

Assessment of parental reinforcement value. To evaluate the previously discussed reinforcement change hypotheses, a simple test of parental reinforcement value was performed at four separate points in the study: at the end of Baseline #1; at the end of Experimental Treatment #1; at the end of Baseline #2; and at the end of Experimental Treatment #2.

The test of reinforcement value is described in detail elsewhere (Gewirtz and Baer, 1958). Briefly, this test requires the child to drop marbles in either of two holes of a wooden box. Both parents observe the child for a 4-min baseline and then both provide their approval following marble drops in the non-preferred hole. After 10 min of this differential attention procedure, the test is concluded and a single parental reinforcer effectiveness score is computed. This score represents a change in the per cent of marble drops in the non-preferred hole from baseline through the differential attention period: more specifically, the median per cent marble drops in the non-preferred hole over the 10-min differential attention period is subtracted from the non-preferred percentage obtained during the fourth minute of baseline.

In summary, it proved possible to evaluate changes in parental reinforcement value as a function of parental use of the contingency management program. If the reinforcement change hypothesis is valid, parental reinforcer effectiveness scores should be higher during the treatment periods than during the baseline periods.

RESULTS

Case No. 1

Billy (age 6) was referred for psychological treatment by his parents because of his consistent tendency to oppose commands set by either parent. According to the parents, he often refused to go to bed on time, refused to eat certain foods, and refused to comply with most everyday requests such as cleaning up his room. Billy also tended to be quite distractible and for some time the parents attributed his oppositional behavior to his "inability to pay attention". At the time of his referral, however, both parents felt that he was also very stubborn. Neither of Billy's two younger siblings presented similar problems.

Billy's first-grade teacher pointed out that he also tended to be fairly oppositional in the classroom. However, she did not consider him to be a serious problem at this point.

Home observations included Billy, his parents, and two siblings. The observations were scheduled on a once-a-week basis during the evening

TABLE 1 Training session data for Billy's parents: number of timeouts used by parents; mean latency per session between Billy's oppositional behavior and parental use of timeout; proportion of parental attention following Billy's oppositional responses.

Sessions	Baseline				Timeout and differential attention					Baseline no. 2		Timeout and differential attention								
	1	2	3	4	1	2	3	4	5	1	2	1	2	3	4	5	6	7	8	9
Number of timeouts used by parents	–	–	–	–	5	7	3	–	–	–	–	5	–	–	–	–	–	–	–	–
Mean latency (in 10-sec units) between oppositional behavior and parental use of timeout	–	–	–	–	5.0	0.8	0.0	–	–	–	–	0.0	–	–	–	–	–	–	–	–
Per cent of parental social attention following oppositional behavior (based on total attention following oppositional and cooperative behavior)	–	–	–	–	15	7	2	–	–	–	–	2	–	–	–	–	–	–	–	–

hours after dinner; during the sessions, the parents were told to keep all the children inside the house.

Interactions between Billy and his parents were infrequent; for the most part, Billy ignored his parents and they ignored him. When interactions did occur they were likely to be parent initiated, generally involving their attempts to curtail his active play or to get him to follow other instructions. Both parents responded to Billy's oppositional behavior by reasoning, arguing with him, or threatening him; on several occasions he was also spanked.

Table 1 describes parental performance during the training sessions. As this table shows, Billy's parents "caught on" to the training procedures rapidly, requiring only four sessions to master the timeout and differential attention technique.

Figure 2 describes Billy's oppositional behavior and parental reinforcer effectiveness scores over all observation sessions. As expected, Billy's oppo-

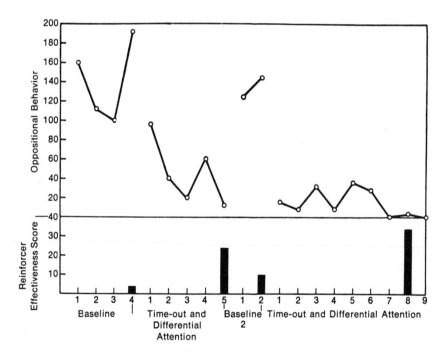

FIGURE 2   Number of Billy's 10-sec oppositional units and parental reinforcer effectiveness scores over baseline and treatment periods. All observations were made during 40-min sessions held once a week in Billy's home. Reinforcer effectiveness scores were obtained through a choice task (see text) conducted at the end of certain observation sessions.

sitional behavior varied in accordance with parental responses to his behavior; frequency counts of oppositional behavior were much lower during treatment sessions than during baseline sessions. Of greater interest, however, are the parental reinforcer effectiveness scores obtained during the various baseline and treatment periods. Parental reinforcement value for Billy was clearly a function of the treatment program; the reinforcer effectiveness scores increased, decreased, and then increased, correlated with the presence and absence of the contingency management program.

Table 2 provides several sources of information. First, it is apparent that the parents varied their differential attention to Billy's behavior in accordance with the treatment program. While they were very attentive to Billy's oppositional behavior during baseline periods, they shifted their attention to cooperative behavior during the treatment periods. Secondly, fluctuations in Billy's oppositional behavior were not due to fluctuations in number of parental instructions. That is, parental instructions were presented at fairly consistent frequencies over all sets of sessions. In addition (although not seen in Table 2), an examination of the pacing of parental instructions within sessions showed little variation over all sessions.

A further examination of Table 2 supports the frequency data of Fig. 2. Notice that the proportion of parental instructions followed, and the latencies between these instructions and cooperative behavior differed between baseline and treatment sessions; as expected from the Fig. 2 data, Billy followed more instructions during treatment periods and with greater speed.

Finally, it is of interest to note that parental use of the timeout procedure decreased markedly over the treatment period. Since Billy's oppositional behavior remained at a low level during treatment, this finding should be considered in connection with parental reinforcer effectiveness scores (Fig. 2). It is possible that Billy's high level of cooperative behavior was maintained primarily by enhanced reinforcement properties of his parent's social attention. While this contention could not be evaluated by the present study, it does seem to be a likely possibility.

A plausible explanation for the increased parental reinforcement value is seen in the data of Table 3. As this table indicates, Billy's spontaneous social approaches to his parents showed marked frequency differences between baseline and treatment sessions. Billy approached his parents more frequently during treatment than during baseline sessions; and, as Table 3 shows, Billy's parents were continuously responsive to these approaches. On the basis of laboratory work by Cairns (1963), these interaction changes could be meaningful. Cairns showed that the strength of a social reinforcer can be increased if it is made contingent upon some aspects of the child's social approach behavior. That is, if the child is first given approval by an adult for dependency behavior, that adult's social attention increases in reinforcement power.

TABLE 2 Observation session data for Billy and his parents: number of parental instructions presented to Billy; number of these instructions followed by Billy; mean latency per session between parental instructions and Billy's compliance; proportion of parental attention following Billy's oppositional responses; parental record of weekly timeouts for Billy.

Sessions	Baseline				Timeout and differential attention					Baseline no. 2		Timeout and differential attention								
	1	2	3	4	1	2	3	4	5	1	2	1	2	3	4	5	6	7	8	9
Number of parental instructions	10	15	12	8	16	19	12	9	13	12	14	19	7	10	16	13	10	18	14	12
Number of parental instructions followed	2	3	4	1	8	15	12	8	13	2	3	19	7	9	16	13	10	18	14	12
Mean latency (in 10-sec units) between parental instructions and cooperative behavior	15.0	25.0	15.2	32.0	3.9	0.4	1.7	3.7	0.8	13.5	10.3	0.6	0.8	1.7	0.4	3.0	3.0	0.0	0.2	0.0
Per cent of parental social attention following oppositional behavior (based on total attention following oppositional and cooperative behavior)	81	72	80	93	46	19	23	10	3	98	96	16	4	0	2	0	1	0	0	2
Weekly timeout (parental record)	–	–	–	–	39	24	7	12	4	0	0	9	4	1	0	3	0	1	0	1

TABLE 3 Billy's spontaneous social approaches to his parents and parental attention following the approaches.

Sessions	Baseline				Timeout and differential attention					Baseline		Timeout and differential attention								
	1	2	3	4	1	2	3	4	5	1	2	1	2	3	4	5	6	7	8	9
Approaches to parents	6	10	4	3	8	19	30	24	33	4	2	50	31	29	51	43	39	53	60	51
Parental attention following approaches	6	8	4	3	8	19	30	23	33	4	2	48	31	29	50	43	39	53	60	51

Possibly, the timeout procedure used in this study increased the likelihood of Billy's social approach behavior by suppressing his most prevalent responses—oppositional behavior. In other words, one might assume that the probability of social approach behavior would be higher for a cooperative child than for an oppositional child. Thus, if Cairns' findings are relevant to the observations presented in Table 3, one would predict an increase in parental reinforcement value. Of course, it could be argued that changes in Billy's social approach behavior were a simple function of increased parental reinforcement value, that these changes had no causal influence on parental reinforcement changes. Obviously, this study raises more questions than it answers.

Case No. 2

Sammy (age 5) was brought to the clinic by his parents because he tended to be quite "destructive" and "extremely stubborn". Both parents found it difficult to obtain cooperation from Sammy and at the time of their referral felt that he, rather than they, controlled household activities. If either parent attempted to enforce their few rules for Sammy, he usually erupted into such violent tantrums that they quickly relented.

Sammy was an only child, born after his mother had suffered a number of miscarriages. Both parents had been extremely concerned about his physical welfare and admitted that they had "spoiled him" by giving him whatever he desired. While they were still very concerned about his welfare, both stated they were "irritated" with him most of the time.

Home observations included Sammy and both parents. The observations were scheduled on a once-a-week basis during the evening hours after dinner; the parents were told to keep Sammy inside the house for all sessions.

As in Case No. 1, interactions between Sammy and his parents were infrequent. Most of these exchanges were verbal and most were initiated by the parents, who attempted to inhibit Sammy's rough play with toys and household furniture. In most instances, Sammy opposed this parental interference, often by whining, crying, or physically fighting the parents. Parental responses to this behavior usually involved reasoning or arguing with him, or bringing out the "belt"; if the latter strategy was not followed by cooperative behavior, the belt was often used, with temporary success.

Table 4 describes the performance of Sammy's parents during the training sessions. Compared to Billy's parents, these people experienced difficulty in mastering the training procedure. Five initial sessions and two post-reversal sessions were required to complete the training requirements; a comparison of the latency and differential attention data between this table and that in Table 1 will describe the difference in training effectiveness for the two sets of parents.

TABLE 4 Training session data for Sammy's parents: number of timeouts used by parents; mean latency per session between Sammy's oppositional behavior and parental use of timeout; proportion of parental attention following Sammy's oppositional responses.

Sessions	Baseline					Timeout and differential attention						Baseline no. 2		Timeout and differential attention						
	1	2	3	4	5	1	2	3	4	5	6	1	2	1	2	3	4	5	6	7
Number of timeouts used by parents	—	—	—	—	—	6	8	4	9	3	—	—	—	3	4	—	—	—	—	—
Mean latency (in 10-sec units) between oppositional behavior and parental use of timeout	—	—	—	—	—	4.7	1.6	3.2	3.5	0.7	—	—	—	1.0	0.0	—	—	—	—	—
Per cent of parental social attention following oppositional behavior (based on total attention following oppositional and cooperative behavior)	—	—	—	—	—	53	14	3	4	2	—	—	—	3	2	—	—	—	—	—

312

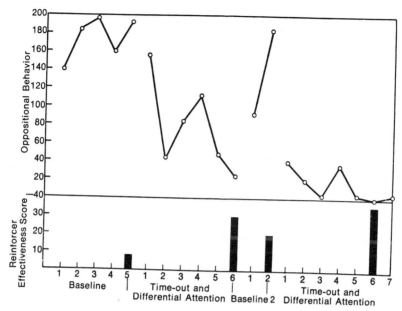

FIGURE 3 Number of Sammy's 10-sec oppositional units and parental reinforcer effectiveness scores over baseline and treatment periods. All observations were made during 10-min sessions held once a week in Sammy's home. Reinforcer effectiveness scores were obtained through a choice task (see text) conducted at the end of certain sessions.

Figure 3 describes Sammy's oppositional behavior and parental reinforcer effectiveness scores over all observation sessions. As expected, Sammy's oppositional behavior varied in accordance with parental responses to this behavior; frequency counts of oppositional behavior were much lower during treatment sessions than during baseline sessions. As was true for Case No. 1, parental reinforcer effectiveness scores for Sammy were clearly a function of the treatment program; the scores increased, decreased, and then increased when they were correlated with the presence and absence of the contingency management program.

Table 5 provides further information on Sammy's behavior and parental reactions to this behavior. It is clear that the parents shifted their social attention from Sammy's oppositional behavior during baseline to cooperative behavior during the treatment sessions. Secondly, fluctuations in Sammy's oppositional behavior were not due to fluctuations in number of parental instructions. Although the number of parental instructions varied over the observation sessions, the variations were not in a direction expected to reduce oppositional behavior. That is, more instructions were

TABLE 5 Observation session data for Sammy and his parents: number of parental instructions presented to Sammy; number of these instructions followed by Sammy; mean latency per session between parental instructions and Sammy's compliance; proportion of parental attention following Sammy's oppositional responses; parental record of weekly timeouts for Sammy.

Sessions	*Baseline*					*Timeout and differential attention*						*Baseline no. 2*		*Timeout and differential attention*						
	1	2	3	4	5	1	2	3	4	5	6	1	2	1	2	3	4	5	6	7
Number of parental instructions	8	14	12	16	15	22	18	19	15	13	17	13	15	20	19	23	14	17	12	16
Number of parental instructions followed	3	2	1	2	3	4	16	14	13	13	17	9	2	19	19	23	14	17	12	16
Mean latency (in 10-sec units) between parental instructions and cooperative behavior	13.3	27.5	25.0	20.0	24.0	15.2	0.6	2.7	4.0	3.9	1.5	3.9	21.5	0.5	1.0	0.1	2.7	0.1	0.0	0.1

TABLE 5 (continued)

Sessions	Baseline					Timeout and differential attention						Baseline no. 2		Timeout and differential attention						
	1	2	3	4	5	1	2	3	4	5	6	1	2	1	2	3	4	5	6	7
Per cent of parental social attention following oppositional behavior (based on total attention following oppositional and cooperative behavior)	77	81	72	88	71	41	38	15	21	8	15	98	95	10	9	0	2	0	0	1
Weekly timeout (parental record)	—	—	—	—	—	40	16	19	20	6	7	0	0	12	1	3	0	1	0	0

315

given during the treatment sessions than during the baseline sessions (as was true of Case No. 1, parental pacing of the instructions within sessions did not vary much over all sessions).

Data from Table 5 also support the frequency data of Fig. 3. Notice that the proportion of parental instructions followed, and the latencies between these instructions and cooperative behavior, differed between baseline and treatment sessions; as expected from the Fig. 3 data, Sammy followed more instructions during treatment periods and with greater speed.

Table 5 also presents the parents' recorded use of the timeout procedure. As in Case No. 1, parental use of the timeout procedure decreased markedly over the treatment period. Thus, in view of enhanced parental reinforcement value, Sammy's frequent cooperative behavior during treatment could have been maintained by reinforcement properties of his parents' contingent social attention.

Again, consistent with Case No. 1, Sammy's social approach responses to his parents were far more frequent during treatment sessions than during baseline sessions; Table 6 describes this finding. Thus, correlational evidence is available to suggest an explanation for increases in parental reinforcement value.

DISCUSSION

The present data lead to two conclusions: (1) parental use of the combined timeout and differential attention program effected dramatic and stable changes in the children's oppositional behavior; (2) parental reinforcement value increased as a function of the above program.

While the first conclusion comes as no great surprise (based on prior research; *e.g.,* Wahler, 1968), the systematic changes in parental reinforcement value present some puzzling questions. First, if parental reinforcement value was initially quite low, why should the timeout procedure be effective? Timeout is conceptualized as removing the child from sources of positive reinforcement, presumably social reinforcement. Therefore, if the parents were ineffective sources of positive reinforcement, the timeout procedure should have had little punishing influence. The fact that the procedure did work may mean that the parents were of significant reinforcement value during baseline or that timeout removed the child from significant sources of non-social reinforcement (*e.g.,* toys or television programs).

Secondly, if parental reinforcement value was initially quite low, what was maintaining the children's oppositional behavior during baseline? This question is also relevant to the earlier study (Wahler, 1968), which showed

TABLE 6 Sammy's spontaneous social approaches to his parents and parental attention following the approaches.

Sessions	Baseline					Timeout and differential attention						Baseline		Timeout and differential attention						
	1	2	3	4	5	1	2	3	4	5	6	1	2	1	2	3	4	5	6	7
Approaches to parents	4	7	2	9	8	7	3	15	17	24	38	6	2	40	28	45	33	51	36	48
Parental attention following approaches	4	6	2	7	8	7	31	15	17	24	38	6	2	40	28	44	33	51	36	47

that eliminating parental social attention contingencies for oppositional behavior did not affect the strength of this response class. A plausible answer to this question involves the definition of oppositional behavior used in these studies. Although oppositional behavior was recorded as a class of responses, it is best described as the absence of cooperative behavior. In other words, the child was considered oppositional if he did not cooperate following parental requests or commands. Apparently, then, oppositional children present behavioral deficits rather than excessive frequencies of specific behaviors. Examined in this light, the relevant question is not one of behavior maintenance but rather of how to account for low frequencies of cooperative behavior. If the parents were in fact poor sources of positive reinforcement, this question poses no problem.

Finally, how did the timeout and differential attention program effect changes in parental reinforcement value? While we have chosen to focus on the previously discussed work by Cairns (1963), it is apparent that other speculations are possible. For example, the parents described themselves as enjoying their children much more after treatment than before treatment. Informal observations supported these descriptions; the parents appeared to talk more frequently with their children, smile more frequently, and have more physical contact with them. It may be, then, that changing the children's behavior through timeout led to changes in parental behavior, changes that were quite reinforcing to the children. This possibility, and that suggested by the work of Cairns, are both subject to empirical tests.

REFERENCES

CAIRNS, R. B. *Antecedents of social reinforcer effectiveness.* Paper read at the biennial Society for Research in Child Development meeting, April, 1963.

GEWIRTZ, J. L. and BAER, D. M. Deprivation and satiation of social reinforcers as drive conditions. *Journal of Abnormal and Social Psychology,* 1958, **57,** 165–172.

HARRIS, F. R., WOLF, M. M., and BAER, D. M. Effects of adult social reinforcement on child behavior. *Young Children,* 1964, **20,** 8–17.

HAWKINS, R. P., PETERSON, R. F., SCHWIED, D., and BIJOU, S. W. Behavior therapy in the home: amelioration of problem parent-child relations with the parent in a therapeutic role. *Journal of Experimental Child Psychology,* 1966, **4,** 99–107.

ROBINS, L. N. *Deviant children grown up.* Baltimore: Williams & Wilkins Co., 1966.

WAHLER, R. G. *Behavior therapy for oppositional children: love is not enough.* Paper read at Eastern Psychological Association meeting, 1968.

RICHARD B. STUART
University of Michigan

Behavioral contracting within the families of delinquents[1]

The technique of behavioral contracting is used to strengthen the control of family and school over the behavior of delinquents. A behavioral contract is a means of scheduling the exchange of positive reinforcements among two or more persons. The use of these contracts is predicated upon four assumptions: (1) receipt of positive reinforcements in interpersonal exchanges is a privilege rather than a right; (2) effective interpersonal agreements are governed by the norm of reciprocity; (3) the value of an interpersonal exchange is a direct function of the range, rate and magnitude of the positive reinforcements mediated by that exchange; and (4) rules create freedom in interpersonal exchanges. The use of a behavioral contract with one delinquent girl is described and analyzed using Markovian methods.

Reprinted from *Journal of Behavior Therapy and Experimental Psychiatry*, 1971, 2, 1–11, with permission of the publisher and the author.

[1] This paper was prepared for presentation at the 78th Annual Meeting of the American Psychological Association, Miami Beach, Florida, 6 September 1970. The research from which this paper was derived was funded by a grant of U.S. 314(d) funds administered by the State of Michigan Department of Mental Health. The author wishes to acknowledge the contribution made to this paper by his colleagues (Drs. Edward Heck, Tony Tripodi and James V. McConnell) and the editorial assistance of Miss Lynn Nilles.

319

Any intervention program intended for use with delinquents must first define a specific subpopulation as a target group. Delinquents may be subdivided according to whether their predominant offenses are or are not classifiable as adult crimes, whether they are initial or chronic offenders, and whether or not they reside in environments replete with constructive resources which can be mobilized to their advantage. For many delinquents [e.g., for 24 per cent of the adolescent male wards of one Michigan county juvenile court (Huetteman, Briggs, Tripodi, Stuart, Heck and Mc-Connell, 1970)], violations of parental authority and other uniquely juvenile offenses (e.g., possession of alcoholic beverages and failure to attend school) constitute the only "crimes" ever recorded. Many engage in chronically dysfunctional interactions with their families and schools, both of which settings contain the rudiments of effective behavioral controls.

A continuum of short- to intermediate-term dispositional goals is available for working with this group (see Fig. 1). Ranging from maintaining the youth in his natural home environment, through a series of semi-institutional settings, to institutionalization in correctional or psychiatric settings, the points along the continuum vary according to the extent to which they provide social structure and make use of natural forces of behavioral control in the community. Recent studies have shown that the more potent the influence of the natural environment throughout treatment, the greater the likelihood that behavioral changes will be maintained following treatment. For example, it has been shown that two groups of delinquents, who spent an average of 131·6 days in psychiatric settings or 91·8 days in correctional settings of every year that they were wards of the juvenile court, actually committed more offenses than another very similar

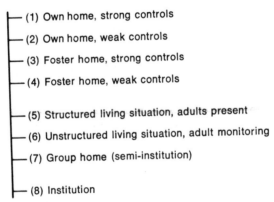

FIGURE 1   Continuum of dispositional goals for the treatment of juvenile delinquents.

group who were not institutionalized (Huetteman *et al.*, 1970). Even stronger support of the need for community treatment is found in a large-scale review of many rehabilitation programs, which concluded with the finding that:

> . . . since severe penalties do not deter more effectively, and since prisons do not rehabilitate, and since the criminal justice system is inconsistent and has little quantitative impact on crime, the best rehabilitative possibilities would appear to be in the community (Harlow, 1970, pp. 33–34).

Community treatment for large numbers of delinquents will be possible only when techniques have been developed which (a) are effective, (b) require comparatively little time for administration, (c) can extend family influence to control behavior in a number of different situations, and (d) can be administered by paraprofessionals. It is suggested that behavioral contracting, to be described and illustrated in this paper, is one technique which meets each of these requirements and can be employed as a tactic in every instance in which efforts are made to strengthen the place of an adolescent in a natural, foster, or group home environment.

RATIONALE

At the core of the effort to use behavioral contracting to combat delinquency are two assumptions. First, it is assumed that the family plays a critical role in the etiology of delinquency when certain dysfunctional family interaction patterns coexist with a paucity of opportunities for acceptable performance in the community (Rodman and Grams, 1967) and when peer pressures are conducive to deviant behavior (Burgess and Akers, 1969). The family may function as a pathogen in two ways. First, the family may model and differentially reinforce patterns of antisocial behavior (Bandura and Walters, 1963). Second, the family may inadequately reinforce prosocial behavior in comparison with the reinforcement of antisocial behavior available in the community. Stuart (1970a) showed that the families of delinquents could be differentiated from the families of nondelinquents on the basis of their low rate of positive exchanges, while Patterson and Reid (1971) demonstrated that interactional patterns of coercion are more common within delinquent families than patterns of reciprocity.

The second assumption is that the family in many instances is a potentially powerful if not the only force available to aid the delinquent in acquiring prosocial responses. Over 15 years ago, Katz and Lazarsfeld (1955) clearly showed that in studies of attitude formation and change the family accounts for over two-thirds of the observed variance. Modern sociologists such as Schafer and Polk (1967) have shown that most social agencies, including schools in particular, are more oriented toward removing than rehabilitating the delinquent. Therefore it is essential to both eliminate the pathogenic elements of the family and to harness its vast power in order to mount constructive programs to aid delinquents.

BEHAVIORAL CONTRACTS

A behavioral contract is a means of scheduling the exchange of positive reinforcements between two or more persons. Contracts have been used when reciprocal patterns of exchange have broken down within families (Carson, 1969; Tharp and Wetzel, 1969) or in efforts to establish reciprocal exchanges from the outset in formal relationships in therapeutic (Sulzer, 1962) and scholastic (Homme, Csanyi, Gonzales and Rechs, 1969) settings. Contracts structure reciprocal exchanges by specifying: who is to do what, for whom, under what circumstances. They therefore make explicit the expectations of every party to an interaction and permit each to determine the relative benefits and costs to him of remaining within that relationship (Thibaut and Kelley, 1959). Furthermore, by making roles explicit for family members, contracts enhance the likelihood that responsibilities will be met, and by postulating reciprocal exchanges within families, contracts contribute to interactional stability. Finally, because privileges and responsibilities are fairly well-standardized across families the execution of behavioral contracts in time-limited, high-pressure settings is quite feasible.[2]

Behavioral contracting with families rests upon four assumptions. First, it is assumed that:

> *Receipt of positive reinforcements in interpersonal exchanges is a privilege rather than a right.*

A privilege in this sense is a special prerogative which one may enjoy at the will of another person upon having performed some qualifying task. For example, states bestow driving privileges upon citizens who qualify for this privilege by passing certain performance tests and by driving with standard prudence. In contrast, a right implies undeniable and inalienable access to a prerogative. Furthermore, a right cannot be denied, no matter what an individual might do. In modern society there are virtually no rights be-

---

[2] Behavior Change Systems (3156 Dolph Drive, Ann Arbor, Michigan 48103) makes available behavioral contracting kits, including code book and computer compatible code forms in addition to standardized materials for use with clients.

yond the right of the individual to think as he may choose. For example, people in a democratic society have the privilege to say what they think, but not to shout "fire" in a crowded theater no matter how hard it is to find a seat.

Within families it is the responsibility of one person to grant the privileges requested by another on a reciprocal basis. For example, an adolescent might wish free time—this is his privilege—and it is his parents' responsibility to provide this free time. However, the parents may wish that the adolescent attend school each day prior to going out in the evening—the adolescent's school attendance is their privilege and it is his responsibility to do as they ask. Privileges may, of course, be abused. Thus a parent might wish to know where his adolescent goes when he leaves home, but if the parents attack the adolescent when they learn of his plans, they have failed to meet their responsibility, i.e., use the information constructively. Thus it is appropriate to consider as a part of the definition of a privilege the conditions for its appropriate use.

A second assumption underlying the use of behavioral contracts is:

Effective interpersonal agreements are governed by the norm of reciprocity.

A norm is a "behavioral rule that is accepted, at least to some degree, by both members of the dyad (Thibaut and Kelley, 1959, p. 129)." Norms serve to increase the predictability of events in an interaction, permit the resolution of conflicts without recourse to power and have secondary reinforcing value in and of themselves (Gergen, 1969, pp. 73–74). Reciprocity is the norm which underlies behavioral contracts. Reciprocity implies that "each party has rights and duties (Gouldner, 1960, p. 169)," and further, that items of value in an interchange must be exchanged on an equity or *quid pro quo* ("something for something [Jackson, 1965, p. 591]") basis. Therefore, inherent in the use of behavioral contracts is acceptance of the notion that one must compensate his partner fairly for everything which is received, that is, there are no gifts to be expected within contractual relations.

A third principle basic to the use of behavioral contracts states that:

The value of an interpersonal exchange is a direct function of the range, rate, and magnitude of the positive reinforcements mediated by that exchange.

Byrne and Rhamey (1965) have expressed this assumption as a law of interpersonal behavior postulating that one's attraction to another will depend upon the proportion and value of positive reinforcements garnered within that relationship. In a similar vein, Mehrabian and Ksionsky (1970) have reviewed many years of social psychological research supporting the conclusion that: "Situations where affiliative behavior increases positive reinforcement . . . induce greater affiliative behavior (p. 115)."

In the negotiation of behavioral contracts, through a process of accommodation (Gergen, 1969, p. 73), each party seeks to offer to the other the maximum possible rate of positive reinforcement because the more positive reinforcements which are emitted, the more will be received. In this sense, each positive offered represents an individual's "investment" in a contract, and each privilege received represents "return on an investment." Therefore a good intrafamilial contract encourages the highest possible rate of mutual reinforcement as represented by the following diagram (Fig. 2) in which CO_{FMA} implies the optimal choice for father, mother and adolescent, $CO_{F/MA}$ the optimal choice for father which the mother and adolescent will accept, etc., and k a value-determining constant.

The fourth and final assumption basic to the concept of behavioral contracting is:

Rules create freedom in interpersonal exchanges.

When contracts specify the nature and condition for the exchange of things of value, they thereby stipulate the rules of the interaction. For example, when an adolescent agrees that she will visit friends after school (privilege) but that she will return home by 6:00 P.M. (responsibility), she has agreed to a rule governing the exchange of reinforcers. While the rule delimits the scope of her privilege, it also creates the freedom with which she may take advantage of her privilege. Without this rule, any action taken by the girl might have an equal probability of meeting with reinforcement, extinction or punishment. If the girl did not have a clear-

$$CO_{FMA} = f[CO_{F/MA} + CO_{M/FA} + CO_{A/FM}] + k$$

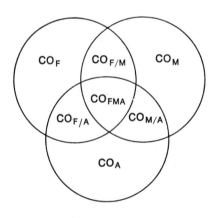

FIGURE 2

cut responsibility to return home at 6:00 P.M. she might return one day at 7:00 and be greeted warmly, return at 6:00 the next day and be ignored, and return at 5:30 the following day and be reprimanded. Only by prior agreement as to what hour would be acceptable can the girl insure her freedom, as freedom depends upon the opportunity to make behavioral choices with knowledge of the probable outcome of each alternative.

Just as contracts produce freedom through detailing reciprocal rule-governed exchanges, so must contracts be born of freedom, since coerced agreements are likely to be violated as soon as the coercive force is removed. Therefore effective behavioral contracts must be negotiated with respect to the following paradigm:

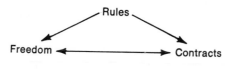

ELEMENTS OF BEHAVIORAL CONTRACTS

ELEMENTS OF BEHAVIORAL CONTRACTS

Good behavioral contracts contain five elements. First, the contracts must detail the privileges which each expects to gain *after* fulfilling his responsibilities. Typical privileges used in behavioral contracts in the families of delinquents include free time with friends, spending money, choice of hair and dress styles and use of the family car for the adolescent. Second, good contracts must detail the responsibilities essential to securing each privilege. Again, in the families of delinquents, responsibilities typically include maintenance of minimally adequate school attendance and performance, maintenance of agreed-upon curfew hours, completion of household chores and keeping parents informed about the adolescent's whereabouts. Every effort is made to restrict privileges to prosocial behaviors and to keep responsibilities to a minimum. The former is necessary if the family is to effectively serve as an agent of social control. The latter is necessary because the parents of teenage children control comparatively few salient reinforcements and must use those which are controlled with sufficient care to maintain desired behavior. If the number of responsibilities is increased without comparable increase in the value of privileges offered, little or no reinforcement will be provided for the new responsibilities and they are unlikely to be met, weakening the general credibility of the contract.

As an added requirement, the responsibilities specified in a family contract must be monitorable by the parents, for if the parents cannot determine when a responsibility has been fulfilled, they cannot know when to properly grant a privilege. Therefore there are some things which are beyond the scope of behavioral contracts, such as where an adolescent goes when he is not at home or whom he sees as friends. The single exception to this rule is the possibility of using school attendance and performance as responsibilities. While it can be argued that classroom behavioral management is the primary responsibility of teachers (Stuart, 1970b), it is often not possible for a behavior modifier to gain access to *any* or all of an adolescent's teachers (Bailey, Phillips and Wolf, 1970), so he may be required to attempt to control behavior in school with reinforcements mediated in the home. When this is done, it is essential to arrange for systematic feedback to be provided by the teacher to the parent describing the teenager's attendance and performance in class. A simple card brought for a teacher's signature every day or every week by the teenager is a sufficient and very practical means of securing this feedback (see Fig. 3).

The third element of a good behavioral contract is a system of sanctions for failure to meet responsibilities. While in one sense the possibility of time out from privileges should be adequate to insure the completion of responsibilities, there are obviously periods in the course of family life when this is not the case. At all times, behavior is under multiple contingency control (Stuart, 1970c), and in certain instances it is more reinforcing to violate the contract and to forfeit a subsequent privilege than to garner the rewards of adhering to the terms of the contract. At these times the existence of sanctions may tip the balance of a behavioral choice to-

---

SCHOOL PERFORMANCE CHART

Name of Student: ....   Date: ....

In order to keep my parents posted on my progress in school, I am asking all my teachers to grade my work in all of my major subjects at the end of each class period. Would you please rate my performance as: A = excellent, B = above average, C = average, D = below average, E = failing.
PLEASE USE INK and initial any corrections. THANK YOU.

Subject	Attendance	Homework	Tests and/or class discussion	Signature

FIGURE 3

ward compliance with contractual obligations. Furthermore, sanctions have an added advantage: they provide the aggrieved party with a temperate means of expressing his displeasure. In families without explicit or understood behavioral contracts, the failure of a child to meet curfew is often met with threats of long-term "grounding". Faced with the threat of not being permitted to go out for weeks on end, the teenager is often persuaded to violate his contract even further and remain out later because the magnitude of the penalty is fixed and not commensurate with the magnitude of his violation.

When sanctions are built into the contract, they may be of two types. One is a simple, linear penalty such as the requirement that the adolescent return home as many minutes early the following day as he has come in late on the preceding day. The second type of sanction is a geometric penalty which doubles or triples the amount of make-up time due following contract violations. It is probably best to combine both types of sanctions, making certain that lateness does not reach a point of diminishing return when it would actually be impractical for the adolescent to return home at all because he would incur no greater penalty for continued absence.

The fourth element in a good behavioral contract is a bonus clause which assures positive reinforcement for compliance with the terms of the contract. Much behavior control within families consists of "negative scanning" (Stuart, 1969) or the extinction of positive responding (by ignoring it) coupled with the severe punishment of negative responding. The effect of this punishment is, of course, to strengthen negative behavior as a consequence of the fact that attention follows negative behavior and does not follow positive responses (Madsen, Becker, Thomas, Kosar and Plager, 1968). To counteract this, bonuses calling for permission to remain out longer than usual, extra money or extraordinary privileges such as the opportunity to have a party or to take a trip with friends are built into contracts as contingencies for extended periods of near-flawless compliance with contractual responsibilities.

When behavioral contracts are well executed, each member of the family is assured of receiving the minimum level of positive reinforcement (privileges) necessary to sustain his participation in the interaction. Furthermore, each party to the agreement is provided with a means of responding to contract violations and each is reinforced for long chains of desirable responses. The contract is not complete, however, unless a means is also built in for keeping track of the rates of positive reinforcements given and received. This is accomplished through feedback systems which serve two functions. First, they cue each individual as to how to respond in order to earn an additional inducement. Second, they signal each person when to reinforce the other. Furthermore, the provision of feedback in this context also sets the occasion for positive comments which themselves strengthen prosocial behavior. The exchange of feedback is facilitated by the use of a behavioral monitoring form calling for each person to check off the fulfillment of his own responsibilities (which includes provision of the privileges of the others).

ILLUSTRATION

A behavioral contract constituted the primary treatment procedure in the management of a 16-year-old girl who was referred to the Family and School Consultation Project by the local juvenile court. At the time of referral, Candy Bremer [3] had been hospitalized as an inpatient at a local psychiatric hospital following alleged promiscuity, exhibitionism, drug abuse and home truancy. Associated with these complaints was an allegation by her parents that Candy engaged in chronically antagonistic exchanges within the family and had for a year done near-failing work in school. Owing to the cost of private psychiatric care, the parents sought hospitalization at state expense by requesting that the juvenile court assume wardship. After initiating this action, the parents were informed by a court-appointed attorney representing their daughter that the allegations would probably not stand up in court. The parents accordingly modified their request to a petition that the court place Candy on the consent docket affording quasi-ward status without termination of parental rights.

At the time of referral, Mr. and Mrs. Bremer were 64 and 61 years old respectively, and both were physically ill—Mr. Bremer suffering from emphysema and Mrs. Bremer from a degenerative bone disease in her hip. Both holding college degrees, Mr. Bremer performed scholarly work at home on a part-time basis while Mrs. Bremer worked as a medical secretary. Candy, the third of their three children, was 20 years younger than her oldest sister. The Bremers resided in a very small ranch-type home which lacked a basement, so privacy could only be found in the bedrooms.

Initially, Mr. and Mrs. Bremer wished to maintain virtually total control over Candy's behavior. They were reluctantly willing to accept her at home but established as conditions that she adhere to a punishing curfew which allowed her out of the home for periods averaging 2 to 3 hours per summer day. Great effort was expended to convince the parents of the need to modify their expectations and to modify a continuous chain of negative interactions. However, when both of these efforts failed, it was decided to execute a behavioral contract anyway, because the problems expected at home seemed less negative than the probable consequences of continued institutionalization and because it was hoped that a more realistic contract could be effectuated as time progressed. Within 3 weeks of the

[3] Pseudonym.

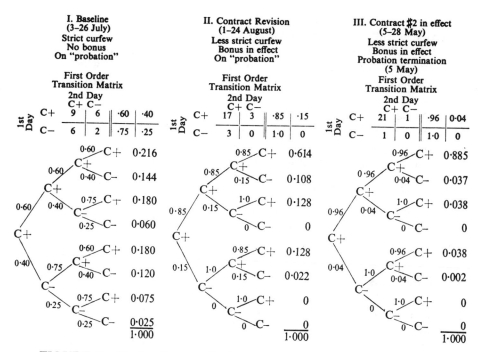

FIGURE 4 Candy Bremer—Curfew maintenance, three 24-day blocks.

start of the contract, Candy was reported to be sneaking out of her bedroom window at night, visiting a local commune and returning home before dawn. It was found that over a 24-day period there were eight major contract violations, and the probability of an extended series of days of contract compliance was quite small[4] (see Fig. 4). While it was deemed

[4] These and subsequent data were evaluated using a Markovian chain designed to make predictions of future behavior based upon observation of past behavior in 24-day blocks. For an extended discussion of this procedure, see Kemeny, Mirkil, Snell and Thompson (1959). In simplified form, the analysis is completed through the following *steps:* (1) write the series of dichotomous observations as a series of +, − notations (+ − − + + − + , etc); (2) count the number of + +, + −, − + and − − sequences, recording the totals in a 2 × 2 table; (3) compute the proportion of + + vs + − and − + vs − − sequences and enter these decimals in the appropriate cells of a 2 × 2 table; (4) draw as many Markovian tree forms as needed following the illustration in Fig. 3; (5) for each + +, + −, − + and − − series, write in the proportions obtained in step 3; (6) multiply all such entries in each series. Checks: (a) entries at each pair of branching alternatives (C+ $\underset{0\cdot4\ \text{C}-}{\overset{0\cdot6\ \text{C}+}{\rule{2cm}{0.4pt}}}$) must total 1·00 (0·6 + 0·4). (b) The probability of all series must total 1·00. *Interpretation.* The obtained values may be interpreted as the probability that each series (e.g. + + − −) will occur, relative to all other series, assuming constant conditions.

vital to introduce more privileges for Candy, it seemed imprudent to do this as a contingency for her having violated her contract in the past. Finally it was decided to do two things. A new contract, which was far more permissive, was introduced (see Fig. 5), accompanied by a new monitoring sheet (see Fig. 6), but a new court order was requested and granted which proscribed Candy from entering the communes. Candy was made to understand that, should she be found in either commune, not she but the commune members would be liable to prosecution for contributing to the delinquency of a minor as they had been officially informed of the limitation placed upon Candy's activities.

As seen in Fig. 4, this modified contract was quite effective, increasing the rate of compliance to the contract terms to a very respectable high rate. When court wardship was terminated and the contract was the sole behavioral prosthesis, Candy's behavior actually continued to improve.

DISCUSSION

Behavioral contracting served as a very useful means of structuring a constructive interaction between Candy and her parents. By removing from the realm of contention the issues of privileges and responsibilities, the eliciters of many intrafamilial arguments were eliminated. When fights did occur, they tended to be tempered by the options available through the contract. The contract itself cannot account for a change in Candy's behavior; but the contract apparently served to assure the use of privileges such as free time and money as contingencies in the truest sense of the term.

The process of negotiating a contract through accommodation of each other's wishes (Gergen, 1969) might have been characterized as an "experience in form" by John Dewey. It appears to have laid the groundwork for a more effective interaction and in this case was adequate in and of itself. In other instances, it is likely that behavioral contracting could profitably be supplemented with interaction training for the parents, tutoring or vocational guidance for the adolescent or financial assistance for the family. The decision about which additional techniques should be employed is discretionary, but it is suggested that behavioral contracting be made a part of every plan to improve the interaction between an adolescent and his parents.

REFERENCES

BAILEY, J., PHILLIPS E. and WOLF, M. (1970) Homebased reinforcement and the modification of predelinquents' classroom behavior. *Proceedings of the*

78th Annual Convention of the American Psychological Association, Vol. 5, 751–752 (Summary).

BANDURA, A. and WALTERS, R. H. (1963) *Social Learning and Personality Development*. Holt, Rinehart & Winston, New York.

BURGESS, R. L. and AKERS, R. L. (1969) A differential association-reinforcement theory of criminal behavior. In *Delinquency, Crime and Social Process* (Edited by CRESSEY, D. R. and WARD, D. A.). Harper & Row, New York.

BYRNE, D. and RHAMEY, R. (1965) Magnitude of positive and negative reinforcements as a determinant of attractions. *J. Pers. Soc. Psychol.* 2, 884–889.

CARSON, R. C. (1969) *Interaction Concepts of Personality*. Aldine, Chicago.

GERGEN, K. J. (1969) *The Psychology of Behavior Exchange*. Addison-Wesley, Reading, Massachusetts.

GOULDNER, A. W. (1960) The norm of reciprocity: A preliminary statement. *Amer. Soc. Rev.* 25, 161–178.

HARLOW, E. (1970) Intensive intervention: An alternative to institutionalization. *Crime and Delinquency Literature* 2, 3–46.

HOMME, L., CSANYI, A. P., GONZALES, M. A. and RECHS, J. R. (1969) *How To Use Contingency Contracting in the Classroom*. Research Press, Champaign, Illinois.

HUETTEMAN, M. J., BRIGGS, J., TRIPODI, T., STUART, R. B., HECK, E. T. and McCONNELL, J. V. (1970) A descriptive comparison of three populations of adolescents known to the Washtenaw County Juvenile Court: Those referred for or placed in psychiatric hospitals, those placed in correctional settings, and those released following hearings. Unpublished manuscript, Family and School Consultation Project, Ann Arbor, Michigan.

JACKSON, D. D. (1965) Family rules. *Arch. Gen. Psychiat.* 12, 589–594.

KATZ, E. and LAZARSFELD, P. F. (1955) *Personal Influence*. Free Press, Glencoe, Illinois.

KEMENY, J. G., MIRKIL, H., SNELL, J. L. and THOMPSON, G. L. (1959) *Finite Mathematical Structures*. Prentice-Hall, Englewood Cliffs, New Jersey.

MADSEN, C. H. JR., BECKER, W. C., THOMAS, D. R., KOSAR, L. and PLAGER, E. (1968) An analysis of the reinforcing function of "sit down" commands. In *Readings in Educational Psychology* (Edited by R. K. Parker). Allyn and Bacon, Boston.

MEHRABIAN, A. and KSIONSKY, S. (1970) Models of affiliative behavior. *Psychol. Bull.* 74, 110–126.

PATTERSON, G. R. and REID J. (1971) Reciprocity and coercion: Two facets of social systems. In *Behavior Modification in Clinical Psychology* (Edited by C. NEURINGER and J. MICHAEL). Appleton-Century-Crofts, New York.

RODMAN, H. and GRAMS, P. (1967) Juvenile delinquency and the family: A review and discussion. In President's Commission on Law Enforcement and Administration of Justice, Task Force on Juvenile Delinquency, *Task Force Report: Juvenile Delinquency and Youth Crime*. Washington, D.C.: U.S. Government Printing Office.

Privileges

General

In exchange for the privilege of remaining together and preserving some semblance of family integrity, Mr. and Mrs. Bremer and Candy all agree to

Specific

In exchange for the privilege of riding the bus directly from school into town after school on school days

In exchange for the privilege of going out at 7:00 P.M. on one weekend evening without having to account for her whereabouts

In exchange for the privilege of going out a second weekend night

In exchange for the privilege of going out between 11:00 A.M. and 5:15 P.M. Saturdays, Sundays and holidays

In exchange for the privilege of having Candy complete household chores and maintain her curfew

Responsibilities

concentrate on positively reinforcing each other's behavior while diminishing the present overemphasis upon the faults of the others.

Candy agrees to phone her father by 4:00 P.M. to tell him that she is all right and to return home by 5:15 P.M.

Candy must maintain a weekly average of "B" in the academic ratings of all of her classes and must return home by 11:30 P.M.

Candy must tell her parents by 6:00 P.M. of her destination and her companion, and must return home by 11:30 P.M.

Candy agrees to have completed all household chores before leaving and to telephone her parents once during the time she is out to tell them that she is all right.

Mr. and Mrs. Bremer agree to pay Candy $1.50 on the morning following days on which the money is earned.

Bonuses and Sanctions

If Candy is 1–10 minutes late	she must come in the same amount of time earlier the following day, but she does not forfeit her money for the day.
If Candy is 11–30 minutes late	she must come in 22–60 minutes earlier the following day and does forfeit her money for the day.
If Candy is 31–60 minutes late	she loses the privilege of going out the following day and does forfeit her money for the day.
For each half hour of tardiness over one hour, Candy	loses her privilege of going out and her money for one additional day.
Candy may go out on Sunday evenings from 7:00 to 9:30 P.M. and either Monday or Thursday evening	if she abides by all the terms of this contract from Sunday through Saturday with a total tardiness not exceeding 30 minutes which must have been made up as above.
Candy may add a total of two hours divided among one to three curfews	if she abides by all the terms of this contract for two weeks with a total tardiness not exceeding 30 minutes which must have been made up as above and if she requests permission to use this additional time by 9:00 P.M.

Monitoring

Mr. and Mrs. Bremer agree to keep written records of the hours of Candy's leaving and coming home and of the completion of her chores.

Candy agrees to furnish her parents with a school monitoring card each Friday at dinner.

FIGURE 5 Behavioral contract.

Days of Month

	1/17	2/18	3/19	4/20	5/21	6/22	7/23	8/24	9/25	10/26	11/27	12/28	13/29	14/30	15/31	16/—
CHORES																
Set table, etc.																
Dishes, kitchen, etc.																
Bathroom																
Vacuum, FR, LR, halls																
Cat boxes																
Other:																
Other:																
CURFEW																
Time leave afternoon																
Phone after school																
Time arrive home from school in afternoon																
Time leave in evening																
Destination approved																
Time return in evening																
Time leave afternoon																
Lateness																
Lateness made up																
BONUS TIME																
Bonus 1 earned																
Bonus 1 spent																
Bonus 2 earned																
Bonus 2 requested																
Bonus 2 spent																

FIGURE 6   Behavioral contract: monitoring form.

SCHAFER, W. E. and POLK, K. (1967) Delinquency and the schools. In President's Commission on Law Enforcement and Administration of Justice, Task Force on Juvenile Delinquency, *Task Force Report: Juvenile Delinquency and Youth Crime*. Washington, D.C.: U.S. Government Printing Office.

STUART, R. B. (1969) Operant-interpersonal treatment for marital discord. *J. Consult. Clin. Psychol.* 33, 675–682.

STUART, R. B. (1970a) Assessment and change of the communicational patterns of juvenile delinquents and their parents. In *Advances in Behavior Therapy, 1969* (Edited by R. D. RUBIN). Academic Press, New York.

STUART, R. B. (1970b) Behavior modification techniques for the education technologist. In *Proceedings of the National Workshop on School Social Work, 1969–70* (Edited by R. C. SARRI). National Association of Social Workers, New York.

STUART, R. B. (1970c) Situational versus self control in the treatment of problematic behaviors. In *Advances in Behavior Therapy, 1970* (Edited by R. D. RUBIN). Academic Press, New York.

SULZER, E. S. (1962) Research frontier: Reinforcement and the therapeutic contract. *J. Counsel. Psychol.* 9, 271–276.

THARP, R. G. and WETZEL, R. J. (1969) *Behavior Modification in the Natural Environment*. Academic Press, New York.

THIBAUT, J. W. and KELLEY, H. H. (1959) *The Social Psychology of Groups*. J. Wiley, New York.

RONALD A. MANN
University of California at Los Angeles

*The behavior-therapeutic use
of contingency contracting
to control an adult behavior
problem: weight control*[1]

*Items considered valuable by the subject and originally his property were sur-
rendered to the researcher and incorporated into a contractual system of prearranged contingencies. Each subject signed a legal contract that prescribed the
manner in which he could earn back or permanently lose his valuables. Specifically, a portion of each subject's valuables were returned to him contingent
upon both specified weight losses and losing weight at an agreed-upon rate.
Furthermore, each subject permanently lost a portion of his valuables contingent upon both specified weight gains and losing weight at a rate below the
agreed-upon rate. Single-subject reversal designs were employed to determine*

Reprinted from *Journal of Applied Behavior Analysis*, 1972, 5, 99–109, with permission of the publisher and the authors. Copyright 1972 by the Society for the Experimental Analysis of Behavior, Inc.

[1] This investigation was partially supported by PHS Training Grant 00183 from
the National Institute of Child Health and Human Development to the Kansas Center
for Research in Mental Retardation and Human Development. This study is based
upon a dissertation submitted to the Department of Human Development, University
of Kansas, in partial fulfillment of the requirements for the degree of Doctor of Phi-
losophy. The author expresses deep appreciation and indebtedness to Dr. Donald M.
Baer for his encouraging support, insightful advice, and helpful suggestions. Special
thanks to Drs. L. Keith Miller and James A. Sherman for their critical evaluations and
suggestions in preparing the manuscript.

the effectiveness of the treatment contingencies. This study demonstrated that items considered valuable by the subject and originally his property, could be used successfully to modify the subject's weight when these items were used procedurally both as reinforcing and as punishing consequences. In addition, a systematic analysis of the contingencies indicated that punishing or aversive consequences presumably were a necessary component of the treatment procedure.

Comparatively few therapeutic techniques displaying generality in natural settings have been developed to deal with the behavior problems of normal non-institutionalized adults. Two major reasons for this are suggested. First, it is difficult for a therapist to discover and/or gain systematic control over relevant consequences of an adult's behavior in its natural settings. Second, even if a therapist did have such control, it would still be difficult to maintain reliable measurement of the behavior. Without reliable measurement, it would be difficult to deliver relevant consequences at appropriate times. Similarly, it would be difficult to assess any changes that might occur in the behavior. Thus, an applied demonstration of a therapeutic change in behavior could be made, but with difficulty.

A recently discussed procedure that may have potential as a technique to remediate adult behavior problems in their natural settings is that of contingency contracting (Homme, 1966; Homme, Csanyi, Gonzales, and Rechs, 1969; Tharp and Wetzel, 1969; Michael, 1970). Its applications as a therapeutic technique, however, have been suggested mainly for use in school settings with children (Homme et al., 1969; Cantrell, Cantrell, Huddleston, and Woolridge, 1969) and in home settings to remediate the behavior problems of pre-delinquent adolescents (Tharp and Wetzel, 1969; Stuart, 1970).

The term "contingency contracting", as it has most commonly been used has meant an explicit statement of contingencies (*i.e.*, a rule), usually agreed upon by two or more people. In other words, it has been a specification of a number of behaviors whose occurrence would produce specified consequences, presumably to be delivered by parents or teachers. It has been amply demonstrated that contingencies can, in fact, change behavior. Nevertheless, little evidence has been gathered to support the notion that the use of contingency contracts will facilitate the remediation of child or adult behavior problems.

The present study attempted to develop a therapeutic technique that would effectively remediate the behavior problems of normal non-institutionalized adults. The basic technique used was that of contingency contracting. The contingency contract used in this study was similar to others that have been discussed, in that it too was an explicit statement of contingencies. However, this contract incorporated a number of additional techniques that were considered necessary to accomplish effectively an applied behavior analysis, and which were relevant to the problems both of gaining systematic control of effective consequences and of maintaining reliable measurement.

In brief, this study attempted to test the applicability of contingency contracting with adult subjects, and to assess the effects of various treatment contingencies on weight reduction. Weight was used as the dependent variable for two reasons: (1) It is a convenient and reliably measurable "behavior", and (2) weight control is a socially important behavior problem.

METHOD

Subjects

Seven women and one man, 18 to 33 yr old, had responded to an advertisement for a "behavior therapy research program of weight reduction". Each subject was required to give to the researcher a signed physician's statement indicating that it would be medically safe for him or her to lose the specified weight agreed upon for this research over the agreed-upon time and at the agreed-upon rate. Furthermore, the physician's statement included an entry indicating whether the subject's physician had prescribed a diet for him. It was made clear to every subject, both verbally and as a written clause included in each contract, that any diet or foods that the subject selected or his physician prescribed would be ultimately the subject's responsibility. With one exception, only those individuals agreeing to lose 25 pounds or more and who had their physician's approval were accepted as subjects. (The one exception was a subject who agreed to lose 16 pounds).

The Contingency Contract

The Contingency Contract was a legal document that incorporated as separate clauses all of the procedures in the weight control program. First, the contract required each subject to surrender a large number of items considered to be valuable to himself. These items were retained by the researcher (a similar technique has been discussed by Tighe and Elliot, 1968). Secondly, the contract prescribed the manner in which the subject could earn back or permanently lose his valuables (*i.e.*, the statement of contingencies). Third, the contract required the subject to be weighed by the researcher at regular intervals. Fourth, the contract stipulated that the researcher, at his discretion, would change the procedures from baseline, to treatment, to reversal, and back to treatment conditions. Thus, the contingencies of the contract could be either continued or temporarily discontinued in order to assess experimentally the causal variables and the efficacy of the contract itself. The details of the experimental conditions were also specified in the contingency contract.

In brief, the contract was a guarantee to the subject that valuables supplied by him would be returned contingent upon meeting the specified requirements, or would be permanently lost if those requirements were not met. It was also a guarantee to the researcher that the subject would be available for measurements and the delivery of consequences at specified intervals.

All individuals interested in losing weight were shown a copy of a contingency contract and given a detailed description of the procedures to be used. The procedures were explicitly characterized as being extremely rigid and severe. The researcher then answered any questions raised by the prospective subjects. Each subject was encouraged to take as much time as he needed to consider whether he should sign the contract. When an individual decided to be a subject in the program, he was asked to nominate a number of objects he considered valuable to himself, either in the form of money and/or personal items (*e.g.*, medals and trophies, clothes, jewelry, *etc.*). It was emphasized to all subjects that the items should be as valuable as possible. The contract was then tailored to each subject's personal specifications, with reference to intermediate and terminal requirements of the program: (1) the minimum number of pounds to be lost cumulatively by the end of each succeeding two-week period (*i.e.*, the minimum rate for losing weight), and (2) the terminal weight requirement. The number of valuables obtained from each subject to be used as consequences depended in part upon the amount of weight that the subject agreed to lose, and the minimum rate at which he agreed to lose it. Finally, the researcher, subject, and one witness signed two copies of the contract. The researcher and the subject retained one copy each.

Three sets of contingencies were specified in the contract: (1) Immediate Contingencies; (2) Two-week Contingencies; and (3) Terminal Contingencies.

The Immediate Contingencies were applied to each cumulative two-pound gain or loss of weight that occurred during the treatment conditions. Any time the subject cumulatively lost two pounds with reference to the final weight measurement of baseline, he received one valuable from the researcher. Each additional two-pound weight loss below the previous weight loss was rewarded with one more valuable, and so on. On the other hand, each cumulative two-pound weight gain (above the subject's lowest recorded weight) was punished by the loss of one valuable. The weight of each subject was always recorded to the nearest half-pound.

The Two-Week Contingencies required the subject to lose a minimum number of pounds by the end of each successive two-week period during the treatment conditions. The two-week periods and their associated minimum weight losses were calculated from the last baseline weight measurement and date. Every two weeks, if this requirement was met, the researcher delivered a bonus valuable. If this requirement was not met, the subject lost that valuable as a punishing consequence. The Immediate and the Two-Week Contingencies were each a single valuable selected unsystematically by the researcher. Subjects never knew in advance which valuable would be used as a consequence.

The Terminal Contingency was a portion of the valuables (or money) delivered to the subject *only* if and when his terminal weight requirement was met. These particular valuables were itemized in the contract as specifically for this purpose, and consequently were never in jeopardy of being lost as penalties (*i.e.,* for weight gains or for not meeting a Two-Week Contingency) nor available to be regained before reaching terminal weight. In addition, the researcher agreed to deliver to the subject all of the other remaining valuables that had not been regained or lost as penalties, whenever the subject reached his terminal weight. However, if at any time the subject decided to terminate the program, then all remaining valuables in the possession of the researcher, including the Terminal Contingency, became the property of the researcher. Thus, the Terminal Contingency helped to ensure that the subject would remain in the program until his terminal weight requirement was met.[2] A clause in the contract stipulated that all items that became the property of the researcher would be disposed of in a manner not personally profitable or beneficial to the researcher. These items were susequently donated to various charities.

It should be stressed that the terminal contingencies were always in effect during every phase of the program (*i.e.,* during baseline, treatment, and reversal conditions). In other words, they were long-term consequences that presumably would operate against the usual outcome of a reversal.

Measurement and Reliability

The contract stipulated that the subject be weighed at a specific time and place every Monday, Wednesday, and Friday of each successive week until his terminal weight was reached. The subjects were weighed on the same medical-type scale throughout the experiment. Both the subject and the researcher independently recorded the subject's weight to the nearest

---

[2] Although the contingency contract did not specify the possibility, the researcher, in fact, would dissolve the contract with the mutual agreement of the subject for special circumstances, and return to the subject the remainder of his valuables.

half pound. However, the consequences were delivered in accordance with the researcher's weight determinations.

Reliability determinations were made on each of the days that the subject was weighed by subtracting the subject's notation of his own weight from the researcher's notation. The range of differences of weight occurring throughout the program was the measure of reliability.

The differences between the subject's and the researcher's weight determinations ranged from plus or minus half a pound. Both the subject and the researcher were in agreement on 95% of the weight determinations.

Procedures

The procedures followed a single-subject reversal design (*cf.*, Baer, Wolf, and Risley, 1968). The design included sequential baseline, treatment, reversal, and treatment conditions (*i.e.*, an ABAB design).

During the baseline condition, the subject's weight was regularly measured; there were no scheduled consequences for weight, except the Terminal Contingency. Baseline data were recorded for approximately two to five weeks, depending upon the stability of the subject's weight. The criterion for stability was a two-week period in which either a subject gained weight, remained stable, or lost no more than one pound per week. The final two-week criterion period was considered baseline.[3] At a time unknown in advance to the subject, the researcher notified the subject that the treatment procedure was beginning. The weight of the subject and the date at the time of this notification were considered the final weight measurement and date of the baseline condition.

During the treatment condition, all three contingencies were in effect: The Immediate, Two-Week, and Terminal Contingencies. Both the Immediate and the Two-Week Contingencies were calculated from the final weight measurement and date of the baseline condition. The treatment condition was maintained at least for four weeks, and often longer, depending upon the stability of the subject's rate of losing weight. At a time unknown in advance to the subject, the researcher notified the subject that the reversal procedure was beginning and that until told otherwise, he could continue losing weight but he would neither receive back valuables for losing weight nor lose valuables for gaining. He was also told that whenever he reached terminal weight, the remaining valuables would be returned. The weight of the subject at the time of this notification was considered the final weight measurement of the treatment condition.

[3] Use of the last 14 days of baseline gives each subject a uniform baseline to facilitate comparisons to other subjects. Fourteen days was the shortest baseline of any subject.

During the reversal condition, the subject continued to be weighed regularly, but there were no scheduled consequences, except the Terminal Contingency, regardless of whether the subject lost weight, gained weight, or remained stable. The reversal condition was maintained for approximately two to four weeks. At a time unknown in advance to the subject, the researcher notified the subject that the second treatment procedure was beginning. The weight of the subject and the date at the time of this notification were considered the final weight measurement and date of the reversal condition.

The second and first treatment procedures were identical. During the second treatment condition, however, both the Immediate and the Two-Week Contingencies were calculated from the final weight measurement and date of the reversal condition.

In summary, items considered valuable by the subject and originally his property were surrendered to the researcher and incorporated into a contractual system of prearranged contingencies. The contract prescribed the manner in which the subject could earn back or permanently lose these items. This complex of contingencies, presumably both of reinforcing and of punishing consequences, was in effect during the treatment conditions. Experiment I assessed the effects of the whole complex of treatment contingencies on weight reduction.

RESULTS AND DISCUSSION

Experiment I

Six of the eight subjects who were in the weight-reduction program participated in Experiment I. The data of one of these subjects have been selected to exemplify the procedures and are presented in Figures 1a and 1b. In these figures, each open circle (connected by the thin solid line) represents a two-week minimum weight loss requirement. Each of the solid dots (connected by the thick solid line) represents the subject's weight on each of the days that he was measured. Each triangle indicates the point at which the subject was penalized by a loss of valuables, either for gaining weight, or for not meeting a two-week minimum weight loss requirement. Only the data of the first four conditions (*i.e.*, baseline, treatment, reversal, and treatment) are considered as Experiment I (Figure 1a). A subsequent experimental manipulation was made with this subject (Figure 1b) and those data were considered as part of Experiment II. This is discussed later. As the data of Figure 1a indicate, this subject gained weight (slightly) during baseline, lost weight during treatment conditions, and gained weight during reversal.

Although the data of this subject were selected as the most orderly to exemplify the procedures, it was representative to the extent that the

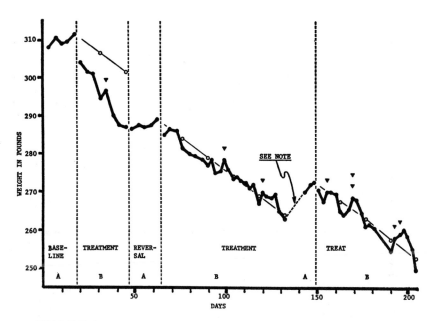

FIGURE 1a A record of the weight of Subject 1 during all conditions. The first four conditions (*i.e.*, Baseline, Treatment, Reversal, and Treatment) were considered as Experiment I. During the Baseline and Reversal conditions, the subject's weight was regularly measured; there were no scheduled consequences. During both Treatment conditions the contingencies of the contract, presumably both of reinforcing and of punishing consequences, were in effect. Each open circle (connected by the thin solid line) represents a two-week minimum weight loss requirement. Each of the solid dots (connected by the thick solid lines) represents the subject's weight on each of the days that he was measured. Each triangle indicates the point at which the subject was penalized by a loss of valuables, either for gaining weight or for not meeting a two-week minimum weight loss requirement. Experiment II begins with the third Treatment condition (continued in Figure 1b). NOTE: the subject was ordered by his physician to consume at least 2500 calories per day for 10 days, in preparation for medical tests.

data of the other subjects, similarly, suggested that the researcher's control of the treatment contingencies were responsible for all losses in weight. That is, most of the subjects gained weight or remained stable during baseline, lost weight during treatment conditions, and gained weight or remained stable during reversal.

A comparison of each subject's rate of losing or gaining weight during each of the first four conditions (*i.e.*, baseline, treatment, reversal, and treatment conditions) is presented in Table 1. These data were calculated

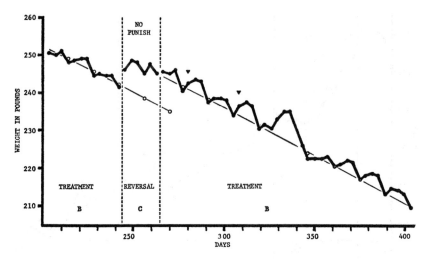

FIGURE 1b   A record of the weight of Subject 1 (continued from Figure 1a). The last three conditions (*i.e.*, Treatment, No Punishment, Reversal, and Treatment) were considered as Experiment II. The Treatment conditions of Experiment II were procedurally identical to those of Experiment I. The No Punishment Reversal condition was identical to the Treatment conditions with the following exception: the punishing consequences were removed; only the reinforcing consequences continued to remain in effect.

for each specified condition (except baseline) by subtracting the final weight measurement of the preceding condition from the final weight measurement of the specified condition. The difference was then divided by the number of weeks that the specified condition was in effect. The baseline data were calculated by subtracting the first weight measurement from the final weight measurement of baseline. This difference was then divided by the two weeks considered as baseline. These calculations yielded an average estimate of the number of pounds lost or gained per week by each

TABLE 1   The average number of pounds lost or gained per week by each subject during each condition of Experiment I (*i.e.*, Baseline, Treatment, Reversal, and Treatment), and Experiment II (*i.e.*, Treatment, No Punishment Reversal, and Treatment). *Subjects 5 and 6 were terminated from the program before a Reversal and second Treatment condition

Experimental condition	Experiment I						$\bar{X}$	Experiment II			$\bar{X}$
	S-1	S-2	S-3	S-4	S-5	S-6		S-7	S-8	S-1	
Baseline A	1.4	0.0	−1.0	0.0	1.0	3.2	0.9	1.5	1.2	−	−
Treatment B	−6.1	−1.7	−2.0	−1.6	−1.3	−1.1	−2.1	−1.5	−1.4	−2.2	−1.7
Reversal A-C	0.8	2.1	4.1	0.4	*	*	1.9	0.4	2.6	1.2	1.4
Treatment B	−2.6	−0.2	−0.5	−1.4	*	*	−1.2	−1.4	−1.5	−1.8	−1.6

subject during each of the four conditions. Only the data from baseline and the first treatment condition are presented for Subjects 5 and 6. Subjects 5 and 6 initially lost approximately 20 pounds during treatment. However, a continuation of scheduled consequences seemed to have no effect on decreasing their weight further. Therefore, both of these subjects were terminated from the program, by mutual agreement.

In all cases except one, the subjects either gained weight or remained stable during the baseline condition. The exception, Subject 3, lost weight during baseline. All of the subjects gained weight during the reversal condition and lost weight during the treatment conditions. Subject 3 lost weight at a greater rate during each of the treatment conditions than during the baseline condition.

A summary assessment of the functions of each of the first four conditions of the program are presented in Figure 2. These data represent the mean weight change in pounds per week that were gained or lost during each of the four conditions. They were calculated by averaging the rates of each subject as listed in Table 1. The baseline and first treatment condition data of Subjects 7 and 8 (Experiment II subjects) were included in these calculations because the baseline and first treatment condition procedures of these subjects were identical to those of Experiment I subjects.

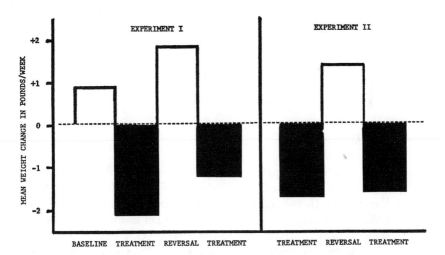

FIGURE 2 Summary assessment of the functions of each condition of Experiment I and Experiment II for all subjects. These data represent the mean weight change in pounds per week gained (+) or lost (−) by all subjects during each of the conditions. They were calculated by taking the means of the average number of pounds lost or gained per week by each subject during each of the conditions of Experiments I and II.

The reversal and second treatment condition data of Subjects 7 and 8 were not included, because the reversal condition of Experiment II differed from that of Experiment I. As Figure 2 shows graphically, the mean weight change during baseline and reversal conditions was +0.9 and +1.9 pounds per week, respectively. Figure 2 also shows the mean weight change during the two treatment conditions was −2.1 and −1.2 pounds per week, respectively.

In summary, Experiment I investigated the applicability of contingency contracting with adult subjects, and assessed experimentally the effects of a complex of contingencies on weight reduction. A single-subject reversal design was used. Almost all of the subjects gained weight or remained stable during the baseline condition, lost weight during treatment conditions, and gained weight or remained stable during the reversal condition. The results suggest that items considered valuable by the subject and originally his property, can be used successfully to modify the subject's weight when these items are surrendered to the researcher and incorporated into a contractual system of prearranged contingencies. Both intra- and inter-subject replications support the generality of these findings. However, Experiment I did not analyze whether the reinforcing consequences, the punishing consequences, or both, were necessary components of the treatment procedure.

Experiment II was an attempt to ascertain whether the presumptive punishing consequences were, in fact, functional as a component of the treatment procedure.

METHOD

Experiment II

Subjects 1, 7, and 8 participated. The procedures were identical to those of Experiment I, with the following exception: during the reversal condition of Experiment II, the reinforcing components of the Immediate and the Two-Week Contingencies continued to remain in effect. The punishing components of the Immediate and the Two-Week Contingencies, however, were removed. In other words, during the reversal condition of Experiment II, the researcher continued to deliver to the subject one valuable contingent upon each cumulative two-pound weight loss. However, if the subject gained weight, he did not lose any of his valuables as a punishing consequence. In addition, the subject continued to receive a bonus valuable contingent upon meeting each two-week minimum weight loss requirement. Nevertheless, no valuables were lost by the subject if he did not meet this requirement. At a time unknown in advance to the subject, the researcher notified the subject that the second treatment procedure was beginning. The weight of the subject and the date at the time of this notification were considered the final weight measurement and date of the reversal condition. During the second treatment condition, both the Immediate and the Two-Week Contingencies were calculated from the final weight measurement and date of the reversal condition.

It should be noted that Subject 1 was used in both Experiments I and II, and consequently was exposed to both types of reversals.

RESULTS AND DISCUSSION

Only the treatment-reversal-treatment portions of the data were considered as Experiment II. The last reversal condition in which Subject 1 participated was procedurally identical to those of Subjects 7 and 8 (see Figures 1a and 1b). Therefore, the last treatment-reversal-treatment condition data of this subject were similarly included in the analysis of this experiment.

During the first and second treatment conditions, all of the subjects lost weight with reference to the final weight measurement of the preceding conditions (*i.e.*, baseline and reversal). During the reversal condition, all of the subjects gained weight with reference to the final weight measurement of the preceding condition.

A comparison of each subject's rate of losing or gaining weight during each of the three conditions (*i.e.*, treatment, reversal, treatment) is presented in Table 1. These data were calculated (in the same manner as for Experiment I) for each specified condition by subtracting the final weight measurement of the preceding condition from the final weight measurement of the specified condition. The difference was then divided by the number of weeks that the specified condition was in effect. These calculations yielded an average estimate of the number of pounds lost or gained per week by each subject during each of the three conditions. In all cases, the subjects lost weight during both treatment conditions and gained weight during the reversal condition.

A summary assessment of the functions of each condition are presented in Figure 2. These data represent the mean weight change in pounds per week gained or lost during each of the three conditions. They were calculated (in the same manner as for Experiment I) by averaging the rates of each subject (*i.e.*, Subjects 1, 7, and 8) as listed in Table 1. As Figure 2 shows graphically, the mean weight change during the reversal condition was +1.4 pounds per week. The mean weight change during each treatment condition was −1.7 and −1.6 pounds per week, respectively. As can be seen in Figure 2, the functions of the reversals in Experiment I and in Experiment II were almost identical.

In summary, Experiment II attempted to ascertain whether the permanent loss of a subject's valuables contingent upon either specified weight gains or losing weight at a rate lower than an agreed-upon rate, was a punishing or aversive consequence. Subjects 1, 7, and 8 lost weight during the two treatment conditions and gained weight during the reversal condition. When the presumably punishing consequences were removed from the procedure (*i.e.*, during reversal), the subjects gained weight even though positive contingencies for losing weight remained in effect (Table 1). The data suggest that the permanent loss of the subject's valuables, when used as consequences are a necessary component of the treatment procedure.

GENERAL DISCUSSION AND SUMMARY

The present research investigated the applicability of contingency contracting with adult subjects, and the effects of a complex of treatment contingencies on weight reduction.

The results suggest that properly designed contingency contracts may be an effective means to control some behavior problems of normal non-institutionalized adults. In this case, being overweight was treated as the behavior problem.

This study demonstrated that items considered valuable by the subject and originally his property, could be used successfully to modify the subject's weight when used as reinforcing and as punishing consequences. Furthermore, a systematic analysis of the contingencies indicated that punishing consequences were a necessary component of the treatment procedure for the three subjects of Experiment II.

The contingency contract used differed from those previously discussed by other investigators (Homme, *et al.*, 1969; Cantrell *et al.*, 1969; Tharp and Wetzel, 1970). Those contracts were essentially an explicit statement of contingencies, usually agreed upon by two or more people. The contingency contract used in this study was also an explicit statement of contingencies, but it incorporated a number of additional features considered salient to its effectiveness.

First, the contract required each subject to surrender a large number of his valuables to the researcher. The subject then could earn back portions of those valuables contingent upon meeting the specified behavioral requirements (*i.e.*, weight losses), or lose valuables if those requirements were not met.

Second, the subject signed the contract in front of witnesses, thus further legalizing the researcher's authority to control the delivery of those valuables as consequences. The researcher also signed the contract, thus obligating him to abide by the terms of the contract.

Third, the contract required the subject to be available for behavioral measurement and the delivery of consequences at specified intervals.

Fourth, the contract included a clause stipulating that the researcher could, at his discretion, experimentally manipulate the treatment variables. Thus, the contingencies of the contract could be continued or temporarily discontinued in order to assess experimentally the casual variables.

Last, the contract was designed as a "behavior trap". A behavior trap, as discussed by Baer and Wolf (1970, p. 321) and Baer, Rowbury, and Goetz (1971), is basically a situation in which, "only a relatively simple response is necessary to enter the trap, yet once entered, the trap cannot be resisted in creating general behavioral change".

In this study, the subject's surrendering of his valuables to the researcher and signing the contract can be conceptualized as the "relatively simple response" required of the subject to enter the behavior trap. Once these responses were made, the subject was in the program (*i.e.*, in the behavior trap), and was required to lose weight steadily (at the agreed-upon rate) or be penalized by the permanent loss of portions of his valuables. Furthermore, the subject could terminate the program, before reaching his terminal weight, only if he forfeited all of his remaining valuables. Thus, the contingencies of this contract presumably acted as a behavior trap by facilitating the subject both to lose weight steadily and to remain in the program until his terminal weight was reached. Still, it should be emphasized that the behavior trap principle was functional only to the extent that the subject did, in fact, surrender items of value.

Although each subject verbally reported which items he considered valuable before surrendering them to the researcher, the definition of valuable in this procedure was still in terms of the effects those items had on the subject's weight. In other words, the items surrendered to the researcher by some of the subjects, could have been valuable (*i.e.*, reinforcing) with respect to affecting some behaviors, but not necessarily as effective with respect to losing weight. This may account, in part, for the variability in the effectiveness of this procedure.

Variability in the effectiveness of this type of procedure may have other sources as well. For example, as a subject steadily loses weight, presumably because of dieting, the probability of consuming larger quantities of food may increase. This increase in probability can then compete with the aversive effects of losing valuables. This type of effect may be facilitated further because the reinforcing effects of eating are immediate while the aversive effects of losing valuables are minimized by the delay in time imposed by this type of procedure.

Before concluding, it should be pointed out that this procedure had some problems, especially as it related to weight control. Unsolicited anecdotal reports from some of the subjects indicated that they had used extreme measures at various times to lose weight rapidly and temporarily in order to avoid aversive consequences. These measures, reportedly, included taking laxatives, diuretics, and doing vigorous exercises just before being weighed. This problem may have occurred because the contract specified that the treatment contingencies be delivered contingent upon specified weight changes rather than the behaviors that can produce those changes. Weight, as a measure, is the result of various other behaviors. The contract neither specified, controlled, nor prescribed the manner in which the subject could arrive at changes in his weight. Therefore, any one of a number of behaviors could have resulted in a reduction of weight. These included appropriate dieting, an increase in exercise, or both, as well as extreme measures such as taking laxatives or diuretics which could avoid aversive consequences, at least on a temporary basis.

Consequently, contingency contracting and other techniques should be used with caution to the extent that these techniques place effective contingencies on the outcomes of various behaviors. It is difficult for a researcher or therapist to anticipate all of the behaviors that can produce a specified outcome or result. And some of the behaviors that can produce such an outcome may be socially undesirable or even dangerous in some cases.

In summary, properly designed contingency contracts may be an effective technique to facilitate remediation of some behavior problems on non-institutionalized adults. The probability of this is increased to the extent that such techniques can facilitate a therapist both in gaining systematic control of effective consequences and in maintaining reliable measurement of the behavior to be changed. The present study met these two criteria and thereby demonstrated the application of contingency contracting with adult subjects. The dependent variable of this study was both a convenient and reliably measureable "behavior". Other behavior problems do not lend themselves as readily to reliable measurement. Smoking, drinking, and stealing, are examples of behaviors that are much more difficult to measure reliably. Nevertheless, as better methods of surveillance and monitoring of these types of behaviors develop, so may an increase in the use of contingency contracting with adult subjects.

REFERENCES

BAER, D. M., WOLF, M. M., and RISLEY, T. R. Some current dimensions of applied behavior analysis. *Journal of Applied Behavior Analysis*, 1968, **1**, 91–97.

BAER, D. M., and WOLF, M. M. The entry into natural communities of reinforcement. In R. Ulrich, T. Stachnick, and J. Mabry (Eds.), *Control of human behavior*, Glenview, Illinois: Scott, Foresman and Company, 1970. Pp. 319–324.

BAER, D. M., ROWBURY, T., and GOETZ, E. The preschool as a behavioral trap: a proposal for research. In C. Lavatelli (Ed.), *The natural curriculum of the child*. Washington, D.C.: National Association for the Education of Young Children, 1971.

CANTRELL, R. P., CANTRELL, M. L. HUDDLESTON, C. M., and WOOLRIDGE, R. L. Contingency contracting with school problems. *Journal of Applied Behavior Analysis*, 1969, 2, 215–220.

HOMME, L. Human motivation and the environment. In N. Haring and R. Whelan (Eds.), *The learning environment: relationship to behavior modification and implications for special education*. Lawrence: University of Kansas Press, 1966.

HOMME, L., CSANYI, A. P., GONZALES, M. A., and RECHS, J. R. *How to use contingency contracting in the classroom*. U.S.A. Research Press, 1969.

MICHAEL, JACK L. Principles of behavior usage. In R. Ulrich, T. Stachnik, and J. Mabry (Eds.), *Control of human behavior*. Glenview, Illinois: Scott, Foresman and Company, 1970. Pp. 28–35.

STUART, R. B. *Behavioral contracting within the families of delinquents*. Paper delivered at the American Psychological Association Convention, Miami Beach, 1970.

THARP, R. G. and WETZEL, R. J. *Behavior modification in the natural environment*. New York: Academic Press, 1969.

TIGHE, T. J. and ELLIOT, R. A technique for controlling behavior in natural life settings. *Journal of Applied Behavior Analysis*, 1968, 1, 263–266.

ELERY L. PHILLIPS
University of Kansas

Achievement place: token reinforcement procedures in a home-style rehabilitation setting for "pre-delinquent" boys[1]

Token reinforcement procedures were designed to modify the behavior of "pre-delinquent" boys residing in a community-based, home-style rehabilitation setting. Points (the tokens) were redeemable for various privileges such as visiting their families, watching TV, and riding bicycles. Points were given by the house-parents contingent upon specified appropriate behavior and taken away for specified inappropriate behavior. The frequencies of aggressive statements and poor grammar decreased while tidiness, punctuality, and amount of homework completed increased. It was concluded that a token reinforcement procedure, entirely dependent upon back-up reinforcers naturally available in a home-style treatment setting, could contribute to an effective and economical rehabilitation program for pre-delinquents.

[1] I wish to thank Montrose M. Wolf for his advice and guidance throughout this research. I am also indebted to Elaine Phillips for assistance in conducting the experiments and in preparing this manuscript. This study is based on a thesis submitted to the Department of Human Development in partial fulfillment of the requirements of the Master of Arts degree. The research was partially supported by a grant (HD 03144) from the National Institute of Child Health and Human Development to the Bureau of Child Research and the Department of Human Development, University of Kansas.

352

CONTENTS

Alternatives are being sought to the placement of juvenile delinquents in large state reformatories. While reformatories are steadily increasing their standards they still have had less than adequate records of success (Block and Flynn, 1966; Berelson and Steiner, 1964).

The current trend away from the reformatory can be seen in the establishment of small home-style, residential treatment programs by individual communities. These often involve a pair of house-parents and from three to eight youths. The adjudicated youths live in these homes, attend the local schools, and continue to participate in their communities.

Achievement Place, the program described in this report, is an example of a home-style, community based, treatment facility. The treatment program at Achievement Place employed a "token economy" based on those described by Cohen, Filipczak, and Bis (1965), and Burchard (1967) for institutionalized delinquents; by Ayllon and Azrin (1965) for institutionalized psychotics; and by Wolf, Giles, and Hall (1968), Clark, Lachowicz, and Wolf (1968), and Birnbrauer, Wolf, Kidder, and Tague (1965) for classroom management.

The aim of the present research was to develop and evaluate the effects of a token economy (based on naturally available reinforcers) in a home-style, residential treatment program for "pre-delinquent" boys.

PROGRAM

Subjects

Three boys who had been declared dependent-neglected by the County Court and placed in Achievement Place served as subjects. The boys, all from low-income families, had committed minor offenses ("thefts", "fighting", and "general disruptive behavior") and had histories of "school truancy" and "academic failure".

Jack was 13 yr old. His school records reported an I.Q. of 85 and a second-grade reading level. Concern had been noted regarding a "speech problem", "poor grammar", "aggressiveness", "poor motivation", and "a general lack of cleanliness".

Don was 14 yr old. School records indicated that academically he was performing two years below his grade placement, but that he had a normal I.Q. rating. Reports from school also described this youth as "possessing an inferior attitude", "rejected" by his classmates, and "aggressive".

Tom, who was 12, was described as having an I.Q. of approximately 120. His disruptive behavior in school had resulted in his being placed in the fifth grade, three years below his level of achievement as indicated by the Iowa Basic Skills Test. School records also noted that he was "dangerous to other children" and "openly hostile toward teachers".

Facilities and Routine

The purpose of Achievement Place was to provide a home situation in the community for boys who had been termed pre-delinquents by local juvenile authorities (boys who had committed only minor offenses thus far, but whom the Court felt would probably advance to more serious crimes unless steps were taken to modify their behavior). The author and his wife were the house-parents.

The daily routine was similar to that of many families. The boys arose at 7 A.M. They showered, dressed, and cleaned their bedrooms and bathrooms. After breakfast, some of the boys had kitchen clean-up duties before leaving for school. After school the boys returned home and prepared their homework, after which they could watch TV, play games, or engage in other recreational activities if these privileges had been earned via the token economy. Some boys were assigned kitchen clean-up duties after the evening meal. Bedtime was 9:30 P.M. Trips, athletic events, and jobs, both around the home and away from the home, were scheduled for weekends and school holidays.

The Target Behaviors and the Token Reinforcement System

Target behaviors were selected in social, self-care, and academic areas considered to be important to the youths in their current or future environment. A further requirement was that a target behavior had to be definable in terms of observable events and measurable with a high degree of inter-observer agreement.

Token reinforcers were used which could be easily and rapidly administered and thus could bridge the delay between the target behavior and the remote back-up reinforcing events. The tokens took the form of points. The boys earned points for specified appropriate behavior and lost points for specified inappropriate behavior. Points were tallied on 3-by-5-in. index cards that the boys always carried with them. Thus, the points could be earned or lost immediately and points later redeemed for the back-up reinforcers.

Items and events which were naturally available in the home and which appeared to be important to the boys were the back-up reinforcers. Access to these privileges was obtained on a weekly basis. At the end of each week the boys could trade the points they had earned that week for privileges during the next week. Some of the privileges are described in Table 1.

The prices of the privileges were relatively constant from week to week, although they were occasionally adjusted as their importance appeared to vary. For example, during the winter the price of television was increased.

The economy of the system (the relationship between the total number of points that could be earned and the total cost of all the privileges) was arranged in such a manner that if a youth performed all the tasks expected of him and lost a minimum of points in fines, he could expect to obtain all the privileges without performing any extra tasks.

There was another set of privileges for "one-of-a-kind" opportunities which had no fixed price but which were instead sold to the highest bidder, auction style. One example was the "car privilege" which entitled the purchaser to his choice of seating in the car for the week. Another auctioned privilege was the opportunity for a boy to obtain authority over the other boys in the execution of some household chore. Each week these managerships were auctioned. The purchaser was made responsible for

TABLE 1   Privileges that could be earned each week with points.

Privileges for the week	Price in points
Allowance	1000
Bicycle	1000
TV	1000
Games	500
Tools	500
Snacks	1000
Permission to go downtown	1000
Permission to stay up past bedtime	1000
Permission to come home late after school	1000

the maintenance of the basement, the yard, or the bathrooms. Each manager had authority to reward or fine the other boys under his direction for their work at the task. The manager, in turn, earned or lost points as a result of the quality of the job done (as judged by the house-parents).

Most of the behaviors which earned or lost points were formalized and explicit to the extent of being advertised on the bulletin board. Rewards and fines ranged from 10 to 10,000 points. Some of the behaviors and approximate points gained are indicated in Table 2.

A few other contingencies were less formalized but still resulted in point consequences. For example, even though there was no formal rule the boys would sometimes earn or lose points as a result of their overall manners while guests were in the home.

EXPERIMENT I:
AGGRESSIVE STATEMENTS

One behavior pattern that had led to the classification of these youths as deviant juveniles had been the "aggressiveness" they exhibited. The terms "aggression" and "aggressiveness" were noted in school records, psychological test reports, Court notes, and in general comments from indi-

TABLE 2   Behaviors and the number of points that they earned or lost

Behaviors that earned points	Points
1) Watching news on TV or reading the newspaper	300 per day
2) Cleaning and maintaining neatness in one's room	500 per day
3) Keeping one's person neat and clean	500 per day
4) Reading books	5 to 10 per page
5) Aiding house-parents in various household tasks	20 to 1000 per task
6) Doing dishes	500 to 1000 per meal
7) Being well dressed for an evening meal	100 to 500 per meal
8) Performing homework	500 per day
9) Obtaining desirable grades on school report cards	500 to 1000 per grade
10) Turning out lights when not in use	25 per light

Behaviors that lost points	Points
1) Failing grades on the report card	500 to 1000 per grade
2) Speaking aggressively	20 to 50 per response
3) Forgetting to wash hands before meals	100 to 300 per meal
4) Arguing	300 per response
5) Disobeying	100 to 1000 per response
6) Being late	10 per min
7) Displaying poor manners	50 to 100 per response
8) Engaging in poor posture	50 to 100 per response
9) Using poor grammar	20 to 50 per response
10) Stealing, lying, or cheating	10,000 per response

viduals who were familiar with the youths. Inquiry into the nature of this "aggressiveness" revealed it to be inferred almost completely from comments the boys emitted such as: "I'll smash that car if it gets in my way" or "I'll kill you". The following experiment describes the house-parents' program to measure and to reduce the aggressive verbal behavior.

PROCEDURES AND RESULTS

"Aggressive" phrases were recorded for the three boys simultaneously for 3 hr each day (one session) while the youths were engaged in woodworking activities in the basement workshop.

Response Definition

Phrases or clauses emitted by the youths were considered to be aggressive statements if they stated or threatened inappropriate destruction or damage to any object, person, or animal. For example, the statement "Be quiet" was not counted as an aggressive response, while "If you don't shut up, I'll kill you" was recorded as an aggressive statement. Over 70% of the aggressive statements were from a list of 19 phrases used repeatedly.

Conditions

Baseline. No contingencies were placed on the youths' responses.

Correction. The boys were told what an aggressive statement was and that such statements were not to be used. A corrective statement by one of the house-parents, such as "That's not the way to talk" or "Stop that kind of talk", was made contingent on the youths' responses. An arbitrary period of approximately 3 to 5 sec was allowed to elapse after a response (or responses) before the corrective comment was made. This meant that a correction did not follow every aggressive statement; sometimes many responses were emitted before a corrective statement was made. The delay interval was employed in order to increase the chance that the boy would have completed his speech episode before correction was administered by the parent.

Fines. A fine of 20 points was made contingent on each response. The fines, like the corrections of the previous condition, were not delivered until approximately 3 to 5 sec had passed without a response. No announcement of this condition was made in advance.

No fines. No fines or corrections were levied on responses. This condition was introduced unannounced. There were occasional threats to reinstate the Fines condition if the rate of responding did not decrease. The threats were worded approximately as follows: "If you boys continue to use that aggressive talk, I will have no other choice but to take away points." These threats were not carried out.

Fines. This condition was identical to the first Fines condition except that fines were 50 points instead of 25. The onset of this condition was announced.

In Fig. 1 it can be seen, by comparing Correction rate with the Baseline rate, that Correction reduced the responding of only one boy, while Fines (20 points per response) produced an immediate and dramatic decline in each youth's aggressive statements. Responses gradually returned when fines were no longer levied but were eliminated when the Fines condition was reinstated. Although the first threat (indicated by the arrows) in the No Fines condition did appear to have a large suppressive effect on the rate of behavior, the last two threats appeared to have much less, possibly due to the fact that the first threat had not been carried out.

Inter-observer agreement about the occurrence of aggressive statements was measured by the use of a second observer during 14 of the 75 sessions. Agreement averaged 92%.

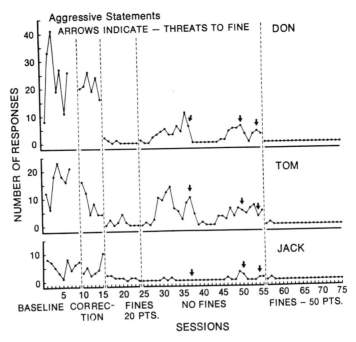

FIGURE 1 Number of aggressive statements per 3-hr session for each youth under each condition.

EXPERIMENT II:
BATHROOM CLEANING

The youths in the home were assigned a number of household chores, such as aiding in the upkeep of the yard and cleaning their rooms and bathrooms. They originally failed to complete these chores in most instances. Programs involving the point system were designed to increase the boys' contribution to the maintenance of these areas. The cleaning of the bathrooms was studied under a number of conditions.

PROCEDURES AND RESULTS

Sixteen cleaning tasks in the bathroom involving the sinks, stools, floors, *etc.* were scored as accomplished or not accomplished. The bathrooms were scored every day between 12:00 and 12:30 P.M., except in the Baseline condition, where recording was done as soon as the boys reported that the cleaning had been completed (usually before noon). Consequences, if there were any, were levied immediately after inspection.

Response Definition

As stated above, the bathroom cleaning was divided into 16 tasks. In order to obtain a high degree of inter-observer agreement, each task had a specified set of criteria to be met in order to be considered accomplished. For example, one of the 16 tasks was described in the following manner:
Floor and Rugs—The floor has to be clear of all objects greater than ¼ by ¼ by ¼ in. and clear of all visible water. If rugs were removed for cleaning, they should be replaced and centered under the sink within one foot of the wall.

Conditions

Baseline. The Baseline condition consisted of instructing all the boys to clean the bathrooms. No consequences were contingent on their behavior other than the instruction that they clean the bathrooms again, if fewer than four of the tasks had been accomplished.

Manager. During the Manager condition one boy was given the responsibility for cleaning the bathrooms daily. He picked the individual, or individuals, to clean the bathrooms each day and then paid or fined the workers (20 points lost or gained per task) according to the quality of their work as judged by him. Later, when the bathrooms were checked by the house-parents, the manager received or lost points (20 points per task). The manager earned points only if 75% or more of the tasks were completed. The privilege of being manager was auctioned each week.

Group. The Group condition consisted of all boys being responsible for cleaning the bathrooms and subject to the same fines. There was no manager. The boys were fined when less than 75% of the 16 tasks were completed. The amount of the fines varied from 25 to 300 points.

Manager. This condition was identical to the first Manager condition.

Group. Identical to the first Group condition except that the fines were 100 points.

Manager. Identical to the first and second Manager conditions.

The point contingencies levied by the manager under the Manager condition were more effective than the fines administered by the houseparents under the Group condition, even when the values of the fines

TABLE 3 Average number of points lost per session by workers and manager under each condition

	Baseline	First manager	First group	Second manager	Second group	Third manager
Worker	0	18	73	13	100	0
Manager	0	64	—	20	—	16

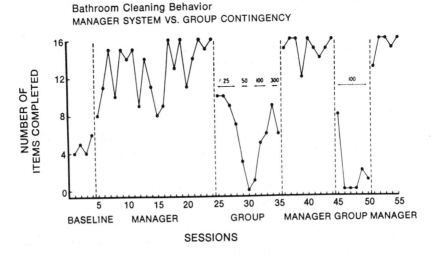

FIGURE 2   Number of tasks accomplished per session for each condition. The numerals above the arrows indicate the possible number of points lost or gained for the sessions indicated by the horizontal arrows.

under the Group condition were greater than those administered by the manager. The greater effectiveness of the Manager condition may have been the result of the differential contingencies for each boy administered by the manager.

Table 3 shows the average number of points lost per boy each day under each condition. Table 3 shows clearly that the managership was not purchased because it was possible to earn a large number of points as a manager. The manager consistently lost more points than the workers he supervised.

Item by item, inter-observer agreement about the accomplishment of the bathroom cleaning tasks for 20 sessions ranged from 83% to 100% agreement and averaged 97%.

EXPERIMENT III: PUNCTUALITY

One of the boys in particular failed to respond to instructions about promptness. This led to an analysis, over a series of behaviors, of the effectiveness of point contingencies on punctuality.

PROCEDURES AND RESULTS

Promptness was recorded for three separate behaviors:

(1) Returning home from school.
(2) Going to bed.
(3) Returning home from errands.

Instructions were posted which stated times to be home from school and to retire to their bedrooms at night. When a boy was sent on an errand the time he was due to return was determined before he departed.

The house-parents recorded the number of minutes late or early up to 30 min.

Conditions

Before Fines. If the boy was late from school or an errand, he was reprimanded by one of the house-parents, "Why are you late? You know what time I told you to be here." Tardiness in going to their bedrooms resulted in a reminder every 10 min, "Go to bed; it's past your bedtime." No other contingencies were involved.

Fines. The youths were fined 20 points for every minute that they were late. Other than being initially informed of the change in contingencies, they were given no reminders or verbal reprimands. The fines were dispensed when the youths returned home or departed for bed. There were no programmed consequences for being early.

Punctuality for school was dealt with first. The termination of the baseline (Before Fines) involving school marked the beginning of the baseline of errands. Completion of the baseline for errands corresponded to initiation of the baseline for bedtime behavior.

The development of Tom's punctuality in all three areas can be seen in Fig. 3. The other two boys had a consistent punctuality problem only at bedtime, and this disappeared at the onset of the Fines condition. The fines were very specific in their effect on the subjects' behavior. Fining tardiness from school had no apparent effect on promptness in returning from errands, and punishing lateness from errands did not seem to produce punctuality at bedtime. Inter-observer agreement was greater than 95% for the 53 checks which occurred throughout the study.

EXPERIMENT IV: HOMEWORK

Failure in school is frequently associated with juvenile delinquency. The school records of the boys sent to Achievement Place all contained ac-

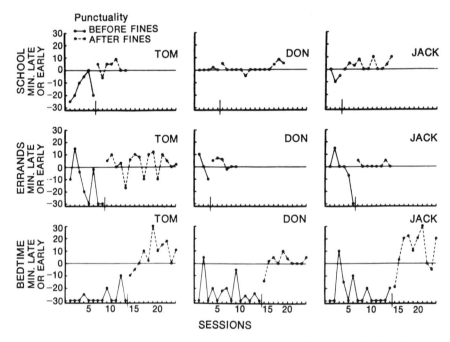

FIGURE 3   Number of minutes early or late before and after the applications of point contingencies. Each youth's punctuality was measured for school, errands, and bedtime.

counts of truancy and lack of academic success throughout the boys' school years. One apparently severe deficiency in their school repertoires involved their failure to prepare routine classroom assignments and homework. This experiment compared the effect of several contingencies on preparation of homework tasks.

PROCEDURES AND RESULTS

The study was carried out during the summer, when the youths were not in school. Daily assignments were described on 3-by-5-in. index cards which were available after 8:00 A.M. each morning. The work was scored at 5:00 P.M. of the same day. Each boy was instructed that failure to pick up an assignment card during the day would result in a fine equal to the number of points he would have received if he had completed the assignment. None of the youths ever failed to pick up his assignment card. The house-parents were available to aid in the preparation of the assignments during two periods each day, 10:00 to 11:00 A.M. and 2:00 to 3:00 P.M.

Response Definition

The assignments were pages out of self-teaching workbooks which required approximately 1 hr to complete. The workbooks used were *The Practice Workbook of Arithmetic*, Grade 5 and 6, Treasure Books, Inc., 1107 Broadway, New York, N.Y., and *The Practice Workbook of Reading*, Grades 2 and 3, also by Treasure Books, Inc.

The assignments, usually two or three pages, were divided into five approximately equal parts on the assignment cards. Each part required an accuracy of 75% to be considered complete. The boys received one-fifth of the maximum number of points, money, or time obtainable for each assignment completed, as explained below.

Conditions

Money. Under this condition each boy could earn 25 cents for each day's assignment if he had completed the assignment with less than 25% errors. The youths had the choice of receiving the money daily or at the end of the week. All three chose the latter, and the amount of money they earned was accumulated on an index card carried by each boy.

Weekly late-time. The boys had the opportunity to earn up to 1 hr of late-time per assignment. Late-time could be spent on the weekends to stay up beyond the youth's normal bedtime (9:30 P.M.). A maximum of 7 hr could be spent by a boy during a weekend and the boys could share their late-time with each other.

Daily late-time. Throughout this condition the boys could use the late-time the same day earned or save it for the weekend.

Points. The points phase allowed the youths to earn 500 points per assignment.

Money. This was the same as the first Money condition.

Points. This was the same as the first Points condition.

Figure 4 shows that the Points condition was by far the most effective in producing homework preparation. Daily Late-Time compared favorably to other conditions. Money, at the one value tested, yielded relatively poor results.

It should be noted that no effort was made to equate the points with the money and it seemed quite likely that at some higher value money would have been as effective as points. It was thought that the low rate of behavior in the first Money condition might have been due to the youths' lack of experience in using money. Thus, after the first condition, an allowance of $1.50 was given each week until the second Money condition (a period of seven weeks). During this interim the youths spent their

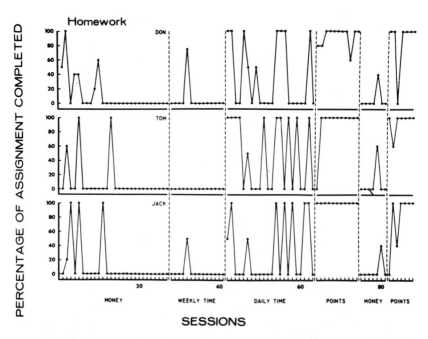

FIGURE 4 Percent of homework assignment completed by each boy under each of several conditions.

money and appeared to understand what could be obtained with money. However, the reinstatement of the Money condition produced no better performance than the original Money condition.

Observer agreement in scoring the assignments was measured for four separate sessions, one in each of the first four conditions. The agreement on the proportion of the assignment completed was 100%.

EXPERIMENT V: "AIN'T"

Poor grammar was an obvious problem for one of the boys. The present study describes a program designed to correct a grammatical problem both with and without manipulation of the point system.

PROCEDURE AND RESULTS

The verbal response "ain't" was recorded for one boy for 3 hr (one session) each day. The 3 hr were not consecutive, nor the time of day consistent. Responses were registered on a silent counter which appeared to be unnoticed by the youth.

Response Definition

It was necessary to differentiate between "ain't" used in normal conversation and the "ain'ts" used in discussions about the incorrect responses. Thus, "ain'ts" used as verbs were considered responses, while "ain'ts" employed as nouns or other parts of speech were not recorded.

Conditions

Baseline. No contingencies were placed on the youth's responses.

Correction. The correction procedure consisted of either house-parent's interrupting the boy's conversation, informing him of his error, suggesting an appropriate alternative, and requiring the youth to repeat the sentence using the correction. The house-parents corrected the mistake in a matter-of-fact manner. The subject's peers were also encouraged to assist in informing the boy of his errors.

Correction and Fines. This condition was identical to the previous phase except that a 20-point fine was levied on each response heard throughout the day. The "ain'ts" from each 3-hr session were recorded as above. Also, the total number of responses fined for the entire day was available by tallying the entries noted on the point card. Again, the other boys were told to inform the house-parents of any responses which occurred when they were not present. These responses were also fined.

Post Check.   One month after the final session of the Correction and Fine condition the response was again recorded for five days (3 hr each day).

As can be seen in Fig. 5, no effect was evident from the Correction condition but when the 20-point fine was made contingent on the youth's behavior, there was an immediate and consistent decline in the frequency of the inappropriate behavior, until, by the end of the second week, the response, "ain't", was eliminated. It was the impression of the house-parents that this effect was not accompanied by any noticeable decline in the youth's overall rate of speech. The dashed line in Fig. 5 indicates the course of the decline in "ain'ts" recorded throughout each day during this condition.

The Post Check condition, 30 days after the elimination of "ain'ts", revealed no trace of the response.

Observer reliability was recorded for over one-fourth of the sessions. The observer recorded data simultaneously with the primary recorder,

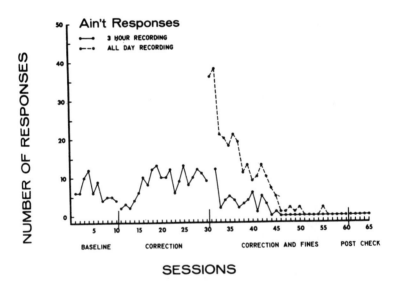

FIGURE 5   Number of responses per day (3-hr session) for one youth under: 1) no consequences (baseline); 2) correction by the house-parents and other boys; and 3) correction and a 20-point fine for each response. Post checks of the behavior were taken 30 days later. The dashed line indicates the total number of responses for the entire day.

but recording was independent. Agreement was never less than 93%, and the overall average was 99%.

DISCUSSION

The token economy (point system), which was designed to deal with a variety of social, self-care, and academic behaviors in the home-style treatment program for pre-delinquent boys, proved to be practicable, economical, and effective. The points seemed almost as convenient to administer as verbal consequences. In the series of experiments presented, the houseparents removed or presented points by requesting the youth's point card and recording the consequence. Subsequent to these studies, the youths themselves have performed the recording tasks equally well. The houseparents have simply instructed the boys to "take off" or "give yourself" points. Cheating has not appeared to be a problem, possibly because of the extremely heavy fine if caught. The privileges for which the points were traded cost nothing, since they were all naturally available in the home as they would be in almost any middle-class home. Since the privileges could be purchased only for a week at a time, they were available over and over again as reinforcers, thus providing an almost unending supply.

The programs involving the point system successfully modified aggressive verbal behavior, bathroom tidiness, punctuality, homework preparation, and poor grammar. The research goals remain of expanding the program to include more boys and more behaviors as well as developing means of transferring the newly established repertoires to the natural contingencies of reinforcement. If these goals can be achieved, token reinforcement procedures should become a basic feature of home-style treatment programs for delinquents.

REFERENCES

AYLLON, T. and AZRIN, N. H. The measurement and reinforcement of behavior of psychotics. *Journal of the Experimental Analysis of Behavior*, 1965, 2, 357–383.

BERELSON, B. and STEINER, G. A. *Human behavior: an inventory of scientific findings*. New York: Harcourt, Brace & World, Inc., 1964.

BIRNBRAUER, J. S., WOLF, M. M., KIDDER, J. D., and TAGUE, C. E. Classroom behavior of retarded pupils with token reinforcement. *Journal of Experimental Child Psychology*, 1965, 2, 219–235.

BLOCH, H. A. and FLYNN, F. T. *Delinquency: the juvenile offender in America today*. New York: Random House, 1956.

BURCHARD, J. D. Systematic socialization: a programmed environment for the habilitation of antisocial retardates. *The Psychological Record*, 1967, **17**, 641–476.

BURCHARD, J. D. and TYLER, V. O. The modification of delinquent behavior through operant conditioning. *Behavior Research and Therapy*, 1965, **2**, 245–250.

CLARK, M., LACHOWICZ, J., and WOLF, M. M. A pilot basic education program for school dropouts incorporating a token reinforcement system. *Behavior Research and Therapy*, 1968, 6, 183–188.

COHEN, A. K. and SHORT, J. F. Juvenile delinquency. In R. E. Melton and R. A. Nisbet (Eds.), *Contemporary social problems*. New York: Harcourt, Brace & World, 1961. Pp. 77–126.

COHEN, H. L., FILIPCZAK, J. A., and BIS, J. S. Case project: contingencies application for special education. Progress Report, U.S. Department of Health, Education, and Welfare, 1965.

GLUECK, S. and GLUECK, E. *Unraveling juvenile delinquency*. Cambridge, Mass.: Harvard University Press, 1950.

McCORD, W., McCORD, J., and ZOLA, I. K. *Origins of crimes: a new evaluation of the Cambridge-Sommerville youth study*. New York: Columbia University Press, 1959.

POWERS, E. and WITMER, H. *An experiment in prevention of delinquency: the Cambridge-Sommerville youth study*. New York: Columbia University Press, 1951.

SCHWITZGEBEL, R. L. *Street corner research: an experimental approach to juvenile delinquency*. Cambridge, Mass.: Harvard University Press, 1964.

SLACK, C. W. Experimenter-subject psychology: a new method of introducing intensive office treatment for unreachable cases. *Mental Hygiene*, 1960, **44**, 238–256.

STAATS, A. W. and BUTTERFIELD, W. H. Treatment of non-reading in a culturally deprived juvenile delinquent: an application of reinforcement principles. *Child Development*, 1965, **36**, 925–942.

THORNE, G. L., THARP, R. G., and WETZEL, R. J. Behavior modification techniques: new tools for probation officers. *Federal Probation*, 1967, June.

WETZEL, R. Use of behavioral techniques in a case of compulsive stealing. *Journal of Consulting Psychology*, 1966, **30**, 367–374.

WOLF, M. M., GILES, D. J., and HALL, R. B. Experiments with token reinforcement in a remedial classroom. *Behavior Research and Therapy*, 1968, 6, 51–64.

6

SCHOOL BEHAVIOR

The scope of contingency control in the classroom is described in a recent review by O'Leary and Drabman (1971) in the *Psychological Bulletin*. Behavior consequences that have been tested include teacher attention (praise and blame) and tokens or points that could be exchanged for candy, toys, privileges, free-time activities, etc. Behavior contracting has also been attempted, with the child actively participating in deciding what behaviors will achieve what consequences.

We present two categories of papers—those aimed primarily at obtaining control of disruptive and non-study behavior and those aimed at programming the child's learning experiences to make his work more effective. It seems natural that when control procedures have achieved a classroom environment more favorable for learning, specific contingencies in the student's interaction with his materials should be investigated. The paper by Lovitt and Esveldt shows an ingenious method for increasing study rate by making payoff magnitude dependent on the quantity of work done. One must be thankful that most students are not yet unionized.

The papers by Birnbrauer, Wolf, Kidder, and Tague and by Wolf, Giles, and Hall combine reinforcement with scheduling of academic materials in small, graded units suitable for frequent monitoring and individualized instruction. The comparative effects of scheduling procedures or of the use of "interesting" teaching materials has not been assessed in any of these studies. These questions are of great interest.

Thomas, Becker, and Armstrong show how well-behaved school children can be made disruptive by dedicated mismanagement of social contingencies. Such studies are rare. Behavior modification procedures are far more frequently designed to *reduce* the incidence of undesirable behavior; they seldom include conditions to *increase* it. Of course, in one sense, any reversal design shows how undesirable behavior can be increased. For example, removal of a token system in the classroom will typically cause misbehavior to rise.

It may seem odd to imagine the normal classroom as an environment fostering pathological behavior. Walker and Buckley present an example of the reality of this incongruity. They established a very high rate of attending behavior in a special school setting through the use of a point system. Attentive behavior fell quickly when the point system was withdrawn. The authors did not attempt to produce good attending behavior under these conditions, however. Instead, they presented a graduated procedure for increasing the time during which attending behavior persisted—from 20 seconds to 10 minutes. The demand on the child in this latter condition was very high—10 minutes in which no nonattending behavior was observed. Then the child was returned to the classroom, his usual school environment; yet performance continued high, at about 90 percent. This is quite an achievement for a "behaviorally disordered" child. However, it may be noted that reliability was not measured during this latter phase of the study, and one may suspect that some relaxation of the requirement for attending may have occurred when the teacher kept the score.

The studies published so far show a rare unanimity in demonstrating measurable control over the target behaviors. The overall effectiveness of contingency management techniques in the schools seems not to be in doubt. Of course there can be no guarantee that a given program will be successful. To emphasize this point we present the article by Kuypers, Becker, and O'Leary, who give several suggestions about procedural matters that are very important to attend to.

Criticism has frequently been directed at the procedures used in behavior modification research in schools on the grounds of their feasibility or desirability in practical settings. The use of tangible reinforcers and even that of social attention as a consequence for "good" study behavior have been criticized. These objections are made on various grounds—that these procedures constitute bribes; that they involve treating the child as an object; that they assault his freedom; that the child will learn he need not study unless rewarded; that the development of the child's joy in learning will be disrupted; that the child should work to please adults and teachers rather than for extrinsic rewards, and that creativity will be stifled are some of them.

Some of these arguments are on moral grounds, and some involve assertions that seem conceivable subjects for empirical study. But there is a romantic tinge to much of this criticism, which appears to regard adult direction and control of children's behavior as objectionable or to prefer that these controls be exercised imperceptively or indirectly.

We prefer to let the data tell us what results we can expect from using behavior modification procedures in the schools. Such research has been used to find solutions for many of the practical problems set for it; and these solutions promise important practical changes in the way we run our schools. The broader social effects of these changes should begin to show themselves soon, now that many schools have begun to use behavior modification methods in their instruction. To this date the results seem socially valuable and progressive. It may be assumed that researchers will be alert to any undesirable effects that may be revealed.

REFERENCE

O'LEARY, K. D. & DRABMAN, R. Token reinforcement programs in the classroom: A review. *Psychological Bulletin*, 1971, 75, 379-98.

TOM C. LOVITT
KAREN A. ESVELDT
University of Washington

The relative effects
on math performance
of single- versus
multiple-ratio schedules:
A case study

This series of four experiments sought to assess the comparative effects of multiple- versus single-ratio schedules on a pupil's responding to mathematics materials. Experiment I, which alternated between single- and multiple-ratio contingencies, revealed that during the latter phase the subject responded at a higher rate. Similar findings were revealed by Exp. II. The third experiment, which manipulated frequency of reinforcement rather than multiple ratios, revealed that the alteration had a minimal effect on the subject's response rate. A final experiment, conducted to assess further the effects of multiple ratios, provided data similar to those of Exp. I and II.

In several recently reported studies, experimental analysis procedures were applied to classroom situations in an attempt to discover the effects of certain variables on different behaviors. They have: (a) described a behavior directly; (b) measured the occurrence of this behavior for an extended period of time; and (c) systematically manipulated a variable in order to analyze its effect.

Reprinted from *Journal of Applied Behavior Analysis*, 1970, 3, 261–70, with permission of the publisher and the authors. Copyright 1968 by the Society for the Experimental Analysis of Behavior, Inc.

The majority of these experimental analyses emanating from classrooms have been concerned with managerial behaviors such as inappropriate talking, disruptive, and out-of-seat behavior (Becker, Madsen, Arnold, and Thomas, 1967; Thomas, Neilson, Kuypers, and Becker 1968). Other reports have described the manipulation of a variable when an academic behavior was the dependent variable (Lovitt and Curtiss, 1969). These studies are representative of current field investigations in that, generally, there is more concern given to the identification of the affecting variables than of the effects of the variables when they are intermittently scheduled.

Studies of contingencies or schedules of reinforcement involving children have been rare. Staats (1965), however, investigated the reading responses of children under several reinforcement schedules and reported that, generally, higher response rates were produced under intermittent schedules. He added that: "Even the child under the variable-ratio and variable-interval schedule responded at a greater rate than the continuously reinforced children . . . (Staats, 1965, p. 45)."

Staats' evidence would tend to corroborate the remarks of Morse (1966), who stated that contingencies of reinforcement are as influential in generating and maintaining behavorial patterns as the reinforcers themselves. Morse also noted that "powerful control of behavior by discriminative stimuli and by reinforcers such as food and water actually develops because they are favorably scheduled events (Morse, 1966, p. 59)."

The present study, which was composed of a series of experiments, was prompted by a boy who responded academically at a very low rate. A previous attempt to accelerate the subject's response rate involved the manipulation of reinforcers by changing the consequences of his academic behavior from contingent time with games and crafts to social time with an adult male. This manipulation did not seem to affect significantly the dependent variable, academic rate.

The study sought to analyze the effects of contingencies of reinforcement on academic performance. To be precise, the purpose of this investigation was to compare performance rate when one reinforcement contingency was scheduled and when several reinforcement schedules were simultaneously available.

The dependent variables were correct and error performance rates on mathematics problems. The consequences or reinforcers for all studies were the same—points that were redeemable for minutes of free time. The independent variable was schedules of reinforcement.

During certain phases of these experiments, only one ratio was available—so many points contingent on correct math responses. In other phases, several ratios or contingency bands were available. During these latter phases, the subject was paid off from one or another ratio, contingent on his rate of responding. If his responses fell below a certain rate he received nothing. However, responses within a higher rate range were reinforced. Moreover, if he responded at a rate within the next higher band, he was paid off at a still higher rate. As the subject's response rate accelerated from one contingency range to the next, he was paid off with increasingly richer ratios.

EXPERIMENT I

Method

The subject was a 12-yr-old boy enrolled in a class for children with behavioral disorders at the Experimental Education Unit of the University of Washington. The material used was the subject's regular mathematics material *Sets and Numbers* (Suppes and Suppes, 1968).

During the 15-day baseline phase, data were obtained 1 hr daily on the subject's rate of responding to the math material. At this time the subject was on a 20:1 reinforcement schedule—1 min of free time in the "high-interest" room (Haring and Lovitt, 1967) contingent on 20 correct mathematics responses.

During the second phase (33 trials), four reinforcement bands were arranged. These new specifications were derived on the basis of the subject's performance during the first (20:1) phase. In order to receive any payoff during Phase 2 (multiple-ratio condition), the subject had to respond beyond his Phase 1 correct rate median of about one per minute.

Response rates higher than one per minute were reinforced at adjusted ratio schedules. The four ratio bands were:

(1) No points if fewer than 60 responses were emitted.
(2) Three points for 60 to 89 responses.
(3) Nine points for 90 to 119 responses.
(4) Fifteen points for more than 120 responses.

The sixtieth, ninetieth, and one-hundred-twentieth responses were marked on the subject's math sheet. These marks served as indicators to the subject only when all of his responses were correct. For example, if the subject passed the sixtieth problem, yet had answered four problems incorrectly, his point accumulation would be derived only from the 56 correct responses.

The ratio of points to responses was "richer" from one ratio band to the next. Within these bands, however, the ratio of reinforcement actually became leaner as the subject approached the next band. For example, as the subject passed into the second band, his 60 responses earned him three points, or a ratio of 20:1. Within the same band, his 89 responses still earned him three points, but now the ratio was 30:1.

The ratio conditions, either single or multiple, were explained to the subject each day. Table 1 describes the four ratio bands in terms of response requirements, rate equivalent, points earned, and the response-per-point or ratio equivalent that were in effect during the multiple-ratio phase.

TABLE 1   Multiple rate contingencies, Experiment I

Responses	Rate/minute	Points earned	Ratio equivalent
0-60	<1	0	0
60-89	1-1.48	3	20:1-30:1
90-119	1.5-1.98	9	10:1-13:1
120-240*	2-4.00**	15	8:1-16:1

*Subject's highest number of correct responses throughout Exp. I.

**Subject's highest rate throughout Exp. I.

In Phase 3, extending over seven trials, the initial contract was reinstated—1 point or 1 min per 20 correct mathematics responses. Throughout the experiment, the teacher calculated the subject's rate immediately after each session. Then, dependent on his rate of correct responses, he received a correspondent number of points that could be redeemed for minutes of free time.

Results

During the first phase, the subject's median response rate was 0.8 per min, in a range from 0.0 to 2.9. His median correct response rate during the multiple ratio stage was 1.7. His range of responding throughout this period was 3.8, extending from 0.2 to 4.0 responses per minute. A median response rate of 0.6 was calculated for the seven-day period when there was a return to initial, single-ratio conditions. The subject's range during this period was 1.3, extending from 0.2 to 1.5 problems per minute. Figure 1 presents the daily response rates throughout the experimental sessions.

Discussion

Although performance appeared to be sensitive to the experimental manipulation of the variable multiple ratios, two procedural matters could have spuriously influenced the findings. First, although the subject's overall

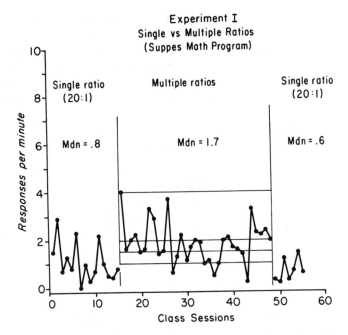

FIGURE 1   Correct mathematics response rate throughout Exp. I where the Suppes Math Program was used and where single and multiple ratios were manipulated. The horizontal lines through the multiple-ratio phase indicate the four contingency bands.

response rate increased when multiple ratio bands were in effect and decreased after the variable was removed, the median difference from condition to condition was not great and the subject's response rate during all experimental phases fluctuated widely. The experimenters believed that this variability in response was partly because the math problems were not always sequentially arranged according to difficulty. The subject worked straight through his Suppes text where the types of problems varied from page to page. For example, on one page, problems such as $63 \div 7 = \Box$ might appear, and on the next page narrative problems might appear. The subject's response rate was obviously affected by the type of problem.

Second, no error rate data were kept for this experiment. Since only correct rate of responding was recorded, it was impossible to determine whether the multiple ratios had any effect on the quality of the performance. Although the subject's correct rate was higher throughout the middle phase than in the first or last phases, the quality of responses (ratio of correct and error responses) was unknown. Because of these procedural concerns, the experimenters decided to conduct a second, more carefully controlled study.

EXPERIMENT II

Method

Since the major concern of this investigation was to assess the variable, multiple-ratio contingencies, and the subject's acquisition of mathematics responses was of secondary importance, the academic material was altered. Rather than require the subject to respond to mathematics material from the Suppes program, as in Exp. I, the subject was now given mathematics problems of the class $49 + 23 =$ _____, where the sum was $\leqq 198$. Mathematics problems of this class were already in the subject's repertoire (Easy Math Program). It was hypothesized that material that was not only within his capabilities, but comparable from problem to problem, would be more sensitive to the experimental variable. It was also decided that error rate, as well as correct rate data, should be gathered.

During Phases 1 and 2, the subject's response-per-point requirement was 20:1 (the same ratio that prevailed during Phases 1 and 3 of Exp. I). In Phases 2 and 4, multiple-ratio bands were imposed. As in Exp. I, the four ratio bands were calculated on the basis of the subject's median performance in the first phase of the experiment. Since the subject's median rate was about three responses per minute during the initial phase of Exp. II, his responses had to exceed that rate to receive points during the multiple-ratio phases. Response rates of fewer than three per minute were not reinforced but rates over three were reinforced with successively richer ratios. For the four ratio bands the following adjusted rate requirements were specified:

(1) No points for 0 to 44 responses.
(2) Three points for 45 to 59 responses.
(3) Six points for 60 to 74 responses.
(4) Fifteen points for more than 75 responses.

Table 2 presents information concerning the multiple ratios, responses required, rate equivalent, points earned, and ratio equivalent.

If the subject responded at a rate of three problems per minute, his payoff would be at a ratio of 15:1, decreasing to 20:1 as his response rate approached four correct problems per minute. Then, if his rate of responding reached four per minute, the ratio would be 10:1.

Each session in Exp. II lasted for 15 min, and, as in Exp. I, the single- and multiple-ratio conditions were explained daily to the subject. Throughout the multiple-ratio phases, the forty-fifth, sixtieth, and seventy-fifth mathematics problems were marked on the subject's worksheet.

TABLE 2   Multiple rate contingencies, Experiment II

Responses	Rate/minute	Points earned	Ratio equivalent
0-44	<3	0	0
45-59	3-3.93	3	15:1-20:1
60-74	4-4.93	6	10:1-13:1
75-126*	5-8.4**	15	5:1-8:1

Subject's highest number of correct responses throughout Exp. II.
**Subject's highest rate throughout Exp. II.*

Results

During the first phase, the subject's median rate of correct responses was 3.1, ranging from 2.0 to 4.5. A median rate of 5.35 correct responses per minute was obtained in the second phase, varying from 4.0 to 7.3 responses per minute. A median correct response rate of 3.9 was calculated for the third phase with responses ranging from 1.7 to 4.4. A median correct rate of 6.4 was obtained for the final multiple-ratio phase. The subject's response rate throughout this last phase varied from 5.5 to 8.4. The data from the four phases are presented in Fig. 2. The ranges of correct responses for the four experimental conditions were 2.5, 3.3, 2.7, and 2.9. This variability was virtually the same as that reported for Exp. I. The error-rate medians for the four phases were 0.2, 0.06, 0.1, and 0.15.

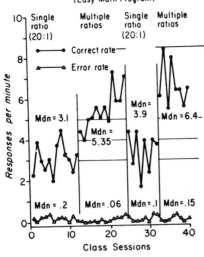

FIGURE 2 Correct and error mathematics response rates throughout Exp. II where Easy Math problems were used and where single and multiple ratios were manipulated.

Discussion

It appears that the multiple ratios of reinforcement served to increase the rate of correct responses. It is also evident that no corresponding rise in error rate occurred. In fact, error rate variance was slight throughout the experiment.

The mathematics items throughout the second experiment were more uniform than those in Exp. I. The altered response rate from condition to condition could therefore be attributed more to the manipulated variable than to an irregular curriculum.

Although the variable—multiple-reinforcement ratios—apparently was effective in altering the subject's rate of mathematics responding, the possibility existed that sheer frequency of reinforcement was at least partially responsible for the performance increase. Figure 3 shows that the subject received much more reinforcement in terms of amount of points during the multiple-ratio phases of Exp. II than during the single ratio phases of the study. In fact, when a comparison is made between the subject's response rate and the rate at which points were dispensed during the second experiment, the patterns were very similar; *i.e.*, when responses

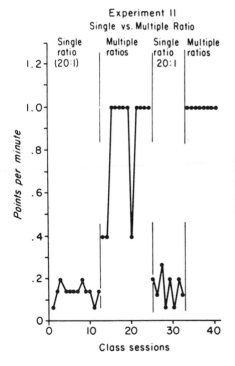

FIGURE 3   Rate of points received per minute by the subject during the four phases of Exp. II.

per minute were high, number of points received was also high (see Fig. 2 and 3).

To determine whether the multiple-ratio condition or frequency of reinforcement was the crucial variable in affecting response-rate differences, a third experiment was conducted in which frequency of reinforcement was the only variable manipulated.

EXPERIMENT III

Method

The first and third phases used the same base ratio as the first two experiments; for 20 correct responses the subject received 1 min of free time. A 5:1 ratio, the highest possible during previous multiple-ratio phases, was scheduled during the second phase of the study. The arithmetic materials were the same as those used in the second experiment (Easy Math Program).

Results

The results of Exp. III, illustrated in Fig. 4, reveal that frequency of reinforcement was apparently only a minimally affecting variable. His median correct rates were 5.65 during Phase 1, 5.9 during Phase 2, and 5.5 during Phase 3. The error-rate medians during the three phases were 0.06, 0.06, and 0.03. The subject's correct rate ranges were 3.2 (4.3 to 7.5), 2.7 (4.7 to 7.4), and 1.3 (5.2 to 6.5) during the first, second, and third phases respectively.

Discussion

As indicated by the data in Fig. 4, the subject's correct rate of responding was but slightly affected by the variable, frequency of reinforcement. Although "easy math problems" were used in both Exp. II and III and the 5:1 ratio was the richest ratio scheduled in both studies, the subject's performance in Exp. II was quite different from his effort in Exp. III. In Exp. II, his median correct rates were much higher in the manipulation phases (2 and 4) than during the control phases; this was not the case in Exp. III.

This difference in response rate between Exp. II and III could be attributed to the fact that during Exp. II, multiple-ratio bands were scheduled, whereas during Exp. III only one ratio was scheduled. It is also possible, however, that this performance difference was the result of

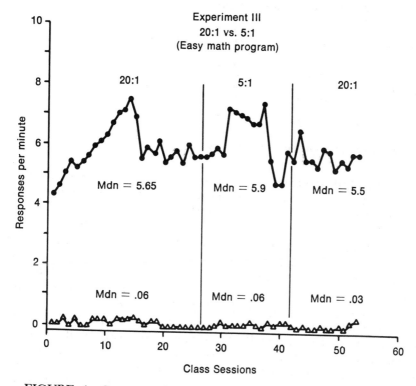

FIGURE 4 Correct and error mathematics response rates during Exp. III where frequency of reinforcement was manipulated.

"marking". During Exp. II, certain problems were marked, thus informing the subject that he had passed from one ratio band to another (if all his answers were correct). It is possible that marking served as a stimulus for accelerated performance. A further experiment was conducted to investigate this possibility.

EXPERIMENT IV

Method

The reason for conducting the fourth experiment was to determine whether marking certain problems to indicate multiple ratios was of itself accountable for the subject's rate increase.

During the multiple-ratio phases of Exp. II, the forty-fifth, sixtieth,

TABLE 3   Multiple rate contingencies, Experiment IV

Responses	Rate/minute	Points earned	Ratio equivalent
0-90	<6	0	0
90-99	6-6.6	6	15:1-16.5:1
100-119	6.7-7-9	8	12.5:1-14.9:1
120-144*	8-9.6**	12	10:1-12:1

*Subject's highest number of correct responses through-
out Exp. IV.
**Subject's highest rate throughout Exp. IV.

and seventy-fifth responses were marked on the subject's math sheets to indicate which schedule of reinforcement would prevail. These marks were included throughout all phases of Exp. IV.

The procedures were the same as those of Exp. II. Responses were reinforced on a 20:1 ratio during Phases 1 and 3, while multiple ratios were in effect in the second and fourth phases. The type of mathematics problems and the length of each experimental session were also the same as before: "easy" materials and 15-min sessions. The ratio conditions, either single or multiple, were explained daily to the subject.

The multiple ratios employed in Phases 2 and 4 were derived in the same way as in Exp. I and II. These rates were based on the subject's average response rate during the initial 20:1 phase, which during Exp. IV, was six responses per minute.[1] In a 15-min session the subject was expected to emit 90 responses (15×6). Therefore, the four differential rate ratios were:

(1) No points for 0 to 90 responses.
(2) Six points for 90 to 99 responses.
(3) Eight points for 100 to 119 responses.
(4) Twelve points for more than 120 responses.

Table 3 presents information concerning the multiple ratios.

Results

During the first phase (Fig. 5), the single-ratio phase, the subject's response rate ranged from 3.9 to 7.4; a median response rate of 6.1. Throughout the 15 sessions of Phase 2, his median rate of responding was 8.1, ranging from 7.5 to 9.6.

When conditions were reversed, the subject's response rate ranged

[1] In Exp. I, II, and IV the first ratio bands were similarly derived. The lowest rate of the first band was comparable to the subject's median rate in the first phase (single ratio) of the experiment. Subsequent ratio bands were rather arbitrarily established.

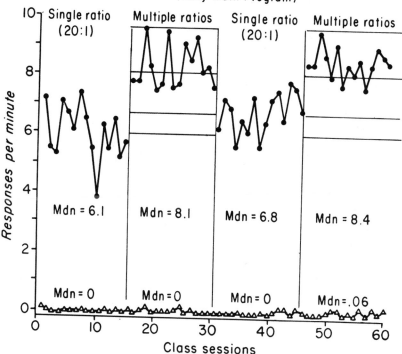

FIGURE 5 Correct and error mathematics response rates during Exp. IV where Easy Math problems were scheduled and where single and multiple ratios were manipulated.

from 5.5 to 7.8. His median rate throughout this phase was 6.8. The fourth phase of Exp. IV, the return to multiple-ratio bands, was characterized by a response range of 1.9 (from 7.6 to 9.5) and a median rate of responding of 8.4. The error-rate medians during the four phases of the study were 0.0, 0.0, 0.0, and 0.06.

Discussion

Apparently, the cue marks used in Exp. II did not influence response rate; for even though the forty-fifth, sixtieth, and seventy-fifth responses were marked throughout the single-ratio phases, his correct rates, during those phases, were lower than during the multiple-ratio conditions. Furthermore, the forty-fifth, sixtieth, and seventy-fifth responses were marked throughout the multiple-ratio phases, when in fact the ratio bands corresponded to the ninetieth, one-hundredth, and one-hundred-twentieth responses.[2] Yet the subject's correct response rate was higher during these phases than when a single ratio was scheduled. It would appear then, that the marks on the pupil's paper, whether they corresponded to ratio changes or not, were totally nonfunctional.

Less variation was observed between the correct-rate medians of Phases 1 and 2, and 3 and 4 of Exp. IV than between the same phases of Exp. II. The differences between the correct medians of adjacent phases in Exp. II were 2.2 and 2.5. The differences in Exp. IV were 2.0 and 1.6. These data could indicate that the subject was perhaps reaching a performance ceiling. As noted earlier, the same materials were used in both experiments. Therefore, the more familiar the subject became with the materials, rate differences between experimental conditions would become increasingly more difficult to obtain.

The subject's gradual increase in response rate may be noted throughout Exp. II, III, and IV by analyzing the data in the single or 20:1 ratio phases. The correct-rate medians during these phases throughout the three experiments were 3.1, 3.9, 5.65, 5.5, 6.1, and 6.8. This acceleration across experiments may also be pointed out by presenting the data from the multiple-ratio phases of Exp. II and IV. The correct-rate medians during multiple-ratio phases through the two experiments were 5.3, 6.4, 8.1, and 8.4.

GENERAL DISCUSSION

The independent variable throughout this study, multiple-ratio contingencies, was a series of ratio bands. This arrangement of ratios was similar to a series of DRH schedules, where successively more rapid response rates are reinforced by correspondingly richer payoffs. However, the similarity between the independent variable in this study and traditional efforts to reinforce high response rates differentially is appropriate for only the lowest portion of each reinforcement band. Since each contingency band represented a range of ratios, the higher the response rate within a band, the higher the reinforcement ratio. It can be argued that it would be most

---

[2] In Exp. I and II, the multiple ratios were derived from the subject's median response rate in the first, single-ratio phase. Since in Exp. IV marks were used in the first phase, before any knowledge of his performance, the same marks were used in the second phase. Therefore the marks in this experiment were not derived from the subject's median rate in the first phase and, correspondingly, did not describe the contingency bands that were in effect during multiple-ratio conditions.

economical, in terms of work expended for points received, for the subject to perform in the lower portion of each contingency band where the schedule is richer. In this series of experiments, the subject did not always behave in such a manner.

As may be noted in Phase 2 of Exp. I, of the 15 times the subject's rate was in the highest payoff band (over two responses per minute) his rates during 10 sessions were no higher than 2.5 responses per minute. It might be said, then, that in this experiment his behavior was very efficient. During Exp. II, Phase 2, the subject responded within 0.5 of the third payoff band twice and within 0.5 of the fourth band three times. Only once in Phase 4 was his response rate within 0.5 of the lower limit of any band. In Exp. IV, Phase 2, when the subject's rates fell within the third ratio band, they were invariably at the top of the band. When his rates fell in the highest band, he responded within 0.5 of the bottom of the band four of the eight times. During the final phase of the experiment the subject's rates, when in the highest payoff band, were within 0.5 of the lower limit six of the 12 times.

When the data from the first multiple-ratio phase of Exp. I, II, and IV were analyzed, it was noted that higher ratio bands generated more pronounced behavioral effects than lower bands. When the subject's responses were analyzed during the four bands of the multiple-ratio phases it was discovered that the subject was paid off more often from the highest rate band than from any of the others. During Phase 2 of Exp. I, the subject's response rate fell three times within the no-payoff band, seven times in the next higher, eight in the next highest, and 15 in the highest. During Phase 2 of Exp. II, his rates fell three times in the next-to-highest and nine times in the highest band, while never falling in the no-payoff or next higher ratio bands. In Exp. IV, Phase 2, the subject was also paid off from only the top two bands—seven times from the next-to-highest and eight from the highest.

Numerous academic, social, and economic situations come to mind that are based on the rather complicated ratios investigated in this report. Circumstances where several reinforcement ratios are available and where the subject must exert more and more effort as he approaches the next ratio are common.

In social organizations like scouting, where several steps or ranks are sequentially arranged, this type of ratio is in operation. When the rank of Life Scout is reached, the scout does not have to increase his behavioral repertoire to retain the rank. But later, as he attempts to pass the skills required of an Eagle, he must first master the easiest tests, then the more difficult. As he approaches the next level of reinforcement, his rate of behavior must increase, although while it is increasing he is still recognized as a Life Scout and is paid off from that level.

A schedule of this type is noted in certain businesses. Civil service employees are also assigned ratings and are paid accordingly. If they wish to advance from one level to the next, they must become more competent, pass tests, or in some way increase their rates of behavior. While these rates are in the process of increasing, however, they are paid off from the initial reinforcement level. Thus, until the next reinforcement band is reached, the civil servant must do more work or more complicated work for the same reinforcement. Only when he is promoted does his reinforcement match his work efforts. And then the process begins all over again.

Rarely in the "real" social and economic worlds are reinforcement levels or promotions linearly related to behavior (too often promotions have no relationship to behavior). These promotions usually occur when a person has greatly accelerated his performance. Once elevated, however, the person's behavioral rate generally stabilizes (post-reinforcement pause).

On the basis of this series of studies it appears that multiple-ratio conditions should be considered an effective variable when the objective is to accelerate academic response rate. Teachers should, however, exercise some caution in scheduling multiple contingencies, as in this study, to accelerate performance. Such contingencies, if associated with reading or arithmetic, when the acquisition of new information is of prime concern, could indeed accelerate responding. However, although the response rate increases, the quality of performance is not necessarily improved; for as correct rate increases, so might error rate. Teachers, therefore, when measuring academic performance, must monitor error rate as well as correct rate and should, in some instances, to influence high-quality performance, associate some contingency with errors.

This study, besides exploring a condition that could serve to accelerate academic performance, also demonstrates a technique for the investigation of other independent variables. Educators, particularly educational researchers, have at least two responsibilities; (a) to arrange circumstances so that pupils acquire new behaviors, and (b) to discover what effects various environmental variables have on behavior.

In setting up experiments, the researcher must consider his objective; is he concerned with the pupil's acquisition of behaviors, or with the discovery of environmental relationships? These objectives are not necessarily the same. If his concern is for the former, measures of the pupil's performance before, during, and after training should be taken to determine the effects of teaching. If the training was successful (the pupil's correct rate increased and error rate decreased), the pupil's behavior is probably irreversible; a reversal condition would therefore serve no purpose.

In such instances, where learning occurs and where an independent variable such as points or tokens is also being manipulated, and if the rate of the measured behavior is altered, the reason for those effects would not be known. If the performance improved, it could be the function of the acquisition of additional skills, the manipulated variable, or some interaction.

However, if the researcher's objective is to ascertain the effects of some environmental condition—arrange situations where the variable is alternately available—he should arrange the setting so that possible effects of that variable can be detected. One way of arranging such conditions was the tactic employed throughout most of the present study—the use of easy or known materials. When the math or reading materials scheduled for a pupil are within his repertory and if a wide rate range of response is possible, the effects of an environmental manipulation on response rate can be isolated from the effects of learning. Such experiments may initially appear as too expensive for the classroom teacher who must be concerned with assisting pupils to acquire dozens of skills. However, unless educational researchers, either in classrooms, laboratories, or clinics, begin to explore the circumstances that may affect learning, the practice of teaching will continue to be nonempirically based.

REFERENCES

BECKER, W. C., MADSEN, C. H., JR., ARNOLD, C. R., and THOMAS, D. R. The contingent use of teacher attention and praise in reducing classroom behavior problems. *Journal of Special Education*, 1967, 1, 287–307.

HARING, N. G. and LOVITT, T. C. Operant methodology and educational technology in special education. In N. G. Haring and R. L. Schiefelbusch (Eds.), *Methods in Special Education*. New York: McGraw-Hill, 1967. Pp. 12–48.

LOVITT, T. C. and CURTISS, KAREN A. Effects of manipulating an antecedent event on mathematics response rate. *Journal of Applied Behavior Analysis*, 1969, 1, 329–333.

MORSE, W. H. Intermittent reinforcement. In W. K. Honig (Ed.), *Operant behavior: areas of research and application*. New York: Appleton-Century-Crofts, 1966. Pp. 52–108.

SUPPES, P. and SUPPES, J. *Sets and numbers*. New York: Singer/Random House, 1968.

STAATS, A. W. A case in and a strategy for the extension of learning principles to problems of human behavior. In L. Krasner and L. D. Ullmann (Eds.), *Research in behavioral modification*. New York: Holt, Rinehart & Winston, 1965. Pp. 27–55.

THOMAS, D. R., NIELSEN, L. J., KUYPERS, D. S., and BECKER, W. C. Social reinforcement and remedial instruction in the elimination of a classroom behavior problem. *Journal of Special Education*, 1968, 2, 291–306.

J. S. BIRNBRAUER
M. M. WOLF
University of Washington

J. D. KIDDER
CECILIA E. TAGUE
Rainier School

Classroom behavior

of retarded pupils

with token reinforcement[1,2]

It was the practice in an experimental programmed instruction classroom to reinforce correct responses with knowledge of results, verbal approval, and tokens. The tokens, check marks, were exchanged at the end of each class for an item from an array of edibles, inexpensive toys, and school supplies. To determine if the token reinforcement was essential to the relatively high levels of accuracy and rates of studying maintained by the retarded pupils, tokens were not dispensed for a period of at least 21 days and were then reinstated. Daily records of items completed, percentage of errors, and disruptive behavior were kept. During the no-token period three general patterns of results were obtained: (1) Five of the 15 pupils showed no measurable change in performance. (2)

Reprinted from *Journal of Experimental Child Psychology*, 1965, 2, 219–35, with permission of the publisher and the authors.

———
1 Paper read by the senior author at the American Psychological Association Convention, Los Angeles, September, 1964. This research is part of a project sponsored by Rainier School (C. H. Martin, Superintendent), the White River School District (Paul Webb, Superintendent) located at Buckley, Washington, and the University of Washington. It was supported in part by NIMH project grant MH-01366 and research grant MH-2232.
2 We are indebted to Mrs. Eileen Argo and to Miss Josephine Grab for their services as assistant teachers, to Mr. John Nonnenmacher for collating the data, and to Dr. S. W. Bijou for his support and advice.

*Six pupils increased either markedly in over-all percentage of errors or suffi-
ciently to reduce progress in the programs.* (3) *Four pupils showed an increase
in percentage of errors, a decline (or considerable variability) in amount of
studying, and an increase in disruptive behavior. Baseline performance was recovered in these 10 pupils when token reinforcement was reinstated.*

Recommendations for maintaining the motivation of pupils to study
usually are limited to (1) preparing materials which are intrinsically reinforcing, i.e., are "interesting," "meaningful," and so on (e.g., Kirk and
Johnson, 1951, pp. 270–271); (2) using materials and procedures which
combine interest value and high probabilities of success, e.g., Montessori
methods (Standing, 1962), Moore's "Responsive Environments" (Pines,
1963), and programmed instruction (Porter, 1957; Skinner, 1958); and (3)
presenting social and/or symbolic reinforcers, e.g., teacher approval, grades,
and stars. Although these methods may provide adequate incentives for
many pupils, they probably do not for many others (Brackbill and Jack,
1958), for example, retarded readers (Walters and Kosowski, 1963),
school drop-outs, and so-called chronic behavior problems. They did not
appear adequate for the retarded pupils attending an experimental programmed instruction classroom (Birnbrauer, Bijou, Wolf, and Kidder,
1965). Had the pupils not been retarded, the poor classroom behavior and
academic progress would have been attributed to the teachers, their methods, and/or low motivation.

In the experiment described here, it was assumed that the last of these
was the case, and a token reinforcement system was introduced. Token
reinforcers are tangible objects or symbols which in and of themselves
probably have little or no reinforcing power. However, they may be exchanged for a variety of other objects which are reinforcing. Therefore,
they should become generalized reinforcers (Skinner, 1953). The tokens in
the present study were check marks which the teachers inserted in book-
lets that the pupils carried. When a pupil accumulated enough check
marks in his booklet, he exchanged them for candy, a small toy, or other
item of his choice immediately after he finished his work for the day. Thus,
all of the pupils were reinforced in the same way during class and yet individual preferences were considered by maintaining a variety of items for
exchange. The effectiveness of token systems has been demonstrated in
laboratory studies by Staats, Staats, Schutz, and Wolf (1962) and by Heid
(1964), and their practical advantages and other features have been discussed by Birnbrauer and Lawler (1964) and by Staats, Minke, Finley,
Wolf, and Brooks (1964).

The purpose of this study was to determine the effects of discontinuing the token system for a relatively long period and subsequently reinstat-

ing it. Throughout the study, the teachers gave approval for appropriate behavior in the manners that were natural to them; they could remove a pupil from class for disruptive behavior; the pupils studied a variety of subjects in each session; and there were opportunities for peer interaction. These conditions made the experimental setting more like ordinary classrooms than laboratories for studies of reinforcement.

METHOD

Subjects

All of the 17 pupils enrolled in the Rainier School Programmed Learning Classroom took part in this study. Fourteen were residents (two were diagnosed as mongoloid; three, familial; and nine, brain-damaged) and three commuted (no clinical diagnoses available). They were all mildly or moderately retarded and were selected for this class because they performed at the first-grade level or below in academic achievement in spite of up to 5 years of previous education at Rainier School.

The characteristics of the pupils were: CA, 8 to 14 years; Peabody Picture Vocabulary Test Mental Age, 4–2 to 8–11; IQ, 50 to 72; California or Metropolitan Achievement Test Grade Equivalents, no score to 1.6 in reading and no score to 1.8 in arithmetic. Nine pupils were first enrolled in this class in September of the year in which this study was conducted; eight had been enrolled during the preceding academic year. Four of the second-year pupils and all of the first-year pupils attended in the morning; the other four second-year pupils attended in the afternoon.

Experimental Design

The study, a within-S design, consisted of three conditions: baseline (B), experimental (NT), and return to baseline (B2), in that order. Since a token reinforcement system had been used during the preceding academic year with eight of the Ss, the baseline conditions (B and B2) included dispensing of tokens; the experimental condition (NT) did not. During B and B2, the following conditions were in effect: (1) Social approval and tokens followed cooperative behavior and correct responses to the instructional materials. (2) Social extinction—i.e., no teacher response—followed incorrect responses and inappropriate, but not disruptive, behavior. (3) A brief time-out period (removal from the classroom) followed disruptive behavior or refusal to comply with instructions. Although no tokens were dispensed during NT, the teachers continued to deliver approval and to administer the time-out procedure in the same fashion as in B and B2.

NT lasted 21 days for the 13 pupils who attended class in the morning and 35 days for the afternoon group of four. (Originally, the study was to be conducted with just the afternoon class to minimize the effects of the study upon other aspects of the research project.) Reinstatement took place on the same day, seven days after the Christmas vacation, for all pupils.

Although we use the expression "days," each pupil attended this class for one to two hours per day. The data include percentage of errors (accuracy), number of items completed on the academic programs (productivity), and the amount of time spent in time-out (index of disruptive behavior).

Classroom Description and General Procedures

Each pupil attended the experimental classroom for one to two hours according to a schedule which ensured that no more than six pupils were present at a time. There was no group instruction or classes as such. Instead, each pupil was given assignments in such areas as sight vocabulary, phonics, reading comprehension, cursive writing, addition, and time-telling. (Most pupils attended other classes in arts and crafts, music, and physical education. This study pertains to their performance in the programmed learning class, the only class in which token reinforcers were dispensed and data collected.) He completed his assignments independently of the activities of the other pupils, either in the classroom proper or in one of the three individual study rooms located at one end of the room.

All of the material was prepared by the staff and was constantly being evaluated and revised as necessary. The pupils' assignments were planned every day on the basis of the previous performance of each individual, with changes being made when the error rate exceeded about 10%. In some programs the pupil was required to repeat sets when this occurred; in others, a simpler form of the program was presented, or the program was dropped temporarily until the difficulty could be found and corrected. In all cases, the teachers attempted to increase the amount of work accomplished per day.

Immediate knowledge of results was built into most programs; in others, it was delayed until the assignment was completed. Assignments required from 5 to 45 minutes. Social reinforcement and token reinforcement (during B and B2 only) were dispensed in either of two ways: (1) When a child studied independently, he indicated that he was finished by raising his hand, and the appropriate reinforcers were given as the teacher scored the work with the pupil. (2) When the program required a teacher's being present—e.g., in sight vocabulary, at the beginning of all programs, and where the type of response or other aspect of a program was changed—a token reinforcer and a social reinforcer were dispensed as each item was completed *correctly*. In September, the second procedure was followed most often; the proportion of independent studying time was increased on an individual basis.

The teachers were one male certified teacher and three female assistants. One assistant had a B.A. in Psychology and had worked in this classroom during the previous year; the other two were recent high school graduates who were trained in the performance of classroom duties by the teacher and the experienced assistant. The teachers applied the contingencies quite skillfully and probably as nearly alike as four humans could. Ordinarily, all four teachers were in the classroom. When they were not working with pupils, they performed such duties as recording data and preparing instructional materials. Children were not assigned to a teacher; whoever was free at the moment scored the completed work and gave the next assignment.

Token Reinforcement Procedures

Each pupil had a folder containing three sheets of paper each divided into squares, his "mark book." The token value of the pages varied according to the number of squares on them, and each folder had a combination of pages, e.g., two 2¢ pages and one 5¢ page. (Three pages of different values were filled concurrently so that the pupil always had partial scores or credit toward a tangible reinforcer.) When the pupil completed his work for the day, completely filled pages were usually exchanged for items from the assortment of back-up reinforcers, which included a variety of edibles, bubble gum, balloons, "caps," stationery and pencils, and trinkets. A few of the pupils saved the value of the pages either toward a more expensive object, which was purchased specifically for them, or toward a trip to town to spend the money. The pupils earned about 2¢ a day in token value. In actual value, they earned about $7 each during the academic year.

The teachers gave a check mark for every correct response to an item, a bonus of 10 marks if an assignment was error-free, and a few marks for being especially cooperative or doing something extra. Marks were made unsystematically on the three pages. Simultaneously, the teachers made such verbal comments as "good," "right," "you did that well." These comments were continued but no tokens or other tangible reinforcers were given in NT.

No attempt was made to formally explain this system to the pupils. Primarily, actual contact with the system was relied upon; and the teachers, especially at the beginning, made a point of saying such things as "Good, you get a mark for that," "Your 2¢ page is almost full," or "You've completed your 5¢ page today—good for you." Also, the number of squares was manipulated to ensure contact even though a pupil might have relatively low productivity. There is no evidence that pupils were aware of this. In about two weeks, it appeared that obtaining marks and particularly completing a page were reinforcing to them.

Time-out Procedures

Talking out of turn, responding incorrectly, cursing, and similar offenses usually were ignored by the teachers. However, if a pupil's offensive behavior was disruptive, he was told to stop and return to work or go "to the hall." If the warning did not result in prompt compliance, the teacher carried out the threat. The pupil was sent to the time-out area, a bare 8 × 22-foot room in the hallway, for 10 minutes, at which time, provided he had been quiet for the preceding 30 seconds, he was given permission to resume his studies. If he did not enter the classroom within 2 minutes, the door was closed for an additional 10 minutes. This practice was also in effect during NT. Examples of behavior that resulted in the application of time-out were refusal to undertake or complete an assignment, talking to or "roughhousing" with another pupil, temper tantrums, and throwing or destroying objects.

(The term "time-out" is an abbreviation of "time-out from positive reinforcement" [Ferster and Appel, 1961]. We prefer the term because it emphasizes that our rationale for using the procedure was to ensure that disruptive behavior was *not* reinforced by peers and/or inadvertently by the teachers.)

Change from Tokens to No-Tokens (B to NT)

On the first day of NT, a teacher made the following announcement: "I wanted you in here all at one time to tell you something. There will be no more marks given. We want you to continue your good work just as you have been doing but you will not get marks." The mark folders and exchange trays had been removed previously. In response to questions the teachers merely replied that "the rules had been changed." (To our own surprise, there was little immediate reaction to this announcement though the mood of the class that day might be described as unenthusiastic. One pupil said that it was not fair and that he would not work any more, but completed his assignments anyway. Others asked teachers later why marks were not being given, but the reply, "the rules have been changed," ended the enquiry. It was as if the announcement had not been comprehended until after the pupils had experienced not receiving marks. The lack of reaction may be attributable in part to the fact that most of these children were institutionalized and in part to the teachers' long-established tendency not to reply to complaints or non-study-oriented conversation.)

On the first day of B2, the mark folders were placed in the previously familiar location. No announcement was made.

Data

The teachers maintained a daily record sheet for each pupil. This showed the assignments that the pupil was to have and contained space for recording the time that the pupil entered class, when he left, the beginning and ending of time-out periods and of each assignment, the total number of items completed, and number of errors made per assignment. Since the time data, except for time-out periods, were only good approximations of how each pupil spent his time in class, we shall present just the items completed, percentage of errors, and the duration of time-out periods.

An item was defined as any question or task culminating in a response that was scored objectively either "correct" or "incorrect." This criterion was met by all of the assigned studies except the cursive-writing exercises. Examples of items were: a sentence and a fill-in question about it; a multiple-choice discrimination problem; $2 + 2 =$; a picture and a set of possible matching words; and the printed direction, "Put 2 spoons in box 4," and an array of objects and numbered boxes. Over the course of this study, items increased in difficulty and tended to become longer. Thus, 100 items in January should have required substantially more and different work than 100 items in September.

Obviously, whether or not a procedure or incentive is "adequate" depends upon one's criteria. In general, we regarded 10% errors as the maximum acceptable level of performance. Although arbitrary and perhaps higher than most teachers require, 10% errors was nevertheless the level that resulted in our revising a program or classroom procedure. To take a specific example, if S exceeded 9% errors on a set in the Sight Vocabulary Program (SVP), he was required to repeat that set. If several Ss "failed" the same set, it was revised. So that the implications of the percentage-of-errors data in this class may be better understood, we shall report the ratio of the number of times SVP sets were "passed" (errors were less than 10%) to the number of times sight vocabulary was included in the pupil's daily assignments. This will be referred to as the "SVP ratio."

RESULTS AND DISCUSSION

Although each pupil reacted to the removal and reinstatement of token reinforcement in a somewhat idiosyncratic way, three general patterns were obtained. (1) Five Ss showed, for all practical purposes, no adverse effects of NT. (2) Six Ss increased in percentage of errors in NT, but continued to cooperate and to complete the same or a greater number of items. (3) Four Ss increased in percentage of errors, accomplished less work, and became serious disciplinary problems during NT.[3] After tokens were reinstated, most of the Ss completed progressively more work and stabilized at levels of percentage of errors that were lower than at any previous time.

The four Ss described under (3) were those who attended class together in the afternoon and had been subjected to 35 days of NT. There were no discernible relationships between CA, IQ, or the type or amount of material being studied and the results obtained.

Figures 1, 2, 4, 5, and 6 show all of the applicable data for selected Ss. The total items completed (productivity), percentage of errors (accuracy), and time-out were compiled for each three-day period S attended class. The SVP ratios cover the experimental period in which shown. If the number of NT days was not divisible by three, the first NT point was obtained by counting backward from the end of NT and prorating the remainder. The B and B2 data were obtained by counting backward from the last day of B and forward from the first day of B2. Thirty days of B2 are shown. The B data includes all of the regular classes after an evaluation that required most of September but varied among individuals. Otherwise, the variability in amount of data resulted from the fact that this study was conducted in a classroom. Pupils were absent and classes were shortened so that the pupils might attend special events. We also excluded a day if the records contained incomplete entries, or if a program ordinarily given was pre-empted by a test or other special activity, e.g., writing a letter. No more than five days were excluded for any pupil for these reasons.

The analysis performed was a visual comparison between each S's performance in NT and that during B and B2. It was concluded that removing token reinforcement had an effect only when there was a change of some duration in either the percentage of errors or the time-out data that would not have been predicted from the B data, *and* when at least the level of performance obtained in B was recovered in B2. The productivity data are shown primarily to indicate that changes in percentage of errors were not due to increases in amount of work. Because of our definition of an item, there was considerable variation in productivity. For example, the sharp declines at A in Fig. 1 do not indicate that S1 was working less diligently, but merely that a program containing fewer but more time-consuming items was presented more frequently. In other words, S1 completed all

---

[3] The data of two Ss were discarded. One was ill during most of the NT period; the other received a change in assignments coincident with the beginning of NT that could not be eliminated as a factor in accounting for the observed changes.

of the work that was assigned on those days. On the other hand, the declines in productivity during NT in Figs. 5 and 6 do mean that the Ss were not completing the work that was expected.

The data of Ss which clearly showed that there was or was not an effect are presented in Fig. 1, S1; Fig. 2; Fig. 4, S3; Fig. 5, S6; and Figure 6. Those that were difficult to classify or open to alternative interpretations are presented in Fig. 1, S2; Fig. 4, S4; Fig. 5, S7.

Figure 1 shows two of the five Ss whose performance appeared to be independent of token reinforcement. Subject 1, the more typical S of this subgroup, steadily increased in amount of studying from the middle of B through NT to the end of B2. He only once made more than 9% errors on SVP and maintained a satisfactorily low level of percentage of errors. Whether the slight rise in errors at the end of NT would have persisted with a longer NT period is, of course, not known. Note that the low point in productivity in B was preceded by a high percentage of errors. This reflects the teachers' efforts to adjust the assignments according to the pupil's performance.

Subject 2 differs from S1 in that she performed more poorly until

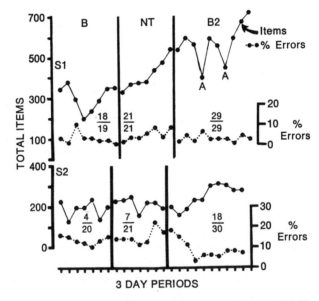

FIGURE 1 Total items completed (left ordinate, solid line) and percentage of errors records (right ordinate, dotted line) of S1 and S2, who exemplify Ss not affected by NT. The ratios are the number of times SVP errors were less than 10% over the number of presentations of SVP in each period. Subject 2's short B period was due to an extended illness in September and October.

about 12 days after the tokens were reinstated. Then, her percentage of errors stabilized at an acceptable level although the amount of work was increased. It is tempting to attribute this improvement to the reinstatement of tokens, but in the absence of an increase in percentage of errors in NT, the data are equivocal.

Subject 1 was 14-years-old, diagnosed as brain-damaged, and one of the second-year pupils. The results were consistent with our impression that S1 was quite sensitive to being correct and receiving approval. Subject 2, a first-year student, was an 11-year-old mongoloid who, in addition to SVP, was receiving primarily pre-reading and pre-arithmetic instruction.

Figures 2 and 4 contain three examples of decreased accuracy during NT, but show no effect upon productivity or degree of cooperation. None of the six Ss represented required the use of the time-out procedure. The NT percentage-of-error levels were from 2 to 6 times higher than those in B and B2.

Subject 5 (Fig. 2) performed satisfactorily in B until he was subjected to a special no-token period (labeled SNT) during which he received tokens for all correct responses except while studying Sight Vocabulary. His percentage of errors immediately doubled and remained at the higher level through a six-day resumption of B and through NT. In B2, S5 attained a remarkably low and stable error rate. Note the attempts by the teachers to increase the amount of work at the beginning of SNT. They were deterred by the higher error rate.

While the percentage of errors shown in Fig. 2 during SNT and NT bordered upon our acceptable 10% level, the higher level of errors had considerable effect upon progress in SVP, as can be seen in Fig. 3. When reinforced with tokens, S5 routinely made fewer than 10% errors on SVP sets. When no tokens were dispensed, he "failed" over 50% of the time.

Three other Ss showed changes in percentage of errors during NT of the order exhibited by S5. This subgroup may be thought of as borderline

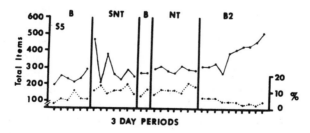

FIGURE 2 Records of S5 prepared as Fig. 1. S5 exemplifies Ss whose percentage of errors increased in NT to the borderline satisfactory level. SNT denotes token reinforcement for all work except SVP.

students. With token reinforcement they maintained at least passing records; without it, they did not.

Subject 3 and S4 (Figure 4) yielded somewhat unique patterns. The accuracy record of each is distinctly worse during NT. There is virtually no overlap between error scores in B (B2) and NT. However, the inverted U-shape of S4's NT data and the fact that much of the change occurred immediately suggest that S4 was affected most by the change in routine *per se* and not necessarily by the absence of token reinforcement. The possibility cannot be ruled out that baseline performance would have been regained without reinstating token reinforcement. Subject 3's data do not suffer from this ambiguity.

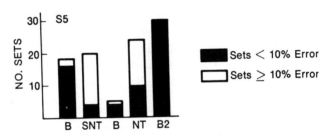

FIGURE 3 A graphic representation of S5's SVP ratios for the experimental periods in Fig. 2. No token reinforcement was delivered for studying SVP in SNT and NT.

Subject 3 was 9-years-old and had the lowest IQ of the pupils, 50. Subject 4 was 10-years-old and had the highest IQ, 72. Subject 5 was 12-years-old and had an IQ of 60. All were diagnosed as brain-damaged.

Figures 5 and 6 show the performance of the four second-year pupils in the afternoon class. They were 10 to 12-years old; three were brain-damaged, and the other was a nonresident who probably would be diagnosed as familial. This group had 35 days of NT. Time-out is plotted for each.

Subject 6, the nonresident, was one of the most capable pupils. This is reflected in (1) his stable 5% error rate except toward the end of NT, (2) his progress in SVP, and (3) the large number of items completed in B2. However, he occasionally required the use of the time-out procedure. During NT, he more often refused to cooperate, interacted with other pupils, particularly S7, and verbally abused the teachers. Consequently, he spent progressively more time in the time-out room and his productivity declined. During the last *three* days in NT, he completed six items, four incorrectly, yielding the terminal 66% error rate. As soon as tokens were

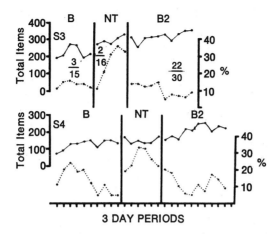

FIGURE 4 Records of *S*s whose percentage of errors increased markedly in NT. Subject 3's NT period is short because of periodic absences. Subject 4 was not studying SVP.

reinstated, his former error rate was recovered and productivity increased. Time-out declined slowly to its former level.

Subject 7's data are presented because of their probable importance to the changes which occurred in S6 during NT. Token reinforcement evidently exerted little control over S7's behavior. The amount of studying was not increased during the year, and time-out was required even beyond the data shown in Fig. 5. About 15 days after tokens were reinstated, S7 went through a period of refusing to attend class, although once he was brought to class his accuracy level was exemplary.

Without token reinforcement, his behavior became worse in all respects. He competed overtly with S6 to be removed from class and engaged in such behavior as hitting, chasing, and shouting at the other boys. Most often, S6 replied. That the disruptive interaction occurred mostly in NT suggests that token reinforcement provided a means whereby the teachers could effectively combat peer reinforcement. Subject 7's relatively good behavior when tokens were being given may *not* have been due to his being reinforced with tokens. Rather, the tokens were sufficiently strong to eliminate peer reinforcement of S7's disruptive behavior. In fact, it was not uncommon for a pupil to tell another in effect to "Leave me alone—I've got work to do." In other words, although the token reinforcement system did not yield the degree of control over S7 that was expected, it did minimize the effects that his behavior had upon other pupils.

Subjects 8 and 9 (Fig. 6) share several common features. Each maintained satisfactory *over-all* accuracy levels in B and B2, often failed SVP

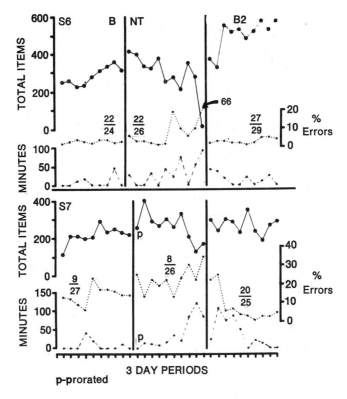

FIGURE 5   Total items completed (left ordinate, solid line), percentage of errors (right ordinate, dotted line) and time-out (left ordinate, dashed line) records of Ss 6 and 7. The final NT percentage of error level of S6 was 66%.

sets, were cooperative during B, and performed erratically in NT. Subject 8's unpredictability is most evident in his NT time-out record, which varies cyclically from no time in three days to as much time as S6 and S7 spent. Subject 9 varied considerably in accuracy. Subject 8's offenses most often took the form of adamant refusals to study, with unquotable verbal behavior. (During NT, the assistant teacher was reminded that S8's behavior for an entire year in a former class had been this way—"he was either an angel or a hellion. You'd never know from one day to another what to expect of him.") Clearly, Ss 8 and 9 were better students with token reinforcement than with only social and intrinsic reinforcement.

These data do not convey the entire picture of the conditions in the afternoon class during NT. The number of warnings increased; these usually sufficed for S9. Often, the time-out room was occupied when it was needed for another pupil, and placing more than one pupil in the

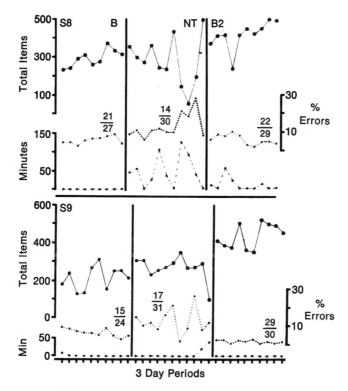

FIGURE 6   Records of Ss 8 and 9 prepared as Fig. 5.

room at a time was not a feasible alternative. Further, it became clear during NT that time-out was not aversive to some pupils and/or that it was losing its aversive properties. The competition between Ss 6 and 7 to be sent out of the room was one indication. Another was the duration of time-out per incident, which was contingent upon *S*'s behavior in the time-out room. In B and B2, each period usually lasted the minimum 10 minutes, whereas the peaks in Figs. 5 and 6 approach the total amount of time in class for three days. It appears that removing a child from a classroom is effective to the extent that it is, in fact, time-out from positive reinforcement. Complying with classroom expectations must be more reinforcing, one way or another, than the alternatives.

The effectiveness of token reinforcement was further increased by taking away a token for each error made. The procedure used was to cross out a previously earned mark. After the page was filled, these had to be re-earned in order to exchange the page for a back-up reinforcer.

Figure 7 shows *S*9's accuracy level while studying sight vocabulary

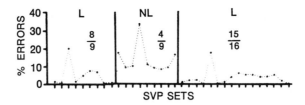

FIGURE 7   Daily percentage of errors record of S9 with token loss (L) and without token loss (NL) for errors on the Sight Vocabulary Program (SVP). SVP ratios are shown for each period. The number of items per set increased systematically from 80 to 100. These data were obtained after the 30-day B2 data in Fig. 6.

with and without loss of a token for each error. With loss in effect, the percentage of errors was halved, and this reduction was sufficient for him to pass the 10% criterion for advancing to the next set almost every day. Like token positive reinforcement, however, loss of tokens for mistakes may not be considered a generally effective technique. Not all pupils showed a corresponding decrease in errors as did S9.

The variability in the findings is consistent with the results of studies comparing the strength of various reinforcers in children (Brackbill and Jack, 1958; Hollis, 1965; Terrell, 1958; Terrell, Durkin, and Wiesley, 1959; Terrell and Kennedy, 1957), and is a consequence of the inability to control the history of the pupils' experiences with the events employed as reinforcers. It is not expected that an unselected, captive group of people will be equally responsive to the same reinforcers when their individual performance is studied. Thus, for some pupils social reinforcement and/or success were sufficient; for S7, both social *and* token reinforcement were weak. The proportions of Ss like S1 and like Ss 6 and 7 undoubtedly differ widely from class to class and school to school.

There are two important points to take into account in interpreting these results. First, the teachers were accustomed to dispensing tokens and believed in their efficacy, for they had not encountered problems like those presented by Ss 6–9 since prior to the introduction of tokens a year earlier. During NT, the teachers reported that all pupils seemed to pay less attention to instructions and correction, and to react more slowly and less enthusiastically. The teachers' enthusiasm also seemed to have decreased. While it is believed that the pupils' behavior changed first, this belief cannot be documented. It would be valuable to replicate this study with teachers who do not routinely use tangible reinforcement and who do not have daily access to the data. However, we see no alternative that will preclude the teachers' changing in response to changes in the pupils' behavior. Indeed, the good teacher must behave this way.

The second factor to consider is that the pupils had received token reinforcement for studying for at least three months before NT started. One could argue that because of the frequent pairing of approval, being correct, and tangible reinforcement, the removal of tokens, i.e., extinction, should have relatively little effect for some time. This view is consistent with the fact that no effect was obtained in 21 days with five pupils, a progressive effect was observed in S3, and a delayed effect was observed in Ss 6–9.

Finally, we should emphasize that the results pertain to a situation in which something that has been a part of the reinforcement complex is abruptly omitted.

To recapitulate:

(1) Five of the 15 Ss included in this analysis gave no measurable indication in 21 days that token reinforcement was necessary to maintain their cooperation and level of accuracy (Fig. 1).

(2) One S (S3) steadily increased in percentage of errors during NT to a level four times that obtained in B and B2; another S (S4) also increased markedly in percentage of errors during NT but may have been responding to the change in routine *per se*. The decreases in accuracy would have been alarming by most standards (Fig. 4).

(3) Four Ss declined in accuracy in NT at least to the point where the effect was educationally significant as measured by their advancing in one program, sight vocabulary (Figs. 2 and 3).

(4) Three Ss (Ss 6, 8, and 9), were clearly more cooperative and more accurate with token reinforcement than without it. In fact, their disruptive behavior in NT was such that dropping them from school would have been in order under ordinary circumstances (Figs. 5 and 6).

(5) The token reinforcement system and programs were not sufficient to bring another S's behavior under sufficient control for him to benefit from education (Fig. 5, S7).

(6) The tokens were sufficiently powerful to contain disruptive peer interactions, substantially reducing the need for time-out procedures.

(7) The effects of loss of tokens for errors ranged from no apparent effect to a considerable increase in accuracy (Fig. 7).

REFERENCES

BIRNBRAUER, J. S., BIJOU, S. W., WOLF, M. M., AND KIDDER, J. D. Programmed instruction in the classroom. In L. Ullmann and L. Krasner (Eds.), *Case studies in behavior modification.* New York: Holt, Rinehart, and Winston, 1965.

BIRNBRAUER, J. S., AND LAWLER, JULIA. Token reinforcement for learning. *Ment. Retardation*, 1964, **2**, 275–279.

BRACKBILL, YVONNE, AND JACK, D. Discrimination learning in children as a function of reinforcement value. *Child Develpm.*, 1958, **29**, 185–190.

FERSTER, C. B., AND APPEL, J. B. Punishment of S$^\Delta$ responding in match to sample by time-out from positive reinforcement. *J. exp. Anal. Behav.*, 1961, **4**, 45–56.

HEID, W. H. Nonverbal conceptual behavior of young children with programmed material. Unpublished doctoral thesis, Univer. of Washington, 1964.

HOLLIS, J. H. Effects of reinforcement shifts on bent-wire performance of severely retarded children. *Amer. J. ment. Defic.*, 1965, **69**, 531–535.

KIRK, S. A., AND JOHNSON, G. O. *Educating the retarded child.* Boston: Houghton-Mifflin, 1951.

PINES, MAYA. How three-year-olds teach themselves to read—and love it. *Harpers*, May, 1963.

PORTER, D. A critical review of a portion of the literature on teaching devices. *Harvard educ. Rev.*, 1957, **27**, 126–147.

SKINNER, B. F. *Science and human behavior.* New York: Macmillan, 1953.

SKINNER, B. F. Teaching machines. *Science*, 1958, **128**, 969–977.

STAATS, A. W., MINKE, K. A., FINLEY, J. R., WOLF, M. M., AND BROOKS, L. O. A reinforcer system and experimental procedure for the laboratory study of reading acquisition. *Child Develpm.*, 1964, **35**, 209–231.

STAATS, A. W., STAATS, CAROLYN K., SCHUTZ, R. E., AND WOLF, M. M. The conditioning of textual responses using "extrinsic" reinforcers. *J. exp. Anal. Behav.*, 1962, **5**, 33–40.

STANDING, E. M. *The Montessori method—A revolution in education.* Fresno: Academy Library Guild, 1962.

TERRELL, G. The role of incentive in discrimination learning in children. *Child Develpm.*, 1958, **29**, 231–236.

TERRELL, G., DURKIN, KATHRYN, AND WIESLEY, M. Social class and the nature of the incentive in discrimination learning. *J. abnorm. soc. Psychol.*, 1959, **59**, 270–272.

TERRELL, G., AND KENNEDY, W. A. Discrimination learning and transposition in children as a function of the nature of the reward. *J. exp. Psychol.* 1957, **53**, 257–260.

WALTERS, R. H., AND KOSOWSKI, IRENE. Symbolic learning and reading retardation. *J. consult. Psychol.*, 1963, **27**, 75–82.

MONTROSE M. WOLF
DAVID K. GILES
R. VANCE HALL
University of Kansas

Experiments
with token reinforcement
in a remedial classroom[1]

This report describes results of the first year of an after-school, remedial educa-tion program for low-achieving 5th and 6th grade children in an urban poverty area. The remedial program incorporated standard instructional materials, mastery of which was supported by token reinforcement. Experimental analyses carried out with individual students showed the token reinforcement to func-tion as such. The effects of the program on the academic achievement and report card grades of the children in the remedial group were found to be sig-

Reprinted from *Behaviour Research and Therapy*, 1968, 6, 51–64, with permis-sion of the publisher and the authors.

———
[1] The authors wish to express their appreciation for the help and encouragement given by Ted Gray, Director of Special Education, Kansas City, Kansas Public Schools; Alonzo Plough, Principal of Grant Elementary School; David Glass, Principal of Stowe Elementary School; and Reverend David Gray, Pastor of Pleasant Green Baptist Church. We are also indebted to Mrs. Janet McCormick and Mrs. Natalie Barge who were the assistant teachers; to Todd Risley and Donald Baer who provided valuable counsel throughout the course of the investigation; to Donald Baer and Stephanie Stolz for their critical readings of the manuscript; and to Dick Schiefelbusch and Fred Girardeau who did a great deal to facilitate this research. The research was partially supported by grants: OEO-KANS CAP-694/1 7-9, Bureau of Child Research, Kansas University Medical Center and NICHHD-HD-00870-(02-03), Bureau of Child Re-search, University of Kansas.

nificant when compared with the gains of a control group who had no remedial program.

Token reinforcement systems have now been used many times to develop and maintain useful human behavior in institutional settings (e.g. Ayllon and Azrin, 1965; Birnbrauer, Wolf, Kidder, and Tague, 1965; Cohen, Filipczak, and Bis, 1965; Lent, 1966; and Staats and Butterfield, 1965). In the present research, we created a token economy designed to develop and maintain the academic behavior of low-achieving children in a community setting. This report describes the results from the first year of an after-school, remedial education program for low-achieving 5th and 6th grade children in an urban poverty area. The remedial program incorporated standard instructional materials, mastery of which was supported by token reinforcement. Experimental analyses of the function of the tokens were carried out with individual students. The effects of the program were evaluated by comparing the academic achievement and report card grades of the remedial group with that of a control group who had no remedial program.

GENERAL PROCEDURES

Students

Pupils from two elementary schools located in a low income neighborhood of Kansas City, Kansas, attended a remedial education program during the summer of 1965, the 1965–66 school year, and the summer of 1966. Fifteen of the 16 students entered the 6th grade and one student entered the 5th grade in the fall of 1965. All of the students had scored at least two years below the norm for their grade level on the reading section of the Stanford Achievement Test (SAT) administered by the public schools during the 1965 spring term which preceded our program.

According to the pupils' school records, their median I.Q. was 88 (range 73–104), median SAT reading grade level score was 3·4, and the median SAT total battery grade level score was 3·6. Their median six-weeks report card grade average from the previous year was 4·1, on a scale where A = 1·0 and F = 5·0.

The program began with five children during the summer of 1965. After 5 weeks, five more children were added. In the fall, one more student[2] (the 5th grader) was enrolled at the beginning and five additional

---

[2] The one 5th grade student was added because her parent refused to let her 6th grade sister attend unless the 5th grader could take part as well. The 5th grade girl was 2 yrs below the norm in her SAT reading score.

students added at the end of the first 6-week period. The last student was enrolled at the end of the second six weeks.

In most instances the children belonged to families of more than five children who received welfare support. In the majority of the homes no father was present.

The children's parents were contacted by a social worker who explained the program and gave the parents the opportunity to have their children attend. All of the parents who were contacted enrolled their children, usually during the first visit. (One parent was visited four times before he made his decision, however.)

Token Reinforcement System

The reinforcement procedure resembled a trading stamp plan (e.g. S & H Green Stamps). Each child was given a folder containing groups of four different-colored pages, each page approximately 3 × 3 in. in size. Blue, yellow, and pink pages were divided into one hundred quarter-inch squares; green pages were divided into sixty ¼ in. squares. After a child completed an assignment correctly, he was given points by the teacher, who marked the squares of the appropriately colored pages with a felt pen.

When a child first joined the program, points were often given after each problem that was worked correctly. As the student acquired a higher rate and more accurate output, the amount and/or difficulty of work required to obtain points was gradually increased. The number of points to be given a child for particular work was decided by the teacher. This decision sometimes was determined partially through negotiation with the child.

Filled pages of points were redeemable, according to their color, for a variety of goods and events: blue pages for weekly field trips, such as circus, swimming, zoo, picnic, sporting events, movies; green pages (the sixty square pages) for a daily snack of sandwich, milk, fruit, and cookie; pink pages for money and items available in the "store", such as candy, toiletries, novelties, and clothing; yellow pages for long range goals which might take several weeks or months to obtain such as clothes, inexpensive watches, and second-hand bicycles. Any child who had accumulated $2.00 worth of yellow tickets was eligible for a shopping trip to local department stores on a designated night of each week.

The face value of a filled page was 25 cents. However, the actual value of a page usually was something less than 25 cents. Many of the field trip events were free to the project, although the children needed from four to eight filled blue pages to be able to go. Also, snacks and store items were purchased wholesale and marked up to approximate typical store prices.

The children received an approximately equal number of points for each of three areas:

(1) Work completed and/or corrected in regular school and brought to the classroom, such as seat work, corrected homework, and tests. For a grade of A the students received 100 points; for B, 75 points; for C, 50 points; and for D, 25 points.

(2) Homework assignments and remedial work completed in the remedial classroom. The number of points given for items in an assignment varied widely as a function of the *characteristics of the items* and *the repertoire of the particular child.* Since these interacted to determine the probability of correct answers and the length of time necessary for completion, both had to be considered beforehand when deciding the point values of items. Values ranged from as little as half a point per item to as high as 20 or 30 points for items that were especially difficult for a particular child.

(3) Six-weeks report card grades. The students were given grades by their regular school teacher in five academic subjects each 6 weeks. For each grade of A most students received 1,600 points; for B, 800 points; for C, 400 points; and for D, 200 points. Three children, however, who had made almost all failing marks the preceding year received double the above amounts.

Materials

A folder of remedial work was always to be found on each student's desk. This folder consisted primarily of exercises in the student's weakest area, graded at an appropriate level of difficulty. The reading materials included the Science Research Associates' *Reading Laboratory* and the *New Practice Reader* by the McGraw-Hill Book Company. The arithmetic workbooks were *Arithmetic for Today* by Chas. E. Merrill Books, Inc.; *The Practice Workbook of Arithmetic* by Treasure Books, Inc.; *Adventures in Arithmetic* by the American Book Company; and *Practice for Arithmetic* of the Lard Law Mathematics series. Language materials included *Individual Corrective English* workbooks by the McCormick-Mathers Pub. Co.; and '3' *in One* workbooks by Chas. E. Merrill Books, Inc.

The students' regular school texts were relied upon for academic materials in the areas of social studies and spelling. When suitable materials could not be found, teachers devised their own materials.

Program

The remedial group attended the classroom each weekday after school for two ½ hr, and on Saturday mornings during the public school year, and each morning except Sundays for 3 hrs during the summer months.

The summer program concentrated on reading, language, and arithmetic deficiencies indicated by the California Achievement Test. With the onset of the public school year, the curriculum also involved work relevant to the ongoing school curriculum. Emphasis was placed on homework assigned by the public school teacher, e.g. solving arithmetic homework, learning spelling lists, writing theme assignments, and preparing social studies projects. After the student completed such assignments, he engaged in remedial work in his deficient areas.

Facilities

The remedial classroom was located in the basement of a church located near the students' elementary schools. Inexpensive card tables served as desks. These were placed along the walls of a large room and were enclosed on two sides by 4 × 4 ft. wooden partitions. Two adjoining rooms were used to keep academic materials and some of the back-up reinforcers (the "store").

Personnel

The classroom was administered by one headteacher and, as the number of students increased, by two more teaching assistants. All are referred to below as instructors. Each instructor worked with five or six students, moving from one to another for short periods of individualized tutoring when necessary. Students were told to raise their hands when they had questions or had materials ready for scoring. There was almost no formal lecturing, however, group participation activities often were led on Saturday morning.

Two Neighborhood Youth Corps employees assisted in the classroom. Their duties included scoring completed assignments, distributing the snack, and exchanging the tokens in the "store" at the end of the day.

EXPERIMENTAL ANALYSIS OF THE TOKEN REINFORCEMENT PROCEDURE

Experimental analysis of the relationship between the rate of certain academic behavior in the classroom and the token system was accomplished in a number of ways. These involved either the modification or discontinuation of the token system and its contingency with achievement.

EXPERIMENT 1

The students usually had a wide choice of materials in the remedial classroom and varied markedly in their selections of these materials. This experiment was to determine whether the choice of materials by two students was at least partially a function of the distribution of the points.

Students

Two boys, identified as KT and AS, both in the 6th grade, were chosen for this experiment. Both had the same remedial instructor; one had a high rate and one had a low rate of completing reading sections in their *New Practice Readers*.

Response

The response consisted of completed units in the *New Practice Reader*. Each unit consisted of a story of approximately 200 words and a set of 12 or 13 questions. Half the questions were designed to test the student's comprehension of the reading material; half were designed to prepare the student's vocabulary for the story in the next reading section. The questions were multiple choice, true-false, and fill-in-the-blank in form. A dictionary was provided for the vocabulary portion. The number of points available for correct answers varied, but a 10 point bonus was given uniformly for a perfect score on either half of the questions. However, no points were given for any half unit if less than 50 per cent of the questions were correct. Also, unless it met the 50 per cent criterion, a half unit was not recorded as a response in the data analysis. In a unit where half was not counted, the other half was still recorded if it met the criterion.

Procedure

For several weeks of class sessions the number of points that the students could obtain from reading the story and answering the questions in the *New Practice Reader* was manipulated as shown in Table 1. For student KT, after 19 days which established a baseline rate against which to compare the effects of subsequent point manipulations, the maximum number of points which could be obtained from each reading unit was changed from 90 to 52 points. After seven sessions, the number was shifted back to 90 points for eight sessions; then again to 52 points for five sessions; and finally back again to 90 points for 10 sessions. Points for student AS were increased from 60 possible points per reading unit to 120 points for 20 sessions and then back to 60 points for six sessions. The differences in design between KT and AS were because AS had never had a rate of reading under previous conditions.

Each of the students was informed about the number of points that he could obtain for correct answers to questions whenever: (1) the number

TABLE 1 Experimental conditions and number of sessions for each subject in Experiment I

Subject	Number of possible points per reading unit	Number of sessions
KT	90	19
	52	7
	90	8
	52	5
	90	10
AS	60	19
	120	20
	60	6

of points were changed, (2) the student inquired about what number of points could be earned, or (3) the student completed an assignment.

Results and Discussion

Experimental manipulation of the number of points earned by reading drastically modified the reading rates of both students, as shown in Fig. 1.

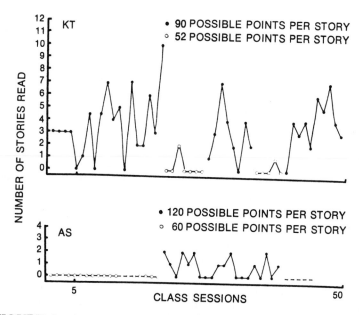

FIGURE 1 A record of completing reading units by two students, KT and AS. Each dot represents the number of units completed during a class session.

Each time KT's points for reading were decreased, his rate fell to almost zero. Doubling the number of points that AS could receive produced a modest rate of behavior, even though he had done no reading during the previous month. The results of Experiment 1 indicated that the points functioned as strong reinforcers for KT and AS.

EXPERIMENT 2

In Experiment 1 there were no observations of the effect of changing reading rate on the rates of other academic behavior. The second experiment was designed to determine the effects of point manipulations on three alternative types of behavior (responses in three workbooks) and, at the same time, to extend the experimental analysis of the token reinforcement system to all of the students in the remedial program.

Students

The second experiment took place during the 2-month summer session which followed the school year program. Eleven students began the summer remedial program 2 days after the spring remedial program ended.[3] The summer program extended over 47 meetings: 39 week-day classes and eight Saturday sessions. Systematic data were recorded only on week-days, since Saturdays were devoted primarily to group participation activities.

Responses

The responses consisted of completed units in any of three standard workbooks: *The New Practice Reader, The Practice Workbook and Arithmetic,* and *Individual Corrective English.* The characteristics of the *New Practice Reader* were described in Experiment 1. The response criterion was the same as in that experiment.

In *The Practice Workbook of Arithmetic* and *Individual Corrective English,* each page was considered to be a unit. Directions were given at the top of the page and the problems to be worked appeared immediately below. The number of arithmetic problems on each page varied from about 40 *regular computations* to about 15 *"story problems."* In the *Individual Corrective English,* a unit consisted usually of 20–25 sentence-items. Each unit involved a topic such as punctuation, proper nouns, or complete and

---

[3] At midyear 16 students were enrolled in the program. However, for various reasons only 11 attended the summer sessions: one girl had married during the spring term, two students were out of town for the summer, one boy was required to stay home and "work" for his mother during the summer, and one student had moved across town and was supposed to ride the bus to class but failed to attend after the first week of summer session.

incomplete sentences. Points were given for each correct sentence-item, regardless of the number of components involved in a particular sentence. A few sections did not follow the above format; for example, one set of directions instructed the student to write a friendly letter. These few sections were deleted in order to keep the remaining units as uniform as possible.

In order for points to be earned or for a response (a completed unit) to be counted in the data, a criterion of 75 per cent correct had to be met for units in both books.

Procedures

Classes during the summer program lasted three hours. The first hour involved a variety of activities such as writing themes and letters, or looking up identification questions in reference books. The third hour consisted of group participation activities such as oral reports, oral reading, and academic games. During the middle hour, the daily experimental session was held. It was described to the students as "free choice time". They were instructed that they could work on any material they pleased but that they would only receive points for working in the three workbooks described above. They were not allowed to work in these books at any other time.

During a baseline period all of the 11 students received the same number of points for working in the three books. Each correct answer in the reader earned 5 points. Each correct arithmetic *computation problem* earned 2 points and each correct arithmetic *"story" problem* earned 5 points. Each correct sentence in the English workbook earned 2 points. The distribution of points, the per cent correct criteria, and the particular workbooks which could be worked to earn points were advertised by a poster in the classroom. When changes in point contingencies occurred the students were told and a 3×5 in. card with the new point schedule was tacked to the wall of their cubicles.

After a student's behavior in the three workbooks appeared to stabilize, the number of points which he could earn in each of the books was shifted in an attempt to increase the rate of the workbook behavior which occurred least frequently. For example, if after five or more sessions a student has steady rates of reading and English but a very low frequency of arithmetic the distribution of points would be shifted in an attempt to increase the rate of arithmetic. On those occasions when the initial shift in the points did not result in an increment, a second adjustment of the points was made. After changes in the workbook behaviors did occur for several sessions, the points were again shifted, either back to baseline values or to new values. Representative records are presented below.

Results

The design of this experiment makes each student a separate and independent miniature investigation. However, the students responded in either of two very typical ways, with one exception. Consequently, the results of two prototypical students and of the single exception, are presented below as a summary of the experimental outcome.

Student GP's baseline response pattern was similar to that of about a third of the students. All of the students recorded responses in the three workbooks during the first few days of the baseline condition. However, the behavior of four of the eleven students (including GP) quickly dropped to zero in two of the workbooks but continued in the third. GP and one other student worked primarily on English, one student did nothing but read, and another worked almost exclusively on arithmetic. When the number of points which could be earned in the workbooks was shifted, their rates of working in the three books shifted correspondingly.

For GP, baseline condition (six sessions) allowed reading responses to earn 5 points (R 5), arithmetic responses to earn 2 or 5 points depending on whether they were computation or story problems (A 2, 5), and English responses to earn 2 points. During these sessions, GP worked primarily on English. His reading and arithmetic rates fell to zero after the second session. These rates are shown in Fig. 2.

Then, for 12 sessions, the points were changed, so that reading responses earned 8 points (R 8) arithmetic responses earned 2 or 5 points (A 2, 5) and English responses earned ½ point (E ½). This produced a substantial increase in reading, no effect on arithmetic, and a significant drop in English.

The point contingencies were then returned for 6 days to the baseline conditions: where reading earned 5 points, arithmetic 2 or 5 points and English 2 points (R 5; A 2, 5; E 2). On this occasion the baseline point value maintained a higher rate of reading and a lower rate of English than previously. The arithmetic rate remained at zero.

The fourth condition, lasting six sessions, changed reading to zero points, arithmetic to 5 or 10 points and English to zero points (R 0; A 5, 10; E 0). During this phase, the first arithmetic in over a month occurred, and reading and English fell to zero.

The final condition was reading at 5 points and arithmetic and English at zero points (R 5; A 0; E 0). It produced a decrease in arithmetic, held English to zero, and reestablished reading.

Student TH was one of seven students who normally worked in at least two of the workbooks. Extensive baselines were taken in some cases. The record of TH was typical, showing the alternation among the workbooks which often occurred.

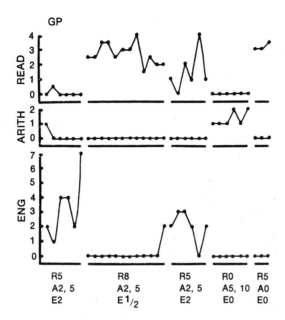

FIGURE 2 A record of student GP's rates of completing units of reading, arithmetic and English in three workbooks. Each dot represents the number of units completed during the experimental hour each class session. The letter and number captions describe the number of points to be earned for reading (R), arithmetic (A) and English (E) under each condition. Two numbers are given for arithmetic; the first for *computation* problems and the second for *story* problems.

TH remained under baseline conditions, where reading responses earned 5 points, arithmetic 2 or 5 points and English 2 points (R 5; A 2, 5; E 2) for 22 sessions. During baseline, TH generally alternated between English and reading, arithmetic remaining at zero after the first day as shown in Fig. 3. By changing the points to zero for reading, 4 or 8 for arithmetic and zero for English (R 0; A 4, 8; E 0) for nine sessions, her arithmetic rate was increased to an average of about 2 units a session; meanwhile, her English and reading rates were consistently zero.

The final condition lasted eight sessions. Reading responses earned 5 points, and arithmetic and English earned zero points. This produced zero rates of arithmetic and English, and a reasonably steady rate of reading.

Student CH was unusual: he worked in all three notebooks for an extended period of time. His baseline condition lasted for 4 weeks. The first change in condition shifted reading to 8 points, arithmetic and English to zero points (R 8; A 0; E 0) which made all his points contingent upon reading. As in the case of GP and TH above, the announcement of

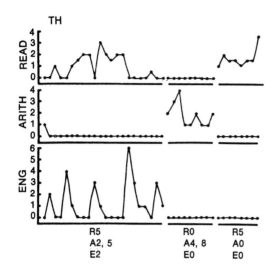

FIGURE 3 A record of student TH's rates of completing units of reading, arithmetic and English in three workbooks during the experimental hour.

"no points" reduced arithmetic and English workbook rates to zero. However, when the baseline condition was reinstated the pattern of behavior observed under the baseline condition (work in all three books) returned only temporarily: he then returned to reading exclusively.

Discussion of Experiments 1 and 2

In every case, shifts in the point contingencies led to shifts in the workbook behavior of the students. Shifts in point values to zero produced immediate cessation of behavior. Lesser shifts produced intermediate and more variable changes. Again, it is clear that the token reinforcement system functioned as such.

There was one type of irregularity that did occur in the data of several of the subjects. As with GP and CH, when the points were shifted to produce a high rate of reading, a return to baseline condition often did not return the reading behavior to its original level. Apparently, exposure to reading changed the operant level of the reading behavior. No similar effect was observed for arithmetic or English.

OTHER CONTINGENCIES

A number of other contingencies were provided in the program. Their functions were not systematically analyzed; however, they did seem to operate as intended. They are included here to provide a complete description of the program.

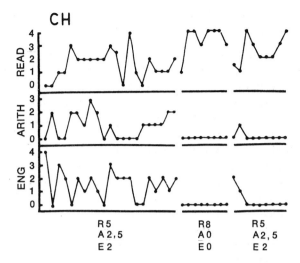

FIGURE 4 A record of student CH's rates of completing units of reading, arithmetic and English in three workbooks during the experimental hour.

Contingency for the instructors. In an effort to encourage maximally effective instruction, a monetary contingency was arranged for the instructors which was linked to the productivity of the students within their charge. Every 6 weeks, for each child whose 6-weeks report card grade average improved over his previous 6-weeks report, a bonus of ten dollars was given to the two assistant instructors.

Contingencies involving further academic work. Favorite subjects or popular academic activities were in some instances reserved for presentation only after completion of work in a less favored subject area. One boy, for example, who asked for Junior High arithmetic materials, was told that as soon as he correctly spelled all of his current spelling words, he would receive instruction in the desired area. Children were often given their choice of activities following the completion of material in a deficient area with less than 5 per cent error.

Academic productivity was often followed by permitting the productive student to instruct other students in their deficient areas. Good students were allowed to check materials completed by other students. Students frequently asked to continue their academic work after the two ½ hr remedial session. For good work, they were given additional assignments to take home.

Contingency for attendance. A 100 point bonus was given each month to every student who had perfect attendance for that period. The bonus was cumulative, in that 200 points were given after two months perfect attendance, 300 after 3 months, and so on.

Contingency for good behavior.   A blackboard containing the names of all the children was placed in front of the classroom. An alarm clock was set to go off at variable intervals during the remedial session, usually about 3 times during the two ½ hr period. Any child who was out of his seat for any reason when the alarm sounded received a mark after his name on the blackboard. Any other disruptive behavior, such as hitting another student, resulted in a mark being placed after the offender's name. At the end of each day, the child with the *fewest* marks received a 60-point award in his ticket booklet. The others received a number of points between sixty and zero, depending upon their position in the hierarchy of blackboard marks. The student with the highest number of marks received no points at all in this way. When more than four marks were received during any one day, some privilege was lost, for example, being denied use of the "store" at the end of the day.

Contingency for report card average improvement.   A party was held shortly after the end of each 6-weeks report card period for all students whose grade average improved over that of the previous 6 weeks. Maintenance of a B average or better also qualified students for the party. The parties consisted of such activities as dining out at a restaurant, camping, and going on an airplane ride.

Contingencies from the regular school teachers.   Teachers in the public school classroom were given the opportunity to give points to, or remove the store privilege from, the students in their classrooms. A form was distributed to the public school teachers on which they could indicate occasions of academic excellence or inappropriate classroom behavior. The children brought the reports to the remedial classroom in sealed envelopes. A report of excellence (the criterion of which was left to the teacher's discretion) resulted in 50 bonus points. A report of inappropriate conduct resulted in denying the use of the store to the student until the following day.

Contingencies for members of the student's family.   Items which could be used as gifts for members of a student's family were available in the store and could be purchased with pink tickets. Shaving lotion, safety razors, shampoo, toys particularly appealing to primary level children, and clothing in a variety of sizes were included. Such gifts were intended to interest the members of the family in the student's academic achievements and his participation in the program.

Contingencies from the natural environment.   Token rewards were often effective in bringing about the acquisition of behavior, but whenever possible the goal of this program was to bring the behavior under the control of the natural consequences of such behavior.

Purchases made either with tickets or real money, and the calculations necessary before the distribution of points, required a functional use of newly acquired arithmetic skills. Reading skills were to some extent maintained by requiring the students to do exactly as the directions of an assignment required in order to receive points for their responses. Comics and other high interest reading materials were made available to the students in a effort to maintain reading skills by consequences other than points.

Contingencies for teams of students. Token contingencies were arranged for subgroups of the students. On Saturdays, group games similar to T.V.'s College Bowl were conducted to encourage cooperation among students as well as to increase group participation skills. Several teams, consisting of two individuals each, competed against one another for a 40-point bonus to be given to the team accumulating the most correct responses. Such members of a team received points for every correct response by either of them. It was necessary for each member of the team to emit at least one correct response in order to qualify for the bonus given to the winning team. The students were permitted to choose their partners. This was done in an effort to place students who responded well in these activities in a situation similar to that of the athlete who does well in games during recess: he is sought out as a hero and a desirable teammate by his peers.

Each group of five or six students who worked regularly with one of the instructors competed with the other two groups in accumulating tests with "A" grades from the public school. An announcement was made to the whole class each time a student brought in such a paper. The "A" paper itself was thumbtacked to one of the partitions at the side of the student's desk. At the end of the week the team receiving the highest number of "A" papers was treated to candy bars of their choice.

EVALUATION OF THE TOTAL REMEDIAL PROGRAM

A primary goal of the program was to help the students make larger than usual gains in their academic skills. In order to evaluate the progress of the students in the program, indications of their academic achievement during the year were compared with those of a control group. The control group went to regular school and had no remedial program at all.

Students

The 6th grade students for the remedial program and for the control group were chosen in the following manner. The names of students were placed in rank order according to their degree of reading deficiency as measured by the SAT. The lowest scoring student was assigned to the remedial classroom group, the next lowest to the control group, etc. This procedure was continued until 15 students had been assigned to each group. As described earlier, for special reasons one 5th grade girl was enrolled in the classroom. A 5th grade girl with the same reading score and a similar report card grade average was added to the control group.

One of the 6th graders in the classroom group was lost during the spring term. She married and dropped out of school and out of the remedial program. The control group had also been reduced to 15 during the spring term as a result of a child moving. Thus the comparisons made at the end of the year involved only 15 students in each group.

The median characteristics of the control group were the same as the remedial classroom group which was described earlier, except that the average 6-week report card grades of the control group was slightly higher, at 3·7, as compared to 4·1 for the classroom group (A = 1·0 and F = 5·0).

Procedures and Results

Stanford achievement test. During each of the preceding two years the median gain made by the experimental and control groups on the SAT administered by the public school had been 0·6 yr. The gains during the year of the remedial program made by the experimental and control groups were compared by using the Mann-Whitney U Test, one tailed (Siegel, 1956). The median gain of the remedial group on the Total Battery of the SAT was 1·5 yr as compared to a median gain of 0·8 yr for the control group. Thus, the rate of gain for the remedial group was almost twice that of the control group. The remedial group gains were significantly greater (at better than the 0·01 level of confidence).

Report card grades. Gains in report card grades of the remedial and control groups were analyzed using the Mann-Whitney U Test, one tailed (Siegel, 1956). The last 6-week report card grade averages of the year of the remedial program, and of the previous year, were compared. The median gain of the remedial group was 1·1 grade points from slightly below a "D" to a "C" average while the gain by the control group was 0·2 of a grade point. The gain of the remedial group was significantly greater (at better than the 0·005 level of confidence).

Attendance. The attendance in the remedial program averaged 85 per cent, with a range from 65–100 per cent, though the program met on Saturdays and most regular school holidays. (The decision to work on regular school holidays was determined by a vote of the students. If a majority voted that the remedial program be held on a holiday, class was conducted on that day. Without exception, the children chose to have class every holiday that a choice was given. The only holidays that class was not held were the Thanksgiving and Christmas holidays—when the instructors somewhat undemocratically chose not to work.)

Cost. The students earned an average of $225.00 in points during the school year. The range among the students was from $167.05 to $278.08. These amounts did not include the cost of the improvement parties. The costs of the points and the improvement parties combined averaged about $250.00 per student during the school year.

DISCUSSION

The results indicate that the students benefited substantially from the remedial program. Not only did they gain, on the average, a full year's advancement in their achievement level; they also gained an additional half year in their previously accumulated deficit.

The comments by the regular school teachers (for what they are worth) suggest that the remedial program benefited the regular school classroom as well. They stated that not only were the children in the program helped, but that the increased participation and "changed attitudes" of the remedial program children increased the productivity of the other children in the regular school classrooms.

Although the control group, on the average, made only about half the gain of the remedial group, individual children in the control group acquired significant gains. One 6th grade boy in the control group made the highest gain in report card grades of all the children. However, perhaps very significantly, some of the control group children regressed in their standard achievement test scores and made lower report card grade averages than the previous year. No child in the remedial group showed any such regression.

The remedial program's effectiveness in maintaining the children's participation was indicated by the high attendance record, and the fact that whenever the opportunity was given them the children chose to attend class on regular school holidays.

The cost of the program, which was substantial, must be contrasted with the long term cost to society in terms of human as well as economic resources lost by not educating these children adequately. The cost could be reduced significantly by utilizing the potential reinforcers which already exist in almost every educational setting. Properly used, such events as recess, movies, and athletic and social activities could be arranged as consequences for strengthening academic behavior.

REFERENCES

AYLLON, T. and AZRIN, N. H. (1965) Measurement and reinforcement of the behavior of psychotics, *J. exp. Analysis Behav.* 8, 357–383.

BIRNBRAUER, J. S., WOLF, M. M., KIDDER, J. D. and TAGUE, C. E. (1965) Classroom behavior of retarded pupils with token reinforcement. *J. exp. child Psychol,* 2, 219–235.

COHEN, M. L., FILIPCZAK, J. A. and BIS, J. S. (1965) *Case project; contingencies applicable for special education.* Brief progress report. Institute of Behavioral Research, Silver Spring, Maryland.

LENT, JAMES R. (1966) *A demonstration program for intensive training of institutionalized mentally retarded girls.* Progress Report, Bureau of Child Research, University of Kansas, February.

SIEGEL, S. (1956) *Non-parametric statistics for the behavioral sciences.* Mc-Graw-Hill, New York.

STAATS, A. W. and BUTTERFIELD, W. H. (1965) Treatment of non-reading in a culturally deprived juvenile delinquent: an application of reinforcement principles. *Child Dev.* 36, 925–942.

DON R. THOMAS
WESLEY C. BECKER
MARIANNE ARMSTRONG
University of Illinois
and Thomas Paine School, Urbana, Illinois

Production and elimination
of disruptive classroom
behavior by systematically
varying teacher's behavior[1]

The effects of teacher behaviors on the classroom behaviors of children were investigated by systematically varying approving (praise, smiles, contacts, etc.) and disapproving (verbal reprimands, physical restraint, etc.) classes of teacher behavior. Measures were taken on both teacher and child behaviors. Each day a sample of 10 children was observed. The subject pool was a class of 28 well-behaved children in a middle-primary public school class. The results demonstrated that approving teacher responses served a positive reinforcing function in maintaining appropriate classroom behaviors. Disruptive behaviors increased each time approving teacher behavior was withdrawn. When the teacher's disapproving behaviors were tripled, increases appeared most markedly in the gross motor and noise-making categories of disruptive behavior. The findings emphasize again the important role of the teacher in producing, maintaining, and eliminating disruptive as well as pro-social classroom behavior.

Reprinted from *Journal of Applied Behavior Analysis*, 1968, 1, 35–45, with permission of the publisher and the authors. Copyright 1970 by the Society for the Experimental Analysis of Behavior, Inc.

[1] The authors wish to thank Urbana School District #116 and the principal of Thomas Paine School, Mr. Richard Sturgeon, for their cooperation. The observers (Loretta Nielson, Barbara Goldberg, Marilyn Goldberg, and Darlene Zientarski) deserve thanks for their conscientious work. This research was supported, in part, by National Institute of Child Health and Human Development Grant HD-00881-05.

Teachers are sometimes unaware of the effects of their actions on the behavior of their students. Many teachers assume that if a child performs disruptive acts in the classroom then the child must have a problem at home, or at the very least, must not have reached a stage of sufficient maturity to function adequately in the school situation. However, an increasing body of evidence indicates that many of the behaviors which teachers find disruptive are actually within their control. A teacher can modify and control the behavior of her students by controlling her own responses.

Contingent use of social reinforcement has been shown to control such motor behaviors as walking, standing, and running (Bijou and Baer, 1963), talking and crying (Kerr, Meyerson, and Michael, 1965; Hart, Allen, Buell, Harris, and Wolf, 1964), and classroom conduct (Becker, Madsen, Arnold, and Thomas, 1967; Zimmerman and Zimmerman, 1962).

Becker *et al.* (1967) worked in public schools with teachers who had problem children in their classes. Behaviors exhibited by the students were observed and the frequency of these behaviors was estimated for each child. Each teacher was taught to use praise, smiles, *etc.* to reinforce good behavior. The rate of appropriate classroom behaviors increased in most cases as soon as teacher approval and recognition were made contingent on such behavior.

The present study evolved from prior research showing the importance of social reinforcement, and Becker's work, which suggests that specific procedures, or definable classes of teacher behaviors can be used by the teacher to increase appropriate classroom behaviors. In order to provide more convincing data on the role of different teacher behaviors, the present study was designed to produce and remove problem behavior in students by systematically varying teacher behaviors in an initially well-behaved class.

METHOD

Subjects

Students. A class of 28 elementary students at the middle-primary level was selected. According to the teacher her class was "a good class, with an above-average distribution of ability and no 'bad' kids." Most of the children were from upper-middle- and middle-income-range families. Ages at the beginning of the study ranged from 6 yr, 11 months to 7 yr, 11 months; I.Q. range (group test) was from 99 to 134.

Teacher. The teacher, age 23, obtained her student teaching experience with a class of "maladjusted" children. In addition, she had 1-yr experience with a class of "slow learners". Preliminary observations indicated that she rarely attended in an approving manner to children who behaved inappropriately, and rarely reprimanded children who were performing their assigned tasks. She volunteered to participate in the study because of its potential contribution to teacher training in the future.

Observation Procedures

The basic data for the study consisted of the relative frequency of occurrence of classes of child behaviors in relation to classes of teacher behaviors utilizing rating schedules to be described. One to three observers were placed in the classroom each morning from approximately 9:15 to 10:00 A.M. while the students were completing reading and reading workbook assignments. To insure obtaining a daily sample of both child and teacher behaviors during the 45-min work period, a 20-min observation time was decided on for both child and teacher observations. Thus, even if only one observer was present, the relevant information could be obtained. This time restriction limited the number of children who could be observed each day. Ten children were selected for observation each morning by drawing numbers from a hat. During Baseline$_1$ and the first No Praise condition a no-replacement procedure was used so that all children had to be observed before a child's number could be drawn a second time. At the start of Baseline$_2$ this restriction was removed. Through the use of a numbered seating chart, the observers recorded the behaviors of selected children in the order in which they were chosen. Five extra numbers were drawn each day to provide observation targets in case one or more of the first 10 subjects drawn were not available for observation. Target children were observed for 2 min each. Each minute was divided into six 10-sec intervals. Observers were trained to record classes of behavior which occurred in a given interval. Recordings were made during the first five intervals of each minute. During the sixth 10-sec interval the observers made notes, checked for synchronization, and/or prepared to switch to a new child. Thus, the daily child observation sample consisted of ten 10-sec observation intervals on each of 10 children.

Teacher behaviors were recorded on a similar schedule, the only difference being that for teacher behaviors each occurrence of a response in a specified class was recorded (frequency measure), whereas for child behaviors a given class of behavior could be rated only once in a 10-sec interval. This difference in procedure was necessitated by the greater difficulty in separating child behaviors into discrete response units. Observers used a clipboard, stopwatch, and a recording sheet which had spaces for 100 observation intervals, guides for computing reliability, and a place for comments.

Undergraduate university students were hired and trained to collect the data. Each observer memorized the definitions of classes of child and teacher behaviors. Pre-baseline training in recording of behavior was carried out in the experimental classroom to allow the children to become accustomed to the presence of the observers. The children were already well adapted to the classroom before observer training was started. Observers were instructed to avoid all interactions with the students and teacher while in the class or on the school grounds. At the scheduled time they would enter the class, walk directly to chairs provided for them, sit down, and begin the observations. A hand signal was used to insure syncronization of observation times. Initially two observers were scheduled to observe on Monday, Wednesday, and Friday, and two on Tuesday and Thursday. When a systematic difference developed between the two sets of observers, one of the Tuesday-Thursday observers was placed on a three-day-a-week schedule to tie the two sets of observations together with reliability checks. Thus, on some days there were as many as three observers in the classroom. The number of observers in the classroom varied from one to three. Due to illness or the need to obtain observations in other classrooms, there were times when only one observer was available. Observers were not informed of changes in experimental conditions.

Classes of Teacher Behaviors:
The Independent Variable

The behaviors emitted by the teacher were defined as belonging to three general classes: (1) Disapproving Behavior, (2) Approving Behavior, and (3) Instructional Behavior. Disapproving and Approving Behaviors were rated only when they immediately followed discriminable child behaviors falling into inappropriate or appropriate classes (see below).[2] Listings were made of the teacher behaviors that could occur within each class.

The general class of Disapproving Behaviors included Physical Contact, Verbal, and Facial subclasses. The subclasses of Physical Behaviors included forcibly holding a child, grabbing, hitting, spanking, shaking, slapping, or pushing a child into position. The Verbal subclass of Disapproving Behaviors included yelling, scolding, raising voice, belittling, or making fun of the child, and threats. Threats included "if-then" statements of loss of privilege or punishment at some future time. For example, the

---

[2] As it turned out, approval following inappropriate behavior occurred only three times and disapproval following appropriate behavior did not occur. Also, this teacher did not make non-response-contingent approval or disapproval comments. Thus, we were dealing essentially with two response-contingent classes of teacher behavior.

teacher might say to the class, "If you don't remain quiet, you will have to stay in from recess." The Facial subclass of Disapproving Behaviors included frowning, grimacing, side-to-side head shaking, gesturing, *etc.*

The general class of Approving Behaviors also included Physical Contact, Verbal, and Facial subclasses. Approving Physical Contacts included embracing, kissing, patting, holding hand or arm of child, or holding the child in the teacher's lap. Approving Verbal comments included statements of affection, approval, or praise. Approving Facial response was rated whenever the teacher smiled, winked, or nodded at one or more of the children.

The general class of Instructional Behavior included any response from teacher to children which involved giving instructions, information, or indicating correct responses.

In addition to recording the above classes of teacher behavior, note was taken of those times when the teacher terminated social interaction by turning out lights and saying nothing, turning her back on the class and waiting for silence, or stopping talking and waiting for quiet.

As noted earlier, the observers recorded every teacher response falling in a given class. Thus, the measures of teacher behaviors are frequency counts.

Child Behaviors: The Dependent Variable

The classes of child behaviors were developed by categorization of behaviors occurring with some frequency in the repertoire of problem children (Becker *et al.*, 1967). It was assumed that certain behaviors, because of their common topography, could be grouped together. Five classes of Disruptive Behavior (Gross Motor, Noise Making, Orienting, Verbalizations, and Aggression) and one class of Appropriate Behavior (Relevant) were defined. Behaviors not specifically defined were rated in a separate category (Other Task). Disruptive Behaviors were essentially behaviors apparently incompatible with good classroom learning conditions.

Included in the category of behaviors labeled as Gross Motor activities were: getting out of seat, standing up, walking around, running, hopping, skipping, jumping, rocking chair, moving chair, sitting with chair in aisle, kneeling in chair, arm flailing, and rocking body without moving chair.

The category of Noise Making was rated with the stipulation that the observers must hear the noise as well as see the noise-making action, and included tapping feet, clapping, rattling papers, tearing papers, throwing books or other objects onto desks, slamming desk top, tapping objects on desk, kicking desk or chair, and scooting desk or chair.

The Verbalization category was rated only when the observer could hear the response. Lip movements alone were not rated. Carrying on conversations with other children, calling out teacher's name to get her attention, crying, screaming, singing, whistling, laughing, and coughing were included in the category.

The Orienting class of behaviors required that the child be seated. Turning of head or head and body toward another person, showing objects to another child, and looking at another child were rated. Looking behaviors of less than 4-sec duration were not rated except for any turn of more than 90 degrees from the desk. When an Orienting response overlapped two rating intervals, and could not be rated in the first interval, because it began too late in the interval to meet the 4-sec criterion, it was rated in the second interval.

Aggression was defined as hitting, pushing, shoving, pinching, slapping, striking with objects, poking with objects, grabbing objects or work belonging to another, knocking neighbor's property off desk, destroying another's property, throwing objects. No judgments of intent were made.

Appropriate behaviors were labeled Relevant and were made more easily identifiable by restricting the observations to a period in the morning when all of the children were preparing reading and workbook assignments. Specific Relevant Behaviors were: looking at the teacher when she was speaking to the entire class or to the child being observed, answering questions of the teacher, raising hand and waiting for teacher to respond, writing answers to workbook questions, looking at pages of text in which reading was assigned. It was required that the entire 10-sec interval be filled with on-task behavior before the Relevant rating was made.

When a child being observed performed a response not defined by one of the categories of Disruptive Behaviors or by Relevant Behavior, a rating of Other Task was made. The Other Task rating was incompatible with Relevant, but could be recorded in the same interval as any or all of the categories of Disruptive Behavior.

When rating the children, the observers were instructed to record each class of behaviors which appeared in an interval regardless of how many other classes had already been recorded in that interval. All five categories of Disruptive Behaviors and the Other Task category were compatible with each other. Relevant Behavior was incompatible with the other categories. No category of behavior was rated more than once in an interval. If a child was conversing with his neighbor, and he made two verbal responses in one interval, this class of behaviors was recorded only once. Thus, each child-behavior measure was a record of intervals in which the response occurred, rather than a count of the number of discrete responses as in the recording of teacher's behavior.

The overall level of Disruptive Behaviors was defined as the percentage of intervals in which one or more Disruptive Behaviors occurred.

Reliability

Two types of reliability were calculated. Reliability I reflects simply the degree to which two observers obtained the same score for each category of behavior during a 20-min observation period. The smaller score is divided by the larger. Reliability I most appropriately applies to the data as reported in Fig. 1, since these are averages for an observation period. Random errors tend to cancel each other out when a score is based on a series of observations and a reliability measure should reflect the gain in accuracy obtained by averaging. For training purposes, and for greater confidence in the accuracy of the observation procedure, a second type of reliability was also calculated (Reliability II). Reliability II required that the same behavior category be recorded in the same interval by each observer to define an agreement. Reliability II was calculated by dividing the number of agreements by the number of agreements plus disagreements.

During the pre-baseline observer training, reliability checks were re-

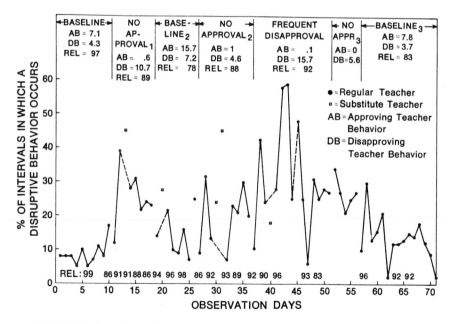

FIGURE 1 Disruptive classroom behaviors as a function of nature of teacher behavior. Data points represent 2-min samples on 10 children each day. Dotted lines cross observations where the regular teacher was absent due to a recurrent illness, including a 10-day hospitalization between Days 39 and 41. The dotted line connecting days 44 and 45 represent the Easter vacation break. The data for Day 26 were taken with the teacher out of the room.

quired for every observation. Before baseline observations were started, consistent reliabilities (Type II) above 80% were required. Reliability I data based on a weighted average of the reliabilities of the child-behavior codes are reported in Fig. 1, as are the average reliabilities by conditions for teacher behaviors. Comparable Reliability II data averaged 82.6% for child behaviors and 83.2% for teacher behaviors. Reliabilities for individual categories are well represented by these averages.

Sequence of Conditions

The first phase of the study (Baseline$_1$) consisted of measuring both teacher and child behaviors. No attempt was made to manipulate teacher behavior.

The second phase (No Approval$_1$) was defined by the absence of Approval Behaviors. The teacher discontinued the use of praise statements and used only contingent Disapproving Behaviors to control the children.

These phases were then repeated (Baseline$_2$, No Approval$_2$). At the beginning of No Approval$_2$ and throughout the rest of the study, the teacher carried a small "supermarket" adding machine with her to count the frequency of Disapproval Behaviors so that she could better monitor her behavior.

The fifth phase of the study, Frequent Disapproval, involved increasing the level of Disapproving Behaviors to approximately three times that given during Baseline$_1$ while continuing to withhold Approving Behaviors.

Phase 6 returned to the lower level of Disapproval (No Approval$_3$) and Phase 7 again returned to the baseline conditions (Baseline$_3$).

The teacher was instructed to maintain experimental conditions throughout the day, not just during the observation period. During the periods when praise was withheld beginning with No Approval$_2$, checks of the daily counts of Disapproving Responses obtained by the teacher with her counter corresponded closely to those which would have been predicted by extrapolation from the observation periods.

RESULTS

The relationships of greatest interest are the effects of presence and absence of Approval Behaviors on Relevant Behaviors and the effects of levels of Disapproval Behaviors on Disruptive Behaviors. Because of a systematic rater bias which entered into the data for Other Task Behavior (discussed later), and therefore also affected Relevant Behaviors incompatible with Other Task, greater emphasis is given to the analysis of Disruptive Behaviors in presenting the results.

Average Level of Disruptive Behavior

In Baseline$_1$ Disruptive Behaviors occurred in an average of 8.7% of the intervals observed. When Approving Behaviors were discontinued (No Approval$_1$), Disruptive Behavior increased to an average of 25.5% (Fig. 1). Approving Behaviors were again provided (Baseline$_2$) and Disruptive Behavior dropped to an average of 12.9%. In order to show more conclusively that the changes in Disruptive Behavior were related to the changes in teacher behavior, Approving Behaviors were again discontinued (No Approval$_2$) and the level of Disruptive Behaviors stabilized near the same level as in No Approval$_1$ condition (average 19.4%). When the Disapproving Behaviors (critical comments) were tripled (Frequent Disapproval), while Approving Behaviors were still withheld, Disruptive Behavior increased to an average of 31.2% with high points far above any observed before. The behavior stabilized, however, near the level at which the two previous No Approval phases had stabilized. When the rate of disapproval was lowered (No Approval$_3$), no great reduction in Disruptive Behavior occurred. The average level of Disruptive Behaviors over No Approval$_2$, Frequent Disapproval, and No Approval$_3$ was 25.9%. At the end of No Approval$_3$, Approval was again added to the low level of Disapproving Behaviors, and Disruptive Behavior dropped to an average of 13.2%, with the trend indicating a level far below this average.[3]

Analysis of Classes of Behavior

Discontinuation of approving behaviors. In reviewing the changes in the individual categories of behavior through the first two withdrawals of Approving Behavior, the majority of the increase in Disruptive Behaviors could be attributed to changes in Verbalization and Orienting categories (Table 1). The mean of Verbalization in No Approval$_1$ was 22.6% due to one extremely high observation on the second day of the condition; however, these behaviors stabilized between 9% and 17% (Fig. 2). Orienting showed a slight decrease across No Approval$_1$ (Fig. 2). The second time Approval was discontinued, Orienting increased across the condition while Verbalization remained relatively stable except for two high observations. Gross Motor behaviors followed the same pattern as

---

[3] A conservative statistical analysis was performed (F test) to compare those three conditions where approval responses were available with those two conditions where approval responses were withdrawn. For this test the Frequent Disapproval and No Approval$_{2+3}$ conditions were collapsed into one condition. In order to insure independence of observations, the average values within each condition were used, thus providing four degrees of freedom. Significant differences were found for Relevant Behavior ($p < 0.01$), Noise Making ($p < 0.05$), Gross Motor ($p < 0.025$), and for the overall level of Disruptive Behavior ($p < 0.01$).

TABLE 1 Average percentages for specific behavior classes for each experimental phase

Behavior classes	Baseline₁	No approval₁	Baseline₂	No approval₂	Frequent disapproval	No approval₃	Baseline₃
Disruptive behaviors[a]	8.7	25.5	12.9	19.4	31.2	26.8	13.2
Gross motor	2.7	6.7	2.0	4.8	12.3	10.4	2.4
Noise	0.9	0.1	0.7	0.09	4.1	4.4	0.9
Verbalization	4.6	22.6	7.7	9.6	7.9	6.0	3.9
Orienting	1.4	6.5	4.1	7.1	11.5	10.2	7.6
Aggression	0.25	0.01	0.2	0.01	0.04	0.04	0.1
Other task	7.0	10.4	5.9	10.7	5.9	4.2	1.2
Relevant	84.1	65.3	83.9	72.1	64.3	69.4	85.6

[a] The addition of percentages for the five classes of disruptive behaviors will usually lead to a sum higher than that reported as percentage of disruptive behaviors, since the latter does not reflect the occurrence of more than one subclass of disruptive behaviors in a given 10-sec interval.

Orienting and Verbalization through No Approval (1 and 2), increasing each time Approving Behavior was discontinued and decreasing when Approving Behaviors were present (Fig. 2).

Noise Making and Aggression followed a pattern through No Approval$_1$ and $_2$ which was distinctly different from the other categories of disruptive behavior. Both of these categories of behavior were already occurring at a low frequency in the Baseline condition (Table 1), but they occurred even less often when only Disapproving Behavior was given.

Increase of disapproving behaviors.   In the Frequent Disapproval condition, Noise Making, Gross Motor, and Orienting all increased (Table 1). Verbalization showed a decline over this condition and continued to decline through the rest of the study.

Changing from a high level of Disapproving Behaviors to a lower level did not markedly change the frequency of the various categories of Disruptive Behaviors relative to their terminal level under the Frequent Disapproval condition.

When Approving Behaviors were again used by the teacher (Baseline$_3$), the frequency of Gross Motor, Noise Making, and Orienting behaviors decreased noticeably (Fig. 2). Verbalization continued to show the steady decrease in frequency which had started in the Frequent Disapproval condition. In Baseline$_3$ Aggression again occurred, but rarely. All Disruptive Behaviors except Orienting dropped to the level of the initial Baseline (or below) during the final Baseline.

Relevant behavior.   Appropriate behaviors were initially high in the classroom (Fig. 2). Behaviors such as getting out of seat to move to a reading group or to check a completed workbook assignment were rated in the Gross Motor category. The requirements for such behaviors, however, remained constant through all conditions so changes in the level of Relevant Behaviors cannot be attributed to changes in classroom requirements. Relevant Behavior decreased each time Approving Behavior was discontinued and increased each time the Approval was reinstated. Relevant Behavior was at a slightly higher level during the final Baseline than during the initial Baseline.

Other task: Behavior not specifically defined.   As indicated earlier, a systematic rater difference was encountered early in the study in rating Other Task behaviors. In Fig. 2 this bias can be seen by contrasting data collected on Days 2, 4, 6, 8, and 10 from one set of observers with that collected on Days 1, 3, 5, 7, and 9 by another set of observers. While an attempt was made to correct this bias by interlocking reliability checks, it is apparent that the bias continued to some extent throughout the study. Since Other Task is by definition incompatible with Relevant Behavior, Relevant Behavior shows the same bias. By looking at Disruptive Behavior,

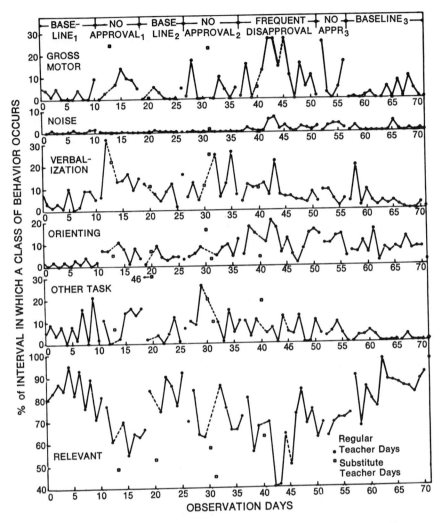

FIGURE 2   Analysis of specific behavior classes by condition. Data points represent 2-min samples on 10 children each day. See notes under Fig. 1.

defined so as to exclude Other Task behaviors, the systematic bias was largely eliminated from the data presented in Fig. 1.

Teacher Behaviors

The behavior of the teacher remained under good control throughout the study. Averages by conditions for Approving and Disapproving Behaviors are given in the upper part of Fig. 1. As the conditions were changed, little difficulty was found in withholding behaviors in the Approving category. Some difficulty was reported by the teacher in regulating the frequency of Disapproving Behaviors while withholding Approving Behaviors, but a partial solution to this problem was found. The teacher found that by carrying a small hand-counter (mentioned earlier) she could more accurately judge the frequency of her critical comments. In the Frequent Disapproval Phase there were days when the children were not emitting enough Disruptive Behaviors for critical comments to be appropriate at the programmed frequency. Rather than make inappropriate comments, the rate of Disapproving comments was adjusted to the frequency of the Disruptive Behaviors. When enough Disruptive Behaviors were available, Disapproving Behaviors were dispensed at a maximum rate of one per minute throughout the day; thus, many of the responses of the children were reprimanded very quickly.

General frequency of instructional comments did not change appreciably across conditions. However, the teacher did increase the frequency with which she would say in a neutral tone whether responses were correct or incorrect in the phases where Approval was not given.

The behaviors characterized as Terminating Social Interaction occurred only twice during the study and were, therefore, not subject to further analysis.

Substitute teachers. Observations taken on the days when a substitute teacher was in charge of the classroom appear in four conditions of the study. The frequency of Disruptive Behaviors increased in the presence of a temporary teacher as long as the regular teacher was in either Baseline or No Approval Behavior phases. When the Disapproving Behavior was being dispensed at a high rate, however, the level of Disruptive Behaviors decreased in the presence of a temporary teacher (Fig. 1).

Day 26. The data for this day were taken while the teacher was out of the room. Since the experimental conditions were not operative, this point should have been omitted altogether.

DISCUSSION

The results indicate that some aspects of the behaviors included in the category of Approving Behaviors were reinforcing for task-appropriate behaviors. The frequency of Relevant Behaviors was high whenever Approving Behaviors followed Relevant child Behavior, and decreased whenever Approving Behaviors were discontinued.

In each change of conditions that involved discontinuation of Approving Behaviors, there appeared a reliable transition effect (observation

Days 11 and 27). This effect may be an example of the typical increase in rate found when a positive reinforcer is removed. In support of this explanation, the teacher reported, "When I stop praising the children, and make only negative comments, they behave very nicely for three or four hours. However, by the middle of the afternoon the whole classroom is chaotic." Since observations were taken during a study period in the morning, the periods of good behavior show up in the data each time a condition was changed. A similar low deviant behavior point occurred at the transition to Frequent Disapproving Behaviors (day 37), but it is not clearly explained. "The children seemed stunned."

Reviewing the individual classes of Disruptive Behaviors brings out certain similarities and differences among the classes. During the first alternations of Baseline with discontinuation of Approving Behaviors, Gross Motor, Orienting, and Verbalization Behaviors increased with discontinuation of Approval, while Noise Making and Aggressive Behaviors remained at the already low frequency. The increases are interpreted as suggesting that some responses in the disruptive classes may be reinforced by peer attention or other environmental circumstances when control through approving teacher responses to incompatible behaviors is withdrawn. For example, Orienting behaviors, such as looking around the room or out the window may be reinforced by seeing other children playing, by observing a custodian cleaning up the schoolyard, or by seeing any of numerous events which have no relationship to the classroom. Observational evidence for this inference was clearest in the Frequent Disapproval phase (below). It is also possible to attribute the increases in Disruptive Behaviors during No Approval$_1$ to the increase in use of Disapproval. However, the data for No Approval$_2$, where Disapproval was held to the Baseline level, would argue that the effect was primarily related to the withdrawal of approval.

Increasing Disapproving Behaviors to a high level produced four days where Disruptive Behaviors were above 40%. Several individual categories of behavior also showed marked changes. The increase in Gross Motor Behaviors was related to an increase in interactions with other students. During the Frequent Disapproval condition, two or three children would make alternate trips to check their workbooks at a table provided for that purpose. Only one child was permitted at the table at a time. During Baseline and No Approval phases, it was rare to see a child make more than one trip to the table; in the Frequent Disapproval phase, some of the children would check their papers several times. Others responded by pushing their papers off of their desks and then getting up to get them. There was a noticeable "pairing off" with two or more children exhibiting the same behaviors.

Another consequence of the Frequent Disapproval phase was a

marked increase in the noise level in the room. A majority of the noises during this period were created by children scooting their desks and chairs. One observer reported, "I waited for a few minutes after the regular observation period was over and counted the noises. During one 40-sec period, I counted 17 separate chair scraping noises. They came in bursts of two or three at a time. It looked as though the kids were trying to irritate the teacher." The noises in "bursts of two or three" seemed similar to the "pairing off" of children noted with the Gross Motor behaviors, and strengthens an hypothesis that reinforcement from peers is one of the elements which accounts for the increase in Disruptive Behaviors during this time. Peer attention cannot be the only element affecting the behavior of the children, however, because the Verbalization category of behaviors showed a constant decrease throughout the Frequent Disapproval condition. The inhibition of Verbalization could be due to interfering emotional responses being elicited by the high level of critical comments by the teacher. More probable, however, is that the children simply talked more quietly to avoid being caught by the teacher. Observers' reports indicate that a substantial number of verbalizations would have been recorded during the Frequent Disapproving Behaviors condition if there had been no requirement that the responses be heard by the observers. The children could be seen to turn their heads, and lip movements could be seen frequently, but the verbalizations could not be heard.

Work by Lovaas, Freitag, Kinder, Rubenstein, Schaeffer, and Simmons (1964) suggests that for some children any adult attention may be reinforcing. Some of the present findings under the Disapproval conditions could also be interpreted as indicating that teacher behavior of the Disapproving variety was positively reinforcing. The level of Disruptive Behaviors during each of the conditions when only Disapproving and Instructional attentions were available does appear to vary with the level of Disapproving Behaviors dispensed by the teacher. Unfortunately, the illness-caused absences and Easter break make the results less clear than hoped. It should be apparent that the effect of Frequent Disapproval on the behavior of the children is not subject to a simple interpretation. Some criticized behaviors decreased, some increased, and several possible controlling stimuli could have been operating with contradictory effects on behavior. It is obviously difficult in a field-experimental study of this complexity to maintain control of all the possibly relevant variables at once.

Another limitation of the present design should be noted. Because of a shortage of observation time under the desired classroom conditions, a sample of 10 children was observed daily. A procedure which included all children each day would have provided a stronger basis for analysis of effects on individuals. A rough analysis of individuals with the present data confirms, however, that an average of 76% of the students made changes in the same direction as the group changes. From Baseline, to No Approval, 81% of the students showed increases in Disruptive Behavior. When Approving Behavior became available, 75% of the students improved within two weeks. Discontinuing Approving Behavior a second time resulted in 78% of the students being more disruptive, while the final addition of Approving Behavior showed an increase in appropriate behavior for 71% of the children. Across condition changes, 5% of the children showed no change on the average, and 19% showed change (usually minor) in an opposite direction. Procedures which permitted specifications of which children were praised or criticized for which behaviors would be needed to clarify fully individual effects. It is quite possible that the children who changed opposite to the group trend were being responded to differently. Of course, there are many ways one can speculate here. In an as yet unpublished study we have shown that praising some children but not others leads to changes in the behavior only for the children who are praised. Results of this sort emphasize the importance of looking at individual contingencies.

Brief mention should be made of the possible ethical considerations involved in producing disruptive behaviors. One needs to weigh the potential gains in knowledge against the short-term or long-term deleterious effects on the children or teacher. On the basis of prior research and the return to baseline after the first No Approving Behaviors condition, the teacher and the experimenters were confident that appropriate behaviors could be readily reinstated at any time it was felt necessary. It may also be reassuring to know that this accelerated middle-primary class did achieve well academically during the year. The children completed all second and third grade work and were all performing on a fourth grade level by the end of the year.

IMPLICATIONS

This further demonstration of the importance of specific teacher behaviors in influencing classroom behavior has a double implication. First, the teacher who uses her Approving Behaviors as immediate consequences for good behavior should find that the frequency and duration of appropriate behaviors increase in her classroom (at least for most children). On the other hand, the teacher who cuddles the miscreant, tries pleasantly to get a child to stop behaving disruptively, talks with a child so that he "understands" what he was doing wrong, or who pleasantly suggests an alternative activity to a child who has been performing inappropriately, is likely to find an increase in the very behaviors she had hoped to reduce. This view of the functional importance of teacher's behavior in creating, maintaining, or reducing classroom behavior problems contrasts sharply with that generated by psychodynamic models of problem behaviors and what to do about them. Work of this sort also suggests a need to re-evaluate the popular cliche about the importance of the interaction of the "personality" of the teacher with that of the child in looking at classroom management procedures.

The suggestive evidence that peer reinforcement (among other stimuli) takes over when social reinforcement is not provided by teacher is given support by the recent work of Wahler (1967). Wahler has shown how preschool children can systematically control the behavior of their peers by differential use of social reinforcement. The more general implication for the teacher is this: unless an effort is made to support desirable classroom behaviors with appropriate consequences, the children's behavior will be controlled by others in ways likely to interfere with the teacher's objectives.

Finally, the possibility that critical comments may actually function to increase some behaviors upon which they are contingent cannot be overlooked. A recent study (Madsen, Becker, Thomas, Koser, and Plager, 1967), gives clear evidence that some forms of critical comment do function to strengthen behavior. The more often a teacher told first graders to "sit down", the more often they stood up. Only praising sitting seemed to increase sitting behavior.

REFERENCES

Becker, W. C., Madsen, C. H., Jr., Arnold, Carole R., and Thomas, D. R. The contingent use of teacher attention and praise in reducing classroom behavior problems. *Journal of Special Education*, 1967, 1, 287–307.

Bijou, S. W. and Baer, D. M. Some methodological contributions from a functional analysis of child development. In L. P. Lipsitt and C. S. Spiker (Eds.), *Advances in child development and behavior*. New York: Academic Press, 1963. Pp. 197–231.

Hart, Betty M., Allen, K. Eileen; Buell, Joan S., Harris, Florence R., and Wolf, M. M., Effects of social reinforcement on operant crying. *Journal of Experimental Child Psychology*, 1964, 1, 145–153.

Kerr, Nancy; Meyerson, L., and Michael, J. A procedure for shaping vocalizations in a mute child. In L. P. Ullman and L. Krasner (Eds.), *Case studies in behavior modification*. New York: Holt, Rinehart, & Winston, Inc., 1965. Pp. 366–370.

Lovaas, O. I., Freitag, G., Kinder, M. I., Rubenstein, D. B., Schaeffer, B., and Simmons, J. B. Experimental studies in childhood schizophrenia— Establishment of social reinforcers. Paper delivered at Western Psychological Association, Portland, April, 1964.

MADSEN, C. H., JR., BECKER, W. C., THOMAS, D. R., KOSER, LINDA, and PLAGER, ELAINE. An analysis of the reinforcing function of "sit down" commands. In R. K. Parker (Ed.), *Readings in educational psychology.* Boston: Allyn and Bacon, 1968 (in press).

WAHLER, R. G. Child-child interactions in free field settings: Some experimental analyses. *Journal of Experimental Child Psychology,* 1967, 5, 278–293.

ZIMMERMAN, ELAINE H. and ZIMMERMAN, J. The alteration of behavior in a special classroom situation. *Journal of the Experimental Analysis of Behavior,* 1962, 5, 59–60.

HILL M. WALKER
NANCY K. BUCKLEY
University of Oregon

The use of positive reinforcement in conditioning attending behavior[1]

Individual conditioning techniques were applied in a controlled setting to increase attending behavior of an underachieving 9-yr-old male subject. The procedure involved: (1) determining a stable response pattern, (2) introducing a treatment variable to establish a high rate of task-attending behavior, (3) measuring the effect of withdrawal of the treatment variable after attaining criterion performance, and (4) transferring control to the classroom. The interval of attending behavior required for reinforcement was systematically increased from 30 sec to 600 sec as the behavior came under experimental control. Manipulating the reinforcing contingencies measurably changed the proportion of attending behavior and the frequency and duration of non-attending events. Once the behaviors were under experimental control, procedures were established to program generalization and to maintain the behavior outside the experimental setting.

Reprinted from *Journal of Applied Behavior Analysis,* 1968, *1,* 245–50, with permission of the publisher and the authors. Copyright 1968 by the Society for the Experimental Analysis of Behavior, Inc.

---

[1] The authors gratefully acknowledge the assistance of Sister Eleanor Barbara from the Christie School in Portland, Oregon, for her efforts in recording data during the experiment.

In the last decade, conditioning techniques have been used effectively to establish a variety of response classes in children (*e.g.*, Patterson, 1965*a*, 1965*b*; Wolf, Risley, and Mees, 1964; Williams, 1959; Hart, Allen, Buell, Harris and Wolf, 1964). Conditioning techniques have been applied to parent-child interactions, hyperactivity, vomiting, stuttering, tantrums, operant crying, and encopresis in order to modify these behaviors in preferred directions. The results of these studies have provided impressive evidence for the efficacy and generality of these techniques.

Two important features of these techniques are that they have been applied under carefully controlled conditions and have focused on the behavior of individual subjects. The application of conditioning techniques in single subject designs permits manipulation of setting events and reinforcing stimuli and the evaluation of treatment effects by (1) establishing stable response rates, (2) introducing a treatment or controlling variable, and (3) withdrawing that variable (after criterion performance) in order to measure its effect upon behavior.

The purpose of the present study was to evaluate the effects of a shaping program for attending behavior of a 9-yr-old subject and to transfer control to the regular classroom.

PROCEDURES AND RESULTS

Subject and Setting

Phillip was a bright (WISC: 116), underachieving male who, upon referral, exhibited a number of deviant behaviors that were incompatible with successful, task-oriented performance in the classroom setting. Phillip was enrolled in the fourth grade and his chronological age at referral was 9 yr 6 months. His deviant behaviors in the classroom reportedly included verbally and physically provoking other children, not completing tasks, making loud noises and comments, coercing attention from the teacher, talking out of turn, and being easily distracted from a given task by ordinary classroom stimuli such as minor noises, movements of others, changes in lighting conditions, and a number of other stimuli common to a classroom setting. A series of observations from the regular classroom (totaling 100 min) indicated that he attended to assignments only 42% of the time.

The subject was enrolled in an experimental class for behaviorally disordered children for two months of the 1966–67 school year. Behaviors which were directly incompatible with appropriate social behavior and successful academic performance gradually decreased in frequency as Phillip's behavior appeared to come under control of the reinforcement contingencies established within the experimental class setting. Our observations indicated that his academic task rate increased markedly and his social behaviors appeared more appropriate and more easily tolerated by his peers. (Walker and Mattson, 1967.) Phillip's distractive behavior, however, continued at a high rate, even though consequences such as teacher approval and points earned for tangible objects were consistently withheld when he was not attending to his assignment.

Phillip's attending behavior appeared to be task-specific (Moyer and von Haller Gilmer, 1955) in that it seemed to vary with the given assignment. He appeared to work well in a programmed reading text (Sullivan Series) but seemed to produce very little from teacher-assigned work such as math problems. His attending behavior continued at a low rate in spite of "treatment", apparently because of the experimenter's inability to manipulate such controlling variables as: a large number of potentially distracting stimuli in the treatment setting, attention from peers for distractive behavior, escape from academic work, and reinforcement from frequent substitute activities (Goldstein and Seigle, 1961). As this behavior was not being controlled effectively in the experimental class setting, an individual conditioning program was designed for administration in a setting where these sources of distractive stimuli could be controlled.

Individual conditioning program. The educational task during baseline and treatment sessions consisted of programmed learning material. The subtraction and addition texts A-B, Lessons for Self-Instruction in the Basic Skills published by the California Test Bureau, were used throughout the conditioning program. The same texts were used in an attempt to control interest and difficulty factors. The programmed texts also reduced the number of task-related questions that the subject had to ask for purposes of explanation and clarification. No feedback was provided about the correctness of responses other than that provided by the text.

The subject participated in 40-min treatment sessions five days a week. The sessions each day were divided into three 10-min time blocks with 3-min breaks occurring after the first and second 10-min block each day. Treatment sessions were conducted in a setting where extraneous stimuli were reduced to a minimum. The setting contained a table, two chairs, a lamp, and the educational task material used by the subject.

After the subject's task rate and attending behavior had stabilized (Sidman, 1960) during baseline observations, the scheduled contingencies were described to the subject before the treatment condition began. The subject was told that when a given interval of time had elapsed, in which no distractions had occurred, a click would sound and the experimenter would enter a single check mark in a cumulative recording form which would indicate that the subject had earned a point. The subject was told that attending to the click represented a distraction and would result in loss of the point for that interval. The subject was allowed to exchange his points for a model of his choice at the conclusion of the treatment period. The number of points necessary for the model (160) was specified to the child when treatment began.

The response measure was established in accordance with Martin and Powers (1967) operant conditioning analysis of attention span. Attending behaviors for the subject involved looking at the assigned page, working problems, and recording responses. Non-attending behaviors were defined as those which were incompatible with task-oriented (attending) behavior. The following observable behaviors were classified as non-attending: (a) looking away from the text and answer sheet by eye movements or head turning; (b) bringing an object into his field of vision with head and eyes directed toward paper (other than pencil, book, and answer sheet necessary for the task); and (c) making marks other than those necessary for the task (*e.g.*, doodling).

During recording, the following notational system was used: (a) Z = beginning of a new attending period, (b) √ = continuation of the same event through successive 10-sec intervals, (c) / = a reinforcement (an audible click indicated reinforcement), and (d) — = subject attended to the click. A sample observation is given in Fig. 1.

The data in Fig. 1 are decoded as follows: 60 sec of attending behavior (interval six) was reinforced; Phillip attended to the sound of the click and immediately lost the point he had earned (interval seven); and non-attending sequence continued through the next seven intervals (interval 14); a new sequence of attending behavior occurred in intervals 15 and continued through 18, followed by 30 sec of non-attending; a new attending behavior began and terminated in interval 22 followed by a distraction (interval 23); attending behavior started in interval 24 and continued through interval 30 with reinforcement being delivered after interval 29.

Before data collection began, the senior author took simultaneous recordings of Phillip's attending behavior with observers who recorded his performance throughout the experiment. Inter-rater reliabilities were calculated by a percent agreement method in which number of agreements were divided by the total number of time intervals. These reliabilities ranged from 0.65 to 0.98. The initial training sessions were terminated

*1	2	3	4	5	6	7	8	9	10	11	12	13	14	15	16	17	18	19	20	21	22	23	24	25	26	27	28	29	30
Z	✓	✓	✓	✓	✓/	--								Z	✓	✓	✓				Z		Z	✓	✓	✓	✓	✓/	✓

*Each time interval represents 10 sec

FIGURE 1 Sample observation form.

when inter-rater reliability was 0.90 or above for five randomly selected time samples (10 min) of attending behavior. Simultaneous recordings were also taken periodically during the treatment process in order to provide a continual check on the inter-observer reliability. Agreement remained at 0.90 or above.

The intervals of attending behavior which met the criterion for reinforcement were: 30, 60, 120, 240, 480, and 600 sec. When Phillip had completed 20 intervals of 30-sec duration in which no non-attending sequences had occurred, the interval length was doubled to 60 sec. Thus, to proceed from one response interval criterion to another, the subject had to produce 10 min of attending behavior, e.g., 20 × 30 sec equals 600 sec or 10 min, or 10 × 60 sec equals 600 sec, or 10 min total. The conditioning program was administered according to the schedule in Table 1.

TABLE 1 Graduated scale for changing response intervals and administering reinforcers.

# of successfully completed intervals	Duration of interval	# of reinforcers received	
		(Events)	(Points)
20	30 sec	20 × 1	
10	60 sec	10 × 2	
5	120 sec	5 × 4	
2.5	240 sec	2.5 × 8	
1.2	480 sec	1.2 × 16	
1*	600 sec	1 × 20	

Completed three intervals to criterion.

During the initial criterion level of 30 sec, one point was administered on 20 separate occasions. In the final criterion interval of 600 sec, a total of 20 points was administered on *one* occasion (at completion of the interval). The reinforcement contingency was withdrawn when the subject had completed three 10-min distraction-free intervals in succession.

As can be seen in Fig. 2, the subject's attending behavior was quite low during the Base Operant Rate Condition, averaging only 33% of the sessions. Introduction of the Reinforcement Contingency Condition immediately increased attending behavior, which grew to average 93% of the sessions. When the reinforcement contingency was withdrawn, under the extinction condition, the attending behavior declined to its original lower level, averaging 44% of the sessions.

In Fig. 3, the response measures of duration and frequency of non-attending events displayed a similar alteration in rate when the experimental variable was manipulated. During Base Operant Rate, the mean duration of non-attending events was 21 sec and the mean frequency was 19

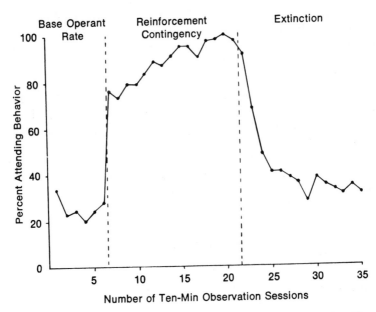

FIGURE 2 Percentage of attending behavior in successive time samples during the individual conditioning program.

non-attending events per 10-min time sample. These rates were reduced to zero by the end of the Reinforcement Contingency period. During extinction, frequency of non-attending behaviors returned to pretreatment levels, but the duration of non-attending behavior rose far above its baseline rate.

Generalization program. When the subject's behavior had returned to baseline levels, after the reinforcement contingency was withdrawn, Phillip was placed on a variable-interval schedule in the regular classroom setting where his behavior was reinforced (on the average) with one point for each 30-min bloc of attending behavior. This 30-min block of time was consistent with the criterion interval for Phillip's attending behavior in the laboratory setting and one which his teacher could reasonably manage in the regular classroom.

A point record form was placed on Phillip's desk each day in the regular classroom. Phillip's teacher was provided with a variable-interval schedule on which she gave one point to Phillip, on the average, of every 30 min of appropriate attending behavior. If Phillip engaged in other than appropriate attending behavior, the teacher was instructed to withhold reinforcement for the interval in which it occurred.

The data describing the results of the generalization program are presented in Fig. 4. After the first 10-min session the program appeared to maintain attending behavior at a high level.

DISCUSSION

As the data in Fig. 2 and Fig. 3 attest, systematic manipulation of the reinforcement contingency during the individual conditioning program produced significant changes in the response measures of percentage of attending behavior and frequency and duration of non-attending behavioral events. Upon withdrawal of the reinforcement contingency, the behavior returned to pretreatment levels, thus indicating that the alteration in behavior was due to the manipulated, experimental variable rather than to the influence of an unknown or chance variable.

Under the generalization program, Phillip reconditioned quickly. As indicated earlier, Phillip was placed on a variable-interval 30-min schedule which delivered reinforcement on an average of once per 30 min for producing task-oriented, distraction-free behavior. The data in Fig. 4 were

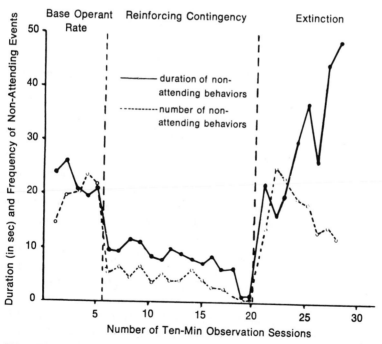

FIGURE 3 Mean duration and frequency of non-attending events per 10-min session during the individual conditioning program.

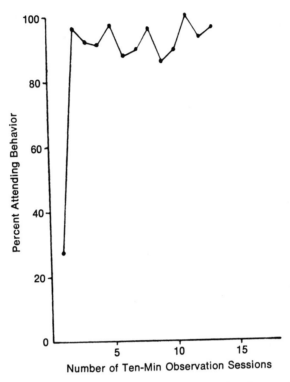

FIGURE 4 Proportion of attending behavior in the regular classroom during the generalization program.

taken in a regular classroom setting where the number of potentially distracting stimuli was much greater than in the controlled setting where the subject was initially conditioned. Each tangible reinforcing event was accompanied by the administration of attention, praise, and social approval from the teacher. It is hoped that in future the higher rates of attending behavior produced by the subject will come under the control of such natural reinforcers as task completion, positive feedback, academic success, and the acquisition of new knowledge.

The functional analysis of Phillip's attending behavior suggests that individual conditioning techniques can be used to acquire efficient, reinforcement control over behaviors which are difficult to modify in regular classroom settings. Once the behavior has been brought under experimental control, procedures can be established to schedule generalization and to maintain the modified performance in settings where maintaining stimuli operate in an uncontrolled fashion. The results of this study appear to have implications for treatment of a variety of subject-specific behaviors which actively interfere with successful academic performance among children in the educational setting.

REFERENCES

GOLDSTEIN, H. and SEIGLE, D. M. Characteristics of educable mentally handicapped children. In J. H. Rothstein (Ed.), *Mental retardation*. New York: Holt, Rinehart & Winston, 1961. Pp. 204–230.

HART, B. M., ALLEN, K. E., BUELL, J. S., HARRIS, F. R., and WOLF, M. M. Effects of social reinforcement on operant crying. *Journal of Experimental Child Psychology*, 1964, 1, 145–153.

MARTIN, G. L. and POWERS, R. B. Attention span: an operant conditioning analysis. *Exceptional Children*, 33 (8), 1967, 565–576.

MOYER, K. E. and VON HALLER GILMER, B. Attention spans of children for experimentally designed toys. *Journal of Genetic Psychology*, 1955, 87, 187–201.

PATTERSON, G. R. A learning theory approach to the treatment of the school phobic child. In L. Ullmann and L. Krasner (Eds.), *Case studies in behavior modification*. New York: Holt, Rinehart & Winston, 1965. Pp. 279–284.

PATTERSON, G. R. An application of conditioning techniques to the control of a hyperactive child. In L. Ullmann and L. Krasner (Eds.), *Case studies in behavior modification*. New York: Holt, Rinehart & Winston, 1965. Pp. 370–375.

SIDMAN, M. *Tactics of scientific research*. New York: Basic Books, Inc., 1960.

WALKER, H. M. and MATTSON, R. H. Identification and treatment of social emotional problems. Interim Report to USOE, May 1967.

WILLIAMS, C. D. The elimination of tantrum behavior by extinction procedures. *Journal of Abnormal and Social Psychology*, 1959, 59, 269.

WOLF, M. M., RISLEY, T. R., and MEES, H. L. Application of operant conditioning procedures to the behavior problems of an autistic child. *Behavior Research and Therapy*, 1964, 1, 305–312.

DAVID S. KUYPERS
University of Illinois

WESLEY C. BECKER
University of Illinois

K. DANIEL O'LEARY
State University of New York at Stony Brook

How to make
a token system fail[1]

A token system was instituted in an adjustment class of six third and fourth graders. The aim of the study was to examine aspects of token systems critical in making them effective. The results indicated a significant degree of improvement in behavior attributable to the token program, but when compared to the highly effective program reported by O'Leary and Becker (1967), it is apparent that an effective program requires more than tokens and back up reinforcers.

Token systems of reinforcement have usually been implemented in classrooms when the available social reinforcers such as teacher praise and approval have been ineffective in controlling the behavior of the children. Token systems involve the presentation of a "token" (e.g., a checkmark) following the emission of specified responses. When the child has accumulated a sufficient number of tokens, he is then able to exchange them for "back up" reinforcers (e.g., candy, toys). The tokens initially function as

Reprinted from *Exceptional Children*, 1968, 35, 2, 101–9, with permission of the authors. Reprinted with permission of The Council for Exceptional Children.

―――
[1] This study was supported by the National Institutes of Health, Grant No. HD 00881-05.

neutral stimuli, and they acquire reinforcing properties by being exchangeable for the back up reinforcers. Teacher praise and approval are often paired with the tokens, in order to increase the effectiveness of praise and approval as conditioned reinforcers. A general goal of token systems is to transfer control of responding from the token systems to other conditioned reinforcers such as teacher praise and grades.

Different investigators have reported upon the success of token systems in controlling the behavior of children in classrooms where the usual social reinforcers were ineffective (Birnbrauer, Bijou, Wolf, & Kidder, 1965; Birnbrauer & Lawler, 1964; Birnbrauer, Wolf, Kidder, & Tague, 1965; O'Leary & Becker, 1967).

Teachers operating successful token programs in these studies have usually been explicitly trained in the systematic use of principles of operant behavior, and much of the success of the programs is most likely due to the general application of principles other than those governing the use of tokens per se. The central aspect of a token system is the pairing of teacher praise with tokens which are backed up by an effective reinforcer. In most effective studies, however, many other procedures have also been used. For example, praise for appropriate behavior and ignoring of disruptive behavior are used at times when tokens are not being dispensed. Time out (or isolation) is often used when intensely disruptive behaviors occur. Systematic contingencies in the form of privileges are often applied throughout the day. The children following the rules are the ones who get to help teacher, to be first in line, to choose an activity, etc. The principle of shaping is also systematically applied. Praise, privileges, and tokens are not administered for achieving an absolute standard of performance, but for improving behavior or for maintaining a high level of acceptable behavior.

The present study is one of several aimed at clarifying the important components of effective token systems. The authors' objective is primarily to make clear to those who might adopt such systems where things can go wrong if a token system is attempted without full consideration of the many variables important to success. The study uses a general procedure which was shown to be very effective when coupled with training in behavior theory, a time out procedure, shaping, and differential social reinforcement throughout the day (O'Leary & Becker, 1967). The present study, however, examines the effectiveness of the token system by itself in a classroom in which no other modifications were made in the teacher's handling of the class. The study approximates what might happen if a teacher read about a token system and tried to use it mechanically without a fuller understanding of those basic principles and supplementary procedures which are often used in successful studies but which are not emphasized or made explicit.

The study was planned to include additional phases to train the teacher in behavior principles; following this, a more effective program would have been established. However, at the request of the teacher, it was necessary to terminate the study prior to its completion. We will come back to this point in the discussion.

METHOD

The subjects who participated in this study were six third grade and six fourth grade children who were described as socially maladjusted. The children were typically assigned to an adjustment class when they showed such behaviors as temper tantrums, fighting, failure to pay attention in class, inability to work on their own, and academic retardation. While the token system of reinforcement was in effect for the entire class, observations were conducted on only three of the children at each grade level—six children in all. Four of the children were selected because they engaged in a high rate of inappropriate and disruptive behavior, and two were selected because the teacher reported a low incidence of highly disruptive behavior in relation to the other class members. Two of the children had previously attended a classroom at another school in which a token system of reinforcement had been used (O'Leary & Becker, 1967).

Observations

The incidence of inappropriate classroom behaviors of the four highly disruptive children was recorded by two undergraduate students during the morning between 9:30 and 11:30. Between 1:00 and 2:00 in the afternoon, three undergraduate observers recorded the behavior of six children who included the four observed in the morning plus two children who were reported by teacher not to show much disruptive behavior. Deviant behaviors were defined as behaviors likely to be incompatible with group learning conditions. Definitions used for six classes of deviant behaviors, and one class of relevant behavior, are as follows:

CODING CATEGORIES FOR CHILDREN

DEVIANT BEHAVIOR

Gross motor behaviors. Getting out of seat, standing up, walking around, running, hopping, skipping, jumping, rocking chair, moving chair, knees on chair. Include such gross physical movements as arm flailing, feet swinging, and rocking.

Disruptive noise. Tapping feet, clapping, rattling papers, tearing papers, throwing book on desk, slamming desk top, tapping pencil or other objects on desk. Be conservative, rate what you hear, not what you see, and do not include accidental dropping of objects or noise made while performing gross motor behaviors.

Disturbing others. Grabbing objects or work, knocking neighbor's books off desk, destroying another's property, throwing objects at another without hitting, pushing with desk. Only rate if someone is there.

Contact. Hitting, pushing, shoving, pinching, slapping, striking with objects, throwing object which hits another person, poking with object. Do not attempt to make judgments of intent. Rate any physical contact.

Orienting responses. Turning head or head and body to look at another person, showing objects to another child, attending to another child. Must be of 4 seconds duration to be rated and is not rated unless seated. Any turn of 90 degrees or more from desk while seated is rated.

Verbalizations. Carrying on conversations with other children when it is not permitted, calling out answers to questions or comments without being called on, calling teacher's name to get her attention, crying, screaming, singing, whistling, laughing, coughing, or blowing nose. Do not rate lip movements. Rate what you hear, not what you see.

RELEVANT BEHAVIOR

Time on task, e.g., answering questions, listening, raising hand for teacher attention, working at assigned task, reading. Must include whole 10 second interval except for orienting responses of less than four seconds duration.

The children were observed in a fixed order for 22 minutes each session, three times a week. Observations were made on a 20 second observe, 10 second record basis. Each observer had a clipboard with a stop watch and a recording sheet. Simple symbols were used to indicate the occurrence of a particular class of behavior. A given class of behavior could be rated only once in an observation interval.

Percentage of deviant behavior was defined as the percentage of intervals in which one or more deviant behaviors occurred. Reliability was checked on the average of once a week, and was calculated by dividing the number of agreements on behavior code and time interval by the number of agreements plus disagreements.

Class Activities

For most of the day the children were in a single classroom with one teacher. During the morning the children's activities consisted of group reading lessons and individual seat work. During the afternoon the first 40 minute period consisted of a group arithmetic lesson and the second 40 minute period consisted of either art or music in another room for the fourth graders and art or spelling for the third graders.

Experimental Phases

Baseline. During the baseline phase, the teacher was asked to handle the children according to her usual techniques and procedures. Observers had recorded the children's behavior for approximately three weeks before the collection of baseline observations was begun. This initial period was instituted in order to allow the children to adapt to the observers' presence in the classroom.

Token reinforcement phase. The following written instructions were given to the teacher and discussed with her. These instructions were used as the basis for the token reinforcement stage.

A. INSTRUCTIONS FOR INITIAL INTRODUCTION OF TOKEN PROGRAM.

1. Prior to the explanation of the token economy to the children, a list of rules should be written on the blackboard and left there while the program is in effect. (The rules worked out with the teacher were: *stay in seats, raise hand, quiet, desk clear, face front,* and *work hard.* For the art period for the third graders the rules were: *quiet, work hard,* and *be polite.*)

2. Explain to the children that they will be rated on how well they follow the rules from 1:00 to 2:30. Spiral notebooks will be attached to their desks, and every rating period the teacher will put a number from 1 to 10 in their notebooks. The better a child follows the rules the higher the number he will receive.

3. By earning points in this way, the children will be able to win prizes. They must have a certain number of points in order to win a prize. Show the children the prizes and explain that 10 points earns a prize from this box (show an example) and 25 points earns a prize from this box. Do not let the children handle the prizes.

4. Emphasize that at all other times when the children are not being rated their behavior will not affect their rating during the afternoon period.

5. Explain to the fourth graders that their other teachers will rate them when they leave the classroom, and that they will have to bring back a slip with their number on it signed by their teacher. If they do not bring back this slip, they will not receive any points that day. Also explain that the other children in the art and music class will not be told about their point system.

6. Emphasize that they will not receive prizes every day, and that sometimes they will have to collect points over two or more days in order to obtain prizes. However, they will be told how long they have to work to earn a prize.

B. GENERAL INSTRUCTIONS FOR OPERATION OF TOKEN PROGRAM.

1. Each day before the rating period, go over the rules with the children. Point out that they can earn prizes, tell them how many points they must have to win different types of prizes, and then show them some of the prizes they can win.

2. When rating a child, point out the rules he followed in order to receive the points he did. "I'm giving you 8 points because. . . ," "I'm not giving you 10 points because. . . ." Also indicate what behaviors could be improved on to earn full points.

3. At all times, except when prizes are being shown to the class or when the children are picking out the prizes they have earned, the prizes should be stored in a location where the children cannot reach them.

4. If the children mention certain types of prizes they would like to be able to earn or if they do not appear interested in any of the prizes available, please notify the investigator as soon as possible.

5. Record points on two pages. One will be picked up each day. Enter ratings from art and music teachers into the book also.

6. Except for the first day of the token program, prizes should be given out at the end of the school day. On the first day give out prizes after the third rating period.

7. The children will be rated from 1 to 10 on how well they follow the classroom rules and behave in class. Rules can be modified or changed, but if this is done, notify the class and put the change on the blackboard.

8. The value of the prize will be changed as the children are required to earn more points to win prizes. The number of points required will be indicated on the appropriate boxes.

9. A child should be very well behaved to earn the highest value prizes. Do not allow the children to try to talk you into giving them more points. Make a judgment and then explain that he earned only so many points, but he can earn more by behaving better.

Two values of prizes were used—one group in the 5¢ to 10¢ range, and one group in the 15¢ to 19¢ range. They included such things as candy, gliders, balls, pencils, and clay.

For third graders ratings were given after each 30 minute period. Since the fourth graders left for art or music during the second 30 minute period, the problem was initially handled by doubling the points earned in the first period and by having the art or music teacher give a rating for that period. After four days the system was changed so that both third and fourth graders were rated after two 40 minute periods. During the first four days prizes were distributed each day. After that they were distributed every other day. The number of points required to earn prizes was gradually increased from 10 to 30 for lower value prizes and 25 to 35 for higher value prizes.

The teacher used her own judgment in making ratings within the guidelines given above. She was informed of how the observers rated the children the first few days of the program, but no attempt was made to determine her ratings. In all other aspects of her behavior, the teacher was expected to continue as she had before.

Baseline two. The token system was withdrawn for two weeks and baseline conditions reestablished. It was during this period that the teacher decided not to continue with the study.

RESULTS

Reliability

During the afternoon observations, interobserver reliability for individual children for the 13 day baseline period ranged from 64 to 98 percent agreement with an average of 80 percent. During the token period the interobserver reliability ranged from 69 to 100 percent with an average of 87 percent. For the second baseline, the range was 68 to 100 percent with an average of 82 percent. The reliabilities for morning observations ranged from 52 to 100 percent with an average of 85 percent.

Group Data

For all six children in the afternoon, the average percentage of deviant behavior during the baseline period was 54. During the token period the average decreased to 27.8 percent and then increased to 41.5 percent when the tokens were removed. The daily averages for the different periods have been plotted graphically in Figure 1. If fewer than four children were observed on any day, then that day was eliminated from the analysis. The single day that a substitute teacher was in the classroom was also eliminated. An analysis of variance, using the average percentage of deviant behavior for each child during each period, indicated that the effects of periods were significant beyond the .01 level ($F = 11.27$, $df = 2$).

The average daily percentage of deviant behavior for the four children observed both in the morning and afternoon is plotted graphically by days for the different periods for both the morning and afternoon observations (see Figure 2). A child had to be observed in both the morning and afternoon for his percentage of deviant behavior to be included in the analyses,

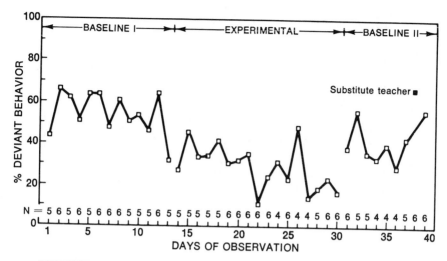

FIGURE 1 Percentage of deviant behavior as a function of experimental conditions for children observed during the afternoon.

and if fewer than three children were observed on any day, then that day was eliminated from the analysis. The average percentage of deviant behavior for the first baseline period was 53.2 for morning and 54.3 for afternoon observations. For the token periods the percentages were 45.0 (A.M.) and 35.5 (P.M.); and for the second baseline they were 58.5 (A.M.) and 50.4 (P.M.). These data show little, if any, generalization of improved behavior from the afternoon period when the token system was in effect to the morning period when the token system was not in effect. No statistical tests were carried out on the generalization data because of wide individual variations in effect. The important results of the study are made clear by examination of the individual graphs.

Individual Data

The individual graphs show that four children (1 through 4, Figure 3) improved considerably under the token system, and two showed at best occasional good days. No consistent individual gains occurred during the morning period when individual data were examined (these graphs are not presented). Of interest is the fact that children 4 and 6 had participated in the earlier program by O'Leary and Becker (1967). Child 5 rarely responded to the new program, and often would not even keep his point book on his desk.

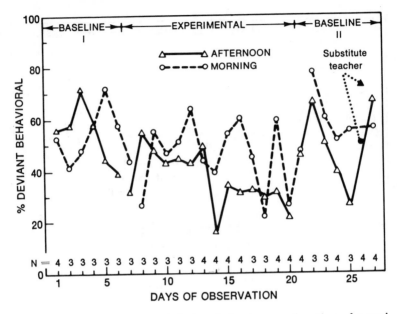

FIGURE 2   Percentage of deviant behavior as a function of experimental conditions for children observed during morning and afternoon.

DISCUSSION

Although an average significant effect of the token program was demonstrated, it is quite clear from the individual graphs and the generalization measures that the program was only marginally effective. Many interpretations are always possible when there is a failure to establish experimental control over behavior; however, a number of the findings when compared with those from the earlier study by O'Leary and Becker (1967) suggest some reasonable conclusions. The reader should first keep in mind that the formal token system was very similar to that used by O'Leary and Becker, including the shift to a two day delay in back up reinforcers after the first four days. The programs were carried out at similar times during the day, on similar children in adjustment classes. In the first study (O'Leary & Becker, 1967) there were more Negro children and the general level of deviant behavior was higher during baseline. The token system in the first study produced a dramatic shift from approximately 80 percent deviant behavior to under 10 percent, and it was effective for all children. Furthermore, although generalization measures were not taken, repeated reports by diverse observers indicated a dramatic change in the behavior of the chil-

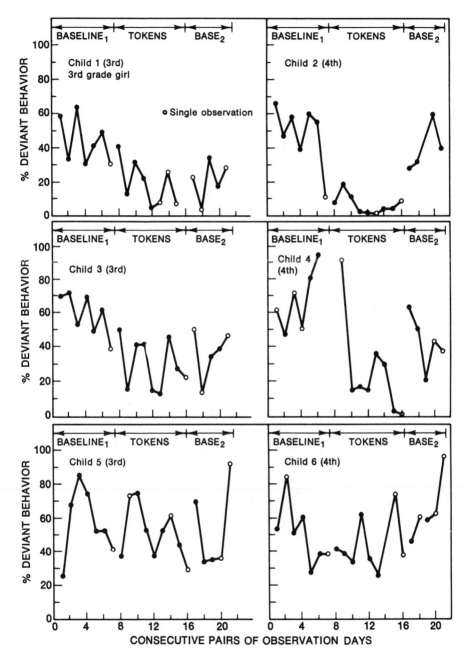

FIGURE 3 Percentage of deviant behavior for individual children based on afternoon observations.

dren throughout the day. Some of the keys to the differences in findings include the following:

1. Tokens or points were given for meeting an absolute standard in the present study, rather than for improvement. A shaping procedure was not used by the teacher. Under these conditions, the two children who were considered by the teacher to be less troublesome to begin with (children 1 and 2) responded very well to the program. While these two children had an average percentage of deviant behavior during baseline approximating that of the other children, it was qualitatively different behavior. Their behaviors involved talking and turning around in their seats rather than fighting, making loud noises, and wandering around the room. It was easy for the teacher to give them high ratings and for them to respond to the reinforcement system. The children who could not as easily meet the standards set by the teacher could have been punished for improved behavior by receiving low point scores. The high degree of variability over days and between children is precisely what would be expected when an absolute standard is applied.

2. No attempt was made to have the teacher systematically apply differential social reinforcement in between the times when points were awarded or at other times during the day. This aspect of the earlier program was probably responsible for much of its effectiveness. Points which are awarded 30 or 40 minutes later are not enough to help a child learn more appropriate behaviors. With effective and continuous use of praise for good behaviors and ignoring of deviant behaviors, immediate consequences can be brought to bear on such behavior, especially when praise has been made important to the children through its pairing with tokens. The lack of generalization effects are most likely due to this difference in procedures. (We had hoped to clearly show this by introducing systematic social reinforcement in the next stage of the experiment.) Observations of the teacher throughout the day indicated that she would intermittently pay attention to deviant behaviors and would often ignore the children when they were behaving well. If paying attention is reinforcing and if ignoring amounts to an extinction condition, these teacher behaviors would be affecting the children in a way opposite to that desired.

3. The teacher in this study was not trained through a workshop in the systematic application of behavioral principles. Such training may be important in knowing how to shape behavior and how to effectively use differential social reinforcement.

4. Some initial difficulties were encountered in getting the fourth graders to respond to the program (children 2, 4, and 6, Figure 3). They typically received high ratings (appropriately given) by their art and music teachers which made it less necessary for them to behave in the classroom to earn points. The point system was eventually changed so

that good behavior in both periods was essential (in the move to 30 points for a lower prize and 35 for a higher one).

5. Another potential problem was that during baseline the teacher considered the level of deviant behavior to be close to an acceptable level. She had a great capacity for tolerating disruptions in the class as long as they did not interfere with her work with an individual child. Also, in making judgments about following the rules, she was much more lenient than our judgment would deem appropriate. Her frame of reference would likely foster the reinforcement of deviant behaviors, as defined in the present study, and leave the level of improvement at a low level.

The authors titled this paper, "How to make a token system fail." In actuality, the system functioned as expected—as far as it went. The minimal token system employed was statistically effective and could not have been much more effective, if differential social reinforcement and shaping must be a central part of a workable system. The real failure in this experiment was the failure to give the teacher sufficient support and information to keep her working with the researchers so that subsequent phases of the study could demonstrate more definitively the importance of additional procedures. The behavior of the morning observers was a particular source of irritation for the teacher. Although instructed to fade into the background, two of them did not. Chewing and cracking gum, talking, and obviously watching the children were among their behaviors found irritating by the teacher. Her warnings were not responded to soon enough, although eventually one of the observers was fired. By then it was too late to save the study. There were other failures in the administration of the study which produced unnecessary irritations for the teacher, such as intruding on her evening and weekend time to discuss problems.

We explicitly point out these problems so that others may profit from our mistakes. Great care should be exercised in selecting and training observers, in providing guidelines for the supervisory staff, and in preparing the teacher for what is coming. While the teacher emphasized the role of the observer's behavior in her decision to stop the study, the study was not stopped until we had withdrawn the token system for about four days. Problem behavior as well as the concerns of the teacher had increased. Although the teacher agreed to let us finish the second baseline period, better preparation of the teacher on our part could have saved the study.

IMPLICATIONS

A token system is usually designed to make more usual social reinforcers effective for children and lead to an elimination of the token system. These objectives involve the use of a complex set of procedures. The findings of this study when contrasted with those from O'Leary and Becker (1967) should suggest to the reader who is interested in applying a token system some of the important procedures which may be missed or not thought important in looking at the literature on token systems. If the token system involves delays in giving tokens or points (to simplify the procedure for the teacher), it is probably very important to use differential social reinforcement at all times. Explicitly, this involves giving praise and privileges for improvement in behavior, and ignoring (rather than criticizing or distracting) children showing deviant behaviors—unless someone is being hurt. In the latter case, withdrawal of all social attention and loss of the opportunity to earn tokens by isolating the child (time out) is the procedure of choice. It is also important to use tokens and praise to shape improved behavior, so that all children can be affected by positive reinforcement. Catch the child being good. Focus on that aspect of behavior which is an improvement (e.g., in seat rather than out, even if not yet working) and reinforce it. Look for sequential steps toward improvement which can be successively reinforced (in seat, not turning and talking to neighbors, desk cleared of excess materials, paying attention, working, working diligently).

A token system is not a magical procedure to be applied in a mechanical way. It is simply one tool within a larger set of tools available to the teacher concerned with improving the behavior of children. The full set of equipment is needed to do the job right.

REFERENCES

BIRNBRAUER, J. S., BIJOU, S. W., WOLF, M. M., & KIDDER, J. D. Programmed instruction in the classroom. In P. L. Ullman and L. Krasner (Eds.), *Case studies in behavior modification*. New York: Holt, Rinehart, and Winston, 1965. Pp. 358–363.

BIRNBRAUER, J. S., & LAWLER, J. Token reinforcement for learning. *Mental Retardation*, 1964, **2**, 275–279.

BIRNBRAUER, J. S., WOLF, M. M., KIDDER, J. D., & TAGUE, C. E. Classroom behavior of retarded pupils with token reinforcement. *Journal of Experimental Child Psychology*, 1965, **2**, 219–235.

O'LEARY, K. D., & BECKER, W. C. Behavior modification of an adjustment class: A token reinforcement program. *Exceptional Children*, 1967, **33**, 637–642.

7

CONTROL OVER
SELF-INJURIOUS
BEHAVIOR

In clinical work with psychotic children, the most upsetting sight one will encounter is that of a child mutilating himself—biting off his fingers, tearing at his shoulder, banging his head against the floor until it bleeds. Such children usually are placed in camisoles (straitjackets) or strapped to a bed in arm and leg restraints (spread-eagled), day after day, month after month, even for years. We say that such children are psychotic, since their behavior is so chaotic, self-defeating, and senseless. One tries to imagine what a disturbed mind, what psychotic confusions must underlie such violence. Such behavior typically leaves the viewer scared, helpless, and filled with pity.

The main point of the two studies in this section is that self-injurious behavior is in fact quite understandable. That is, it is lawfully related in a predictable manner to certain environmental events. When we have clarified these relations and can control these behaviors, then we can say we understand the behavior.

The reinforcement control over self-destruction is very striking in both the studies we report here, a fact that leads one to suspect that self-destructive behavior is operant behavior. It is operant behavior when it is controlled by its consequences, and the studies show that one can strengthen and weaken self-destructive behavior by presenting and withdrawing rein-forcers. The first time we demonstrated reinforcement control over self-destruction was reported in an earlier study (Lovaas *et al.*, 1965). That study also points to another (derived) form of control, namely S^D (dis-criminative stimulus) control. In fact, the studies demonstrate how highly discriminated the self-destructive acts can be. The child did not waste any blows, so to speak, but hurt himself only in those situations where it was most likely that he would be attended to. Such stimulus control gives fur-ther evidence of the operant nature of self-injurious behavior.

The decision to punish a child who hurts himself so terribly is not an easy one to make. But if punishment helps the child and if other methods are not available, then punishment is less difficult for the therapist or par-ent to contemplate. Notice that the "natural" thing to do, to express love and concern contingent on self-destruction, makes it worse. These findings point to a better definition of love than a mere description of a person's behavior toward another. To punish a child who hurts himself in order to end his pain may be a loving act. To fondle and comfort a child contin-gent on his hurting himself may worsen his condition; and such an ex-pression of "love" can be called destructive.

The Peterson and Peterson study is a natural corollary to the study by Lovaas and Simmons. Granted that one may be able to stop self-injurious behavior through the application of aversive stimuli, but is there a more humane way to treat the problem? Our aim must be to create an environ-ment that will produce, with the least pain, a complete and happy person. Aversive stimulation, therefore, must be viewed as an intervention valuable only for its efficiency in stopping such a behavior. If we can accomplish this aim without adding to the child's pain, we should certainly do so.

REFERENCE

Lovaas, O. I., Freitag, G., Gold, V. J. & Kassorla, I. C. Experimental studies in childhood schizophrenia: Analysis of self-destructive behavior. *Journal of Experimental Child Psychology*, 1965, 2, 67–84.

O. IVAR LOVAAS
JAMES Q. SIMMONS, M.D.
University of California at Los Angeles

Manipulation
of self-destruction
in three retarded children[1]

The study attempted to isolate some of the environmental conditions that controlled the self-destructive behavior of three severely retarded and psychotic children. In the extinction study subjects were placed in a room where they were allowed to hurt themselves, isolated from interpersonal contact. They eventually ceased to hurt themselves in that situation, the rate of self-destruction falling gradually over successive days. In the punishment study, subjects were administered painful electric shock contingent on the self-destructive behavior. (1) The self-destructive behavior was immediately suppressed. (2) The behavior recurred when shock was removed. (3) The suppression was selective, both

Reprinted from *Journal of Applied Behavior Analysis*, 1969, 2, 143–57, with permission of the publisher and the authors. Copyright 1969 by the Society for the Experimental Analysis of Behavior, Inc.

[1] These studies were supported by PHS Research Grant No. MH-11440 from the National Institute of Mental Health. Aspects of this manuscript were presented with the purpose of illustrating the use of aversive stimuli in behavior therapy work, at the Miami Symposium on the Prediction of Behavior: Aversive Stimulation, Marshall R. Jones (Editor), University of Miami Press, 1968. We express our appreciation for the help of the nursing staff at the Neuropsychiatric Institute at UCLA, and to the large number of students from the Department of Psychology who assisted in the project. We are particularly indebted to Mrs. Kathy Burnett, M.A., R.N., and Michael Clowers, of Southern Illinois University, for their valuable assistance in these studies.

465

across physical locales and interpersonal situations, as a function of the presence of shock. (4) Generalized effects on other, non-shock behaviors, appeared in a clinically desirable direction. Finally, a study was reported where self-destructive behavior increased when certain social attentions were given contingent upon that behavior.

A significant number of children, who are diagnosed as psychotic or severely retarded, manifest, at one time or another in their lives, self-destructive behavior. This behavior consists primarily of "head-banging" (against walls and furniture), "arm-banging" (against sharp corners), beating themselves on their heads or in their faces with their fists or knees, and biting themselves on wrists, arms, and shoulders. In some children, the self-destructive behavior can be severe enough to pose a major problem for the child's safety. Thus, one can frequently see that such children have removed large quantities of flesh from their bodies, torn out their nails, opened wounds in their heads, broken their noses, *etc.* Such severe forms of self-destruction often require restraints, either in the form of camisoles ("straitjackets") or by tying the child's feet and arms to his bed. Sometimes the self-destructive behavior may be sporadic, at other times it is long-lasting, necessitating such prolonged use of restraints that one can observe structural changes, such as demineralization, and shortening of tendons, and arrested motor development, secondary to disuse of limbs.

Such children pose major problems for both their parents and the personnel who care for them. First of all, there is the immediate threat to the child, either directly through tissue damage or indirectly through infections. There are secondary problems associated with self-destructive behavior which center on the curtailment of growth, psychological and otherwise, in the child who has to be restrained. Finally, the self-destructive child poses major psychological problems for those who take care of him, in the form of anxiety, demoralization, and hopelessness. The authors know of no treatment that effectively alleviates self-destructive behavior. The most common form of treatment consists of some combination of drugs and supportive, interpersonal therapy, and occasional electro-convulsive therapy. There is no evidence to demonstrate that any of these forms of treatment are effective. Conceivably, some treatments could make the child worse. There are no systematic studies that would support either outcome.

Finally, clinically speaking, such violent self-destruction forms an expression of a most severe psychotic state. If self-destruction is an expression of a psychosis, then an understanding of the events that affect self-destruction should throw some light on the psychosis itself.

An earlier paper (Lovaas, Freitag, Gold, and Kassorla, 1965a) reported an attempt to study self-destructive behavior in a systematic manner. Data were presented which indicated that the self-destructive behavior showed a great deal of lawfulness which could be accounted for by considering the self-destructive behavior as learned social behavior.

The present paper seeks to clarify further the variables that control self-destructive behavior. On the suggestion from the first study that such behavior is learned social behavior and is maintained by social reinforcement (*e.g.*, attention), the following relationships could be expected to exist: (a) one should observe a decrease and eventual disappearance of self-destructive behavior if the social consequences were withheld (that is, self-destructive behavior should extinguish); (b) one should observe an increase in self-destructive behavior if that behavior resulted in social reinforcement; and (c) the delivery of aversive stimuli, contingent upon such behavior, should serve to suppress it.

Punishment by the use of aversive stimuli or extinction through withdrawal of effective reinforcers ("ignoring") involves purposefully exposing the child to pain and raises ethical problems of what to do. In addition to punishment and extinction procedures, we could have attempted to check the pathological behavior by establishing incompatible behavior. A previous study (Lovaas *et al.*, 1965a) found that self-destructive behavior could be suppressed by building incompatible behaviors. Perhaps this would be the most humane procedure, since it involves exposing the child to minimal pain. However, the children to be treated here came from, and were to be returned to, state hospitals where maintaining incompatible behaviors was judged unfeasible. The wards were understaffed (a particular nurse having to deal with as many as 20 children) and were staffed by personnel unfamiliar with reinforcement procedures. In fact, the failure of the ward environment to provide reinforcement for alternative behaviors (coupled with the attention paid to the self-destruction) may have originally created, maintained, and increased the self-destruction. The viable alternatives, then, center on extinction by "ignoring" *versus* suppression with severe aversive stimulation. The potential therapeutic value of this intervention, once the children were returned from our clinic to the state hospitals, will be discussed after the data on aversive stimulation has been presented.

METHOD

The three children reported here were obtained by requesting that two of the state hospitals in Southern California point out their worst cases of self-destructive children. We then requested transfer of the first three children referred to the Neuropsychiatric Institute at UCLA. These children were all known, in their respective hospitals, from among thousands of children for the severity of their self-destructive behavior. The children were hospitalized at UCLA for the explicit and limited purpose of investigating their self-destructive behavior.

The three children, John, Linda, and Gregg, can be described as follows. John was an 8-yr-old boy with a diagnosis of severe mental retardation (IQ = 24). There was no known organic basis for his retardation. He had no speech and showed only a very limited understanding of language, such as simple commands. He would visually attend to adults, but in general had minimal social behavior. He did not imitate, was not toilet trained, and did not dress himself. At various times in his life he had evidenced severe psychotic behaviors, such as smearing and eating of feces, drinking from the toilet bowl, mouthing of objects, rocking, etc. He had no play behavior. His self-destructive behavior started when he was 2 yr old. A medical examination at the time he was three noted that "his fists and knuckles were used to bang the temple and forehead area to a degree in which bruising and contusions are resulted". Apparently his parents were initially partly successful in suppressing self-destructive behavior by teaching incompatible behaviors. For example, during one of his psychological examinations, at age five, his mother had him hold a cup in each hand to prevent him from hitting himself. The self-destructive behavior worsened over time and caused the parents to hospitalize him at the age of seven. For six months before this study he had been in continuous restraints on both legs and arms. He would become extremely disturbed and refuse food if the restraints were removed. At this point in his development he needed complete care in feeding, hygiene, and all other aspects of his functioning. He had been on a combination of tranquilizers during his prior hospitalization with no visible effect on his self-abusive behavior. When admitted to UCLA, he had multiple scars all over his head and face. He was extremely agitated, kicked and screamed, and in general appeared extremely frightened and out of control, with a heart rate exceeding 200. Two days after hospitalization, he had settled down to the hospital routine, and the agitation and fear were seemingly gone but would reappear as soon as he was taken out of restraints.

Linda was 8 yr old at the time of hospitalization at UCLA. She had an IQ of 33 and was diagnosed as mentally retarded, etiology unknown. She evidenced some psychotic features, primarily in the form of self-stimulatory behavior. She had no speech and her understanding of speech was limited to correct responses to primitive commands. She had a viral infection at the age of two, at which point she stopped walking for three months and subsequently evidenced a bizarre gait. She was not toilet trained, could not feed herself, and in general needed complete nursing care. Unlike John, she resisted affectionate contact. She had bilateral cataracts, thought to be congenital, and was effectively blind. Her self-destructive behavior went back to her seventeenth month, and had become so severe that she had been kept in continuous restraints for 1.5 yr before her admission to UCLA. When she came to UCLA her left ear was bleeding, she had multiple scabs on both ears, and multiple bruises on both legs. Unlike John, she did not seem apprehensive upon admission, and her heart rate was within normal range, although she laughed excessively and inappropriately. She wore wrist restraints, tied around her thighs in such a fashion as to prevent her from hitting her ears. To prevent her knees from reaching her head, and thereby damaging herself, she had been placed on her abdomen while in bed, where she would lie quietly for most of the day, flopping her foot up and down rhythmically.

The third child, Gregg, was 11 yr old. He was diagnosed as having craniostenosis with motoric impairment and severe retardation ($IQ = 13$). He had been hospitalized since the age of 3.5 yr. As a child he was described as hyperactive and irritable. He was not toilet trained and could not dress himself. His self-destructive behavior started when he was 2 yr old. He had spent most of the two preceding years in restraints, tied on legs and arms to the four corners of his bed. He appeared unable to walk and was confined to a wheelchair. He had shortened Achilles tendons and some demineralization secondary to disuse. When placed on the floor he would stand still on his toes, hunched over, with his back bent, but it was judged physically possible for him to walk. He did not talk, but evidenced considerable delayed echolalia, particularly when upset. His social development was as limited as his intellectual, although he enjoyed physical contact, such as tickling and stroking. Upon admission to UCLA, he had about the same amount of scar tissue on his face and scalp as had Linda and John. Our informal probes revealed that none of the children responded appropriately to the word "no". It is important to note that these children came from, and would return to, settings where available treatments had failed and probably would continue to do so. Unless an effective technique was discovered, in all likelihood these children would remain self-destructive.

All experiments were conducted in sparsely furnished wardrooms that contained a bed, chest of drawers, a chair, and an occasional table. Some of these rooms had adjoining observation rooms connected by one-way mirrors and sound equipment, permitting observation and recording of the child's behavior. Recordings were made on a button panel, where each button corresponded to a particular behavior, the panel being wired into an Esterline Angus multiple pen recorder. A more detailed account of this observation technique has been given in a previous paper (Lovaas *et al.*, 1965*b*). The observers were instructed to depress the button corresponding to a particular behavior and keep it depressed for the duration of that behavior. Three observers were randomly assigned to record at various times throughout the study, so as to rule out changes in the recordings being associated with peculiarities in any one observer. The observers met with experimenters, who defined the behaviors in the presence of the child. If the observers did not exceed 90% agreement on any one behavior before the actual recordings, they were trained to do so. In no instance did the training exceed 1 hr. If agreement was not achieved in that time, the response was redefined.

The following behaviors were recorded (although all behaviors were not recorded in any one study): *Self-destructive behavior* was particularly unambiguous in its occurrence. The child would strike his head with his fists or hit his head against the side of the bed, the blows generating considerable noise; the observers agreed that this would have caused considerable pain to them had they done likewise. Their agreement in recording this behavior exceeded 95%, without training. Two additional behaviors were recorded, in an attempt to measure more generalized changes which might help determine whether a particular form of intervention, such as aversive stimulation, should be employed. In particular, changes were recorded in withdrawal from attending adults. The adult would attempt to maintain close physical proximity to the child (less than 1 ft) and reestablish that contact as soon as the child moved away. *Withdrawal* was scored when the child was in the process of moving away from the adult [certain instances of this behavior were quite unambiguous, such as the child struggling to get off the adult's lap (*cf.* John on lap), or to withdraw a hand (*cf.* Linda during walk)]. An instance of emotional behavior, *whining,* was also recorded. The child would emit an annoying, screeching sound, without tears, and without communicating sadness or apprehension, but rather anger.

The three studies performed on these children, extinction through removal of interpersonal consequences, suppression by the use of painful shock, and increasing self-destruction through attention, are presented separately.

Extinction Study

If the self-destructive behavior had been originally shaped by its effect on the social environment and if the maintenance of the behavior was dependent upon its producing social effects or consequences, then the removal of such consequences should weaken, and eventually stop, the self-destruction. That is, the behavior should extinguish. We had previously attempted extinction, in an informal manner, on another self-destructive boy, Rick (attending personnel were instructed not to give him attention when he hit himself, and to leave his room if he started self-destruction while they

were present). Rick eventually did stop hitting himself under this arrangement, but the reduction in self-destruction was not immediate, and even
took a turn for the worse when the extinction was first initiated, causing
considerable bleeding and apparent physical discomfort. We feared, therefore, for the children's safety, and decided not to expose Linda to this treatment (her ears were already badly damaged), limiting the extinction to
John and Gregg.

Extinction was carried out in a small, 12 by 12 ft experimental room
with a bed and occasional furniture. The experimental room was connected to an adjoining observation room by one-way screens and sound
equipment. The extinction sessions were conducted in the morning, on
consecutive days. Each session lasted for 1.5 hr. The child was placed on
the bed and his restraints removed; then the attending adults left the child
alone. An observer in the observation room recorded each act of self-
destructive behavior.

Figure 1 shows the extinction data on John and Gregg in terms of
total frequency over days of extinction. The abscissa gives successive days
of extinction and the ordinate gives the total number of self-destructive
acts on any one day. John started with a high rate of 2750 self-destructive
acts in the first 1.5 hr of extinction, declining to zero by the tenth session.
John hit himself almost 9000 times before he quit. The data on Gregg are
consistent with those of John: from a high of more than 900 self-destructive acts during the early part of extinction, his rate fell gradually to a low
of 30 acts during the last part of extinction. It was different from John's
in two respects: Gregg took more sessions for extinction and showed more
irregularity. Actually, only the first 17 days of extinction represented "true"
extinction, since certain experimental manipulations were superimposed
upon the extinction from Session 18 on. These are discussed more fully in
the subsequent section.

We have replicated the extinction operations on other institutionalized children, with similar, but not as intense, self-destructive behaviors
as those of John and Gregg. In each instance, the self-destructive behavior
showed a very gradual drop over time, being particularly vicious in the
early stages of extinction. Our data are consistent with those reported by
others. For example, Wolf, Risley, and Mees (1964) observed a similar
cessation of tantrumous and self-destructive behavior in an autistic child
when the child was isolated from interpersonal contact contingent upon
such behavior.

In summary, we can conclude that although extinction seemingly
works, it is not an ideal form of treatment because the large amount of
self-destructive behavior during the early stages of extinction subjects the
child to much apparent discomfort. For some children extinction is ill-
advised because the self-destructive behavior is severe enough to pose a

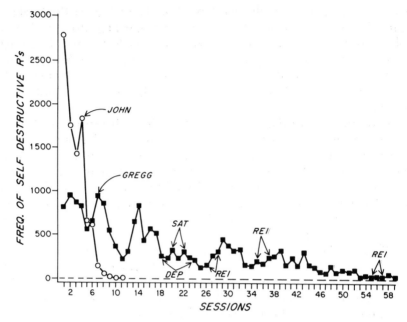

FIGURE 1 Extinction of John's and Gregg's self-destructive behavior, over successive days of extinction, during 90-min sessions with total number of self-destructive acts on any one day given on the ordinate. SAT stands for satiation, DEP for deprivation, and REI for reinforcement.

high risk of severe or fatal damage, for example in children who bite themselves, tearing tissue. Another disturbing feature of the extinction data pertains to the highly situational nature of effectiveness: while the self-destructive behavior fell to zero in the room used for extinction, it remained unaffected in other situations (these data are presented below). It is likely, therefore, that the child has to undergo extinction in a variety of situations. In view of these considerations, it was judged appropriate to investigate punishment (painful electric shock) as a way to suppress this behavior.

Punishment Study

While John received extinction for self-destructive behavior in the first situation, the bedroom, we recorded his self-destruction in two other situations, referred to as "John during lap" and "John during room". In the first situation, "John during lap", John's restraints were removed, and the attending nurse sat him sideways on her lap; placing one arm behind his back for support and the other on his knees. Although he was allowed as much freedom of movement as possible, he was not allowed to get off her lap. These observations took place in the same ward, but in a different room from that used during his extinction. They were made on a daily basis, each observation lasting 5 min. In addition to recording the frequency of his self-destructive behavior, a record was also kept of the amount of time that he attempted to avoid the nurse (defined as struggle to get off her lap) and the amount of time whining.

The data on John during the lap sessions are presented in the upper half of Fig. 2. The abscissa gives the days, the kind of experimenter (one of four adults) present during that particular session, and condition: [S (shock)]. The ordinate gives either frequency of self-destructive behavior or per cent of time that John was avoiding and whining during the session.

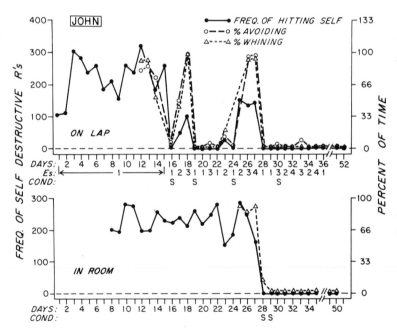

FIGURE 2 Frequency of John's self-destructive behavior and the percentage of avoiding adults and whining, as a function of shock. Data are presented for two situations: daily 5-min sessions "on the lap" (upper half), and daily 10-min sessions "in the room" (lower half). The ordinate gives the particular experimenter (attending adult) present, condition (cond.) which shows when shock (S) was administered, and days, which are the same for the two situations, enabling comparison between the two situations. Shock was given by Experimenter I on Days 16, 19, and 24, and by Experimenter 3 on Day 30, in the lap situation. It was given on Days 28 and 29 in the room.

(Because of mechanical failures in the apparatus, some data are missing for some sessions.) The first 15 days were used to obtain his base rates. As can be observed, his rates stayed about the same over these 15 days, neither improving nor getting worse. It is important to note that the extinction of John's self-destructive behavior in the experimental room, as presented in Fig. 1, was going on during this time, and while he had reached Session 10 in the lap situation, he was effectively extinguished in the experimental room. The extinction, then, did not generalize to this situation. Punishment, in the form of a 1-sec electric shock, was delivered by a hand-held inductorium ("Hot-shot", by Hot-shot Products Company, Inc., Savage, Minnesota). The inductorium was a 1-ft long rod, with two electrodes, 0.75 in. apart, protruding from its end. The shock, delivered from five 1.5-v flashlight batteries, had spikes as high as 1400 v at 50,000 ohms resistance. It was definitely painful to the experimenter, like a dentist drilling on an unanesthetized tooth, but the pain terminated when shock ended. As soon as (within 1 sec) the child hit himself, the experimenter, holding the inductorium, reached over and applied it to the child's leg. The punishment (S in the figure) was introduced in Session 16 with dramatic results. John received a total of 12 shocks distributed over Sessions 16, 19, 24, and 30. There was a two-week span between Sessions 36 and 51, and it can be observed that his rate was low, even without shock, after that time period.

Two additional observations are of interest. The first pertains to the generalizations of the suppression effect across experimenters. Up to Session 29, he was punished only by Experimenter 1. The suppression effected by Experimenter 1 generalized only partly to the other experimenters. By Sessions 25, 26, and 27 it can be observed that his rate of self-destructive behavior with the non-punishing adults was climbing alarmingly. In other words, he started to form a discrimination between the adult who punished him for self-destruction, and those who did not. In Session 30, Experimenter 3 also punished John for self-destruction, with the effect of producing generalization across other experimenters.

The second observation of interest pertained to the generalization of the shock effects to behaviors that were not punished. As self-destructive behavior was brought down by shock, John avoided the attending adult less and also whined less. Apparently, avoiding, whining, and self-destructive behavior fell within the same response class. These data indicated that the side effects of punishment were desirable. Informal clinical observations further confirmed the finding (John was observed by some 20 staff members), the nurse's notes reporting less distance and less fussing.

Perhaps the most significant changes that took place in John after he was freed from restraints were the ones we were unable to quantify. He was removed from restraints and shocked at 9 A.M. He appeared extremely frightened and agitated (apparently not by the shock, but from the absence of restraints). He sat slumped on the floor, close to the wall and underneath the washbasin in a corner of his room. At 9:25 he moved out from the wall, peeked into a cupboard in the room, and then darted back to his original place of departure. He repeated this behavior at 9:40 and 9:50. At 10:00 and 10:30 he moved, in very gradual steps, from his room into the corridor and adjoining room. He became very rambunctious, running up and down the hallway, seemingly insatiable. Freedom from restraint also permitted him many other apparently reinforcing discoveries: that first afternoon he allowed himself a full hour of scratching himself, a luxury he had not been allowed while his hands were tied behind his back. He had been so self-destructive that it had been almost impossible to give him a bath in a tub. Freed of self-destructive behavior, he behaved much like a seal when he was placed in a tub, screaming in happiness and scooting underneath the water with his face up and eyes open.

The hallway and the bath were immediately adjacent to the location in which he was shocked, and maintained the suppression. The effect of shock did not generalize to rooms some distance away (*e.g.*, in another part of the ward) from the punishment situation. For example, it did not generalize to the other situation where we kept a record of his self-destruction, called "John during room". In this situation, he was left free to wander around a small dormitory room, in the company of two or three adults. The sessions lasted for 10 min each, and were conducted once each day; during this time the rates of his self-destructive behavior and his whining were recorded.

Data from this study are presented in the lower half of Fig. 2. The days along the abscissa in the lower half correspond to those in the upper half, so that his behaviors in the two situations can be readily compared. Twenty days (Days 8 through 27) of pre-experimental measurements were obtained. They show that his self-destruction was essentially unaffected by what occurred in the lap situation, where his self-destruction had been essentially eliminated by Day 16. (It should be pointed out that the pre-experimental sessions in Fig. 2, as in Fig. 3 and 4, approximate extinction sessions, since self-destruction was left unattended. Apparently, 10 min sessions were too short for extinction, probably reflecting the thinness of the schedule of reinforcement, less than VI 10-min, which had supported the self-destruction in the past.)

He was given two 1-sec shocks on Days 28 and 29. This brought his self-destructive behavior down to zero and retained it at that level until the end of the experiment, some 18 days later. At the same time as his self-destructive behavior was decreasing, whining also disappeared. In general, these data are identical to those observed during the first shock session, except that fewer shocks were necessary to suppress the behavior.

At the end of this last experiment, shock was introduced in all other situations. It is notable that John was effectively freed from self-destructive behavior after five shocks in other (on the ward and on the street) situations. In other words, it was possible to achieve suppression of his self-destructive behavior in a large variety of situations using only a few shocks.

We attempted to study the effect of shock on Linda's self-destructive behavior in the same manner as John had been studied. The effect of shock on Linda was observed in two situations. The first situation, "Linda during room", consisted of 5-min sessions, one session per day. The data from this experiment are presented in the upper half of Fig. 3. The abscissa gives number of days, kind of experimenter (one of five) present during that session, and conditions. The first 15 days served as base-rate measures. There was considerable variability in these sessions, but they showed neither a worsening nor an improvement in her self-destruction. Experimenter 1 administered a 1-sec shock (S) to her while at the same time

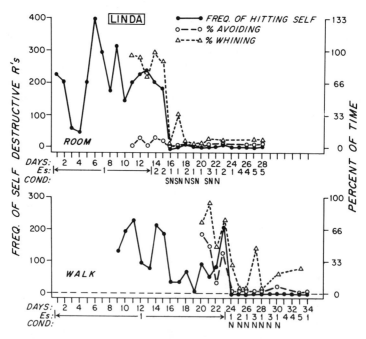

FIGURE 3 Frequency of Linda's self-destructive behavior and the percentage of avoiding adults and whining, as a function of shock (S) and of "No" (N). Data are from two situations: daily 5-min sessions "in the room" (upper half), and daily 5-min sessions "on the walk" (lower half). The days in the two situations are the same, enabling comparison between situations.

she gave the patient a loud "no" (denoted by the letter N on the abscissa). She received one shock on each of Days 16, 17, 19, and 21, and it is apparent that her rate fell to zero or near-zero immediately, with the shock effects generalizing across experimenters. During Days 18 and 22, she received merely the word "no". "No" had been tested for suppressing properties for Linda before its pairing with shock (on Days 14 and 15) and was demonstrated to be neutral (*i.e.*, ineffective).

One can observe the same change in non-punished behaviors with Linda as was the case with John: there was a substantial decrease in both avoiding of the attending adults and whining after shock was administered.

The other situation in which Linda was studied is referred to as "Linda during walk". In these sessions the experimenter and Linda walked together up and down a corridor for a 5-min period. The experimenter held Linda's hand; if Linda pulled away, which was scored as avoiding, the experimenter would let her go and then reestablish hand-to-hand contact. We were particularly interested in whether the word "no", which had been paired with shock during the room sessions, had acquired suppressing properties.

The data are presented in the lower half of Fig. 3. The abscissa shows which experimenter was attending to her. The days correspond to those in the upper half of the figure (Room sessions) so that her behaviors in the two situations can be readily compared. In addition to keeping track of her self-destructive behavior and her whining, avoiding behavior, defined as pulling away from the experimenter's hand, was recorded. The first 15 days (9 through 23) served as baseline. As we had already observed with John, there was no effective generalization from shock in the room (Day 16 on) to the walk situation. On Days 16 through 21, a loud "no" was given contingent upon self-destructive behavior, and it served to bring that behavior to zero level. The effects generalized across experimenters (4 and 5). The correlated behavior changes were the same as in the other studies reported: a concurrent suppression of whining and avoiding behavior.

Gregg was the last child with whom we observed the effect of shock under these controlled conditions. He was studied during one situation referred to as "Gregg during wheelchair". These sessions took place one week after extinction and the accompanying seven sessions of reinforcement for self-destruction (to be discussed later) had been completed. The sessions lasted for 2.5 min. He was placed in a standard wheelchair on one side of the experimental room (he was placed in a wheelchair because he did not walk). His self-destruction was so violent that the arms of the chair had to be padded. An attending adult sat directly in front of and facing him.

The data on Gregg in the wheelchair are presented in Fig. 4. The first 11 sessions served to establish the base rate, and produced no apparent

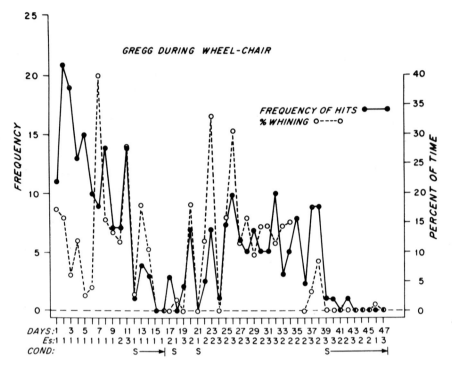

FIGURE 4 Gregg's self-destructions and whining, during wheel-chair sessions, as a function of shock (S) and the attending adult (E) who delivered shock. Each session ran 2.5 min.

change in his behavior. He was given shock by Experimenter 1 in each of Sessions 12, 13, and 14. His self-destruction was almost immediately suppressed during these sessions. Experimenter 2 and Experimenter 3 did not punish him at this time and it can be observed that his self-destructive behavior increased in their presence over the next several sessions (Sessions 22 through 38). In other words, he formed a discrimination between Experimenter 1 and other experimenters, as had John (Fig. 2). He was punished with shock by the other experimenters starting at Session 39 and the result shows an unambiguous drop in self-destruction. It was consistent with the data obtained on Linda and John, *i.e.*, as self-destructive behavior was brought down by the use of shock, there was a concomitant drop in whining. In the case of Gregg, we also recorded his physical contact with the attending adults and his vocalizations, but these were not systematically related to the experimental operations or correlated with the other behaviors.

In the case of both Gregg and John (Fig. 4 and 2 respectively) we replicated the effect of the noxious stimulus in a single subject design. Considering also the replication across subjects and situations, we no doubt are dealing with a reliable phenomenon.

Additional data on self-destruction, from more casual recording procedures, support the data on John, Linda, and Gregg. One of the most severe cases seen was Marilyn.[2] She was a 16-yr-old child diagnosed as retarded (moderate range) with psychotic features. She had been hospitalized for the previous 2 yr, and had been self-injurious since she was 2 yr old. The referring complaint centered on the parents' inability to control her self-destructive behavior. During her 2 yr of hospitalization she had been kept in a camisole in an attempt to prevent this behavior. When removed from the camisole, or when she removed the camisole herself by using her teeth, she would bite her hands so severely that at one time the little finger on her right hand had to be amputated to the first joint. She would similarly, with her teeth, remove her nails by their roots. She was also a head-banger; her scalp was covered with scar tissue. She would fall to the ground without apparent reason, scream, and occasionally aggress toward others by biting them.

Her base rate of "spontaneous" injury was very low, and in that way different from the other children's. That is, self-destructive acts were highly discriminated: she would mutilate herself only whenever the experimenter gave her affection, such as comforting her or praising her (33 self-injurious behaviors out of the 36 such interactions with her before shock). The first session lasted for about 2 hr; half way into the session she was given shock for self-destructive behavior. A total of five shocks (on the first, fourth, fifth, and fifteenth presentation of the affectionate interaction) brought her biting and head-banging to zero, and it remained at zero-level for the rest of the session. The suppression data on Marilyn were virtually identical to the others.

Because of the extreme severity of her self-injurious behavior, Marilyn demonstrated why it is impossible to place such a child on extinction. Marilyn could have inflicted serious self-injury or even killed herself during the extinction run.

While the immediate generalized behavior change due to shock was very favorable, there is some reason to believe that her aggression toward other children on the ward increased at a later time. Apparently, the reinforcers that maintained the self-destructive behavior were still operative, and since she did not develop a more acceptable behavior form, which seems to be the case in most children, and was not explicitly trained to

[2] Thomas Ball, Ph.D., Chief Psychologist at Pacific State Hospital in Pomona, California, and Lawrence Dameron, Ph.D., formerly on the staff at Pacific State, had the major responsibility for the research with Marilyn.

behave otherwise, she returned to a form of behavior which also yielded large quantities of attention.

The data on shock can be summarized as follows. First, the use of shock, given contingent upon self-destructive behavior, brings about an immediate cessation of that behavior. Second, the effect of shock appears specific to the situations in which it is administered. If a child is shocked in one room, and not in another, or by one person and not another, he sometimes will form a discrimination between these situations. Finally, both in the changes that we were able to record objectively and in the clinical observations, there was every evidence that the side effects of punishment, instead of being undesirable, were judged to be therapeutically desirable.

Worsening the Self-Destructive Behavior

It is apparent from the data presented above that considerable changes can be effected in destructive behavior, either by extinction or punishment. That there must be other variables that control self-destructive behavior is apparent on inspection of the great amount of variability present in all our baselines. Consider, as an example, the variability in the extinction data on Gregg, which was presented in Fig. 1. Within a matter of three or four days, his rate of self-destruction fell from more than 900 (Session 7) to less than 300 (Session 11) and then increased to more than 800 hits per session. Such large shifts in amount of self-destructive behavior surely must be related to powerful variables and it is, therefore, appropriate to search for them.

We had some reason to suspect that these fluctuations in self-destructive behavior were caused by changes in the kinds of nursing care received on any one day. In particular, the early peaks in self-destruction occurred on Mondays, and we knew that the nursing personnel who cared for him over the weekend approached him differently from those who cared for him during the week. The nature of this difference was unknown, however, and could be a function of deprivation of interpersonal relationships, satiation of such relationships, or an undue amount of attention being paid to his self-destruction. Of course, a large number of other dimensions in interpersonal relationships could be responsible for the rise and fall in his self-destructive behavior.

In an attempt to identify some of the sources responsible for the magnitude of his self-destructive behavior, certain probes were initiated. First, we considered that deprivation of attention was responsible for a rise in self-destruction. Therefore, he was placed on a 24-hr period of social deprivation before Sessions 18 and 24 (DEP in Fig. 1). Essentially, Gregg was left alone in his room except for being changed and fed. He would lie the entire day on his bed in restraints, much as a typical day in a state hospital. The rate of self-destructive behavior after these deprivation operations was not different, however, from other days. To check further on the effectiveness of such operations of availability of social stimulation, we instigated two days of social satiation. During the 24-hr periods before Sessions 20 and 22 (SAT also in Fig. 1), Gregg was given continual attention during his waking hours, such as being talked to, touched, tickled, hugged and kissed, walked, and generally stimulated an excessive amount. However, there was no significant change in his self-destructive behavior accompanying such periods of social stimulation. We concluded, therefore, that the availability of interpersonal stimulation (*per se*) had no appreciable effect upon his self-destruction.

One form of nursing intervention of particular interest to us centered on the nurse's reaction to the child when he was self-destructive. We observed that the great majority of nursing personnel would be particularly likely to interact with him contingent upon his self-destruction. Anyone who has been around self-destructive children has experienced an urge to attend to such children when they hurt themselves, in an attempt to nurse their suffering. In fact, nursing personnel, as well as parents, are typically given explicit directions by the doctors and nurses in charge of the case to respond to self-destructive behavior with warmth and "understanding", attempting to reassure the child that they are in attendance, that he need not be afraid, and other words and gestures to that effect.

We tested the effects of this kind of intervention during Sessions 26 and 28 (REI in Fig. 1). Half an hour into the session, an adult would enter the room contingent upon Gregg's self-destructive behavior, hold Gregg's hands and say in a pleading voice, "don't do that, Gregg, everything is OK", and other comments to that effect. This contact lasted for approximately 30 sec, at the end of which the attending person would again leave. The adult would appear on the average of every third time Gregg hit himself. If one considers Sessions 25 through 34, it looked as if his self-destructive behavior temporarily worsened (acquisition followed by extinction). We replicated these operations (REI) in Sessions 35 and 37. Again, there seemed to be some worsening of his self-destructive behavior following these operations. However, when these operations were reintroduced a third time during Sessions 55 and 57, we did not replicate the observations.

On the basis of these data, we entertained the possibility that his self-destructive behavior was under the control of the attention paid to that behavior, but that the attention he did receive was a rather weak consequence which lost its reinforcing properties over time: that is, it lost its reinforcing properties as its S^D properties extinguished. This led us to investigate whether there were other consequences that would lead to greater control over his self-destruction.

The day after the last extinction day (Session 59 in Fig. 1), we obtained a new base rate of Gregg's self-destructive behavior in the same situation where he had undergone extinction. The new base rate data are presented in Fig. 5 as cumulative curves. Numbers 1 and 2 refer to the first and second 10-min sessions that formed the base rate of self-destruction: he was left to hit himself and no one did anything about it. The number 3 refers to the third 10-min session where approach was changed as follows. On an average of every fifth time that Gregg hit himself, we would take him out of the crib for about 30 to 60 sec and, in addition to comforting him, would allow him to play with some drawers, closet doors, and wooden blocks, which we knew that he liked to play with. On the average of every fifth reinforcement, we would take him for a 5-min walk

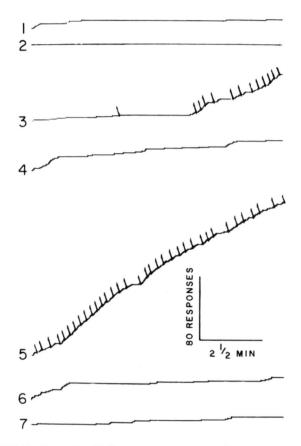

FIGURE 5 Gregg's self-destruction, as cumulative response curves, over successive sessions (1 through 7). The upward moving hatchmarks in Sessions 3 and 5 mark delivery of sympathetic comments, play, *etc.*, contingent on self-destruction.

(with the experimenter's physical assistance) from his bedroom to the day room. Again, Gregg very much enjoyed to be taken for a walk. This 10-min reinforcement period (referred to as number 3 in Fig. 5) was followed by a 10-min extinction session (number 4 in Fig. 5). This extinction session was similar to the pre-experimental operation denoted with number 1 and 2. The next day, we again gave attention and play contingent upon self-destructive behavior (number 5 in Fig. 5). Finally, we ended with 2 hr of extinction with the first 10 min and the last 10 min presented as 6 and 7, respectively.

It is apparent that this approach, trying, in a sense, to "understand" what Gregg wanted and to give it to him when he was self-destructive, is a very dangerous form of treatment. His rate went up the first time we did this (number 3) and climbed alarmingly the second time (number 5). In fact, the attending adults agreed that if we had continued to attend to his self-destruction, we could have hurt him badly. This could have been true particularly if we had given attention contingent upon larger and larger amounts of self-destruction, as might happen when a parent or attendant becomes "used to", or adapted to, a particular level of self-destructive behavior.

This finding was consistent with one reported earlier (Lovaas *et al.*, 1965a) where a child's self-destructive behavior worsened when we attempted to communicate sympathy and reassurance contingent upon such behavior. Such therapy is typically prescribed for such children when the therapist attempts to address himself to the alleviation of some internal pathology, such as anxiety, for which the self-destruction is seen as an expression. Reinforcing attention is also likely to be given spontaneously by adults, since it is extremely difficult to withhold expressions of concern when a child appears to hurt himself. If our data are reliable, then it is such expressions which keep the child in restraints. Said differently, in this instance the expression of "love" contingent upon self-destructive behavior benefits only the giver.

The great majority of studies on treatment attempt to isolate the conditions under which a particular problem can be alleviated. There is also some value in attempting to assess whether aspects of current treatments do in fact worsen the patient's condition. Ideally, such studies help change old treatments.

DISCUSSION

Our data can be summarized as follows. Two procedures effectively terminated the self-destructive behavior. The first procedure, carried out with two of the children, involved an extinction paradigm, whereby the child was allowed to hurt himself, isolated from personal contact. In both these instances, the self-destructive behavior was terminated. Our data are consistent with those obtained by Risley *et al.* (1964), who used extinction procedures to reduce the self-destructive behavior of a 3.5-yr-old boy. Additional data which support this kind of intervention have been reviewed by Gardner (1967).

This procedure of withdrawing or making potential reinforcers unavailable has an undesirable attribute, in that it is not immediately effective and temporarily exposes the child to the danger of severe damage from his own self-destruction, which is particularly intense during the early stages of the extinction run. In some cases of severe self-destruction, it is ill-advised to place the child on extinction. Marilyn (reviewed above), for example, could have inflicted serious self-injury or possibly even killed herself during an extinction run.

We reported five studies, carried out on three children, in which we observed an immediate suppression of self-destructive behavior when aversive stimuli were given contingent upon that behavior. This finding is consistent with data from previous work with aversive stimuli (Lovaas, Schaeffer, and Simmons, 1965) which reported the suppression of tantrums and self-destruction in two 5-yr-old autistic boys. Risley (1968), Tate and Baroff (1967), and others (as reviewed by Bucher and Lovaas, 1967) have reported similar findings.

The effects of shock appear to be specific to the situation in which shock is used, with respect to both physical locales and attending adults. This implies that if punishment to suppress self-destruction is to be maximally therapeutic (*i.e.*, durable and general) it has to be administered by more than one person, in more than one setting. Our data amply suggest that each child would revert to self-destruction as soon as he returned to the treatment settings from which he came, unless his treatment under those conditions was made consistent with our procedures. The children, in other words, formed discriminations. Figure 2 illustrates how quickly such discriminations can come about. Again, our previous work and the work of others (*e.g.*, Risley, 1968; Hamilton and Standahl, 1967) is consistent on the highly discriminated stimulus control of shock. We observed also that the children did not become generally fearful of the adults who administer the punishment, but showed fear of the adult only when the adult gave signs of disapproval (looking angry and verbalizing anger, as he does when he administers punishment) or when they are in the act of self-destruction. That observation also supports the specificity of the shock-effects. Most likely, such discriminations come about because of the adults' differential treatment. Should the adult administer only punishment, then it seems likely that the child would become generally fearful of him. However, the adult who administered punishment for self-destruction was asso-

ciated with the child in a number of situations, as a caretaking and parental person, administering love when the child acted appropriately. Watson
(1967) made this point explicitly in discussing punishment effects.

One of the surprising findings on the use of shock pertains to the immediate increase in socially directed behavior, such as eye-to-eye contact
and physical contact, as well as the simultaneous decrease in a large variety
of inappropriate behaviors, such as whining, fussing, and facial grimacing.
Such response generalization has also been reported by others: Risley
(1968) made specific efforts to record some of these. Hamilton, Stevens,
and Allen (1967) described their children, after punishment, ". . . to be
more socially outgoing, happier, and better adjusted in the ward setting . . ." (p. 856). White and Taylor (1967) reported, as a consequence
of shock, that their patients ". . . appeared to be more aware of and interact more with the examiner . . ." (p. 32). We reported similar findings
in an earlier study (Lovaas *et al.*, 1965c). We have a filmed record that
quite dramatically portrays the changes in John.

Some of these behavioral changes might occur for rather "mechanical"
reasons: that is, it is difficult for a child who whines to smile simultaneously. It is easier for a child, removed from the restraints of his bed, to
come into contact with more rewarding aspects of his environment, *etc.*
Some of the beneficial changes will be specific to certain children. For
example, the suppression of self-destruction (largely head-banging) in
Linda permitted surgery for her cataracts, with resultant alleviation of her
restricted vision. Some of the behavioral changes accompanying shock
probably occur because reinforcements have been given to the child for
behaving appropriately when faced with aversive stimuli in the past.
Finally, certain behaviors may be elicited by shock as an unconditioned
stimulus: that is, certain kinds of stress, fears, or pains may call forth
socially oriented behavior at a purely biological level. A number of interesting questions await research in that area.

Although the immediate "side-effects" of punishment point in a
desirable direction, one should be less optimistic about long-term behavioral change under certain conditions. We can supply few data which
exceed a couple of months follow-up, and in the case of only two children
have we had the opportunity to conduct follow-ups for as much as 1 yr,
while the suppression of self-destruction was being maintained. It seems
reasonable that if social reinforcement controlled the self-destructive behavior in the first place, then that reinforcement, being unaltered in
strength through punishment operations, should retain the power to build
other, equally undesirable, behaviors. If the child had to go to such extremes as self-destruction to gain some attention from his attending adults,
then it seems but reasonable that these adults, unless they were taught to
respond to more appropriate behavior, would repeat themselves and begin

shaping some similarly alarming behavior, such as feces smearing or eating, aggression toward other children, *etc.* Within reinforcement theory terms, the suppression of one behavior may be discriminative for a large number of other behaviors, some more and some less desirable than the suppressed one.

These children have demonstrated, through their self-destruction, that they will apparently withstand considerable pain to get attention, and that they may have considerable experience with pain adaptation. To avoid selecting a neutral shock, or a weak one to which the children could adapt quickly, we have used a strong shock which guaranteed quick suppression. By a strong shock is meant a shock which the experimenters experienced as definitely painful (smarted like a whip, or a dentist drilling on an unanesthetized tooth), and to which the subjects gave every sign of fear and apprehension. The question is sometimes raised as to how, in view of the much more severe pain associated with self-destruction (*e.g.*, pulling own nails out with teeth), the shock works in the first place. We can offer two guesses in this regard: the child has not had an opportunity to adapt to shock, nor has the shock been associated with positive reinforcement, both of which may have occurred with the painful stimuli generated by the self-destruction.

REFERENCES

BUCHER, B. and LOVAAS, O. I. Use of aversive stimulation in behavior modification. In M. R. Jones (Ed.), *Miami symposium on the prediction of behavior 1967: aversive stimulation.* Coral Gables, Florida: University of Miami Press, 1968. Pp. 77–145.

GARDNER, J. E. Behavior therapy treatment approach to a psychogenic seizure case. *Journal of Consulting Psychology,* 1967, **31**, 209–212.

HAMILTON, H., STEPHENS, L., and ALLEN, P. Controlling aggressive and destructive behavior in severely retarded institutionalized residents. *American Journal of Mental Deficiency,* 1967, **71**, 852–856.

HAMILTON, J. and STANDAHL, J. *Suppression of stereotyped screaming behavior in a profoundly retarded institutionalized female.* Unpublished paper, Gracewood State School, Georgia, 1967.

LOVAAS, O. I., FREITAG, G., GOLD, VIVIAN J., and KASSORLA, IRENE C. Experimental studies in childhood schizophrenia: analysis of self-destructive behavior. *Journal of Experimental Child Psychology,* 1965, **2**, 67–84. (*a*)

LOVAAS, O. I., FREITAG, G., GOLD, VIVIAN J., and KASSORLA, IRENE C. A recording method and observations of behaviors of normal and autistic children in free play settings. *Journal of Experimental Child Psychology,* 1965, **2**, 108–120. (*b*)

LOVAAS, O. I., SCHAEFFER, B., and SIMMONS, J. Q. Experimental studies in childhood schizophrenia: building social behavior in autistic children by the use of electric shock. *Journal of Experimental Research Personnel,* 1965, **1**, 99–109.

RISLEY, T. The effects and side effects of punishing the autistic behaviors of a deviant child. *Journal of Applied Behavior Analysis,* 1968, **1**, 21–35.

TATE, B. G. and BAROFF, G. S. Aversive control of self-injurious behavior in a psychotic boy. *Behavioral Research Therapy,* 1966, **4**, 281–287.

WATSON, L. S. Application of operant conditioning techniques to institutionalized severely and profoundly retarded children. *Mental Retardation Abstracts,* 1967, **4**, 1–18.

WHITE, J. C., JR. and TAYLOR, D. Noxious conditioning as a treatment for rumination. *Mental Retardation,* 1967, **6**, 30–33.

WOLF, M., RISLEY, T., and MEES, H. Application of operant conditioning procedures to the behavior problems of an autistic child. *Behavioral Research Therapy,* 1964, **1**, 305–312.

ROBERT F. PETERSON
University of Illinois

LINDA R. PETERSON
Illinois State Department of Mental Health

The use of positive reinforcement in the control of self-destructive behavior in a retarded boy[1,2,3]

Severe self-destructive behaviors in an 8-yr-old boy were observed to change as a function of treatment procedures which included both primary and secondary reinforcers and a brief walk across the room. The presentation and withdrawal of a blanket also appeared to exert considerable control over the frequency of self-destructive behaviors. The results were discussed in terms of environmental control through self-injurious behaviors and the development of the blanket as a reinforcing stimulus.

One of the most severe problems observed in young children involves self-inflicted physical injury. Disturbed children have been observed to

Reprinted from *Journal of Experimental Child Psychology*, 1968, 6, 351–60, with permission of the publisher and the authors.

---

[1] The present paper is based on a report delivered to the Society for Research in Child Development, New York, March 30, 1967.

[2] This research was supported in part by grants from the Children's Bureau (Training for Nursing in Mental Retardation, 306) and the National Institute of Mental Health (MH 12067) and was carried out while both of the authors were at the University of Washington.

[3] The authors acknowledge their debt to Mr. Frank Junkin, Superintendent, and the staff of Fircrest School whose cooperation made this study possible, and would like to thank Dr. Sidney Bijou for his helpful criticism of this manuscript.

488

strike various parts of their bodies against hard surfaces or hit themselves until tissue injury results. Recently, investigators have become interested in studying self-destructive behaviors from a general behavior theory point of view, and have suggested techniques which may control them. For example, Allen and Harris (1966) investigated severe scratching in a 5-year-old girl. They found that by teaching the child's parents to attend to incompatible behaviors they were able to eliminate the scratching. Similarly, Lovaas, Freitag, Gold, and Kassorla (1965) analyzed self-abusive behaviors in a schizophrenic girl and likewise found the behavior to be influenced by social reinforcement. Using a brief period of isolation as a "time-out" from reinforcement, Wolf, Risley, and Mees (1964) reduced tantrum behaviors which involved self-slapping, hair pulling, and head banging.

Aversive stimulation has also been used to control self-injurious behaviors. Both Tate and Baroff (1966) and Lovaas, Freitag, Kinder, Rubenstein, Schaeffer, and Simmons (1964) suppressed self-destructive responses in psychotic children for several months by employing contingent electric shock.

Despite their effectiveness in controlling some undesirable behaviors, techniques involving the application of aversive stimuli (punishment) have certain disadvantages. As Azrin and Holz (1966) have pointed out, social relationships may be disrupted. The punished individual may avoid the person administering the aversive stimuli and may also aggress against him or others nearby. Furthermore, for social and ethical reasons, many professionals have been extremely reluctant to use punishment as a form of educational or clinical treatment.

The present study was designed to explore the use of positive reinforcement in the control of self-destructive behavior. A second concern involved an assessment of the functional properties of a blanket that seemed to play a significant role in the behavior of the S.

SUBJECT

The S was an 8-year-old boy who had been admitted to a state institution at the age of 6 because he was unmanageable at home. At the time of the study, S was not toilet trained, had no speech, but was ambulatory. He would respond to a variety of commands such as "come here," and could feed himself. Due to his behavorial problems it was not possible to assess his skills with conventional psychological procedures. Most of the day S lay or rocked on his bed, wrapped in a small quilt. Often he carried a blanket with him when not on his bed. When not so engaged, S displayed violent self-injurious responses, slapping the side of his head or leg with either hand, hitting his hand against his teeth, or banging his forehead against his forearm. He also struck his head and hands against chairs, tables, and walls. The S cried loudly but tearlessly when behaving in this fashion. These responses were so forceful that his face, arms, and legs were covered with bruises, scabs, abrasions, and on occasion, open wounds.

PROCEDURE

The study was conducted in a small room which contained three tables and a few chairs. S was seen from one to 11 times a week with a typical session lasting 15 minutes. Sessions coincided with mealtime (lunch and/or supper) and portions of food were used as reinforcers. The S sat on one side of a table, the E on the other, with a tray of food between them.

The study was divided into five stages: the base line period, the first and second experimental periods, the reversal period, and a third experimental period.

Base Line Period

The base line period consisted of 12 observations on the ward and five in the experimental room, both with and without the blanket. Because of the severity of the child's behavior the observation periods were limited to 5 minutes each. Self-destructive behavior was defined as those responses which involved striking one part of the body with another. Behaviors which involved striking objects were excluded.

Observer reliability in recording these behaviors was assessed by the E and a second O in sessions 7, 17, and 18. It was obtained by comparing the respective scores of two observers during each 30-second interval of recording. For any given interval where a difference in scoring occurred, the smaller score was subtracted from the larger to obtain a difference score. These difference scores were summed over all intervals. The smaller scores in each interval were also summed over all intervals. Reliability was computed by dividing the sum of the smaller scores by the sum of the difference scores plus the sum of the smaller scores. The result was multiplied by 100. The average reliability for all three sessions exceeded 95%. A slightly higher reliability figure was obtained when reliability was computed over the total session without regard for differences within 30-second intervals.

First Experimental Period

During this part of the study, reinforcement in the form of food (one-quarter teaspoon) and the word "good" were given contingent upon a 3- to 5-second interval of no self-injurious responses. Whenever a self-injurious response did occur, the *E* took the food from the table, turned away from the child, and began counting silently. If no self-destructive behavior occurred during the next 10 seconds, *E* then turned back to the child, said "good," and gave him a bit of food. Attempts were made to lengthen the interval between self-injurious responses. This procedure continued for 10 sessions (Sessions 18–27 inclusive).

Second Experimental Period

In order to reduce further the rate of self-destructive responses, the previous procedure was altered. Reinforcement was still given following a brief interval of any behavior other than self-destructive (excluding the striking of objects) but the time between responses was not increased nor was the food removed. Instead, S was given verbal and gestural instructions, contingent upon a self-destructive response, to walk across the room (a distance of 12 feet) and sit in a chair. If no self-injurious responses occurred while walking to the chair, the *E* immediately went to the child and reinforced his behavior with "good" and food. If self-destructive behaviors did occur, S was again instructed to walk across the room. This procedure was continued until he had walked from one chair to another without a self-injurious response. (It should be noted that the S was free to engage in self-destructive behavior at all times. Walking in no way hindered him from doing so.) In addition, S was taught to indicate which particular part of his meal (potatoes, meat, beans, etc.) he would like to eat by pointing to it. Thus, after a brief interval of no self-injurious behavior, the *E* said, "Show me what you want" waited until S pointed or gave some indication, and fed it to him.

Reversal Period

Following the second experimental period, the reinforcement operations were again modified beginning in Session 64. The S was now instructed to walk from one chair to another not as a consequence of a self-injurious response, but until such a response occurred. When this happened the *E* immediately reinforced the behavior. These operations then, are exactly the reverse of those in the previous Experimental Period. Because these procedures were in effect for only a brief period (3 sessions), they might be more accurately viewed as a behavorial "probe," which was designed to study the effects of the changed contingency on self-injurious behaviors.

Third Experimental Period

During this part of the study, reinforcement contingencies were identical to those in the Second Experimental Period. S was instructed to walk across the room following a self-destructive response. If further responses did not occur, the E said "good," and gave him a bit of food. If self-injurious behaviors were displayed during the walk, S continued walking until he had crossed the room without injuring himself.

RESULTS

Reduction in Self-Destructive Behavior

The overall changes in self-destructive behavior can be seen in Fig. 1 which shows the rate of behavior while the child was in the experimental room without his blanket. During the base line period the behaviors ranged between 21.6 and 32.8 responses per minute. Although there was a drop in self-injurious behaviors following the introduction of the treatment procedures, there was also considerable variability. The response rate ranged from 5.3 to 24.6 responses per minute. The mean number of responses per minute during the first experimental period was 14.2. This contrasts with a mean rate of 26.6 responses per minute during the base line.

The Second Experimental Period began with Session 28, and the introduction of new procedures. Response rate dropped from the previous

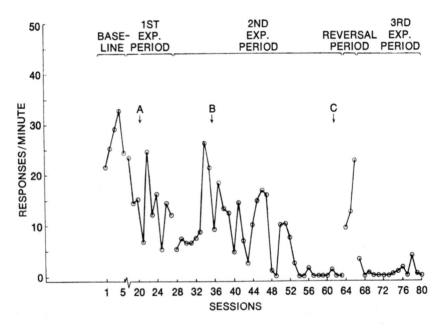

FIGURE 1 Rate of self-injurious behavior during successive sessions.

session and after remaining relatively stable for six sessions became extremely variable. There was a gradual reduction in the rate of self-destructive behaviors over the next 20 sessions. Ultimately, the responses disappeared.

Two sessions prior to the beginning of the Reversal Period (point C on Fig. 1) the E was changed. A second E was needed because the first E was no longer available. The new E did not appear to affect the rate of self-destructive behavior.

During the Reversal (probe) Period all experimental contingencies were altered. The S was instructed to walk across the room; however, the instruction was not contingent upon self-injurious behavior. The results may be seen in Fig. 2 which shows the child's responses during successive minutes of the three reversal sessions. Seven minutes elapsed before a self-destructive response occurred. This response was reinforced while subsequent self-injurious responses were only occasionally reinforced. This intermittent reinforcement resulted from the E's attempts to reinforce those behaviors which appeared to be least harmful to the child, e.g. slapping his leg. The response rate rose to a high level almost immediately. A comparison of all three reversal sessions shows an increase in the acceleration of self-injurious behaviors from the first through the third sessions. Figure 1 shows that the average response rate rose to 9.5 in Session 64, increased to 12.6 in Session 65 and reached 23.2 responses per minute in Session 66.

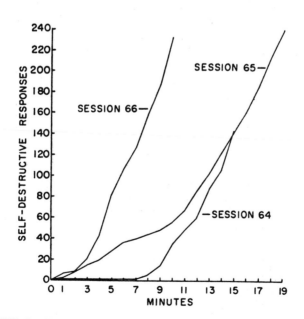

FIGURE 2   Frequency of self-destructive behavior in three reversal sessions.

When the contingencies were returned to those of the previous experimental period, the rate of self-destructive behavior dropped to 3.2 responses per minute in Session 67 and remained at or near zero thereafter.

Subsequently, attendants reported that S engaged in fewer self-destructive behaviors while on the ward and spent more time with other children. Such reports should be viewed skeptically, however.

Effect of Manipulating the Blanket

Figure 3 shows how closely the blanket controlled S's behavior. During the base line, the blanket was presented and taken from S according to a series of 30-second intervals. The intervals were programmed in such a way that S held the blanket for a minimum of 30 seconds on some occasions and a maximum of 60 seconds on others. He was allowed to keep the blanket a total of 2½ minutes out of each 5-minute observation period. Typically, the loss of the blanket produced self-destructive responses while repossession of the blanket caused a fairly abrupt cessation of responding.

Figure 4 shows the effect of the blanket over the entire base line period. In the experimental room, S's rate of self-destructive behavior ranged from 22 to 32 responses per minute without the blanket and 9–19 responses per minute with the blanket. Stimulus control was even greater when S was lying or sitting on his bed in the ward. Here, when deprived of the blanket, self-destructive behaviors occurred at a rate of 20–42 per minute; when allowed to keep the blanket, the range of injurious responses was from 0 to 24 responses per minute. During seven of the 12 sessions on the ward, no self-destructive behavior was observed while S was in possession of the blanket.

The S also cried when engaging in self-destructive behaviors. Figure 5

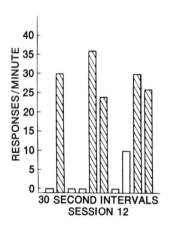

FIGURE 3   The effects of blanket deprivation and blanket possession on self-destructive behaviors within a single session. Striped columns = without blanket; white columns = with blanket.

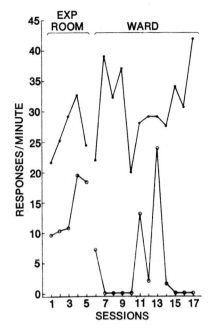

FIGURE 4 Rate of self-injurious responses during periods of blanket possession and blanket deprivation. Open circles = with blanket; solid circles = without blanket.

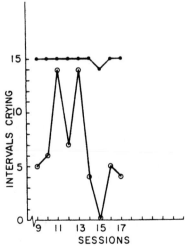

FIGURE 5 Intervals crying during periods of blanket availability and unavailability. Open circles = with blanket; solid circles = without blanket.

shows the rate of crying from Sessions 9 through 17. (Data on this behavior was not obtained before Session 9). Crying was defined as a loud high-pitched sound of more than a 2-second duration. Figure 5 shows a high rate of crying (measured in 10-second intervals) when deprived of the blanket. Over all 9 sessions the rate of crying was some 56% lower when S kept his blanket. However, crying was not as closely controlled by the blanket as was self-injurious behavior.

DISCUSSION

Although it is clear that the term "good" coupled with food did function as a positive reinforcer for S, the interpretation of the walking procedure is open to discussion. Since it was possible to expand the interval between injurious responses from a few seconds to as long as the entire session after instituting the walking response, it may be that the use of this procedure gave the child a behavior which functioned to mediate the minimal period between self-abusive behaviors needed for reinforcement to occur (Ferster and Skinner, 1957). It is also possible that walking functioned as a punishing stimulus which delayed reinforcement (Azrin and Holz, 1966). The effects of the walking procedure cannot, however, be separated from the effects of reinforcement. Further analysis is needed to estimate just how much and in what way this operation contributed to the reduction in self-destructive behavior.

In contrast, the role of the blanket seems somewhat clearer in that it appeared to function as a powerful reinforcer. When deprived of it, S would reach for it or attempt to retrieve it. Sometimes he would accept a second blanket while on other occasions only the original would do. The loss of the blanket did produce an immediate display of self-injurious behavior. The S's behavior in this situation is similar to that of the child reported by Lovaas, et al. (1965). These investigators found that the withdrawal of reinforcement from a previously reinforced response was the discriminative stimulus for self-destructive behavior. In S's case it was not obvious just what response the blanket was reinforcing. Holding the blanket did *not* prevent S from engaging in self-destructive behavior. He would occasionally hit himself while under the blanket or even through the blanket. Bijou and Baer (1965) have noted that a blanket may develop the properties of a generalized reinforcer. This may result from the blanket being discriminative for skin temperature changes, for rest and sleep, and being a source of tactual stimulation, all of which may be reinforcing. For S, the blanket may also have been discriminative for periods of time where few stimulus events produced self-destructive behaviors. Such a condition may have given the blanket additional reinforcing properties.

Although the blanket exerted strong control over S's behavior early in the study, this control was reduced by the end of treatment. Unfortunately, no data which would allow quantitative comparisons were obtained. However, it was possible to remove the child's blanket without producing immediate self-destructive behaviors as before. Nevertheless, S, like the comic strip character, Linus, preferred to keep his blanket with him much of the time, perhaps for the "security" it provided.

Both prior to and during most of the present study, S received drugs (thioridazine and chlorpromazine) except for the period covered by Sessions 21 through 36 inclusive, (see points A and B in Fig. 1). Despite this complication no relationship between the presence or absence of medication and the rate of self-destructive behavior was observed. In addition, the results of the reversal period clearly show that the medications were not responsible for the changes in self-destructive behavior.

It should be apparent that by engaging in self-destructive behavior a child may exert considerable control over his environment. It is possible therefore, that the development and strength of self-injurious responses may be at least partially dependent upon the presence and effectiveness of alternative behaviors which can also be used to influence the environment. If so, maximum therapeutic gain might be achieved by integrating procedures designed to expand the child's behavioral repertoire along with procedures for the control of self-destructive behavior.

REFERENCES

ALLEN, K. EILEEN, AND HARRIS, F. R. Elimination of a child's excessive scratching by training the mother in reinforcement procedures. *Behaviour Research and Therapy*, 1966, 4, 79–84.

AZRIN, N. H., AND HOLZ, W. C. Punishment. In W. K. Honig (Ed.) *Operant behavior: areas of research and application*. New York: Appleton, 1966.

BIJOU, S. W., AND BAER, D. M. *Child development: the universal stage of infancy*. Vol. II. New York: Appleton, 1965.

FERSTER, C. B., AND SKINNER, B. F. *Schedules of reinforcement*. New York: Appleton, 1957.

LOVAAS, O. I., FREITAG, G., KINDER, M. I., RUBENSTEIN, D. B., SCHAEFFER, B., AND SIMMONS, J. B. Experimental studies in childhood schizophrenia: Developing social behavior using electric shock. Paper read at American Psychological Assoc., 1964.

LOVAAS, O. I., FREITAG, G., GOLD, VIVIAN J., AND KASSORLA, IRENE C. Experimental studies in childhood schizophrenia: Analysis of self-destructive behavior. *Journal of Experimental Child Psychology*, 1965, 2, 67–84.

TATE, B. G., AND BAROFF, G. S. Aversive control of self-injurious behavior in a psychotic boy. *Behaviour Research and Therapy*, 1966, 4, 281–287.

WOLF, M. M., RISLEY, T., AND MEES, H. Application of operant conditioning procedures to the behavior problems of an autistic child. *Behaviour Research and Therapy*, 1964, 1, 305–312.

8

ACHIEVEMENT OF APPROPRIATE STIMULUS CONTROL

As we pointed out in the Introduction, much research in behavior modification has been aimed at showing changes that can be achieved by manipulating the reinforcement conditions that affect the child's behavior. The explicit use of such techniques is hardly novel; it is as old as human history. But we hope that the demonstration of their power has been surprising and enlightening to our readers. In addition to manipulating *consequent* (reinforcing) stimuli, one can also manipulate *antecedent* (evoking, eliciting) stimuli. The differential responsiveness of humans and animals to changed environmental circumstances is so obvious as to pass almost unnoticed as a potential technique for behavior change.

Learning to use subtle, available environmental cues as guides to behavior and reinforcement is an important part of the child's progress toward intellectual maturity. Learning to read, for example, may be conceptualized as the acquisition of discriminative responding to minute, printed cues. The elaboration of this skill obviously is of immense importance for the child's development. We do not know a great deal about how children learn to use cues; yet most children are expected to master them. Fortunately, discrimination learning has been the subject of extensive investigation in recent years, particularly since the concept of attention was revived in learning research.

We present here three examples of this work. The study by Touchette is one of a number that shows that quite simple learning—for example responding differentially to the location of a small black square on a white background—may. be almost impossible using trial–and–error training methods (in which correct responses are rewarded and others are not.) Such simple learning need not be difficult, however, if the discrimination is built up from other abilities the child already possesses. We now know enough not to attempt to teach calculus before arithmetic. The desirable sequencing of training materials is fairly well understood in this area. However, it is often difficult for educators to distinguish between what children *can* learn and what they *do* learn. Moreover it is not appropriate for us to draw conclusions about the upper limits of what they can learn until we can be assured that the training techniques being used are the best available. Judgments about children's learning capabilities, however, are commonplace. Touchette shows that we cannot talk of a child's capabilities while ignoring the skill with which he is being tutored.

A second interesting point made by Touchette is that preliminary trial–and–error learning made the task more difficult for the child who was then trained using the gradual stimulus change procedure. Failures in trial–and–error learning led to more failures in the subsequent procedure. This result resembles the phenomenon of "helplessness," which is observed in animals given training in avoiding shock. After a series of unavoidable shocks, learning to avoid often is much more difficult. Perhaps many children whose rate of acquisition of new intellectual skills seems inordinately slow have been similarly afflicted with damaging prior reinforcement histories.

The success of Touchette's training points to the possibilities of developing programs based on these gradual shaping principles for teaching self-care, social skills, language, and so on to retarded (or normal) children. The development of such programs is an important research area.

Touchette interprets the difficulty in learning he explores as due to an inflexibility in shifting from those stimulus elements that the child uses to guide his responding and toward others that may be more successful and that could increase the child's access to reinforcement. For example, a child may be occasionally rewarded in a discrimination task if he always chooses the right-hand stimulus, but the reward available for following a color or form cue may be much greater. The failure to find this greater reinforcement schedule is a failure to acquire adaptive behavior.

The study by Lovaas, Schreibman, Koegel, and Rehm shows a somewhat surprising finding: if you reinforce the autistic child for responding to a complex stimulus input (a tone, a light, a touch), then *all* of that input does *not* become functional in controlling his behavior. It is as if the child selects certain aspects of the stimulus input while he ignores others. This phenomenon is called overselective attention (or stimulus overselectivity). If he attends to the visual cues, he ignores the auditory ones; if one wants the child to attend to the auditory cues, he should make sure the visual cues are removed. This study suggests the possibility that cues may "interfere" with each other and that for autistic children, such interference may be unusually severe. It is important to know about these matters, because we are always concerned with how much the child is learning about his environment.

The article by Koegel and Schreibman elaborates on the problems associated with shifts in stimulus control (i.e., behavior being shifted from one input to another), with particular reference to overselective attention and its application to prompt and prompt-fading procedures. Only insofar as we become aware of the psychotic child's deviant perceptual functioning can we begin to construct those learning environments in which he also can learn. The Koegel-Schreibman article suggests some new and more helpful procedures in teaching autistic children. Similar considerations may well apply to many other children with learning difficulties.

PAUL E. TOUCHETTE
Joseph P. Kennedy, Jr. Memorial Laboratories

The effects
of graduated stimulus change
on the acquisition
of a simple discrimination
in severely retarded boys[1]

Methods were compared for teaching severely retarded boys to discriminate the position of a 0.75-in. black square and to press the response key closest to it. Seven boys were given trial-and-error training; one learned the task. The six boys who did not learn were presented with a program of graduated stimulus changes. All but one acquired the performance, and he was under appropriate control during the program. When he reached the criterion stimuli, he reverted to a position-based response learned during trial-and-error training. Six similar subjects were presented with graduated stimulus training alone. All six learned the criterion discrimination with few or no errors. Both groups were tested for retention of the criterion performance 35 days after training was completed. Two boys who had near-perfect criterion discrimination performances showed no signs of retention after 35 days. These boys had a history of trial-and-error training.

Reprinted from *Journal of Experimental Analysis of Behavior*, 1968, 11, 39–48, with permission of the publisher and author. Copyright 1968 by the Society for the Experimental Analysis of Behavior, Inc.

[1] The author wishes to thank Drs. Murray Sidman, Douglas Porter, and Sheldon White for their assistance and to acknowledge the cooperation of the following personnel to the Walter E. Fernald State School: Malcolm J. Farrell, Superintendent; Hugo Moser, Director of Research; Elizabeth Cassidy, Matron. This research was supported by P. H. S. Research Grant NB 03535 from the National Institute of Neurological Disease and Blindness.

Recent studies of discrimination learning have indicated that a significant number of severely retarded children fail to learn even simple discriminations, despite carefully programmed contingent reinforcers. Barrett (1965) found no learning in seven of 25 retarded subjects, and deviant response patterns in 11 others, after as much as 16 hr of differential reinforcement. Other studies have reported this finding in the form of subjects who were discarded from experimental samples for failure to learn (Ellis, Girardeau, and Pryer, 1962; House and Zeaman, 1958, 1960; Orlando, 1961).

Errors may be defined as responses to a stimulus not related to the reinforcement contingencies in a learning situation. Spence (1936), Harlow (1959), Krechevsky (1932), Skinner (1948) and others have pointed out that stimuli not specified as "relevant" to the correct response frequently come to control behavior during "normal" discrimination learning. Retardates who do not learn, or who adopt deviant response patterns, may differ from normal in that they continue under the control of some irrelevant property of the experimental situation long after more efficient behavior has been developed by those who learn. Barrett and Lindsley (1962) found ". . . initial differential responding of a 'superstitious' nature . . . and marked response stereotypes . . ." (p. 428) in trial-and-error learning by institutionalized retardates.

Errors have long been assumed to be a necessary part of the learning process. However, several experimenters have demonstrated that discriminations can be learned without errors (Schlosberg and Solomon, 1943; Terrace, 1963a, 1963b; Moore and Goldiamond, 1964). In the above studies, the experimenters initiated training by reinforcing a stimulus-response relation which already existed or which was easily acquired. The controlling stimuli were then gradually changed to approximate more and more closely those appropriate to the discrimination to be taught. By maintaining appropriate stimulus-response relations throughout training, responses based on stimuli not directly related to reinforcement were eliminated.

The present study sought to determine whether a procedure designed to maintain stimulus control throughout training can be effective in teaching severely retarded subjects who have already demonstrated no learning under differential reinforcement conditions. Subjects with and without histories of trial-and-error training are compared.

METHOD

Subjects

Fourteen retarded boys, permanent residents of the same ward at the Walter E. Fernald State School, served. Ages ranged from 9 to 16 yr, and duration of institutionalization from 5 to 13 yr. All subjects had been diagnosed as severely retarded with some organic brain disorder. The boys demonstrated little or no verbal behavior. Several were able to respond appropriately to a few simple instructions. Detailed information on individual subjects is given in Table 1. For the purposes of this study, the 14 subjects were ranked according to their current accomplishments by four psychologists and two teachers who had been in close contact with the boys for 18 months or more. The children are identified throughout the study by their rank number. The coefficient of Concordance (Kendall's W) for the internal consistency of the rank-order ratings was 0.85 (significant beyond 0.001). Their I.Q. scores were of little value for differentiating the boys, since the test-retest variation was as great as the variation in score from subject to subject.

Apparatus

The subjects sat in an area approximately 9 by 8.5 by 7 ft, lit by soft, indirect light. The wall facing the subject contained a response and display matrix consisting of three 3.75-in. square Polacoat Plexiglas panels, mounted in an aluminum plate. No dividing strips separated the two response keys from the center display panel (Fig. 1). The two outside panels (keys) were hinged at the top and in contact with heavy-duty microswitches at their lower edge. The center panel was fixed in place. It was occasionally touched by subjects exposed to the programmed sequence, and to minimize feedback, responses to it were not recorded.

The stimulus projection apparatus was a Model 550 Kodak Carousel 35mm slide projector, mounted behind the response panel. A motor-oper-

TABLE 1   Data on individual subjects from institution records

Relative rank	Age (years) at admission	Age (years) current	Mean I.Q.	Diagnosis
1	1	13	45	Kernicterus
2	3	11	43	Chronic brain syndrome
3	4	14	27	Familial microcephaly
4	4	13	41	Familial microcephaly
5	1	14	30	Mongolism
6	3	15	31	Neonatal anoxia
7	7	12	45	Mongolism
8	5	16	27	Mongolism
9	5	13	31	Cerebral palsy
10	4	9	42	Mongolism
11	6	11	34	Mongolism
12	1	11	42	Mongolism
13	1	14	27	Mongolism
14	1	13	35	Mongolism

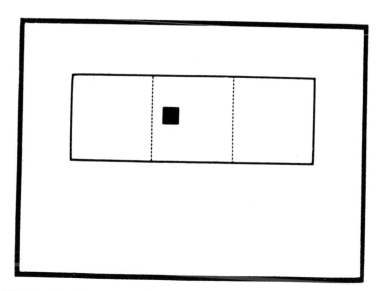

FIGURE 1 Experimental apparatus, subject's view.

ated shutter interrupted light from the projector during the interval between trials. Each slide contained the stimuli for all three panels for a
given trial. Below the panels was a strip of five photocells keyed by holes
punched in the lower portion of the slide. These photocells served to de-
code the correct key position for each trial. Light falling on the photocells
was not visible to the subject. A similar apparatus has been described by
Hively (1964).

Stimuli for the several programs were manufactured by photograph-
ing a mock-up of the apparatus front panel. Kodak high-speed Ektachrome
type B film was used. Background colors (including black) were Color-
Aid paper. Progressive changes in brightness and color were made by adding or removing layers of Bourges overlays, placed over the stimuli to be
photographed.

Pilot data indicated that position-based responses were the most
probable type of error pattern. The sequence of correct key-positions was
designed so that no more than two consecutive trials required a response
in the same position. Repeated presses of the position which was correct
on the previous trial would have been reinforced only 35% of the time.
Further pilot data indicated that the children did not learn the sequence
or portions of it either under trial-and-error or programmed training conditions.

The last slide in the tray of 40 activated a photocell which automatically stopped the session. When this occurred, the slide tray was man-

ually recycled and the session continued until the appropriate number of trials had been given (see below). Recycling the tray by hand rarely took longer than the normal intertrial time of 5 sec.

Responses were recorded on a 20-channel Esterline Angus operations recorder which provided a running account of the onset of trials, location of the correct key, and latency of all responses during and between trials. This apparatus was housed in a plywood container surrounded by sound-insulating materials. "White" noise also helped to mask extraneous sounds.

After every correct response, a Gerbrands M&M dispenser mounted to the right of the stimulus display operated and chimes sounded. The candy dropped into a 5 by 3 by 1 in. Plexiglas tray at the base of the dispenser. During a session the room was dimly lit, but subjects had no difficulty in locating the candy.

PROCEDURES

The initial objective was to determine whether subjects who failed to learn a discrimination under trial-and-error training conditions could be taught that same discrimination by a programmed sequence of stimuli. The preliminary training and criterion discrimination common to all subjects and both training procedures are described first.

Preliminary Training

Before each child was brought into the experimental chamber for the first time, an M&M candy was placed in the tray below the dispenser. All children discovered the candy soon after sitting down to face the matrix of keys. Subsequent operations of the dispenser made sufficient noise to attract their attention to the tray. The procedure of preloading the dispenser with an M&M was continued throughout the experiment. It served to reinforce the child's entering the room, sitting down, and orienting toward the apparatus.

The boys were then taught to press whichever response key was illuminated. The most expedient combination of verbal instructions, demonstration, and guidance was used to get the child to press the key initially. After this initial response, key-pressing was quickly established by the programmed reinforcement contingencies.

At this point, the correct stimulus was a brightly lit red key. The other key and the center panel were dark. In a dimly lit room, the single bright key was the dominating visual stimulus. Once key-pressing had been established, the children were allowed to press the keys while the correct key changed from side to side in a predetermined sequence. A candy was dispensed and a chime sounded after each correct response. Pretraining was considered complete when a child had made eight successive correct responses. All children met this criterion in fewer than 20 trials.

Criterion Discrimination

During each trial, the center (display) panel contained a single black 0.75-in. square. This square was displaced 0.5 in. from either the left or right margin of the panel (see Fig. 2, part E). Proximity to the square determined which outside response key was correct.

A trial began when the display panel and the two keys were illuminated, and ended when the subject applied sufficient pressure to close the switch behind the key closest to the square. Reinforcement (candy, chimes, projector cycle) followed responses to the correct key. If both keys were pressed simultaneously (within 0.5 sec of each other), the trial was terminated and reinitiated after 5 sec. With the exception of "simultaneous" responses, all trials ended with a correct response. An intertrial interval of

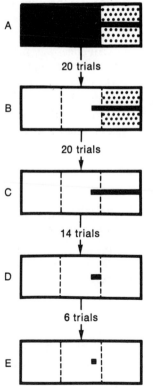

FIGURE 2   Schematic representation of the major stages in the programmed sequence of graduated stimuli. Although the correct key is shown on the right, its position actually varied according to a predetermined sequence. The dotted backgrounds in parts A and B represent solid red fields. Transitions from one stage to the next were carried out in small, gradual steps (see text for details).

5 sec, during which the panels were dark, followed each correct response. Incorrect responses were recorded, but produced no contingent event. This correction procedure was used throughout the experiment.

The criterion discrimination with correction served as a teaching procedure for subjects who received trial-and-error training and as a test procedure to assess the effects of the alternate training method described below.

Programmed Stimulus Sequence

The major stages in the programmed sequence of graduated stimuli are presented in Fig. 2. Part A represents the initial training slide. It consisted of a black display panel, a black response key (shown on the left) and a red key containing a black horizontal line. Through the first 20 trials, the black response key and display panel became progressively lighter until they were fully bright, as shown in B. In the next 20 trials, the red background was gradually desaturated until all of the panels were white, as shown in C. In the next 14 trials, the black line was gradually shortened until it was entirely on the center panel, as shown in D. In the next six trials, the line continued to shorten, approximating the 0.75-in. black square which served as the criterion stimulus, shown in E.

Each step followed the preceding step and the sequence was never reversed. A correct response always advanced the next slide in the sequence. The criterion discrimination procedure used the same stimuli on each trial, varying only the position of the stimulus on the display panel.

The empirical procedures used to develop this instructional program were similar to those described by Hively (1962) and Sidman and Stoddard (1966).

Sequence of Training Procedures

Two groups of subjects were each presented with a different sequence of training procedures. The subjects had comparable ratings and I.Q. scores. The objective of this group comparison was to determine what effect, if any, a history of trial-and-error training might have on performance during the programmed sequence, the criterion test, and the retention test.

"Trial-and-Error" Group

Seven subjects (2, 3, 4, 7, 8, 9, 13) were given trial-and-error training on the criterion discrimination. Duration of training was arbitrarily limited to 320 trials (four sessions).

Two subjects (7, 8) were given an additional 320 training trials (a total of 640) to determine the effects of extended practice.

All subjects who had not learned the discrimination after the above training (2, 4, 7, 8, 9, 13) were then given the programmed stimulus sequence to determine if this type of training would affect preformance. Immediately after completing the graduated stimulus sequence, the subjects were given 40 criterion trials identical to those which had preceded the programmed stimuli. Thirty-five days later, the criterion discrimination test was applied once again in order to assess retention.

"Program" Group

Seven subjects (1, 5, 6, 10, 11, 12, 14) were given the programmed sequence of stimuli directly after preliminary training. Immediately following the programmed sequence, 40 criterion trials were presented. Thirty-five days after training was completed, the criterion test was reapplied to assess retention.

RESULTS

Trial-and-Error Training

The initial experimental question was whether the square, displaced to either side of the center panel, would come to control the key-pressing responses of the severely retarded subjects given trial-and-error training.

Seven subjects were given the criterion discrimination and were rewarded for responses on the key closest to the square. One subject learned the criterion discrimination, six failed to learn. Figure 3 shows the course of training. The left-hand portion of the records in Fig. 3 shows the frequency of correct responses and errors in each of the consecutive 40-trial sequences under differential reinforcement contingencies. In six cases, there was no evidence of learning or any indication that acquisition was imminent after 320 trials.

To appraise the effects of extended practice, two boys (7, 8) were given an additional 320 trials, for a total of 640. They continued to show no significant deviations from 50% correct. No response patterns were related to the repetitive 40-trial sequence of key positions.

One clear error pattern emerged during trial-and-error training. Subject 7 developed a right-key position preference. Figure 4 shows the development of this preference during the first 120 training trials. No noticeable change occurred during the next 520 trials. Subject 7 continued to initiate more than 90% of the trials with a response on the right key.

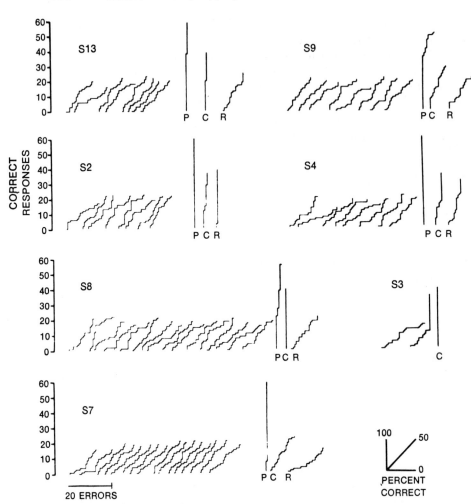

FIGURE 3 Cumulative correct responses (each step up) and errors (each step to the right) for each of the 40-trial sequences during trial-and-error training, during the programmed stimulus sequence (P), the criterion test (C), and the retention test (R). Only the first response in each trial is plotted.

Programmed Stimulus Sequence

The trial-and-error procedure provided a group of subjects who had demonstrated no tendency to learn under these conditions. It was thus possible to ask whether the graduated stimulus sequence would affect performance of the "non-learners."

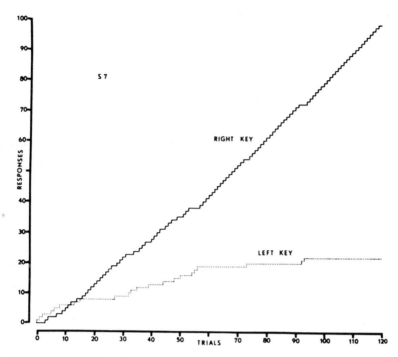

FIGURE 4 Development of a position-based response during trial-and-error training, Subject 7.

The six subjects who had not learned the criterion discrimination under trial-and-error conditions were given a 60-trial instructional program. The portion of the records designated P in Fig. 3 shows cumulative correct responses and errors during the sequence of programmed stimuli. Five subjects made few or no errors; Subject 9 made several in the latter part of the program. The portion of the records designated C in Fig. 3 represents the frequency of correct responses and errors during the 40 criterion discrimination trials which followed the instructional sequence. Four subjects (13, 2, 4, 8) improved from chance responding to 85% or better accuracy. Subject 9 improved to 72.5% accuracy, while Subject 7 did not show any increase in the number of correct responses emitted during the criterion test.

During the last half of the trial-and-error training, Subject 7 picked the right key first on more than 95% of the trials. During the programmed stimulus sequence, however, there was no evidence of a position preference. He made only one error in these 60 trials. While the programmed visual stimuli successfully maintained control over this subject's responding, the position habit returned when the criterion stimuli were presented after the program was completed.

Program Subjects

Seven boys who had been magazine trained and taught to press a lighted key (1, 5, 6, 10, 11, 12, 14) were presented directly with the programmed stimulus sequence and then the criterion discrimination test.

The objective of establishing a group which received no trial-and-error training was to determine what effect, if any, trial-and-error training might have had on the first group's performance during the programmed sequence, criterion, and retention tests.

Subject 12 was dropped from the experimental group when it was discovered that he was nearly blind. He made only three errors in the first 45 program trials, but exhibited no evidence of control by the programmed stimuli after trial 45. No other child had ever had difficulty with this portion of the program. Similar results were obtained on a second presentation. An opthalmologic examination revealed bilateral mature cataracts, with scars on the left pupil and cornea, the result of surgery performed in infancy. In terms of his behavior on the ward, this nearly blind child was not readily discernible among those with their vision physically intact. He had, in fact, been considered one of the brighter, more alert boys on the ward. This accidental discovery of a severe visual impairment made it clear that the level of visual functioning normally displayed by the subjects in their daily routine was even lower than originally suspected.

Figure 5 includes a trial-by-trial account of the Program (P) and Criterion test (C) performances of the remaining six Program subjects. Only one boy (6) dropped below 90% accuracy during the programmed sequence of stimuli. During the 100 training and test trials, this group's median error frequency was 5, while the maximum was only 11. Thus, the worst subject in this group was 89% correct during training and testing. These records revealed no systematic error patterns across or within subjects. The programmed sequence of graduated stimuli maintained nearly perfect stimulus control while bringing these severely retarded boys under the control of the final stimuli in only 60 trials.

Retention Tests

All 12 boys were retested 35 days after the program and criterion test were completed. The retention test consisted of 40 criterion trials under the same correction procedure used before. Criterion performances may be contrasted to retention test performances in Fig. 5. Table 2 shows the criterion and retention test scores expressed in terms of per cent correct.

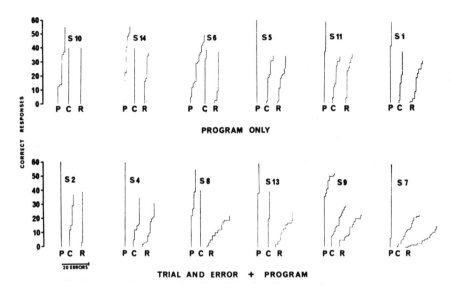

FIGURE 5 Cumulative correct responses (each step up) and errors (each step to the right) for both groups during the programmed stimulus sequence (P), the criterion test (C), and the retention test (R). Only the first response in each trial is plotted.

Subjects 8 and 13 in the Trial-and-Error group, who had nearly perfect criterion test performances, showed virtually no retention. Their retention test performances were not significantly different from chance. Subject 1 in the Program group suffered the largest loss after 35 days, dropping from 92.5 to 75% correct. His retention score was, however, still significantly above a chance performance (P < 0.001). Thus, two boys in the Trial-and-Error group lost all that they had learned after near-perfect original performances. In the Program group, all subjects but one showed excellent retention, and that one boy was still demonstrating the controlling relation between the experimental stimuli and his responses. It should be noted that the boys in both groups had learned the discrimination by means of the program, and differed from each other only in their earlier training.

DISCUSSION

These data indicate that retarded children, who show no signs of learning a discrimination by trial and error, can be taught by a program of graduated stimulus changes. The data further suggest that a history of trial-and-

TABLE 2 Comparison of criterion and retention test scores

Subject number	Criterion test % correct	Retention test % correct
8	100.0	55.0*
13	97.5	62.5*
2	92.5	97.5
4	87.5	77.5
9	72.5	57.5*
7	57.5*	37.5*
10	100.0	100.0
14	100.0	90.0
6	97.5	92.5
1	92.5	75.0
11	85.0	87.5
5	85.0	85.0

Scores marked with an asterisk were not significantly different from chance (50%) $P < 0.01$.

error training may interfere with acquisition and retention of a discrimination. These findings support and extend those of Sidman and Stoddard (1967).

Sidman and Stoddard (1967) reported that retardates, presented initially with a criterion test under trial-and-error conditions, were better able to learn when presented with a programmed instructional sequence. Several subjects in each of their groups (4 of 9 subjects with a history of trial and error, 3 of 10 subjects with no training history) failed to get through the instructional sequence. In this study, subjects similar to those used by Sidman and Stoddard, all completed the program of graduated stimulus changes with few or no errors. A possible reason for this difference lies in the pre-training procedure employed. All subjects were initially taught to discriminate a lighted red key from a dark key to a criterion of eight successive correct responses. This procedure guaranteed that each subject was familiar with the apparatus, had no major topography problems, and was under the control of the stimuli which initiated the instructional program. In contrast, Sidman and Stoddard (1967) presented subjects initially with program slides or criterion trials. They initiated training with a procedure and stimuli which might in no way control the behavior of the subject. Each procedure was then terminated when a criterion of five successive errors on the same slide was met. Thus, it was possible for subjects to get through several procedures without ever having come under the control of the stimuli presented on the keys. If this occurred, and it seems likely that it did, the programmed instructional sequence was doubly taxed. It then became necessary to establish, for the first time, appropriate stimulus control in subjects who were likely to have come under the control of inappropriate aspects of the experimental environment.

Training procedures which do not immediately establish control by appropriate stimuli can result in the acquisition of stimulus-response relations which interfere with the establishment of control by the designated aspects of the experimental environment.

The data from Subject 7 illustrate this point. After pretraining, Subject 7 was presented with 640 criterion trials under differential reinforcement and rapidly acquired a position habit. When he was switched to the program, control by the experimental stimuli was reestablished. He made only one error during the 60-trial program which gradually approximated the criterion stimuli. However, when the stimuli were made identical to those which had been present during trial-and-error training, Subject 7 reverted to his position-based response. This subject responded to the training stimuli by pressing the "correct" key but responded to the criterion stimuli by always pressing the right-hand key. This breakdown of control at the very last step of the program suggests that the subject "recognized" the 0.75 in. square and emitted the response pattern which had been adventitiously reinforced in the presence of this stimulus during trial-and-error training. It seems unreasonable that altering the width of the black area on the key by 0.125 in. would cause such a dramatic change in the subject's behavior, were it not for his previous exposure to the criterion stimuli.

Subject 7's position-based responses might be described as "discriminated errors" in that they signaled his discrimination of the criterion stimuli from the training stimuli. It seems likely that the three Sidman and Stoddard (1967) subjects who went through the initial stages of the instructional program with relatively little difficulty, but returned to making errors as the criterion stimuli reappeared, were making some form of discriminated errors.

The remaining five trial-and-error subjects in the present study did not develop any identifiable error patterns in the presence of the criterion stimuli. This could have been a result of the extreme simplicity of the visual display. The 0.75-in. square was the only stimulus presented on the display-response panels which varied from trial to trial during the criterion procedure. Thus, when this singular visual stimulus did not gain control, the basis for responses was not apparent. There were, however, several indications that these subjects were under the control of some properties of the display-response panels; their continued accurate response topography, and the absence of responses between trials, *i.e.*, when the keys were dark.

In the group of six subjects with a history of trial-and-error training, four showed some difficulty in acquiring or retaining the discrimination.

Since none of the members of the group without this training history showed these effects, it seems likely that the trial-and-error training had deleterious effects even in those cases where the adventitiously reinforced response patterns were not obvious. The nature of the interaction between subject and environment in a trial-and-error procedure precludes the accurate specification of historical variables. However, the magnitude of the effects observed in these children suggests that research should be directed to identifying historical variables which affect acquisition, transfer, and retention of stimulus control.

In a visual discrimination problem where "correct" responses are differentially reinforced, the contingencies set by the experimenter do not exclude inappropriate observing behavior. Thus, responses can be reinforced regardless of what the subject is observing. The conditions under which reinforcement is delivered may be sufficient to shape superstitious control. In normal subjects, superstitions frequently appear during discrimination training, but they are replaced by more efficient behavior (Krechevsky, 1932; Harlow, 1959). In the retardate, superstitious controlling relations generated early in discrimination training frequently seem to prevent the development of any appropriate controlling relation. The occurrence of spurious controlling relations cannot be avoided even with the most careful application of reinforcement in a trial-and-error procedure (*cf.* Reynolds, 1961). However, if training is initiated by reinforcing a stimulus-response relation which already exists, or is easily established, it may then be possible to shift the stimuli towards those which comprise the criterion discrimination, while maintaining control of responses by specified and appropriate aspects of the training environment.

Tedious though it may be to establish a graduated series of training stimuli which insure the continuity of stimulus control, the startling effectiveness and economy of the program, once perfected, amply justify the work necessary to develop it. Further, some retardates who give the appearance of being untrainable, may in fact be the victims of training techniques which generate perseverative error patterns. For them, a programmed graduated stimulus training procedure may provide the only means for discovering their true potential.

REFERENCES

Barrett, B. H. Acquisition of operant differentiation and discrimination in institutionalized retarded children. *Amer. J. Orthopsychiat.*, 1965, **35**, 863–885.

Barrett, B. H. and Lindsley, O. R. Deficits in acquisition of operant discrimination and differentiation shown by institutionalized retarded children. *Amer. J. ment. Def.*, 1962, 67, 424–436.

ELLIS, N. R., GIRARDEAU, F. L., and PRYER, M. W. Analysis of learning sets in normal and severely defective humans. *J. comp. physiol. Psychol.*, 1962, 55, 860–865.

HARLOW, H. F. Learning set and error factor theory. In, S. Koch (Ed.), *Psychology: A study of a science*, Vol. 2. New York: McGraw-Hill, 1959. Pp. 492–537.

HIVELY, W. A. Programming stimuli in matching-to-sample. *J. exp. Anal. Behav.*, 1962, 5, 279–298.

HIVELY, W. A. A multiple-choice visual discrimination apparatus. *J. exp. Anal. Behav.* 1964, 7, 387–389.

HOUSE, B. J. and ZEAMAN, D. Visual discrimination learning in imbeciles, *Amer. J. ment. Defic.*, 1958, 63, 447–452.

HOUSE, B. J. and ZEAMAN, D. Visual discrimination learning and intelligence in defectives of low mental age. *Amer. J. ment. Defic.*, 1960, 65, 51–58.

KRECHEVSKY, I. "Hypotheses" in rats. *Psychol. Rev.*, 1932, 39, 519–532.

LASHLEY, K. Preliminary studies of the rat's capacity for detail vision. *J. genet. Psychol.*, 1938, 18, 123–193.

MOORE, R. and GOLDIAMOND, I. Errorless establishment of a visual discrimination using fading procedures. *J. exp. Anal. Behav.*, 1964, 7, 269–272.

MORSE, W. A. and SKINNER, B. F. A second type of "superstition" in the pigeon. *Amer. J. Psychol.*, 1957, 70, 308–311.

ORLANDO, R. The functional role of discriminative stimuli in the free operant performance of developmentally retarded children. *Psychol. Rec.*, 1961, 11, 153–161.

REYNOLDS, G. Attention in the pigeon. *J. exp. Anal. Behav.*, 1961, 4, 203–208.

SCHLOSBERG, H. and SOLOMON, R. Latency of response in a choice discrimination. *J. exp. Psychol.*, 1943, 33, 22–39.

SIDMAN, M. and STODDARD, L. Programming perception and learning for retarded children. In, N. Ellis (Ed.), *International Review of Research in Mental Retardation*, Vol. 2. New York, Academic Press, 1966. Pp. 152–207.

SIDMAN, M. and STODDARD, L. The effectiveness of fading in programming a simultaneous form discrimination for retarded children. *J. exp. Anal. Behav.*, 1967, 10, 3–15.

SKINNER, B. F. "Superstition" in the pigeon. *J. exp. Psychol.*, 1948, 38, 168–172.

SPENCE, K. W. The nature of discrimination learning in animals. *Psychol. Rev.*, 1936, 43, 427–449.

TERRACE, H. Discrimination learning with and without "errors." *J. exp. Anal. Behav.*, 1963, 6, 1–27 (*a*).

TERRACE, H. Errorless transfer of a discrimination across two continua. *J. exp. Anal. Behav.*, 1963, 6, 223–232 (*b*).

O. IVAR LOVAAS
LAURA SCHREIBMAN
ROBERT KOEGEL
RICHARD REHM
University of California at Los Angeles

Selective responding
by autistic children
to multiple sensory input[1]

Three groups of children (autistic, retarded, and normal) were reinforced for responding to a complex stimulus involving the simultaneous presentation of auditory, visual, and tactile cues. Once this discrimination was established, elements of the complex were presented separately to assess which aspects of the complex stimulus had acquired control over the child's behavior. We found that: (a) the autistics responded primarily to only one of the cues; the normals responded uniformly to all three cues; and the retardates functioned between these two extremes. (b) Conditions could be arranged such that a cue which

Reprinted from *Journal of Abnormal Psychology*, 1971, 77, 211–22, with permission of the authors. Copyright 1971 by the American Psychological Association, and reproduced by permission.

[1] This investigation was supported by United States Public Health Service Research Grant 11440 from the National Institute of Mental Health. The authors express their appreciation for the help of: James Q. Simmons, Associate Program Director of Clinical Training for the Mental Retardation Center, Neuropsychiatric Institute, University of California, Los Angeles; Thomas Ball, of the Department of Psychology, Pacific State Hospital, Pomona, California; and Norbert Rieger, Superintendent of Children's Services, Camarillo State Hospital, Camarillo, California. They are grateful to B. Henker, W. E. Jeffrey, and I. Maltzman for their helpful comments on an earlier draft. They also wish to thank Bodil Sivertsen for her assistance in this research.

The essentials of this paper were presented at the Annual Meeting of the National Society for Autistic Children, San Francisco, California, June 24–27, 1970.

had remained nonfunctional when presented in association with other cues could be established as functional when trained separately. The data failed to support notions that any one sense modality is impaired in autistic children. Rather, when presented with a stimulus complex, their attention was over-selective. The findings were related to the literature on selective attention. Since much learning involves contiguous or near-contiguous pairing of two or more stimuli, failure to respond to one of the stimuli might be an important factor in the development of autism.

The unresponsivity of autistic children serves as one of the main criteria for their diagnosis. This unresponsiveness is typically apparent in a child during the first year of life when he behaves as if he were blind and deaf, causing his parents to seek professional opinion. Kanner (1944) describes such behavior in one of his patients as follows:

> When spoken to, he went on with what he was doing as if nothing had been said. Yet one never had the feeling that he was willingly disobedient or contrary. He was obviously so remote that the remarks did not reach him. [p. 212].

Rimland (1964, cf. pp. 94–96) has presented several other illustrations of such unresponsivity. Description of the phenomenon points to a large variability which can be observed within a particular modality. For example, it may be impossible to observe a response in these children to a very loud (100-db.) sound, yet they may respond excessively to a barely audible siren. The child who behaves as if he does not see the person who greets him, or other objects in his environment, may spot a sugar-coated corn flake some 20 ft. away. There also exists some speculation (Rimland, 1964) that the unresponsiveness may vary across modalities, such that visual, auditory, and pain stimulation are less likely to elicit a response than tactual, gustatory, or olfactory stimuli.

An example from our own laboratory serves to illustrate how such unresponsivity interferes with these children's treatment. We attempted to teach mute autistic children language by beginning with a program on the teaching of verbal imitation (Lovaas, Berberich, Perloff, & Schaeffer, 1966). We have tried to facilitate such imitations by providing the child with visual cues as well as auditory ones. Thus, the child can clearly see the teacher's face when she presents the various sounds, such as "mm," which has auditory and visual cues quite distinct from "ah." The child will learn under these conditions; that is, he comes to reliably emit the vocal response in apparent imitation of the teacher. Following this, the teacher presents the sounds while the child is looking away, or while she is purposely covering her face. Strikingly, the child remains mute. He only attended to the visual cues. It is as if he had never heard the sounds despite thousands of trial exposures.

Figure 1 presents an example from a large number of such instances in our speech training program. The figure is based on data from a patient, Johan, an 8-yr.-old mute boy diagnosed as a "textbook example of autism." He was trained to imitate the sound "ah" with full visual exposure to the teacher's face. Percentages of correct reproductions (*S*'s "ah" to *E*'s "ah") are given on the ordinate, and trials are given along the abscissa. The *S* had 1,180 trials preceding those which are plotted here, but his performance reflected no learning until after 1,400 trials. At this point he improved, and by Trial 1,740 he gave an onlooker the impression that he was listening to *E* and imitating what he had heard. However, when *E* removed the visual cues associated with the sound (Trials 1760–1780, 1800–1820, and 1840–1860), *S*'s performance fell to zero. It is as if he had never heard *E*'s voice.

The insert in the figure shows the same loss when visual cues are removed from the training of Johan's second sound, "mm." Eventually, as in the case of gutteral sounds (e.g., "g," "k") without distinct visual components, the child learns to discriminate (imitate) the auditory cues. This acquisition is very slow. These observations raise several questions. Are the children particularly unresponsive to auditory cues? Are they unresponsive to auditory cues when these are presented together with visual cues? Do

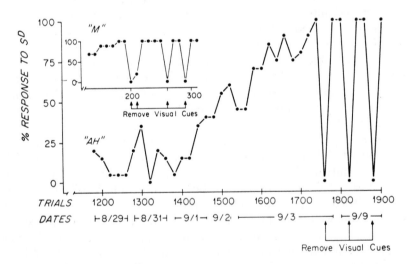

FIGURE 1   Acquisition of "Ah" and "Mm" trained with auditory and visual cues. (Percentages of correct reproductions of *E*'s presentations are plotted on the ordinate with trials plotted along the abscissa. Arrows indicate trials where visual cues were removed.)

they have difficulty attending to any one cue in a multiple cue input, etc.?

The clinical observations that these children respond to cues in a particular modality on one occasion while not responding to these cues on another occasion have led to inferences regarding deficiencies in attentional, rather than sensory, mechanisms. These deficiencies in attentional mechanisms have been given a central, explanatory role in the child's failure of cognitive, social, or emotional development. For the reader who feels that there may be a similarity between attentional deficit in adult and childhood schizophrenia, excellent reviews of theories of attentional deficit in adult schizophrenia have been provided by Buss and Lang (1965), Lang and Buss (1965), and Feigenberg (1969).

There are two main etiologies which have been proposed to underlie the attentional deficiencies in autism. One of these is based on developmental models and draws heavily on Sherrington's work (1906). He postulated a transition from near-receptor dominance in lower organisms to far-receptor dominance in higher organisms. He considered, furthermore, that the far receptors are prerequisite for the development of complex psychological processes. This conceptualization has been employed by Goldfarb (1964) in his postulation of a distorted hierarchy of receptor dominance in autistic children, with motor-tactile orientation dominating auditory and visual inputs. Subsequent experimental studies (cf. Schopler, 1966) have failed to verify the propriety of this model in describing receptor orientation in autistic children.

The other proposed etiology of these attentional deficits is based on hypothesized deviations in their social history and draws heavily on psychodynamic formulations. The children's primary difficulty is seen to arise from inadequate early mother-child interactions, with a consequent failure in the development of perceptual activity, or it may be selective, largely restricted to social stimuli. As was the case with the developmental theories based on Sherrington's work, there has been a similar failure for research to confirm psychodynamic interpretations.

Much of the empirical work here has been carried out by Hermelin and O'Connor (summarized by Hermelin, 1966) and usually involved exposing the children to various stimulus displays, obtaining preferences for certain inputs as a function of the amount of their visual or tactual attending behavior. The conclusion which can be drawn from these studies is that, in contrast to normals, autistic children look less at the experimental stimuli, but do not selectively avoid social ones. Young (1969) found that they may attend proportionately less to complex, incongruous stimuli.

Although descriptions of visual attending behavior, which comprise the bulk of research in this area, may provide leads in understanding the psychopathology, such studies are quite inferential. That is, they require a model which relates visual attending to learning, or to some other behavior change. This is feasible since a person can visually attend to an environment without learning anything about it. Receptor orientation is necessary, but not sufficient, for learning. Viewed in that context, a discrimination learning situation may be a superior procedure for the study of attentional deficits, since it incorporates learning. We have employed such a procedure in the study we shall describe below.

The situation we constructed was as follows: the child was reinforced for responding in the presence of a stimulus display and was not reinforced for responding in the absence of that display. One can argue that the child attends to (is controlled by) certain stimuli when independent variation of these stimuli is associated with concurrent change in the child's behavior. We employed a multidimensional stimulus display, that is, a display which contained auditory, visual, tactual, and temporal cues. The study was designed such that, after the child's behavior was brought under the control of the display, separate components of that display could be presented singly so as to assess to which aspects the child was responding. One could then find out if certain components of the display were more functional than others, how many components had become functional, whether certain components had failed to acquire any function, etc.

METHOD

Subjects

We ran three groups of Ss. The autistic group consisted of five boys and one girl, with mean CA of 7.2 yr. (range of 4–10 yr.). These children had been diagnosed by agencies not associated with the experiment. Four of the Ss were mute and would utter only unintelligible sounds without communicative intent. They gave sporadic response to the most elementary commands (e.g., "sit down," "close the door"). They were untestable on standard psychological tests. Two of the Ss were not toilet-trained, and other social and self-help skills were minimal. For example, they did not dress themselves; they did not play with toys; and they did not play with peers. Three had early histories of suspected deafness. They were in-patients, and in all likelihood faced permanent hospitalization. In short, they were extremely regressed and fell within the lower third of the psychotic continuum. The fifth child, Danny, differed from the rest in that he was echolalic, expressed simple demands, and was behaviorally more advanced so that he remained at home and made a marginal adjustment to a class for severely retarded children. Like the others, he would frequently act as if he did not see or hear adults. All Ss demonstrated bizarre self-stimulatory behavior (stereotyped motor acts).

The second group contained five mentally retarded children, four boys and one girl, with a mean CA of 8 yr. (range of 7–10 yr.) and a mean MA of 3.7 yr. (range 3.5 to 4.0 yr.). Four of these Ss were institutionalized. Two had been diagnosed as Mongoloid, two as retarded due to birth trauma, and one as retarded from an unknown genetic origin. One of the retarded Ss had a history of suspected (but unconfirmed) deafness, while all other Ss had displayed normal responsiveness to external stimulation.

A normal control group consisted of five children with mean CA of 6.4 yr. (range of 6.0–7.5 yr.). These Ss, two boys and three girls, were obtained from parents working at the university.

Apparatus

The S was seated in a 7 × 8 ft. experimental room in front of a 2½-ft.-high table holding a box with a 3-in. bar protruding from its front. The box also housed a Davis Model 310 universal feeder which delivered candy, potato chips, etc., to S through a chute at the left side of the box. Sound equipment and one-way vision screens connected the experimental room to an observation room from which E would present the various experimental manipulations. The experimental room was lighted by a 40-w. light, giving a dim illumination level of .50 ftc. The room was sound attenuated.

We employed four kinds of stimuli. (a) A visual stimulus, which consisted of a 150-w. red floodlight, was mounted on the ceiling behind S's back and out of his view. This light raised the room illumination level from .50 to 2.50 ftc. as measured by a Weston illumination meter, Model 756 (these readings were made on the front panel of the box which faced S). (b) An auditory stimulus, consisting of white noise, was fed from a tape recorder into a speaker located above S. The noise level generated was 63 db. (measured by a General Radio Co. sound-level meter, Type No. 1551-B, set at 20-kc. weighting). Since white noise consists of all frequencies, the possibility of Ss being differentially sensitive to particular frequencies was eliminated. (c) A tactile stimulus was applied by forcing air into a blood pressure cuff fastened around S's left calf. The cuff was attached by a rubber tube to an automobile tire pump operated by E. The arrangement allowed E to deliver a rather discrete tactile pressure (20 mm. of mercury), retain that pressure for the desired interval, and instantly remove (deflate) it. (d) A temporal cue was arranged by presenting all the stimuli for a 5-sec. interval every 20 sec. That is, S could obtain reinforcement simply by hitting the bar as a function of time elapsed since last reinforcement (a temporal cue) rather than on the basis of the three other cues.

The S was run in two kinds of sessions, training and testing. During training sessions, he was taught a discrimination where his bar presses were brought under the control of the stimulus complex. During the subsequent test sessions, he was presented with the various components of the stimulus complex to assess which one(s) had acquired functional control.

Training

The S was seated before the bar and instructed that if he pressed it he would get candy. If S failed to respond to the instructions, E prompted the response manually. As soon as S had emitted two unassisted bar presses within 1 min., he was left alone in the experimental room and presented with the S^D (stimulus complex). The S^D was presented for 10 sec. or until it was terminated by a single bar press. When S had responded to the S^D on three successive presentations, the duration of the S^D period was gradually decreased in 1-sec. units to the ultimate 5-sec. S^D interval. At the same time, the reinforcement schedule was gradually changed from FR-1 to FR-4. In the final stages of training, S would eventually respond with a burst of four bar presses within the 5-sec. S^D period. The fourth bar press terminated the S^D. S^Δ was set to last for 20 sec. When S failed to give any evidence of decreased rate of response during the S^Δ interval after the first training session, E would deliver a loud "no" over the intercom contingent on such response. All steps, including the onset and timing of the S^D and S^Δ intervals, operation of the feeder, recording of the bar presses, etc., were carried out automatically through Davis relay programming equipment and a Davis Model CRRC 133 cumulative recorder. Session lengths, which varied between 20 and 50 min., were determined by the length of time it required S to obtain 36 reinforcements (which emptied the dispenser). The Ss received not more than two sessions per day, not more than 3 days apart. The discrimination training was considered complete, and test trials were begun, when S had completed two consecutive sessions in which at least 90% of his bar presses fell within the S^D interval.

Testing

Upon completion of the training phase, each autistic and retarded S received 10 test sessions. Testing for the normal Ss was terminated after two successive tests showing 100% response to the auditory, visual, and tactile cues. The test sessions were of the same duration as the training sessions and were distributed such that S received no more than two tests a day nor less than one every third day. In the test trials, the single stimuli were randomly interspersed between training trials (trials with all the stimulus components present) except that: (*a*) each test trial was always preceded and followed by at least one training trial, and (*b*) E did not run more than three training trials in a row. The density of the training trials helped to maintain the discrimination. The S was reinforced if he responded correctly on a test trial. To test for temporal discriminations, the S^Δ interval was altered from 20 to 10, 15, 25, and 30 sec. The intervals with presentations occurring prior to 20 sec. potentially provided evidence for responses to individual stimuli in the absence of the normal temporal cue. The intervals greater than 20 sec., however, allowed S to respond on the basis of a temporal cue without the influence of the external stimuli. The S received, on the average, seven presentations of each individual stimulus in a test session. The temporal intervals were randomly selected among the 10, 15, 25, and 30 sec. Altogether, he received approximately 70 test trials on any one stimulus, distributed over 10 sessions.

RESULTS

There was a great deal of variability in the acquisition of the discrimination. The normal Ss learned to respond to the complex input within a matter of minutes. The retarded Ss required, on the average, less than five 30-min. training sessions, while the autistic group required approximately twice as many sessions as the retardates. One autistic child, Leslie, was run for a total of 3 mo., five sessions a week, and still could not maintain the discrimination (she responded less than 80% of the time to the S^D, and had large bursts of S^Δ responding). Her discrimination of the complex input was so poorly maintained that tests for component control were meaningless; hence her data are not included.

Once S had learned to discriminate the stimulus complex, the main question became centered on which stimuli within the complex were controlling his responding. The S's responding to the separate components will be presented as a percentage derived from the number of actual responses to a given stimulus over the total number of opportunities to respond to that stimulus. For example, if in a particular test session S gave eight bar presses to the tactile stimulus, and that stimulus was presented eight times during that session, which would allow for 32 possible responses (4 responses per presentation), his score would equal 25%. This value is used as an index of S's sensitivity to a particular stimulus element. There will be no discussion of the temporal cue since no evidence for a temporal discrimination was observed for any of the Ss.

The most general conclusion which can be made from the data is that autistic Ss respond primarily to one stimulus component, retardates to two, and normals to all three. We derived this conclusion from a statistical analysis which was carried out as follows: we divided the Ss' responses into three levels—high, medium, and low—on the basis of the amount of responding to the separate stimuli. High was the stimulus component to which S responded most (was most functional), medium was the next most functional, and low the least functional. The magnitude of these differences was tested as follows. If there was no significant difference in the amount of responding between these levels, then it could be inferred that S had not responded differently to the three stimuli. On the other hand, a significant difference between these levels would indicate differential control by the stimulus components. For example, a significant difference between high and medium and a lack of difference between medium and low would indicate that only one cue had acquired control.

The statistical analysis was performed on the first test session only. We limited the analysis to this test session because with additional sessions S received increasing reinforcement for responding to single cues.

Table 1 shows the analysis of variance. There was a significant ($p < .01$) interaction between diagnosis (autistic, retarded, and normal) and level of responding (high, medium, and low). There was no significant difference in regard to overall level of responding. A Newman-Keuls test on the means enabled a closer analysis of the individual populations. The result of that analysis has been presented in Table 2.

TABLE 1   Analysis of variance on level of responding to the single cues

Source	df	MS	F
Diagnosis (D)	2	1217	.548
Ss within groups	12	2218	
Level of responding (L)	2	9487	43.1*
D X L	4	1677	7.62*
L X Ss within groups	24	220	

p < .005.

TABLE 2   Results of the Newman-Keuls Test on the mean levels of responding for autistic, retarded, and normal Ss

Ss	Level of response	p<
Autistics	High vs. medium	.05
	Medium vs. low	ns
	High vs. low	.01
Retardates	High vs. medium	ns
	Medium vs. low	.01
	High vs. low	.01
Normals	High vs. medium	ns
	Medium vs. low	ns
	High vs. low	ns

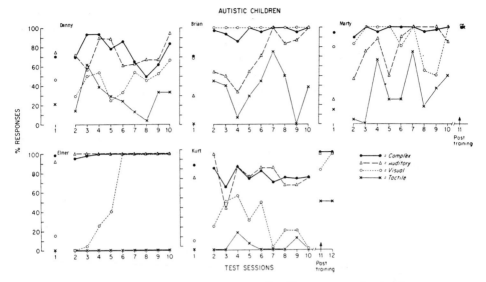

FIGURE 2 Test sessions for the autistic Ss. (Percentages of correct response to the stimuli are plotted on the ordinate and test sessions are plotted along the abscissa.)

As Table 2 shows, there was no significant difference in the amount of responding to the separate stimuli for the normal Ss. The normals gave no evidence for a preference among the cues, or that they were selectively attending to some cues and not others. For the autistics, the significant difference between the high and medium cues and lack of significant difference between the medium and low cues show the dominance of one cue. The retardates differ from the autistics in that they responded to two of the cues. They did not show a significant difference between the two most functional cues (high versus medium), while the difference between these cues and the third one (medium versus low) was significant.

The data from all the test sessions for the autistic Ss are presented in Figure 2. Percentages of correct responding are presented on the ordinate, while the test sessions are plotted along the abscissa. It is perhaps best to split these data into two parts. The first part can be limited to Test Session 1 and provides data on which cues had acquired control over S during training, when he was reinforced for responding to the stimulus complex. The second part of the data provides information about change in S's responding to the separate stimuli with continuation of testing conditions, when S was reinforced for responding to the separate presentations of these stimuli.

If we inspect the data from Test Session 1 in Figure 2, we observe that the performance on only one of the single cues lies close to the complex cue, and the response to the remaining two cues is very weak or absent altogether. This is clearly shown in regard to the tactile cue for all Ss. It is also apparent in Elmer and Kurt's minimal response to the visual cue, while Marty and Brian responded minimally to the auditory cue.

If we now look at the data with continuation of testing (Session 2 on), one can observe much variability in Ss' response to the separate stimuli. Elmer's record is the least variable. He was initially under auditory control only, but as he received reinforcement for responding to the separate presentation of the visual cue, that cue acquired control. Similar effects can be observed in Brian's and Marty's records. They were initially under visual control and later began responding to the auditory stimulus. This effect, however, is unpredictable. Thus, despite Kurt's reinforcement for responding to the visual cue, that cue eventually ceases to control him. Similar failures of separate elements to acquire control, despite reinforcement for responding in their presence, can be observed in Danny's response to the visual cue, and in Brian's, Marty's, and Danny's response to the tactile cue.

Since we were testing for the possible acquisition of temporal cues, we could not maintain the conditions for the suppression of S^{Δ} responding. One may therefore question whether response to the least functional cue(s) reflects control by that cue, or random responding. We attempted to answer this question by examining the correlation between S^{Δ} responding preceding an S^D trial and response during that trial. This analysis was performed on the data of three of the autistic Ss. For each S, we correlated S^D and S^{Δ} to the two least functional stimuli and to the complex stimulus. This was done for five of the tests of each of the three Ss. Of the 45 correlations, only 6 were significant. However, these 6 were based on few observations, thus increasing the possibility of the analysis reaching significance by chance. We therefore concluded that S^{Δ} responding was not an important factor in determining S's level of responding to the least functional stimuli.

At the end of the test sessions, we took the cue which had not become functional in the earlier training (visual for Kurt, tactile for Marty) and attempted to establish it as functional by presenting it repeatedly with a variable S^{Δ} interval. Thus, in contrast to the test sessions, reinforcement could only be obtained by responding to the nonfunctional cue since none of the other cues were presented. Upon reaching criterion, S was reintroduced to the test sessions as before. The data from this training are presented as Posttraining Trial 11 for Marty on the tactile cue and Posttraining Trials 11 and 12 for Kurt on the visual cue. When the previously nonfunctional cues are trained separately, they do acquire control.

Data from the normal Ss are presented in Figure 3. The normal Ss differed from the autistics in three ways. First, they quickly acquired the discrimination and, second, their data show little variability. Third, while the autistic Ss responded differentially to certain components of the complex, the normals responded uniformly to all. Four of the normal Ss appeared to have formed a pattern discrimination, treating the separate components as different from the complex. With continuation of testing, this discrimination is broken, allowing for a demonstration of the equal control acquired by the separate cues.

Individual responding of the retarded Ss is presented in Figure 4. David's (Mongoloid), Tony's (genetic origin), and Colleen's (birth trauma) responding conform to the statistical analysis (Table 1) in that their response to two of the cues parallels their response to the complex. By the end of testing, Jeffrey's (only outpatient) record resembles a normal child, while Roberto's (Mongoloid) graph most closely resembles that of an autistic in that he responded to only one of the cues. These children,

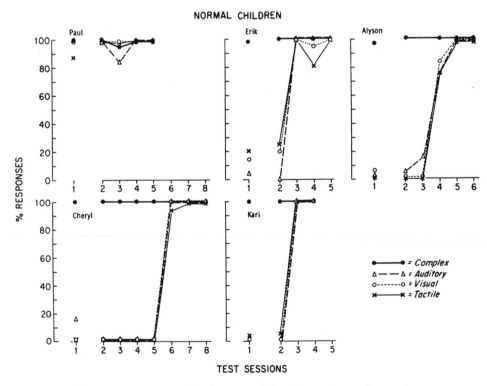

FIGURE 3   Test sessions for the normal Ss. (Percentages of correct response to the stimuli are plotted on the ordinate and test sessions are plotted along the abscissa.)

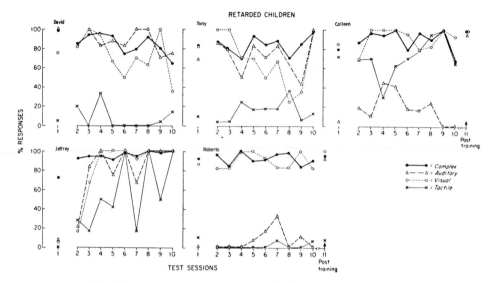

FIGURE 4   Test sessions for the retarded Ss. (Percentages of correct response to the stimuli are plotted on the ordinate and test sessions are plotted along the abscissa.)

like most retardates, present heterogenous behavioral repertoires, and we have no way of accounting for the variability in their performance.

At the end of testing, we trained a nonfunctional stimulus separately (the auditory stimulus for Colleen and Roberto) in the same manner as we had for the autistic children. The data are presented in Session 11 for both children. The separate training established the cues as functional and allows us to rule out more easily understood problems in sensory deficiency.

DISCUSSION

Three groups of children were reinforced for responding to a complex stimulus involving the simultaneous presentation of auditory, visual, and tactile cues. Once this discrimination was established, elements of the complex were presented separately to assess which aspects of the complex stimulus had acquired control over the child's behavior. We found that (*a*) the autistics responded primarily to only one of the cues; the normals responded uniformly to all three cues; and the retardates functioned between these two extremes. (*b*) Conditions could be arranged such that a cue which had remained nonfunctional when presented in association with other cues could be established as functional when trained separately.

Our data failed to support notions that any one sense modality is impaired in autistic children, or that a particular sense modality is the "preferred" modality. Our data can perhaps best be understood as the autistics' problem of dealing with stimuli in context, a problem of quantity rather than quality of stimulus control. One can call this a problem of *stimulus overselectivity*.

There are some obvious qualifications which one has to impose upon these data. One pertains to the potentially unstable nature of Ss' responding with increased exposure to the training stimuli. This is left unclear in our experiment, since the stimuli were taken out of context and presented singly (from Test Session 1 on). But one may observe different results with different amounts of training prior to testing.

Perhaps the most important qualification centers on the choice of Ss and the bases of their diagnoses. It is noteworthy that we have worked with the most regressed of autistic children, and that different results may have been obtained had we used children who were more advanced, having, for example, speech development. This problem may be even more pronounced with the retarded Ss who show much heterogeneity. Roberto, for example, though he was diagnosed as retarded, responded like an autistic.

Similarly, we may qualify our data in regard to the *intensity* of the stimuli. Prior to the experiment we attempted to correct for unequal subjective intensities by choosing intensities which college students had rated as having "equal impact." It would have been more ideal to have autistic Ss perform this task, but that would be extremely difficult to do. The results could also be a function of the particular *kind* of stimuli we employed. Perhaps it is the tactile cue which blocks response to other cues. One can also think of other qualifications, such as Ss' motivational level, except that the retarded Ss appeared motivated, yet show parts of the deficiency. Training under more stress, however, as when the child is anxious or inhibiting self-stimulation, may wipe out the effect.

Although these results could be interpreted in several ways, the data conform closely to a selective attention, or stimulus selection, hypothesis. Selective attention refers to the process in which an organism, when presented with multiple cues, attends to, or comes under the control of, only a portion of the available stimuli. This fact has led to the distinction between "nominal" or perceived stimulus variables which consist of the total set of available elements and "functional" or effective stimuli which are those elements actually controlling behavior.

There has been a great deal of research on this differentiation, and excellent reviews of such research are available in recent texts by Fellows (1968) and Trabasso and Bower (1968). A comprehensive presentation will not be attempted here, but a short comment is appropriate.

Long ago, Pavlov (1927) found that the conditioned response to one element (the dominant) of a complex stimulus was as large as the response to the complex, leaving the response to the other elements negligible. Warren (1953) taught monkeys to discriminate between two objects differing in size, color, form, two, or all three of these dimensions. He found that although learning was facilitated by the inclusion of more relevant cues, the color cue alone was the most dominant. Similar results have been reported in other studies with animals (Harlow, 1945; Warren, 1954) and with children (Suchman & Trabasso, 1966). Studying nursery and kindergarten children, Suchman and Trabasso found that when color, size, and form cues were simultaneously available for discrimination, younger children preferred the color cue while the older children preferred the form cue. Working within the operant training paradigm presented here, Reynolds (1961) trained two pigeons to discriminate two white forms on differently colored backgrounds (red or green). In extinction test periods, it was found that one pigeon responded only to the white form and the other pigeon responded only to the colored background. Orlando (1961) reported similar instances of stimulus selection in the learning of retarded children. In a task in which a cue for S^D and S^Δ periods was employed, he found that one of these cues was not only sufficient, but exclusively functional in maintaining the discrimination.

There have been various mechanisms thought to underlie selective responding in normals. Sometimes the underlying mechanism is considered genetic, in that a particular cue emerges as the dominant for the great majority of members within a species. One can also manipulate learning experiences in such a fashion as to render a cue dominant. Both Kamin (1968) in a classical conditioning paradigm and Trabasso and Bower (1968) in a redundant relevant cue (RRC) paradigm have demonstrated blocking effects, finding that a first-learned cue blocks the learning of another relevant cue which was added during overtraining.

"Stimulus blocking" is said to occur when attention to one stimulus in a complex stimulus situation blocks or inhibits the attention to another cue also present. Trabasso and Bower (1968) suggested that the observed dominance or selection in RRC tasks could be due to the blocking of a slower learned cue by a faster learned cue when both cues are present from the beginning of training. They see overshadowing as resulting when an S by chance responds to a particular cue and because he is reinforced does not broaden his learning to the other relevant cues.

One conclusion from all the work on normal children using RRC procedures is that normal children display stimulus selection and thus often come under the control of only a portion of the available stimuli. It is important, therefore, to use a control group of normal Ss to better assess selective responding in autistics. Our failure to observe selective responding in the normal children, which others so often report, was probably based on the nature of the task. In most RRC tasks all the elements fall within one modality, rather than being distributed across modalities as was the case in our study. We also kept the number of stimuli small. Levine (1967) and Eimas (1969) have presented data which suggest that by the time normal children have reached the age of the Ss in this experiment, they will generally attend to about three or four simultaneous cues during discrimination learning. In contrast to the normal children, the autistic children showed an extreme degree of stimulus selection, leaving large segments of their environment essentially neutral.

Perhaps the first questions to be raised by this study regard a more accurate description of the stimulus overselectivity. For example, one may wonder whether the selectivity is a function of the kinds and number of cues in the complex stimulus; whether it is present also when all cues are presented in one modality; or whether it also presents itself when the cues are nonoverlapping but closely spaced in time. Studies are now in progress in our laboratory to investigate some of these questions.

The second line of questions deals with assessing some of the mechanisms which may underlie stimulus overselectivity. Perhaps the autistics tend to respond only to one cue because of a failure in "switching" behavior. Lindsay, Taylor, and Forbes (1968) and Treisman (1969) have suggested that normals seem to attend to only one stimulus component at a time and analyze complex cues by very rapidly switching attention to different aspects of the complex, going quickly through sets of "alternative analyzers." Autistics may not adequately sample stimuli, but settle on one stimulus which "blocks" the others. The problem with this line of reasoning can be easily seen when one considers the possibilities that inadequate switching may result in stimulus blocking, or, conversely, that stimulus blocking may result in inadequate switching. Either direction seems equally plausible.

A third line of questions may be directed toward a better description of stimulus selectivity among groups with different pathology. We included a retarded group to help isolate those peculiarities associated with autistic functioning. The retarded Ss showed less stimulus selectivity than the autistics. They also showed less behavioral deficiency (higher IQ scores, social adjustment, etc.). Perhaps future research will suggest that this kind of discrimination task differentiates between children with different degrees of behavioral deficiencies.

It may be of interest to speculate on how our findings may relate to the pathology in autistic children. Before we present this speculation, two considerations must be made. First, the pathology in autism is so profound and extensive that it is unlikely any one finding will provide insight into it all. Second, the speculations we make presuppose that our inference of stimulus overselectivity best describes the data. Additional studies will be needed to strengthen this inference.

Implications for Understanding Autism

A necessary condition for much learning involves a contiguous or near-contiguous presentation of two stimuli. Such contiguous stimulus presentations are clearly present in classical conditioning when the CS is presented in close proximity to the UCS. In fact, this is a necessary condition for optimal learning. Contiguous presentations are also present in those aspects of operant conditioning where one seeks a shift in stimulus control. In these instances the training stimulus is presented simultaneously with a prompt. Since this contiguous presentation of two stimuli involves presenting the child with a stimulus complex, it may be assumed that the autistics' response to one of these stimuli is blocked, overshadowed, or otherwise has failed to occur. Let us consider some of the implications of this assumption for certain kinds of learning.

1. One can consider that the acquisition of most human behavior, like language, interpersonal, and intellectual behavior, is based on the prior acquisition of conditioned reinforcers. A failure in this acquisition would lead to a failure in behavioral development (Ferster & DeMyer, 1962). If it is the case that conditioned reinforcers acquire strength by contiguous association with primary ones, then our finding should help to further describe the failure for such conditioning to take place in autistic children (Lovaas, Freitag, Kinder, Rubenstein, Schaeffer, & Simmons, 1966).

2. The autistic child's failure to give appropriate affect is well-known. The mechanisms for establishing appropriate affect may well be very similar to those involved in establishing conditioned reinforcers: contiguous presentation of two stimulus events which enables the affect, elicited by one of these events (the UCS), to be elicited by the other (the CS).

3. Many autistic children have topographically elaborated speech (echolalia), but it appears without "meaning." One can argue that the speech exists without meaning to the extent it has an impoverished context. The acquisition of a context for speech probably involves a shift in stimulus control. To the extent that this involves simultaneous presentations of auditory with visual, tactile, or some other cue, one may expect that the autistic child would "overselect" and fail to learn.

4. From a consideration of the data in Figure 1, which illustrates the difficulties in the establishment of imitative behavior, it is also possible that such stimulus overselectivity as we have described might contribute

importantly to the autistic child's failure in the acquisition of new behavioral topographies. In fact, the usual way we train new skills is to "aid" the child by adding large numbers of extra cues to the training situation. This, of course, may be exactly what makes it so difficult for the autistic child to learn what we want him to.

5. Whenever one postulates blocking of incoming stimuli, learning as well as performance should be impaired. Stimulus overselectivity may also be a factor which underlies the sporadic, highly variable nature of these children's responses to already functional stimuli. A number of other possibilities suggest themselves, which probably are best discussed in light of more extensive data.

REFERENCES

Buss, A., & Lang, P. Psychological deficit in schizophrenia. I. Affect, reinforcement, and concept attainment. *Journal of Abnormal Psychology*, 1965, **70**, 2–24.

Eimas, P. Multiple-cue discrimination learning in children. *Psychological Record*, 1969, **19**, 417–424.

Feigenberg, I. Probabilistic prognosis and its significance in normal and pathological subjects. In M. Cole & I. Maltzman (Eds.), *A handbook of contemporary Soviet psychology*. New York: Basic Books, 1969.

Fellows, B. J. *The discrimination process and development*. London: Pergamon Press, 1968.

Ferster, C. B., & DeMyer, M. A method for the experimental analysis of the behavior of autistic children. *American Journal of Orthopsychiatry*, 1962, **32**, 89–98.

Goldfarb, W. An investigation of childhood schizophrenia. *Archives of General Psychiatry*, 1964, **11**, 620–634.

Harlow, H. F. Studies in discrimination learning in monkeys. VI. Discriminations between stimuli differing in both color and form, only in color, and only in form. *Journal of General Psychology*, 1945, **33**, 225–235.

Hermelin, B. Recent psychological research. In J. K. Wing (Ed.), *Early childhood autism*. London: Pergamon Press, 1966.

Kamin, L. J. Attention-like processes in classical conditioning. In M. R. Jones (Ed.), *Miami Symposium on the Prediction of Behavior, 1967: Aversive stimulation*. Miami: University of Miami Press, 1968.

Kanner, L. Early infantile autism. *Journal of Pediatrics*, 1944, **25**, 211–217.

Lang, P. J., & Buss, A. H. Psychological deficit in schizophrenia. II. Interference and activation. *Journal of Abnormal Psychology*, 1965, **70**, 77–106.

Levine, M. The size of the hypothesis set during discrimination learning. *Psychological Review*, 1967, **74**, 428–430.

Lindsay, P. H., Taylor, M. M., & Forbes, S. M. Attention and multidimensional discrimination. *Perception and Psychophysics*, 1968, **4**, 113–117.

LOVAAS, O. I., BERBERICH, J. P., PERLOFF, B. F., & SCHAEFFER, B. Acquisition of imitative speech in schizophrenic children. *Science*, 1966, **151**, 705–707.

LOVAAS, O. I., FREITAG, G., KINDER, M. I., RUBENSTEIN, B. D., SCHAEFFER, B., & SIMMONS, J. Q. Establishment of social reinforcers in schizophrenic children using food. *Journal of Experimental Child Psychology*, 1966, **4**, 109–125.

ORLANDO, R. The functional role of discriminative stimuli in free operant performance of developmentally retarded children. *Psychological Record*, 1961, **11**, 153–161.

PAVLOV, I. P. Lectures. In, *Conditioned reflexes*. Oxford: University Press, 1927.

REYNOLDS, G. S. Attention in the pigeon. *Journal of the Experimental Analysis of Behavior*, 1961, **4**, 203–208.

RIMLAND, B. *Infantile autism*. New York: Appleton-Century-Crofts, 1964.

SCHOPLER, E. Visual versus tactual receptor preference in normal and schizophrenic children. *Journal of Abnormal Psychology*, 1966, **71**, 108–114.

SHERRINGTON, C. S. *The integrative action of the nervous system*. London: Cambridge University Press, 1906.

SUCHMAN, R. G., & TRABASSO, T. Color and form preference in young children. *Journal of Experimental Child Psychology*, 1966, **3**, 177–187.

TRABASSO, T., & BOWER, G. H. *Attention in learning*. New York: Wiley, 1968.

TREISMAN, A. Strategies and models of selective attention. *Psychological Review*, 1969, **76**, 282–299.

WARREN, J. M. Additivity of cues in visual pattern discrimination by monkeys. *Journal of Comparative and Physiological Psychology*, 1953, **46**, 484–488.

WARREN, J. M. Perceptual dominance in discrimination learning in monkeys. *Journal of Comparative and Physiological Psychology*, 1954, **47**, 290–292.

YOUNG, S. Visual attention in autistic and normal children: Effects of stimulus novelty, human attributes, and complexity. Unpublished doctoral dissertation, University of California, Los Angeles, 1969.

ROBERT L. KOEGEL
University of California, Santa Barbara

LAURA SCHREIBMAN
Claremont Men's College

The role of stimulus variables in teaching autistic children[1]

Although research in behavior modification has presented considerable information on the reinforcement variables involved in establishing new behaviors, relatively little is known about the roles of the stimulus variables involved. Investigators have generally assumed that processes such as transfers in stimulus control take place naturally. For example, in teaching a child to read a new word, a teacher may present an added stimulus—a *prompt* (e.g., a picture)—to elicit a correct response to the new stimulus word. In such teaching, the assumption is made that when the prompt is removed, the child will continue to respond correctly to the new training stimulus. This assumption, however, is without empirical verification. That we desire such shifts to occur is no reason to assume that they will.

The literature reviewed below suggests that transfers or shifts in stimulus control do not always take place. Furthermore, whether a transfer takes place or not appears to be a function of the characteristics of the

[1] The autism research reported in this paper was supported by United States Public Health Service Research Grant 11440 from the National Institute of Mental Heath. Manuscript preparation was also supported in part by State of California, Department EHA, Part B (Title VI-B) #42-00000-0000832/025, administered by the County Superintendent of Schools, Santa Barbara, California.

537

stimuli involved as well as of the learning characteristics of the child being taught. These variables are considered separately.

STIMULUS CHARACTERISTICS

Prompting a correct response generally entails presenting an additional stimulus to bring about correct responding to a training stimulus. For example, a teacher may prompt a child by pointing to a red-colored block while simultaneously instructing the child to touch the red block. Thus, several stimuli are simultaneously presented to the learner (the pointing finger, the red block, and the teacher's voice). Research in discrimination learning suggests that there are certain conditions under which the presentation of such multiple stimuli will be detrimental to learning. Two phenomena, "overshadowing" and "blocking," are particularly relevant to this point. Comprehensive reviews of research on both these phenomena have been provided by Fellows (1968), Trabasso and Bower (1968), and Sutherland and Mackintosh (1971). A brief summary of this research is presented below.

Overshadowing refers to the failure of one of two or more simultaneously presented stimuli to acquire control over responding as a function of the presence of another stimulus. In particular, the presence of a strong relevant cue retards learning about a weak relevant cue and often suppresses such learning completely. Lovejoy and Russell (1967) have provided an illustrative example of overshadowing in the area of animal discrimination learning. They trained two groups of rats on a two-choice simultaneous discrimination. On each trial, one alternative was a vertical line, the other a horizontal line; one was black and the other white. Response to the vertical line was rewarded for both groups. For one group, however, black-white was also a relevant cue; for the other group, it was irrelevant. When the easy, black-white cue was relevant, learning about the relatively difficult orientation cue (vertical-horizontal) was suppressed. That is, under these conditions the presence of an additional stimulus was detrimental to learning.

Overshadowing also exists in the human learning literature. For example, Anderson and Faust (1967) performed an experiment in programmed instruction, teaching English-Russian word pairs. For one group the correct stimulus was prompted by underlining, but for the other group no prompt was provided. On a recall test, the group who learned the same pairs without any prompt recalled significantly more word pairs. Moreover, many of the prompted subjects reported that during the training they answered the questions on the basis of the prompt alone without attending to the relevant prompted cue at all. As in the animal learning example above, the presence of an additional cue was detrimental to learning.

Another phenomenon that appears to be detrimental to transfers in stimulus control is stimulus *blocking*. Blocking occurs when a learner is pretrained to respond to one stimulus and is then trained on another discrimination with both the first and a new stimulus relevant. In this situation the new stimulus either totally fails to acquire control or acquires very little control compared to when it is trained alone. One of the most classic examples of the blocking phenomenon has been provided by Kamin (1968), using rats as subjects. He paired one stimulus (a light or a tone) with the onset of shock and showed that in later trials, presentation of that stimulus would suppress bar pressing. He then presented a second stimulus (again a light or a tone) simultaneously with the first for an additional number of reinforced (shock) trials. Finally, he tested the first and second stimuli separately for suppression effects. Under these conditions, the stimulus added after pretraining did not acquire suppressing effects. That is, acquisition of control by the second stimulus was blocked by the presence of the pretrained stimulus.

Trabasso and Bower (1968) have reported similar results with human subjects. After subjects had learned a discrimination between cards containing different letters, an additional letter was made relevant for 32 overtraining trials. None of the subjects came under the control of the added stimulus. The earlier pretraining blocked the acquisition of the added letters. This experiment also illustrated an important distinction between a learner noting a stimulus and coming under the control of that stimulus. Each subject in the above study was required to name aloud all of the letters on the display before responding. Thus, although each subject noticed the added cue, nevertheless they did not come under its control.

CHARACTERISTICS OF THE LEARNER

Stimulus control is not only determined by the characteristics of the stimuli and their presentation. One must also consider the learning characteristics of the organism under control. That is, independent of the general effects of selective responding, certain abnormalities in the sensory functioning of the learner may also affect transfers in stimulus control. For example, there is a growing body of research indicating that autistic children have an attentional deficit that would lead to particular problems in the area of stimulus control.

One of the most characteristic features of autistic children is their unresponsiveness to external stimulation. An autistic child may be oblivious to the point at which he will not respond to his name or to a loud sound.

He may walk past a person or object in his environment as though it were not there. Such behavior has caused observers to describe these children as "living in a shell" or "in another world." This unresponsiveness is often so severe that the children are suspected of being blind or deaf. Although they are unresponsive, this unresponsiveness is selective and variable in nature. For example, a child who does not respond to his name or to a loud sound may react violently to the turn of a newspaper page or turn toward the sound of a rustling candy wrapper. The child who behaves as if he were blind may sight a small piece of candy several feet away or become engrossed in staring at a shiny doorknob.

Recent research on the characteristics of this unresponsivity has pointed to abnormalities in the way such children learn about their environment. Relating autistic sensory deficit to learning, Lovaas, Schreibman, Koegel, and Rhem (1971) employed a discrimination task in an attempt to see how these children use incoming sensory information in order to learn. In that study, groups of autistic, retarded, and normal children were trained to press a bar in the presence of a complex stimulus composed of the simultaneous presentation of visual (red floodlight), auditory (white noise), and tactile (pressure on leg) cues. Once this discrimination was established, the elements of the complex stimulus were presented singly to assess the amount of control exerted by each cue over the child's behavior. It was found that the autistic children characteristically responded to only one of the stimulus components. In contrast, the normals responded uniformly to all three cues. The retardates responded at a level between these two extremes. The authors discuss these results in terms of the autistic child's problem of "stimulus overselectivity," whereby he is overselective in his response to multiple stimuli and has difficulty dealing with stimuli in context.

In a subsequent study, Lovaas and Schreibman (1971) investigated the possibility that such overselectivity was due to "flooding" or overstimulating the child by presenting input from three modalities. In this study only two stimuli, a light and a sound, were used (in the same paradigm as before). The results were consistent with those of the previous study. The autistic children, unlike the normals, showed stimulus overselectivity in that they characteristically responded to only one of the cues. However, the overselectivity effect was not as strong as when three modalities were employed. In this second study two of the nine autistics did respond to both stimuli.

Stimulus overselectivity has also been found when the stimuli fall within one modality. Koegel and Wilhelm (1972) trained autistic and normal children to discriminate a card with two stimuli (e.g., a girl and a house) from another card with two different stimuli (e.g., a bicycle and a tree). After this discrimination was learned, the individual stimuli were tested for their control over the child's responding. Twelve of the fifteen autistic children responded on the basis of only one of the cues, while twelve of the fifteen normals responded to both of the cues.

Such stimulus overselectivity is also evident when one tries to treat these children. Lovaas, *et al.* (1971) cite, as an example, the problem of teaching verbal imitation to a mute, autistic child. To facilitate acquisition of imitation, a therapist generally provides visual as well as auditory cues. Thus, when the therapist presents the auditory stimulus to be imitated, the child is also presented with the visual stimulus of mouth movements. Since the different sounds have distinct visual as well as auditory components, the child is presented with two relevant cues. The child's learning curve then appears to indicate that he is learning to imitate. However, when the therapist removes the visual cues by covering her mouth as the sound is presented, the child no longer responds. He has selectively responded to the visual stimulus of the therapist's mouth movements and has learned nothing about the sound.

This research indicates that autistic children are under extremely narrow stimulus control. The most important implication of this overselective responding is that it is likely to retard or prevent learning. Most learning depends on the contiguous or nearly contiguous presentation of stimuli. In classical conditioning paradigms, the CS (conditioned stimulus) is presented closely to the UCS (unconditioned stimulus). In operant conditioning paradigms, contiguous presentation of stimuli occurs when one seeks to achieve a transfer in stimulus control as when one presents a prompt. Thus a failure to respond to multiple cues would lead to a failure to learn. This is consistent with the kinds of problems one often encounters when trying to teach these children with prompts. In prompting, it is frequently very difficult or impossible to achieve a shift in stimulus control from the prompt to the training stimulus. For example, the behavior of the mute autistic child cited in the Lovaas, *et al.* (1971) study was controlled solely by the visual cues of the therapist's mouth movements (prompt) rather than by the auditory (training) stimulus.

With respect to using prompts, then, the above literature suggests that if the learner is pretrained to respond correctly to a given cue, and if this cue is then used as a prompt (presented simultaneously with new training stimuli), one might expect that the presence of the (pretrained) prompt may block the acquisition of the training stimuli for both autistic and normal subjects. Furthermore, since autistic children have been shown to be overselective in their response to multiple stimuli, one might expect that the presence of a prompt would be particularly detrimental to the acquisition of new discriminations for these children.

In order to test these hypotheses, an experiment was conducted (Koegel, 1971) in which autistic and normal children were trained on discrimination problems with and without the use of prompts. The number of discriminations acquired under each of these conditions was then used as a measure of the effectiveness of each procedure.

In the first part of the experiment, two groups of eight normal children each were trained to respond differentially on a red-green color discrimination. After acquiring the color discrimination, each of the two groups was trained on four new discriminations (hexagon versus octagon; X versus O; high-pitched tone versus low-pitched tone; and a low intensity tone versus a high intensity tone). One group was trained on each of these discriminations with a no-prompt (trial and error) procedure. The other group was trained with a prompt procedure, in which the pretrained color stimuli were used as prompts (presented simultaneously with the new training stimuli) in order to bring about correct responding to these training stimuli. The prompts were then gradually faded (by desaturating the color) until the children were presented with only the training stimuli alone. If the children then responded correctly to the training stimuli, one could say that the children had transferred from control by the prompt stimuli to control by the training stimuli. The results, however, showed that while each of the eight children in the no-prompt (trial and error) condition acquired all four of the new discriminations, the children in the prompt condition acquired only an average of 3.1 (range 2–4) of the discriminations. This difference between the number of discriminations acquired by the prompt and no-prompt groups was highly significant according to the median test ($p < .005$). Furthermore, all of the children in the prompt group who failed to acquire discriminations were able to acquire these discriminations when subsequently trained with a no-prompt (trial and error) procedure. Thus, the presence of the prompt stimuli proved to be detrimental to the acquisition of new discriminations for normal children.

Since the literature reviewed above suggests that autistic children would show an even greater deficit than normal children when prompts are used (since the prompt procedures require attention to multiple stimuli), the second portion of the experiment was designed to compare the relative effectiveness of using a prompt with normal versus autistic children. A group of eight autistic children participated in discrimination training according to exactly the same procedures as the normal children. A comparison of the autistic versus the normal groups showed that using the prompt procedure, the normal children acquired an average of only 3.1 (range 2–4) discriminations per child compared to an average of only 1.2 (range 1–3) discriminations per child for the autistic children. This difference between autistic and normal children was also highly significant according to the median test ($p < .02$). Furthermore, autistic children who failed to acquire the discriminations with a prompt procedure were able to acquire all of the discriminations when subsequently trained with a no-prompt procedure.

In summary, this first experiment showed that the presence of additional stimuli to prompt correct responding was detrimental to the acquisition of new discriminations for both autistic and normal children. That is, although the children responded correctly when the color prompt was present, they frequently ceased to respond correctly when the prompt was removed. Prompting was, however, significantly more detrimental for the autistic children than it was for the normal children. Given that these children are overselective in their response to stimuli and that such overselectivity precludes the use of typical prompting techniques, it remains to develop effective techniques that work around their unique problems.

Although blocking and overshadowing inhibit transfers in stimulus control, another phenomenon, "transfer along a continuum," facilitates such transfers. Transfer along a continuum refers to a process by which a difficult discrimination is trained by first providing training on an easier discrimination, then by gradually increasing the difficulty of the discrimination until the criterion discrimination is reached. For example, Lawrence (1952) demonstrated that with rats a difficult light gray versus dark gray discrimination was more efficiently trained by first training the Ss on an easy black-white discrimination, then by gradually increasing the difficulty of the discrimination along intermediate steps until the difficult (light gray versus dark gray) discrimination was acquired. It should be noted that in "transfer along a continuum" the subject does not respond to simultaneously presented multiple cues. Rather, he is trained to respond to a prompt that may be considered to be an exaggerated version of the training stimulus. This exaggerated stimulus is then gradually transformed into the training stimulus.

We reasoned that if autistic children are overselective, responding to only one component of a complex stimulus, then it might be effective to prompt the children to respond correctly to a given stimulus by exaggerating that stimulus and using transfer along a continuum as the procedure to fade the prompt. In this case, the prompt lies within the relevant stimulus and does not require the child to respond to multiple cues.

The purpose, then, of the second experiment (Schreibman, 1972) was to test whether using a within-stimulus prompt and transferring control along a continuum would facilitate stimulus shifts, as compared with using an extra-stimulus prompt and transferring control across a continuum. In this experiment two prompting procedures were used. They include: (1) provision of an added stimulus as an *extra-stimulus prompt*. This prompt represented the typical type of prompt used in teaching situations. It required that the child respond to both the prompt and the training stimuli in order to achieve a transfer of stimulus control. This prompt was systematically faded to determine if such a transfer could be accomplished. (2) Provision of a *within-stimulus prompt* that involved emphasizing the relevant component of the training stimulus. This prompt was also faded by systematically withdrawing this emphasis. It was hypothesized that if a prompt within the dimension of the training stimulus itself was provided by exaggerating the relevant part of the stimulus, fading this kind of prompt would be effective since it did not require the child to respond to simultaneously presented multiple stimuli.

A single-subject design was employed in which six autistic children were each trained on four difficult discrimination tasks. Two of the tasks involved visual stimuli consisting of forms drawn on cards, and two involved auditory stimuli consisting of two-syllable nonsense words. For each of these tasks there was only one component of the stimuli that was relevant to the discrimination. Thus for each auditory discrimination, the first syllable remained the same, and only the second syllable differed (was relevant). For example, one auditory discrimination was nolä versus nolé. For each visual discrimination the forms were identical except for one feature. Thus one of the visual discriminations consisted of a stick figure with one arm raised versus a stick figure with one arm lowered.

The Ss were first trained on each discrimination to determine if they could learn the task without a prompt. If they did not acquire the discrimination, they were presented with the prompt conditions. To provide the extra-stimulus prompt for the visual tasks, E pointed to the correct card. This prompt was faded by gradually presenting the pointing prompt at greater distances from the training stimuli. The within-stimulus prompt involved presenting the relevant component of the form discrimination alone. For example, just the arms were presented, then the rest of the figures gradually were faded in. For the auditory discriminations the extra-stimulus prompt consisted of a buzzer presented contiguously with the correct stimulus. This buzzer prompt was faded by decreasing its intensity. The within-stimulus prompt involved emphasizing the relevant component (syllable) and gradually reducing this emphasis. For example, just the second syllable was presented alone (é versus ä), and then the first syllable gradually was faded in. The order of presentation of the conditions was balanced.

The results can be summarized as follows: (1) the Ss usually failed to learn the discriminations without a prompt. Of twenty-four discriminations only eight were learned during the unprompted pretraining. This indicates that even if most prompts typically are not effective with autistic children, some discriminations are too difficult for them to acquire without a prompt. (2) The Ss always failed to acquire a previously unlearned discrimination when the extra-stimulus prompt was employed, although they usually did learn a previously unlearned discrimination when the within-stimulus prompt was employed. Thus, discriminations that were not acquired either without a prompt or with an extra-stimulus prompt could be acquired only when the within-stimulus prompt was used. (3) These findings were independent of which modality (auditory or visual) was required for the discrimination.

SUMMARY AND CONCLUSIONS

In determining the functional properties a stimulus will have in controlling a behavior, one must consider both the manner of stimulus presentation and the learning characteristics of the behaving organism. In our discussion we have provided evidence that the probability of a particular stimulus coming to control a response depends on the context in which it appears. Thus, phenomena such as "overshadowing" and "blocking" serve to reduce the amount of stimuli controlling a response. In addition, we have presented evidence that autistic children characteristically respond to only one component of a complex stimulus—that is, they operate on a very restricted range of stimulus control. These observations illustrate that reduced stimulus control can be a function of both stimulus and organism variables.

We reasoned that the difficulty one often encounters when attempting to achieve transfers in stimulus control with autistic children (as with the use of prompts) might be explained by stimulus overselectivity. The results of the two experiments we have described indicate that, indeed, prompts interfere with learning in autistic children when they require response to simultaneously presented multiple cues. However, this problem can be alleviated by utilizing another phenomenon, transfer along a continuum, which allows for prompting within the relevant dimension of a training stimulus. Thus, the autistic child is not required to respond to multiple stimuli.

These results illustrate that an understanding of the variables governing stimulus control can lead not only to an understanding of response patterns (such as autistic overselectivity) but also to the development of specific procedures that incorporate this understanding for teaching purposes. As the experiments summarized here show, knowledge of the very limited stimulus control under which autistic children function led to developing a prompting procedure that takes advantage of their selective response.

In the case of autistic children, the learning characteristics of the child and the manner of stimulus presentation play important parts in determining whether or not prompting will be effective. Perhaps these variables are important for other types of stimulus shifts as well. Many learning situations require functional control by multiple stimuli. Emotions acquired through classical conditioning require response to a contiguously presented CS and UCS. The acquisition of the meanings of words requires attention to the verbal stimulus of a teacher's voice as well as to the referent of the word being spoken. Perhaps a knowledge of variables affecting the acquisition and transfer of stimulus control may improve the techniques used to bring about the acquisition of these and other behaviors.

REFERENCES

ANDERSON, R. C. & FAUST, G. W. The effects of strong formal prompts in programmed instruction. *American Educational Research Journal*, 1967, 4, 345–52.

FELLOWS, B. J. *The Discrimination Process and Development*. London: Pergamon Press, 1968.

KAMIN, L. J. Attention-like processes in classical conditioning. In M. R. JONES, (Ed.), *Miami Symposium on the Prediction of Behavior, 1967: Aversive Stimulation*. Miami: University of Miami Press, 1968.

KOEGEL, R. Selective attention to prompt stimuli by autistic and normal children. Unpublished doctoral dissertation, University of California, Los Angeles, 1971.

KOEGEL, R. & WILHELM, H. Selective responding to multiple visual cues by autistic children. Submitted for publication, 1972.

LAWRENCE, D. H. The transfer of a discrimination along a continuum. *Journal of Comparative and Physiological Psychology*, 1952, 45, 511–16.

LOVAAS, O. I. & SCHREIBMAN, L. Stimulus overselectivity of autistic children in a two stimulus situation. *Behaviour Research and Therapy*, 1971, 2, 305–10.

LOVAAS, O. I., SCHREIBMAN, L., KOEGEL, R., & REHM, R. Selective responding by autistic children to multiple sensory input. *Journal of Abnormal Psychology*, 1971, 77, 211–22.

LOVEJOY, E. & RUSSELL, D. G. Suppression of learning about a hard cue by the presence of an easy cue. *Psychonomic Science*, 1967, 8, 365–66.

SCHREIBMAN, L. Within-stimulus versus extra-stimulus prompting procedures in discriminations with autistic children. Unpublished doctoral dissertation, University of California, Los Angeles, 1972.

SUTHERLAND, N. S. & MACKINTOSH, N. J. *Mechanisms of Animal Discrimination Learning*. Academic Press, 1971.

TRABASSO, T. & BOWER, G. H. *Attention in Learning*. New York: Wiley, 1968.

AUTHOR INDEX

SUBJECT INDEX